TOXICOLOGY

A Case-Oriented Approach

TOXICOLOGY

A Case-Oriented Approach

John Joseph Fenton

CRC PRESS

Boca Raton   London   New York   Washington, D.C.

Library of Congress Cataloging-in-Publication Data

Fenton, John Ph.D.
    Toxicology : a case-oriented approach / John Fenton.
        p. cm.
    Includes bibliographical references and index.
    ISBN 0-8493-0371-0 (alk. paper)
    1. Toxicology--Case studies. I. Title.
    [DNLM: 1. Toxicology--Case Report. Poisons--Case Report. QV 600 F342t 2001]
RA1219 .F46 2001
615.9'07—dc21
                                        2001035682
                                          CIP

Visit the CRC Press Web site at www.crcpress.com

© 2002 by CRC Press LLC

No claim to original U.S. Government works
International Standard Book Number 0-8493-0371-0
Library of Congress Card Number 2001035682
Printed in the United States of America   2 3 4 5 6 7 8 9 0
Printed on acid-free paper

Preface

This book is an outgrowth of the author's experience teaching a toxicology course for 12 years at West Chester University and his interactions with physicans and laboratory toxicologists for 24 years in the Crozer Keystone Health System. These experiences provided valuable insights into the needs both groups have for an enhanced understanding of toxicology in the laboratory and in the emergency department. Accordingly, the present volume was written in hopes of meeting the requirements of both physicians and laboratory toxicologists by presenting the analytic and clinical aspects of toxicology.

Many excellent books are available that address the diagnosis and treatment of the overdose patient. Other fine volumes, intended for a scientific audience, have been written that provide test methods and explanations of instrumental modalities for toxicology testing. The present book is the only one, to the author's knowledge, that speaks equally to both audiences, the caregiver and the analytical scientist. The reader will find that this book, although less clinical than medical toxicology texts, and less chemical than analytical works, is, nevertheless, heavily vested in both clinical and analytical aspects of toxicology. Scientists can provide better test results if they understand the problems of the clinician. Physicians can employ the laboratory more effectively if they understand the nature, power, and limitations of toxicology testing. We hope that this book will meet these needs.

Case studies are a popular and effective means of teaching concepts. Pedagogic research has shown that people tend to remember information that is presented in the form of case studies. Students also enjoy the narrative approach characteristic of such studies. Accordingly, the present volume features a very large number of case studies, all of which are cross-referenced to the clinical literature. They were selected for their interest and their ability to teach important aspects of toxicology. The reader is challenged in each case to identify an unknown toxin and may, in fact, make the identification on the basis of his/her knowledge of symptoms, physical properties of toxins, and so on. The level of medical knowledge required to fully understand each case presented here is not insignificant. Some students who have very little clinical experience will find them very challenging. It is the author's belief, however, that even without a complete understanding of every aspect of each clinical history presented here, one can derive a great deal of benefit by reading the case studies and trying to answer the questions and problems.

The author has endeavored to maintain the reader's interest in other ways as well. For example, many interesting anecdotes from the history of toxicology are found throughout the text. The alleged arsenical poisonings of Napoleon and of President Taylor, the probable mercury overdose of Isaac Newton, and the hemlock ingestion of Socrates are just a few examples of the many famous facts or fiction that are part of the history of toxicology. Such events teach us about the nature of life in the past and the specific dangers that toxins presented to our ancestors.

The author wishes to thank the many who have contributed to his teaching and toxicology experiences. It has always been a pleasure working with young people as they start their careers in science. I have also been continuously impressed by the dedication and effort that the toxicology staff at Crozer Keystone Health System brought to their jobs everyday. In their company and that of many other members of the hospital staff we learned toxicology in the "real world."

John Fenton, Ph.D.
Philadelphia

Dedication

---

to Marjorie

Table of Contents

1 History of Toxicology

CONTENTS

ANCIENT TIMES

The history of poisons dates to earliest times. Ancient man undoubtedly observed toxic effects in nature partly on a serendipitous basis as, for example, when he noted a harmful or fatal effect follow the casual ingestion of some plant or animal product by one of his fellow tribesmen. But serendipity was not the only mechanism of discovery. Assuredly, man experimented with natural products in an effort to improve his arsenal of weapons, the better to achieve success when waging war with his enemies.

Modern toxicology is characterized by extremely sophisticated scientific investigation and evaluation of toxic exposures of all kinds. To a large degree this has been made possible by the widespread application of computers to analytical equipment. Coupled with other chemical and electronic innovations modern instruments can detect quantities of toxins that are much smaller than those that could be measured in the past. Analytic methods are not only highly sensitive but they are also capable of extreme specificity so that compounds can be implicated in poisoning episodes to the near certain exclusion of other highly similar compounds. In the course of this text the reader will learn to appreciate the sophistication and application of technologies such as chromatography-mass spectrometry, inductively coupled plasmas, and many of the novel ways that antibodies have been employed to allow rapid and sensitive drug detection.

In modern times most poisoning episodes relate to synthetic products. Obviously, at an earlier and simpler time before technology permitted us to make better toxins, plant extracts and animal poisons were the poisons of choice. The Egyptian manuscript known as the Ebers Papyrus, approximately 1500 B.C., tells us that arsenic, lead, antimony, mandrake, hemlock, opium, aconite, and some other plant products were known for their poisonous properties even at that early time. Ancient poisons were used as weapons, but a unique feature of ancient use was the often ceremonial character of their application. Some poisons were ordeal agents, i.e., they were provided to a victim as an alleged means of deciding guilt or innocence. If the accused survived the exposure to the poison, the gods were smiling upon him and affirming his innocence.

More than 16,000 years before Christ, the Masai tribe of Kenya used poisons in darts and arrows to increase the lethality of their weapons and assure successful hunting. Among those arrow tip toxins was strophanthin, a cardiotoxic agent derived from plants indigenous to Kenya. Nor was the concept of arrows dipped in poison limited to Africa. In ancient India, as recorded in Rg Veda, an Indian text of 1100 B.C., aconitine was employed to charge arrows. The Greeks used hellebore, as described by Homer, in the same manner. The Romans dipped their arrows and darts into the blood of serpents. This practice is related by Ovid who lived from 43 B.C. to 18 A.D.

Ultimately, attempts were made to introduce a modicum of organization into the growing knowledge of poisons. These rudimentary efforts at classification included the division of poisons into those which are slow acting such as arsenic vs. fast-acting substances like strychnine. Dioscorides, a Roman physician, divided poisons according to their origin as vegetable, mineral, or animal.

Among the animal poisons, snake venom was, not surprisingly, best known. Nicander, a Greek of the second century B.C., experimented with snake venom and the poisons of other animals. He used prisoners as his unwilling subjects. Cleopatra is arguably among the most famous of the earliest victims of animal poisons. History records that she took her own life by allowing an asp to bite her.

Plants probably are the largest source of poisons from the perspective of the sheer number and variety of toxins and this is true even in modern times. The ancients took note of the toxic properties of plants. Theophrastus, writing in the fourth century B.C., described many poisonous plants in *De Historia Plantarum*. Some of the nations of antiquity such as Athens, used plants, e.g., hemlock, for official executions. Socrates was a victim of this practice as described in *Phaedo*, a work of Plato. As mankind became aware of the deadly nature of some plants such as hemlock, henbane, hellebore, etc., knowledge of their euphoric and abusable properties also spread. Opium and cannabis were two such plants well-known to the ancients.

Heavy metals caused very many problems in former centuries, problems which have not fully dissipated despite the higher level of modern knowledge. Lead, mercury, arsenic, and antimony were the major agents among metals which caused toxicity in ancient times. Lead was probably the most problematic. It may have, in the opinion of some scholars, been a major factor in the fall of the Roman Empire. The Romans not only used lead heavily in plumbing, but also in the preparation of food. Wine was exposed to leaden vessels for long periods because the Romans preferred the sweet taste which resulted.

No one knows what the first historical instance of deliberate poisoning for murderous purposes was; however, by the time of Rome, poisoners were very busy and regularly employed by those in power. The emperor Sulla proclaimed the Lex Cornelia in 81 B.C. By its provisions, a noble person who was guilty of poisoning would be exiled. A low-born poisoner would be given to wild beasts in the Coliseum. Locusta was a famous poisoner of antiquity. Among her many victims was the emperor Claudius. Locusta dispatched Claudius with arsenic or mushrooms, the exact nature of the poison not being clear from surviving historical documents. Locusta also poisoned Nero's stepbrother, Brittanicus, as part of an effort to control succession to the throne. The emperors were not fools and knew that death by poison was a constant occupational threat to anyone who aspired to such a high position. One way to minimize this threat was to employ tasters who sampled the food before the emperor. In the case of Brittanicus, legend has it that Locusta heated the food so intensely that the victim had to wait before eating it although the taster ate it while still hot. While the food was cooling, Locusta slipped in the toxin at the propitious time.

ANTIDOTES

Ancient man had such fear of poison that he made attempts from the earliest times to lessen their effects. The expectation that an antidote, i.e., a specific cure, could be found or designed was part fanciful dreaming but part observation. In other words, scientists of the time noted that some animals were partially or fully immune to toxins which would kill others. Among men there was a great difference in apparent susceptibility to poisons, generating the belief that unknown factors might be discovered that would convey protection.

In Homer's *Odyssey*, Ulysses is advised to take "moli." This may be an extract of Galanthus, now known to contain an inhibitor of cholinesterase. In turn, Ulysses would be exposed to deadly plants like *Datura stramonium*, if famine struck on his journeys. Moli, if it does mean Galanthus, would indeed be protective against ingested Datura. This might be the first recorded reference to an antidote.

King Mithridates VI of Pontus (132 to 63 B.C.) lived in a region where poisoning was even more common than in other parts of the Roman Empire. Accordingly, he dedicated himself to discovery of a universal antidote. He worked long before the days of informed consent and so his experiments could be freely performed on slaves and criminals whose objections to such treatment fell on deaf ears. The concoction which the king eventually prepared was called a mithridatum. It is said that he took it every day. Perhaps it had some effect because he lived to be 69, well beyond the expected longevity of the time. Legend has it that he tried to commit suicide in later life, but the poison he now took to end his life had no effect because of his long years of mithridatum use. He died by the sword as told by Galen, the great physician of the ancient world.

The universal antidote of Mithridates was called a mithridatum. A more common term for universal antidote in the ancient world was theriac. The theriac of Andromachus (68 to 37 B.C.) was more famous than the mithridatum. Andromachus was the chief physician to Nero and prepared his theriac with the usual assortment of incredible materials including viper flesh, squills, opium, and 70 other substances. The inclusion of opium suggests why this theriac was considered effective. This theriac surivived the test of time and was still in use during the eighteenth century. Despite the abundant superstition that was prevalent during much of the history of Andromachus's theriac and those of others, there is a possibility that theriacs did more good than harm. It is only a possibility, however, and we shall never know the answer to this question with exactitude.

Charms were also proposed and employed to ward off the ill effects of poisons. Unicorn horns were, perhaps, most famous in this regard but toadstones and bezoar stones were also popular. A toadstone is an inorganic inclusion found in the head of a toad and alleged to extract poison from a bodily site when held in its proximity. Unicorn horns came into vogue in the fourth century B.C. Because there were no unicorns, one might reasonably question the very existence of unicorn horns. In actuality, they were narwhal tusks or rhinoceros horns. Merely drinking water from the horn was said to confer protection. Remarkably, the pre-scientific era was not completely without studies to explore the alleged properties of theriacs and charms. Thus, a study of 1593 showed that unicorn horns would have some protective value on dogs poisoned with arsenic. It was not clear, however, as to whether the study was conducted in an objective, controlled manner.

Bezoar stones were stomach or intestinal calculi made of calcium phosphate which deposited around a gallstone or other foreign material. Goats, cows, and apes were their sources. The stones were used in multiple ways but always to prevent or treat poisoning. It is, perhaps, not surprising that man would bestow some measure of reverence on an object which arose from the body in an unusual manner and endow it with supernatural characteristics.

MIDDLE AGES

As was true of most aspects of human development, little occurred in relation to toxicology during the Dark Ages, between the Fall of Rome and the earliest stages of the Renaissance. A landmark event in toxicology was the appearance of a book by Moses Maimonides (1135–1204), Treatise on Poisons and their Antidotes, in 1198. Predictably, a lot of his book supported ineffective or dangerous practices. He did, however, discuss suctioning to remove superficial poisons and emesis to reduce poison uptake. For many poisons he provided accurate descriptions of the specific symptoms associated with exposure to them.

An important figure in toxicology is Paracelsus (1493–1541) whose real name was Theophrastus Bombastus von Hohenheim. Like many of his contemporaries he was mired in superstition and half truths but still must be credited with greater recognition of the true nature of medical problems than the vast majority of other medieval physicians. Paracelsus recognized that the basic nature of poisons was chemical and not supernatural. His greatest contribution is his teaching that the dose makes the poison, an important fact that most modern people do not understand. Paracelsus stated, "What is there that is not poison? All things are poison and there is nothing without poison. Solely the dose determines that a thing is not a poison."

POISONERS

Poisoners of the Middle Ages are better known in history than their colleagues of antiquity. Murder by administration of poison reached an art form by the fifteenth century. One could go to school to learn this trade and the very best practitioners of the art in Venice were called the Council of Ten. Like contemporary hit men they conducted their trade for profit when hired to do so.

The Borgia family of Florence has been given credit for an especially high level of knowledge in this context. A mixture called la cantarella, whose true nature is not known, was the usual vehicle of their murderous activity. La cantarella may have contained arsenic and phosphorus. Pope Alexander VI, Rodrigo Borgia, and his son, Cesare, are alleged to have killed many members of the nobility and the church with la cantarella.

Catherine de Medici, queen of France (1547–1559), brought poisoning skills from Italy to France. It is said that she learned a great deal about poisoning by experimenting with the sick, poor, and criminal. Several political poisonings were ascribed to her actions. Other celebrated practitioners of this art during the late Middle Ages included Madame Giulia Toffana, executed in 1719, and murderer of more than 600 victims. Toffana dispatched her victims with arsenic trioxide. French women who murdered with poison included Marchioness de Brinvilliers and Catherine Deshayes, who were executed just 4 years apart in the late seventeenth century. De Brinvilliers was not limited to one poison but used mercury bichloride, arsenic, lead, copper sulfate, and antimony. Deshayes specialized in family planning and executed 2000 infants and an uncounted number of husbands. She is alleged to have used a mixture of aconite, arsenic, belladonna, and opium. Because she practiced sorcery, she was burned at the stake as a witch.

ADVANCES IN TOXICOLOGY

In the late eighteenth century there lived a French physician named Bonaventure Orfila. Such were his contributions to the growth of scientific knowledge in toxicology that he has been called the Father of Modern Toxicology. Proclaiming that investigations of deaths were too important to be left to dabblers he emphasized that toxicology must be a separate science and autopsy and chemical analysis must be its foundation. He wrote a text which went through five editions and was truly a landmark in scientific history, Traite des Poisons (1814).

During the nineteenth century, written works on toxicology contributed greatly to the systematic growth of the science. European and American scientists wrote texts which improved the chemical and medical understanding of poisons. Sophisticated methods (for the time) were developed to confirm the presence of toxins. Because arsenic was such a common means of murder, it became the focus of early analytic work. No fewer than three scientists developed methods to test for arsenic. James Marsh, Hugo Reinsch, and Max Gutzeit gave their names to methods some of which are still in use today. At this same time in history, medical science began to explore pharmaceuticals in a more rigid and systematic manner. Great scientists, especially in France and Germany, made contributions to the understanding of human physiology and drug interactions within the body.

THERAPY

By the sixteenth century, rudimentary efforts were being made to study poisoning therapy in a scientific manner removed from the veil of superstition and witchcraft that had characterized the practice of treatment and prevention in earlier centuries. Secundus designed a stomach pump in 1769. In 1805, Philip Physick, an American surgeon, employed the pump to attempt gastric lavage. He washed out the stomachs of two children who had ingested opium. Edward Jukes, a British surgeon, was more systematic. He did animal experimentation and, when he was ready, he practiced on himself. Jukes swallowed a lethal dose of opium and pumped his own stomach. He experienced some minor effects and the experiment was a success. Scheele (1773) and Lowitz (1785) described the nature of charcoal adsorption. Some time later, in 1813, a French chemist, M. Bertrand, realized that charcoal, because of its high affinity in binding a wide assortment of chemicals, might have medical value in treating poisoning. He heroically ingested an overdose of arsenic trioxide mixed with charcoal and survived. A French pharmacist, Touery, conducted a similar experiment in 1831, only this time the audience was the French Academy of Science. Touery survived ten times the lethal dose of strychnine thanks to the adsorptive properties of charcoal.

MODERN TOXICOLOGY

In common with other practical sciences toxicology grew at a regular rate from the late nineteenth century to the present time. Society recognized its value as the drug industry grew and more people suffered toxic reactions to drugs. Other stimulating factors contributing to toxicologic growth in modern times are the high number of suicides, the many toxic manifestations arising from pesticides, synthetic chemicals, and other modern chemicals, and the parallel growth in the science of analytical chemistry.

Modern toxicology is characterized by extremely sophisticated scientific investigation and evaluation of toxic exposures of all kinds. To a large degree this has been made possible by the widespread application of computers to analytical equipment. Coupled with other chemical and electronic innovations, modern instruments can detect quantities of toxins that are much smaller than those that could be measured in the past. Analytic methods are not only highly sensitive, but they are also capable of extreme specificity so that compounds can be implicated in poisoning episodes to the near certain exclusion of other highly similar compounds. In the course of this text the reader will learn to appreciate the sophistication and application of technologies such as chromatography-mass spectrometry, inductively coupled plasmas, and many of the novel ways that antibodies have been employed to allow rapid and sensitive drug detection.

THE PROBLEM OF POISONING

How extensive is the problem of poisoning? The dimensions of this medical and national problem may be inferred from several sources. Data are maintained in various forms by the American Association of Poison Control Centers, by the Drug

Abuse Warning Network (DAWN), and by medical examiners, to name just a few sources.

A survey of hospital emergency departments by DAWN showed an increase of heroin-related admissions on the order of 44% (21,400 to 30,800) in just 12 months (mid-1992 to 1993). Cocaine-related incidents increased in the same year from 57,700 to 61,000, an increase of 5.7%. Methamphetamine, phencyclidine, and marijuana all rose in relation to emergency department visits during this period by 61, 45, and 19%, respectively.[1]

DAWN also reveals that use of illicit and potentially harmful substances on the part of pregnant women is widespread, as statistics based on the entire nation show here:[1]

	Percent of Pregnant Women Who Used Substance During Pregnancy	Estimated Number of Pregnant Users
Cigarettes	20.4	820,000
Alcohol	18.8	756,900
Prescription sedatives or analgesics	11.2	449,000
Marijuana	2.9	119,000
Prescription tranquilizers	1.4	55,400
Cocaine	1.1	45,000
Any illicit drug	5.5	221,000

Medical examiner data are revealing in regard to the number of deaths associated with specific drugs. These data show that the largest reporting 26 metropolitan areas had 5628 total drug-related deaths in 1990 and this figure grew to 7485 by 1993, a growth in such deaths of 33% in just 3 years. Medical examiner data are broken down on the basis of each drug: 76 drugs are mentioned at least 10 times, with cocaine the number one drug in associated fatalities with 3910 cocaine-related deaths from these 26 municipalities. Heroin/morphine were reported in 3805 cases while alcohol, in third place, had 3444 mentions.[1]

POISON CONTROL CENTERS

Poison Control Centers, with their mission of providing helpful information and tracking the national incidence of poisoning, have the most extensive data bank on overdose and poisoning. Each year they publish an extensive review of the previous year's national experience in dealing with the poisoning epidemic.[2,3] By 1996 there were 67 Poison Control Centers (PCC) in the United States. It is estimated that these centers serve 232 million people. In 1996 the number of requests for help reached 2,155,952. When subdivided by age, the number of calls related to poisoning and suspected poisoning incidents involved a heavy preponderance of pediatric ingestions (Figure 1.1). Over 39% of calls were for children 3 years of age or younger and 53% for children under 6. Less than 25% of PCC requests for help involved adults over 20 years of age.

Reasons for Overdose: Nonfatalities
Unintentional Exposure

General	76.4%
Therapeutic error	4.6
Bite/sting	3.6
Item misuse	2.9
Food poisoning	2.2
subtotal	89.7%

Intentional Exposure

Suicide	7.7%
Misuse	1.4
Abusive use	1.2
subtotal	10.3%

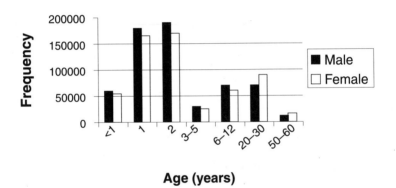

Age (years)

FIGURE 1.1 Age distribution of all poisonings.

Among this massive total of over 2 million exposures, the total of fatalities was only 726. Although most calls seeking help for poison exposures were for pediatric subjects, children under 6 years old comprised only 4% of fatalities; 61% of deaths were in the 20- to 49-year-old bracket (Figure 1.2).

Evaluating the reasons for poison exposure, PCC found that most non-fatal overdoses were unintentional (89%), including ignorance of toxicity, accidents during use, therapeutic error, and food poisoning. The number of fatal intoxications, however, included a major fraction of intentional overdoses. Only 110 of 726 fatalities were unintentional (15.1%), whereas 554 (76%) were deemed to be intentional and 152 were abuse or misuse, which is also labeled as intentional overdose.

One of the more amazing findings in PCC data is that 164,085 calls were in regard to a poison exposure for suicidal purposes. Despite this impressive total, only 358 calls were logged in relation to a successful suicide. This wide disparity between threatened and actual suicides is partly due to the doubt-laden mindset of the suicidal patient, but also reflects the simple fact that successful suicides will often occur without any contact with the PCC.

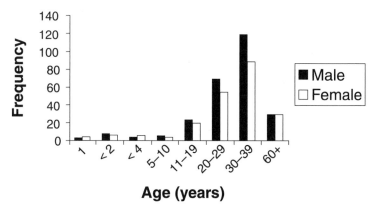

FIGURE 1.2 Age distribution of fatal poisonings.

Suicidal Overdose

7.7% (150,000) of all poison calls
54% (410) of all fatal overdoses

PCC try, insofar as is possible, to evaluate the outcome for each toxic exposure. Outcomes are classed as no effect, minor effect (minimally bothersome problem which resolved rapidly), moderate effect (not life-threatening but treatment is required), major effect (signs or symptoms which are life-threatening or resulted in significant residual disability), and death. From this perspective, the 2,000,000+ exposures had no effect 24% of the time; minor, 18.8%; moderate, 4%; major, 0.4%; and death, 0.03%. The remaining 56% of exposures were not followed up for various reasons, but most were deemed to constitute only a minor risk for significant injury.

Medical Outcome

No effect	24.0%
Minor effect	20.1
Moderate effect	4.1
Major effect	0.4
Death	<0.1

(No follow up, toxicity unlikely = 48.2%)

The majority (73.6%) of these exposures could be treated at the site of poisoning, usually in the home. However, 288,011 patients were treated in healthcare facilities and released. Those admitted to a critical care unit numbered 60,065 patients, 2.8% of the total exposures. An additional total of about 200,000 patients were referred to some level of medical care. A significant number were lost to follow up or refused referral advice. These large numbers suggest the huge economic dimensions of the poisoning problem.

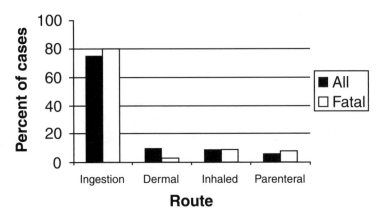

FIGURE 1.3 Route of bodily exposure in PCC-reported poisonings.

Data on the specific interventions employed are interesting. Only dilution of the poison or irrigation was used in about 1,000,000 cases. Activated charcoal was tried in about 150,000 exposures. Other remedial steps were as listed here:

Cathartic	104,447
Gastric lavage	65,554
Ipecac	39,376
Whole bowel irrigation	1912
Hemodialysis	839

Antidotes were used approximately 22,000 times. The large majority of such applications were for N-acetylcysteine (9707) or naloxone (7172).

Of great interest are those substances which are most problematic from the perspective of frequent occurrence and largest number of lethal exposures. The 10 substances or classes of substances most frequently encountered are as follows:

Substance	Number	Percent
Cleaning agents	221,261	10.3
Analgesics	208,305	9.7
Cosmetics	184,799	8.6
Plants	113,619	5.3
Cough/cold meds	106,823	5.0
Bites/envenomation	95,283	4.4
Pesticides	86,912	4.0
Foreign bodies	84,392	3.9
Topicals	77,269	3.6
Food products	73,947	3.4

The categories with the largest number of deaths are as follows:

Drug/Category	Number
Analgesics	228
Antidepressants	146
Stimulants/street drugs	120
Cardiovascular drugs	102
Alcohols	89
Sed./hypnot./antipsychotic	83
Gases/fumes	49
Chemicals	36
Anticonvulsants	25
Insecticides/pesticides	20

INTERPRETATION OF PCC DATA

Data collected by PCC are of great value to healthcare planners and others interested in disease trends and anxious to plan public health policy in the most effective manner. No other single source appears to be as thorough as the database of the PCC in regard to overdose and exposure to all manner of toxins.

Yet there are significant hazards in reading PCC data without an adequate understanding of the manner in which these data are collected and the consequent limitations associated with it. Many other incontrovertible sources indicate, for example, that the incidence of drug-associated suicide is much higher than PCC data suggest. Similarly, data from medical examiners show that deaths from drugs of abuse are much more common than one could ever suspect from PCC data. Therefore, one is wise to regard the following factors when using PCC data to evaluate the degree of poisoning.

1. PCC data are based on calls to the PC centers for assistance. Many patients are overdosed on common drugs like digoxin. When these patients present to emergency departments, there is a strong possibility that the attending physician, being familiar with the drug, will be fully aware of the appropriate treatment. The PCC will not be contacted. We expect, therefore, that PCC data must understate the incidence of overdose by drugs with which physicians are familiar.
2. Some drugs, perhaps cardiac drugs in particular, are taken by patients whose health may already be significantly compromised. It may be difficult to sort out a symptom as being due to drug overdose or the patient's underlying condition. Even if the patient is actually experiencing an adverse drug reaction, the morbidity associated with the reaction is likely to be intensified by the patient's pre-existing poor health. Some drugs, therefore, appear to cause greater toxicity as a function of the type of patient who is using them. Another example of this phenomenon would be tricyclic antidepressants. Such drugs are manifestly dangerous. Their

toxicity, however, is probably overstated because they are used by depressed patients many of whom are suicidal.

3. Drugs of abuse are likely to be under-reported because users of such substances are less likely to call the PCC for any number of reasons. Such persons will usually seek immediate medical help or will try to avoid medical care altogether.

4. Many drug-related deaths are discovered after the fact or when it is too late to help the victim. The PCC will not be contacted in such an incident and their data will thereby understate drug-related deaths, whether suicidal or accidental.

REFERENCES

1. Leikin, J.B. and Paloucek, F.P., Poisoning and Toxicology Handbook, 2nd ed., 1996, Lexi-Comp, Inc., Hudson, Ohio.

2. Litovitz, T.L. et al., 1995 Annual Report of the American Association of Poison Control Centers Toxic Exposures Surveillance System, *Amer. J. Emerg. Med.*, 14, 487–537, 1996.

3. Litovitz, T.L. et al., 1996 Annual Report of the American Association of Poison Control Centers Toxic Exposures Surveillance System, *Amer. J. Emerg. Med.*, 15, 447–500, 1997.

Questions and Exercises

1. Look up the September 2000 edition of the American Journal of Emergency Medicine. This edition is devoted entirely to toxicology. Peruse the data from Poison Control Centers on incidents of poisoning in the United States during the previous year. List:
   • Antidotes used and the number of times each was used
   • The distribution of fatalities vs. age of victim
   • The route of exposure in reported poisonings

2. Review at least three descriptions of fatal poisonings which appear in this edition of the journal described in question 1. For each incident, list the toxin, the probable dose, any intervention which might have been helpful, and the reason why the fatality occurred.

3. Check the Internet and other references to complete your knowledge of the history of toxicology. Describe one of the following:
   • Growth in the knowledge of substances which cause cancer
   • Improvements in the control of airborne pollutants such as lead
   • Improvements in workplace safety by chemical hazard control

2 Measuring Toxicity

CONTENTS

QUALITATIVE DESCRIPTIONS OF TOXICITY

There are many ways to express the relative toxicity of a substance. In one of the simplest methods, toxins have been divided into six groups (Table 2.1).

There are several shortcomings in the above qualitative description of relative toxicity. One such weakness is the width of each category. A second problem is the imprecision of the terminology. The term supertoxin, for example, is not clear.

An alternative semi-quantitative description which has the advantage of showing the extremes of toxicity is depicted in Table 2.2. This shows that the lethality of known substances can vary over an incredibly wide range of 10 orders of magnitude, extending from ethyl alcohol (which is not entirely innocuous) to botulinus toxin.

These categorizations are helpful only in providing an approximate idea of relative toxicity. While they allow one to appreciate relative magnitudes of toxicity, they avoid the inherent complexity of the subject.

The LD_{50} is the main statistic used in most toxicology studies. It is described in greater depth below. For now, it is sufficient to state that it represents the dose of a toxin which will kill 50% of a group of test subjects. While this is a valuable quantity to be aware of it is inadequate in terms of fully understanding the inherent danger present in certain substances. For one thing, the LD_{50} describes only one end-point, death. Organ damage, cancer induction, and other dangers present in substances, while they are less serious outcomes than death are, nevertheless, extremely undesirable. If a substance has a low LD_{50}, we suspect that it is also dangerous to health in exposures below the LD_{50}. While this is usually true, it does not clearly define the problem. In other words, there are many substances to which we are exposed in amounts well below the LD_{50}. If the exposure is several orders of magnitude less than the LD_{50} we might, perhaps, feel entirely safe. This is inappropriate because the potential for health damage to a degree which falls short of killing a subject cannot be predicted on the basis of the LD_{50}. A second problem with the LD_{50} is that it has a large uncertainty associated with it even in the prediction

TABLE 2.1
Relative Substance Toxicity

Rating	Toxicity	LD_{50}^{a} (rat,oral) (mg/kg)	Adult human (oral LD)	Example
1	Essentially safe	>15,000	> 1 quart	Water
2	Slightly toxic	5000–15,000	> 1 pint	Ethanol
3	Moderately toxic	500–5000	>1 ounce	Aspirin
4	Very toxic	50–500	1 tsp.–1 ounce	Dieldrin
5	Extremely toxic	5–50	Few drops	Parathion
6	Supertoxic	<5	1–2 drops	Nicotine

^{a} LD_{50} = amount which causes death in 50% of a population (see discussion below).

TABLE 2.2
The Extremes of LD_{50} of Selected Chemicals

Chemical	LD_{50} (mg/kg)
Ethanol	10,000
Sodium chloride	4000
Ferrous sulfate	1500
Morphine sulfate	900
Phenobarbital	150
Picrotoxin	5
Strychnine	2
Nicotine	1
Tubocurarine	0.5
Tetrodotoxin	0.1
Dioxin	0.001
Botulinum	0.00001

Note: Most values are based on rats; ethanol and sodium chloride were measured in mice; dioxin is based on guinea pigs.

of the outcome that is measured, death. This is because LD_{50} must be determined in animals. When the data are collected, they are extrapolated to humans. Is it reasonable to assume that a substance which is especially toxic to rats will also be very toxic to humans? Usually this assumption is correct but only in a very approximate manner. If there is reason to believe that a particular test organism has a large biochemical difference from humans in regard to the disposition of some toxin, then we must be very wary in extrapolating animal data to humans for that substance. An excellent example is dioxin. This name refers to a series of compounds, the major one of which is 2,3,7,8-tetrachlorodibenzo-para-dioxin (Figure 2.1).

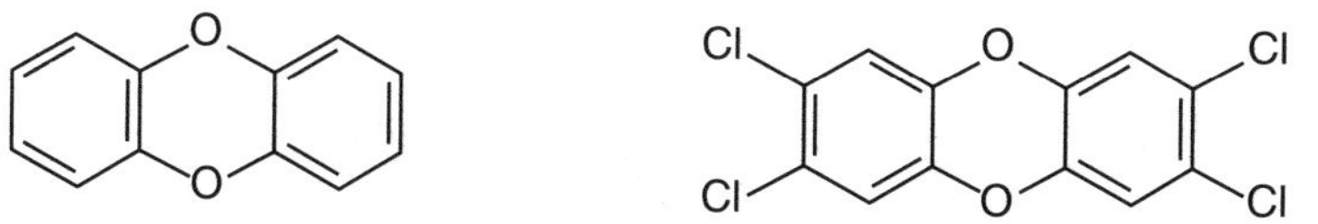

DIOXIN **2,3,7,8 TETRACHLORO-DIBENZO-P-DIOXIN**

FIGURE 2.1 Structures of dioxin and tetrachlorodioxin.

Dioxin has been described by some self-proclaimed experts as the most danger-ous chemical known to man. This statement is probably true for guinea pigs (the most dangerous chemical known to guinea pigs). The LD_{50} of dioxin for guinea pigs is about 0.6 µg/kg; however, for hamsters, the figure is 3000 µg/kg. The difference in these two numbers is a staggering example of inter-species differences. What is the LD_{50} for man? This is not known. Still, when a fertilizer plant exploded in Italy, many farm animals were killed in the surrounding area as dioxin descended upon them from the skies. The only demonstrated effect in humans, however, was chlo-racne, a severe skin rash. Dioxin was actually tested on volunteer prison inmates who received large applications of the chemical to their skin. Again, no toxicity other than chloracne was noted. Table 2.3 describes the harm done by acute vs. chronic (long-term) exposure to dioxin to humans and to animals. It will be noted that little is known about effects in humans and the table indicates only that there is a minimal risk at low exposure. Dioxin may be a carcinogen but this suspicion has not been proved conclusively.

LD_{50} values are published for many toxins for humans. Again, it is important to realize that these data are approximate for many reasons:

1. No human experiments have been done.
2. One source used for such data is deaths which occurred by accidental or suicidal exposure. Often the size of the dose is not known precisely and has to be estimated. The database from this source is usually small. Whether or not the victim was also exposed to a second or third agent is often not taken into account.
3. Additional circumstances which may have rendered the victim more or less susceptible or resistant to the toxin are often not known.

As a result of these factors, LD_{50} values published for humans have very high uncertainties. The same may be said for blood concentrations published as repre-senting overdoses. Although such data are helpful, their use is often problematic as, for example, when a decedent is found with a low level of some toxin in his blood and no other cause of death is apparent.

EXPOSURE LIMITS

A clearer idea of toxicity might be provided by certain statistics determined by agencies charged with protecting public health. The American Council of Government

---

TABLE 2.3
Effects of Dioxin in Humans and in Animals

Acute Exposure

1 ng/kg/day	Possible risk of cancer in humans
>20 ng/kg/day	Developmental defects in animals only
>500 ng/kg/day	Death in animals only

Chronic Exposure

5 pg/kg/day	Possible risk of cancer in humans
200 pg/kg/day	Liver injury in animals only
5000 pg/kg/day	Reproductive toxicity in animals only
10,000 pg/kg/day	Death in animals only

Industrial Hygienists (ACGIH) reviewed the literature and history of workplace toxic exposures over many years starting after World War II. From its in-depth studies, it published limits of exposure which enable one to estimate the inherent toxicity of various substances. ACGIH proposed threshold values that represent exposure levels above which employees and others would suffer injury from toxins. Perhaps its major statistic is the TWA or threshold weighted average, the exposure level for a standard 8-hour day, 40-hour work week. In other words, an average individual exposed to a toxin at a level greater than the TWA for a 40-hour week would be expected to experience a toxic response. If the exposure was below the TWA, no injury would be expected unless an additional factor was present. An example of such a factor would be prolonged exposure. If someone were exposed to only 90% of the TWA but for 120% of 40 hours (48 hours) in a week, the weighted result would exceed the TWA.

The following formula explains this:

$$\text{TWA} = \frac{\text{Expos. time A} \times \text{Conc. A} + \text{Expos. time B} \times \text{Conc. B} + \text{Expos. time C} \times \text{Conc. C...}}{\text{total time of work shift}}$$

In 1972 the Occupational Safety and Health Administration (OSHA) introduced the term Permissable Exposure Limit (PEL), which amounts to an updated TWA and may differ from the TWA because it comes from a different agency, is not based on the same studies, and may be more recent.

Other exposure limits have also been published. One important statistic is the IDLH, the concentration at which there is **I**mmediate **D**anger to **L**ife and **H**ealth. This statistic, developed by NIOSH (National Institute for Occupational Safety and Health) and EPA (Environmental Protection Agency), represents a level that may cause injury even from a very short duration exposure. Two similar statistics have also been used in this context: STEL, the short-term exposure limit, and TLV-C, Threshold Limit Value-Ceiling. The former, the STEL, is an individual's exposure limit over the brief time span of 15 minutes. It recognizes the fact that many toxins can cause damage from short-term, relatively high level exposure. In some situations the PEL may be misleading. An individual might be below the PEL because they

TABLE 2.4
Examples of Toxic Exposure Limits

Substance	Odor Threshold	PEL-TWA	TLV-TWA	TLV-C	IDLH
Acetone	13–20	1000	750		20,000
Ammonia	25–48		25		500
Arsine		0.05	0.05		6
Benzene		1–10	1		2000
Carbon disulfide	0.1	4	10		500
Carbon monoxide		35	50		1500
Chlorine	3.5	0.5	0.5		30
Chloroform	85		10		
Formaldehyde		3	1		100
Gasoline	25	300	300		
Hydrogen chloride	1–5			5	100
Hydrogen fluoride	0.03 mg/m^3	3		3	20
Hydrogen sulfide	10		10		300
Methylene chloride	160–620	500	50		5000
Methyl mercaptan	1.6 ppb		0.5		400
Sulfur dioxide	1	2	2		100
Toluene	0.17	200	100		
Xylene	0.05	100	100		

Note: All figures are in parts per million (ppm) unless otherwise stated.

are away from a toxin for part of the day. Nevertheless, the duration of his or her actual exposure is long enough to be injurious. Some toxins are so dangerous that a ceiling has been set, the TLV-C, which must not be exceeded for any period of time, no matter how short (Table 2.4).

There are many interesting features of the published limits as set forth in Table 2.4. It is noteworthy that the PELs and TLVs usually agree or, at least, are not notably different. Some exceptions exist such as carbon disulfide where the TLV is 2.5 times the value of the PEL. Methylene chloride is another interesting exception where the PEL is 10 times greater than the TLV, perhaps related to the relatively recent belief that methylene chloride is a suspect carcinogen. It is also worth commenting on the odor thresholds. People rely on their sense of smell to inform them of airborne hazards. It is noteworthy, however, that there is no correlation (nor should one be expected) between the odor threshold and the danger threshold. For the majority of toxins, their characteristic odors are detectable at much lower concentrations than the levels required to cause harm. This is true despite the low regard that humans have of their sense of smell and the fact that human sense of smell is, indeed, inferior to most animals'. Note, for example, that people can smell methyl mercaptan at the vanishingly low level of 1.6 ppb but the TLV is 0.5 ppm (500 ppb). For some toxins, such as methylene chloride, the permissable exposure limit is less than the odor threshold so that injury may be occurring in the absence of one's ability to recognize the odor of this chemical.

DETERMINATION OF LD_{50} AND GRAPHICAL REPRESENTATIONS

The LD_{50}, also called the median lethal dose, is the dose of a toxin that kills 50% of the tested population. This statistic is the best way to express lethality because it avoids the extremes. In other words, some animals are very sensitive to particular toxins whereas other animals are very resistant. Focusing on the median of a population gives the best and most realistic assessment of a substance's inherent toxicity. LD_{50} may be measured by providing a series of doses to a group of animals, usually the laboratory rat, the white Norway rat.

Dose is usually described in mg/kg of body weight unless a higher or lower mass unit is appropriate for a relatively harmless or relatively toxic substance. At least 10 animals are exposed at each of six doses. The grade of the material is usually technical (95% pure) because a grade of higher purity does not simulate the most likely exposure in real-life situations. In addition, a solvent and route of exposure (oral, inhalational, etc.) which are reasonable for the substance under study must be chosen.

Animals of similar weight are selected, fasted for one overnight, and randomly assigned to treatment groups. Doses are applied starting from a negative control, i.e., animals which receive the solvent only. Increasing doses are then given. It is common to perform such experiments in ascending order, i.e., progressively larger doses of toxin, to minimize the possibility of problems caused by carryover of the toxin from one dose to the next in the delivery instrument. Volumes of toxin must be small, less than 2.0 mL. This is done to minimize false conclusions that may be due to a high volume of solvent rather than to the toxin's effects. The animals are followed for an appropriate period of time and all results are tabulated. Numerical outcome is plotted in one or both of two methods: a graph of cumulative mortality vs. log dose (Figure 2.2) or a histogram of incremental deaths vs. log dose (Figure 2.3).

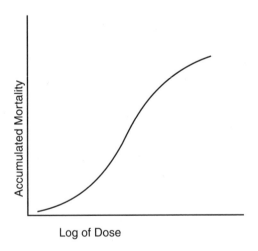

Log of Dose

FIGURE 2.2 Cumulative mortality vs. log dose.

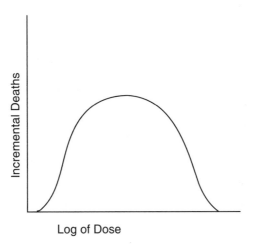

FIGURE 2.3 Incremental deaths vs. log dose.

TABLE 2.5
Sample Data from an LD$_{50}$ Experiment [a]

Dose of Toxin (mg/kg)	Mortality	Cumulative Mortality	Increm. Deaths	Log Dose
1	1	1	1	0
2	3	4	2	0.301
5	6	10	3	0.699
10	18	28	12	1
15	22	50	4	1.176
20	23	73	1	1.301
25	26	99	3	1.398
50	30	129	4	1.699
100	31	160	1	2

[a] Number of subjects = 40 in each category.

For example, assume that the data shown in the first two columns of Table 2.5 were collected in an experiment. Then the data are transformed as shown in the last three columns of the table and these three columns are plotted. The graph shown in Figure 2.4 results when cumulative mortality is plotted vs. log of dose and the LD$_{50}$ can be read from the graph as equal to the antilog of the point on the x-axis which corresponds to 50% mortality on the y-axis. In the example represented by data in Table 2.5 the answer for LD$_{50}$ is 20 mg/kg. In the second method, incremental deaths are plotted vs. log dose and a histogram is constructed (Figure 2.3). If the resulting histogram has a Gaussian shape (normal distribution), then the LD$_{50}$ equals the antilog of the x value under the center of the histogram (Figure 2.4). This method will generally not be satisfactory unless a large number of specimens are tested.

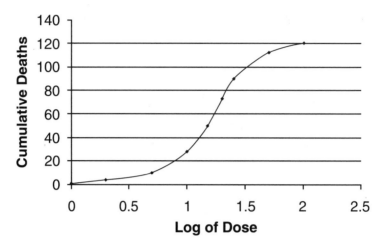

FIGURE 2.4 Graphical assessment of LD_{50}.

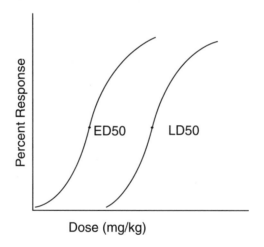

FIGURE 2.5 LD_{50} vs. ED_{50}.

Otherwise, the data may not have a Gaussian distribution simply because of variability in plotting of data.

ED_{50} AND LD_{50}

The concept of LD_{50} has been explained. An analogous concept is that of ED_{50} (median effective dose) which means the concentration of a drug at which 50% of a population of patients are effectively treated. This could be determined in an experiment which is similar to that just described for LD_{50}. Figure 2.5 shows ED_{50} and LD_{50} plotted on the same set of axes. One final useful concept is the therapeutic index. This entity is merely the LD_{50} divided by the ED_{50}. Upon consideration it will be recognized that the therapeutic index is equivalent to a safety margin. If the therapeutic index is high, it means that the LD_{50} is high, the ED_{50} is low, or both are true. This is a good situation because it means that there is a wide gap between doses that provide therapeutic effect and doses that are toxic. The opposite situation, one in which the therapeutic index is low, is bad because a small increase in dosage could cause toxicity. Drugs which have low therapeutic indices must be highly regulated when given to patients. Part of the strict control over the application of these drugs therapeutically is to measure blood concentrations regularly so that one may be certain that the patient is not reaching a potentially toxic blood level.

UNITS IN TOXICOLOGY

Concentrations studied in toxicology are the same as those used in other branches of science. Units such as mg/L are common. In toxicology, however, very low concentrations are often studied. Therefore, µg/L and ng/L are more frequently found than mg/L. It has also become popular to describe concentrations not just in the customary mass-per-volume units but often in the jargon of parts per million, parts per billion, and so on. The student of toxicology frequently needs to convert from these two systems for expressing concentrations. The table below provides the appropriate conversion factors:

Units	Abbrev. Unit	Aqueous Solution	Air
1 part per million	1 ppm	1 mg/L	$40.9 \times MW \ \mu g/m^3$
1 part per billion	1 ppb	1 µg/L	$40.9 \times MW \ ng/m^3$
1 part per trillion	1 ppt	1 ng/L	$40.9 \times MW \ pg/m^3$

EXAMPLE

An aqueous solution contains trichloroethylene at 8 ppm. What is this in mass units?

Solution:

$$1 \text{ ppm} = 1 \text{ mg/L} = 1 \ \mu g/mL$$

$$8 \text{ ppm} = 8 \times 1 \text{ mg/L} = 8 \text{ mg/L or } 8 \ \mu g/mL$$

Some explanation of these factors is in order because their origins are not immediately apparent. Pure water weighs 1 kg/L. Therefore, 1 part in a million of 1 L of water is 1 kg/1,000,000 = 1 mg. We conclude that 1 ppm is 1 mg/L. Also, because water = 1 g/mL, then 1 µg (1 g/1,000,000 µg/g) in 1 mL of water must equal 1 part per million. It is conventional when speaking of dissolved compounds that 1 ppm is understood to mean 1 part by <u>weight</u> in a million parts of water. One ppb is intuitively less concentrated than 1 ppm by a factor of 1000. Therefore, if 1 ppm equals 1 mg/L we expect that 1 ppb will equal 1 mg/L divided by 1000 or 1 μg/L. The situation with substances contained in air is more complicated because, by convention, 1 ppm, 1 ppb, etc., are understood to represent 1 molecule per million molecules of air, one molecule per billion molecules of air, and so on. Parts per million or billion, etc., are not based on weight. The derivation is as follows:

$$1 \text{ liter} = 10^3 \text{ cm}^3$$

$$1 \text{ meter}^3 = 100 \text{ cm} \times 100 \text{ cm} \times 100 \text{ cm} = 10^6 \text{ cu cm}$$

$$1 \text{ meter}^3 = 10^6 \text{ cu cm}/10^3 \text{ cu cm/L} = 10^3 \text{ liters}$$

At 25°C

$$\text{molar volume} = 22.4 \times 298/273 = 24.45 \text{ liters/mole}$$

$$\text{or } 1 \text{ meter}^3 = 10^3 \text{ liters}/24.45 = 40.9 \text{ mole gas}$$

EXAMPLE

For sulfur dioxide, the molecular weight is 64 g/mole.

Thus, 1 ppm = $40.9 \times 64 \ \mu g/m^3 = 2617 \ \mu g/m^3$

Note that this is a markedly different result than that which would have been found if the convention was to stick with absolute weight units:

1 m³ air = 40.9 moles ($28 \times 0.8 + 32 \times 0.2$) = 1177.9 g = mass of 1 cu meter of air

1 ppm of sulfur dioxide on a mass basis = 1177.9 μg/m³

1 ppm on a molecule basis is, as shown above, equal to 2617 μg/m³

The latter answer is, by convention, taken to be correct.

Problems

1. The EPA states that a sample of contaminated air contains chlorine at 50 ppb. What is this in mg/cu meters?
2. Table 2.4 shows that the odor threshold for methyl mercaptan is 1.6 ppb. What is this in ppm? What is it in ng/L?
3. Cocaine metabolite is found in a urine specimen at a concentration of 160 ng/mL. What is this in ppm? in ppb?

4. If aspirin is therapeutically effective in the average patient at a blood concentration of 10 mg/dL and the lethal blood level is 100 mg/dL, what is the therapeutic index for aspirin?

5. A new drug is studied and the following data are collected in rats in an effort to determine the LD_{50}. Use these data to calculate the LD_{50}:

Dose (mg/kg)	Mortality
2	1
4	2
8	3
12	7
15	8
20	9
50	16
100	20

3 Therapy

CONTENTS

The primary goal of this book is to understand toxicology from a scientific perspective. It is not intended to be a guide toward treatment, an area which is covered in much greater detail in other fine texts. Therefore, this chapter deals with treatment in a brief manner with the emphasis on the scientific aspects of the therapy of poisoning.

Stages in Work-Up of Suspected Poisoning

Evaluation
    Stabilization
    History and physical
    Toxidrome?
    Laboratory testing
Management
    Decontamination
    Enhanced elimination
    Administration of antidote

APPROACH TO TREATMENT

The first step in the treatment of a potential poisoning is the stabilization of the patient. The attending physician must assure that the patient's vital functions are protected before he/she becomes concerned about the probable identity of the offending agent. Securing the airway and ensuring cardiopulmonary function must receive the highest priority. Vital signs must be recorded frequently. Oxygen should be administered to any patient with respiratory distress or altered mental status. Continuous ECG, pulse oximetry, and establishment of IV access are necessary early steps for the patient who is delirious, stuporous, or comatose. Pulse oximetry measures pulse rate and the degree of oxygen saturation of hemoglobin. While this technique is valuable, the treating physician must remember that results reported by pulse oximetry may not reflect the patient's actual status.

Cautions about Pulse Oximetry

Falsely elevated by
  • Fetal hemoglobin
  • Carboxyhemoglobin
Falsely depressed by
  • Methemoglobin
No indication of carbon dioxide levels
No indication of cellular utilization of oxygen

Patients with altered mental status must be considered for possible administration of oxygen, glucose, thiamine, flumazenil, and/or naloxone. Oxygen should be given unless there is unequivocal evidence of adequate oxygenation. Glucose should be provided for any patient with altered mental status if the serum glucose is less than 80 mg/dL or if the glucose level is unknown due to delayed testing. Glucose infusion to a patient with a pre-existing hyperosmotic load will intensify the intracranial pressure; however, this factor is minor compared to the harm done by delaying glucose for a patient with severe hypoglycemia. Thiamine should be provided when a patient is evidently malnourished and is receiving glucose. Naloxone (Narcan) is recommended for any patient for whom clinical evaluation suggests a history of opiate use. Because naloxone has a very short half-life (1 hour) it may be necessary to continuously re-dose the patient with this narcotic antagonist, especially if the opiate which the patient used was a long-acting one. Alternatively, Nalmefene (Revex), a newer opioid antagonist with a prolonged half-life of 8 to 10 hours, may be more effective. Flumazenil (Romazicon) is an antagonist of the benzodiazepines. It can completely reverse a coma within 1 to 2 minutes when the coma is due solely to benzodiazepine poisoning. Some emergency physicians do not employ it because benzodiazepine overdose is usually mild and because of possible problems related to its use. On the other hand, benzodiazepine use and abuse are very common, so flumazenil may have a place in emergency treatment of overdose.

Problems Related to Flumazenil Administration

Possible withdrawal seizures in the chronic benzodiazepine abuser
Breakthrough seizures in patients with underlying seizure disorder
Seizures in tricyclic antidepressant overdose since TCAs lower seizure threshold
Cardiac arrhythmias in patients with multiple drug overdose

When attempting to stabilize the overdosed patient the treating physician may encounter seizures as a major complicating factor. Many overdoses cause seizures as one of their most problematic features. Benzodiazepines are often effective in treating seizures. Two unique situations are seizures induced by theophylline or isoniazid. The former may not respond to benzodiazepines and phenobarbital or dialysis may be necessary. For isoniazid overdose, pyridoxine is usually effective.

HISTORY AND PHYSICAL EXAMINATION

Taking a good history is possibly more important for drug overdose than for other medical problems, but is also more difficult. Determine the mode of exposure (inhalation, ingestion, etc.), state of the toxin (solid, liquid, gas), quantity, time of exposure, and other circumstances. All of this information may help to estimate the patient's risk for morbidity and mortality. Remember, however, that history from an overdosed patient is not likely to be accurate. The patient may deny suicidal or illicit drug-taking behavior. The testimony of family and friends of the victim may be more accurate than that of the victim.

Physical exam should be comprehensive and focus on respiratory abnormalities, abnormal pulse rate or blood pressure, CNS aberrations, GI disturbances, cardiac irregularities, and skin disorders.

It is usually helpful to consider the possibility of classifying the patient as one of the known toxidromes. A toxidrome is a constellation of symptoms or a syndrome of characteristic features associated with some drug or class of drugs. Recognition of a toxidrome can help with the selection of therapeutic steps, especially administration of an antidote if one is available. Recognition of a toxidrome also will allow for faster initiation of therapy than waiting for laboratory results. There are problems associated with the concept of diagnosis based on categorizing into toxidromes. A clinician must be very cautious and observant. Further, if a patient has been using multiple drugs or presents at a significant time lapse since ingestion, it may not be possible to accurately determine the class of agents which caused the overdose. Following is a description of the major toxidromes:

Anticholinergic Toxidrome

Signs

Tachycardia	Myoclonus	Delirium
Dry skin	Urinary retention	Seizures
Dilated pupils	Decreased bowel sounds	Coma
Raised body temperature	Agitation	

Mnemonic

Hot as a hare, Blind as a bat,
Dry as a bone, Red as a beet,
Mad as a hatter

Anticholinergic Toxidrome (Continued)
Toxins that Cause Anticholinergic Syndrome

Antihistamines	Antipsychotic drugs	Plants:
Antiparkinson drugs	Antidepressants	Jimsonweed
Atropine	Antispasmodics	Amanita
Amantadine	Muscle relaxants	

Sympathomimetic Toxidrome
Signs

Delusions	Hyperpyrexia	Hyperreflexia
Paranoia	Diaphoresis	Hypertension
Tachycardia	Mydriasis	Seizures

Note: Distinction from anticholinergic: diaphoresis and no urinary retention are characteristic of sympathomimetic; dry skin and absent bowel sounds more likely in anticholinergic.

Toxins that Cause Sympathomimetic Toxidrome

Cocaine	Amphetamine	Methamphetamine
Decongestants		
Phenylpropanolamine,		
Ephedrine, Pseudoephedrine		

Note: Caffeine and theophylline show similar physiological signs but differ from the sympathomimetics because they do not cause manic or hallucinatory symptoms.

Opiate Toxidrome
Signs

Hypotension	Respiratory depression	Bradycardia
Hypothermia	Altered mental status	Meiosis
Decreased bowel sounds		

Note: Seizures secondary to hypoxia, trauma, multiple drugs, or hypoglycemia.

Toxins that Cause Opiate Toxidrome

Morphine	Heroin	Codeine
Synthetic opiates	Semi-synthetic opiates	

Note: Check for needle tracks. Reversal of symptoms with naloxone is essentially diagnostic.

Cholinergic Toxidrome

Signs

Confusion	Agitation	Tremors
CNS depression	Delirium	Coma
Seizures	Meiosis	Tachycardia
Hypertension	Fasciculations	

Mnemonic

SLUDGE (Salivation, Lacrimation, Urination, Defecation, Gastrointestinal sounds, Emesis)

Toxins that Cause Cholinergic Toxidrome

Organophosphate insecticides	Carbamate insecticides	Pilocarpine

Hallucinogenic Toxidrome

Signs

Perceptual distortions
Depersonalization
Lack of reality sense

Toxins that Cause Hallucinogenic Toxidrome

Amphetamines	Cannabinoids	Cocaine	Phencyclidine

Sedative-Hypnotic Toxidrome

Signs

Sedation	Stupor	Delirium
Loss of CNS function	Confusion	
Coma	Apnea	

Drugs that Cause Sedative-Hypnotic Toxidrome

Anticonvulsants	Ethanol	Methadone
Antipsychotics	Fentanyl	Methocarbamol
Barbiturates	Glutethimide	Opiates
Benzodiazepines	Meprobamate	Tricyclic antidepressants

MANAGEMENT

DECONTAMINATION

This term refers to removal of the toxin from the patient, either from clothing or the physical environment of the patient, or from inside the body of the person affected. If some of the poison is adhering to the patient's clothing or in any other manner he is still physically capable of further exposure, then the patient must be removed from the toxic environment or have his contaminated clothing taken from him.

Decontamination more commonly refers to efforts made to reduce the load of toxin in the stomach or intestine prior to its absorption into the blood. This kind of intervention is theoretically valuable because of the customary interval between ingestion and absorption. In the case of sustained release preparations or slowly absorbed toxins, gastrointestinal decontamination should be especially beneficial. This therapy is, nevertheless, very controversial. In the case of certain substances, it is clearly contraindicated. It should not be attempted for highly volatile hydrocarbons which can be aspirated into the lung during decontamination. This leads to pneumonitis and a worsened situation. Decontamination of corrosives such as acids and bases should not be attempted either because of possible perforation of stomach or esophagus.

Methods of GI Decontamination

Induction of emesis
Lavage
Activated charcoal
Whole bowel irrigation

EMESIS (VOMITING)

This is typically induced with syrup of ipecac, which causes vomiting by acting on the chemoreceptor trigger zone. Ipecac is an extract of Brazil root and contains emetine and cephaline. On average, 30% of a toxin load will be removed by emesis with ipecac if the emetic is given within 1 hour of ingestion of toxin. Ipecac should not be given when the specific toxin is from the classes mentioned above for which emesis constitutes a greater hazard within the GI tract than the toxin. Ipecac may not be given to a patient with altered mental status because of the high risk of aspiration. It also is usually not employed within the ED itself because of the value of charcoal therapy, i.e., ipecac induces emesis and, therefore, interferes with the mixing of charcoal and toxin. If it is desirable to administer charcoal for purposes of binding the toxin within the GI tract, the ipecac delays the time at which charcoal may be given.

Ipecac is relatively innocuous despite the fact that cephaline is cardiotoxic. The amounts used in poisoning therapy are too low to constitute a cardiac threat; however, there are cases of persons who abused ipecac by using it in a bulimic manner and such persons exhibited cardiac arrhythmias. There are also a number of cases of

Munchausen-by-proxy (a disorder in which a parent or other caregiver poisons or, in another manner, undermines a child's health in order to attract attention to themselves) in which babies manifested cardiac symptoms secondary to a parent secretly administering ipecac to them. In general, a much greater problem for these babies was the failure to thrive associated with the chronic vomiting brought on by the ipecac.

OROGASTRIC LAVAGE

This method consists essentially of rinsing the patient's stomach with water or saline lavage solution by means of a tube inserted through the patient's mouth or nose. Once the tube is in place and solution delivered, a syringe is attached to the tube and the stomach contents are suctioned. It is of some value when initiated within 1 hour of ingestion of the toxin. If the patient does not have a gag reflex, then lavage may result in stomach contents being aspirated into the lung with potentially catastrophic consequences. In that case, endotracheal intubation with a cuffed endotracheal tube protects the airway from aspiration. Placement of the tube is difficult and any indication of problems such as cyanosis suggests that the tube has entered the larynx rather than the esophagus. The lavage process is continued until the return solution is clear and free of any evidence of the presence of further toxin.

ACTIVATED CHARCOAL

The theory behind the use of charcoal is that it binds many chemicals and prevents their absorption into the bloodstream. Instead, the toxin–charcoal complex ideally passes through the GI tract and is excreted together with the feces. A 10:1 charcoal-to-toxin ratio is usually provided and charcoal administration may be repeated several times at 3- to 4-hour intervals if necessary.

Charcoal Binding

Some Substances Bound to Charcoal
   Arsenic, cocaine, digitalis, tricyclic antidepressants, salicylates, isoniazid, mercuric chloride,
      theophylline, acetaminophen, nicotine, parathion, phenothiazines, phenytoin, alcohol,
      propoxyphene, many others
Some Substances not Bound
   Lithium, iron, potassium

It is difficult to accurately generalize but, to a first approximation, charcoal binds well to nonpolar drugs and toxins and binds poorly to polar substances.

WHOLE BOWEL IRRIGATION

This relatively new process essentially consists of flushing the entire GI tract with the intention of drastically reducing transit time and, therefore, limiting the opportunity for toxins to be absorbed into the bloodstream. A polymeric material, polyethylene glycol (Golytely, Colyte) is employed which prevents a net transfer of molecules between the irrigating fluid and the blood during the process. Whole bowel irrigation is continued for approximately 5 to 6 hours or until the effluent from the rectum has the same characteristics as the fluid being instilled. This procedure is especially valuable for toxins such as lithium or iron which are not removed by charcoal. Obviously, in common with other methods for decontamination, it must be employed soon after the toxin exposure has occurred.

ENHANCED ELIMINATION

An acid or base load may be provided to a patient and will result in change in the urinary pH. If a substance is present in the blood and it has a pK near the pH of the blood, then this manipulation may change the charge status of the substance. This is shown by the following equations:

$$\text{Acidify Blood} \rightarrow \text{Increased } H^+ \text{ concentration} \tag{3.1}$$

$$\text{Drug}^{(-)} + H^{(+)} \rightarrow \text{DrugH}^{(0)} \text{ (uncharged drug)} \tag{3.2}$$

$$\text{DrugH}^{(0)} + OH^{(-)} \rightarrow \text{Drug}^{(-)} \text{ (negatively charged drug)} \tag{3.3}$$

This technique is also called ion trapping and depends on the fact that charged species are less likely to cross biological membranes. Thus, if the urine is rendered alkaline, an acidic drug such as salicylic acid is converted to a salt within the kidney. This is illustrated by Eq. 3.3. The salicylate anion which carries a negative charge is now more prone to remain in the renal filtrate than to be reabsorbed back into the blood. In other words, it is more rapidly excreted from the body. Converting urine to an alkaline pH is, therefore, an effective means for enhancing the elimination of acids such as salicylates, barbiturates, methotrexate, and others. Conversely, it is possible to increase the acidity of the urine and thereby increase the charged character of drugs which are basic. Basic drugs such as tricyclic antidepressants or phencyclidine can be excreted more rapidly by acidifying the urine. This is not recommended, however, because the benefits of improved elimination usually are more than offset by the deleterious effects of the blood acidosis on cardiac and CNS function.

DIALYSIS AND HEMOPERFUSION

Dialysis is the process in which the blood is circulated through a bath in which a semipermeable membrane separates the components of the blood from the constituents of the dialysis fluid (Figure 3.1). In dialysis the various substances in blood will diffuse across into the dialysis bath provided that they are small enough (low molecular weight) to transit the membrane and their concentration is lower in the bath than in blood. Many factors relate to the potential effectiveness of dialysis. Tissue binding of the toxin, high volume of distribution for the toxin, and high molecular weight are three factors which diminish the efficacy of dialysis. Lithium, methanol, isopropanol, salicylates, theophylline, and ethylene glycol are examples

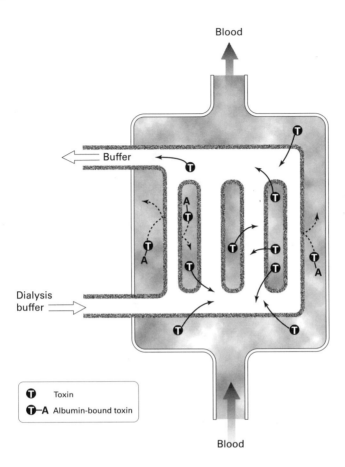

FIGURE 3.1 Dialysis.

of substances which respond well to this therapy and are quite rapidly removed. A toxin which does not respond is digoxin. This is due to the fact that digoxin is largely tissue bound. Because very little of this drug is found in the blood, it makes sense that treatment of the blood to affect its removal would not be especially efficacious.

Dialysis can be conducted with an external bath, in which case it is known as hemodialysis. It can also be carried out in the patient's peritoneal cavity (peritoneal dialysis). The latter form is easier to set up and does not require as much instrumentation; however, the rate of toxin removal is much slower by peritoneal than by hemodialysis.

Hemoperfusion is a process in which the blood is pumped through an external cartridge (Figure 3.2). It has the advantage of rapidly exposing the blood to a filtering device and is theoretically faster for removal of toxins. The cartridge used may contain charcoal or some other adsorbent. Hemoperfusion can be effective for toxins that are sluggish in responding to dialysis due, for example, to their protein binding in serum or their relatively high molecular weights.

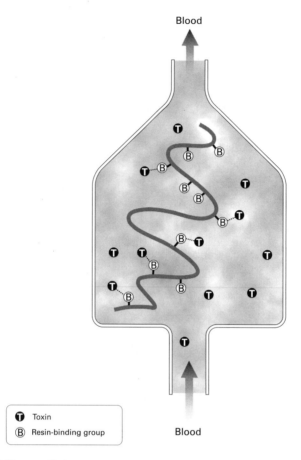

FIGURE 3.2 Hemoperfusion.

Some Drugs Removed by Dialysis

Acetaminophen	Fluoride	Methanol
Aluminum	Formaldehyde	Methotrexate
Amphetamine	Iodides	Methyldopa
Antimony	Isoniazid	Oxalic acid
Calcium	Isopropanol	Phenobarbital
Carbamazepine	Lithium	Potassium chloride
Disopyramide	Magnesium	Quinidine
Ethylene glycol	Meprobamate	Theophylline

ANTIDOTES

Once the toxin has reached the biological receptor it is very difficult to provide any further specific treatment other than supportive care. The one exception to this statement is use of antidotes when available. This term is understood to mean a medicinal intervention that is specific to a toxin and is effective only for that toxin or others closely related to it. The term is sometimes used loosely when applied to a substance that acts indirectly and weakly on the mechanism of some toxin. Some would prefer defining an antidote as any substance that raises the lethal dose of a toxin. This is a looser definition which does not require that the antidote be specific in any manner.

An antidote might appear to be the ideal treatment for poisoning. It sometimes is. However, no antidote is completely without side effects. Many are only semi-specific. All must be given in a timely manner. In view of the many conditions relating to the administration of antidotes, it is perhaps not surprising that they are given with relative infrequency. According to the American Association of Poison Control Centers (AAPCC), antidotes were employed in only 0.9% (16,536 times among 1,713,462 cases) of the poisoning incidents about which they were contacted in 1990. The frequency of use rose to 1.3% of cases by 1993. The ten antidotes used most frequently are as follows:

N-acetylcysteine
Naloxone
Atropine
Deferoxamine
Antivenins
Ethanol
Hydroxycobalamin
Digibind
Pralidoxime

It is useful to subdivide antidotes into four classes: chemical, receptor, dispositional, and functional. Chemical antidotes react with the poison, resulting in formation of a compound with lesser toxicity or reduced absorbability. An example is calcium chloride for oxalic acid poisoning. This antidote forms calcium oxalate when it reacts with oxalic acid and the calcium oxalate has low solubility which effectively limits its toxicity. Metal chelating agents are also examples of this type of antidote. Receptor antidotes compete with the poison for receptor sites. Naloxone, for example, reverses opiate-induced respiratory depression by binding to receptors and, thus, displaces the opiate from the receptor. Physostigmine also belongs to this category, in a manner of speaking. It inhibits the activity of cholinesterase. This action limits the poisonous effects of atropine and other anti-cholinergic compounds, which extends the activity of cholinesterase to harmful limits.

Dispositional antidotes reduce the amount of toxin available to tissues. They can do this in various ways including altering absorption, metabolism, distribution, or excretion of toxic agents. Acetaminophen is potentially extremely toxic and exerts its detrimental action by forming a toxic metabolite. The antidote, N-acetylcysteine, a dispositional antidote, limits the supply of this toxic metabolite by converting it to a nontoxic form.

Functional antidotes are antagonists. They have no direct action on the toxin itself nor on its action. However, they act on one biochemical system to offset the actions of a second biochemical system, the latter being the one affected by the toxin. As an example, the toxicity of many drugs or insect stings includes an immunological reaction which can reach anaphylactic proportions as the victim experiences severe breathing difficulties from bronchoconstriction. Epinephrine can reverse this by causing bronchial dilation with the restoration of normal breathing.

The Poison Control Centers include the compounds listed below among their clinically useful antidotes. They are mentioned briefly here and discussed in greater depth in the relevant portions of this text.

Antidote	Poison	Comments
Acetylcysteine	Acetaminophen	Must be given < 24 hours post-ingestion; activated charcoal absorbs antidote
Amyl nitrate	Cyanide	Provide immediately; converts hemoglobin to methemoglobin which becomes cyanide sink
Antivenin	Snake venom	Polyvalent antiserum raised against common rattlesnakes; binds venom *in vivo*
Atropine	Organophosphate	Causes anticholinergic activation which counters cholinergic activity of insecticide
Calcium EDTA	Lead	Chelating agent
Calcium gluconate	Hydrofluoric acid	Forms insoluble, non-absorbable fluorides
Deferoxamine	Iron	Very high affinity for iron; discontinue therapy when urine color returns to normal
Digoxin immune Fab	Digitalis and other cardiac glycosides	Synthetic antibody raised for medicinal purposes
Dimercaprol	Arsenic, some other metals	Chelating agent; reacts with adjacent sulfhydryls
Ethanol	Methanol, toxic alcohols	Competitive inhibitor of metabolizing enzyme
Flumazenil	Benzodiazepines	Receptor antagonist
Glucagon	Calcium channel	Some activity with beta blockers and hypoglycemic agents
Leucovorin	Methotrexate	A form of folic acid
Methylene Blue	Methemoglobin inducers	Stimulates alternative oxidative pathway
Naloxone	Opiates	Receptor antagonist
D-penicillamine	Arsenic, other metals	Chelator
Physostigmine	Atropine, anticholinergics	Acts on the neurotransmission by acetylcholine at the synapse agents
Pyridoxine	Isoniazid, some mushrooms	
Succimer	Lead, arsenic, mercury	Chelating agent

Questions and Exercises

1. See a case study at the end of a chapter in this book. Correlate each aspect of the patient's history and treatment with the stages described for work-up of a poisoning in this chapter.
2. See the case study, "Mass Casualty or Bugs All over Me," at the end of Chapter 25. Compare this patient's presentation to the various toxidromes discussed in this chapter and decide which toxidrome matches symptoms most closely.
3. A patient is poisoned by amphetamine. Should attempts be made to adjust the pH of his urine as part of his treatment? Explain. Another patient is overdosed with digoxin. Should this patient's urine be pH adjusted?

Case Study 1: Child Abuse or Mother Abuse?

A 3-month-old baby was brought to the emergency department by his parents who described the child's refusal to feed, lethargy, and rapid breathing rate. The child was not responding to physical stimulation and was found on laboratory testing to have severe acidosis, pH equal to 7.02, anion gap elevated at 26.3, and bicarbonate depressed to 3 mmol/L. The child also had hypoglycemia and was positive for urinary ketones. Further testing included blood cultures and routine drug screening.

At this point what are possible <u>toxicologic</u> explanations of these findings?
a) Salicylate poisoning
b) Acetaminophen overdose
c) Ethylene glycol or several other volatiles
d) Tricyclic antidepressants

The findings are, of course, too few to draw definite conclusions. Acetaminophen and tricyclics are very unlikely because they do not cause, as one of their primary features, a metabolic acidosis. Some of this child's findings are consistent with salicylates although the degree of acidosis is extreme for salicylates, which cause mixed respiratory alkalosis-metabolic acidosis. Ethylene glycol poisoning is a possibility. None of the presenting symptoms, as briefly as they have been described up to this point, is inconsistent with ethylene glycol poisoning.

The additional routine drug screening was negative. However, an independent laboratory reported acetone at 215 mg/L and ethylene glycol at 180 mg/L. Because the parents could not explain the baby's exposure to ethylene glycol, the child was removed from them and placed in protective custody.

Two months later, the child was brought to the emergency department by foster parents when he vomited, experienced muscle spasms, and hyperventilated. The major finding upon laboratory evaluation was severe acidosis with pH at

6.9. The child appeared close to death but was resuscitated with endotracheal intubation and bicarbonate. The commercial laboratory reported an ethylene glycol of 911 mg/L at this time. A second commercial laboratory confirmed the finding of ethylene glycol. Despite treatment for ethylene glycol overdose (dialysis and ethanol infusions), the child's condition deteriorated and he expired 3 days later. One of the commercial laboratories also tested a baby bottle allegedly used by the biologic mother who visited the baby 3 days before the last hospitalization. When this bottle was positive for ethylene glycol the mother was arrested, incarcerated, and charged with first degree murder.

The mother went to prison while pregnant and delivered her second child while incarcerated. This child was placed in foster care. Two weeks later this baby exhibited the signs which had been characteristic of the deceased brother, namely, severe acidosis and obtundation. This prompted an extensive work-up which revealed that both children suffered from the same inherited metabolic disease, methylmalonic acidemia.

Questions

Q1. A laboratory error occurred in which another compound was mistaken for ethylene glycol. This compound was
   a) Propylene glycol
   b) Ethanol
   c) Propionic acid
   d) Methylmalonic acid
Q2. This error could have been prevented by
   a) A more specific method, such as gas chromatography-mass spectrometry
   b) Extreme attention to detail
   c) Confirming the result by additional analytic steps
   d) Confirming the result by additional evaluation of the known signs of ethylene glycol poisoning
   e) All of the above
Q3. The biochemical lesion in this inherited disorder is
   a) Deficiency of methylmalonyl CoA racemase
   b) Deficiency of propionyl CoA carboxylase
   c) Deficiency of methylmalonyl CoA mutase
   d) Deficiency of branched-chain amino acid precursors

Answers and Discussion

Q1. (Answer = c) In the disease in question large amounts of methylmalonic acid are formed and much of this compound decomposes to propionic acid. In two different GC systems employed, propionic acid has a retention time fairly close to that of ethylene glycol. On one column the relative retention time is 0.69 for ethylene glycol vs. 0.64 for propionic acid relative to the internal standard, propylene glycol. On the second column the relative retention times (RRT) are 0.49 for ethylene glycol and 0.55 for propionic acid. These are close enough to cause confusion. It is noteworthy, also, that many patients have significant serum concentrations of propylene glycol arising from medications that have a base of propylene glycol. Therefore, propylene glycol could also be mistaken for ethylene glycol under some chromatographic conditions.

Q2. (Answer = e) Three different laboratories made this very serious misidentification.[1] A laboratory specializing in metabolic disease eventually clarified the issue. It seems clear that the problem arose because of the similar retention times. However, they were sufficiently different that detailed evaluations of chromatograms should have raised questions about the putative identification. Further, if authentic ethylene glycol had been added to the patient's specimen and it was then re-chromatographed, two peaks would appear, a clear indication that the original serum did not contain ethylene glycol. Gas chromatography-mass spectrometry would have distinguished these two compounds because the identification is not based merely on retention time, and the spectra of ethylene glycol and propionic acid are different. Routine volatiles analysis in most laboratories is, however, not conducted by GC-MS. Perhaps the patient should have been evaluated further by gas chromatography for ethylene glycol metabolites and by urine analysis for calcium oxalate dihydrate crystals to confirm ethylene glycol poisoning. In view of the serious nature of the penalty being imposed on the mother, a stronger case was desirable prior to her jailing.

Q3. (Answer = c) Valine, threonine, isoleucine, and methionine are catabolized to propionyl CoA, which is converted to methylmalonyl CoA and then to succinyl CoA, which enters the Kreb's cycle. Deficiencies of methylmalonyl CoA mutase prohibit the normal metabolism of these amino acids. Methylmalonic acid accumulates to a large extent in the blood of victims of this disease. It may be spontaneously degraded to propionic acid, large amounts of which were found in the blood and urine of this child.

REFERENCE

1. Shoemaker, J.D. et al., Misidentification of propionic acid as ethylene glycol in a patient with methylmalonic acidemia, *J. Pediatr.*, 120, 417–421, 1992.

4 The Role of the Laboratory in Diagnosis and Treatment of Poisoning

CONTENTS

CURRENT PRACTICES

There is a wide disparity in the emphasis placed on toxicology testing in modern hospitals. Some hospitals have extensive toxicology testing with relatively sophisticated instruments that are dedicated to the detection and measurement of poisons. Many others do little or no testing for poisons except for those toxins that are very common or a part of routine medical practice. This latter group of laboratories would test, for example, for digoxin, a cardioactive drug that is often involved in overdoses. Such labs might also test for the most common drugs of abuse. These tests would be urine-based, qualitative, and usually less than 100% specific. Why is there little uniformity among healthcare institutions in regard to the extent of their test menus? This is, to some extent, a function of the specific mission of the medical center. For example, an urban institution located where drug abuse is a severe problem would be more likely to develop elaborate toxicology laboratory facilities. Further, the directors of laboratory facilities do not always agree on what the precise role of drug testing should be. Opinions differ. Some pathologists and laboratory scientists have great faith in the ability of the toxicology laboratory to help the attending physician. Other laboratory directors are of the opinion that limited medical resources are better directed at other areas.

Drug-testing technologies employed in clinical laboratories range all the way from thin-layer chromatography to high-performance liquid chromatography with mass spectrometer detectors (see Chapter 13 for a comprehensive discussion of these techniques). Smaller laboratories with modest offerings in toxicology testing usually limit themselves to immunoassays for drugs of abuse and such tests are conducted on large analyzers. The advantages of this approach are that testing is automated and rapid. Results are, therefore, readily available and there is no strain on laboratory personnel resources. In addition, because drugs of abuse are so widespread this testing yields a high percent of positive findings. One step up in complexity is the use of thin-layer chromatography (TLC). This technology allows the laboratory to look for a much wider array of possible toxins. TLC may be inexpensive to run and will detect many of those drugs found in poisoning cases. It is not easily mastered, however, and is costly from the perspective of technologist time. For many drugs, TLC has a high detection limit, i.e., small quantities are not detected. This rarely is a major problem in clinical toxicology because overdosed patients usually have substantial quantities of drugs in their body fluids.

Some hospital laboratories employ relatively advanced instruments such as gas or liquid chromatographs sometimes coupled to mass spectrometer detectors. With this type of sophisticated equipment very advanced testing is possible. Determination of blood concentrations of virtually any organic compound is possible. This kind of testing is, however, usually not rapid and requires highly trained personnel. Very significant expense is associated with this approach to toxicology testing. One automated system has been developed that uses liquid chromatography in an automated testing platform. As such it reduces the training problem and increases the rapidity of testing, but the cost of this system may not be justified for every overdose case.

VALUE AND LIMITATIONS
OF LABORATORY TESTING

In this section we focus on the studies that have been done to pinpoint the best way to use a toxicology laboratory. One's initial attitude might be that the more laboratory testing the better. One might think that the physician treating an overdose is operating in a vacuum and can use all the help that is available. It might further be assumed that laboratory identification of the responsible toxin will "break the case," enabling the physician to provide the appropriate antidote, predict the outcome, and care for the patient in a much more effective manner.

Upon further thought, however, one might recall that not many antidotes are available, often the toxin is known from history (e.g., a parent might bring in the empty pill bottle found by the bedside), and the doctor knows how to treat the patient's symptoms irrespective of what particular stimulus caused those symptoms. We need to ask at this point, therefore, whether the laboratory is valuable and how it should be used. Clinical outcome studies can cast light on this question and help one to plan the most intelligent use of toxicology testing.

LABORATORY ACCURACY OR ERROR

Some studies suggest that the toxicology laboratory should not be used because there is simply too much error in testing and results are not reliable. In one study[1] toxicology specimens were split among three commercial laboratories with orders for comprehensive toxicology testing including identification and quantification of toxic agents. The study claimed that drugs responsible for the patient's overdose were identified in only 50 to 70% of cases. Moreover, the laboratories differed significantly among each other in regard to the quantitative results. This older study may have had some value in showing the uncertainty related to toxicology testing. It was, however, unduly critical in other ways. The authors claimed that the laboratories were wrong if they did not agree with the patient's subsequent testimony about the exact drug that was used. Patient credibility should not be assumed when many of these overdose patients are suicidal, depressed, etc. The authors of this study were also critical when laboratories failed to identify a drug even if the laboratory did not test for that particular drug on a regular basis. A study by Soslow in the *Annals of Emergency Medicine*[2] also was critical of laboratory accuracy. That study noted agreement between the history of an ingestion and laboratory findings in only 59% of cases. It seemed that the laboratory is guilty of many false negatives. Again, this conclusion is very dubious because it is based on the facile assumption that the patient's testimony is reliable, and if it contradicts a laboratory finding, then the laboratory is incorrect.

The issue of laboratory accuracy is a legitimate one. The studies quoted thus far were done in 1981, a time when toxicology testing was less accurate than it is today. The contemporary quality of laboratory accuracy is quite high. Laboratory equipment is very sophisticated and regulatory agencies are constantly monitoring the accuracy of toxicology testing. A national study commissioned by the American Association for Clinical Chemistry in 1987 evaluated the performance of toxicology testing and found an overall accuracy rate of 99.2%.[3] In this study, 47 laboratories across the United States were recruited for participation. The commonly tested drugs of abuse, amphetamines, cannabinoids, cocaine, opiates, and phencyclidene were tested. Out of 1847 test results 1833 were correct. Only 1 false positive and 13 false negatives were found.

In 1996 proficiency testing programs of the College of American Pathologists (CAP) showed true positive rates between 55% (chlorpheniramine) and 94% (amphetamine). Amphetamine accuracy was much higher because it is tested very often. Uncommon drugs such as chlorpheniramine may be misidentified. Further CAP data show that quantitative testing for drugs of abuse yields coefficients of variation between 8% for amphetamine and 12.9% for marijuana metabolite. These data show that drug quantitation is conducted with excellent accuracy with coefficients of variation (CV) being generally low; for example, 96% of the labs testing cocaine metabolite gave results within 18% of an average value of 373 mcg/mL.

It may legitimately be concluded that drug-testing accuracy is good and much better than it was in the 1980s. Testing is of the highest quality for drugs that are the objects of frequent testing and is less accurate for uncommon drugs. Accuracy is diminished in inexperienced laboratories or by those that fail to be attentive to detail and quality control.

OUTCOME STUDIES

The best way to examine the clinical value of toxicology laboratories is to conduct outcome studies, i.e., evaluation of patient outcomes as a result of the availability of drug test results. A logical method for evaluating the value of drug testing is to ask if the laboratory test findings were useful in improving patient care. Alan Brett[4] reviewed the records of overdose patients treated in a large medical center. Reviewing 3 years experience he found a 47% agreement between laboratory results and clinical impression, i.e., the laboratory confirmed a suspected drug in 47% of cases. In 52% of cases, the laboratory found a result that differed from what was already known from the patient's history. It might, perhaps, be thought that the lab is invaluable because most of the time (52%) new findings emerged from its investigation. Brett's study asked, instead, about the frequency with which these additional toxicological data were of value. Surprisingly, he found that only 3 patients were treated differently as a result of the drug findings and none of the 3 appeared to have a difference in medical outcome as a result of the toxicology tests. In his study 30 of the patients were poisoned with an agent for which an effective antidote exists. Nevertheless, the toxicology result was found to be non-contributory because that antidote had already been started or else the concentration of the offending agent, e.g., acetaminophen, was below the level at which the antidote is recommended. This study concluded that identification of unsuspected drugs may or may not be helpful depending on the use that the attending physician makes of the laboratory.

Brett and co-workers[5] also did a study of overdose patients in which they classified the study patients as low risk or high risk, the latter classification being applied under <u>any</u> of the following circumstances:

Patient needs intubation
Patient has seizures
Patient has no response to verbal stimuli
$pCO_2 > 45$ torrs
Any arrhythmias
Secondary or tertiary AV block
QRS > 0.12 seconds
Systolic pressure < 80 mm

None of 151 patients originally classified as low risk developed a high-risk finding. During hospitalization 7 patients did develop a high-risk condition but they all had a prior classification of high risk for one of the above symptoms. Brett did not find that patients could be effectively triaged into a high- or low-risk category on the basis of toxicology data. The above symptoms were much more important than the identity of the toxin ingested by the patient. It was concluded that use of the above predictive criteria would have eliminated over 50% of intensive-care days. Treatment of overdose, including triaging of patients, depended mostly on symptoms and was largely independent of laboratory findings.

A recent study by Belson and co-workers[6] is valuable in casting light on the question of what resources should be devoted to toxicology testing. Belson did extensive testing of a large population of pediatric patients who were treated in an urban medical center over an 18-month period. A comprehensive toxicological analysis was performed on 444 patients whose emergency room presentation suggested the possibility of drug overdose. The term comprehensive meant testing in serum for acetaminophen, salicylates, and ethanol and in urine for the following classes of abused drugs: benzodiazepines, cocaine, amphetamines, opiates, phencyclidine, and barbiturates. It also included testing by automated high performance liquid chromatography (HPLC) with a method that will detect any drug from a group of 550 potential toxins. Basically, the results from this truly comprehensive approach were compared with the results from a limited toxicology screen. The limited screen equals the comprehensive analysis except that the automated HPLC is not included. Belson found that a high proportion of his patients (51%) were positive for at least one drug. Further, the most common positive findings in children 6 to 18 years old were ethanol (18%), cocaine (8%), acetaminophen (7%), and narcotics (5%). In the vast majority of patients (97%), toxins were suspected by history or physical examination, were present on the limited screen, or were judged to be clinically not significant. In the remaining 3% (7 of 234 positive screens) the drug finding was deemed to be clinically significant and was found only on the automated HPLC part of the comprehensive screen. These 7 findings appeared to be the payoff for the trouble and expense associated with the additional testing that this laboratory included in its comprehensive screen. Unfortunately, however, patient management was not affected by the positive finding in any of these 7 patients. The authors claim that the automated HPLC part of the comprehensive screen cost $16,000 to perform on all of the 444 patients in the study. This works out to $2315 per positive finding but, as noted above, there was no clinical value in this finding. One might conclude from this study that extensive and random screening may not be of value. On the other hand, there may have been some value to positive or negative findings that was not recognized by those tracking the data, a different group from the physicians who initially treated the patients. It is also possible that some of the results lost their value because they were not found early enough or were not transmitted to physicians in a timely manner. As it stands, however, this study suggests that random testing is of little or no importance in a clinical toxicology setting. Testing should be focused and rationally based if it is to be of value.

The above-cited studies suggest a minor role for toxicology testing in the evaluation of the overdosed patient. This is due to a number of reasons including the fact that doctors must often treat symptoms irrespective of their cause, and the difficult and time-consuming nature of broad-based drug testing in contrast with the clinical need to intervene rapidly. Most of the problems identified in the studies quoted above have to do with the shortcomings of drug screening. Screening is problematic because it tries to do too much, i.e., identify one toxin among literally thousands of possible agents. The number of potential toxins is much greater than the ability of any one protocol to identify even a significant fraction of them. In fact, the availability of comprehensive screens creates an illusion in the physician's mind that the laboratory is actually able to definitely rule out a toxin as the cause of the patient's symptoms. Physicians must be aware of the limited ability of their laboratory's drug screen. Sometimes they fail to consider this. On the other hand, studies on the contribution of the toxicology laboratory in relation to measuring levels of specific toxins show, on the whole, that directed testing of this sort (in contrast to screening) can be beneficial provided that the specimen is collected at the correct time and the toxin is one with serum concentrations that correlate with symptoms, prognosis, etc.

The laboratory, in the sense of the full spectrum of clinical laboratories, is absolutely indispensable in the treatment of the overdosed patient. Toxicology testing is less important than one might have expected but other laboratories are vitally needed. Toxic overdoses are often medical emergencies because they provoke dramatic and extensive metabolic alterations in bodily chemistry. Therefore, chemistry, coagulation, blood gases, and other laboratories provide data the physician must have in order to treat the numerous metabolic abnormalities which usually accompany drug overdose.

THE STRUCTURE OF CLINICAL
TOXICOLOGY TESTING

It has been argued above that random screening is not an effective approach to the problem of laboratory involvement in care of the overdosed patient. What tests should be included in a hospital's repertoire and how rapidly should the laboratory provide such testing results? Three knowledgeable sources have published responses to this question and they provide the lists shown here for STAT (i.e., immediate) testing in the context of possible drug overdose:

LIST 1[7]	LIST 2[8]	LIST 3[9]
Iron	Iron	
Acetaminophen	Acetaminophen	Acetaminophen
Methanol	Methanol	Methanol
Methemoglobin	Methemoglobin	Methemoglobin
Carboxyhemoglobin	Carboxyhemoglobin	Carboxyhemoglobin
Salicylates	Salicylates	Salicylates
	Ethylene glycol	Ethylene glycol
Theophylline	Theophylline	
	Lithium	Lithium
Arsenic	Iron binding capacity	
Barbiturates	Digoxin	
Lead	Ethanol	
	Osmolality	

The lists above may be regarded as compilations of the most important toxicology tests, and those tests should be provided locally. Results from them should ordinarily be reported in 1 hour or less. A review of the above recommendations shows a high degree of agreement among these experts but some surprising variability. For example, one opinion supports lead and arsenic as critical analytes that should be eligible for STAT testing, but other experts do not agree. Also, only one of the three experts believes that iron binding capacity, digoxin, ethanol, and osmolality should be included in this critical grouping.

What are the criteria to be considered when making a decision about the importance of offering a particular test within one's laboratory? A critical principle in laboratory medicine must be kept in mind here. If a test result alters therapy in a critical way, then that test is, by necessity, a critical one. Another factor is lethality of the toxin. If exposure to a substance causes only minor symptoms then we can feel free to exclude that test from our menu. A second consideration is the availability of an antidote. If an effective antidote or other treatment is available, then the knowledge that a patient's symptoms are due to a specific toxin is of great value because it directly guides the physician's intervention. A third factor is the relative informational content supplied by the patient's presentation. This refers to the ability of the history, physical examination, etc. to guide the patient's care without any help from the laboratory. If the patient has a severe cardiac arrhythmia, for example, and a specific medication would always be given to counter this arrhythmia, then the laboratory identification of the toxin is irrelevant to the subsequent steps taken by the treating physician. On the other hand, if the patient's presentation is misleading, the laboratory might be quite helpful. For example, acetaminophen may cause mild symptoms such as nausea. A finding of high amounts of acetaminophen in the blood of a nauseous patient changes the treatment plan totally. A fourth factor is the presence or absence of a pharmacokinetic relationship between the laboratory finding and its clinical significance. By this we mean that a positive drug finding may be coincidental to a patient's presentation. A positive urine screen result for antidepressants can be due to normal therapeutic use of antidepressants and may not explain symptoms that the patient is currently manifesting. A high serum level of a phenothiazine may be due to the patient's tolerance to these drugs and may not be associated with some problem that the patient is currently experiencing. A fifth factor is the frequency with which a particular toxin is ordered for testing. For example, if a laboratory is asked to test for ethylene glycol 2 or 3 times a year, then it probably makes no sense to do the test in house. Even if rapid results are needed, the laboratory is not likely to conduct this test in a competent manner because its personnel lack sufficient experience in doing the test.

Why were the specific tests listed here selected for inclusion? Iron is chosen because it is common in overdose and because the clinical presentation is likely to overstate the severity of the poisoning. Intense GI irritation and hypotension occur, which collectively often suggest that the patient's situation is worse than it really is. Nevertheless, iron toxicity is often life-threatening. A quantitative serum level can help to sort things out. Acetaminophen is selected for the opposite reason. Severe overdose may appear to be mild when first observed but there is a risk of hepatic failure if antidotal therapy is not begun. Methanol is dangerous because its toxicity is due more from its metabolites than from methanol itself. Thus, the most critical symptoms are delayed and laboratory help in recognizing a severe overdose is likely to be beneficial. Methemoglobin must be confirmed by a laboratory test in order to distinguish this cause of cyanosis from other causes. Serum concentrations of salicylate are critical because salicylate poisoning is a common occurrence and early symptoms do not correlate well with prognosis. Theophylline levels are valuable because there is a narrow margin between a safe dose and a toxic dose and a patient may have minor symptoms that can abruptly escalate to major problems such as respiratory and cardiac arrest. A high level is sometimes a major prognostic factor for severe toxicity. Carboxyhemoglobin must be measured because carbon monoxide is a relatively common toxin and CO concentration is suggestive of the severity of exposure.

The testing opinions of several experts have been presented above. The present author suggests still a fourth set of tests and rules for the ideal use of the toxicology laboratory. The following list is intended to meet almost all of the needs of the attending physician and at the same time be realistic in regard to the economic and technical limitations placed on the laboratory:

    Screens that should be STAT eligible
        Urine: marijuana metabolite, cocaine metabolite, amphetamines, opiates,
            phencyclidine, benzodiazepines, and barbiturates
        Serum: acetaminophen, salicylates, ethanol
    Therapeutic drug levels that should be STAT eligible
        Phenytoin, digoxin, theophylline, lithium
    Therapeutic drug levels that should be offered but not STAT
        Aminoglycosides, anticonvulsants (except phenytoin), antiarrhythmics
    Miscellaneous tests that should be STAT
        Carboxyhemoglobin, methemoglobin, iron
    Tests that should be sent to commercial laboratories
        Methanol, ethylene glycol, isopropanol

How is this last list justified? The drugs of abuse and over-the-counter analgesics that are recommended for STAT testing are very common in overdose situations. Many fatalities have been seen with these drugs. Therapeutic drugs that are often measured in the serum are potentially very toxic, especially those listed here for STAT service. Carboxyhemoglobin, methemoglobin, and iron are common enough and of proven clinical value. They can be done by highly automated and inexpensive test methods. Finally, alcohols other than ethanol should be sent to outside laboratories unless the hospital laboratory is located in an area where these substances are commonly found. That is rarely the case. Because the tests are rarely ordered and difficult to conduct it makes sense to send them to a laboratory accustomed to this type of analysis. Some contend that physicians need immediate results in order to decide whether a patient should be started on hemodialysis. The fact is, however, that a decision to dialyze is best based on the overall condition of the patient, not merely on a laboratory number.

Questions

1. It is impossible for clinical laboratories to provide immediate test results for highly specialized tests that are conducted on complex instruments. Discuss the problems that physicians have in treating patients if they are

not informed by the laboratory in a timely manner about the identity of overdosed drugs.

2. What characteristics dictate whether or not a toxicology test should be available on an immediate basis?
3. Compare the advantages of ordering comprehensive drug screens with the concept of ordering tests on a selective basis.
4. For each of the following tests list several reasons why or why not the test should be included in those offered by a toxicology laboratory in a clinical setting. Which, if any, should be available STAT?

   Iron
   Iron binding capacity
   Acetaminophen
   Methanol
   Benzodiazepines
   THC (marijuana metabolite)

REFERENCES

1. Ingelfinger, J. et al., Reliability of the toxic screen in drug overdose, *Clin. Pharmacol. Ther.,* 29, 570–575, 1981.
2. Soslow, A., Acute drug overdose, *Ann. Emerg. Med.,* 10, 18–21, 1981.
3. Frings, C.S. et al., Status of drugs-of-abuse testing in urine under blind conditions: an AACC study, *Clin. Chem.,* 35, 891–894, 1989.
4. Brett, A.S., Implications of discordance between clinical impression and toxicology analysis in drug overdose, *Arch. Int. Med.,* 148, 437–441, 1988.
5. Brett, A.S., Predicting the clinical course in intentional drug overdose, *Arch. Int. Med.,* 147, 133–137, 1987.
6. Belson, M.G. and Simon, H.K., Utility of comprehensive toxicologic screens in children, *Amer. J. Emerg. Med.,* 17, 221–224, 1999.
7. Done, A.K., The toxic emergency, *Emerg. Med.,* 2, 91–98, 1977.
8. Bryson, P.D., The role of the laboratory, in *Comprehensive Review of Toxicology,* 2nd ed., Aspen Publishers, Rockville, MD, 1989, 43–52.
9. Weisman, R., The toxic emergency — Using the toxicology lab, *Emerg. Med.,* 9, 243–248, 1984.

5 Introductory Toxicokinetics

CONTENTS

The nature of poisoning is intrinsically related to the basic physiological processes that the human body employs to handle drugs. Thus, one must appreciate essential pharmacological principles for a better understanding of toxicology.

The biochemical and physiological handling of drugs by the human body is called pharmacokinetics. In brief, pharmacokinetics is what the body does to the drug. It may be regarded as only slightly less important than pharmacodynamics, what the drug does to the body. Pharmacokinetics is of critical importance relating as it does to factors such as the length of time that a drug stays in the body, the manner of elimination, and so on. All new drugs are subjected to comprehensive pharmacokinetic evaluation. For a drug to be clinically beneficial it must not only have the appropriate pharmacological activity but it must also have pharmacokinetic characteristics that do not render it inappropriate.

Toxicokinetics is a subdivision of pharmacokinetics that is concerned with the impact of toxins on normal body–drug interactions. Knowledge of toxicokinetics enables one to understand individual factors that enhance or reduce toxicity. Toxicokinetics helps to explain why some people survive large quantities of a particular toxin whereas others succumb to a much smaller amount. It is obviously impossible to conduct controlled studies in humans on overdose. Therefore, much of the data on poisonings is anecdotal and based on particular cases. Those data are not perfect because exact amounts of toxin and exact times of exposure are not usually known.

The four major areas involved with the body's handling of drugs in therapeutic or toxic amounts are absorption, distribution, metabolism, and elimination. This brief review will describe each. The aim of this chapter is understanding the importance of these areas and the concepts associated with them (volume of distribution, half-life, etc.) and their impact on the toxicity of specific substances.

OVERALL DRUG DISPOSITION

The disposition of a drug within the body is shown in Figure 5.1. For an ingested medication, the drug enters the stomach, usually dissolves, and is absorbed into the blood. Drugs circulate in the vascular compartment in an equilibrium mixture of free and protein-bound forms. Usually the proportion of a drug that is bound is high if the drug has a highly polar character. However, drugs bind to protein not only by ionic attractions but by nonpolar forces, as well. Therefore, uncharged drugs may

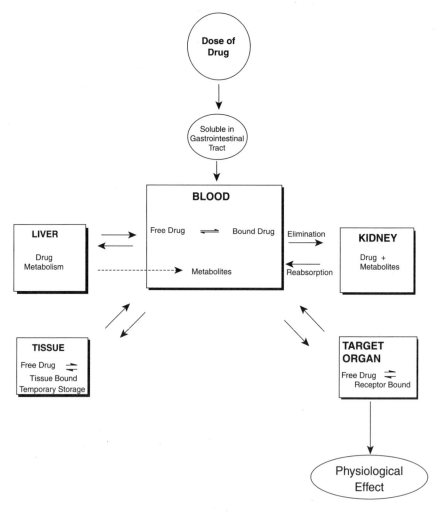

FIGURE 5.1 Distribution of drugs within the body.

also exist, to some extent, in a protein-bound form. Some fraction of drug is taken up by the liver, the major site of biotransformation. Simultaneously, some fraction of the dose enters tissue; for example, very nonpolar drugs and nonpolar drug metabolites are stored for varying intervals in adipose (fat) tissue. They re-enter the blood from the adipose tissue depending on equilibrium. If the concentration of drug and metabolite within the blood is high, as would be the case for a chronic drug user, then the equilibrium favors continued adipose tissue storage. The phenomenon of tissue storage explains why urine testing is positive for some drugs a long time after a person may have discontinued their use. The drug continues to re-enter the blood and from there enough of it is transferred to the urine to give a positive test result. Some drug also enters the renal circulation, the point of final exit from the body for most drugs. As blood courses through the kidneys, drug is constantly being transferred to urine for release from the body. Finally, some drug does what it is intended to do — it binds to a biological receptor and influences bodily physiology. Although this is the main reason why a drug is taken, to improve a physiological function, much of an ingested dose never reaches the intended target within the body. A variable percent of the dose is not absorbed or it is converted to an inactive metabolite or excreted by the kidney before it has an opportunity to exert the intended pharmacological effect.

ABSORPTION

There is no toxic effect from a substance unless a threshold amount of it comes in contact with vulnerable bodily areas. The toxin must enter the body via the oral, intravenous, inhalational, or other routes. If a drug is administered by the intravenous route, it is physically placed in the vascular space and 100% of the dose, of necessity, reaches the blood. On the other hand, if the drug is absorbed by the oral route, something less than 100% of the dose reaches the blood. Drug solubility is variable so the bioavailability, that fraction of the dose entering the blood, is less than 100%. Two factors that are quantitatively related to bioavailability are the area under the concentration curve (AUC) and the peak serum level. The AUC is the integrated space measured by plotting concentration of drug vs. time. AUC is the best measurement of bioavailability, and allows us to calculate the fraction of the drug or toxin that entered the blood. Peak serum level is important to know and will sometimes correlate with the symptoms of drug exposure. However, the peak level may not accurately reflect total drug exposure in a clinical situation because it is a single result, a snapshot of drug concentration in the blood at one given moment in time only.

Figure 5.2 shows the absorption characteristics of an average drug. Consider the problem of inferring the peak level of that drug by taking a slice parallel to the ordinate and estimating the total drug in the blood from that slice. The estimate will be correct only if the curve has known dimensions, e.g., Gaussian character, and if one knows the specific location along the abscissa at which the sample is taken. This is the problem that often arises in real emergency overdose situations. The laboratory reports a blood concentration and the physician assumes it is a peak level. However, the result may not be reflective of the patient's true status because the

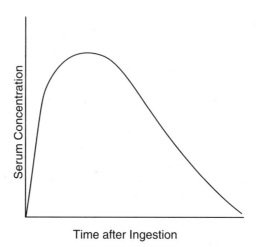

FIGURE 5.2 Change of serum concentration as a function of time after ingestion.

clinician does not know the time of ingestion or, if the time is known, the sample is still inappropriate because some other factor has shifted the concentration curve relative to the time axis. Examples of possible other factors include patient or drug-specific characteristics that alter the expected rate of drug absorption.

TOXICOKINETICS AND BIOAVAILABILITY

The normal absorption behavior and, therefore, the normal bioavailability of a drug may change drastically when that drug is ingested in overdose quantities. Iron is a good example. When taken therapeutically, the absorption of iron is limited by a selective uptake process. However, in overdose amounts, the iron overloads this selective uptake control mechanism and is absorbed in large and potentially toxic amounts. Other examples include ethyl alcohol and salicylates that may paralyze the pyloric sphincter and delay their own absorption, especially when taken in large doses. This factor is potentially beneficial to the patient because gastric lavage may be employed at a time long after ingestion, when these drugs would normally be expected to have already undergone absorption. Some materials, such as aspirin, meprobamate, and others, form bezoars, concretions that can remain in the stomach for long periods, and continue to be slowly absorbed into the blood. Bezoars behave like giant sustained-release tablets. The overdose behavior of the drugs just described is not easily predicted and laboratory results will be difficult to interpret because of unusual absorption behavior.

FIRST-PASS METABOLISM

Some drugs are strongly taken up and metabolized by the liver almost to the point of being fully metabolized in their first pass through the liver. This phenomenon is known as first-pass metabolism. Examples of drugs that are subject to extensive first-pass metabolism include morphine, heroin, and other narcotics. Whenever first pass occurs to a substantial degree, as it does with these narcotics, the drug achieves only a low blood level from oral administration. It must be given by a parenteral (non-oral) route in order to achieve an acceptable level of potency. When given by injection, a high percent of the dose reaches intended receptors before passing through the liver. If ingested, however, the liver is the first organ that the drug encounters as it passes through the bloodstream. It is also important to note that in overdose a drug subject to first-pass metabolism may achieve a higher than expected serum level. Enzymes responsible for first-pass metabolism may become saturated by high doses. In other words, a higher than usual fraction of the drug reaches receptor sites causing more toxic manifestations than expected.

DISTRIBUTION

Distribution is the dispersion of the drug among the various organs or compartments within the body. The drug may remain largely within the blood, within fatty tissue, or at a multitude of other possible locations. An extremely useful concept, the apparent volume of distribution (Vd), has been devised to describe the distribution of the drug. Vd is the volume into which the drug appears to distribute and it is calculated from the dosage and the concentration of drug in the blood.

$$Vd = D/(Cp \times k)$$

where:
     Vd = volume of distribution
      D = dose
    Cp = plasma level
      k = kg body weight

For example, assume that 100 g of alcohol are ingested by a man who weighs 70 kg and the blood level is found to equal 2.38 g/L. The Vd is calculated as equal to 0.6 L/kg or 42 liters (0.6 × 70). This figure is approximately equivalent to the total volume of body water in a 70 kg man (men are about 55% water) and is in keeping with the fact that alcohol distributes evenly throughout body water.

Vd for various drugs ranges from about 5% of body volume to as high as 400 L. The latter figure is much greater than anyone's total body volume and we see, therefore, that Vd is an artificial concept. It is, nevertheless, of great value in describing one characteristic of a drug: whether the drug tends to be found primarily in the bloodstream or is more likely to be found at other tissue sites.

Vd depends partly on the lipid vs. water solubility of a drug. Thus, water-soluble drugs have low volumes of distribution, i.e., they tend to remain in the blood as would be expected from their solubility characteristics. If they are water soluble, then they should stay in the aqueous medium of the blood. Fat-soluble drugs, by contrast, are expected to bind to cell membranes, adipose tissue, and other fat-rich areas. In addition, Vd also relates to whether a drug is protein bound. Drugs that are charged, especially positively charged, tend to bind to serum proteins. In their protein-bound state they form large macromolecular complexes that are too large to cross biological membranes. Thus, they remain confined to the bloodstream.

Pathological states may also change Vd. Thus, a drug may have an unexpected Vd in a patient who has impaired renal or cardiac function. Depending on the exact disease from which a patient suffers, the Vd may be higher or lower than that in a normal individual.

Because Vd mathematically relates blood concentration to dosage it may be employed in interpretation of laboratory results. For example, it may be used to estimate the quantity of drug ingested when a quantitative laboratory result is available. As a corollary, the blood concentration may be estimated if reliable dosage information is available from history. This may be helpful if the laboratory test result is not available and a physician needs to quickly estimate the blood level. A physician can also double check a laboratory result by a quick calculation if there is a suspicion that a laboratory result was uninformative, having, for example, been based on a specimen collected too early or in some other inappropriate manner.

Because Vd may be useful for providing an estimate of dosage, it follows that it can help estimate the amount of antidote to be given. This would be true only if the particular toxin is one for which an antidote is available and one in which antidotal therapy should be based on quantity ingested. Antidotes are sometimes given based on symptoms rather than blood levels of the responsible toxin.

Vd is able to indicate whether there is any value in trying to enhance elimination as, for example, by dialysis. Drugs with high Vd are not confined to the vascular compartment. Dialysis of the blood, therefore, does not reach the major fraction of the drug because it is hidden away at receptor sites. If Vd is high, therefore, enhanced elimination will probably be fruitless.

Vd is helpful in the context of drug monitoring. It helps to predict whether the practice of drug measurement in blood will have any clinical value. Drugs with high Vd are not present in the blood to any extent and it follows, therefore, that tests on blood specimens may give an inaccurate picture of total body burden of the drug. In other words, one must measure blood content of drug because it is impractical to measure organ content, but the drug produces symptoms depending on the organ content. In actuality, the key feature of drug monitoring from the perspective of correlation between concentration and symptoms is that an equilibrium exists between the drug at the receptor and the drug's concentration in the blood. This equilibrium, furthermore, is more likely to exist for a drug with low Vd; drugs with this property, therefore, are good candidates for drug monitoring by measurement of blood concentration. Psychotropic drugs such as tranquilizers, antidepressants, antipsychotics, mood-altering agents, etc., create their effects by binding at sites within the central nervous system. Because the CNS is quite remote from the blood, such psychotropic agents are frequently not suitable subjects for therapeutic drug monitoring.

Table 5.1 consists of a list of drugs that have been recommended for therapeutic drug monitoring because studies show that the concentrations of these drugs correlate with overdose-induced symptoms. Knowing the concentration of the drug in plasma is clinically useful. Column 1 of the table shows a list of drugs for which the opposite is true. Column 1 drugs should not be monitored because the drug level is frequently

TABLE 5.1
Volumes of Distribution of Selected Drugs

Plasma Level Correlates with Effects		Plasma Levels Unrelated to Effects	
Drug	Vd	Drug	Vd
Acetaminophen	0.9 L/kg	Amphetamine	4.4 L/kg
Aminoglycosides	0.25	Alprazolam	1.6
Digitoxin	0.6	Amitriptyline	8
Ethanol	1.0	Chlorpromazine	>8
Ethylene glycol	0.8	Cocaine	2.3
Ibuprofen	0.2	Heroin	25
Methotrexate	0.75	Indomethacin	0.9
Salicylates	0.15	Phencyclidene	6.2
Averages	0.58		7.05

unrelated to symptoms of overdose, degree of toxicity, prognosis, etc. The table also shows the Vd for each drug and average Vd for each column. The average value of Vd for drugs that are good candidates for monitoring is 0.58 L/kg, whereas the same statistic for inappropriate candidates for monitoring is 7.05 L/kg. Thus, the hypothesis that low Vd indicates that a drug level is probably valuable is supported by the data in this table.

FREE AND BOUND DRUGS

Volume of distribution depends, among other factors, on the extent of the protein binding of a drug. When a drug binds a protein the drug becomes part of a macromolecular complex that is trapped by its large size within the bloodstream. The drug is pharmacologically inert, that is, unable to act at a site outside of the blood while in this bound form. However, the drug, whether in this bound form or not, is measured by most analytical methods. In other words, when a laboratory test is performed, the total drug (bound plus free) is usually measured. Because only the free form is active but the laboratory result expresses the total drug concentration, the result is misleading if a patient has an abnormal free fraction. For example, phenytoin is normally 10% free. Total phenytoin is usually reported and can be correctly interpreted if this 10% free is highly reproducible from person to person. It will not be, however, if the patient has an abnormal protein concentration or an acid-base imbalance. A patient with low albumin lacks adequate binding protein and will have a higher-than-expected free fraction. Such a patient could be phenytoin toxic even though a laboratory result shows the total phenytoin concentration to be within the recommended range. Acid-base imbalance also affects the phenytoin free fraction because the binding protein changes its charge state as the pH of the plasma changes. As the protein's overall charge is altered, its affinity for phenytoin (and the binding fraction that relates to this) is also altered.

Therefore, a drug level is not fully interpretable for a drug which undergoes extensive protein binding unless the bound (inert) and free (active) fractions are known. Measurement of the free fraction is often clinically preferable especially for drugs with high degrees of protein binding such as phenytoin. The drug's free fraction is likely to increase in overdose. For example, 10% of phenytoin is usually free but in overdose the amount of phenytoin may be high enough to saturate protein-binding sites so that more than 10% may be free and active. Physicians may request assays for free drug levels if they suspect that a patient's total drug concentration may not be representative of the active drug.

ELIMINATION

Eventually, unless the patient dies, all drugs are removed from the body. The major excretory organs are the liver and the kidney, although other organs also have lesser roles in drug elimination. If a drug is reasonably polar in structure, then it tends to pass into the urine in a more or less efficient manner. Nonpolar drugs are efficiently reabsorbed in the renal tubules and would circulate continuously in the blood, theoretically for weeks or even months. To prevent this long-term occupation of the body by a foreign chemical, the liver has developed an ability to convert nonpolar drugs into polar ones, which are then excreted. Drug toxicity will be greater if the patient has some degree of hepatic disease and is ingesting a drug that depends on the liver for its removal. Similarly, a patient with renal impairment should, in general, avoid drugs that depend on the kidney for their elimination. Vd also relates to the site of elimination because water-soluble drugs are usually polar and, as mentioned above, renally eliminated. Such drugs also usually have low volumes of distribution.

Drug elimination is capable of analysis by kinetics in the same way that chemical reactions are kinetically understood. There are three types of drug kinetics (pharmacokinetics), each of which has its own type of kinetic, time vs. concentration, plot (see Figure 5.3). When the concentration of the drug in plasma declines with time and the rate of the elimination also slows, the elimination process is said to be first order. In this situation the rate is a function of the concentration of the substance being eliminated. This is characteristic of a toxin that is primarily eliminated by the renal route. An example of a drug eliminated by first-order pharmacokinetics is lithium.

The kidney has a high capacity for elimination and so the rate is determined, not by the kidney, but by the toxin's concentration. A certain fraction of drug is eliminated per unit time. Therefore, the remaining drug becomes progressively less and the same fraction of a smaller total amount of drug means a slowing rate of elimination. Zero-order elimination is characterized by the plot of concentration vs. time being a straight line. This means the rate of elimination is not influenced by concentration. The toxin or drug is eliminated at a constant rate irrespective of whether there are small or large amounts of it. This is characteristic of hepatic elimination, the route of elimination for nonpolar drugs. The rate of zero-order elimination depends on the availability of hepatic enzymes and these are limited. At enzyme saturation, which occurs usually at a low drug concentration, the reaction rate is maximal. The concentration of metabolizing enzyme, not the concentration of toxin, is the major factor in setting the rate of elimination. An example of a drug that is removed by zero-order kinetics is acetaminophen.

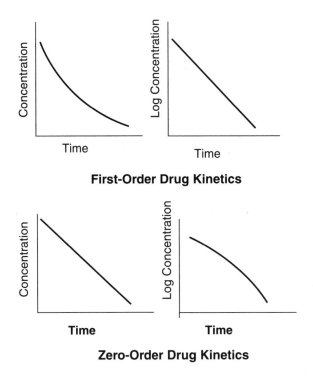

FIGURE 5.3 Linear and log plots of elimination behavior.

Some drugs, such as alcohol, follow Michaelis-Menten kinetics. This is a mixture of zero- and first-order pharmacokinetics. At a high concentration of drug the rate of elimination is dictated by the concentration of the fully saturated enzyme. At this concentration zero order prevails and elimination is not related to drug concentration; the elimination rate is constant. At a certain drug concentration, the amount of drug or toxin is too low to saturate the metabolizing enzymes. Beyond that point the reaction rate is a function of the concentration of toxin. The rate becomes first order.

The elimination behavior of a drug is most simply described by its half-life, the time needed for a drug's concentration to be cut by one half. Short half-life means that a drug is removed efficiently. Perhaps it has characteristics that cause rapid loss in the kidney or perhaps it is subject to metabolism by an enzyme that is present in an especially large amount. Whatever the reason, the fact of a short half-life is clinically important. It means that the patient may survive because the symptoms will not last for a long time. If the half-life is short enough, the treating physician may be able to wait out the drug effects until recovery is complete. This assumes, of course, that toxicity is not so great that death or serious injury occurs during the brief time that the drug is in the patient. An added point about half-life is important: For some drugs the toxicity is greater if the half-life is shorter. For example, secobarbital is much more toxic than phenobarbital as shown here:

	$t_{1/2}$	Lethal Plasma Level
Secobarbital	24 hr	1 mg/dL
Phenobarbital	82	12 mg/dL

Both have the same actions but secobarbital has a shorter half-life and greater toxicity at lower plasma levels. The apparent reason for this is that secobarbital is less polar and able to more readily enter the central nervous system. Thus, a higher percent of a secobarbital dose will enter the CNS compared to phenobarbital and greater harm will be done.

SUMMARY

Drugs are poisonous because they interact with normal bodily biochemistry in a deleterious manner. Biochemistry and pharmacodynamics explain the basic reasons why some compounds are toxic. Pharmacokinetics is an additional dimension of the toxicity process inasmuch as it explains why poisoning is more or less intense than expected in specific cases. Pharmacokinetics takes into account individual-specific factors that should be considered for a deeper understanding of toxicology. Some of the major points that pharmacokinetics teaches and that enable us to understand unexpected laboratory findings include:

1. For an ingested drug, bioavailability is that portion of the dose that is actually absorbed. This fraction may be greater or less than normal in overdose situations.
2. Orally ingested drugs are transported by the bloodstream directly to the liver. For those with extensive liver uptake, drug metabolism may be extensive resulting in achievement of very low blood levels. This first-pass effect can be overcome largely by injection or inhalation, rather than oral ingestion, of the drug.
3. Volume of distribution is possibly the most important pharmacokinetic parameter. It indicates whether a drug is to be found primarily in the blood or in another bodily site.
4. Volume of distribution is affected by many factors:
   - It may be higher in overdose
   - It suggests that drug testing is worthwhile if the Vd is low
   - It enables calculation of a dose from a blood level or vice versa
5. Drugs are often found bonded to protein in the blood to some extent. Only the free, nonbonded portion is active. Most laboratory tests give answers for the total drug concentration. The free concentration is important when the patient has protein-binding abnormalities such as a low protein concentration in the plasma.

6. Drugs are eliminated from the body according to fairly predictable kinetic models. The sites of elimination are the kidney and the liver. Kinetics of elimination may change in overdose.
7. Half-life, the time during which a drug's concentration drops by one-half, may change in overdose.

Problems in Toxicokinetics

1. Five drugs have the following volumes of distribution:

Drug	Vd
A	0.4 L/kg
B	12 L/kg
C	30 L/kg
D	30 liters
E	0.2 L/kg

a) Which of these is likely to be a good candidate for therapeutic drug monitoring?
b) Which of these might be effectively removed from the body by dialysis as an overdose treatment?
c) Which of them are most likely to be polar?
2. Calculate the patient's blood concentration from the following data:

Patient's weight	165 pounds
Vd of drug	0.7 L/kg
Dose ingested	90 mg

3. The graph in Figure 5.2 shows the blood levels in the blood of a patient who overdosed on a drug. The patient is brought to the emergency department 4 hours after ingestion and the physician draws blood for concentration determination at that time. Discuss any problems related to interpretation of the result on the part of the physician.
4. Drug A has Vd = 10 L/kg and drug B has Vd = 0.5 L/kg. Each of these is taken by a patient in renal failure. All else being equal which drug is more likely to cause toxicity?

Case Study 1: The Value of Pharmacokinetics

A 45-year-old white male, a known chronic alcoholic, was admitted to the hospital for ingestion of an alcohol 20 hours previously. His family reported that he consumed about 2.5 liters of windshield wiper solvent containing 30% (volume/volume) of an alcohol that was not immediately identified. When admitted, the patient was unconscious, had a severely depressed body temperature of 32°C, and his pupils were fixed and dilated. Diastolic blood pressure was low at 45 mm. Several abnormal chemistry values were noted including bicarbonate of 6 mEq/L; glucose, 225 mg/dL; anion gap, 46; pH, 6.76; and serum osmolality, 465 mOsm/kg. Formic acid level in serum was 270 mg/L. Ophthamology consult resulted in a finding of papilledema. The patient also had a creatine kinase level of 4,600 U/L, which increased to 38,500 by the second day of hospitalization.

Treatment for this patient consisted of a 100-gram loading dose of ethanol followed by continuous ethanol infusion at 25 g/hr. Intravenous sodium bicarbonate was administered for the acidosis. Because this was a very severe overdose and alcohols are eliminated by dialysis, hemodialysis was conducted for 5.5 hours. It is common to find that this treatment lowers alcohol efficiently, but there is a rebound after it is discontinued. Therefore, a second or third course of dialysis may be necessary. Dialysis is often continued until the patient reaches a serum concentration of 30 mg/dL. To determine if this has been reached one can continuously sample blood and test for the alcohol. A better idea is to calculate the half-life in blood during dialysis and, from this quantity, calculate the time required to reach the desired end-point. This method requires only 2 blood tests for the alcohol rather than continuous serial testing.

What is the probable identity of the alcohol?
    a) ethanol
    b) methanol
    c) isopropanol
    d) ethylene glycol

Gas chromatography resulted in a finding of methanol at a concentration of 265 mg/dL. The presentation is consistent with methanol or ethylene glycol but not the other two alcohols. The severe acidosis this patient experienced is not usually found with ethanol or isopropanol. The formate level is the most specific indication that the offending agent is methanol because formate is produced from methanol and not from ethylene glycol.

The following formulas are known from pharmacokinetics:

$$k = (1/t)(\ln C1/C2)$$

$$\text{half-life} = t_{1/2} = \ln 2/k$$

$$C_{max} = C(\text{init})e^{-kt}$$

$$Vd = \text{dose}/Cp$$

where:

> k = elimination rate constant
> t = time
> C1 = concentration at time 1
> C2 = concentration at time 2
> C_{max} = maximum concentration
> $C_{(init)}$ = concentration at start
> Vd = volume of distribution
> Cp = plasma concentration

Questions

Q1. What is the half-life of methanol during dialysis if the patient had a serum methanol of 265 mg/dL at the start of dialysis and 65 mg/dL after 5.5 hours?
  a) 2.7 hours
  b) 24 hours
  c) 1.2 hours
  d) 2 days

Q2. How many grams of methanol did the patient ingest?
  a) 12 g
  b) 324 g
  c) 585 g
  d) 1.1 kg

Q3. The half-life of methanol in the absence of dialysis has been shown to equal 15.1 hours. This patient's initial serum methanol concentration was 265 mg/dL. The maximum (peak) serum level can be calculated from an equation above. This patient's highest serum methanol was
  a) 664 mg/dL
  b) 265 mg/dL
  c) 481 mg/dL
  d) 1240 mg/dL

Q4. Volume of distribution is a critical pharmacokinetic property that equals the dose divided by the serum concentration. For methanol, what is its value in this 220-pound man?
  a) 0.65 L/kg
  b) 0.88 L/kg
  c) 2.1 L/kg
  d) 3.6 L/kg

Answers and Discussion

Q1. (Answer = a) The elimination rate constant, k, equals the fraction of a dose that is eliminated per unit time. In this case, t = 5.5 hours, C1 = 265 mg/dL, C2 = 65 mg/dL. Thus, k = 0.26. Knowing k, one can calculate half-life which is found from the second formula given ($t_{1/2}$ = ln 2/k) to equal 2.7 hours. This is an increase in the elimination rate over normal by a factor of almost 6.

Q2. (Answer = c) From the history given, the patient drank 2.5 liters of 30% (volume/volume) methanol. Thus, 2500 mL × 0.3 = 750 mL of methanol. This volume multiplied by the density of methanol (0.78 g/mL) gives a total of 585 grams of methanol.

Q3. (Answer = a) From the half-life of methanol in the absence of dialysis (15 hours), one can calculate an elimination rate constant of 0.0459. In the formula for maximum serum level, therefore, k = 0.049, t = 20 hours, and C(init) = 265 mg/dL. Therefore, maximum concentration equals 664 mg/dL.

Q4. (Answer = b) Dose was determined in Q3 to equal 585 grams. Blood level at peak was estimated to equal 664 mg/dL. Vd is, therefore, 88.2 liters. Vd is more accurately expressed in terms of L/kg. The man weighed 220 lbs. or 100 kg so the Vd for methanol is 88.2 L/100 kg = 0.88 L/kg.

References

1. LeGatt, D., Frequent determination of methanol in serum not needed for monitoring hemodialysis therapy of methanol ingestion, *Clin. Chem.*, 34, 1371–1372, 1988.
2. Burns, A.B. et al., Use of pharmacokinetics to determine the duration of dialysis in management of methanol poisoning, *Amer. J. Emerg. Med.*, 16, 538–540, 1998.

Case Study 2: The Impaired Driver

An automobile was traveling down an isolated rural road at a slow rate. A driver and his passenger were in the vehicle that swerved unsteadily from side to side along the highway. The vehicle was spotted by a state highway patrol officer who stopped the car because of the erratic manner in which it was moving down the road. The officer noted the odor of alcohol on the breath of the driver. He also found a plastic packet containing vegetative matter that he presumptively identified as marijuana. The driver was given a field sobriety test and, upon doing poorly, was taken to a hospital where blood and urine were collected for further toxicological examination.

Subsequently, the following results were reported by the laboratory:

Blood alcohol	135 mg/dL
Urine drug screen	Positive for THC–COOH (marijuana metabolite)
Blood THC	0.6 ng/mL
Blood THC–COOH	40 ng/mL

Questions

Q1. Does alcohol interfere with normal driving ability?
   a) Invariably interferes irrespective of the blood concentration
   b) Interference starts at 20 mg/dL and increases in an approximately linear manner with concentration

    c) Has no effect on hardened drinkers regardless of the blood concentration

    d) Usually has a minor impact that can be intensified by additional drugs

Q2. This driver's blood alcohol

    a) Is slightly below the common legal limit

    b) Is above the legal limit but the serum alcohol would be lower

    c) Is well above the common legal limit

    d) Must be interpreted with respect to other factors before legal implications can be known

Q3. Does marijuana use have any relation to safe driving ability?

    a) Marijuana usually improves alertness and driving ability

    b) Marijuana by itself cannot interfere with safe driving

    c) Marijuana plus alcohol is a greater hazard than either alone

    d) Marijuana is much more of a hazard than alcohol

Q4. Is this driver impaired by marijuana?

    a) Absolutely: the positive finding of urinary THC–COOH proves impairment

    b) Definitely: positive blood and urine findings support each other in proving impairment

    c) Yes: the high level of THC–COOH in the blood is unequivocal

    d) Maybe: the active agent is at a very low level in the blood

Q5. Cone and Huestis[1] have developed an equation that allows estimation of time of marijuana use on the basis of plasma concentrations of THC and THC–COOH:

$$\log h = 0.576 \log \mathrm{THC-COOH/THC} - 0.176$$

$$h = \text{hours since marijuana use}$$

From this equation and data provided in this case how long ago did this subject smoke marijuana?

    a) 1 hour

    b) 4 hours

    c) 7 hours

    d) 24 hours

Answers and Discussion

Q1. (Answer = b) Alcohol is clearly a cause of multiple accidents and is fully capable of impairing driving ability. Various figures are derived from studies but the consensus is that a blood alcohol greater than 100 mg/dL involves a heightened risk of automobile accidents on the order of about 8-fold greater than in an alcohol-abstinent state. At a blood level of 200 mg/dL, the elevated risk is equivalent to 20 times that of zero blood alcohol. As a consequence, states have passed laws known as "per se" statutes. These statutes amount to a presumption of impairment if the blood alcohol exceeds the legal limit, irrespective of the driver's apparent intoxication status at the time of police evaluation.

In this case the driver had a blood level of 135 mg/dL. This is well above the legal limit in the United States where most states use a limit of 100 mg/dL. At the present time the vast majority of laboratories have testing methods for alcohol that are very specific and precise. If the specimen was handled and tested according to accepted forensic procedures, then this result of 135 mg/dL could not be challenged seriously as possibly being due to some other substance, nor could it credibly be claimed that it actually was less than 100 mg/dL.

Q2. (Answer = c) Legal limits for blood alcohol vary among the states in the United States. Some permit up to 0.10% (100 mg/dL) and others have a limit of 0.08%. A new federal law requires all states to use the 0.08% limit by 2003. This person's level of 135 mg/dL was equivalent to 0.135%. It is noteworthy that statutes are written in terms of blood levels and some laboratories test serum rather than whole blood. If serum is tested, one must bear in mind that blood levels are approximately 10 to 15% lower than serum collected at the same time.

Q3. (Answer = c) Most studies show that marijuana is a driving hazard when used by itself and that it intensifies the degree of impairment when used with other drugs, including alcohol. At low levels of marijuana use a driver may act more cautiously while driving; however, cautious driving does not compensate for abnormal perception, slowed reactions, and other effects. Studies also show that a combination of marijuana plus alcohol is more dangerous than either alone. Although marijuana use should be avoided while driving, it appears to be significantly less dangerous than alcohol as a cause of high-risk driving.

Q4. (Answer = d) The effect of marijuana on driving is a more ambiguous issue than the effect of alcohol. On the whole, it appears that marijuana does impair driving ability. This conclusion is complicated, however, by the fact that drivers who have recently used marijuana tend to be more aware of their impaired status than alcohol-impaired drivers. They will frequently, therefore, drive more slowly. Nevertheless, they are at elevated risk, have slowed reaction time, are easily confused by changing traffic situations, and lack normal judgment.

The relationship between blood or urine concentrations of marijuana and its metabolites and degree of driving impairment is significantly more complicated than the equivalent situation with alcohol. A positive urinary marijuana is very uninformative because marijuana metabolites are known to be excreted by the kidney over long periods of time. There is documented evidence of individuals who discontinued marijuana use but remained positive by urine testing for more than 1 month. This is particularly likely if the person used marijuana chronically prior to discontinuation of drug usage. In this case, therefore, the positive urine finding may have no bearing on the driver's potential impairment.

Blood testing is more informative but still may not always indicate whether or not a driver is impaired by marijuana. This is due to the kinetics of marijuana in the human body. For example, if marijuana is smoked, the active agent, tetrahydrocannabinol (THC), reaches a peak concentration rapidly. Its blood level is approximately 100 to 200 ng/mL within 15 minutes of smoking and declines to values as low as 1 to 5 ng/mL in 4 hours. The subject may still be impaired to some degree even after the blood level of THC approaches detection limits of laboratory testing. Therefore, the finding of a very low concentration of THC in blood does not mean necessarily that the marijuana was used a long time ago nor does it mean that the subject is not impaired because THC concentration is low. Furthermore, one cannot estimate the time of marijuana use on the basis of blood concentration. This is because chronic users tend to have a small amount of THC in the blood at all times. This THC is re-entering the blood from adipose tissue storage sites. Therefore, if one finds a concentration of THC in the range of <2 ng/mL in a subject's blood it could indicate that the person smoked marijuana recently (4 to 6 hours ago) and drug metabolism has driven the concentration down to a very small amount. It could also be indicative, however, of regular use but not necessarily in the past 2 days. In the former case the subject would be impaired. In the latter case, he would not be impaired.

Q5. (Answer = c) Direct application of this equation yields a result of 7.5 hours. This must be regarded as the best estimate of actual time of use. However, because inter-individual variability is so high, the 95% confidence interval around this time estimate extends from 2 to 20 hours.

References

1. Cone, E.J. and Huestis, M.A., Relating blood concentration of tetrahydrocannabinol and metabolites to pharmacologic effects and time of marijuana usage, *Ther. Drug. Monit.*, 15, 527–532, 1993.
2. Chesher, G., Alcohol and other drugs in road crashes. What does pharmacokinetics have to do with it? *Alcohol, Drugs, and Driving*, 1(1), 1–20, 1985.
3. Chesher, G., The effects of alcohol and marijuana in combination: a review, *Alcohol, Drugs, and Driving*, 2(3), 105–119, 1986.
4. Agurell, S.L. and Hollister, L.E., Pharmacokinetics and metabolism of Δ-9 tetrahydrocannabinol: relation to effects in man, *Pharmacol. Rev.*, 2, 61–77, 1986.

FOR FURTHER READING

1. Rosenberg, J. et al., Pharmacokinetics of drug overdose, *Clin. Pharmacokin.*, 6, 161–192, 1981.
2. Weisman, R.S. et al., Pharmacokinetics and toxicokinetic principles, in *Goldfrank's Toxicologic Emergencies*, fifth ed., Appleton and Lange, Norwalk, CT, 1994, 85–99.

3. Tilstone, W.J. and Stead, A.H., Pharmacokinetics, metabolism, and the interpretation of results, in *Clarke's Isolation and Identification of Drugs*, second ed., The Pharmaceutical Press, London, 1986, 276–305.

4. Opheim, K. and Raisys, V., Therapeutic drug monitoring in pediatric acute drug intoxications, *Ther. Drug. Monit.*, 7, 148–158, 1985.

5. Watson, I., Practical clinical pharmacokinetics, *J. Int. Fed. Clin. Chem.*, 4, 35–39, 1992.

6. Warner, A. et al., Drug abuse testing: pharmacokinetic and technical aspects, in *Ther. Drug Monit. Toxicol.*, 8, 1–11, 1986.

7. Gibaldi, M. and Levy, G., Pharmacokinetics in clinical practice, 1. Concepts, *JAMA*, 235, 1864–1867, 1976.

8. Gibaldi, M. and Levy, G., Pharmacokinetics in clinical practice, 2. Applications. *JAMA*, 235, 1987–1992, 1976.

6 Biotransformation

CONTENTS

INTRODUCTION

The term biotransformation is sometimes used to describe the conversion of drugs and other toxins into metabolites, i.e., biochemical breakdown of the drug. It is a process with critical importance for several reasons. In the first place, the rate of biotransformation is important for estimating the toxicity of a specific ingestion. If a toxic molecule, for example, is rapidly metabolized to a nontoxic metabolite, it may, for that reason, have a lower toxicity because the drug is cleared rapidly from the body. On the other hand, metabolites of some drugs are more toxic than the primary drug itself. When this is true, as for example, with methanol or acetaminophen, knowledge of the metabolic transformation is important for understanding the poisoning process and for designing effective therapies. Last, knowledge of metabolites is important when interpreting laboratory results relating to drug concentrations. This is particularly true for drugs of abuse as we shall see later in this text.

The purpose of biotransformation, from the perspective of involved organs, is to alter structure and, therefore, alter properties. In particular, xenobiotics (foreign molecules) are usually made more polar, which expedites their excretion from the body.

Broadly speaking, biotransformation is divided into Phase I and Phase II reactions. In Phase I reactions the toxin is oxidized or reduced and a new functional group is usually introduced; for example, hydroxyl or alkyl groups may be added to the substrate. In Phase II reactions a new prosthetic group, e.g., sugars, sugar acids, sulfate groups, or others are attached, usually to the functional group which was introduced during Phase I.

PHASE I REACTIONS

Monooxygenations of xenobiotics are the major type of Phase I reaction. They are also called mixed-function oxidations. One atom of a molecule of oxygen is accepted by the substrate while the other oxygen atom is reduced to water.

A summary of this process is shown here:

$$RH + O_2 + NADPH + H^+ \rightarrow NADP^+ + ROH + H_2O$$

There are two different classes of enzymes which belong to the category of monooxygenases (or mixed function oxidases, also called microsomal oxygenases) and, therefore, carry out the process depicted here. The cytochrome P_{450} system is the larger of the two categories and actually is composed of over 400 different enzymes, all of which carry out the general reaction indicated above. These reactions are basically similar in the role played by molecular oxygen and the movement of electrons, but substrates and products come from different chemical classes. A multiplicity of enzyme reactions are possible; some of which are shown below:

Enzyme	Some Known Substrates
Epoxidation, hydroxylation	Aldrin, benzo alpha-pyrene
N-,O-,S-dealkylation	Methylmercaptan, atrazine
N-,S-,P-oxidation	Chlorpromazine
Desulfuration	Parathion
Dehalogenation	Carbon tetrachloride, chloroform

Details of some of these reactions are illustrated in the reaction outlines shown below (Figures 6.1–6.3).

The ultimate carcinogen in tobacco smoke is benzo (alpha) pyrene 7,8-diol-9,10-epoxide. Its formation by a Phase 1 reaction is shown here (Figure 6.2).

Biotransformation, whether completed by the P_{450} system or some other biotransforming enzyme is rarely a simple process. A single metabolic transformation does not usually occur but, instead, a xenobiotic is subject to several different processes concurrently. An example is the metabolism of chlorpromazine (Figure 6.3). Which

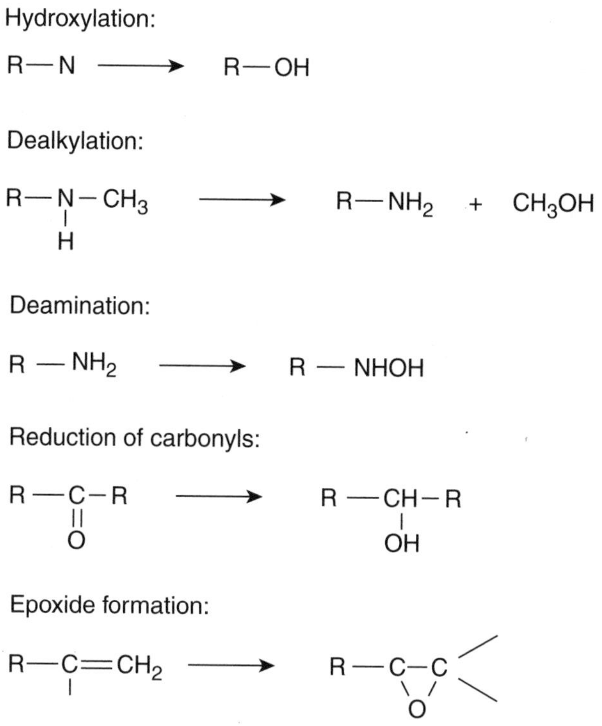

Hydroxylation:

$$R-N \longrightarrow R-OH$$

Dealkylation:

$$R-\underset{\underset{H}{|}}{N}-CH_3 \longrightarrow R-NH_2 + CH_3OH$$

Deamination:

$$R-NH_2 \longrightarrow R-NHOH$$

Reduction of carbonyls:

$$R-\underset{\underset{O}{\|}}{C}-R \longrightarrow R-\underset{\underset{OH}{|}}{C}H-R$$

Epoxide formation:

$$R-\underset{\underset{|}{}}{C}=CH_2 \longrightarrow R-C-C\underset{O}{\diagdown\diagup}$$

FIGURE 6.1 Some Phase 1 reactions that occur in biotransformation.

specific metabolic products form is related to the enzymes that are present. It is usually also dependent to some extent on the concentration of the xenobiotic.

SITE OF BIOTRANSFORMATION

The major organ that carries out Phase I conversions is the liver and the major site within the liver is the endoplasmic reticulum of the liver cell. Because components of the endoplasmic reticulum appear in the microsomal fraction when cell homogenates are separated into fractions by ultracentrifugation, these cytochrome P_{450} enzymes are also called microsomal oxygenases. Although most microsomal oxygenase activity occurs in the liver, the distribution of these enzymes is extensive. Other organs which contain them, in approximate descending order of enzyme activity, are lungs, kidney, adrenal cortex, gut, spleen, heart, and muscle.

FLAVIN-CONTAINING MONOOXYGENASE

The second kind of monooxygenase enzymes is known as the flavin-containing monooxygenases (Figure 6.4). This is a much smaller group than the P_{450} system, but it has the same basic reaction mechanism and is dependent on NADPH and molecular oxygen. Flavin monooxygenases catalyze the breakdown of secondary and tertiary amines, some sulfur compounds, organophosphorus compounds, and others. Examples of their activity are

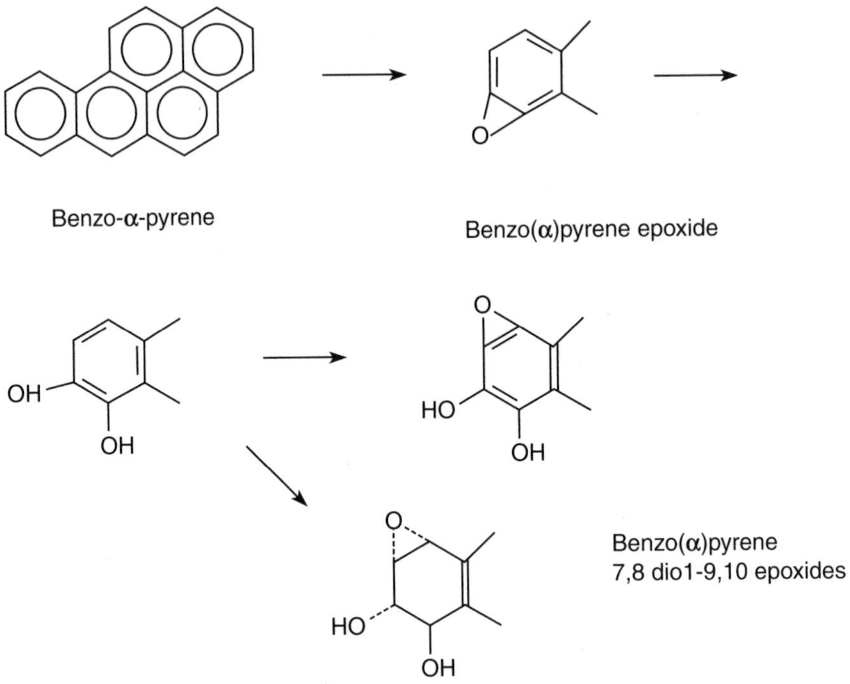

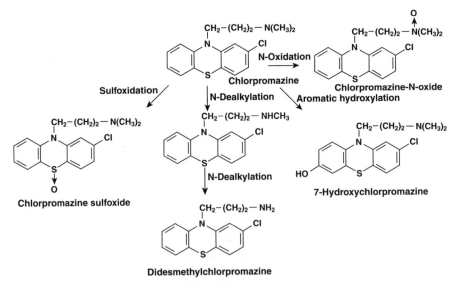

Benzo-α-pyrene
Benzo(α)pyrene epoxide
OH
OH
HO
OH
O
HO
OH
O
Benzo(α)pyrene
7,8 dio1-9,10 epoxides

FIGURE 6.2 Biotransformation of benzo (α) pyrene to carcinogenic products.

Chlorpromazine
N-Oxidation
Chlorpromazine-N-oxide
Sulfoxidation
N-Dealkylation
Aromatic hydroxylation
Chlorpromazine sulfoxide
N-Dealkylation
7-Hydroxychlorpromazine
Didesmethylchlorpromazine

FIGURE 6.3 Variety of reactions involved in chlorpromazine metabolism.

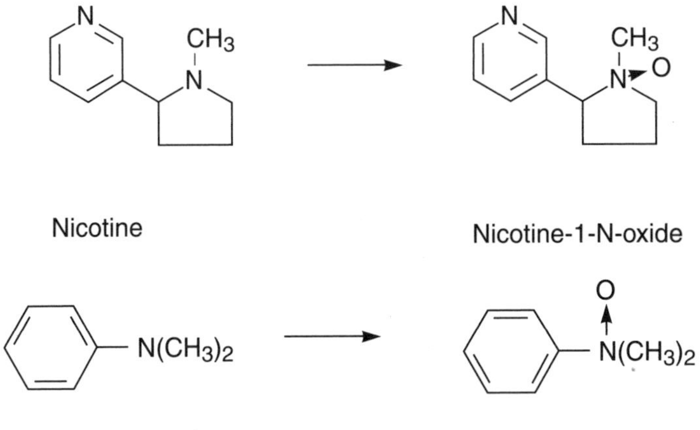

FIGURE 6.4 Some Phase 1 reactions carried out by flavin-containing monooxygenases.

Nicotine → Nicotine-1'-N-oxide

Dimethylaniline → Dimethylaniline/N-oxide

INDUCTION OF MICROSOMAL ACTIVITY

It was discovered in the 1960s that the concentration of cytochrome P_{450} enzymes is not constant. It is variable and these enzymes are increased or induced in the presence of certain other chemicals. This is a significant observation because it means that the effect of a drug is somewhat dependent on another drug and the duration of effect can be substantially shortened or prolonged when a patient takes more than one drug at a time. This is a critical factor that must be borne in mind by physicians when dosing patients or when attempting to interpret laboratory data in relation to blood concentrations of therapeutic agents.

For example, a concentration reported by the laboratory may be lower than expected on the basis of pharmacokinetic calculation. The explanation of the discrepancy could be that an enzyme involved in metabolism is at a higher than expected concentration.

Some examples of chemicals that induce the cytochrome P_{450} system are listed below:

Inducers of the Cytochrome P_{450} System	
Barbiturates	Imipramine
Chloral hydrate	Morphine
Chlordiazepoxide	Nicotine
Diphenhydramine	Phenylbutazone
Ethanol	Phenytoin
Halothane	Propoxyphene

There are also chemicals that inhibit the cytochrome P_{450} system. Some from this group are chloramphenicol, carbon disulfide, carbon tetrachloride, and bromobenzene. They exert an inhibitory effect by competitively binding to cytochrome P_{450}, inhibiting its synthesis, or inactivating or destroying the enzyme and/or its subcellular location.

OTHER FACTORS ALTERING NORMAL BIOTRANSFORMATION

Induction or inhibition of biotransforming enzymes are only two factors that can change the normal course of xenobiotic metabolism. Other factors that may enhance or delay drug elimination include

Factor	Comment
Diet	For example, some metal deficiencies may decrease metabolism
Hormones	For example, growth hormone or thyroxine increases metabolism
Age	Newborns and geriatric individuals usually have slower metabolisms
Genetics	Enzyme levels are, to some degree, genetically determined
Disease	Multifactorial, especially hepatic disease

OTHER PHASE I REACTIONS

Other Phase I processes are known. For example, alcohol dehydrogenase is a biotransforming enzyme which metabolizes ethanol, methanol, isopropanol, or ethylene glycol. (See Chapter 14 on alcohols.) Molybdenum-based hydroxylases are responsible for oxidation of purines, methotrexate, and other drugs. Esterases are metabolic enzymes that catalyze the transformation of several toxins, e.g., parathion (see Figure 6.13 below).

PHASE II REACTIONS

Phase II processes add a substituent to the substrate and thereby increase its size and molecular weight. Most of these reactions increase the polarity of the substrate and enhance its elimination. Methylation and acetylation are exceptions that may decrease both the substrate's polarity and its solubility in water.

GLUCURONIDATION

In these reactions a glucuronidase enzyme adds glucuronic acid to a substrate (Figure 6.5), e.g.,

$$\text{Morphine} + \text{UDP-glucuronic acid} \xrightarrow{\text{Glucuronyl transferase}} \text{Morphine glucuronide}$$

This enzyme is, like the cytochrome P_{450} system, subject to induction, often by the same compounds that induce the P_{450} enzymes. Interestingly, alcohol inhibits

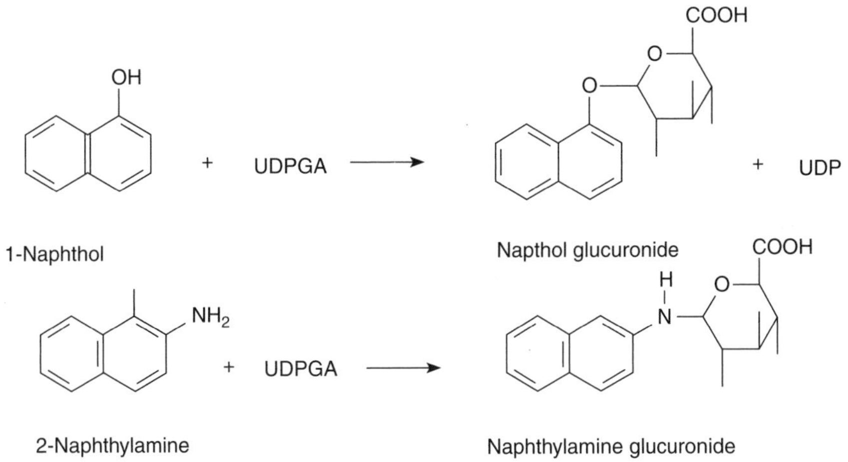

FIGURE 6.5 Examples of glucuronidation reactions. Formation of products from substrate plus UDP glucuronic acid.

glucuronidation by decreasing the availability of NAD^+ as the metabolism of alcohol leads to large amounts of the reduced coenzyme, NADH. In turn, the shortage of oxidized NAD^+ interferes with synthesis of UDP-glucuronic acid, a process that requires NAD^+. Products of glucuronidation have relatively high molecular weights (e.g., morphine diglucuronide has a molecular weight of 655 daltons) and are, therefore, prone to excretion in the bile because they can readily transfer from the liver cell into the blood. Morphine monoglucuronide and diglucuronide are found in much larger quantities in bile than in urine.

GLUTATHIONE CONJUGATION

Glutathione, a tripeptide, may be attached to substrates by the enzyme, glutathione-S-transferase. A further reaction sometimes occurs in which glutamic acid and glycine are lost from the glutathione and the remaining amino acid, cysteine, is acetylated. The resulting product is a mercapturic acid metabolite (Figure 6.6).

In the example shown, the acetylamino group of acetaminophen is conjugated. Three enzymes participate in the breakdown of the glutathione conjugated product. In the case of acetaminophen acting as substrate, the final product is the mercapturic acid conjugate of N-acetyl-p-benzoquinoneimine (NAPQI). A diverse array of functional groups including alkyl, aryl, N-hydroxy, and others are possible substrates for this reaction. As was the case with P_{450} and glucuronyl transferase, glutathione-S-transferase is subject to enzyme induction. The major purpose of this enzyme appears to be the control of reactive electrophiles. Such electrophiles are present naturally or from metabolism and have a deleterious effect upon the body. Glutathione is a strong nucleophile and will, therefore, readily react with and inactivate foreign electrophiles.

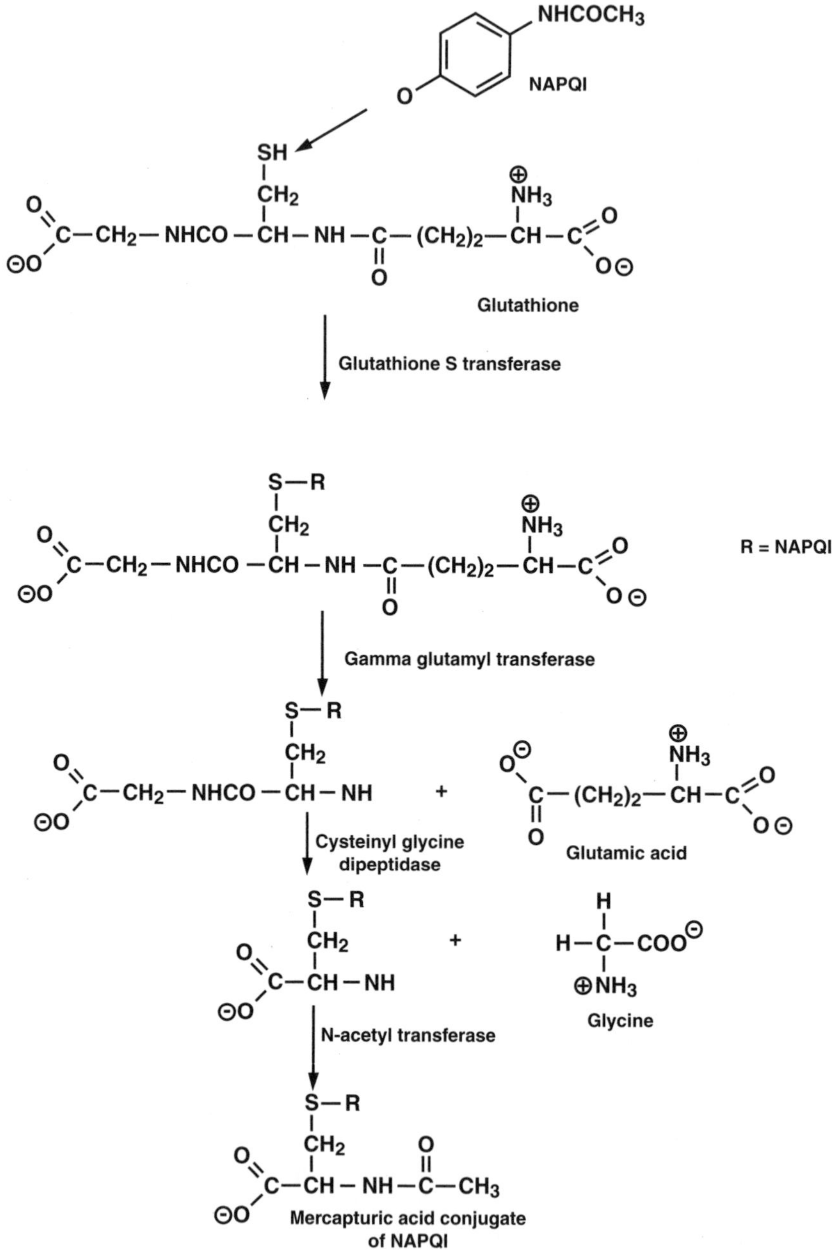

FIGURE 6.6 Complete transformation of acetaminophen metabolite by reaction through the glutathione cascade.

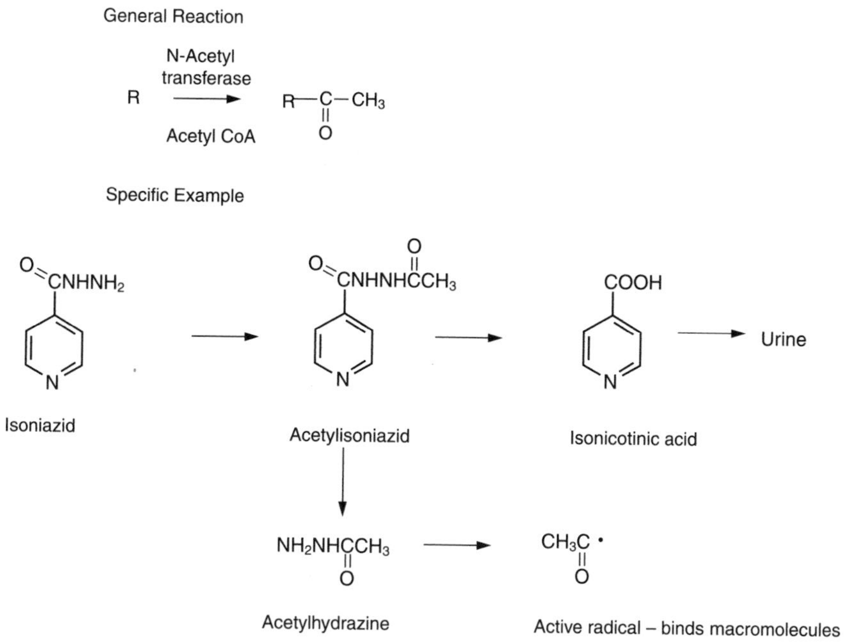

FIGURE 6.7 Acetylation reactions as exemplified by isoniazid acetylation.

ACETYLATION

In this reaction a cytoplasmic enzyme uses the common acetyl donor, S-acetyl CoA, to conjugate hydroxyl, amino, sulfhydryl, or other groups of several substrates (Figure 6.7). This enzyme is widespread in tissues and exists in many isoenzyme forms, the distribution of which is genetically determined to some degree. Chemicals which induce or inhibit this enzyme are known.

SULFATE CONJUGATION

The enzyme involved in sulfate conjugation is known as a sulfotransferase or a sulfokinase and it conjugates sulfate to alcoholic, amino, or phenolic groups of xenobiotic substrates (Figure 6.8). The coenzyme PAPS, phosphoadenosine phosphosulfate, contains an activated form of sulfate which assures that the transfer of sulfate is energetically favored. These enzymes also exist in isoenzyme forms. Generally speaking, sulfation does not occur to a large extent partly because of the small pool of sulfate present in the cell. A corresponding group of enzymes exists that are known as sulfatases and essentially reverse the sulfate conjugation. Such classes of reversing enzymes are also known for most of the Phase II processes that are discussed here.

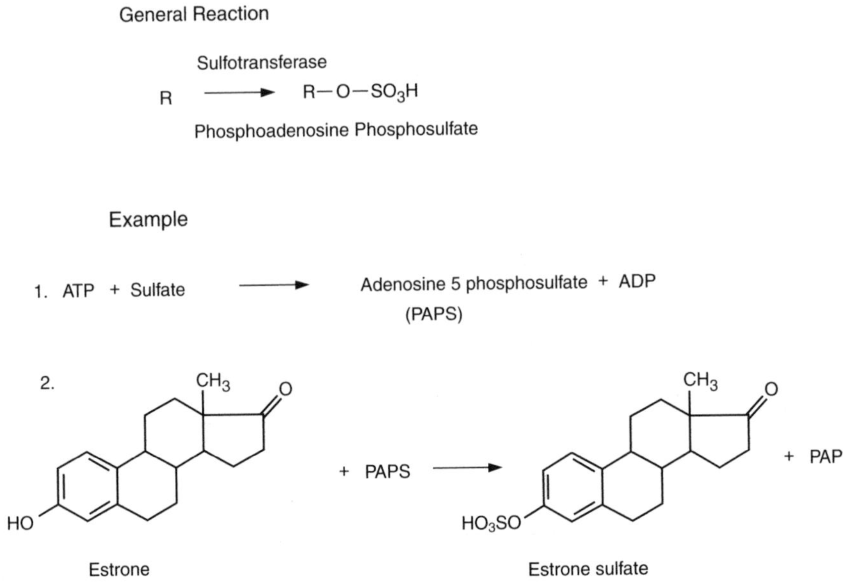

General Reaction

Sulfotransferase

$$R \xrightarrow{\hspace{1.5cm}} R-O-SO_3H$$

Phosphoadenosine Phosphosulfate

Example

1. ATP + Sulfate $\longrightarrow$ Adenosine 5 phosphosulfate + ADP
(PAPS)

2. + PAPS $\longrightarrow$ + PAP

Estrone   Estrone sulfate

FIGURE 6.8 Sulfation conjugations as exemplified by estrogen sulfation.

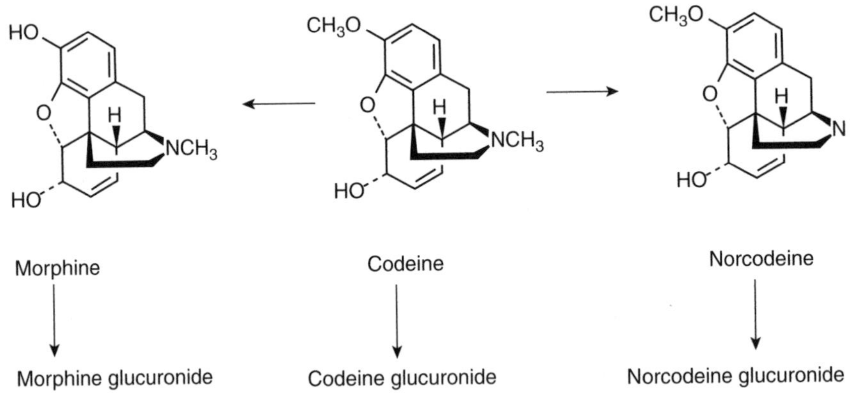

Morphine   Codeine   Norcodeine

Morphine glucuronide   Codeine glucuronide   Norcodeine glucuronide

FIGURE 6.9 Aspects of codeine metabolism.

SOME EXAMPLES OF APPLIED
BIOTRANSFORMATION KNOWLEDGE

CODEINE: METABOLISM TO MORPHINE

Codeine is very similar in structure to morphine. One of the metabolic reactions involving codeine is O-demethylation that produces morphine. Morphine, therefore, appears in the urine of a codeine user. Consequently, a toxicologist testing for opiates in urine may find morphine. The problem is that morphine also comes from heroin.

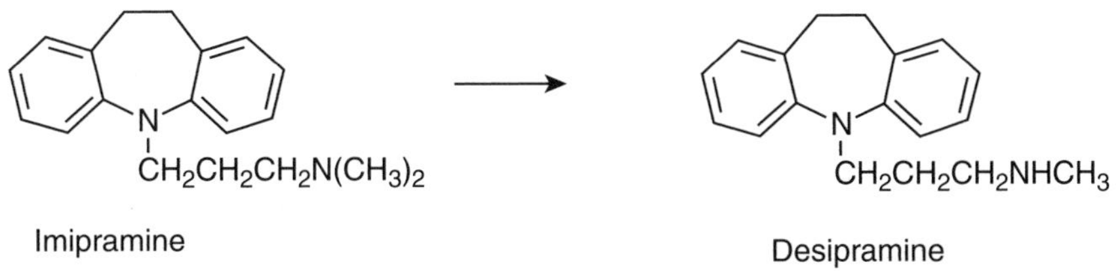

FIGURE 6.10 Dealkylation of imipramine to an active product, desipramine.

Codeine is more widespread in medicinal products and is less subject to abuse than heroin or morphine. Therefore, this particular metabolic behavior of codeine sometimes presents a dilemma in interpreting drug test results. This quandary is not always resolvable. The concentration of morphine is usually much greater if the drug taken was morphine or heroin. Near the end of the metabolic process, however, codeine users may actually have more morphine in their urine than codeine.

IMIPRAMINE: CONVERSION TO DESIPRAMINE

Imipramine is an antidepressant drug. It is frequently useful clinically to measure the amount of this drug in blood in order to determine whether a patient's symptoms may be due to too much imipramine in the blood. Conversely, a patient who is not responding to the drug may not be taking it as prescribed and his/her physician needs to document the noncompliance by showing the absence of the drug from the blood. Importantly, if only imipramine is measured the result may be misleading because its N-dealkyl-metabolite, desipramine, also has antidepressant activity (Figure 6.10). One is obliged to measure both drugs in order to accurately assess the total antidepressant activity that is present in the blood.

POPPY SEED DEFENSE

Persons who abuse heroin (diacetylmorphine) have the heroin metabolite, morphine, in their urine (Figure 6.11). Those consuming poppy seeds found in many foods including poppy seed bagels or poppy seed cake are ingesting a small but detectable quantity of morphine that will appear in the urine. Since heroin itself is quickly metabolized to morphine and does not appear in the urine, heroin abuse usually is recognized by the appearance of morphine in urine. One cannot easily distinguish an abuser of heroin from someone who is ingesting a food that contains morphine. A solution is to look for another metabolite of heroin, monoacetyl morphine. This metabolite is produced from heroin but not from morphine. The finding of monoacetylmorphine in urine is evidence of heroin and not morphine use.

METHAMPHETAMINE: METABOLISM TO AMPHETAMINE

One of the reactions found in methamphetamine biotransformation is N-demethylation. Because amphetamine and methamphetamine differ only in respect to the N-methyl group, the loss of this group produces amphetamine from methamphetamine (Figure 6.12). Methamphetamine is somewhat difficult to confirm in urine

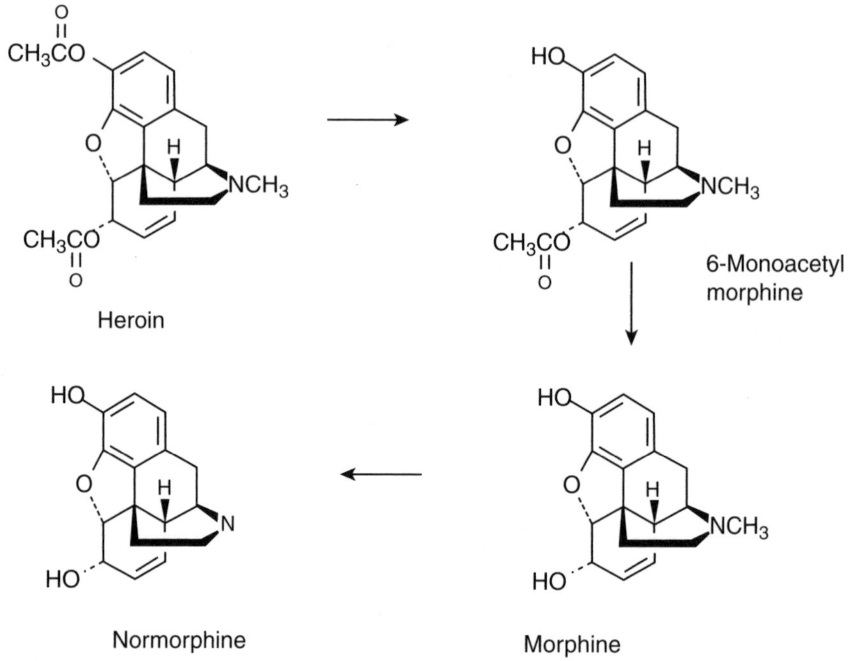

FIGURE 6.11 Metabolic conversion of heroin to morphine and normorphine.

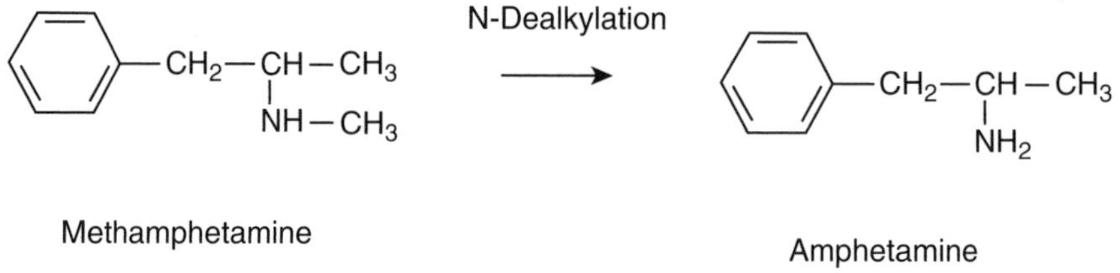

FIGURE 6.12 Formation of amphetamine from methamphetamine.

because of the existence of many very similar but legitimate pharmaceutical compounds. Therefore, confirming the presence of amphetamine in a specimen also containing methamphetamine strengthens the prior contention that the urine contained methamphetamine.

BENZODIAZEPINES: GLUCURONIDATION AND ITS IMPACT ON DRUG SCREENING

Benzodiazepines (e.g., Valium (diazepam) and Librium (chlordiazepoxide)) are commonly prescribed minor tranquilizers, sedatives, and anticonvulsants. They are a large class of compounds and also undergo extensive metabolism, with glucuronidation often being the last step in the biotransformation. Most immunoassays for benzodiazepines involve antibodies raised against a common benzodiazepine metabolite, oxazepam. However, because most oxazepam excreted into the urine is actually

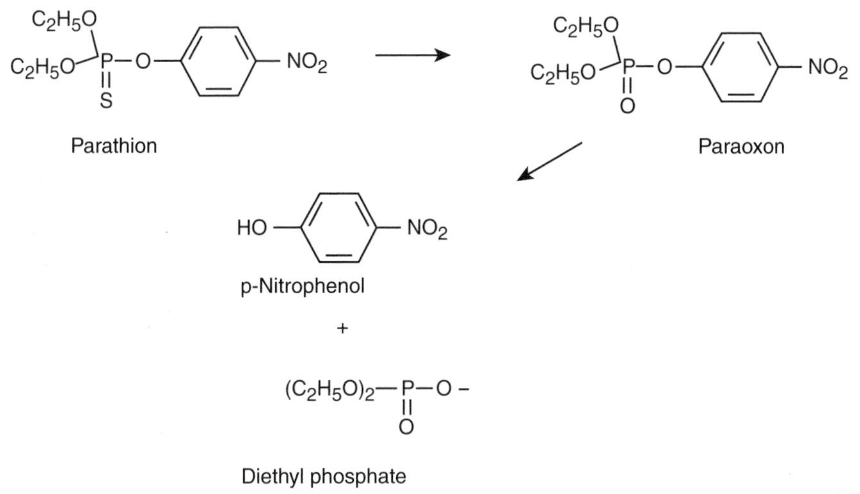

FIGURE 6.13 Parathion activation and inactivation.

oxazepam glucuronide, the immunoassay does not always perform well. The antibody has less reactivity with the oxazepam glucuronide, the actual metabolite present in urine. Some research has shown that pretreatment of the urine specimen with glucuronidase, which liberates the metabolite from binding with glucuronide, improves the sensitivity of the method.

PARATHION ACTIVATION AND INACTIVATION

Parathion, an organophosphate insecticide, undergoes several reactions, one of which (desulfuration) activates it to a toxic enzyme inhibitor, paraoxon. Another biotransformation reaction, ester hydrolysis, converts parathion or its active intermediate to inactive products (see structures, Figure 6.13). This insecticide has some species specificity because the ester hydrolysis reaction of inactivation occurs more readily in mammals than in insects. There are four possible outcomes in biotransformation of a xenobiotic, all of which are illustrated by parathion. The xenobiotic can be metabolized to a nontoxic compound, to a toxic compound, or it may be activated and then inactivated, and, last, it may bind to some biological receptor and exert a pharmacological effect.

Questions

1. Naphthylamine and estrone, a feminizing hormone, are both capable of biotransformation by sulfation. Show the complete reactions for the sulfation of these compounds.
2. Aldrin is biotransformed by a Phase I reaction of epoxidation. Show the chemical equation for this process using structural formulas.
3. Methylmercaptan and atrazine are two compounds that undergo Phase I metabolism by N, O, or S-dealkylation. Show the equations for these processes.

4. Figure 6.3 shows some of the metabolic transformations that occur with chlorpromazine. Give the structures of the products listed in this figure.

5. Discuss the significance of the phenomenon of enzyme induction in relation to laboratory measurement of drug concentration in plasma. Does enzyme induction invalidate such measurements? Is drug concentration measurement of no importance for a patient who has significant levels of enzyme induction?

6. How is laboratory testing able to counter the poppy seed defense?

Case Study 1: Drug Metabolism in Forensic Toxicology

A 30-year-old man was driving a motor vehicle when his car went out of control and struck a tree. The driver was rushed to a hospital where he was treated intensively for 24 hours. Eventually, however, he expired from injuries sustained in the accident. His body was transferred to the county morgue and an autopsy established that death was due to the motor vehicle accident and no other cause. However, a toxicological exam completed on body fluids showed the presence of a substance, sodium pentobarbital, that is sometimes used as an abused drug.

This driver had a life insurance policy that listed his wife as beneficiary and contained a double indemnity clause. The policy paid double if death was due to an accident. One of the conditions of the policy was that the double indemnity would not be paid if death was suicidal. The insurance company alleged that his death was due to the accident that was, in turn, related to the decedent's use of barbiturates. The accident would not have occurred, they claimed, if he had not been under the influence of barbiturates while driving the car. From a legal perspective this was suicide because the decedent had contributed toward his own death by driving while under the influence of a drug of abuse, barbiturates.

The wife of the decedent sued the insurance company, claiming that she was being defrauded of her lawful right to the full value of her husband's policy. Experts for the insurance company, however, contended at trial that barbiturates are depressants and have approximately the same effect on driving as alcohol. Witnesses for the laboratory defended their work which unequivocally supported the finding of sodium pentobarbital in the decedent's body.

Is it possible that the victim of this accident was not under the influence of drugs when the accident occurred?
   a) Yes, it may have been a laboratory error.
   b) The analytic work may have been flawless but maybe the specimen was mixed up with a different one.
   c) The patient may have received the barbiturate as a medication in the hospital.
   d) The test was positive but the amount was not measured. Without quantification the result is not meaningful.

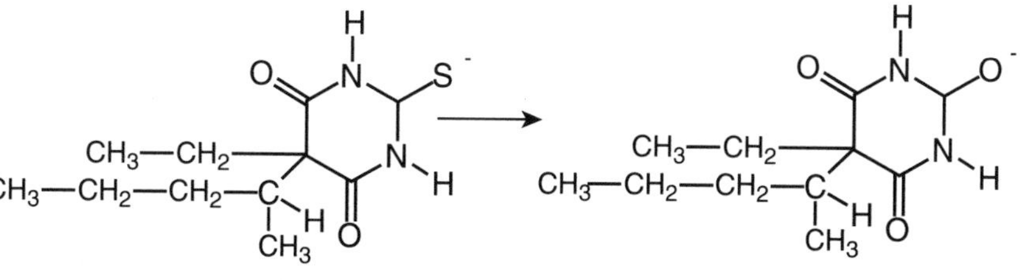

Pentothal (Thiopental)   Pentobarbital

FIGURE 6.14 Conversion of pentothal to pentobarbital.

To settle these issues the surviving spouse hired an attorney who hired a toxicologist. The toxicologist reviewed the hospital records and noted that many drugs were given to the victim during his short hospitalization. Included among them was 100 mg of sodium pentothal (Thiopental), an ultrashort-acting barbiturate that is used as an anesthetic and induces sleep within 20 seconds of IV injection. Thiopental is also employed in the treatment of cranial injury to lower intracranial pressure and reduce oxygen utilization. There was no record, however, of the patient having been given sodium pentobarbital.

The question of whether the patient had driven under the influence of barbiturates was still a puzzle until the toxicologist reviewed the metabolism of sodium pentothal. This drug is a sulfur-containing barbiturate and such drugs are primarily metabolized by conversion to oxybarbiturates. The oxybarbiturate that corresponds to Thiopental is pentobarbital (Figure 6.14). Moreover, the latter has a much longer half-life and is the primary form in which pentothal appears in urine. Conclusion: There was no evidence that the decedent had driven under the influence of a substance that would undermine his ability to control a motor vehicle. The high probability is that postmortem drug findings were due to medications that were given after the accident.

7 Hepatic Toxicity

CONTENTS

The liver is frequently a site for damage from toxic chemicals. Part of its suscepti-bility to toxic damage is because orally ingested materials go directly to the liver via the portal vein. Therefore, the toxin reaches the liver in a relatively concentrated form. Moreover, most metabolic reactions for toxins occur in the liver and the toxin is, therefore, concentrated in the liver. Included among these reactions is activation, in which the pre-toxin is converted from an inactive to a toxic form.

LIVER STRUCTURE AND FUNCTION

Liver cells are called hepatocytes. They are arrayed in rows which are adjacent to sinusoids, spaces that are supplied by branches of the portal vein and hepatic artery and which, in turn, supply the hepatocytes with solutes from the blood (see Figures 7.1 and 7.2). Solutes arriving through the sinusoids bathe the hepatocytes which, in turn, absorb many dissolved particles. Products of liver cell activity exit the hepatocytes by one of two drainage mechanisms. These products may enter the aforementioned sinusoids or they may drain into bile canaliculi. Bile acids as well as many products of toxin metabolism move from the liver cell into the tiny bile channels, the canaliculi, and these merge into larger ducts, eventually forming the bile duct which drains into the upper part of the small intestine, the duodenum. Along the way from liver to duodenum, bile may be temporarily sequestered in the gall bladder.

    The liver is seen, therefore, as a structure composed primarily of actively metab-olizing cells, the hepatocytes, which are highly exposed to fresh blood and nutrients

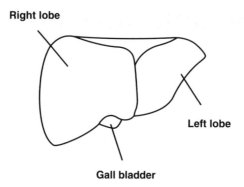

FIGURE 7.1 Gross structure of the liver.

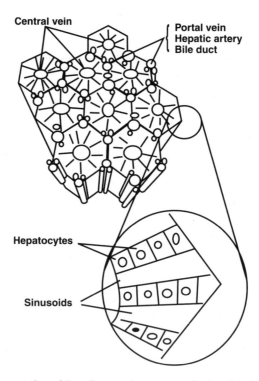

FIGURE 7.2 Representation of the microscopic structure of a liver lobule showing blood and bile channels.

from the portal vein and the sinusoids. These cells are also readily able to excrete their products into two different excretory systems, blood or bile.

The liver carries out many metabolic processes. One of its major functions is a role in glucose metabolism in which glucose is converted to glycogen for storage following a carbohydrate meal. Between meals the liver responds to hypoglycemia (low blood sugar) by glycogenolysis, the re-conversion of glycogen back to glucose to maintain normal blood glucose levels. The liver also may supply glucose by gluconeogenesis, the synthesis of glucose from amino acids or other sources. Lipid metabolism depends intimately upon the liver. Thus, many lipoproteins, proteins which conduct lipids throughout the blood and are found in adipose tissue and other areas, are manufactured in the liver. Lipoprotein precursors are transported to the liver and various types of metabolic processes result in the formation of many classes of lipoprotein. Liver cells have a central role in protein metabolism. Most of the albumin in blood arises from the liver. Amino acid interconversions occur within the liver. Finally, the urea cycle is found within the liver. In this cycle, ammonia, which arises from the deamination of amino acids, is processed into the innocuous product, urea, which makes its way to the kidney for excretion into the urine.

Other activites which occur partly or entirely in the liver include the synthesis of some blood-clotting factors, antibody synthesis, metabolism of xenobiotics (foreign chemicals), synthesis of bile acids (emulsifiers that promote lipid absorption), and storage and synthesis of fat-soluble vitamins.

LIVER INJURY

The types of liver injury that may occur depend on the identity of the liver toxin, the degree of exposure (massive vs. slight), and whether the exposure is acute or chronic.

Fatty Liver

This is an abnormal accumulation of fat in the liver caused by alcohols, carbon tetrachloride, and several other agents. Excess synthesis or inadequate secretion of lipids from the liver may be responsible. Ethanol itself is believed to cause fatty liver, with up to 50% of the total liver mass becoming fat, by blocking the secretion from the liver of triglycerides. Other evidence, however, suggests that ethanol acts instead by increasing fatty acid synthesis. In the face of excess substrate (NADH that arises from the oxidation of ethanol) more lipoprotein product will be formed. This hypothesis is supported by the finding of low lipoprotein levels in the blood of chronic ethanol users who have fatty liver. Other hepatic toxins may act by inhibiting the synthesis of the protein moiety of very low density lipoprotein (VLDL). Without its protein moiety, VLDL particles could be trapped in the liver and contribute to fatty liver. Conversely, some act by limiting, not the synthesis of lipoprotein, but the joining of the individual substituents of VLDL into an aggregate particle. A summary of potential mechanisms of fatty liver is as follows:

1. Reduction in synthesis of protein portion of lipoprotein
2. Failure in joining protein and lipid substituents
3. VLDL transport into cells is impaired
4. Decrease in synthesis of phospholipid portion of VLDL

Fatty liver is not necessarily a pathological finding, by itself, but is often the first step in eventual large-scale liver disease.

Diagnosis of Fatty Liver

In order to document that a patient has fatty infiltration of the liver, fine-needle aspiration followed by histological examination is necessary. In other words, a very narrow-bore needle is inserted through the chest wall and into the liver. A specimen is drawn from the liver into the needle. In the laboratory the specimen is stained and examined under the microscope for the characteristic appearance of fat globules within the tissue structure.

LIVER CELL NECROSIS

Necrosis means cell death. Necrosis can be very limited, in which case it is referred to as focal. If it is widespread, it is called massive necrosis and can be life-threatening. Necrosis also is sometimes described as zonal or diffuse, terms which denote degrees between merely focal vs. massive. Viral or bacterial infection, as well as biochemical toxicants, can be causes of hepatic necrosis. The proximate event in necrosis may be one of the following: binding of reactive metabolites to proteins (e.g., acetaminophen, see separate discussion); lipid peroxidation with associated membrane destruction (see below); defects in protein synthesis; or changes in Na^+, K^+, or Ca^{2+} homeostasis. The specific cause of cell death from a hepatic toxin usually is not known definitively. Calcium is thought to be involved frequently with the cell's death because high levels of calcium are found in the intercellular environment at the time of death. Further, membrane damage, such as occurs with exposure of hepatocytes to many toxins, may change the membrane's ability to control the location of intercellular calcium. Shifts in calcium stores may be causes of cell death or merely found in association with necrosis.

Many biochemical tests are available for evaluating the degree of liver impairment, i.e., the relative number of necrotic cells. Among the best of these markers are the enzymes, alanine aminotransferase (ALT) and aspartate aminotransferase (AST). In the event of liver cell necrosis, these enzymes are sensitive indices of the extent of necrosis; for example, in necrosis associated with viral hepatitis, AST can rise from a normal of 20 International Units per liter to more than 10,000 IU/L. They are, however, not specific, and elevations of these enzymes occur from causes other than liver injury. Serum elevations of bilirubin, especially of the direct, i.e., conjugated, variety are also usually indicative of hepatic disease.

CHOLESTASIS

This term refers to the blocking of the flow of bile. It may arise on a microscopic basis from disruption of the normal hepatic architecture which occurs when hepatocytes die. Alternatively, it may occur from a macroscopic abnormality such as a hepatic tumor. In any case, the outcome is some degree of jaundice (yellow discoloration of the skin) and the disruption of normal biliary flow. Many drugs including some tranquilizers, antidepressants, and hormones are capable of causing cholestasis.

Enzyme tests on blood serum may demonstrate a cholestatic process. Among the enzymes that tend to rise in cholestasis are alkaline phosphatase, gamma glutamyl transferase, and 5′ nucleotidase. Enzyme tests are not entirely accurate in distinguishing between necrosis and cholestasis. However, the enzymes listed here generally rise more prominently in a cholestatic disorder than in a necrotic one.

CIRRHOSIS

This is the deposition of fibrous tissue, collagen, usually on a chronic basis, in various parts of the liver. As the normal hepatocytes are replaced by collagen there is a progressive impairment in liver functions such as drug detoxification and other hepatic metabolic processes. Blood and biliary flow also are affected. The best example of a toxicant causing cirrhosis is ethyl alcohol, although other chemicals may also cause this disorder. There is no specific chemical test for cirrhosis. The diagnosis is suspected on the basis of the patient's history and can be confirmed by microscopic evaluation of a needle biopsy.

HEPATITIS

This term literally means inflammation of the liver. It is caused mainly by viruses and may be diagnosed on the basis of highly specific serological tests that distinguish among hepatitis A, B, C, and D. Hepatitis A is extremely common and has affected more than 50% of the populations of many large urban areas. Inflammation of the liver may also arise from chemicals and, as was true of cirrhosis, alcohol is a common cause of chemically induced hepatitis. Chemical hepatitis is significantly less common than viral hepatitis. Hepatitis is characterized by dramatic elevations of AST and ALT, up to 1000× the upper limit of normal. Interestingly, the disease may be further differentiated on the basis of the ratio of these two enzymes. Viral hepatitis is suggested by greater elevations of ALT, approximately twice the levels of AST. In the case of alcoholic hepatitis the ratio is reversed, i.e., AST is about twice the elevation of ALT. This is consistent with the characteristically more malignant character of alcoholic hepatitis because the AST is a membrane-bound enzyme and will be liberated into the blood as a marker of cell injury only when cell damage is more extensive.

CARCINOGENESIS

Chemical toxicants may produce liver cancer, primary hepatoma, in humans. However, this type of cancer is rare in the United States. It is common in parts of Asia where primary hepatomas are due to viral infection in the liver. Liver tumors in the United States population, by contrast, are usually secondary to the spread of cancer from a different primary site. Natural chemicals that have been implicated in liver cancer include aflatoxin, safrole, and cycasin. Aflatoxin B1 is produced by a fungus and grows on grain. It is known to be converted by the cytochrome P_{450} system to a reactive epoxide (Figure 7.3). This epoxide, in turn, can bind to DNA and change the properties of the genetic material. Synthetic chemicals that may cause liver cancer include vinyl chloride, employed industrially to produce polyvinyl chloride (Figure 7.4). Workers exposed to vinyl chloride in industry produced an unusually large number of angiosarcomas, a tumor which is rare in other settings.

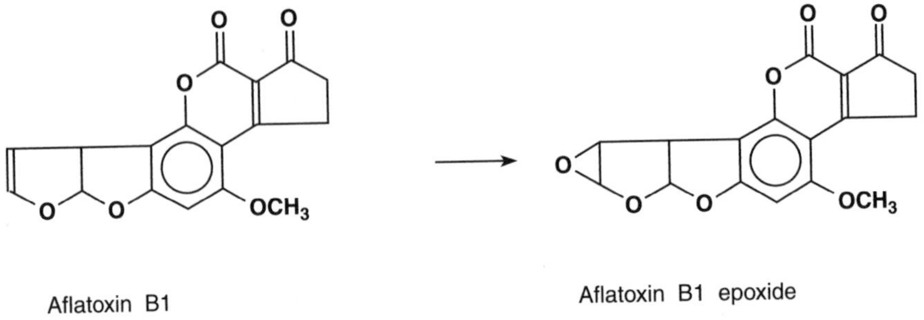

FIGURE 7.3 Aflatoxin and its conversion to a carcinogen.

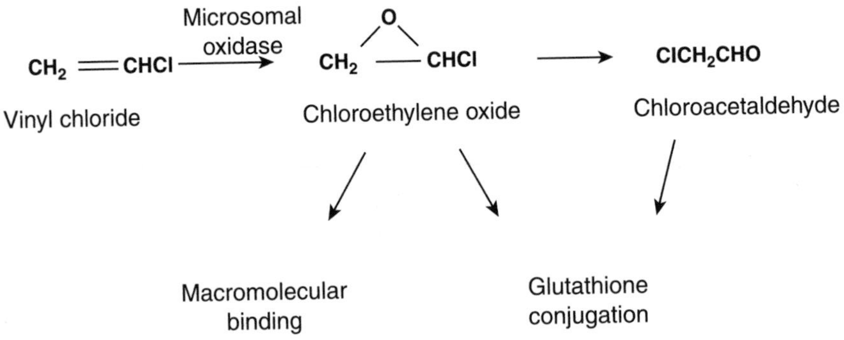

FIGURE 7.4 Vinyl chloride metabolism.

SPECIFIC HEPATIC TOXINS

ACETAMINOPHEN

Acetaminophen is a popular over-the-counter pain reliever that also has anti-inflammatory and antipyretic properties. It is usually a safe drug unless taken in large quantity or when used by individuals whose alcohol drinking behavior is excessive. The mechanism of acetaminophen toxicity is an excellent example of liver pathology. Figure 7.5 shows the metabolism of acetaminophen. It is important to note that several metabolic fates are possible for acetaminophen but over 90% of the drug is excreted as conjugates with glucuronic acid or sulfate. In normal use, less than 5% of acetaminophen will be converted to a reactive electrophilic metabolite, N-acetyl-p-benzoquinoneimine (NAPQI). That portion which is converted to NAPQI will be inactivated readily by reduced glutathione under normal conditions. However, when NAPQI accumulates, it is toxic and binds to nucleophilic macromolecules in the hepatocyte causing cell necrosis. If high amounts of acetaminophen are ingested, then the glutathione detoxification mechanism is overwhelmed. NAPQI achieves high concentrations.

The role of alcohol in the whole process is interesting. Alcohol induces the P_{450} oxidase system enzymes. Therefore, a relatively larger quantity of the acetaminophen will take the metabolic pathway to NAPQI. Alcoholics have suffered acetaminophen overdose on as little as 4 acetaminophen tablets per day.

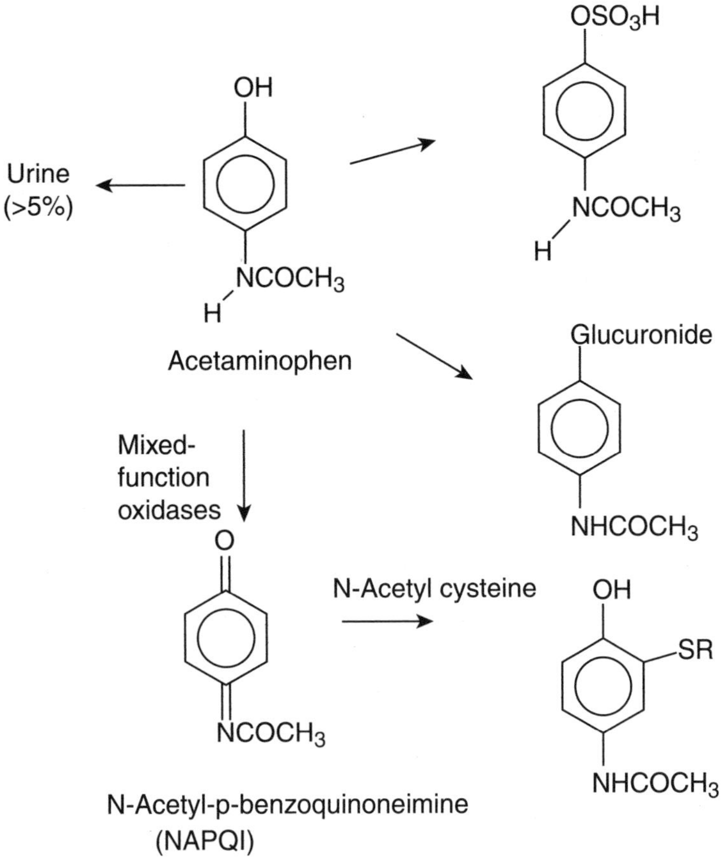

FIGURE 7.5 Metabolism of the analgesic, acetaminophen, and formation of its toxic metabolite.

Knowledge of the acetaminophen metabolic pathway has suggested possible points at which to prevent its potential toxicity. Clearly, enhancing the amount of glutathione should reduce hepatic damage because it is the consumption of glutathione which permits the NAPQI toxin to accumulate. If glutathione drops below 30% of normal, then toxicity occurs. Glutathione itself, however, cannot be given intravenously because it is unable to enter the hepatocyte. N-acetylcysteine (NAC) is an effective antidote if given within 24 hours of ingestion and, preferably, within 16 hours. It is efficacious in several ways. NAC is converted to cysteine which, in turn, increases the amount of active glutathione. NAC also replaces glutathione in effecting the conversion of NAPQI to the nontoxic cysteine conjugate. Finally, NAC provides substrate for the sulfation of acetaminophen and, insofar as acetaminophen becomes conjugated to sulfates, there will be less of it converted to NAPQI.

Biochemical knowledge of acetaminophen is an excellent example of the significance of this information in understanding the mechanism of toxicity and in designing ways to counter that toxicity.

The laboratory is valuable in assisting the physician in treating acetaminophen overdose. Most importantly, the serum concentration of acetaminophen can be measured and is related to the patient's risk of liver injury and liver failure. The laboratory also helps to identify persons with drinking histories who are at risk of acetaminophen overdose despite consuming relatively small amounts of acetaminophen. These alcoholic patients have extremely high levels of AST enzyme when they present to the emergency department. In other words, patients with a history of acetaminophen use are at elevated risk if AST is above normal. They are candidates for antidotal therapy even if the serum acetaminophen is normal.

CARBON TETRACHLORIDE

This compound also may damage the liver and, like acetaminophen, it is not the compound itself but a derivative of it that is damaging. Free radicals are formed from carbon tetrachloride by the action of oxidase enzymes on it. The products of free radical action are conjugated dienes which arise from lipid peroxidation. Although the toxicity of carbon tetrachloride by this mechanism is not proved beyond any doubt, several lines of evidence support it. First, carbon tetrachloride exposure can be shown to be specifically damaging to membranes, which also are known to be sites for free radical attack. Second, administration of antioxidants limits damage caused by carbon tetrachloride. Antioxidants are also known to reduce free radical formation (Figure 7.6). Reactive free radicals have a small radius of action (due to high reactivity); thus, damage is centered in the centrilobular region where the activating enzymes are present in the largest amount. The peroxy radical is believed to be the main cause of lipid peroxidation.

Questions and Exercises

1. Describe the theories of fatty liver formation.
2. What is the difference between necrosis and cholestasis?
3. Discuss the distinctions among hepatitis, cirrhosis, and carcinogenesis.
4. Outline the metabolism of acetaminophen with a sketch of your own design.
5. Show the reactions that are believed to be involved in the toxicity of carbon tetrachloride by a free radical reaction.
6. List laboratory tests that are suitable for the diagnosis of
   Fatty liver
   Cholestasis
   Liver cancer
   Hepatocyte necrosis

Case Study 1: The Liver Spot

A 42-year-old white male received an annual physical examination with routine laboratory testing. An elevated alkaline phosphatase was found in the biochemical

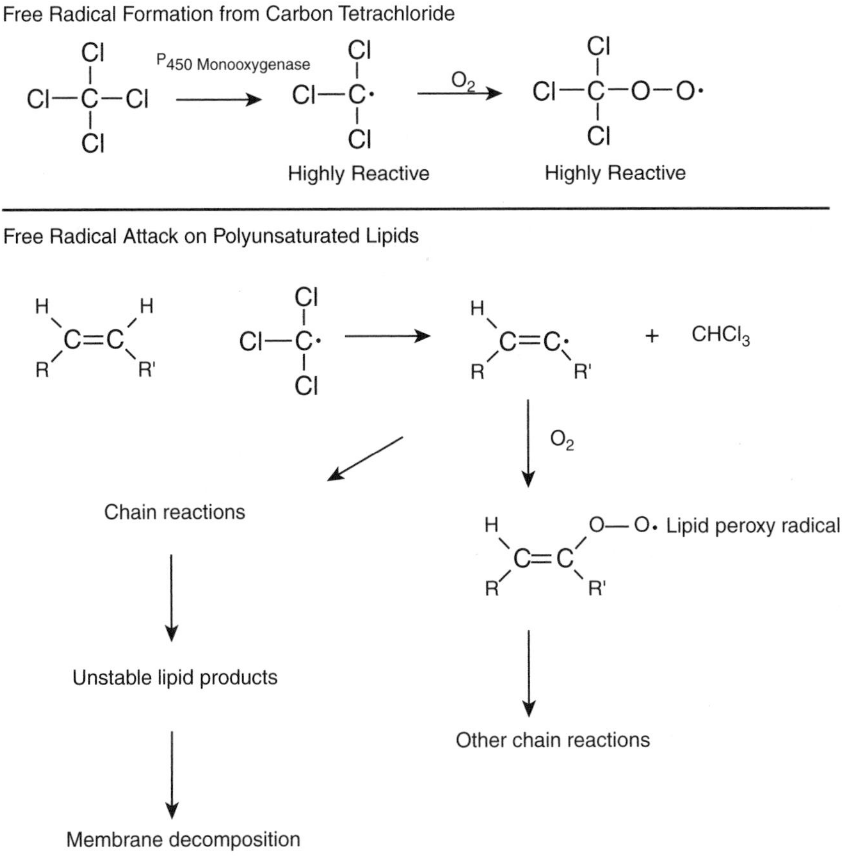

Free Radical Formation from Carbon Tetrachloride

Free Radical Attack on Polyunsaturated Lipids

FIGURE 7.6 Formation of reactive free radicals from carbon tetrachloride and proposed mechanism for membrane damage by free radicals.

screen. Because of this finding, his blood chemistry testing was repeated 3 months later at which time his total bilirubin was also noted to be elevated. His physician, therefore, ordered a liver scan that showed mottling of the right lobe. The interpretation of this finding was that the patient had either cirrhosis or a tumor in his liver.

An employment history revealed that the patient was an employee of a plastics production plant and had worked there for 20 years. More specifically, he believed that the plant made a polymer and he had frequently cleaned vats in which polymer formation occurred.

What toxin was the patient probably exposed to?
   a) CCl$_4$
   b) Methane
   c) Vinyl chloride
   d) Ethanol

The chemistry laboratory data from this patient are consistent with a liver disorder, although the exact nature of the problem cannot be known from blood work alone. The liver scan was somewhat more specific so we can infer that the patient's work brought him into contact with a toxin that may cause liver cancer (hepatoma) or cirrhosis. The employment history is very significant because it relates to plastics production. Upon further investigation it was determined that this man was heavily exposed to vinyl chloride in his workplace where polyvinyl chloride was manufactured. The monomer, vinyl chloride, is a known carcinogen.

Based on the findings from the liver scan the man was admitted for extensive evaluation. Hepatic artery angiography gave findings consistent with a tumor in the right lobe of the liver. This prompted a laparotomy that revealed a 4-cm tumor mass in the right lobe and many smaller nodules throughout the liver. Upon pathological examination the 4-cm mass was determined to be an angiosarcoma. Hepatic fibrosis and cirrhosis were also widespread in the liver. Surgery for resection of the more affected right lobe was considered but it was thought to be too hazardous because of the diseased condition of the rest of the liver. The patient was started on adriamycin, 60 mg/m^2 of body surface area IV every 3 weeks. It was also decided to monitor the patient with liver function tests and liver scans on a periodic basis. The patient tolerated the chemotherapy with moderate abnormalities in blood tests including platelets that dropped to 80,000/mm^3 and leucocyte counts as low as 2000/mm^3. During subsequent check-ups the patient remained approximately the same. Cyclophosphamide therapy was, however, substituted for adriamycin. One year later the patient died from a massive hemorrhage in his abdomen that resulted from a rupture of an angiosarcomatous cyst in his liver. Autopsy showed widely disseminated cancer not only throughout the liver, but also in lymph nodes, lung, and head.

Questions

Q1. Adriamycin is beneficial in higher doses. Why was the dose limited and a substitution for cyclophosphamide made?
   a) Patient did not respond to adriamycin.
   b) Adriamycin is cardiotoxic.
   c) Patient had widespread chemical abnormalities following the therapy.
   d) Patient had a myocardial infarction from this agent.

Q2. This patient had an earlier history of heavy alcohol consumption. Is this significant?
   a) No, because alcohol causes cirrhosis as the only liver finding.
   b) Yes, because alcohol causes cancer more frequently than vinyl chloride and may be the real agent in this case.
   c) Yes, because alcohol may exacerbate the risk of cancer.
   d) This question must be answered on a patient-by-patient basis.

Q3. What percent of individuals with high levels of vinyl chloride exposure are expected to develop hepatic angiosarcomas?

a) 100%
b) 1%
c) 12%
d) 0.1%

Q4. What is responsible for the carcinogenicity of vinyl chloride?
a) Vinyl chloride changes the host DNA.
b) Vinyl chloride is converted to a simple hydrocarbon.
c) Metabolism forms reactive metabolites from vinyl chloride.
d) Vinyl chloride is converted to a known carcinogen, methylene chloride.

Answers and Discussion

Q1. (Answer = b) Adriamycin, in common with virtually all chemotherapeutic agents, has high potential toxicity. In the case of this drug, the limiting toxicity is cardiac. More drug might have been beneficial in attacking the tumor but it would likely have been cardiotoxic. There was no mention in his history of chemical abnormalities nor of myocardial infarction during his treatment for the angiosarcoma.

Q2. (Answer = c) Alcohol is responsible for a range of liver pathology. Heavy drinking causes fatty liver that may progress to hepatitis that may progress to cirrhosis. Some small number of alcoholics develop liver cancer. The specific pathology resulting from alcohol is not predictable but it is certain that alcoholism correlates with risk of hepatic cancer. A history of alcohol abuse puts this patient in a higher risk category. Whether this is merely additive to the risk that arises from vinyl chloride exposure or whether it is greater than the additive risk predicted from each factor independently is not known. This patient drank excessively and required hospitalization on 3 occasions over the previous 5 years for alcohol abuse.

Q3. (Answer = c) Studies show that about 1 in 8 of workers who are heavily exposed to vinyl chloride develop angiosarcoma. Those who manually clean the polymerization tanks have the highest risk. There is no cure for this disease other than liver transplant which is contraindicated if the disease is metastatic at the time of diagnosis. The relationship with vinyl chloride exposure as the causative agent is also based on extensive workplace studies. It is confirmed by many laboratory animal exposure studies.

Q4. (Answer = c) Although there is not absolute certainty on this point the best evidence suggests that vinyl chloride is converted to reactive metabolites. One line of evidence supporting this hypothesis is that there is an enhanced mutagenic response in *Salmonella typimurium* exposed to vinyl chloride when microsomal enzymes are present.

Reference

1. Berk, P. et al., Vinyl chloride-associated liver disease, *Ann. Internal Med.,* 84, 717–731, 1976.

Case Study 2: Hazards of Hazardous Waste Removal

Three workers, charged with removal of old chemicals from a closed factory that had once manufactured chlorofluorocarbons, were handling several large barrels of a sweet-smelling liquid. The room in which they worked was hot and poorly ventilated. One of the workers, a 24-year-old man, removed his respirator because he had been drinking the night before and had a hangover. He mentioned that he could work more efficiently without the respirator. Shortly after, all three workers complained of dizziness, headache, and nausea.

They reported to an emergency department where physical exams showed no abnormalities for the two workers who had not removed their respirators, a 40-year-old man and a 32-year-old, 6-week-pregnant woman. The younger man, however, was ataxic and confused. He was held for observation whereas his co-workers were discharged. After 6 hours the patient became sicker with nausea, vomiting, diarrhea, and abdominal pain. Based on his history of exposure, he was given gastric lavage and activated charcoal. N-acetyl cysteine was provided intravenously for its antioxidant activity. His disorientation intensified and he was febrile and had an elevated pulse rate at 140 per minute. Two days after admission he remained febrile and laboratory studies now demonstrate hepatic and renal impairment:

Creatinine	2 mg/dL
AST	80 U/L
Total bilirubin	2.4 mg/dL
Prothrombin time	15 seconds
Urinalysis	2$^+$ proteinuria

What is the toxin that the patient was exposed to?
  a) Carbon tetrachloride
  b) Hexane
  c) Ethanol
  d) Methanol

The patient was poisoned by merely being in an area containing a waste material, presumably an organic compound used in the synthesis of chlorofluorocarbons. Methanol and ethanol are not sufficiently toxic to produce severe symptoms just from this form of casual contact. They would have to be ingested. Hexane has a high vapor pressure and one could be injured simply by breathing fumes of hexane. Renal and hepatic findings are possible but not likely. Hexane does not have a sweet odor. Carbon tetrachloride is the most suspect agent because it might be expected to be found in this setting, has a sweet odor, and is known to cause hepatic, renal, and CNS symptoms.

Other symptoms that the patient exhibited during his first 2 days of hospitalization included weakness, lethargy, stupor, and restricted vision. He experienced a moderate coma on the day following admission. This gradually resolved as did most of the CNS signs over the ensuing 5 days.

With supportive care the patient eventually recovered. He was discharged and cautioned strongly about finding a different job. He was also counseled to discontinue drinking alcohol.

Questions

Q1. Why is alcohol an important factor in a patient exposed to carbon tetra-chloride?
   a) It is an additional hepatotoxin.
   b) It induces enzymes that promote the conversion of CCl_4 to a toxic product.
   c) Both of the above.
Q2. What effect will this exposure have on the fetus of the pregnant worker?
   a) Severe impact because the fetus is very young.
   b) No effect because the exposure was minimal.
   c) No effect because these enzymes have not yet formed in a 6-week-old fetus.
   d) The greatest concern is the carcinogenicity of CCl_4.
Q3. One of these exposed workers had a history of hepatitis B.
   a) Unrelated to this exposure because the virus does not make free radicals.
   b) Only relevant if it were a recent exposure to virus.
   c) Hepatitis B is not relevant, but hepatitis A is important in this context.
   d) The previous history of viral hepatitis means an enhanced risk of hepatic carcinoma.

Answers and Discussion

Q1. (Answer = c) This patient admitted that he drank nine beers the night before his exposure to carbon tetrachloride. He began work, therefore, with his liver already somewhat compromised by a well-known toxin, alcohol. Carbon tetrachloride would be at least additive as an hepatotoxin. More importantly, CCl_4 is exhaled or metabolized. The fraction that is metabolized is most harmful and forms trichloromethyl free radical. Metabolism is by the inducible P_{450} enzyme system. This system is induced by alcohol so a person who drinks it will have a higher amount of enzyme and, therefore, make more of the injurious trichloromethyl free radical. The free radical has multiple deleterious actions including destruction of cell membranes in many organs.
Q2. (Answer = c) Carbon tetrachloride is lipophilic and will, therefore, cross the placenta or other membranes. Studies show, however, that it is not injurious to animals in the early stages of pregnancy. This is thought to be because enzymes needed for the conversion of carbon tetrachloride to

active free radicals do not appear in the fetus until the latter stages of pregnancy.

Q3. (Answer = d) Multiple episodes of liver injury, whether chemical or viral in nature, are cumulative; that is, they increase the risk of chronic liver disease including hepatocellular cancer.

Reference

Agency for Toxic Substances and Disease Registry, Carbon tetrachloride toxicity, *Am. Fam. Physician,* 46, 1199–1207, 1992.

8 Renal Toxicology

CONTENTS

There are two kidneys located in the middle of the back. Each is supplied with blood by a branch of the descending aorta called the renal artery. Blood is filtered by the kidneys and the filtered product, urine, is passed to the urinary bladder via the ureters. Each kidney (Figure 8.1) contains about 1,000,000 functional units known as nephrons. The basic structure of these nephrons is depicted in Figure 8.2.

RENAL FUNCTION

The major function of the kidneys is elimination of waste from the blood. However, many other important activities are carried out by this organ, including metabolic processes (although less than the number carried out by the liver). The kidney also plays a central role in controlling acid-base balance. When there is an acid-base imbalance in the blood, renal compensation can partly offset the effects of excess acid or base by regulating the rate at which bicarbonate is excreted into the urine. The kidney also can contribute to hydrogen ion homeostasis by producing glutamine from glutamic acid. This is its major method for dumping excess hydrogen ion during episodes of metabolic acidosis. Hormonal activities of the kidney include synthesis of renin (blood pressure regulation), erythropoietin (red cell production), and 1,25-dihydroxyvitamin D3, the most active form of vitamin D, for the absorption and retention of calcium in the body.

The kidney is especially susceptible to the effects of toxins for several reasons. In the first place, it receives a disproportionate amount of blood flow. One might expect that the blood flow to the kidney would be small because the kidneys weigh less than 5 lbs. each. However, they actually receive 25% of the total blood flow, undoubtedly because of their important function in relation to clearing the blood of waste. In addition, the very fact that the kidneys are responsible for concentrating

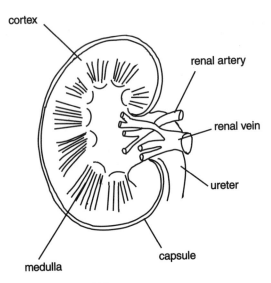

FIGURE 8.1 Gross anatomy of the kidney.

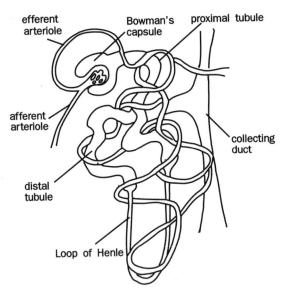

FIGURE 8.2 Illustration of a nephron, basic unit of the kidney.

substances in preparation for excretion means that substances, including toxins, reach much higher concentrations within the kidney than within the bloodstream. Last, renal toxicity is intensified because the kidney, like the liver, is capable of converting inactive pre-toxins into toxic substances.

The elimination activity of the kidney is achieved by several structures within the nephron: glomeruli, proximal tubules, and distal tubules. Blood filtration starts within the glomerulus. All of the solute within blood that has molecular weight less than approximately 40,000 Da is passed through the glomerular membrane into the tubules. About 120 mL per minute or 180 L per day of blood are treated in this manner. Glomerular filtration is a very simple, passive process governed by the pressure of the blood (slowing in the presence of low blood pressure or low blood volume) and the size of the particles to be filtered.

The body's way of filtration is accomplished most efficiently by rapid transfer of almost every small molecule to the glomerular filtrate and then gradual reabsorption back into the blood of those substances needed for normal biochemistry (Figure 8.3). Thus, the filtrate flowing through the proximal tubules is subjected to close scrutiny and valuable substances are selected for absorption back into the blood. Glucose and amino acids are among the substances salvaged at this point. It is noteworthy that biochemicals become concentrated at this stage and, therefore, toxins may be especially deleterious to the proximal tubules based on their relatively high concentrations in this region. Both active and passive absorption processes are involved in tubular reabsorption. However, passive absorption is usually found for xenobiotic materials. When absorption is passive it favors nonpolar, i.e., lipophilic, compounds because they are better able to transit the lipid-rich cell membrane. This is an example of the chemical principle that like dissolves like. Similarly, compounds biotransformed to lipophilic ones by hepatic or renal metabolism also have a higher likelihood of re-entering the blood. While the proximal tubule cells are busy extracting compounds from the glomerular filtrate, and thereby sparing them from excretion, they are also engaged in secretion of other substances. Thus, one sees that the activity of cells in the proximal tubules is highly sophisticated and acts by several mechanisms to regulate the final composition of the filtrate, the fluid destined for elimination from the body.

In tubular secretion the sulfate and glururonide conjugates of xenobiotics are actively transferred from blood into the glomerular filtrate. Other acids and bases are also objects of tubular secretion. This process, when it occurs in a passive manner, is very much influenced by pH. See the discussion of ion-trapping in Chapter 3.

to proximal tubule

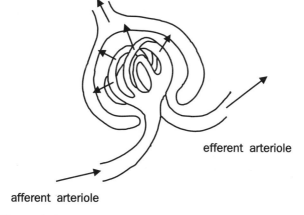

efferent arteriole

afferent arteriole

FIGURE 8.3 The renal glomerulus.

NEPHROTOXICANTS

METALS

Metals, particularly heavy ones, are capable of causing kidney damage. The specific site of damage is usually the proximal tubules and cell death or impairment results. At a biochemical level metals bind to sulfhydryl groups on proteins found in membranes or in enzymes, and thereby interfere with normal function leading to various degrees of reduced function or death. At least one metal, mercury, is believed to have one additional deleterious action, namely, constriction of blood vessels with a consequent reduction of blood flow and oxygen supply to renal tissue.

Chromium has a different effect from mercury. It inhibits glucose reabsorption by damaging the proximal convoluted tubule, the site of glucose re-uptake. Chromium toxicity depends greatly on the oxidation state of chromium. If the oxidation state is 3+, the chromium is relatively nontoxic and is absorbed to a very limited degree. When the oxidation state is 6+, however, the chromium is reduced by intracellular enzymes. In the process, free radicals are formed and disrupt many cellular processes.

Lead is a heavy metal which is taken up by proximal tubule cells. Within these cells lead interferes with mitochondrial biochemistry. The cell has some ability to detoxify lead and appears to do this to some degree by forming inclusion bodies of lead bonded to acidic proteins. Such bodies, which appear before lead toxicity starts, may be seen as microscopic inclusions within the cell.

Cadmium (atomic weight = 112.4, density = 8.6 g/mL) is somewhat different from other metals, being a common cause of kidney damage. It has a very long half-life in the human body, approximately 15 years and, thus, even low degrees of exposure may eventually result in significant and toxic accumulations. Metallothionein, a protein that primarily binds zinc, is synthesized within the kidney in response to high concentrations of cadmium. The metallothionein then binds cadmium and the resulting complex is taken up by renal lysosomes presumably as a protective mechanism. However, some cadmium will be released as the lysosomes become saturated and nephrotoxicity, especially to proximal tubular cells, results.

The kidney has some capacity to reduce the impact of heavy metals upon it. One mechanism of protection involves the transfer of metals into the subcellular structures known as lysosomes. This transfer occurs by several mechanisms and results in sequestration of the metal in a relatively innocuous form. It is an effective protective device provided the concentration of metal is not so high as to overwhelm lysosomal storage capacity.

ANTIBIOTICS

Many antibiotics have at least some degree of nephrotoxicity. Prominent among those that do are the aminoglycosides, a group that includes gentamycin, kanamycin, sisomycin, and streptomycin (Figure 8.4). The mechanism of their nephrotoxicity is not clear but may be indirect in the sense that their toxicant actions arise as a consequence of the kidney's method of eliminating them. They carry a plus charge and are filtered by the glomerulus, reabsorbed in the proximal tubule by binding to

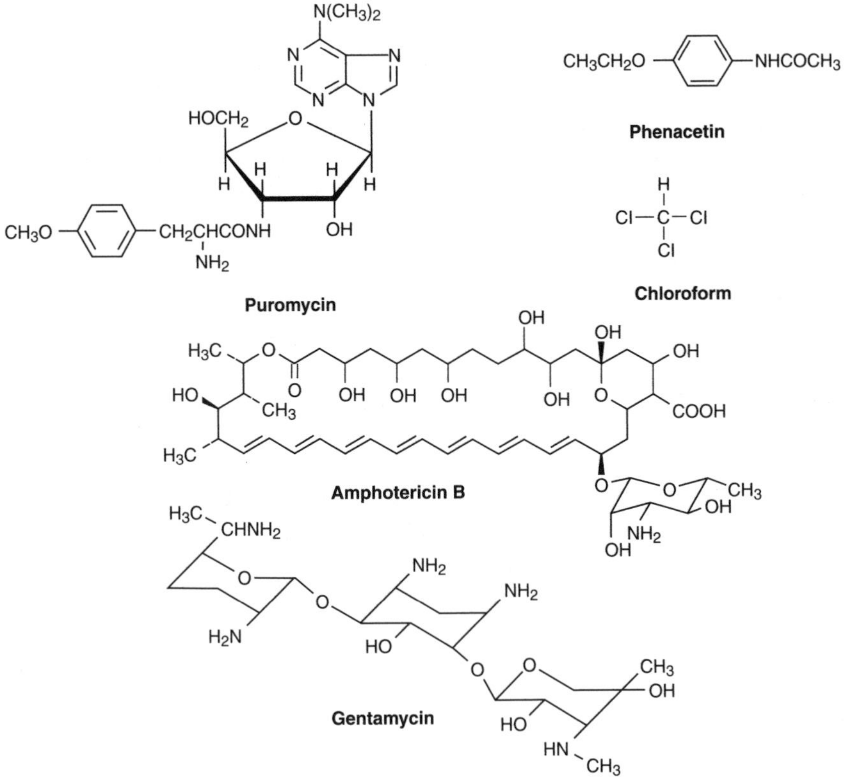

FIGURE 8.4 Structures of some known nephrotoxins.

negatively charged phospholipids on membranes, and taken up by lysosomes. When the lysosomal capacity is exceeded, the lysosomes rupture and release hydrolytic enzymes that produce cell death. The concentration of liposomal enzymes in urine correlates with the degree of renal damage. Other theories about aminoglycoside renal toxicity relate to inhibition of phospholipases or effects on mitochondrial function.

Puromycin is another antibiotic with nephrotoxic action. It reduces the negative charge on the glomerular membrane which causes the excretion of large anions including proteins. In turn, this leads to elevated urinary protein, proteinuria. Puromycin also specifically damages kidney cells known as podocytes. This causes an increase in filtration of particles that are normally too large to pass into the filtrate.

AMPHOTERICIN B

Although an antibiotic, amphotericin B is discussed separately because it acts in a manner that is dissimilar to other members of its class. This drug has a nonspecific effect on the kidney. It is a surface-active agent that binds to membrane phospholipids and thereby disrupts the integrity of cell membranes. Normal cell permeability is affected. This toxicity is not kidney-specific and would be expected in any organ in which the amphotericin B achieved high enough concentrations.

HALOGENATED HYDROCARBONS

These molecules are likely to damage kidney tissue in the same manner in which they affect the liver. They are thought to be activated by cytochrome P_{450} oxidases producing free radicals which can then attack cell organelles such as cell membranes. Halogenated hydrocarbons like chloroform may covalently bind renal tubular cell proteins and thereby disrupt the normal activity of those proteins.

ANALGESICS

Aspirin and phenacetin damage the medulla, the inner structure of the kidney where many of the loops and collecting ducts are located. They also affect the blood vessels, which may be the reason the medulla is secondarily affected. In other words, aspirin inhibits prostaglandin synthesis, thus reducing vasodilation with an eventual effect on kidney function.

ASSESSMENT OF KIDNEY INJURY BY BIOCHEMICAL TESTING

The kidney's ability to filter blood depends primarily on the health of the nephron and, within the nephron, on the integrity of the glomerulus. Glomerular filtration, therefore, is the best index of filtering ability. The best measure of filtration, in turn, is clearance, i.e., the removal of waste chemicals from blood per unit time. Good renal function equals the ability to clear waste chemicals effectively from the blood. Clearance is expressed in units of milliliters per minute and equals the volume of blood that is cleared per minute. A normal result in humans is approximately 120 mL/min. Individuals with serious impairment may have clearances of only 20 mL/min or less. These figures are based on the clearance of creatinine, a waste product of muscle metabolism. Of various chemicals that have been tested as candidates for determining the glomerular filtration rate, creatinine is regarded as the best chemical to measure. It is not perfect because some creatinine is transferred to the urine by tubular secretion and, therefore, it is not strictly accurate to regard all urinary creatinine as being due to glomerular filtration. Nevertheless, creatinine clearance is very close to an exact estimate of the true glomerular filtration rate. The formula for creatinine clearance is

Creatinine clearance =

(urinary creatinine concentration × urine volume)/(serum creatinine × collection time)

where:
   Urinary creatinine is in mg/dL.*
   Serum creatinine is in mg/dL.*
   Urine volume is in mL.

---

* Any concentration unit is acceptable as long as it is the same for both urinary and serum creatinine.

Collection time is usually 24 hours. Enter it as 1440 minutes. A shorter collection time is not advisable and increases the imprecision of the result. The result for creatinine clearance is expressed in mL/min. Whereas creatinine clearance estimates glomerular function, other tests are available to assess the health of other parts of the nephron.

TESTS FOR TUBULE FUNCTION

Tests for tubular function are not as simple nor as reliable as the creatinine clearance is for glomerular filtration. Renal markers (indicator chemicals) that are indicative of tubular disease rather than glomerular disease include Beta-2-microglobulin, a low-molecular-weight protein excreted in high amounts in urine when renal tubules are injured. Another useful marker is N-acetyl-beta-D glucosaminidase. This is an enzyme normally found in the cell lysosome, a subcellular structure that serves as a storage site. When the cell is damaged, some of the lysosomal enzymes are released into urine.

Questions

1. Describe four physiological functions of the kidney.
2. Contrast nephrotoxicity of antibiotics vs. that due to halogenated hydro-carbons.
3. Calculate creatinine clearance for a person with the following data:

Serum creatinine	3.5 mg/dL
24-hour urine volume	450 mL
Urine creatinine	1.41 g/day

This person has normal body surface area. Is this person's creatinine clearance within the normal range?

Case Study 1: The Bright Orange Crystals

A high-school chemistry student brought home some orange crystals for his science project. Unfortunately, they were not stored in a safe area and the student's 2-year-old brother ingested approximately 1 gram of the crystals. The child immediately vomited an orange-tinted material and his parents brought him to a local emergency department. Gastric lavage was attempted and ascorbic acid was provided intravenously. The patient was then transferred to a large, regional children's hospital. Vital signs at this time (3 hours post-ingestion) showed normal temperature and blood pressure and moderate elevations of pulse and respiratory rate. Liver enzymes, renal function tests, and coagulation studies were all within normal limits.

The child's condition deteriorated and he required intubation. He was given ascorbic acid as a continuous intravenous infusion. Diuretics were provided and a double volume exchange transfusion with 1.6 liters of whole blood was conducted. The patient exhibited some improvement from these therapeutic steps. Soon thereafter, however, the child became anuric and renal tests showed elevations of urea and creatinine. He became hypotensive and developed pulmonary edema. It was decided to initiate hemodialysis when peripheral edema became marked but this was discontinued after 3 hours as a result of increasing hypotension. Laboratory studies now revealed progressive deterioration of liver function and decline in coagulation status.

The patient continued to receive aggressive supportive care but died 48 hours after the original ingestion. At autopsy the larynx was eroded with submucosal necrosis. The entire upper gastrointestinal tract was hemorrhagic and ulcerated. There was also extensive necrosis of the liver and the kidneys. Adrenal cortex was hemorrhagic and the brain was somewhat swollen.

What were the orange crystals that the child swallowed?
>   a) Sodium salicylate
>   b) Ammonium dichromate
>   c) Citric acid
>   d) Barium sulfate

Sodium salicylate is a medicinal agent similar to aspirin. It can be toxic but only in amounts much larger than 1 gram. Citric acid and barium sulfate are also toxic in relatively high amounts; neither is orange colored nor is significantly toxic in a 1-g quantity. Barium sulfate is quite insoluble so very little will be absorbed into the circulation. Ammonium dichromate is a very toxic orange-colored chemical. Chromium is present in this salt in the more toxic 6+ oxidation state.

Questions

Q1. Why was ascorbic acid given?
>   a) It lessens the absorption of chromium VI (6+).
>   b) It reduces chromium VI to III (3+)within the gut or blood.
>   c) It may prevent renal failure that occurs from chromium toxicity.
>   d) All of the above.

Q2. Why is chromium VI toxic?
>   a) It selectively inhibits metabolic enzymes found in the liver.
>   b) It interferes with aerobic oxidation of glucose.
>   c) It undergoes intracellular reduction that forms free radicals.
>   d) It undergoes intracellular oxidation with a decrease in available free radicals.

Q3. What was this child's cause of death?
>   a) Chromium-induced liver failure
>   b) Chromium-induced renal failure

c) Chromium-induced cardiac failure

d) Widespread organ dysfunction

Q4. This child's plasma chromium concentration peaked at 4163 mcg/L. How does this compare with normal levels?

a) Slightly above normal

b) 10-fold greater than normal

c) 100-fold greater than normal

d) >1000-fold greater than normal

Answers and Discussion

Q1. (Answer = d) Ascorbic acid is a potent reducing agent. It has been shown to convert chromium VI to chromium III in the gut and in the bloodstream. When this conversion occurs in the gut, it is beneficial because it leads to a reduction in chromium absorption. Chromium VI is absorbed 20-fold more extensively than chromium III. In the blood, chromium III binds to protein and the resulting complex is excreted in the urine.

Q2. (Answer = c) Some of the absorbed chromium VI is reduced to chromium III which is, in turn, excreted. There is a limited capacity for this reduction and the excess chromium VI enters cells and produces free radicals as it undergoes intracellular reduction. Lipid peroxidation, with its associated cell membrane destruction, is just one of the deleterious effects of free radical formation.

Q3. (Answer = d) This child had apparent hepatic toxicity as indicated by elevations of liver enzymes and by a finding of an enlarged liver. His kidneys were impaired as indicated by his failure to produce urine and the development of azotemia (increase in serum levels of nitrogenous waste products). The effects of chromium were not limited to these organs, however, as evidenced by the widespread necrosis that was noted at autopsy. Multi-organ failure is expected when the mechanism of a toxin's action is very general as in this case, namely, the destruction of cell membranes by lipid peroxidation.

Q4. (Answer = d) Normal plasma levels of chromium are less than 0.05 mcg/L of plasma. The concentration in this patient was 4163 at its peak, or more than 80,000 times greater than normal. This was indeed a massive overdose despite the fact that the total amount ingested was just 1 gram.

Reference

Meert, K.L. et al., Acute ammonium dichromate poisoning, *Ann. Emerg. Med.*, 24, 748, 1994.

Case Study 2: The Dangers of Special Nutrients

A 33-year-old white woman experienced severe fatigue and malaise for 2 weeks that intensified over the previous 3 days. She came to an emergency department complaining of the above symptoms plus fever, nausea, and abdominal pain. Because of a history of depression she had received paroxetine and fluphenazine for many months but she discontinued these drugs 2 weeks earlier. At the time of this admission she was off all medications except an over-the-counter "natural product" for weight loss. Although she weighed only 90 lbs and was 5 ft 3 in. tall, she was trying to lose weight and had succeeded to the extent of a 10-lb. loss over the past 2 weeks. Later on she was diagnosed with an eating disorder and psychiatric counseling was begun.

At this time her blood pressure was low at 94/62, heart rate was elevated, and temperature slightly low. Sclera were icteric. Clinical findings plus laboratory data revealed a host of abnormalities including anemia, hemolysis, hepatic dysfunction, renal failure, and thrombocytopenia. Relevant laboratory data are

Hemoglobin	6 g/dL
Platelets	15,000/mm^3
AST	1274 U/L
ALT	992 U/L
Bilirubin	3.7 mg/dL
LDH	7879 U/L
BUN	152 mg/dL
Creatinine	5.3 mg/dL
Urine output	150 mL/day

Because of the hemolysis and low hemoglobin, preliminary diagnoses of thrombotic thrombocytopenic purpura or hemolytic uremic syndrome were made, but the patient had no fever nor mental status changes and other findings were not consistent with these diagnoses. During the first 3 days of hospitalization the patient's hepatic function improved. Her renal function, however, remained poor. She had proteinuria, glycosuria, and red and white cells in the urine. She was, therefore, dialyzed repeatedly. Her urine output began to increase by the 11th day after admission.

Her illness was eventually traced to a metal in her over-the-counter diet aid. What is a possible identity of this metal?

a) Lead
b) Mercury
c) Chromium
d) Sodium

Sodium in the metallic form is too reactive to be present. As a cation it is very nontoxic and is, of course, widespread in commercial products. Lead and mercury are well-known to be very toxic and their inclusion in medicinal products is rare and, on those occasions when they are present, it is in very low amounts. One cannot, of course, absolutely rule out the accidental inclusion of lead or mercury in a specific batch or bottle of a medicinal. Chromium is an essential element. It is also a popular nutritional supplement particularly in the form of chromium picolinate. In this form it is represented as contributing to effective weight loss, lower blood sugar, and improved cholesterol profile. The recommended daily allowance is 50 to 200 μg. This lady was using 1200 to 2400 μg per day of chromium picolinate for at least the previous 4 months. Normal chromium plasma concentrations equal 0.1 to 2.1 μg/mL (Chromium VI) and her plasma concentration was 4.6 μg/mL 24 hours after admission. Her high level of chromium consumption is believed to be the cause of her many symptoms at admission.

This patient was finally discharged after 26 days of hospitalization with a final diagnosis of liver and renal disease due to chromium toxicity. One year after discharge her liver and kidney function were normal on the basis of serum biochemistry testing.

Questions

Q1. What is the oxidation state of chromium in chromium picolinate?
   a) Trivalent (+3)
   b) Divalent (+2)
   c) Hexavalent (+6)
   d) Negative (2-)
Q2. This patient had an increase in blood chromium after hemodialysis. Other patients have had decreases with dialysis. An explanation is
   a) The patient experienced volume contraction.
   b) Covert ingestion of chromium picolinate continued.
   c) Tissue-bound chromium was redistributed into the blood.
   d) A laboratory error occurred.
Q3. Another chromium poisoning was reported in which the patient died from ingestion of 1 g of ammonium dichromate. Why did our patient survive 2400 μg/day for many months?
   a) The dichromate salt is more toxic on a weight-for-weight basis.
   b) The dichromate poisoning was a much greater amount of toxin.
   c) Ammonium salts are more toxic.
   d) The dichromate patient may have had a smaller body mass.
   e) All of the above.

Answers and Discussion

Q1. (Answer = a) Chromium can have many different oxidation states from –2 up to +6. Its specific oxidation state is very important. Hexavalent chromium is considered to be 100 times more toxic than trivalent chromium. It causes many industrial problems in addition to cancer. Trivalent chromium has very low solubility; although present in yeast, meat, and whole grains, it is absorbed only to the extent of 1%. It is believed to be essential for normal glucose metabolism because patients on long-term parenteral nutrition who were chromium deficient had insulin resistance, hyperglycemia, and glycosuria.

Q2. (Answer = c) Volume contraction means that the patient became less hydrated so that solutes such as chromium were dispersed in a smaller volume of blood. This is a common phenomenon but would not explain a change as large as the 50% increase that she experienced. Moreover, repeated episodes of hemodialysis could not lower the chromium. Covert ingestion was highly improbable because family members turned in her bottles of chromium picolinate to the attending physicians. Laboratory error was ruled out on the basis of repeat analysis and confirmation by alternate methods. It is known that chromium achieves tissue levels up to 100 times greater than blood levels. In the case of chronic poisoning those tissue levels would be expected to be very high. Hemodialysis would cause a redistribution of chromium from tissue storage sites into the blood.

Q3. (Answer = e) In ammonium dichromate the chromium is in the hexavalent state. Ammonium salts would be more toxic but this would not be a major consideration. The patient who died from the dichromate was, in fact, only 2 years old and weighed 22 lbs. Finally, 1 g is greater than the total burden of chromium to which the first patient was exposed. She ingested 2400 µg/day for up to 150 days for a total chromium burden of 0.36 g (as picolinate). One gram of ammonium dichromate caused the patient's death in 48 hours due, primarily, to hypotension caused by extensive ulceration and hemorrhage. This patient suffered renal and hepatic failure but it was more likely due to the corrosive action of ammonium dichromate rather than a specific hepatotoxic or nephrotoxic action of chromium. It is of interest that this patient received exchange transfusions and ascorbic acid as a prospective antidote.

Reference

Cerulli, J. et al., Chromium picolinate toxicity, *Ann. Pharmacother.*, 32, 428–431, 1998.

9 Cardiac Toxicity

CONTENTS

The cardiovascular system delivers oxygen and other nutrients to the 300 billion cells that make up the human body. It also removes waste materials to lungs, kidneys, and other destinations for disposal from the body. Other functions such as a role in neuroendocrine control are also part of its activities. In an approximate sense, it has two components: a hollow, muscular pump, the heart, and a system of large and small elastic vessels.

Some knowledge of cardiac anatomy and physiology is needed to understand the nature of toxic activity by especially cardiotoxic chemicals. The heart is found between the lungs in the middle of the chest somewhat skewed (2/3) toward the left of the breastbone. The bottom left corner of the heart is tilted forward and comes close to the surface of the body. A normal heart weighs approximately 200 to 400 grams and equals two clenched fists in volume. Cardiac anatomy includes four chambers whose walls are composed of muscle, the myocardium. The chambers are separated from each other by structures called septa. Blood flows between the chambers through openings that are controlled by valves.

The basic concept of cardiac blood flow begins with blood returning to the heart in the venous system from remote areas of the body, where it enters the right atrium. From there the blood is pumped past the tricuspid valve into the right ventricle. The tricuspid valve has three cusps, or leaflets. Like the other valves found between chambers, it keeps the blood flowing forward. It opens to allow flow when the right atrium contracts and then it snaps shut, thereby preventing backward flow when the right atrium relaxes. The tricuspid valve has strong chords of fibrous tissue, chordae tendineae, that anchor the valve to the ventricular wall. When the right ventricle contracts small muscles in the ventricular wall, papillary muscles pull the chordae tendineae and thus prevent them from flopping too far back. At that point, blood cannot regurgitate into the right atrium but must follow the progression from the right ventricle into the pulmonary circulation. On its way into the pulmonary artery the blood passes the pulmonary valve. Blood is then returned to the heart after being oxygenated. It re-enters the heart at the left atrium which, in turn, pumps the blood by muscle contraction into the left ventricle. Again, a valve separates the two chambers. The valve that functions between left atrium and left ventricle is the mitral valve. This is a cone-shaped funnel resembling the triangular headdress worn by ecclesiastics, the miter; hence, the name, mitral valve. The mitral valve has two highly mobile leaflets that open and close rapidly. Finally, the blood, having arrived in the major chamber, the left ventricle, is pumped from there into the main circulation. The first vessel it enters is the aorta. The valve located between the left ventricle and the aorta is a semilunar valve, so named because of its crescent-shaped cusps. There are several semilunar valves and the specific name for this one is the aortic valve. It is forced open when the left ventricle contracts and blood is propelled into the main circulation. As the left ventricle relaxes, back pressure in the aorta causes the aortic valve to close. The left ventricle does more work than the other chambers by a wide margin. Its walls are, therefore, more than 14 mm thick. This is greater than the thickness of the right ventricle by a factor of two- to threefold. The lungs are very close to the heart and the walls of pulmonary vessels are less resistant than those of the aorta. Therefore, the right ventricular wall has a relatively small muscle mass compared to the left ventricle. (See Figure 9.1.)

The heart is lined on each side by a protective membrane. The smooth membrane on the inside of the heart is called the endocardium, and the outside is covered by a two-layered sac called the pericardium or pericardial sac. The pericardium is connected to the heart muscle on its inner layer, while the outer layer of the pericardium anchors the heart in place by its connections to the vertebral column with ligaments, and to the diaphragm and other organs. A lubricating fluid is found within the pericardial sac reducing friction that would otherwise arise from the intensity of heart beats. The coverage provided by the pericardial sac is thorough, so that in the event the heart were to leak blood, the sac would fill and provide a counter pressure that would effectively prevent the heart from refilling after a pumping step. This life-threatening event is called a cardiac tamponade.

The heart is the hardest working muscle in the body and, therefore, has a high demand for oxygen. This demand is satisfied by two coronary arteries that arise from the aorta and run around the outside of the heart. Each of these arteries branches

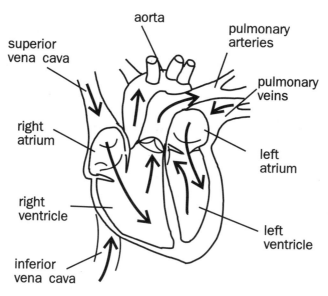

FIGURE 9.1 The heart and its chambers in relation to systemic circulation.

into smaller vessels and capillaries that supply blood to each fiber in the heart. The rate of blood flow through the coronary arteries is, predictably, associated with the level of physical activity of the body. It can increase by 500% under conditions of extreme exertion. The increased blood flow is associated with both a higher cardiac output and dilatation of the coronary arteries.

CONDUCTION SYSTEM

Heart rhythm is regulated by electrical currents. A microscopic bundle of specialized cells, the sinus node, is the key agent in overall control of heart rhythm. It is called the heart's natural pacemaker. The sinus node is found in the upper right corner of the heart and is the usual source of electrical impulses to the heart. Because any part of the heart muscle has an inherent ability to generate electrical impulses, another part of the cardiac conduction system can take over impulse generation in the event that the sinus node becomes impaired. From the sinus node impulses usually transmit through muscle fibers of the atria to the atrioventricular node found in the area at the juncture of the right atrium and right ventricle. Impulses continue from the atrioventricular node along the bundle of His and the Purkinje fibers. These structures are simply fibrous paths specialized for efficient conduction of electric impulses. Eventually, impulses reach the muscles of the right and left ventricles.

OVERALL CARDIAC ACTIVITY

The above description of impulse conduction and an understanding of the activity of each chamber and valve allow one to appreciate the events in the complete cardiac cycle. Electric activity, on the order of just one millionth of an ampere, coordinates the rhythmic contraction of the heart. There are two phases. Diastole is the phase in which the heart's ventricles are relaxed. This is about 67% of the entire cardiac cycle. Systole is that interval during which blood is pumped from the ventricles. It lasts for about 33% of the cycle.

Normal diastole occurs as follows. The sinus node generates an electric impulse that causes the atria to contract. The tricuspid and mitral valves are open. Blood is pumped from the atria into the ventricles. When this diastolic phase ends, the impulse has reached the ventricles and they are now ready to contract. During the systolic phase, the ventricles contract and close the tricuspid and mitral valves. As the pressure in the ventricles rises, the pulmonary and aortic valves are forced open and blood is pushed into the pulmonary artery and the aorta. As this phase ends, the ventricles relax, blood backs up from the pulmonary artery and the aorta, and the pulmonary and aortic valves are shut by back pressure. As the pressure in the ventricles is now lower than the atria, the tricuspid and aortic valves open again and a new cycle starts. All of the events associated with the cardiac cycle occur approximately 70 times each minute or more than once a second, depending on the heart rate of the individual person. The lub-dub sound, as it is often called, corresponds to one cardiac cycle composed, in turn, of two sets of contractions.

The cardiac output is the name given to that volume of blood pumped by the right ventricle in 1 minute. This logically depends on the heart rate and also the volume of blood dispensed with each contraction. The latter is called the stroke volume and it equals about 50% of the blood within the left ventricle. Stroke volume is an important clinical parameter and its decrease is an ominous finding indicative of developing heart failure.

CARDIAC FUNCTION AND TOXICITY:
GENERAL PRINCIPLES

Many chemicals cause structural and/or functional abnormalities in cardiac function. Factors that dictate the severity of toxicity include the concentration of the chemical, its inherent toxicity, and the duration of exposure. In particular, because cardiac tissue is intrinsically very excitable it is a sensitive target for toxic responses. Toxins may cause arrhythmias by altering impulse formation or conduction. Other toxins may alter contractile function directly, for example, by a cytotoxic mechanism, or indirectly, by an electrical disturbance. Metabolic alterations may also be caused by a toxin and these alterations are manifested by contraction and/or conduction abnormalities. Some toxin-induced aberrations in cardiac activity can be repaired, but the repair mechanism itself may be an additional part of the toxin's detrimental action.

Cardiotoxicity can be both acute and chronic in nature. Acute cardiac injury carries a high risk because of the indispensable character of heart action. Mechanisms associated with chronic injury have become better understood in recent years. Aspects of chronic cardiac injury include alterations in myocardial cell excitability, activation of pre-toxins, failed chemical detoxification, accumulation of an active toxin, and extension of toxic pharmacological effects. Later in this chapter specific toxins are discussed and a better understanding of these various mechanisms will be possible.

BIOCHEMICAL MECHANISMS

From the perspective of biochemistry, toxicity to myocardial tissue may relate to one or more of several abnormal changes. These can, in turn, be classified into four categories; ionic changes, energy alterations, membrane disturbances, or cellular defense changes.

IONIC CHANGES

Ionic changes can be detrimental to cardiac tissue. The normal functioning of the myocardium depends largely on the ionic composition of local intracellular and intercellular fluids. Calcium, for example, is critical in the contractile process. This central ion also influences enzyme actions, hormone message transfer, and other membrane-related activities. A change in calcium ion concentration can have a great effect on normal cardiac function. In fact, some have proposed that accumulation of intracellular calcium is the major event in the final stages of cell death. In this context, several cardiotoxins that are discussed more fully below relate to increased calcium ion concentration and myocardial cell injury. These include catecholamines, medicinal agents like doxorubicin, and halogenated anesthetics.

Sodium is another ion that is central to cardiac contractility. Depolarization of cardiac and other cells occurs due to a massive influx of sodium ion. Here, too, toxic actions of a number of cardiac agents are associated with a specific interference in normal intracellular sodium activity. Alkaloids like batrachotoxin, grayanotoxin, and aconitine, all natural products, increase resting sodium permeability and thereby affect the heart and also other nervous system activity. Conversely, many antiarrhythmic agents inhibit the sodium current in myocardial cells. It seems that calcium and sodium ions are the ones whose concentration changes have the greatest influence on heart activity. Several others, however, such as potassium, iron, and manganese, also can influence cardiac activity.

ENERGY CHANGES

Some toxins affect cardiac activity by reducing the availability of energy by means of modifying mitochondrial function. In this context it should be mentioned that the heart is especially vulnerable to energy perturbations because it has very limited storage of energy and, conversely, has a great need for uninterrupted energy flow. Some toxins impair energy flow by attacking the mitochondrion of myocytes. Various outcomes result, including depletion of high energy phosphates, reduction in the cell's ability to deal with oxidative damage, and calcium overload within the cell. One agent that may inhibit intracellular energy flow is calcium. When calcium is present in high amounts in the heart cell, it accumulates in the mitochondria. One of its effects at that location is the uncoupling of oxidative phosphorylation. Cyanide and carbon monoxide affect the energy currency of every cell but, as mentioned earlier, the heart is especially involved because of its high energy demands.

MEMBRANE CHANGES

Some cardiotoxins derive their deleterious effects by specific actions on the myocyte membrane. These actions are multi-targeted and may include some directed at mitochondria, plasma membranes, lysosomes, or sarcoplasmic reticulum. Within those particular structures the specific type of membrane action may involve disruption of energy flow, intracellular calcium accumulation, activation of hydrolytic enzymes, or altered contractility of heart muscle. This topic is expanded under the discussion of specific cardiotoxins (see below).

FREE RADICAL FORMATION

The energy demands of cardiac pumping require that oxidative phosphorylation supplies most of the needed energy. Utilization of molecular oxygen leads to the formation of highly reactive oxygen-derived free radicals. There are mechanisms in place that inactivate many of the free radicals produced by metabolism and, thus, protect cells from oxidative injury. Components of the antioxidant defense system include glutathione-glutathione peroxidase, superoxide dismutase, catalase, ascorbic acid (vitamin C), and alpha-tocopherol (vitamin E). It is beyond the scope of the present discussion to expand on the actions of each of these antioxidant mechanisms; however, one must emphasize that some cardiotoxins act at the level of interference in this normal method for oxidant removal. Again, specific examples are discussed below.

CLASSIFICATION OF CARDIOTOXINS

Cardiotoxicity is not amenable to a simple system of classification. Instead, a wide variety of agents may have toxic action on the myocardium. Some of the better known are antidepressants of the tricyclic category; antineoplastic agents such as adriamycin, antibiotics, alcohols, anesthetics; and heavy metals. Cardiac drugs become cardiotoxins when taken in large doses. Some of the members of this category that have been involved in many cases of toxicity are digoxin (and other digitalis glycosides), quinidine, beta-adrenergic-receptor agonists, beta-adrenergic-receptor antagonists, and some antihypertensive agents. What follows is a discussion of the mechanisms of some cardiac toxins.

SPECIFIC CARDIOTOXINS

Catecholamines

Norepinephrine, epinephrine, and a synthetic analog, isoproterenol, can be cardiotoxic (see Figure 9.2). The normal function of the first two members of this category is to activate alpha and beta receptors, leading to a variety of actions, especially elevation of blood pressure and increased cardiac output. Isoproterenol is a relatively selective beta-receptor agonist. The cardiotoxicity of these compounds is believed to be associated with exaggeration of their normal pharmacological actions. It may be manifested in a variety of symptoms such as arrhythmias, tachycardia, ventricular fibrillation, hypertension, and even myocardial necrosis. It seems

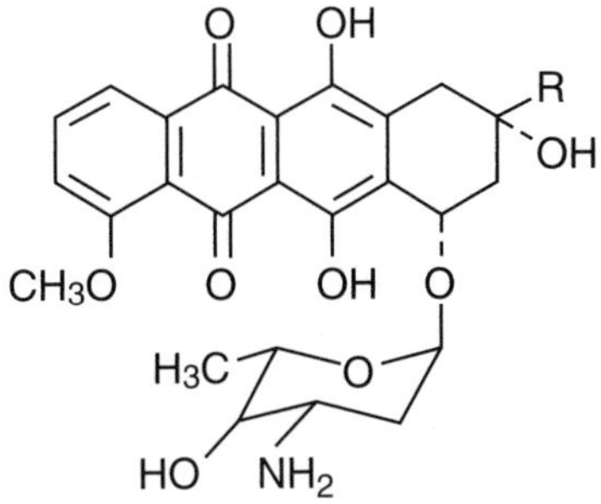

Adriamycin (R = $COCH_2OH$)
Daunorubicin (R = COCH)3

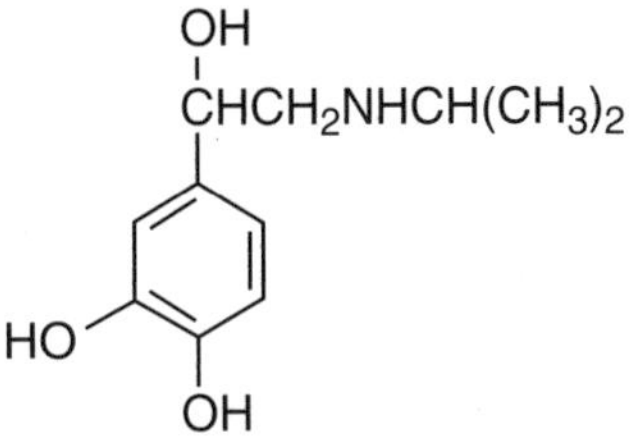

Isoproterenol

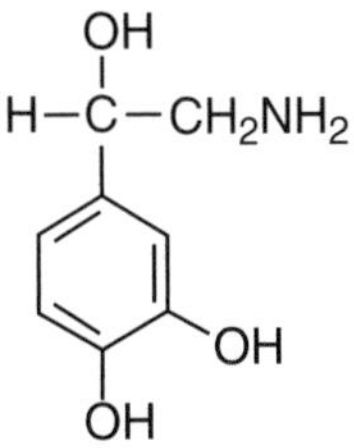

Norepinephrine

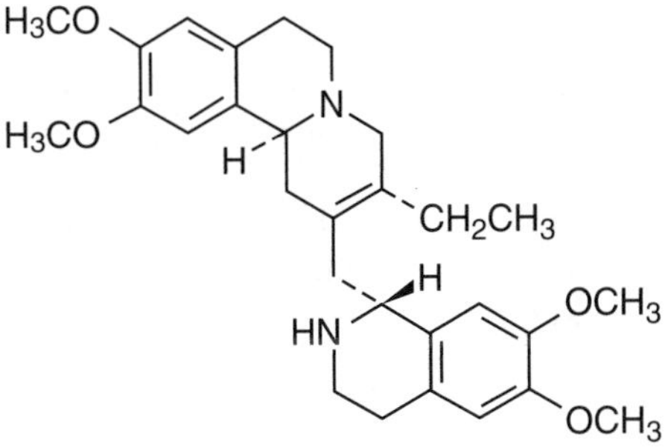

Emetine

CH_3CH_2OH Ethyl alcohol

FIGURE 9.2 Structures of some cardiotoxins.

that only isoproterenol can be toxic to the extent of causing a myocardial infarction-like syndrome. Because of this drug's ability to cause necrosis of myocytes it has been employed in research on the pathophysiology of myocardial infarction. The point of attack of isoproterenol upon the myocyte is not understood clearly but most research suggests that the sarcolemma, the myocyte cell membrane, is undermined by catecholamines. Because the sarcolemma is responsible for maintenance of ionic homeostasis and cellular integrity, catecholamines are believed to compromise the permeability of the sarcolemma. An outcome of this is an influx of calcium. In experimental animals there is clear evidence of calcium accumulating in the heart after administration of isoproterenol. Therefore, calcium overload, as alluded to earlier, is believed to be the cause of the cardiac damage related to isoproterenol and other catecholamines. Calcium channel blockers are a relatively new category of cardiac drugs and their discovery was related to an increased awareness of the dangers of intracellular calcium as noted in research on catecholamines.

Cancer Chemotherapy

Antibiotics belonging to the anthracycline class have a well-known cardiotoxicity. Doxorubicin (adriamycin) and daunorubicin are prominent in this regard. They are potent cancer chemotherapeutic agents but their antitumor use is limited because of their cardiotoxic effects. The effects of these drugs on the heart are recognizable histologically and manifested by muscle cell necrosis, loss of contractile elements, and swelling of mitochondria. Why these effects occur is not clearly understood but the following theories have been proposed.

Oxidative Stress

Anthracycline antibiotics may cause lipid peroxidation. It is suggested that they enter the mitochondria and undergo a one electron reduction to their semiquinones. Thereafter, there is redox cycling that leads to the generation of several reactive oxygen species. Peroxidative injury occurs to membranes and subcellular organelles. The heart is especially prone to this kind of injury because of the low levels of antioxidants within it. This oxidative stress theory is supported by the effect of iron chelators. Such chelators bind iron and reduce anthracycline toxicity. Because iron works in other organs by potentiating oxidative stress, this finding suggests that such stress is also at work in the case of the anthracyclines. However, contradictory to this theory, is a significant body of evidence from trials in which common antioxidants such as tocopherol and ubiquinone were of no help in reducing cardiac damage associated with doxorubicin.

Calcium Changes

Changes in the calcium content of various parts of the heart occur. These changes are, however, not consistent and, although it seems that calcium disposition in the heart is clearly affected by doxorubicin, the exact nature of the change is not clear. Thus, some evidence shows an increased content of calcium within the ventricle. Other data show early mitochondrial calcium depletion, followed by calcium deposition at a later time within the mitochondrion. Doxorubicin has altered calcium conductance in muscle of experimental animals. In summary, anthracyclines appear to have several effects on calcium. How these are related to cardiac injury from this group of antibiotics is not clear.

Energy Fluxes

Laboratory experiments show some distinct inhibitory actions of doxorubicin in enzymes involved in mitochondrial oxidative metabolism. For example, succinate dehydrogenase-coenzyme Q reductase and NADH oxidase-coenzyme Q reductase are clearly affected in beef heart mitochondria. Cytochrome c oxidase is inhibited when doxorubicin covalently binds a membrane cardiolipin that is a necessary component of mitochondrial electron transport. Any of these actions on energy-related enzymes could disrupt the ability of the heart to carry out oxidative metabolism.

Alcohols

Alcohols can affect the heart differently depending on whether the exposure is in an acute or chronic manner. Acutely, alcohols reduce the contractile force of the heart, with higher molecular weight alcohols having a greater toxicity than smaller ones like methanol. In the case of long-term or chronic exposure, the heart muscle is damaged (cardiomyopathy) eventually resulting in heart failure. Cardiomyopathy associated with long-term ingestion of alcohol was once thought to be a result of factors other than an inherent toxicity on the part of alcohol itself. For example, beri-beri heart disease is due to thiamine deficiency, and this may be secondary to alcoholism because alcohol damages the GI mucosa and decreases vitamin absorption. Other types of malnutrition are not uncommon in heavy drinkers and these, too, sometimes lead to cardiomyopathy. Another factor is the presence of impurities in alcohol. For example, an outbreak of heart failure was found once to be due to cobalt present as a contaminant in beer. The cobalt, not the alcohol, was the culprit in that incident.

Ultimately, however, it has been demonstrated that cardiomyopathy may arise from alcoholism even in the presence of adequate nutrition and the absence of other toxins in the alcoholic drink. Alcoholic cardiomyopathy is usually reversible with many of the signs of this disorder declining with abstinence from alcohol. Alcoholic cardiomyopathy is manifested as hypertrophy of the heart with a decrease in muscular activity. Electrocardiograms are usually abnormal. Multiple microscopic findings are noted. Myofibrils are decreased in number and have lost some of their usually high degree of organization. Mitochondria are swollen and fewer in number. Lysosomes, subcellular organelles containing digestive enzymes, are present in above-average abundance. Other histological findings are present.

The pathological picture of alcoholic cardiomyopathy is well-known but the basic biochemical causes of the cellular observations are not fully understood. Thus, it is known that alcohol affects the phospholipids and proteins of cell membranes. The fluidity of membranes eventually decreases due to an alteration in the types of lipids present in the membrane. As the membrane becomes more rigid it may act toward calcium in an abnormal manner with abnormal uptake of calcium and, associated with this, changes in the normal calcium-associated excitation. An alternative hypothesis is that acetaldehyde, the first product of alcohol metabolism, inhibits protein synthesis and calcium uptake by the myocyte. Amounts of acetaldehyde are usually very low from alcohol ingestion but the small amounts found may still be capable of these effects.

Emetine

This alkaloid is a natural product whose commercial presence is limited to ipecac syrup. As described in Chapter 3, it is recommended as a means of inducing vomiting to reduce absorption of other toxins. Emetine is toxic in its own right but only when used on a chronic basis. Two situations in which this has occurred are ipecac use by individuals suffering from bulimia and in the context of child abuse. Emetine has been shown to accumulate in the heart and cause histopathological changes and abnormal electrocardiograms. As with many other toxins, the exact mechanism of toxicity is not clear but it probably relates to an impairment in myocardial energy production.

Metals

Lead is toxic to multiple organs. Due to its nonspecific binding to the sulfhydryl group of enzymes it is especially damaging to metabolically active organs such as the heart. As a divalent cation it may also compete with calcium, leading to disturbances in calcium homeostasis. Cobalt is cardiotoxic and blocks slow channels which also leads to abnormal calcium activity. Cadmium is directly toxic to the myocardium and has the additional toxic features of inducing atherosclerosis and hypertension.

Carbon Monoxide

Short-term exposure to even low doses of carbon monoxide is well-known to be life-threatening. Apart from this type of toxicity, CO is also capable of causing vascular injury, intimal layer injury from acute exposure, and atherosclerotic lesions from long-term exposure. Interestingly, CO toxicity is enhanced by co-ingestion of a lipid-rich diet. Part of the intimal injury and the atherosclerotic lesions may be due to the hypoxic effects of carboxyhemoglobin formation. It is thought that these specific lesions also are due partly to the formation of metal–ligand complexes with CO and iron and/or copper in myoglobin, cytochrome c oxidase, and other proteins. Such complexes compete with molecular oxygen and result in impairment in normal cellular functions.

Questions

1. Describe the features of cardiac anatomy and physiology that render the heart susceptible to certain types of toxins.
2. List and describe four types of cardiac toxicologic changes. What is the basis for injury to cardiac activity in each case?
3. Describe three theories as to why some cancer chemotherapeutic agents may be toxic.
4. In what sense may alcohol be cardiopathic? Is alcohol neutral or even beneficial to heart action?

Case Study 1: Delayed Cardiotoxic Activity

A 60-year-old white woman was admitted to the hospital with symptoms consistent with congestive heart failure (CHF). For 1 month she experienced dyspnea on exertion, orthopnea, and edema in her lower extremities. On admission, blood pressure was 120/88 mm; pulse, 110 bpm; respirations, 22/minute; and normal body temperature. Rales could be heard in the base of her lung and there was dullness to percussion at the left lung base. Other symptoms consistent with CHF were jugular venous distension, cardiomegaly by chest X-ray, and pretibial edema. Echocardiography showed diffuse reduction in heart motion. Cardiac catherization revealed an enlarged left ventricle, mitral regurgitation, and reduced cardiac output. A right ventricular endomyocardial biopsy was performed showing, on light microscopy, interstitial fibrosis, loss of contractile elements, and the formation of vacuoles in the myocardial cells.

Past medical history was significant for stage IIIB lymphoma diagnosed on lymph node biopsy 14 years earlier. At that time the patient was treated with radiation. She went into remission from this cancer for 6 years and then presented with cervical adenopathy. Biopsy showed a diffuse histiocytic lymphoma and it was decided to treat her with a mixture of chemotherapeutic agents. The patient appeared to recover fully and was disease free while followed in an Oncology Clinic for the following 7 years.

What is a reasonable suggestion for the cause of her current cardiac disease?
a) Elevated norepinephrine
b) Alcohol
c) Carbon monoxide
d) Doxorubicin

All of the suggested responses are feasible from the perspective that all are known cardiac toxins. Most of them are not in this woman's history, however, and the exact symptoms that each of them would cause do not match up exactly with those manifested by this patient. The exception is doxorubin, a cancer chemotherapeutic agent. Closer scrutiny of the specific chemotherapeutic agents that were administered to her revealed that doxorubicin was among them. It is also known that cardiac toxicity from this agent is usually delayed, i.e., does not manifest until sometime, usually 1 to 6 months, after the discontinuation of cancer chemotherapy. A delay of this magnitude (at least 7 years) is, however, extreme. Nevertheless, there is no doubt that this patient's CHF is related to doxorubicin because of the specific histological findings in the endomyocardial biopsy.

The patient was treated with diuretics that cleared her peripheral edema and pleural effusion. On discharge she was counseled to continue using diuretics and topical nitrates. With extensive management on an outpatient basis, there was no recurrence of her CHF symptoms over a 2-year follow-up period.

Questions

Q1. Could this patient's cardiac symptoms be due to the radiation she received?
 a) Radiation has no cardiac effect.
 b) Radiation shows the same exact picture as anthracycline antibiotics.
 c) Radiation can cause myocarditis that is distinguishable from her findings.
 d) The intensity of radiation administered to her has no harmful effects.

Q2. Are there any predictive factors to guide the physician oncologist who is using doxorubicin to minimize the patient's risk?
 a) Eventual CHF is more likely in female patients.
 b) Eventual CHF is more likely if the drug is used alone.
 c) CHF is a high risk if the dose of doxorubicin is high.
 d) Patients with advanced cancer have greater subsequent incidence of CHF.

Q3. What is the nature of congestive heart failure?
 a) Formation of plaques that interrupt blood flow to the heart wall.
 b) Spasms in the coronary arteries that lead to necrosis of tissue.
 c) Loss of the normal integrity of the mitral valve.
 d) Gradual weakening of the heart muscle with enlargement as a compensation.

Q4. What is the mechanism for doxorubicin toxicity?
 a) Oxidative stress
 b) Calcium changes
 c) Impairment of normal energy producing pathways
 d) Unknown

Answers and Discussion

Q1. (Answer = c) Radiation is able to increase the risk of subsequent anthracycline toxicity and also may induce cardiac injury in its own right. Radiation does not usually injure the heart but when it does, it is most likely to cause myocarditis. In any case, the microscopic appearance of the heart biopsy in this patient is quite specific for doxorubicin injury to the exclusion of other possible causes.

Q2. (Answer = c) The incidence of cardiomyopathy is greater than 30% among patients who receive a dose of more than 600 mg/m². Approximately 4% of all patients receiving this drug develop an overt cardiomyopathy and as many as 70% suffer at least a small degree of reduction in cardiac function. Therefore, the oncologist must make sure that the patient receives the minimum dosage despite the fact that doxorubicin is often effective as an anti-tumor agent and more would be given were it not for this dose-limiting cardiomyopathy.

Q3. (Answer = d) Congestive heart failure is a disease primarily associated with muscle weakness. This contrasts with myocardial infarction, which is mainly due to occlusion of a coronary artery by a plaque and an associated thrombus. Because the heart muscle is weakened in CHF, cardiac output is low. Hypertrophy results as a compensatory response. High pressure in the extremities and in the lungs occurs because of cardiac congestion. Peripheral edema and pulmonary edema are often noted.

Q4. (Answer = d) The suggested responses to this question are all possible and each is supported by some research evidence. A final answer is not possible on the basis of evidence collected currently, so the actual mechanism is not fully known. Review the discussion of this topic in this chapter.

References

Gottlieb, S.L. et al., Late, late doxorubicin cardiotoxicity, *Chest,* 78, 880–882, 1980.

Davis, L.E. and Brown, C.E., Peripartum heart failure in a patient treated previously with doxorubicin, *Obstet. Gynecol.,* 71, 506–508, 1988.

Freter, C.E. et al., Doxorubicin cardiac toxicity manifesting seven years after treatment, *Amer. J. Med.,* 80, 483–485, 1986.

Case Study 2: The Penalties of Vice and the Rewards of Virtue

A 60-year-old man visited his family physician with complaints of weakness and swelling in his extremities that had been present intermittently over the past 3 months. The diagnosis of congestive heart failure was made on the basis of a reduced left ventricular ejection fraction (11%) as determined by radionuclide ventriculography. In addition, the left ventricle was noted to be severely hypokinetic. A thallium stress test was negative for myocardial infarction or ischemic injury. However, cardiac catherization showed extensive coronary artery disease. Three coronary vessels each manifested 80% occlusion. Past social history was significant for up to 4 martinis ingested each day for 15 years. The patient was started on diuretics, digoxin, nitrates, and calcium channel blockers.

What toxin caused this patient's findings?
   a) Carbon monoxide
   b) Alcohol
   c) Probably not toxicologically related, associated with his occlusive disease
   d) Tobacco

This patient was a nonsmoker. There was no history of exposure to carbon monoxide. Congestive heart failure can occur following an ischemic event. This patient did not, however, have evidence of a previous infarction. His stenosis should not induce CHF. The alcohol is strongly suspected in this case as the cause of the CHF. This suspicion could be greatly enhanced if subsequent abstention from alcohol led to an improvement.

The patient resolved to improve his health status. He discontinued his martini lunches and 8 months later his ejection fraction improved to 29% at rest, 36% after 12 minutes of exercise. The hypokinetic character of his wall motion persisted. After 18 months of abstention from alcohol, ejection fraction was up to 61% at rest and 74% after exercise. This time, cardiac catherization showed no wall-motion abnormalities.

Questions

Q1. How does one know that the improvement (greatly improved ejection fraction and normal wall motion) was due to abstention from alcohol?
   a) Drinking was the only factor that was changed.
   b) A discontinuation of drinking behavior always cures CHF.
   c) The associated improvement in occlusive disease.
   d) Anatomical studies demonstrated reductions in alcohol-related damage.

Q2. Alcoholic cardiomyopathy may be due to
   a) Toxic effects of additives that are sometimes present in alcoholic beverages.
   b) Direct toxicity of alcohol or its metabolites, i.e., acetaldehyde.
   c) Nutritional deficiencies often found in alcoholism.
   d) All of the above.

Q3. What is the expected outcome in untreated alcoholic cardiomyopathy?
   a) It is a mild disorder with complete recovery being the rule.
   b) It is usually severe, but recovery depends almost entirely on medication.
   c) In actuality, almost half of patients die within 3 years.
   d) It can be treated effectively with newer medications.

Answers and Discussion

Q1. (Answer = a) It is indeed difficult to prove that an improvement is necessarily due to one specific factor. In this case, however, the patient stated definitely that he did not change exercise habits nor dietary behavior except for the abstention from alcohol. Questioning and testing did not reveal any other change that could account for this great improvement in cardiac function. Also, other similar case reports demonstrate unequivocally that abstention from alcohol can reverse heart failure.

Q2. (Answer = d) At one time alcohol was thought to be innocuous to the heart. This belief was based on finding multiple examples of cardiac damage in association with other factors such as nutritional deficiencies, toxic contaminants, etc. It has been shown, however, that alcohol itself is damaging to the heart when used chronically, even in the absence of one of these other factors.

Q3. (Answer = c) Very good drugs are available for the treatment of heart failure and, if it is caused by chronic alcoholism, then abstention from alcohol is a critical aspect of therapy. Since many patients are unable to discontinue drinking, however, up to 42% of those with alcoholic cardiomyopathy die within 36 months.

References

1. Nethala, V. et al., Reversal of alcoholic cardiomyopathy in a patient with severe coronary artery disease, *Chest,* 104, 626, 1993.
2. Stollberger, C. and Finsterer, J., Reversal of dilated to hypertrophic cardiomyopathy after alcohol abstinence, *Clin. Cardiol.,* 21, 365–367, 1998.
3. Hackel, A.J. et al., Idiopathic dilated cardiomyopathy, *Clin. Cardiol.,* 17, 270–272, 1994.

Case Study 3: A Puzzling Case of Relentless Emesis

A 5-year-old white child was admitted to the hospital for evaluation of vomiting and diarrhea that had begun 10 days earlier and was, by the parent's testimony, unresponsive to any treatment. The child continued to exhibit symptoms of GI distress while in the hospital. Testing for the most common causes of chronic vomiting was conducted but this patient was negative for stool cultures, stool exam for ova and parasites, and viral stool cultures. Abdominal ultrasound, small bowel biopsy, upper GI contrast study, and other evaluations were all normal. On the 10th hospital day parenteral nutrition was started through a peripheral intravenous line. A nasojejunal tube was employed starting on the 18th day of hospitalization and enteral feedings were begun in place of the parenteral nutrition. Five days later the patient showed tachycardia with an irregular heart rhythm. Blood pressure at that time was 90/50 and heart rate was 130 beats per minute. Chest X-ray showed that the heart was enlarged compared to the admission film. Diffuse T-wave inversion was observed on two leads in the ECG. Echocardiogram also demonstrated a large left atrium and thickened septum. Creatine kinase and lactate dehydrogenase were elevated to three times the upper limit of normal. A skeletal muscle biopsy was performed. Electron microscopy was markedly abnormal.

What toxin could be responsible for this child's symptoms?
   a) Emetine
   b) Nortriptyline
   c) Adriamycin
   d) Ethanol

The major findings in this case were continuous GI distress manifested by nausea and vomiting and a delayed onset of cardiac symptoms long after the primary GI problem was established. Only emetine, among the choices listed above, would present this picture. Emetine is found together with cepheline in ipecac.

About 3 weeks into this child's hospitalization the nursing staff found a bottle of syrup of ipecac in the patient's bedside drawer. The mother's coat pocket also contained three bottles of ipecac. Although she denied giving ipecac to the patient, her responses to inquiries about why she was carrying this substance were inconsistent and strongly implied dishonesty on her part. The mother also had a long history of drug abuse and so was challenged about medicating her child with ipecac. After this confrontation the patient's vomiting and diarrhea abruptly stopped. By the 7th week of hospitalization the child's electrocardiogram had improved markedly. He was discharged after 53 days of inpatient care and was normal on outpatient physical examination 8 months later.

Questions

Q1. What is the name for this disorder?
   a) Stevens-Johnson syndrome
   b) Clark's disease
   c) Munchausen's syndrome by proxy
   d) Von Wernike encephalopathy

Q2. What biochemical action is attributed to emetine?
   a) Impaired myocardial cellular respiration
   b) Abnormal carbohydrate metabolism
   c) Inhibition of the citric acid cycle
   d) All of the above

Q3. Why were cardiac symptoms delayed until after the GI symptoms stopped?
   a) Emetine always attacks the GI system first.
   b) Cardiac toxicity results from chronic emetine exposure and takes time to develop.
   c) GI symptoms are protective of the heart.
   d) Emetine cardiac toxicity began immediately, but GI signs distracted physicians from recognition of it.

Q4. Which is not a sign of emetine toxicity?
   a) Nausea and vomiting
   b) Hypotension
   c) Tachycardia
   d) Hyporeflexia
   e) All of these signs may be seen

Answers and Discussion

Q1. (Answer = c) Baron Munchausen was a nineteenth-century German aristocrat who was allegedly addicted to the habit of making preposterous claims about his own activities and achievements. In other ways as well, his behavior was said to be bizarre. Munchausen syndrome by proxy refers, therefore, to the bizarre behavior of care-givers who poison their children. Because the object of the activity is another person, "proxy" is part of the name.

Q2. (Answer = d) A large body of research shows that emetine has numerous metabolic actions. Although these actions are not restricted to the myocardial cell, the effect on those specific cells may be more drastic because of the high demand for energy within the myocardium. The drop in available energy leads to myofibrillar degeneration and the lysis of myocytes.

Q3. (Answer = b) The temporal relationship between the discontinuation of one set of symptoms and the start of a different, cardiac set of symptoms is coincidental. Emetine gradually undermines the integrity of cardiac function and this impairment is not recognized until a certain point is reached and the disease becomes symptomatic.

Q4. (Answer = e) Emetine causes GI, cardiovascular, and neuromuscular signs. Miscellaneous findings also include dehydration, hyponatremia, and fever. All of these symptoms, in addition to others, are possible.

References

Ho, P.C. et al., Rapidly reversible cardiomyopathy associated with chronic ipecac ingestion, *Clin. Cardiol.,* 21, 780–783, 1998.

Schneider, D.J. et al., Clinical and pathologic aspects of cardiomyopathy from ipecac administration in Munchausen's syndrome by proxy, *Pediatrics,* 97, 902–906, 1996.

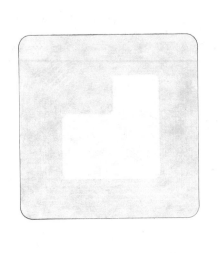

10 Neurological Toxicity

CONTENTS

The nervous system is very vulnerable to many toxins because of its central and delicate role in the overall control of bodily activities. Within the nervous system a number of actions contribute to coordinated control. First, sensory organs evaluate the environment and relay the collected information to other parts of the nervous system. The motor system responds to external and internal stimuli. Integration of information is a third part of the nervous system's activity and involves thinking, learning, and memory.

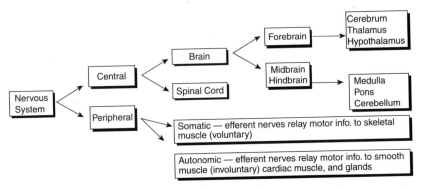

FIGURE 10.1 Basic structure of the nervous system. Somatic (voluntary NS) = efferent nerves that relay motor information to skeletal muscles. Autonomic (involuntary NS) = efferent nerves that relay motor information to smooth muscle, cardiac muscle, and other glands.

ANATOMY AND PHYSIOLOGY OF THE NERVOUS SYSTEM

Figure 10.1 shows the divisions within the nervous system.

CELLS IN THE NERVOUS SYSTEM

Neurons

Cells in the nervous system that are capable of neurotransmission (Figure 10.2). They may be as much as 1 m in length. Dendrites are processes extending from neurons and transferring information <u>into</u> the neuron body. Multiple dendrites are usually found in each neuron. Axons are structures that carry information <u>away</u> from the neuron. Each neuron has only one axon. "Nerve" refers to a collection of several integrated neurons.

Glial Cells

These are supporting cells intended to contribute indirectly to the function of neurons. There are several types of glial cells:

Oligodendroglial cells. Cells that form myelin within the CNS. Myelin, in turn, is a material that surrounds neurons and insulates them, reducing the loss of nerve message transmission that might occur if the neurons were in intimate contact with other neurons and other cell types. Myelin also increases the speed of nerve impulse transmission.
Schwann cells. Cells that form myelin within the peripheral nervous system.
Microglia. Phagocytic cells in the CNS that help to reduce infection by trapping microorganisms and other foreign material.
Astrocytes. Structurally supporting cells especially in the formation of the blood–brain barrier.

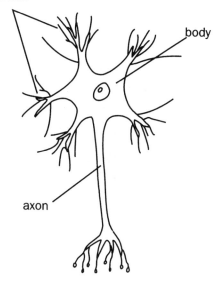

FIGURE 10.2 A neuron.

THE NERVOUS SYSTEM AND SUSCEPTIBILITY TO TOXINS

Several factors make this particular system, the nervous system, more prone to damage from toxins than some other bodily systems. In the first place, neurons have a very limited ability to regenerate. Thus, once a neuron is damaged by a toxin the damage is likely to be irreversible. Second, nerve cells have a rather large surface area that increases their susceptibility to attack for the simple reason that more area is exposed. Third, the nervous system, perhaps more than other physiological processes, depends for its normal activity on a high degree of integrated activity. A toxin could, therefore, attack in a very localized region but still have a massive overall impact on the organism because it disrupts this highly delicate and integrated network.

PROTECTION FOR THE NERVOUS SYSTEM

The nervous system is protected, as are other bodily systems, by the usual protective mechanisms of the body, including skin and other outer protective layers, immune system, etc. An additional source of protection not present in other areas is the blood–brain barrier. Structurally, this barrier consists of tight packing of endothelial cells that line the capillaries in the brain. Endothelial cells always line capillary vessels but usually are arranged loosely so that substances can diffuse between them. This is less likely in the CNS. The barrier also is formed by astrocytes wrapping around the endothelial cells thus reinforcing their tight packing (Figure 10.3). The effect of the barrier is to reduce, not eliminate, the entry of toxins into the CNS. Low molecular weight, lipid-soluble, nonpolar molecules may still penetrate this type of structural barrier. Specific active transport systems also exist. Although these

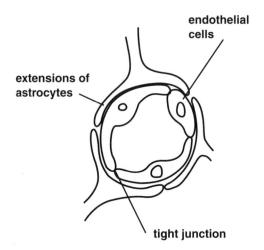

FIGURE 10.3 Blood–brain barrier.

active systems are intended for the uptake of needed nutrients, they sometimes are employed by toxins as a means of forcing entry into the CNS. A kind of metabolic blood–brain barrier also exists. It consists of high levels of enzymes strategically located at the blood brain interface to modify toxins as they enter the CNS. Therefore, although the barrier has been penetrated, the effect of such compromise is greatly diminished because the toxin is converted to a nontoxic (or much less toxic) form.

Other points that are important about the blood–brain barrier are the following. It is less well established in some regions of the CNS (specifically, the pituitary and the hypothalamus), and the peripheral nervous system. These areas are, in general, more susceptible to toxic damage. Some toxicants, such as lead, are deleterious because they harm the CNS and also the blood–brain barrier. They have a type of cumulative action in which chronic exposure becomes progressively more harmful because the barrier becomes less of a barrier with continued attack. As time passes smaller amounts of lead can do as much or more harm because the effective concentration they reach in the CNS is higher. The blood–brain barrier is also less protective in neonates because it has not developed fully at this stage of life. Finally, the barrier will obviously prevent the passage of all molecules with certain structural features regardless of whether the molecule in question is beneficial or harmful. Conversely, drug antidotes or other medications that are polar or of high molecular weight are likely to have a great deal of trouble trying to enter the CNS.

MANIFESTATIONS OF NEUROTOXICITY

Because the nervous system has such extensive control over physiological processes, a wide variety of symptoms may accompany injury to any part of the nervous system. Motor effects can occur, including tremor, lack of coordination, and abnormal activity ranging from paralysis all the way to convulsions. Mood alterations are possible including excitability, depression, irritability, etc. Cognitive effects are observed and these would include loss of memory, confused behavior, and difficulty with speech or learning. Sensory damage might be manifested by problems in vision, hearing, or pain perception. Finally, neurological disorders not specifically associated with motor, cognition, mood, or sensory change might occur. These more nonspecific or whole-body symptoms include fatigue, loss of appetite, stupor, and narcosis.

SPECIFIC INTERFERENCE WITH NORMAL NEUROLOGICAL ACTIVITY

There are several ways to classify toxin activity within the nervous system. In this chapter we divide neurotoxicity into the following five categories: toxins that affect electrical conduction, toxins that harm the nerve cell body, toxins that attack myelin, toxins with action against the axon, and toxins affecting neurotransmitters. Although these categories are not entirely mutually exclusive they do provide a means for comprehensive understanding of the types of neurotoxicity.

TOXINS AND ELECTRICAL CONDUCTION

Recall that the basic function of the nervous system is to transmit information, by way of nerve impulses, between various sections of the body. A nerve impulse should be thought of as comprising two kinds of transmission: first, electrical conduction, the movement of the impulse as an electric wave along a membrane; and, second, synaptic transfer, the propagation of the impulse in a slower, chemical rather than electrical, manner. Synaptic transfer occurs at specific and relatively few sites. These processes, which collectively add up to a nerve impulse, should be evaluated more closely and we need to examine how they can be affected by various neurotoxins.

A neuron has a membrane potential, an electric voltage difference across its membrane, which can be varied continuously along the neuron's length and thereby constitute an impulse. The voltage or potential is based on opening of ion channels. As channels open an action potential builds to a point at which it is self-sustaining. When this occurs this membrane potential rapidly changes from -70 to $+30$ mV. This self-sustaining change in membrane potential is called depolarization. It spreads rapidly across the entire neuron membrane as a neural message or impulse. Immediately after a section of membrane has become depolarized (and thereby sent its message), it reverts to a polarized state by changes in the status of ion channels.

What is the physical basis for the membrane's potential? There are more negatively charged ions inside the cell than outside of it in the extracellular fluid. Inside the cell are many large, and therefore non-diffusible, protein anions. These proteins are permanently inside the cell and contribute to the excess negative charge inside. Furthermore, there is also an uneven distribution of small ions across the membrane. Potassium ions are located preferentially within the cell. The reason for the higher intracellular concentration is primarily the existence of a sodium–potassium pump. This energy-driven pump drives three sodium ions out of the cell while simultaneously pumping two potassium ions in. Once inside, potassium ions may leak out slowly through specific potassium ion channels that remain partly open. Their concentration normally favors an intracellular location, however, because of the continuous action of the sodium–potassium pump and the attractive force of the intracellular

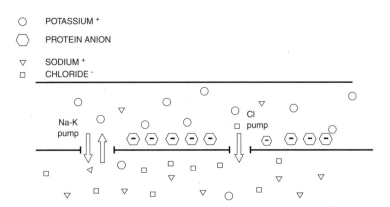

FIGURE 10.4 Depiction of neuron membrane and distribution of charges.

protein anions described earlier. Sodium ion also is distributed unequally. It is, as mentioned, extruded from the cell by the pump. Sodium tends to remain outside in a resting neuron because channels through which it might otherwise re-enter all are closed tightly. Thus, the sodium concentration is much higher outside the cell.

Chloride ion is another species that is unevenly distributed. Like sodium, chloride favors an extracellular location. A negatively charged intracellular protein would work to reduce intracellular chloride by electronic repulsion. A chloride pump is also active and its normal activity is the expulsion of chloride. In summary, uneven distributions of sodium, potassium, chloride, and protein all contribute to a negative membrane potential.

The channels that exist in the neuronal membrane are specific to each ion. They are called voltage-gated because the membrane potential, i.e., the voltage across the membrane, affects the status of these channels with respect to whether they are open or closed. The opening of these channels is said to depolarize the membrane. See Figure 10.4 which depicts this process.

To summarize electrical conduction, a potential or voltage exists across a nerve cell membrane. This potential changes during the propagation of an electrical impulse. The initial event in this change is the opening of sodium channels which reduces the negativity of the potential in the region where this occurred. Then more of these voltage-gated sodium channels open. Eventually (in a few microseconds), the potential changes from a resting value of –70 to +30 mV. This is depolarization and it spreads rapidly across the entire membrane. Then repolarization begins. Sodium channels close and potassium channels open. The membrane potential is restored. While this restoration is in progress the neuron is refractory, which means that it cannot conduct an impulse. Very shortly, however, the resting status is re-achieved and the process is ready to begin again if necessary.

Many natural and some synthetic toxins act at a point in the electrical propagation of the nerve impulse. Tetrodotoxin, from the puffer fish (Fugu or *Lagocephalus scleratus*), blocks electrical conduction. Puffer fish is a delicacy in the Japanese diet and chefs must cautiously prepare it in a manner that excludes the tetrodotoxin-containing fish parts from ending up on the plate. In fact, in Japan, chefs must be certified by the government before they are permitted to prepare puffer fish for consumption by their customers. There is very little toxin in muscle but levels in liver may be as high as 10 mg/g. The LD_{50} of this toxin in mice is only 300 μg/kg. Therefore, consuming only a tiny quantity of liver is fatal if humans are as susceptible as mice. The toxin also is found in fish skin, gonads, and intestine. Despite the high level of preparation that is required of chefs who make this delicacy, there are approximately 50 deaths each year in Japan from this source.

Tetrodotoxin is able to bind to a region on the outside of the neuron membrane and block sodium channels. Interference with the function of any of the voltage-gated channels would, of course, terminate or drastically slow down normal electrical conduction. Studies of patients poisoned with tetrodotoxin show motor conduction velocities of 25 to 30 m/s vs. a normal rate of greater than 47 m/s. Because of blockade of the voltage-gated sodium channels the affected region takes longer to reach the threshold, which decreases conduction velocity or the threshold may not be reached in which case the amplitude of the action potential is reduced. The symptoms of poisoning from tetrodotoxin are somewhat predictable. The onset is very rapid, within 5 minutes of consumption of the fish. The victim is weak, experiences feelings of numbness, and becomes paralyzed. Initially, consciousness is retained despite the presence of paralysis. Eventually, the patient becomes comatose. Even smooth muscle cannot function and this leads to circulatory collapse because the victim's blood vessels are flaccid and cannot support the maintenance of adequate blood pressure. Death is usually associated with respiratory paralysis and circulatory failure. If medical intervention is fairly rapid, the victim can survive by the administration of medication to support blood pressure and by mechanical ventilation. There are natural diseases that mimic tetrodotoxin poisoning. In hyperkalemic periodic paralysis the patient experiences partial paralysis because he/she has a congenital defect in the structure of the sodium channel of the neuron. Paralysis is the expected symptom that such patients experience.

A second, very potent toxin that acts at the level of electrical conduction is saxitoxin. It is produced by marine microorganisms called dinoflagellates, specifically a type known as *Gonyaulax catenella*. In the food chain, dinoflagellates are eaten by fish and shellfish, some of which are injured or killed by saxitoxin. Certain fish species are unaffected by saxitoxin but eventual consumption of the fish by humans only means that the toxin's activity spares the fish but kills the human. Saxitoxin is sometimes called mussel poison, clam poison, or scallop poison because, in human affairs, it usually goes from the dinoflagellate to the mussel, clam, or scallop and then to humans. The dinoflagellates are associated with red tides, the appearance of which signals the danger of probable shellfish poison. Saxitoxin blocks sodium channels and produces symptoms that are similar to those observed in tetrodotoxin poisoning. Because of the characteristic symptoms, this type of shellfish poisoning is often called paralytic shellfish poisoning. Saxitoxin blocks neuromuscular transmission in the motor axon and muscle membrane but does not affect the end-plate. It suppresses conduction in the atrioventricular node and inhibits the respiratory center. Both the specific symptoms and the timeframe of onset are very similar to tetrodotoxin and the distinction between these two agents may have to depend on the history of what the patient ate.

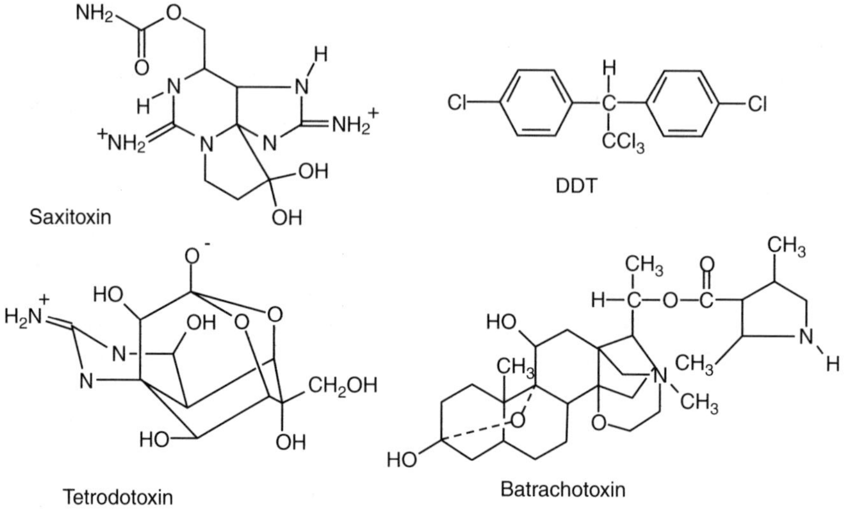

FIGURE 10.5 Some neurotoxins that interfere with nerve impulse electrical conduction.

Batrachotoxin is a neurotoxin found in some animals including certain species of frogs. It is found in the skin of five species of the genus, *Phyllobates*. Its name comes from a Greek root, *batrachos*, which means frog. Ancient man discovered its poisonous character many centuries ago and employed it as an agent into which arrows were dipped to increase their lethality. Batrachotoxin increases the sodium permeability for entry into the neuron, and it does this by prevention of sodium channel closure. This is a selective and irreversible increase in sodium permeability. The normal voltage gradient cannot be established because the gradient depends on the usual distribution of all ions across the neuron membrane. This agent presumably binds at the sodium channel and may exert its toxic effect from either inside or outside of the membrane. It is highly potent and a fatal human dose is estimated to be as small as 200 µg (LD_{50} in mice = 2 µg/kg).

Organochlorine insecticides including the well-known DDT (dichloro-diphenyl trichloroethane) also interfere with electrical conduction in nerves. They delay the closing of sodium channels and alter the movement of potassium across the neuronal membrane. Their exact site of action is not known but this disruption of normal sodium channel activity is clearly capable of reducing neuron communication and causing abnormal electrical activity. (See Figure 10.5.)

TOXINS THAT ATTACK THE NERVE CELL BODY

Many agents are found within this category. Some of them are metals such as mercury, lead, manganese, and aluminum. Common agents that have this activity include cyanide. More exotic compounds that are able to attack the neuron cell body include domoic acid and MPTP (methyl-phenyl-tetrahydropyridine). Cyanide is deleterious for the simple reason that neurons have very high metabolic rates. In the presence of cyanide the electron transport system is inhibited and adenosine tri-phosphate energy substrate becomes available only from glycolysis. This supplies an entirely inadequate amount of energy for survival and neurons are among the first cells to suffer from this deprivation.

Metals bind to structural proteins and enzymes in neurons. There are multiple binding sites with sulfhydryl groups among the most favored. As a result of this binding the normal structure and activities of the neuron become impossible and the cell body undergoes necrotic changes (see Chapter 18 on metals for more extensive discussion of metal toxicity). A different mechanism may be responsible for the damage caused by manganese to those who work in the mining of this metal. Some of these miners develop a Parkinson-like syndrome (uncontrollable shakes, espe-cially of extremities). Victims of this manganese-induced illness are found to have destruction of some dopaminergic neurons. The loss of such neurons also occurs in idiopathic Parkinson's disease and in this disease it is mainly localized in a brain region called the substantia nigra. One hypothesis states that manganese toxicity is due to its ability to oxidize dopamine. Cell death may follow when the cells cannot be stimulated by their normal interaction with dopamine.

MPTP (methyl-phenyl-tetrahydropyridine) is a neurotoxic agent that attacks the neuron cell body and causes cell death. This compound has appeared in street drugs and was found to be an unintended contaminant in designer drug preparations of MPPP, a synthetic narcotic. The MPTP contaminant caused Parkinsonian symptoms in young people and also caused the death of dopaminergic neurons in the substantia nigra. This drug-induced type of Parkinson's disease appeared to simulate the natural form in virtually every way and even responded to classical Parkinson's medications.

Research eventually demonstrated that MPTP crosses the blood–brain barrier and is taken up by specific astrocytes. They metabolize it to methylphenylpyridinium (MPP⁺), a reaction catalyzed by monoamine oxidase (Figure 10.6). The astrocytes transfer the MPP⁺ to dopamine neurons and cause their destruction possibly by oxidative damage to their mitochondria.

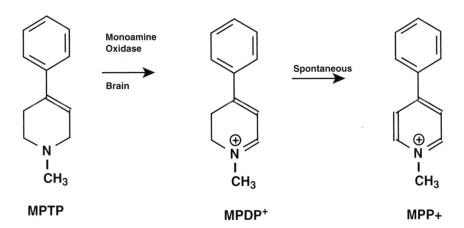

FIGURE 10.6 Conversion of MPTP to MPP⁺.

A neurotoxic agent that has been involved in a number of shellfish poisonings is domoic acid. This toxin is able to cause neuron death and patients who died after consuming contaminated mussels demonstrated neuron necrosis or cell death on autopsy. Neuron loss from domoic acid, as observed in the postmortem examination, was most prominent in the hippocampus and amygdaloid nucleus. In a Canadian outbreak of this type of shellfish poisoning, surviving patients were tested by positron emission tomography (PET). This technology is able to measure glucose metabolism in areas of the brain. PET showed that the decline in glucose metabolism correlated with decline in memory and that the decreased glucose utilization was confined to two brain regions, the amygdala and the hippocampus. The PET findings, therefore, confirmed the autopsy results described above. In other words, there was decreased glucose metabolism because many of the neurons in the specific brain regions were destroyed by domoic acid. The domoic acid found in the mussels came from a form of marine vegetation, *Nitzschia pungens*, a diatomaceous member of the phytoplankton community.

Domoic acid caused a most peculiar form of toxicity. It produced gastrointestinal symptoms and an unusual neurologic syndrome in its victims. Patients experienced severe GI symptoms with nausea, vomiting, and diarrhea within 1 day of mussel consumption and neurologic symptoms within 2 days. The neurologic aspects included coma and seizures but the most persistent finding was memory loss. This memory loss was of long duration and so severe that some patients could not recognize family members. Domoic acid is less potent that many other shellfish poisons and the most severely affected patients in the outbreak had consumed up to 300 mg. No traces of the toxin are found in blood or spinal fluid only 48 hours after ingestion. The toxin, therefore, appears to have a short half-life. Its effects, however, are very long term.

Figure 10.7 shows the structures of domoic acid, kainic acid, and glutamic acid. Structural analogies are suggested by this figure and it has been shown that all three compounds may bind at the same sites. It is known that some drugs bind to receptors for the neurotransmitter, glutamate, and these compounds, by binding in this manner, can cause neuronal death. The term excitotoxicity has been coined for this phenomenon and it refers to the fact that these drugs excite glutamate receptors and cell death eventually occurs from this excitation. Kainic acid and domoic acid are two such excitotoxins that bind to glutamate receptors. The structural similarities among these molecules are presumably the reason for the binding. Domoic acid, like kainic acid, is thought to bind on the post-synaptic dendrite near the synapse where it causes excessive glutamate release or prevents glutamate absorption from the pre-synaptic axon. This action of domoic acid on glutamate definitely promotes convulsions and at least part of the resulting neuron death is due to the effect of the convulsions. A more specific action of domoic acid in causing cell death also is involved but the details of that mechanism are not known.

TOXINS THAT ATTACK MYELIN

Recall that an insulating substance called myelin covers neurons in the central and peripheral nervous systems. Myelin is similar to the membranes of most cells as it

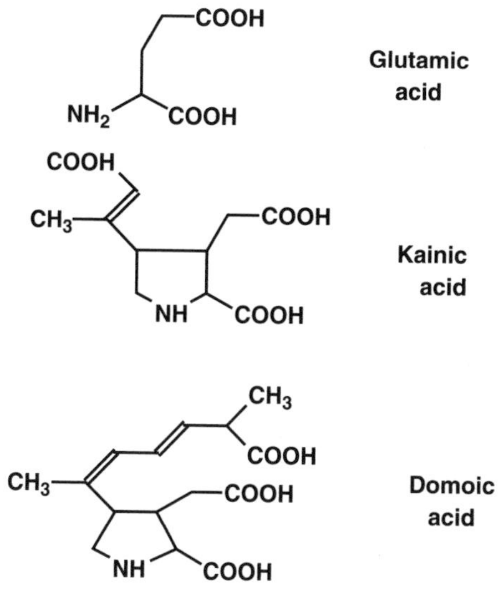

FIGURE 10.7 Domoic acid, a neuron cell body toxin, and its structural relationship to kainic acid and glutamic acid.

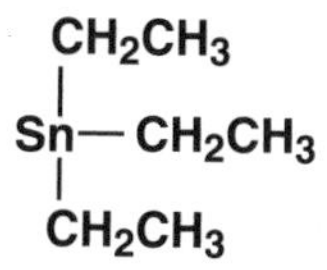

FIGURE 10.8 Structures of myelin toxins.

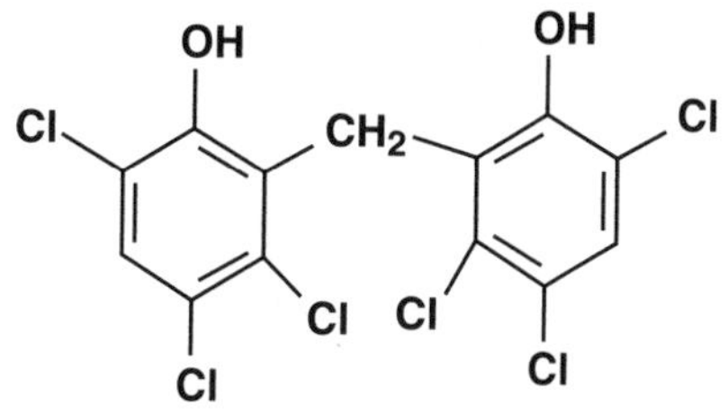

is composed primarily of cholesterol, phospholipids, and sphingolipids. Myelin represents another target for toxins in the nervous system and damage to myelin is similar in effect to damage to electrical conduction. There is a delay or reduction in action potentials. Numbness, weakness, and paralysis may result.

One compound that damages myelin is triethyl tin (Figure 10.8). It is very lipid-soluble and binds to sites on myelin. The result is splitting of the myelin and the appearance of fluid-filled spaces, vacuoles, in the myelin. In rats, triethyl tin causes a decrease in conduction velocity in peripheral nerves and brain damage with reduction in cerebral blood flow and glucose uptake. The awareness of triethyl tin as a myelin toxin dates back to 1954 when over 1000 people were poisoned by triethyl tin that was a contaminant of an antibacterial preparation.

Tellurium, the metallic element, causes a demyelinating polyneuropathy in laboratory rats fed a diet rich in this metal. The exact mechanism of this toxicity is not clear but it is known that tellurium inhibits squalene epoxidase, an enzyme. This

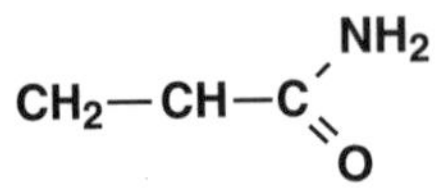

Acrylamide
(2-propenamide)

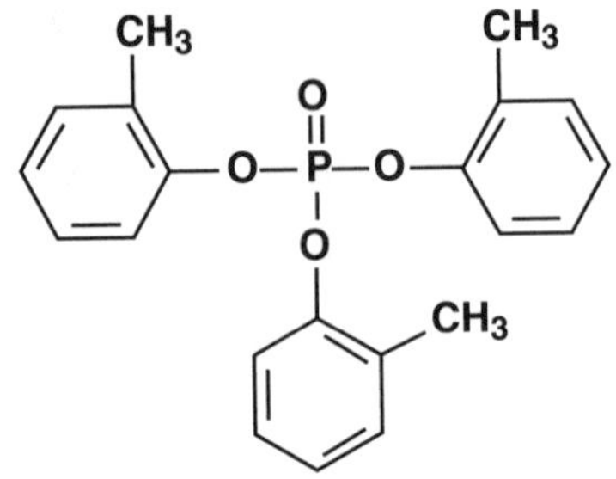

Tri-ortho cresyl phosphate
(TOCP)

FIGURE 10.9 Structures of some axon neurotoxins.

enzyme is, in turn, involved in the metabolic pathway that leads to cholesterol. Tellurium, therefore, lowers cholesterol including that which is needed for normal myelin synthesis.

Hexachlorophene (HCP) is remarkably similar to triethyl tin as a myelin toxin. The usual function of HCP is as an antibacterial applied to the skin. Some infants treated with HCP, however, subsequently developed signs of central and peripheral neuropathy of the kind associated with myelin damage. These children developed white-matter vacuolation (empty spaces) in the brain stem and cerebellar hemispheres following exposure to HCP. The children experienced lower extremity weakness and cerebral edema that was occasionally fatal.

TOXINS THAT ATTACK AXONS

Toxins are known that attack either the part of the axon near the neuron body, the proximal axon, or the remote part, the distal axon (Figure 10.9). The axon is less susceptible to toxins than the cell body in one sense; it has very limited metabolic functions. The axon derives needed molecules by transport down the length of the axon from the neuron body. This may involve a transfer of several feet as, for example, for some motor neurons of the spinal cord. Axonal proteins such as enzymes or structural materials move down the axon from the cell body by a process called slow transport. This is well-named for the rate is only about 1 mm/day. By contrast, a fast transport mechanism exists in which substances are transferred as much as 400 times as fast. This is the method by which membrane components are transferred down the axon. Some toxins such as virus and tetanus toxin are thought to enter the axon and be transferred up to the cell body by fast transport. Subcellular structural elements such as microtubules, microfilaments, and neurofilaments are believed to form a track along the axon through which fast transport occurs. Pathological injury to axons are more common in the peripheral nervous system and the resulting neurological damage is called a neuropathy. Most axonopathies involve the distal axon. When they occur they usually are evidenced by swelling, damage to mitochondria, accumulation of neurofilaments, and disintegration of myelin. Either acute or chronic exposure to some toxicants may cause distal axonopathies.

It is believed that some distal axonopathies are due to prior damage to the neuron cell body. The injured cell body cannot supply the distal axon with needed nutrients and axonal damage is the result. Alternatively, axon damage may result from a direct insult to the axon.

Axon-associated neuropathies include "Ginger Jake paralysis." This term refers to a neurological disorder that struck about 50,000 adults at the height of Prohibition, "The Noble Experiment," in the United States. This occurred in 1930–1931 when the federal ban on alcohol sale or use was at its height. The Prohibition Bureau permitted the sale of Jamaica Ginger Extract as a headache remedy and digestive aid. This material, however, contained 60–80% alcohol. It was common for people to buy the extract, mix it with soda, and consume the resulting cocktail. The problem occurred when unscrupulous distributors ran out of the ginger oleoresin, a flavoring agent normally added to Jamaica Ginger. They substituted, in one large batch, tri-ortho-cresyl phosphate (TOCP). This material is widely used as a liquid plasticizer. From the perspective of the purveyors of Jamaica Ginger extract TOCP was ideal because it was cheap, soluble in alcohol, and conveyed a taste that was similar to the customary taste of the extract. Victims of TOCP suffered the so-called "Jake leg" or "Jake walk" because they developed spinal cord damage and permanent (or minimally reversible) partial paralysis. Studies showed that TOCP caused an axonal neuropathy that attacked primarily large muscle groups. The axon-damaging mechanism of TOCP is not entirely clear. However, this compound is an organophosphate, i.e., an inhibitor of acetylcholinesterase. It is believed to cause organophosphate-induced delayed neuropathy (OPIDN). Further, in this disease, TOCP is thought to bind, not acetylcholinesterase, but a neurotoxic esterase. The exact nature and role of this neurotoxic enzyme have not been clarified. Nevertheless, the dimensions of this specific toxicological event were catastrophic and highlight the dangers of unregulated distribution of food materials to the public.

Acrylamide is a substance that blocks slow, possibly fast transport, too, and this blockade causes axonal degeneration. Acrylamide monomer is a white crystal solid used extensively in industry for the production of polyacrylamide. The monomer is neurotoxic whereas the polymer is considered to be harmless. It has been absorbed by inhalation, dermal absorption, and ingestion. Those exposed to it in industry are believed to absorb it mainly through the skin. Environmental contact with it has been from ingestion of groundwater that became contaminated. The neurotoxicity of acrylamide is manifested by paresthesias, numbness, peeling and sloughing of skin, and muscle weakness. In severe cases more extreme signs such as ataxia, weakened deep tendon reflexes, and muscle atrophy are found. If nerve fibers are biopsied, there is a loss of myelinated fibers and axons are noted to be swollen with masses of neurofilaments. The same biopsy picture is found from carbon disulfide, n-hexane, and methyl n-butyl ketone. The last two compounds share the property of being metabolized to 2,5-hexanedione, the proximate cause of the axonal neuropathy (Figure 10.10). Long-term exposure to any of these solvents, commonly found in glues and cleaning fluids, causes accumulation of neurofilaments in the distal part of the axon followed by myelin disintegration.

Carbon disulfide is used heavily in fumigation and in rayon synthesis and is neurotoxic. It causes axon loss in both central and peripheral nervous systems.

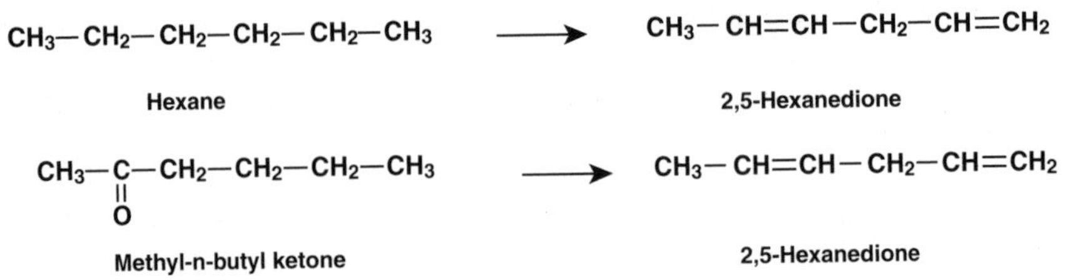

CH₃—CH₂—CH₂—CH₂—CH₂—CH₃ ———→ CH₃—CH=CH—CH₂—CH=CH₂

Hexane   **2,5-Hexanedione**

CH₃—C—CH₂—CH₂—CH₂—CH₃ ———→ CH₃—CH=CH—CH₂—CH=CH₂
  ‖
  O

Methyl-n-butyl ketone   **2,5-Hexanedione**

FIGURE 10.10 Biotransformation of some hydrocarbons to an axonal neurotoxin, hexanedione.

Parkinsonian symptoms (especially tremor) are found in addition to sensory loss and cognitive decline.

TOXINS THAT ATTACK SYNAPTIC FUNCTION

A synapse is a space between the axon of one neuron and the dendrite of a second. They also are located between neurons and muscle cells and between neurons and glands. Usually, the electrical impulse traveling down the axon stimulates the release of a chemical called a neurotransmitter from the end of the axon. This neurotransmitter diffuses across the synaptic space and binds a special receptor on the other side of the synapse (postsynaptic membrane). Binding to the special receptor affects the membrane potential of the postsynaptic membrane and allows the neural message to continue through the nervous system.

Receptors may be excitatory or inhibitory. When neurotransmitters bind to excitatory receptors, ion channels are opened. Cations such as sodium enter the cell and the membrane potential becomes a little less negative. After a few milliseconds the original potential is restored. When a large number of neurotransmitters cross the synapse together, however, very many sodium channels open and the membrane potential drops to the point at which an action potential is generated and the message passes on. In the case of inhibitory neurotransmitters, their binding to receptors on the postsynaptic membrane opens potassium and chloride channels. Potassium exits the cell in larger numbers and chloride entry is enhanced. The membrane potential becomes more negative from this process and the action potential is, therefore, less likely. The propagation of the nerve impulse is prevented or, at least, rendered less probable.

There are many different neurotransmitters in various regions of the nervous system. Usually, each neuron makes and releases only one specific neurotransmitter. Many toxins act on neurotransmitters to interfere with normal synaptic transmission. In this manner these toxins have a neurotoxic action. Following is a discussion of the important neurotransmitter, acetylcholine, and several compounds that affect its action. These include botulinum toxin, nicotine, muscarine, curare, and atropine. Also discussed are biogenic amines as neurotransmitters and the impact of certain drugs of abuse, such as amphetamine, on their activity. Finally, several amino acids serve as neurotransmitters. The actions of strychnine and tetanus toxin as inhibitors of glycine neurotransmitter behavior are discussed as examples of toxins that affect the amino acid type of neurotransmitter.

Acetylcholine

Acetylcholine (AC) is the most abundant neurotransmitter. It is found in many synapses in the autonomic nervous system (related to involuntary muscle movement), in neurons that control voluntary muscle movement, and in many parts of the central nervous system. AC is stored in the neuron in subcellular vesicles and released from the axon into the synapse when a rapid influx of calcium occurs from an action-potential-induced change in membrane potential.

Botulinum Toxin

Botulinum toxin has the unenviable distinction of being probably the most toxic substance known to man with an LD_{50} in the ng/kg range. It impedes the formation of functional AC vesicles thus reducing the amount of AC that can be released during the depolarization of a motor neuron. It causes, therefore, a presynaptic problem. The toxin is a protein of 150 kD size that is cleaved into two smaller chains. One chain, of 100 kD size, is involved in neuron binding and promotes the intracellular penetration of the toxin. The other chain, 50 kD, obstructs neurotransmitter activity in other ways.

Eight serotypes of botulinum toxin have been identified. They are manufactured by *Clostridium botulinum,* a Gram positive bacillus. The term botulus means sausage and refers to an outbreak of the disease in Germany in the eighteenth century in which many died from contaminated sausage. The microorganism is anaerobic and grows in sealed containers. Many cases of botulinum exposure involve home-canned foods. In addition, some victims are wounded and their wounds become infected with *Clostridium* which then produces toxin *in vivo*. In infants, consumption of honey may lead to botulinum poisoning from *Clostridium* present in the honey. This source is thought not to be a hazard in adults because of the very small amounts of *Clostridium* likely to be present in honey.

One could predict the symptoms of botulinum poisoning on the basis of bodily functions that depend on AC. Neurons that use AC are immobilized and the victim experiences muscle weakness (AC involved in voluntary muscle action), paralysis (AC acts at the neuromuscular junction), and autonomic effects such as nausea, diarrhea, and blurring of vision (AC acts in the autonomic nervous system). The earliest signs of poisoning are paralysis around the eyes and weakness of the facial muscles. Nerve conduction studies reveal low amplitude muscle action potentials. The suspicion of botulinum poisoning can be confirmed by injecting a sample of the patient's serum into a mouse. If the mouse undergoes paralysis and then dies, the diagnosis of botulism is confirmed.

As stated, poisoning with botulinum often results from contaminated food. Cases have been reported in which the victims ate smoked fish, cheese sauces, and many other food products. Since 1982 botulinum toxin has also been used as a medicinal for the treatment of a variety of musculoskeletal disorders. For example, one patient received regular injections of botulinum toxin into the lacrimal gland to reduce pathological tear secretion. Her profuse tear production had occurred as the aftermath of a viral infection of the eye. The localized paralysis of the lacrimal gland was effective in preventing excessive tears. In cases like this the medication may diffuse away from the injection site. When this happens ptosis and diplopia may result. Not surprisingly, therefore, use of a substance as potent as botulinum toxin, in a therapeutic manner, is not without danger.

Nicotine

Acetylcholine neurotransmitter is said to be found in cholinergic synapses, so named after the neurotransmitter itself. In actuality, AC receptors can be subdivided further into those sensitive to nicotine and those that respond to muscarine. Nicotinic receptors are located in autonomic neurons and on skeletal muscle. Muscarine-responding receptors are at neurons of the parasympathetic system where such neurons attach to smooth muscle or glands. These two compounds, nicotine and muscarine, are cholinergic agonists in the sense that they bind to their respective receptors and cause the same effect as if AC were released into the synapse. Nicotine (methylpyridylpyrrolidine) is, of course, the addictive agent of tobacco. Nicotine in the appropriate area of the CNS has psychoactive actions. Because nicotine acts directly at many synapses, one can surmise correctly that it is a potentially neurotoxic agent. Moreover, nicotine is rapidly absorbed through skin and lungs. There are deaths on record due to ingestion of nicotine as a pesticide and even by exposure through the skin. It directly stimulates the nicotine subset of CNS and peripheral AC receptors. Moderate poisoning is said to produce symptoms of cholinergic excess (described in Chapter 17, under pesticide poisoning). These include miosis, salivation, urination, defecation, emesis, and increased pulmonary secretions. The cause of these symptoms is parasympathetic stimulation. In large-dose exposure a short-lived stimulation is followed rapidly by neuromuscular blockade related to persistent membrane depolarization. If death occurs, the most common mechanism is respiratory arrest due to peripheral neuromuscular blockade and cardiovascular collapse.

Muscarine

Muscarine is analogous to nicotine in that it is able to mimic the actions of acetylcholine in certain cholinergic neurons. This compound is found naturally in some mushrooms such as *Amanita muscaria, Clitocybe dealbata, C. illudens,* and others. Muscarinic effects on the autonomic nervous system are similar to effects produced from nicotine and are summarized by the acronym SLUD: salivation, lacrimation, urination, and defecation. Because muscarine is a quaternary ammonium compound it does not cross the blood–brain barrier and effects are more peripheral than central for this reason.

Curare

Some compounds are toxic because they antagonize the actions of acetylcholine. They behave like nicotine only in the sense that they bind to the postsynaptic receptor. Once they are bound there, however, they block the receptor and prevent the action potential in the postsynaptic neuron. Curare is a nicotinic antagonist. This compound is famous for use as an arrow poison by South American Indians. One of the major sources of curare is the South American plant *Chondrodendron tomentosum.* Curare is a mixture containing d-tubocurarine. By blocking the nicotinic receptor motor, weakness up to the point of paralysis is induced. Death may occur from paralysis of the diaphragm, the muscle that permits breathing. Today, poisoning by curare is as likely to occur by a medical error as from some other source. The hypotension and respiratory failure that it causes are treatable if intervention is rapid. Neostigmine acts as an antidote for curare poisoning. Blocking at the ganglia causes low blood pressure and reduced heart rate. Today, curare has been purified and is used frequently in surgery; for example, it has been employed as a muscle relaxant prior to tracheal intubation.

Atropine

Atropine is a highly potent compound that acts as a muscarinic blocker. It is found in numerous plants including Jimsonweed and *Atropa belladonna*, deadly nightshade. Exposure to atropine blocks muscarinic receptors and prevents their normal action of innervating parasympathetic neurons of muscles and glands. The symptoms that occur from atropine overdose are tachycardia, pupillary and bronchiolar dilation, and decreases in secretions and in peristalsis. At the level of the CNS, atropine causes excitation at low doses but depression at large doses. Hallucinations often accompany atropine abuse and, for this reason, some persons deliberately have employed large amounts of it as a drug of abuse.

Scopolamine

Scopolamine, structurally analogous to atropine (see Figure 10.11), is found in many species of plants, and has actions that are nearly identical to those of atropine. It has a notorious history of being employed by thieves to render their victims unconscious and amnesiac. At the present time, it is described as a national problem in Columbia where it is known as burundanga. Criminals sprinkle the highly potent scopolamine into the victim's food and wait for the person to achieve a zombie-like state. At that point, the victim is powerless to resist his assailant. Not only is scopolamine capable of causing profound sedation but there is often an amnesiac aftermath that only makes it more desirable as a means of perpetrating crime.

One other class of compounds that interferes with cholinergic nerve transmission at the level of the neurotransmitter AC are the organophosphates. These compounds have been used primarily as insecticides but to some extent also as chemical warfare agents in the form of nerve gases. They are extremely toxic with LCt_{50}s as low as 10 mg/min/m^3 (for the poison gas called VX). This is the airborne concentration that will kill 50% of a population of persons exposed for one minute. By contrast, the highly toxic hydrogen cyanide has an LCt_{50} of 5000 mg (min)/m^3. Discussion of the organophosphates will be saved for the chapter on pesticides, later in this volume.

Biogenic Amines

A second group of neurotransmitters is the biogenic amines. These are compounds that contain a basic amine group usually as part of an aliphatic chain attached to a benzene ring. Prominent among these neurotransmitters are norepinephrine, epinephrine, dopamine, serotonin, and histamine. High amounts of biogenic amines are found in the CNS. Amphetamine, popularly known as speed, causes some of its

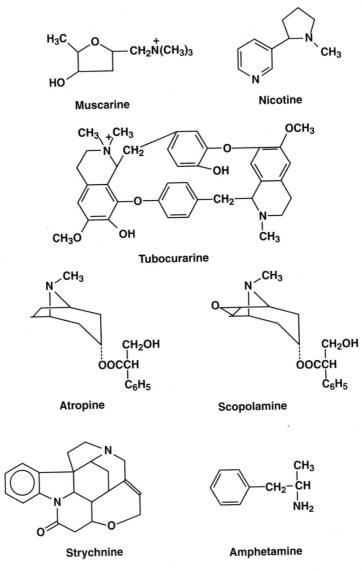

FIGURE 10.11 Structures of some neurotoxins that interfere with synaptic transmission.

effects by increasing the release of one biogenic amine, norepinephrine. Analogous to the two kinds of cholinergic receptors, nicotine and muscarine, there are two kinds of receptors for some biogenic amines, alpha and beta receptors.

Amphetamine is an alpha and a beta agonist, i.e., it stimulates both of these receptor types. It has, therefore, at least 2 mechanisms of action. Pharmacologists have taken advantage of knowledge about alpha and beta receptors to design a large number of drugs that block them and produce a myriad of pharmacological actions.

GABA

Several other neurotransmitters belong to a third class of amino acid neurotransmitters. Gamma aminobutyric acid (GABA) is an important member of this class that acts as an inhibitory neurotransmitter at specific receptors. GABA release from the presynaptic membrane and binding at the postsynaptic side causes an increase in chloride permeability. Chloride enters the neuron in larger amounts and the membrane potential becomes more negative. The important class of drugs known as benzodiazepines act by potentiating the chloride transfers caused by GABA.

Glycine

Glycine is also found as an inhibitory neurotransmitter and is largely confined to the spinal cord and brainstem. Strychnine is a drug that owes its action to the binding and blocking of the postsynaptic glycine receptor. Strychnine is an alkaloid found in the seeds of an Indian vine, *Strychnos vomica*. It has been used as an insecticide. An excitatory effect is induced in the CNS from this drug due to the prevention of glycine uptake on the postsynaptic membrane of inhibitory neurons. As a consequence, the strychnine-poisoned individual is extremely sensitive and minimal sensory stimulation can trigger widespread muscle contractions. The excitatory action extends to the medulla so the individual has enhanced sensations of touch, smell, hearing, and sight. Vomiting and hyperthermia are other clinical manifestations.

Tetanus Toxin

Tetanus toxin also acts on the inhibitory neurons that use glycine as neurotransmitter. It also causes convulsions and spasms in a manner very similar to strychnine. A common name for one of these symptoms is lockjaw. Indeed, victims of tetanus often are unable to open their jaws because of muscle spasms. This is only one of myriad symptoms that include multiple, painful, and generalized spasms that can occur with only the very slightest tactile stimulus.

Clostridium tetani, an anaerobic, gram-positive bacillus, produces at least two exotoxins. One of these, tetanospasmin, enters alpha motor neurons through the motor endplate at the site of infection and elsewhere. The infection is often a deep puncture wound that is ideal for the development of the organism since it is an anerobe. Many years ago, tetanus was common because the causative organism is present almost everywhere. The advent of immunization has reduced the incidence of this illness to less than 100 cases per year in the United States.

Questions

1. State several reasons why the nervous system is especially susceptible to toxins.
2. Describe the normal mechanism for electrical conduction in the nervous system. Why is the action of tetrodotoxin harmful to this system?
3. Describe the toxicity of domoic acid. How is its structure related to compounds normally present in the nervous system?

TABLE 10.1
Summary of Neurotoxins
**Interfere with Propagation
of Electrical Impulse**

Tetrodotoxin
Saxitoxin
Batrachotoxin

Attack Neuron Cell Body

Heavy metals
Cyanide
Methyl phenyl tetrahydropyridine (MPTP)
Domoic acid
Kainic acid

Attack Myelin

Triethyl tin
Tellurium
Hexachlorophene

Attack Axons

Tri-ortho-cresyl phosphate
Acrylamide
Carbon disulfide
n-Hexane
Methyl-n-butyl-ketone

Affect Synaptic Transfer

Botulinum toxin
Muscarine
Nicotine
Atropine
Scopolamine
Curare
Strychnine
Tetanus toxin

---

4. Compare and contrast the mechanisms of toxicity of acrylamide and TOCP.
5. Name four toxins that impede the normal activity of acetylcholine at the synapse. Discuss the specific mechanisms of action for each toxin.
6. Which toxins act at inhibitory neurons? Explain the proposed mechanism of action of strychnine.

Case Study 1: The After-Dinner Delicacy

A 23-year-old man, who weighed 176 pounds, ate a large meal and afterward consumed a very small piece of fish as a kind of after-dinner delicacy. The amount of this fish was estimated to be only 0.25 oz. Ten minutes after eating the fish he experienced a sensation of tingling in his mouth. This was rapidly followed by dizziness, fatigue, headache, tightness in his throat and chest, nausea, and vomiting. His legs weakened and he collapsed, unable to bear his own bodyweight. He was in the company of two companions each of whom also ate tiny quantities of the fish and suffered similar symptoms. The 23-year-old man was rapidly transported to an emergency department where his vital signs were as follows: blood pressure, 150/90; heart rate, 117 beats per minute; respirations, 22 per minute; temperature, 99.3°F.

Which of the following poisons is most likely in this case?
   a) Domoic acid
   b) Saxitoxin
   c) Batrachotoxin
   d) Tetrodotoxin

A major factor in this case is the source of the poison, namely, a fish rather than shellfish or other source. Of additional interest is the speed of the victim's response, just a few minutes. The symptoms are suggestive of a neurotoxin that is aimed primarily at the peripheral nervous system. All of these features are characteristic of tetrodotoxin, which is found in puffer fish. It blocks sodium conductance and electrical transmission in skeletal muscles. Symptoms are not primarily reflective of the CNS. Physicians, relying mainly on the patient's history and clinical presentation, correctly diagnosed the problems of these patients as being due to fugu. They were given gastric lavage and then activated charcoal. Hydration was provided to restore fluid balance that had been disrupted due to intense vomiting. No specific antidote is available so therapy had to be essentially supportive only. Symptoms eventually resolved and the patients were discharged without any apparent permanent effects.

Questions

Q1. Tetrodotoxin is known to cause death in 60% of persons who consume it. Why did these three persons survive?
   a) Possible wrong diagnosis.
   b) The fish was decayed and the toxin had been destroyed.
   c) They ate parts of the fish that were low in toxin.
   d) They ate very little puffer and received fast medical care.

Q2. Where does puffer fish come from?
   a) Japanese waters
   b) China
   c) South America
   d) Shallow water of tropical and temperate zones
Q3. What is the cause of death in tetrodotoxin poisoning?
   a) Diaphoresis
   b) Convulsions
   c) Bradycardia
   d) Respiratory muscle paralysis
Q4. Based on data provided in this chapter and assuming that this man had eaten puffer fish liver, what fraction of a fatal dose would he have ingested?
   a) About 20%
   b) About 300%
   c) About 1%
   d) 3000%

Answers and Discussion

Q1. (Answer = c or d) The toxin is very heat stable and it is unlikely that these people ate old or contaminated fish. The diagnosis was absolutely correct. It is possible that they ate parts low in toxin because the distribution of toxin in the fish is very irregular. It is also true that they were saved by the relatively small amount of fish eaten and by rapid medical care including gastric lavage.

Q2. (Answer = d) Although the puffer is favored by the Japanese, the fish is not limited to the waters in the region around Japan only. They have a relatively wide distribution and are commercially exported from China, Japan, Mexico, the Phillipines, and Taiwan.

Q3. (Answer = d) Victims of tetrodotoxin usually die within 6 to 24 hours of eating the puffer and the usual cause of death is respiratory failure because they cannot breathe and circulatory failure because blood vessels cannot constrict to maintain normal blood pressure.

Q4. (Answer = b) This man weighed 176 pounds or 80 kg. Extrapolating from animal data, 24 mg is a lethal dose for someone of this body weight. Consumption of 0.25 oz. (7 g) provides 70 mg of toxin. This is 290% of a fatal dose. We are forced to conclude from this calculation that this man did not eat fish liver, the most toxic form of puffer fish.

Reference

Morbidity and Mortality Weekly Review from the CDC, Tetrodotoxin poisoning associated with eating puffer fish transported from Japan to California, 1996. *J. Amer. Med. Assoc.*, 275, 1631, 1996.

Case Study 2: The Poisonous Shellfish

A 68-year-old man was admitted to the hospital 4 hours after eating 0.50 lb. of steamed, shelled mussels. He complained of nausea and vomiting and was very confused. His neurologic examination was very abnormal and demonstrated the patient's confusion and disorientation. Focal abnormalities were absent. Biochemical testing of blood and spinal fluid gave results within normal limits. Testing for infectious microorganisms was negative. Computerized tomography of the head was normal but diffuse abnormalities were seen on the electroencephalogram.

The most likely toxin at this point is
   a) Tetrodotoxin
   b) Saxitoxin
   c) Domoic acid
   d) Batrachotoxin

On the basis of the patient's history, Answers a and d can be ruled out because his exposure was to shellfish. Tetrodotoxin comes from puffer fish and batrachotoxin is found in frogs. Clinical findings are consistent with domoic acid, however, because it characteristically causes a GI picture that evolves into a primarily neurological problem. Tachycardia (pulse, 160) and severe hypotension (70/0 mm Hg) developed several hours after admission. He was transferred to Intensive Care where he underwent multiple episodes of labile blood pressure and arrhythmias. He also had pulmonary edema and profuse respiratory secretions that required frequent suctioning. He sank into a deep coma and exhibited unusual eye movements with disconjugate gaze. His multiple abnormalities resolved very gradually and he was finally discharged after 86 days of hospitalization. At that time, however, his short-term memory continued to be severely impaired.

Questions

Q1. Which of the following diseases does not arise from eating contaminated mollusks?
   a) Paralytic shellfish poisoning
   b) Domoic acid toxic encephalopathy
   c) Neurotoxic shellfish poisoning
   d) Tetrodotoxin poisoning
Q2. The metabolism of which biochemical is most influenced by the presence of domoic acid?
   a) Glutamic acid
   b) Acetylcholine
   c) Dopamine
   d) Norepinephrine

Answers and Discussion

Q1. (Answer = d) The first three answers are types of shellfish poisoning. The last answer is correct since tetrodotoxin arises from consumption of the poisonous parts of puffer fish.

Q2. (Answer = a) Domoic acid is known as an excitotoxin because it binds to glutamic acid receptors in neurons (i.e., it excites glutamic acid receptors) and may cause excessive glutamate release and associated convulsions. Death may result from this disturbance of normal glutamate metabolism.

References

Perl, T.M. et al., An outbreak of toxic encephalopathy caused by eating mussels contaminated with domoic acid, *N. Engl. J. Med.,* 322, 1775–1780, 1990.

Teitelbaum, J.S. et al., Neurologic sequelae of domoic acid intoxication due to the ingestion of contaminated mussels, *N. Engl. J. Med.,* 322, 1781–1787, 1990.

Case Study 3: The Poisoned Fishermen

Six fishermen were at sea aboard a fishing boat in the Georges Bank area, off the Nantucket coast in the waters near the northeastern coast of the United States. The fishermen ate a meal of blue mussels (*Mytilus edulis*) that had been harvested from deep water. Approximately 1 hour after eating the mussels, symptoms started including numbness around the mouth, paresthesias of extremities, vomiting, tingling in the tongue, numbness of face, throat, and tongue, and edema around the eyes. All six experienced lower back pain 1 day after the ingestion that persisted for 3 additional days. The fishermen reported to a hospital emergency room but not until 10 hours after the exposure because they were at sea when the event occurred. Four were treated and released whereas two had to be admitted for 3 days.

What toxin was most likely encountered in this ingestion?
  a) Saxitoxin
  b) Domoic acid
  c) Tetrodotoxin
  d) Batrachotoxin

Again, the last two mentioned responses are not possible on the basis of history. The fishermen became sick after eating mussels. Both saxitoxin and domoic acid are toxins that originate from shellfish. Domoic acid is characterized, however, by a slow recovery with persistent loss of memory. These two findings are not consistent with the case presented here. Saxitoxin, also called paralytic shellfish poison, was suspected and several other cases were reported to public health authorities at the same time and in the same place as the incident reported here. The mussels not eaten by the fishermen were tested and found to contain saxitoxin at 24,400 µg/100 g of raw mussels and 4280 µg/100 g of cooked mussels. Saxitoxin is soluble in hot water so much of the toxin leaches from the mussels into water during cooking.

Exposure to saxitoxin usually causes symptoms that are more severe than those experienced by the fishermen. Three weeks after the incident described here a Native Alaskan consumed 30 steamed clams while on a fishing boat. He shortly thereafter complained of numbness and tingling around his mouth, face, and hands. Within 3 hours of the shellfish meal he suffered a cardiopulmonary arrest during which he expired. Cause of death was proven to be saxitoxin on the basis of measurements of the toxins in the clams and his stomach contents.

Questions

Q1. What toxin is most closely related to saxitoxin in effects?
   a) Tetrodotoxin
   b) Domoic acid
   c) Methyl phenyl tetrahydropyridine
   d) Batrachotoxin
Q2. How is nerve transmission affected by saxitoxin?
   a) Axonal damage.
   b) Neurotransmitter concentration declines.
   c) Neuron body is destroyed.
   d) Electrical transmission is affected.
Q3. Neurologic testing of victims of saxitoxin poison is most likely to show which?
   a) An increase in conduction velocities.
   b) Shortening of distal motor latencies.
   c) Significant decrease in nerve conduction velocity.
   d) Shortening of sensory motor latencies.

Answers and Discussion

Q1. (Answer = a) Saxitoxin is very similar to tetrodotoxin in regard to the three-dimensional structure of each molecule, the mode of action of each toxin on the nervous system, and the symptoms experienced by victims of either toxin. A major difference is, of course, the source of the toxin.
Q2. (Answer = d) Saxitoxin impacts the electrical transmission of nerve messages by an effect on the sodium channels at the cellular and subcellular level.
Q3. (Answer = c) As expected, studies of the nerve conduction velocity by electromyography on victims of saxitoxin poisoning show a significant decrease in conduction velocities. Slowed conduction results from a cumu- lative delay along the length of the axon as the normal movement of

sodium, needed to establish a voltage difference, is impeded. Nerve conduction studies also show a marked prolongation of distal motor and sensory latencies.

References

Anon., Paralytic shellfish poisoning – Massachusetts and Alaska, 1990, *Morbidity and Mortality Weekly Report,* 40, 157–160, 1991.
Long, R.R. et al., Paralytic shellfish poisoning: a case report and serial electrophysiologic observations, *Neurology,* 40, 1310–1312, 1990.

Case Study 4: The Burned Boy

A 10-year-old boy was badly burned when a small gasoline engine exploded near him. Twenty-five percent of his body surface area suffered partial thickness burns. His initial treatment included application of dressings over the burned areas. They were soaked with pHisoHex™. For 9 days following admission to the hospital he was exposed to this antibacterial agent on a frequent basis. At that time, his temperature rose but bacterial cultures were negative. The child developed lower extremity weakness and became confused. These neurological signs progressed and he became apneic 2 weeks after the injury. He was resuscitated and blood was drawn for studies:

Na^+	124 meq/L
K^+	3 meq/L
Cl^-	80 meq/L
BUN	15 mg/dL
Arterial pH	7.45

His respirations again decreased. He showed no deep tendon reflexes nor response to pain. The child died on the 15th day of hospitalization.

What toxin may have caused the neurological aspects of this child's disease?
   a) Hexachlorophene
   b) Tetrodotoxin
   c) Tellurium
   d) Triethyl tin

The child's death was unexpected because he was admitted to the hospital for a very treatable burn injury. His prognosis had been excellent. The specific symptoms that he manifested were not consistent with organ failure related to burns. A reasonable suspicion is that he reacted to a medicinal agent. pHisoHex contains hexachlorophene and this is known to be toxic to myelin. None of the other possible answers is consistent with the history of the child's treatment or possible exposures in the hospital.

Autopsy showed satisfactory progress in burn wound healing. Also noted were cerebral swelling with elevated brain weight. There was edema of gray and white matter. Findings were similar to those seen in brains of laboratory animals exposed to large amounts of HCP.

Questions

Q1. What biochemical aberration results from HCP exposure?
   a) Uncoupling of mitochondrial oxidative phosphorylation
   b) Blockade of sodium channels in neurons
   c) Inhibition of squalene epoxidase
   d) Inhibition of electron transport
Q2. What blood concentration of HCP is toxic?
   a) >1 μg/mL
   b) >1 ng/mL
   c) >10 μg/mL
   d) >1 mg/mL
Q3. Which is true of HCP?
   a) It is a bacteriostatic agent with antibacterial action against *Staphylococcus*.
   b) Burns have been shown to decrease HCP absorption.
   c) It has a blood half-life of about 10 days.
   d) Its major toxicity is interference with normal blood coagulation.

Answers and Discussion

Q1. (Answer = a) At the subcellular level, HCP uncouples oxidative phosphorylation. This explains the patient's elevated body temperature because the metabolism of glucose produces heat rather than chemical energy in the form of adenosine triphosphate (ATP), when uncoupling occurs. One effect of this uncoupling is degradation of myelin in neurons.
Q2. (Answer = a) The effect of HCP on oxidative phosphorylation has been demonstrated at concentrations less than 1 μg/mL in blood or less than 1 μg/g in brain and other tissue. The patient described in this case had tissue levels from a low of 2.1 μg/mL in blood to as high as 6 μg/g in fat.
Q3. (Answer = a) HCP is a valuable topical antibacterial that protects patients against infection, a leading cause of complications and death after burn injury. However, burns increase absorption of this potential neurotoxin by a factor of 2.5 in laboratory animals and presumably in humans, as well. The agent is usually safe and its customary safety is enhanced by its short half-life of 10 hours. In this patient, however, dosing was probably too frequent in view of the high amounts found in blood and other tissues. It seems that HCP was absorbed by this patient, stored in skin, distributed by blood, and deposited temporarily in body fat. The overall body burden of HCP was sufficient to cause death.

Reference

Chilcote, R. et al., Hexachlorophene storage in a burn patient associated with encephalopathy, *Pediatrics,* 59, 457–459, 1977.

Case Study 5: The Recovering Alcoholic

A 22-year-old woman had become a severe alcoholic for the preceding 5 years. She presented to a treatment center and consented to aversion therapy with disulfiram. This medication, also known as tetraethylthiuram disulfide or Antabuse, is an inhibitor of acetaldehyde dehydrogenase. As a consequence, if a patient drinks alcohol while on this drug his or her metabolism of alcohol will stop at acetaldehyde. Nausea results from the relatively large amounts of this compound that appear in the blood. She complied well with a regimen of 250 mg disulfiram daily for 6 months and was alcohol free for this period. In her 7th month of disulfiram treatment, she noticed numbness first in the lower part of both legs and then in her hands. She also started having trouble walking and climbing stairs. Neurological examination confirmed her complaint of leg weakness. Sensation was impaired to the midthigh. Her gait was abnormal. Nerve conduction studies were abnormal including denervation in the distal leg muscles.

She discontinued disulfiram treatment and, 3 months later, showed marked improvement in sensory detection and in strength. A nerve biopsy was obtained. Conduction studies on the biopsy specimen showed reduction in amplitude of potential. Light and electron microscopy showed degeneration of axons and swelling of axons due to accumulation of neurofilaments.

Q1. What agent may be responsible for this patient's neurological impairment?
   a) Carbon disulfide
   b) Acrylamide
   c) Methyl n-butyl ketone
   d) Any of the above

Responses a–c are toxic in the manner described in this case and all have been responsible for the exact presentation that this woman displayed. To decide among them one has to investigate the history of toxic exposures. It was ultimately determined that carbon disulfide was the immediate agent causing her symptoms.

Questions

Q1. What part of the neuron is attacked by carbon disulfide?
   a) Axon
   b) Neuron cell body
   c) Dendrite
   d) Myelin sheath

Q2. How did this patient come into contact with carbon disulfide?
   a) She may have worked in a CS_2-related industry.
   b) CS_2 is common in many consumer products, but some persons are unaware of its dangers.
   c) It arose from the disulfiram that she employed as a medication.
   d) It was probably a contaminant of alcohol that she was abusing.
Q3. Why is carbon disulfide toxic to nerve tissue?
   a) It chelates metals that are needed for enzymes to function.
   b) It forms toxic peroxides.
   c) It inhibits glycolytic enzymes.
   d) Exact mechanism of biochemical action is not known.

Answers and Discussion

Q1. (Answer = a) Carbon disulfide attacks the axon as demonstrated by axonal damage seen in electron microscopy of nerve tissue. It is referred to as a "dying back" axonopathy, which means that it starts by injuring the distal parts of the axon and then progresses toward the proximal part.

Q2. (Answer = c) There is nothing in this patient's history to support any of the suggestions presented here except for the known fact that disulfiram is metabolized to carbon disulfide (Figure 10.12). Disulfiram is first reduced by glutathione reductase to diethyldithiocarbamate. In a second step, this compound is transformed into diethylamine and carbon disulfide. Disulfiram toxicity, therefore, is equal to carbon disulfide exposure plus some drug reactions that are due to the disulfiram, itself. Disulfiram toxicity is manifested by skin rash, drowsiness, headache, and occasional psychotic reactions. These signs are not due to carbon disulfide but to the drug itself or some other metabolite. If a person drinks alcohol in spite of concurrent use of disulfiram they will experience a wide range of symptoms including tachycardia, severe headache, hypotension, tachypnea, and fainting. Several deaths have been reported in association with simultaneous use of alcohol and disulfiram.

   That carbon disulfide as a metabolite is sufficient to cause neurotoxicity is supported by studies that show levels of this metabolite in blood as high as 14 mg/L from disulfiram therapy.

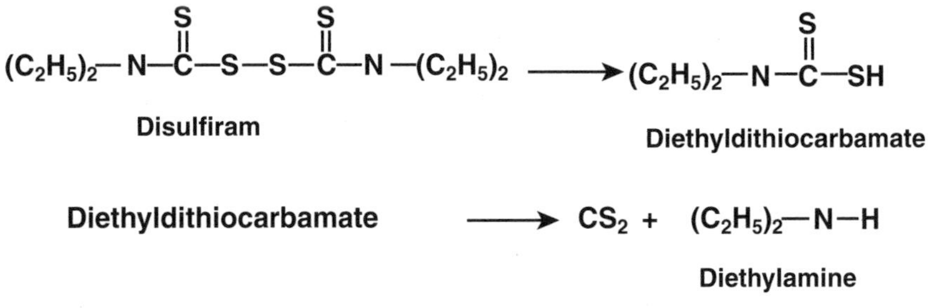

FIGURE 10.12 Biotransformation of disulfiram to carbon disulfide.

Q3. (Answer = d) The reason why this particular compound, carbon disulfide, should be neurotoxic is not known exactly. Speculation centers on a probable role in energy metabolism. If CS_2 interferes in the production of energy in neural tissue the resulting energy deficit would lead to the disruption of normal neuron integrity.

References

Ansbacher, L.E. et al., Disulfiram neuropathy: a neurofilamentous distal axonopathy, *Neurology,* 32, 424–428, 1982.

Peters, H.A. et al., Extrapyramidal and other neurologic manifestations associated with carbon disulfide fumigant exposure, *Arch. Neurol.,* 45, 537–540, 1988.

Case Study 6: The Satanic Cult

A 17-year-old male was under house arrest in the home of his parents for drug-related offenses. When he created a serious domestic dispute with his parents, they felt a need to call the police. When the police arrived, the young man stated, "You should not have called them. I told you they would never take me alive!" He then rapidly swallowed a brown liquid from a test tube. Parents learned later that a fellow member of a Satanic cult to which this boy belonged had given him the liquid as a means of suicide if he thought it necessary. The boy vomited and collapsed within 2 minutes. No pulse was recognized, so police performed CPR. Advanced cardiac life support was provided in about 6 minutes. Epinephrine converted the patient from asystole to ventricular fibrillation. Orotracheal intubation and defibrillation produced sinus tachycardia with normal blood pressure. On arrival at an emergency department the patient was in a coma, with elevated pulse rate and reduced blood pressure. Pupils were fixed and dilated. Bowel sounds were absent. Extremities were flaccid and there was no response to deep pain. Mechanical ventilation was begun. Dopamine was started with improvement of blood pressure to 120/60. Gastric lavage was carried out with normal saline followed by instillation of 50 g of activated charcoal. Detectives arrived with a bottle labeled "Pesticide" that contained material that resembled what the patient had drank.

What neurotoxin did this patient ingest?
   a) Strychnine
   b) Nicotine
   c) Saxitoxin
   d) Tetrodotoxin

The wide range of symptoms that this patient exhibited cannot be clearly associated with one toxin at this point. It is especially difficult to make an identification because it appears to be a massive overdose that immediately caused a cardiac arrest. Therefore, many of the patient's signs were secondary to the complications accompanying the arrest. Among the choices given nicotine fits the picture of an immediate and catastrophic response. The other agents, which come from food (saxitoxin and tetrodotoxin), do not fit the history seen here. Strychnine would also not be expected to react as quickly. The solution the patient drank was tested and found to contain nicotine at 870 mg/mL. Serum levels of nicotine in the patient equaled 13,600 ng/mL, an amount that greatly exceeds a lethal level. It was estimated that the patient consumed 5 g of nicotine. By comparison, 60 mg is thought to equal the LD_{50}, although some believe that the LD_{50} is probably higher than this.

Chest X-ray showed bilateral infiltrates indicative of aspiration pneumonitis from the patient's extreme vomiting. In ICU the patient had multiple grand mal seizures and developed cerebral edema. EEG showed no cortical function. Severe hypotension occurred 30 hours after the poisoning. The patient expired at 64 hours post-ingestion. The cause of death was believed to be anoxic brain injury.

Questions

Q1. Which is not expected as a sign of nicotine poisoning?
   a) Hypertonicity
   b) Seizures
   c) Weakness
   d) Diaphoresis

Q2. What amount of nicotine is present is a single cigarette?
   a) 20 µg
   b) 20 mg
   c) 500 mg
   d) 10 nanograms

Q3. What treatment should be instituted for children who ingest cigarettes?
   a) Atropine as antidote
   b) Gastrointestinal decontamination
   c) No intervention is needed
   d) Ipecac

Q4. What is the best substance to evaluate in urine to document smoking?
   a) Nicotine
   b) Cotinine
   c) Nicotine epoxide
   d) Nicotine-1'-N-oxide

Answers and Discussion

Q1. (Answer = a) Due to neuromuscular blockade, hypotonicity rather than hypertonicity is expected in nicotine overdose.

Q2. (Answer = b) A single cigarette has from 10 to 20 mg of nicotine compared to an average cigar that contains approximately twice as much. How can cigarettes be used so extensively if the quantity of nicotine is so near the alleged lethal amount of nicotine of 60 mg? Some of the nicotine is lost in sidestream smoke and some is incinerated. Further, the value of 60 mg is probably something of an underestimate.

Q3. (Answer = b) Children ingesting cigarettes are in danger of slow nicotine absorbtion. Avoid Ipecac because the child might seize from nicotine and aspirate vomitus. Other forms of gastrointestinal decontamination should be attempted.

Q4. (Answer = b) Cotinine, an oxidized form of nicotine, is generally measured in urine to evaluate a person's smoking status. It is better to measure cotinine than nicotine because only 5% of smoked nicotine is excreted into the urine. Further, the average urinary concentration of nicotine in a smoker is 1.2 mg/L vs. an average cotinine concentration of 9.2 mg/L. The sensitivity of cotinine assay is, therefore, better than that of nicotine.

Reference

Lavoie, F. and Harris, T., Fatal nicotine ingestion, *J. Emerg. Med.,* 9, 133–136, 1991.

Case Study 7: The Dead Farmer

A 32-year-old man who worked as a farmer awakened his wife at 5 a.m. one morning and announced that their barn was on fire. The two of them rushed to the barn to remove valuable equipment before it was destroyed by the fire. As they fought the fire and waited for assistance from the local fire fighters, the farmer vomited and experienced several convulsions. His wife tried in vain to help him and reported later that when she touched her husband he only went into additional convulsions. He eventually became cyanotic and then unconscious. The fire company found him with no pulse and they successfully provided cardiopulmonary resuscitation. On arrival at the hospital he seemed much better, without cyanosis, with good vascular perfusion, and with sinus tachycardia. He did, however, continue to seize but this was controlled with diazepam administration, induction of paralysis, and mechanical ventilation. Arterial blood gases showed a severe metabolic acidosis with pH of 6.6 and pCO_2 of 7.91 kPa.

He was in renal failure and was transferred to a dialysis unit. At this time a probable diagnosis is
a) Carbon monoxide
b) Malathion
c) Strychnine
d) Alcohol overdose

On the basis of his exposure to a fire immediately before symptoms started, the initial diagnosis was carbon monoxide poisoning. Seizures were the most significant feature of his presentation and they can be found in CO poisoning. Seizures would not usually be such a major aspect of the illness, however. Quite soon the laboratory reported a carboxyhemoglobin result of 2% and this was regarded as proof that the patient's symptoms were not related to CO. Alcohol could be ruled out because the seizures were not preceded by stuporous, alcoholic-type behavior. An important clue to this patient's problem was the report from his wife that a mere touch from her sent him into further seizures. This response is characteristic of strychnine. The suspicion of strychnine was reinforced by the fact that strychnine is found as an insecticide on many farms. Additional studies on this patient revealed a creatine kinase of 1500 U/L and urinary crystals. The urinary crystal finding suggested the possibility of ethylene glycol poisoning. Gas chromatography showed no alcohols, however, and X-ray diffraction revealed that the crystals were not calcium oxalate, the kind that arises from ethylene glycol exposure.

Thin layer chromatography finally revealed that the patient had strychnine in his urine. GC/MS confirmed this finding with major ions at 334, 162, and 120, all characteristic of the electron impact spectrum of strychnine.

The patient was continuously dialysed and mechanically ventilated but he died on the 6th day of hospitalization. Examination of the patient's social history suggested suicide since he often complained of marital conflict and financial worries.

Questions

Q1. Which induces symptoms similar to those of strychnine?
   a) Tetanus toxin
   b) Amphetamine
   c) Botulinum toxin
   d) Tri-ortho-cresyl phosphate
Q2. What is the mechanism of strychnine action?
   a) It demyelinates neurons in the extremities.
   b) It inhibits acetylcholine release.
   c) It blocks the inhibitory neurotransmitter, glycine.
   d) It causes an axonopathy.
Q3. What is the significance of elevated creatine kinase and myoglobin in the blood of patients with strychnine poisoning?
   a) They are signs of cardiac injury.
   b) They are classical markers of neurotoxicity.
   c) They indicate the beginnings of renal impairment.
   d) They are indicative of muscle damage.

Answers and Discussion

Q1. (Answer = a) Tetanus toxin has the same target as strychnine, i.e., the inhibitory neurotransmitter, glycine. There is a difference. Strychnine blocks the uptake of glycine at the postsynaptic receptor site in certain motor neurons in the spinal cord. Tetanus toxin also causes hyperexcitability but it does so on the presynaptic side. It blocks the release of glycine within the inhibitory neuron. The convulsions induced by both are, not surprisingly, very similar.

Q2. (Answer = c) As stated above, strychnine interferes with normal activity of the inhibitory neurotransmitter, glycine. In doing so it produces spasms of the abdominal muscles, muscle twitching, and spastic paraplegia. The hyperexcitability induces convulsions, hyperthermia, and opisthotonus (an arched position of the body in which the victim lies on his back but only the head and feet are in contact with the floor or bed). Severe cases are associated with cessation of breathing.

Q3. (Answer = d) The enzyme, creatine kinase, and the protein, myoglobin, are both elevated with muscle damage. Myoglobin, but not creatine kinase, also is raised when renal impairment occurs. The patient with strychnine poisoning suffers muscle damage from the severity of his convulsive behavior.

References

Burn, D.J. et al., Strychnine poisoning as an unusual cause of convulsions, *Postgrad. Med. J.,* 65, 563–564, 1989.

Nishiyama, T. and Nagase, M., Strychnine poisoning: natural course of a nonfatal case, *Am. J. Emerg. Med.,* 13, 172–173, 1995.

11 Pulmonary Toxicology

CONTENTS

The primary role of the pulmonary system is to exchange gases, pass oxygen into the blood, and remove waste carbon dioxide. Without oxygen the organism must live anaerobically, depending on biochemical processes that provide less than 10% as much energy as is available from oxygen-driven metabolism. The lungs are responsible for gas exchange. If they and the other components of the pulmonary system are healthy, gas exchange can go forward. Getting oxygen into the blood is only one aspect of oxygenation, however. Because oxygen is fairly insoluble in blood, an adequate supply of competent red blood cells is also a critical aspect of efficient tissue oxygenation. Other roles for the pulmonary system include participation in acid-base balance, defense of the organism against infection, and the production of intelligible speech. The pulmonary system may also constitute a route for the invasion of the body by toxins.

BASIC PULMONARY ANATOMY AND PHYSIOLOGY

Anatomy of the pulmonary system is often divided into the conducting area, structures which transfer gases to and from the innermost regions of the lungs, and the respiratory part, the localized region of gas exchange (Figure 11.1). The nose is the first component of the conducting area. The nostrils are adjacent to the nasal cavity, a space surrounded by bony structures. It is divided approximately in two by the nasal septum. Two protective mechanisms found in the nose consist of ciliated epithelial cells and goblet cells that secrete mucus. The cilia and mucus work together to trap particulates that enter the body through the nose. This filtration process tends to remove microorganisms and some components of smog. Additional activities associated with the nose are smell, warming of air, and modulating the voice to give it a nasal quality. Behind the nasal cavity lies the pharynx, a structure that also communicates with the oral cavity and the esophagus.

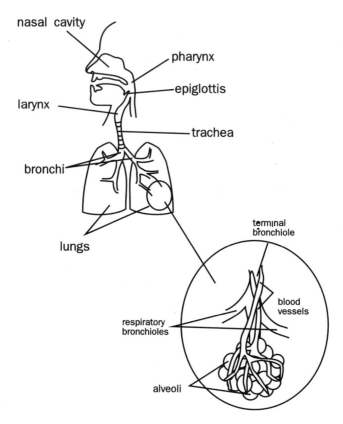

FIGURE 11.1 Lungs and related pulmonary structures.

Beneath the pharynx is the larynx, a cartilaginous structure with a mucous membrane lining. The center of the larynx is open and folded and the folds vibrate as air passes over them. These folds are known as the vocal cords. Sound modulation is achieved partly by varying the tension of the cords by muscles connected to them. The size of the laryngeal opening can also be changed, further modulating the sound of the voice. A critical tissue flap called the epiglottis is placed above the larynx. It closes over the larynx during swallowing to prevent food from entering the larynx. A cough is a reflex response to irritation of the larynx. While coughing the larynx is temporarily closed and air is forced upward. Pressure rises and the eventual outcome is that the larynx re-opens with the expulsion of the irritant that produced the cough.

The trachea is the next section of the pulmonary anatomy. This structure also is composed mainly of cartilage, is flexible, and is lined with mucous membranes. Air passes through the trachea and thence into the right and left primary bronchi. While passing through these bronchi the air is within the lung itself. Progressive branching is now the rule with the primary bronchi branching out to secondary bronchi, secondary bronchi branching into smaller structures called bronchioles, and bronchioles branching into terminal bronchioles. Finally, these branch into respiratory bronchioles that end in alveoli, tiny sacs from which gas passes into and out of the blood. From the trachea to the terminal alveolar sac there are 23 branching events. Three hundred million alveoli are found in each lung. Cartilage content decreases as the diameter of these pulmonary tubes decreases and the cartilage is replaced by smooth muscle. Bronchioles are completely encircled by smooth muscle that sometimes undergoes spasms in the disorder known as asthma.

The branching pattern, together with the microscopic structure of the alveoli, provide a huge surface area across which gas exchange may occur. In an adult human this surface equals the size of a tennis court in area.

The alveoli consist simply of a single layer of epithelial tissue on top of a thin layer of elastic fibers. Within the epithelial tissue three types of cells are found: Clara cells that are metabolically active in biotransformation of chemicals that enter the lung, Type I cells that make pulmonary surfactant, and Type II cells that also manufacture surfactant. A deficiency of surfactant is often found in infants who are premature, especially those delivered more than 6 weeks early. It also can be deficient in some adult diseases. Surfactant deficiency renders breathing very difficult and is associated with respiratory distress syndrome. Adjacent to each alveolus are capillaries that arise from the branching of the pulmonary arteries. Millions of alveoli are in the most intimate proximity with miles of capillaries to expedite the critical process of gas exchange. The capillaries exit the lungs while merging to form pulmonary veins by which oxygenated blood is returned to the heart.

GAS EXCHANGE

The process of normal breathing involves the action of two muscles. The diaphragm, a dome-shaped muscle, is at the floor of the thoracic cavity, the region within the chest that holds the lungs. The external intercostal muscles are attached to the ribs. Breathing occurs when the diaphragm contracts, changing from a dome to a flat muscle. The size of the thoracic cavity thereby becomes enlarged. At the same time the external intercostals contract and make the ribs move upward, also increasing the size of the thoracic cavity. As the lung volume increases, pressure in the lung must decrease. This low pressure provides the motive force for air to enter the lungs.

The lung is actually covered by a membrane, the parietal pleura; the walls of the thoracic cavity, in close proximity to the lungs, are covered by the visceral pleura. The pleural cavity, which is filled with liquid, is located between the two kinds of pleural membranes. Among the functions of the pleural cavity is lubrication so the oft-repeated motions of breathing occur in a smooth manner. Obviously, a hole in one of these membranes may allow air into the pleural cavity. This is known as a collapsed lung and breathing will be enormously difficult if not impossible because the critical pressure difference disappears.

Expiration, or breathing out, is more or less the opposite of inspiration, breathing in. During the expiration phase pressure within the lungs is greater than the external pressure, with the pressure difference arising from a decreased lung volume. The process, however, is passive. Because the lungs are elastic they automatically contract in volume as the muscles relax.

Respiratory physiologists measure various aspects of the breathing cycle and the resulting values may be indicative of some pathological states (Table 11.1). A

TABLE 11.1
Tests in Physiology and Chemistry and Their Meanings
Summary: Tests in Spirometry

TV	Tidal Volume	Normal volume during sedentary breathing
IRV	Inspiratory Reserve Volume	Added air that is inhaled with effort
ERV	Expiratory Reserve Volume	Added air that is exhaled with effort
VC	Vital Capacity	Maximal air breathed (TV + IRV + ERV)
RV	Residual Volume	Air volume always remaining in lungs (Total lung volume = RV + VC)
RR	Respiratory Rate	Breaths per minute
MV	Minute volume	Volume of air breathed per minute (MV = RR × TV)
FEV_1	Forced Expiratory Volume	Volume of air forcibly exhaled per second after maximum inhalation

spirometer is an instrument for testing breathing. It measures, among other variables, the tidal volume (TV). This is the normal volume of air breathed in or out in normal sedentary breathing. Additional measures of pulmonary activity by the spirometer include the volume that can be inhaled with effort (the inspiratory reserve volume, IRV) or volume exhaled with effort (the expiratory reserve volume, ERV). The maximum air that can be breathed is called the vital capacity and this is equivalent to TV + IRV + ERV. Because of the nature of the lungs with innumerable passages and huge numbers of alveoli, it is impossible to completely empty the lungs of all air. The residual volume (RV) is that amount of air that always remains in the lungs. Total lung capacity equals vital capacity plus RV. Other useful values include the respiratory rate which, of course, equals the number of inspirations per minute. The volume of air that moves in and out per minute is called the minute volume. Minute volume is equal to respiratory rate times tidal volume. Forced expiratory volume (FEV_1) is an important respiratory variable that equals the volume of air one can forcibly exhale in one second after maximum inhalation. The total volume forcibly exhaled is the FVC, the forced vital capacity. Normal individuals exhale 80% of the air in the first second. In other words, FEV_1 equals 80% of FVC.

In the broadest sense, pulmonologists divide lung disease into two types of conditions. Restrictive conditions are associated with decrease in elasticity of lung tissue that leads to a reduction in maximum flow rate and a reduction in total volume exhaled. An example of a restrictive disease is pulmonary fibrosis. The second type of condition is obstructive disease such as asthma, chronic bronchitis, or emphysema. In obstructive disease, there is an obstacle to air flow. In restrictive disease, both FEV_1 and FVC are reduced, but the FEV_1/FVC% is normal or even increased. It is said that the hallmark of restrictive disease is reduction in lung volumes. Measurement of lung volumes enables one to assess the severity of restrictive disease. As stated above, obstructive disease is manifested by a decrease in expiratory airflow. In these conditions the FEV_1 is reduced much more than the FVC causing a low FEV_1/FVC%. Thus, measurement of these parameters enables a physician to improve diagnostic accuracy. In some patients, however, there is a mixed disease pattern that complicates interpretation of spirometric findings.

TABLE 11.2
Pulmonary Disease and Spirometry

Condition	Examples	Spirometric Results
Restrictive	Pulmonary fibrosis	FEV_1 reduced
		FVC reduced
		FEV/FVC% normal or elevated
Obstructive	Asthma	FEV_1 reduced more than FVC
	Chronic bronchitis	FEV/FVC% decreased
	Emphysema	

GAS GRADIENTS

Gases diffuse between the alveoli and the bloodstream. To accomplish this they need only cross a Type I alveolar cell and a flat endothelial cell of the blood capillary vessel. Gases diffuse according to differences in concentration as expressed by their partial pressures. Thus, the partial pressure of oxygen is high and the partial pressure of carbon dioxide is low in the alveolus. Because the magnitudes of these partial pressures are exactly opposite within the blood (relatively high pCO_2 and low pO_2), the gradient favors movement of oxygen into and carbon dioxide out of the blood. Deep within the body the gradients are, again, reversed. Carbon dioxide is a product of cellular respiration and leaves the tissue to enter the blood. Oxygen is needed within the cells and is usually present in them in low partial pressures. Thus, oxygen leaves the blood while carbon dioxide leaves the cells. Because oxygen is a nonpolar molecule, very little of it can dissolve in an aqueous medium such as blood. On the other hand, the demand for oxygen is very high. The solution to this problem is hemoglobin which carries about 98% of the oxygen present in the blood.

PULMONARY FUNCTION AND TOXICITY

The pulmonary system is able to protect the body from some toxicants. It is also the point of attack for others, either because they naturally enter the body through this route or some aspect of pulmonary biochemistry renders the lung especially vulnerable to their effects. Two kinds of substances enter the body by inhalation: gases and particulates. Particulates are greater in size than gases and are suspended in air rather than being dissolved in it like true gases. Particulates form heterogeneous mixtures with air. They are not uniformly distributed in air the way oxygen and nitrogen are uniformly dispersed.

The lungs are self-protective in a number of ways. Cilia and mucus in the pharynx and larynx trap particles and direct them upward by ciliary action. Eventually these particles reach the mouth from which they can be swallowed or expectorated. Macrophage cells patrol the alveoli and they also consume particles that have escaped the first line of defense, the cilia and mucus described above. Some toxins, such as tobacco smoke, are deleterious to the body not only directly by organ injury but also indirectly by undermining the normal protective mechanisms. They increase the viscosity of mucus and inhibit ciliary action. Both of these effects limit the organism's ability to capture and eject toxins from the pulmonary system. Some toxins harm macrophage and thereby lead to an increased susceptibility to infection. Some antibody-producing cells are also found in the lungs and they can be effective in resisting infection by antibody synthesis. The type of antibody found in the lung is called secretory antibody and is composed of immunoglobulin A, a protein type distinctly different from the major antibody types found in the blood. Protecting the lung against invasion is so critical that the body has evolved additional mechanisms. When Type I cells are injured, Type II cells are ready to divide and replace the injured cells with new Type I cells. Clara cells contain many enzymes for biotransformation and, therefore, inactivation of some toxins begins as soon as the toxin has entered the lung.

Factors Affecting Penetration of Gases and Particulates

Certain physical characteristics of substances, especially solubility and size, have a great impact on their pulmonary toxicity. For example, if an airborne gas is water soluble and is inhaled, it will be expected to dissolve into the aqueous material that comes from the cells that line the upper airway. This protects the lower airway because soluble gases never make it into the deep recesses of the lung. On the contrary, insoluble gases have a greater chance of penetrating deeply into the lung.

Size is the major factor influencing the depth of penetration of particulates. The largest such materials, those above 5 μm in diameter, settle onto the walls of the upper airway, the nasal cavity and pharynx. Medium size particles, 1–5 μm in size, stay suspended in the inhaled air as deep as the trachea where the air moves slowly, and this results in sedimentation of these particles onto membranes. The smallest particulates, those less than 1 μm in diameter, can be carried all the way into the alveoli.

ACUTE PULMONARY TOXICITY

Acute pulmonary toxins (Figure 11.2) may cause a number of effects within the respiratory tract. First, they may simply irritate the tract. Irritation is characterized by an increase in mucus secretion and may provoke coughing. Irritants also often cause contraction of the smooth muscle that surrounds the bronchioles. This is known as bronchoconstriction. Swelling may accompany bronchoconstriction. The combined effect is a narrowing of the airway and a decrease in the availability of air. Sulfur dioxide is an example of a potent bronchoconstrictor.

Inflammation is a second and sometimes more severe insult to the system. In inflammatory injury the blood vessels in the vicinity of the lungs experience an increase in permeability and immune cells congregate in the damaged area. The change in blood vessel permeability eventually results in fluid leaving the blood vessels and entering the airway, a phenomenon called pulmonary edema. Many agents, such as sulfur dioxide and nitrogen dioxide, can cause pulmonary edema. The fluid increases the work of breathing since it constitutes a barrier to the transit of gases across the alveolar membrane. In extreme cases, it leads to asphyxia and

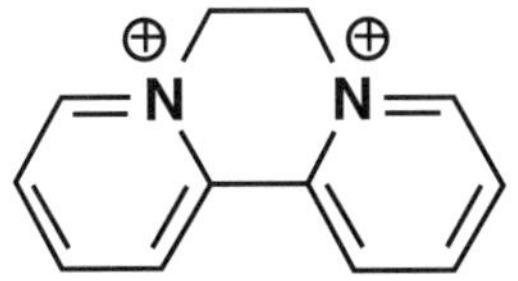

Diquat

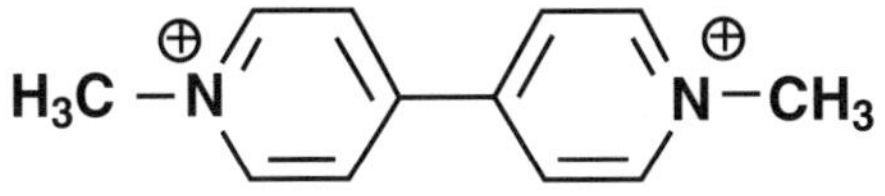

Paraquat

SO_2 **Sulfur dioxide**

NO_2 **Nitrogen dioxide**

O_3 **Ozone**

FIGURE 11.2 Structures of some acute pulmonary toxins.

death. The normal pulmonary hydrostatic pressure is low at 15 mm Hg. The colloid osmotic pressure of blood is greater than this at 25 mm. Therefore, the net force favors retention of fluids in the blood. Edema results when the cell permeability is lost and liquids equilibrate between the blood vessels and the alveolar space Another cause of edema is increase in pulmonary pressure so that the hydrostatic pressure in the pulmonary vessel is greater than the oncotic pressure so fluid enters the alveolus.

One final effect of pulmonary toxins is necrosis, or cell death, from specific toxins. For example, ozone, a very strong oxidant, damages cells probably by the process of lipid peroxidation. Concentrations as low as 1 ppm have caused pulmonary edema and cell necrosis in laboratory animals. During hot summer days the weather service issues ozone alerts when the concentration of this material reaches dangerous levels. Another agent that causes necrosis of pulmonary cells is paraquat, an herbicide. Paraquat and diquat are herbicides that destroy plant tissue by mere contact. They are inactivated by contact with soil, a property that is advantageous because it limits their persistence in the environment. The fatal dose of paraquat has been estimated to be as low as 4 mg/kg although it is generally reported as about 20 times this value. Whereas its exact mechanism of action is not known, it does accumulate in Type II cells and is believed to inhibit the enzyme, superoxide dismutase. This results in generation of free radicals, lipid peroxidation, and eventual destruction of lung tissue. Paraquat initially produces a local corrosive action including hemoptysis and ulcerations at the site of ingestion. Liver, renal, and cardiac damage are noted in about 2 days. Pulmonary symptoms are the major clinical finding after 3 days, with pulmonary fibrosis and edema being associated with low arterial oxygen tension. Respiratory failure eventually occurs as a prelude to death.

Still another example of a pulmonary toxicant that probably oxidizes lung tissue is nitrogen dioxide. When inhaled it reaches the deep recesses of the lungs because it does not irritate the upper airway. However, it extensively damages pulmonary tissue while provoking a toxic pneumonitis and pulmonary edema. Because it is produced from the burning of fossil fuels we may expect that its presence will be ubiquitous although usually below amounts that would produce symptoms. Many interesting episodes of poisoning with this agent have occurred. On one occasion a coin collector inadvertently dumped a large number of coins that were 96% copper into a tray containing 50% concentrated nitric acid. Not recognizing any danger, he then breathed the gas emitted from the mixture. Twelve hours later he was admitted to the hospital with complaint of dyspnea. Examination revealed pulmonary edema and hypoxemia. He recovered after several days of treatment with steroids. It was subsequently recognized that nitrogen dioxide had poisoned him. It was formed by the following reaction:

$$Cu + 4HNO_3 \rightarrow Cu(NO_3)_2 + 2NO_2 + 2H_2O$$

On another occasion 24 men were refueling an intercontinental ballistic missile when an accident led to the spillage of 49,000 liters of nitrogen tetroxide, a dimer of nitrogen dioxide. Two of the men died, after experiencing dyspnea, pulmonary edema, hypoxia, and other respiratory symptoms. This overdose was so massive, however, that chemical burns were a greater problem than the toxicity due to nitrogen dioxide in this case.

CHRONIC POISONING WITH PULMONARY TOXICANTS

The term "chronic" refers to injury arising from repeated exposure to a disease cause and the time frame of the organ damage is over a relatively long period. Cancer is a good example of a disease process that usually occurs from chronic conditions. Both obstructive and restrictive pulmonary conditions may occur from chronic injury. Asthma is a chronic condition that is induced by sensitivity to many different chemicals. Toluene diisocyanate (Figure 11.3) is a chemical that causes chronic asthma and also causes the patient to be more sensitive to other chemical asthma-causing agents. The bronchoconstriction characteristic of asthma is only one of the hypersensitivities found with airway disease. A hypersensitivity pneumonitis is a chronic condition associated with dyspnea, fever, and chills. Chronic exposure to some irritants provokes an immune reaction especially in the lower airways. Mold or fungi found on food cause hypersensitivity pneumonitis in many persons. If the exposure is sufficiently prolonged and concentrated, it leads after many years to fibrosis. This is a restrictive condition in which macrophage cells are activated so

$$Mg_6(Si_4O_{10})(OH)_8$$ **Asbestos (one form)**

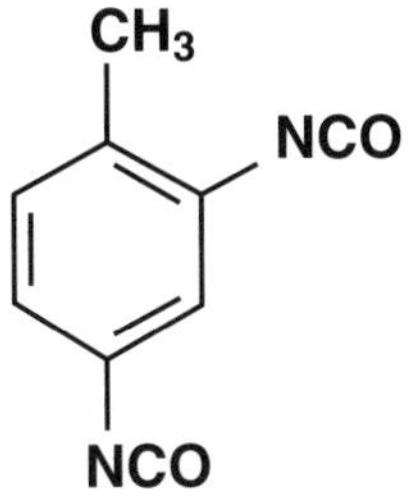

Toluene diisocyanate

FIGURE 11.3 Structures of some chronic pulmonary toxins.

frequently that they cause inflammation from their chemical products. The inflammation then causes the activation of fibroblasts, cells that reproduce and synthesize collagen, the protein of connective tissue. Within the confines of the lung the collagen causes restriction, reduces tissue elasticity, and interferes with ventilation and blood flow.

Fibrosis also may arise from silicate exposure, a condition called silicosis. Here again the macrophage cells are the proximate cause of fibrosis. They attempt unsuccessfully to engulf and eliminate silicates but the effort merely leads to the demise of the macrophage. Enzymes are released from macrophage cells. The enzymes cause inflammation. Fibroblasts proliferate and collagen is deposited as fibrous tissue. Pulmonary tissue destruction causes a reduction in pulmonary function.

Chronic bronchitis is a well-known affliction characterized by a chronic cough related to excessive secretion of mucus from more or less continuous exposure to some toxicant. Cigarette smoking or living in a region with poor air quality are examples of situations that lead to the development of chronic bronchitis.

One specific type of silicate, asbestos, causes asbestosis, an inflammatory condition that is very similar to silicosis. Asbestos also leads to lung cancer, either the common form found in epithelial cells, or a rarer form, mesothelioma, which is not curable and is found almost solely in association with asbestos. A virtual hysteria has gripped the public over asbestos and massive amounts of money have been poured into asbestos abatement programs.

Questions

1. Make a list of at least five tests used in spirometry. Define each test. For the listed tests describe the clinical interpretation given to abnormal findings.
2. List at least three normal mechanisms employed by the lungs and associated pulmonary structures to reduce susceptibility to the actions of toxins.

3. Compare and contrast the actions of paraquat and nitrogen dioxide on the human pulmonary system.
4. How do chronic toxins affect the pulmonary system such that their activities provoke a long term rather than an acute toxicity?
5. What are the diseases caused by asbestos? Among the various forms of asbestos, which are carcinogenic? What are the chemical and physical features of those types of asbestos that make them carcinogenic?

Case Study 1: A Different Kind of Hockey Injury

A 17-year-old hockey player was admitted to the hospital one morning because of difficulty in breathing and repeated hemoptysis. No immediate explanation for his problem was apparent. He had no history of pulmonary disease nor was he a smoker. On the afternoon of the previous day he played hockey in an indoor rink. At that time he experienced a cough and diffuse chest pain, complaints that were also made by several other players. By midnight he suffered from dyspnea, dizziness, and headache.

At the time of admission his temperature was normal but his respirations were elevated and heart rate was increased to 95 beats per minute. Auscultation of the chest revealed crackles on both sides and the peak expiratory flow rate was only 350 L/minute (normal mean is 640 L/min). Arterial blood gases showed severe hypoxemia (pO_2 = 6 kPa, pCO_2 = 5.7 kPa). Hemoglobin saturation was 81%. Both carboxyhemoglobin and methemoglobin were in the normal range. White blood cell count was elevated at 17,100 and C-reactive protein equalled 57 mg/L (normal < 10 mg/L). Chest X-ray showed infiltrative lesions in the parenchyma.

If his symptoms were due to a pulmonary toxin in the hockey arena what is its possible identity?
   a) Carbon monoxide
   b) Nitrogen dioxide
   c) Sulfur dioxide
   d) Chlorine

Insufficient evidence is presented to form an exact opinion. However, carbon monoxide is highly unlikely because the patient's carboxyhemoglobin was normal. Further, his symptoms are not exactly consistent with carbon monoxide. A chlorine or sulfur dioxide spill would not be expected in this environment. In addition, both of these gases have low odor thresholds so that someone should have reported an unusual odor. Nitrogen oxides are emitted by internal combustion engines including the machines that re-cover the ice (the Zamboni). If the instrument was malfunctioning and/or the ventilation was very poor, it is possible that nitrogen dioxide achieved toxic levels. Symptoms displayed by this patient are consistent with NO_2. This gas was subsequently determined to be the cause of the patient's symptoms.

The boy was given steroids and transferred to ICU. In the ICU steroids and oxygen therapy were continued. Over the following 4 days his condition improved to the point that he could be discharged. Spirometric testing 1 month later showed that he had completely returned to normal.

Questions

Q1. What factor increased the player's risk of pulmonary poisoning?
    a) Poor physical condition
    b) Intense physical exercise
    c) Playing in a cold environment
    d) Prior existence of pulmonary disease
Q2. Measurement of the air within the arena after operation of the ice resurfacer gave levels of nitrogen dioxide of 2400 µg/m³. What is this in ppm?
    a) 1.3
    b) 5.6
    c) 103
    d) 8000
Q3. How does NO_2 damage the lung tissue?
    a) By irritating the mucus membrane
    b) By blocking the upper airway
    c) By reducing the compliance of lung tissue
    d) By oxidation of lung tissue
Q4. What is the significance of elevated C-reactive protein?
    a) It distinguishes poisoning from a natural disease state.
    b) It indicates muscle injury.
    c) It signifies a cardiac complication.
    d) It is a sensitive test for inflammatory disease.

Answers and Discussion

Q1. (Answer = b) Respiratory rate increases during exercise. An intense sport such as ice hockey will cause a greatly increased minute volume. This is equivalent to exposure to a much higher concentration by a sedentary subject. Pre-existing pulmonary conditions would be important but there is no record of such a condition in this patient. Asthmatics, in particular, are extremely prone to the harmful effects of pulmonary irritants (see below).
Q2. (Answer = a) 2400 µg/m³ = 1.3 ppm. This is well above the 1 hour air quality standard in Sweden (where this incident occurred) of 110 µg/m³. Bronchoconstriction can occur in normal subjects at 5000 µg/m³ and in those with asthma at just 500 µg/m³. Bronchial hyperactivity may occur in normal subjects at 2000 µg/m³ and in asthmatics at just 10% of that level.

Q3. (Answer = d) Nitrogen dioxide is not irritating to the mucus membrane partly because of its insolubility in water. This adds to its insidious and toxic character by not warning the inhaler of the danger. It is a powerful oxidant and is used as such for diversified purposes including rocket fuel. Nitrogen dioxide is believed to produce free radicals and this leads to lipid peroxidation by a familiar and common mechanism. After membrane lipids become oxidized they are susceptible to destruction. Nitrogen dioxide is also the acid anhydride of nitric acid so this corrosive acid is formed when NO_2 is in the presence of water. Tissue destruction would, of course, be expedited by the availability of nitric acid.

Q4. (Answer = d) The concept of a generic marker of poisoning is, of course, nothing more than a fanciful notion. There are, on the other hand, markers of cardiac or muscle injury. C-reactive protein is not among them. This test is indicative of inflammation. It is greatly elevated in this patient because the injury to the respiratory tract causes inflammation. By the same token, inflammation usually responds to steroid treatment and this patient was successfully treated with steroids.

References

Karlson-Stiber, C. et al., Nitrogen dioxide pneumonitis in ice hockey players, *J. Intern. Med.*, 239, 451–456, 1996.

Kriskandan, K. and Pettingale, K.W., Numismatist's pneumonitis. A case of nitrogen dioxide poisoning, *Postgrad. Med. J.*, 61, 819–821, 1985.

Yockey, C.C. et al., The McConnell missile accident – Clinical spectrum of nitrogen dioxide exposure, *J. Am. Med. Assoc.*, 244, 1221–1223, 1980.

Case Study 2: The Deadly Defoliant

A 59-year-old man, weighing 165 pounds, was despondent and decided to commit suicide. He ingested a material he found in his garden shed. The bottle of the ingested material was labeled as 20% Gramoxone® and the volume the man swallowed was approximately 60 mL. Upon arrival at an emergency department the patient was noted to have erythema in his pharynx as his only physical finding. He complained of a burning sensation in his mouth and throat. Blood gases and other laboratory values were all unremarkable except for a slight elevation of the enzyme, alanine aminotransferase. Electrocardiogram and chest X-ray were all within normal limits.

Based on the history of ingestion his attending physician decided to conduct digestive tract decontamination. Stomach contents were aspirated and 100 g of charcoal were administered. After 25 minutes the charcoal was removed and gastric lavage repeated. Activated charcoal was given again. The patient was then started on 6 hours of hemodialysis. Finally, antioxidant therapy was begun with deferoxamine and N-acetylcysteine. The patient remained in good condition until the 4th day after admission when chest X-ray began to show abnormalities. Bilateral infiltrates were also noted in the pulmonary bases by computed tomographic scan. Lung capacity was reduced. Hypoxemia, with partial pressure of oxygen equal to 63 mm, was found.

At this time we would infer that the toxin present in Gramoxone is
    a) Malathion
    b) Ozone
    c) Paraquat
    d) Nitrogen dioxide

Malathion is a pesticide with cholinergic properties. It provokes the SLUD syndrome (see Chapter 17) which is not seen in this patient. Ozone and nitrogen dioxide are relatively insoluble gases. If present in the liquid they would be there in low concentrations. Paraquat is a suspect because it could be present in a garden shed as a defoliant. There is a characteristic delay in the appearance of respiratory symptoms when paraquat is ingested such as this patient manifested. Furthermore, when symptoms do appear they are usually pulmonary in nature. On his 4th hospital day this patient began to exhibit signs of poisoning by a pulmonary toxin.

The pulmonary findings were indicative of moderate impairment of gas exchange. They slowly resolved but did not return to normal until 16 days after admission. During his hospitalization the patient suffered acute renal failure demonstrated by creatinine of 5.6 mg/dL and creatinine clearance of 11.8 mL/min. He also experienced hepatic injury manifested by elevations of all liver enzymes.

Pulmonary, renal, and hepatic function all returned to normal and the patient was discharged from intensive medical care. He was transferred to a psychiatric ward where he underwent treatment for 3 additional months.

Questions

Q1. Gramoxone has a density of 0.97 gram/mL. What dosage of paraquat did this patient consume?
    a) 155 mg/kg
    b) 2 mg/kg
    c) 1 g/kg
    d) 23 μg/kg
Q2. The LD_{50} of paraquat is variously stated as being equal to 4–80 mg/kg. Why did this patient survive an amount that is much greater than the published LD_{50}s?
    a) He vomited shortly after the ingestion.
    b) Some patients are genetically resistant to this toxin.
    c) The toxin had decomposed while stored in the garden shed.
    d) Treatment was initiated expeditiously and an appropriate antidote was given.

Q3. What is the rationale for administering deferoxamine (DFO)?
   a) DFO forms an inactive complex with paraquat.
   b) Iron is needed for paraquat toxicity and DFO chelates iron.
   c) DFO converts paraquat to diquat.
   d) DFO prevents paraquat uptake by the lung.
Q4. What are the symptoms of massive paraquat ingestion?
   a) Slow onset pulmonary fibrosis without other signs
   b) Progressive pulmonary fibrosis with increasing dyspnea and hypoxemia
   c) Corrosive injuries of the GI tract with shock and acute respiratory failure
   d) Initially hepatic failure followed by complete renal failure

Answers and Discussion

Q1. (Answer = a) This patient weighed 165 pounds which equals 75 kilograms. The appropriate calculation is as follows:

$$60 \text{ mL} \times 0.97 \text{ g/mL} \times 20\% = 11.64 \text{ g}$$

$$11.64 \text{ g}/75 \text{ kg} = 155 \text{ mg/kg}$$

Q2. (Answer = d) Some formulations of paraquat contain an emetic that causes vomiting to occur following an ingestion, suicidal or otherwise. This sample did not contain an emetic and there is no record of the patient vomiting. No specific genetically based protections are known and the toxin is usually fairly stable in solution although labile after being spread onto soil. The patient's survival seems to be due to early and aggressive treatment. The attending physicians were aware of the identity of the toxin and knew that it was usually fatal. They also employed two effective antidotes. Part of the therapy included hemodialysis that was clearly very effective. Blood levels of paraquat were at 30 µg/mL before hemodialysis and dropped to 0.03 µg/mL at the end of dialysis, 6 hours later. According to a study of Proudfoot[1] this patient's first level of 30 µg/mL is usually predictive of a fatal outcome.

Q3. (Answer = b) Several studies[2] have shown that both iron and copper have essential roles in the toxicity of paraquat. Mice treated with DFO survived high doses of paraquat and, conversely, loading animals with iron and then providing paraquat led to enhanced mortality. The DFO rendered any local iron unavailable for paraquat.

Q4. (Answer = c) Massive paraquat ingestion causes a rapid onset of corrosive injuries. Pulmonary edema and hemorrhage result. The patient may die rapidly from blood loss and associated hypotension. In the case of lesser doses, the lung is the primary target organ and it is slowly incapacitated by a developing fibrosis. The specific impact of paraquat on the lung has not been fully understood but it has been shown that paraquat does enter lung cells with high affinity and against a concentration gradient.

References

1. Proudfoot, A.T. et al., Paraquat poisoning: significance of plasma paraquat concentrations, *Lancet,* 2, 330–332, 1979.
2. Kohen, R. and Chevion, M., Paraquat toxicity is enhanced by iron and reduced by desferrioxamine in laboratory mice, *Biochem. Pharmacol.,* 10, 1841–1843, 1985.

Additional Reading

L'heureux, P. et al., Survival in a case of massive paraquat ingestion, *Chest,* 107, 285–289, 1995.

12 Drug Testing: Screening

CONTENTS

Toxicology tests have often been divided into two major categories: screening tests and confirmation tests. Drug screening refers to the practice of testing for drugs by methods that are rapid and comprehensive (many drugs are included). Screening tests are sensitive but not necessarily specific. Screening is done for several reasons. In the first place, drug screening is done in place of testing for one specific substance when there is little or no prior knowledge of what drugs, if any, may be present in a specimen. In that case, testing for one drug is likely to be of no value because of the high probability that the result will be negative. If, on the other hand, one has an effective way of looking for many drugs simultaneously, chances of success are much greater. Screening, therefore, is thought of as a rapid check for the presence of some toxic material. In addition, screening provides additional evidence for a positive result when it is used together with a follow-up test (confirmation test) for demonstrating the presence of the drug. In other words, the conclusion that a drug is present in a specimen is less subject to rejection if its presence has been shown by both a screening method and an additional test, which is called a confirmatory method.

The screening method should be based on a different principle than that which underlies the confirmatory method. If the methods are the same or similar, they are subject to the same kind of interference. For example, if the drug is shown to be present by a test method based on antibodies and this is confirmed by a second method which also employs antibodies, the positive result is not as convincing because a contaminant causing a false positive by interfering with the antibody in the first method may do the same thing in the second method. An acceptable sequence of screening and confirmation might include, for example, immunoassay for screening followed by chromatography, especially gas chromatography-mass spectrometry, for confirmation. These two approaches are based on entirely different scientific principles.

The screening method, in addition to being of a different nature than the confirmatory method, should also have a relatively low detection limit. If it lacks sensitivity, an unacceptably large number of false negatives will result. The screening method should be specific but absolute specificity is not necessary because the confirmatory method will be used for further testing. If a false positive is found from the screening test, it causes no major problem because the result is not reported until the confirmatory test is finished and corroborates the screening result. The only harm done by a poorly specific screening test is it creates additional labor by requiring a confirmatory test on a specimen that is actually negative. The confirmatory method must have absolute specificity, if possible. It is very rare that both the screening and confirmatory results are positive and incorrect. This is a very bad situation and test systems must be carefully designed to prevent this from ever occurring.

SCREENING METHODS

THIN-LAYER CHROMATOGRAPHY

The basic concept in the major form of thin-layer chromatography (TLC) is that the components of a mixture can be separated from each other because they differ in regard to polarity. Molecules can be described as differing over a vast range in terms of their dipole moments. Thus, when they are allowed to partition between a polar medium and a less polar medium they often separate clearly, with the more polar molecules from the mixture associating with the polar phase of the TLC system and the nonpolar molecules remaining in the nonpolar phase. A good example is shown in the illustration here of the actual separation between cocaine and cocaine metabolite, benzoylecgonine, in a TLC method (Figure 12.1). Cocaine, which is relatively nonpolar, is more attracted to the relatively nonpolar moving phase, the TLC solvent. The moving phase contains 85% ethyl acetate, a very nonpolar solvent. The nonpolar cocaine is only weakly attracted to the relatively polar stationary phase, the thin-layer plate packing, usually silica gel. Benzoylecgonine is much more polar than cocaine since it has a carboxyl group. In the partitioning system described, benzoylecgonine prefers to associate with the relatively polar stationary phase. It hardly moves and ends up near the origin of the plate. After the mixture components have been separated by partitioning between the stationary and mobile phases, they can be detected by spraying with reagents that impart color when viewed by visible or ultraviolet light.

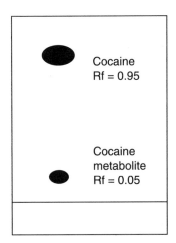

FIGURE 12.1 Thin-layer chromatographic separation of cocaine and cocaine metabolite.

Sample Preparation before TLC

The specimen (usually urine) must be pre-treated prior to being placed on the thin-layer plate. This pre-treatment consists of transferring the specimen from an aqueous to an organic phase and concentrating it. These steps can be accomplished together either by solid-phase extraction or solvent–solvent extraction.

The need for concentration of the specimen is not immediately obvious but is critical nonetheless. Imagine, for example, that a specimen contains phencyclidine (PCP) at a concentration of 100 ng/mL and 10 μL will be spotted onto the TLC plate. The sample spotted must be small in area or else it will diffuse and eventually result in a very wide spot that overlaps other components. If 10 μL are directly spotted, the total PCP in the spot is 100 ng/mL × 0.01 mL = 1 ng. This is too small a quantity to be detected after spraying the spot with a colorimetric reagent. However, if 10 mL of urine, which would contain 100 ng/mL × 10 mL = 1000 ng of PCP, is extracted, dried down, and reconstituted in 50 μL of organic solvent, 10 μL of that solvent would contain 200 ng of PCP; 200 ng equals the original result of 1 ng multiplied by the concentration factor of 10 mL/50 μL = 10,000/50 = 200. This much PCP would be readily visible after spraying.

As mentioned above, the extraction of sample from aqueous to organic phase allows it not only to be concentrated but also dried rapidly. Once in the organic phase the sample may be spotted onto the thin-layer plate and then the solvent will quickly evaporate because of the low boiling points characteristic of organic solvents.

Specimen Extraction

Drugs can be extracted into an organic phase by pH adjustment (if necessary) followed by shaking with an appropriate organic solvent. For example, amphetamine, shown below in Figure 12.2, may exist as the free base or the salt form. The primary amine group of amphetamine has a pK of 9.9. At pH greater than 9.9, therefore,

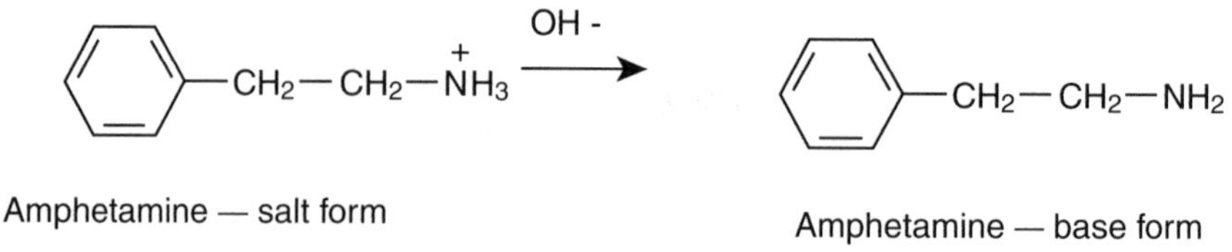

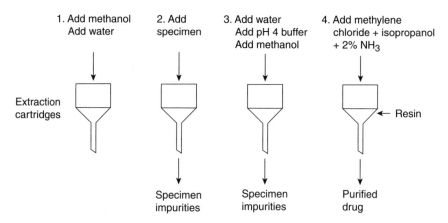

FIGURE 12.2 Behavior of amphetamine in neutral or alkaline solution.

FIGURE 12.3 Solid phase tubes and procedure for solid-phase extraction.

amphetamine exists mainly as the free base. At pH greater than 12 it is almost entirely in the uncharged form of amphetamine base. Moreover, the free base is more soluble in nonpolar solvents than in water. The situation is the opposite for the salt form (e.g., amphetamine hydrochloride) which is more soluble in water than in nonpolar solvents such as methylene chloride or hexane. In summary, if amphetamine is treated with alkali to raise the pH and then mixed with methylene chloride, it will be extracted into the methylene chloride. Once in the methylene chloride the solvent can be removed by drying down.

Solid-phase extraction is a variant on the solvent–solvent extraction just described. In this approach one employs small tubes packed with a mixed bed resin. The resin binds the drug or drugs present in the specimen. Other impurities percolate through the solid-phase tube. The tube is then rinsed with a solvent that releases the drug from the resin allowing it to collect in a relatively pure form within the organic material that rinsed it from the resin. The process is depicted in Figures 12.3 and 12.4.

Which method is preferable for purposes of preparing the specimen, solvent–solvent extraction or solid-phase extraction? The former is usually less expensive and involves less equipment and fewer procedural steps. More solvent is employed, however. Solid-phase extraction often gives a cleaner product and is more compatible with automated sample preparation which is becoming more common. Solvent–solvent extraction may be more applicable to sample preparation for TLC screening

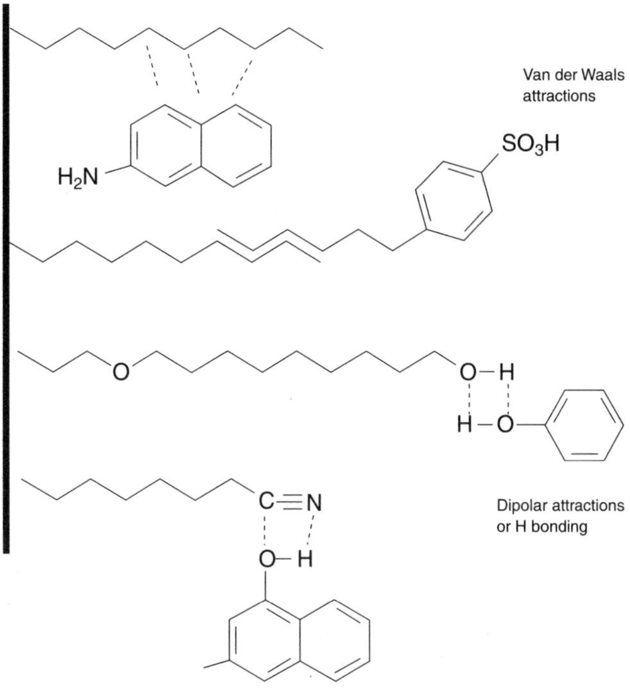

FIGURE 12.4 Some side-chains present in solid phase tubes.

because it allows one to begin with a very large specimen, e.g., 30 mL. Solid-phase methods typically employ a specimen that is much smaller. An indication that both methods work well, however, is the current widespread use of both within state-of-the-art toxicology laboratories.

Evaluation of TLC for Drug Screening

TLC has been used extensively for evaluating specimens from patients with coma of unknown etiology or patients presenting with other signs of drug overdose. It is valuable in this context because of its relatively unique ability to test for a very large number of drugs at the same time. When the physician or the laboratory are uncertain about the identity of an offending agent, TLC may be useful for identifying literally hundreds of drugs in the course of a single analysis. There are, however, limitations to the concept of drug screening. In a few laboratories multi-component drug screening is conducted with gas chromatography. This requires expensive equipment and probably is less specific than TLC for this particular application. One other method for drug screening is an automated liquid chromatographic system known as the Remedi™ (BioRad). The Remedi™ is an instrument with highly sophisticated analytic and computerized components and is able to identify drugs on the basis of their retention times on the liquid chromatographic column and their ultraviolet or visible spectra. Cost per analysis is, however, very high.

The advantages and disadvantages of TLC are summarized in the table below:

Advantages	Disadvantages
Simultaneous analysis of many drugs	Slow (2- to 3-hour test time)
Inexpensive	Subjective
No instrument required	Difficult to learn
	High detection limits for some drugs

A commercial TLC method known as Toxilab® eliminates some of the disadvantages of TLC and is a widely used method for clinical applications. It is commercially designed to reduce the complexity of TLC. Because it is heavily supported with learning materials, specific prepackaged reagents, etc., the low cost advantages of noncommercial methods are not present with Toxilab®.

IMMUNOASSAYS

Drug screening may be completed with the use of commercially prepared diagnostic kits that are based on antibodies. It is important to recognize that the value of antibodies in biological specimens is founded on the fact that the matrix of biological materials is very complex. Thus, testing for specific substances almost always requires tedious separation of the components of interest. If the toxins being tested are not separated from the urine matrix, the chances are very high that something else will interfere in the assay reaction, thereby causing a falsely elevated or lowered result. Antibodies provide an option. Because of their characteristically high specificity (especially for monoclonal antibodies), tests may be conducted in which no separation step is required. For that reason, immunoassays, i.e., tests based on antibodies, can be rapid and amenable to automation.

It is significant that some laboratory-accrediting organizations require laboratories to use immunoassay methods for drug screening in a pre-employment setting. These agencies prohibit using TLC for this purpose. They have several objections to TLC and foremost among these objections is the subjectivity of the method. They believe that an inexperienced user of TLC could easily misidentify a substance and falsely label it as a drug of abuse. As a result, a job applicant would be unjustly treated and lose an opportunity for securing a job. It is worth mentioning that most laboratories would prefer to use immunoassay anyway, because of the easily automated nature of immunoassays vs. the basically manual nature of TLC analysis.

IMMUNOASSAY METHODS

EMIT

One of the most commonly employed immunoassay methods is EMIT (Behring Diagnostics). EMIT stands for enzyme multiplied immunoassay technique. Methods such as EMIT are popular mainly because they are readily placed on automated instruments and are, thus, extremely convenient and rapid to run. The technology

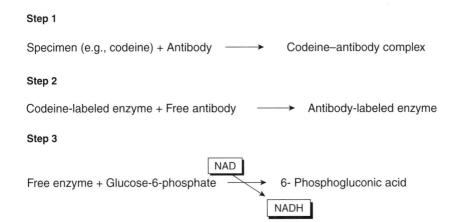

Step 1

Specimen (e.g., codeine) + Antibody $\longrightarrow$ Codeine–antibody complex

Step 2

Codeine-labeled enzyme + Free antibody $\longrightarrow$ Antibody-labeled enzyme

Step 3

Free enzyme + Glucose-6-phosphate $\longrightarrow$ 6- Phosphogluconic acid

NAD

NADH

FIGURE 12.5 Enzyme multiplied immunoassay technique.

of EMIT is complex; however, that complexity is irrelevant to the user who can employ the method in a reliable and simple, straightforward manner. The mechanism of the EMIT method is illustrated in Figure 12.5.

In step 1 an aliquot of the specimen is mixed with an antibody that is specific for the drug being tested. For example, the antibody could be prepared against codeine and would therefore complex with codeine or, to some degree, cross-react with other members of the opiate class of drugs. In step 2 a reagent is added that contains an enzyme with codeine bonded near the active site of the enzyme. If all of the antibody became complexed in step 1, then there is no reaction in step 2, i.e., the codeine-labeled enzyme remains unchanged. On the other hand, if the specimen does not contain an opiate, nothing happens in step 1. In that case, the antibody would be available in step 2 for complexing with the codeine that is bonded to the enzyme. Finally, in step 3, an enzyme substrate is added. The customary enzyme reaction occurs but only if the enzyme did not complex with antibody. If enzyme did complex with antibody, the presence of the antibody in the vicinity of the active site prevents the substrate from reaching the active site. In that case, no reaction can occur.

The actual enzyme employed in EMIT is glucose-6-phosphate dehydrogenase. The substrate is glucose-6-phosphate and the co-enzyme is NAD^+. The reaction produces the reduced form of NAD; namely, NADH, which absorbs light at 340 nm. The amount of absorbed light is proportional to the amount of NADH formed which, in turn, is proportional to the original concentration of drug within the specimen. Note, however, that a simple linear relation between NADH concentration and drug unknown concentration does not exist. Instead, each molecule of drug produces an amplified response because it activates the enzyme in the reagent. Thus, the method is called enzyme multiplied. Without the enzyme multiplication, the detection limits of the method would be much inferior to what they actually are.

EMIT can be run in a qualitative manner in which a calibrator is tested and its change in absorbance is recorded. Next, an unknown specimen is run (or an entire batch of unknowns by an automated analyzer) and the specimen is positive if the

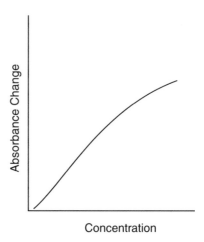

FIGURE 12.6 Sample EMIT standard curve.

absorbance change in the unknown exceeds the absorbance change in the calibrator. Alternatively, EMIT can be made semi-quantitative or quantitative by running a series of calibrators and preparing a standard curve. The curve has approximately the shape shown in Figure 12.6. These curves typically are not subject to simple mathematical analysis and several iterations are necessary before a satisfactory equation is derived that allows conversion of absorbance changes into concentrations.

Critique of EMIT	
Advantages	**Disadvantages**
Rapid	Not usually specific to a single drug
Simple to use	Reagents are expensive
Objective	Each drug group is analyzed separately
Low detection limits	Not amenable to analysis of macromolecules
Amenable to automation	(Not usually a disadvantage for drugs)

Specificity of EMIT or any other immunoassay method depends on the quality and specific nature of the antibodies employed in the process. As a result, there is a wide range of specificities being exhibited by different immunoassay products. However, given the particular nature of the drugs being tested most of these immunoassay products are reasonably similar. For example, all are fairly specific for cannabinoids or cocaine metabolite. As a consequence, a positive screen result for cannabinoids or cocaine metabolite is rarely incorrect and is usually confirmed as positive by gas chromatography-mass spectrometry. Conversely, most immunoassay products for morphine also react with codeine, hydrocodone, hydromorphone, and several other compounds. A positive immunoassay result for morphine is really a positive for opiates and the specific opiate present has to be determined by another method.

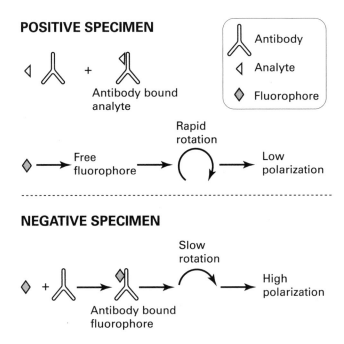

FIGURE 12.7 Mechanism of FPIA.

Fluorescence Polarization Immunoassay (FPIA)

FPIA is another immunoassay method developed for many analyses, including therapeutic and abused drugs, by the Abbott Diagnostics Corporation. It resembles EMIT inasmuch as each drug group has a separate reagent kit and specificity of the product is determined by the antibody. Another feature in common with EMIT is that the mechanism of the method is fairly complex but the user can, nevertheless, operate the instrumentation without a full understanding of the theory. FPIA is a competitive binding assay and works by the following reaction (Figure 12.7):

Drug-Fluorescein reagent +

Drug in specimen $\xrightarrow{\text{Antibody (limiting)}}$ Antibody-Drug-Fluorescein + Antibody-Drug

     Drug in the patient sample competes with a fluorescein-labeled drug in the reagent for a limited number of antibody binding sites. If the patient specimen contains high amounts of drug, then the antibody associates mainly with drug from the patient. Most of the fluorescent material remains unbound to antibody. In that case the fluorescent material is bonded to a small molecule, its molecular rotation is rapid, and the polarization of the fluorescent signal is low. Conversely, if the concentration of antibody-drug-fluorescein is high, as when patient specimen is negative, the large antibody molecule affects the rotational speed of the fluorescent tag. High polarization results. An inverse relationship exists between drug concentration in the patient's specimen and the amount of fluorescence polarization (Figure 12.8).

Critique of FPIA

Advantages	Disadvantages
Partly automatic	Limited number of reagent vendors
Easy to use	Relatively high reagent cost
Semiquantitative	Slow throughput
Low detection limits	
Good specificity	
Good reagent shelf-life	
(i.e., reagents last a long time)	

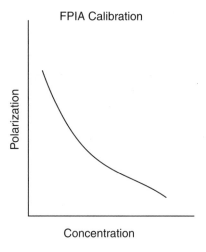

FIGURE 12.8 FPIA calibration curve.

Triage®

Triage is a recent product that in the opinion of some experts represents a new and growing trend within the drug testing industry. It is a point-of-care device, which means the test is highly portable, does not require an instrument or any specialized accessories, and can be conducted in almost any environment by easily trained personnel. Triage is produced by Biosite Diagnostics, San Diego, CA. The platform for the method consists simply of a card which is about 12 square inches.

Procedure

1. Pipet 140 µL of specimen onto the card.
2. Incubate at room temperature for 10 minutes.
3. Transfer the reaction mixture (140 µL) to a different part of the card.
4. Add 3 drops of wash solution.
5. Read the result after 5 minutes.

A positive result consists of a colored band in an area that corresponds to each of 7 different drug classes. If the drug-specific region has no colored bar, then the specimen is negative for that drug. Triage contains controls as an integral part of the product. Thus, there are positive and negative bars which verify that the card is working correctly.

Mechanism

How does the card give a colored bar whenever the specimen contains a drug? Like many other immunoassays, Triage reagent contains each drug in a form that is labeled by being bound to a detector molecule. The drug plus the detector molecule (a colored molecule or chromophore) is called a drug conjugate. During incubation this conjugate is liberated from a monoclonal antibody bound to it if there is drug in the specimen competing with the conjugate for antibody binding sites. Therefore, a positive specimen contains a drug that displaces drug-chromophore during the incubation phase. This drug-chomophore migrates to the site of the colored bar where it binds to a second monoclonal antibody and produces the visible colored bar.

Evaluation of Triage System

Triage is highly specific and rivals other laboratory-based products in assuring that false positives from interfering materials are almost nonexistent. It is immensely simple to use and, therefore, the training burden is minimal in preparing personnel to work with this product. Because it has only a few procedural steps errors would be very infrequent, unless the user is inordinately careless with the test card. Triage is at the forefront of new point-of-care testing devices intended for a testing environment other than a laboratory, although in some cases it is used in laboratories, also. Triage, in common with most point-of-care devices, is most sensible when used with a small number of specimens. If an analyst has a large workload, this product is not the most reasonable approach for completion of the task. It is also extremely expensive compared to other reagents that are intended for application within large, highly automated analyzers.

Available Triage Tests and Analytical Cut-Offs (ng/mL)	
Phencyclidine	25
Benzodiazepines	300
Cocaine	300
Amphetamines	1000
Tetrahydrocannabinol	50
Opiates	300
Barbiturates	300

CEDIA (Cloned Enzyme Donor Immunoassay)

The CEDIA method is a recent approach to antibody-based testing that shows the wide variety of possible approaches and the ingenious techniques that have been developed.

Mechanism

CEDIA is similar to EMIT in the sense that an enzyme is used that is activated only if drug is present in the specimen and the signal produced is magnified by the continuous reaction of each enzyme molecule, once it has been activated. Using recombinant DNA technology, the manufacturers of this product have produced two inactive fragments of the enzyme, beta-galactosidase. One inactive fragment of the enzyme is conjugated to the drug being tested. The reaction system consists of an antidrug antibody, one inactive enzyme fragment, the specimen, and the second inactive fragment to which a drug molecule has been linked. If drug is present in the sample, it forms a complex with the antibody and then the inactive enzyme fragments will spontaneously reassociate and produce active enzyme. In the assay format a substrate will be cleaved and a chromophore results that is measured with a spectrophotometer. On the contrary, in the absence of drug in the specimen the drug on the conjugate forms a complex with the antibody eliminating the possibility of active enzyme. As is true of EMIT, the amount of active enzyme and the measured absorbance change are proportional to the amount of drug present in the sample.

Protocol

This is a fully automated testing method and reagents are prepared in a straightforward manner. The specific steps of testing depend on the analyzer rather than the CEDIA method.

Evaluation of CEDIA

The CEDIA method has performed well in actual practice. Again, its specificity is as superb as that of the other antibody-based methods described above, being a function of the excellent and carefully selected antibodies employed rather than a function of the CEDIA mechanism itself. It is rapid and easily automated. It is superior to EMIT in regard to the linearity of the method, i.e., higher concentrations of drug may be reliably quantified if one wishes to do so. In the EMIT method, by contrast, the calibration curve flattens out at a low drug concentration. CEDIA, therefore, is applicable to any instrument for which manufacturer's specifications are available.

The specificity of CEDIA is illustrated by the following data that are excerpted from manufacturer's publications:

Drug	Concentration Tested (ng/mL)	% Cross Reactivity
Nitrazepam	300	100
Alprazolam	138	205
Chlordiazepoxide	2000	13
Diazepam	110	247
Lorazepam	208	122
Glucuronide	10,000	1.4
Nordiazepam	150	211
Oxazepam	275	107
Triazolam	138	191

Questions and Problems

1. You are setting up a program for testing of drugs subject to abuse. What factors are important in selecting a testing method? Based on those factors, which of the screening methods described in this chapter is the best choice?

2. Thin-layer chromatography is not acceptable as a screening method in the National Laboratory Certification Program, a stringent program for accrediting laboratories for testing of specimens primarily for employment applicants. What do you suppose are the objections to this method by NLCP?

3. Contrast the testing needs of a clinical laboratory operating within a hospital and intended to assist physicians in handling drug overdose with the needs of a large commercial laboratory that is operating for profit and evaluates urines for possible drugs of abuse from job candidates.

4. Ten mL of urine are extracted by a solvent–solvent method which has 75% recovery. The extract is dried entirely and reconstituted in 200 uL of solvent. One tenth of this final volume is spotted onto a thin-layer plate. What is the absolute amount of morphine on the plate if the original specimen contained morphine at 5000 ng/mL?

5. Below are absorbance changes at 340 nm for drug calibrators tested by an EMIT method. Two unknowns were also tested under identical conditions:

Specimen	ΔA
Cocaine metab, 100 ng/mL	0.13
200 ng/mL	0.24
400 ng/mL	0.42
600 ng/mL	0.54
800 ng/mL	0.59
Unknown #1	0.29
Unknown #2	0.60

Discuss what conclusions can be made about the probable content of the unknowns.

6. You are designing a method for analysis of acetylsalicylic acid (ASA) from urine. You need to separate the aspirin from the aqueous urine and redissolve it in organic solvent. The pKa for ASA is 3.5. How could it be transferred to organic solvent?

Case Study 1: The Indiscreet Physician

Two teenage boys were driving home from a party late one evening when their car skidded on an icy road and came to a stop in a roadside ditch. The boys sustained minor injuries that necessitated medical care at a nearby hospital. In the hospital, one of the boys was noted to have a bruise on his head, among other cuts and contusions, and appeared to be slightly disoriented. He also required 7 stitches for a deep cut to his face. In view of the head bruise, his treating physician was concerned about a possible cranial injury. The boy's behavior, however, also may have been due to the very late hour or some alcohol or drug used at the party. The physician ordered a routine drug screen and an X-ray to evaluate the head injury.

The X-ray was normal but the drug screen results were as follows:

Drug	Result
Opiates	Negative
Phencyclidine	Negative
Marijuana metabolite	Negative
Cocaine metabolite	Negative
Amphetamines	Positive
Barbiturates	Negative
Benzodiazepines	Negative

The boy's apparent disorientation resolved and, in view of other negative findings, he was discharged from the hospital. The following day the parents of this boy contacted their family doctor for follow-up and asked if further treatment such as removal of stitches was needed. The family doctor said that he would review the chart for the ED admission and get back to them. The doctor did so and commented to the parents that their son did not appear to need further treatment but that he would like to speak with them in a regular office visit. Two days later, on the occasion of this visit, he expressed his concern about the boy's use of drugs of abuse, particularly a hard drug such as amphetamine. He further expressed his belief that this was a matter of urgency since we are "not dealing with a small matter like alcohol or marijuana."

At home the distraught parents spoke to their son who vehemently denied using any drugs of abuse. The ensuing argument became very heated and the son even directed verbal abuse toward his parents. The son's denials were so fervent, however, that the mother contacted her doctor again inquiring as to whether he was certain about the drug test.

Are there any innocent explanations for the positive drug finding?
   a) The lab may have mixed up his specimen with a different one.
   b) The test may have been nonspecific.
   c) The instrument may have malfunctioned.
   d) The technologist may have misread the result.
   e) All of the above.

All of the above (e) is correct. Of all the suggested answers, however, nonspecificity is the most likely. Most screening tests for amphetamines actually test for many sympathomimetic amines. These include some very common medications such as phenylpropanolamine, ephedrine, pseudoephedrine, and so on. The boy in this case may have been using an over-the-counter medication for a cold, allergy, or the flu. Phenylpropanolamine and the other listed drugs are popular decongestants. The fact that these drugs give positive results is probably a desirable outcome from the point of view of clinical toxicology. That is, these drugs can produce clinical effects and it is important to notify physicians that sympathomimetic drugs are present when a doctor is trying to explain a patient's symptoms. If, however, a screening test is intended to show only illicit drug use, then selection of a more specific assay is desirable.

The doctor should not assume that positive amphetamines means only illicit drug use. The laboratory should also emphatically indicate in the test report that the test result is for clinical purposes only. If the result is to be used for forensic purposes, it must be confirmed by an unequivocal, highly specific method.

There are now cases on record where a party sued the physician and the laboratory for damages caused by careless use of laboratory data. A suit might be brought in a case such as the above alleging that great harm was done to family harmony.

13 Confirmatory Tests in Toxicology

CONTENTS

In toxicology testing, specimens found to be positive by a screening test are often re-run by a second method called a confirmation test. This appears to be redundant, but there are many justifications for this practice. In the first place, an additional positive by a second method constitutes more compelling evidence that the specimen does, in fact, contain the drug in question. Toxicology findings are often legally or medically critical and the need for accuracy is paramount. Therefore, two tests that reinforce each other are a powerful argument in favor of the drug's presence. Second, a screening method often is automated whereas confirmatory assays are usually too complex to be automated. Assuming that less than 10% of specimens are usually positive, it is economically efficient to do the rapid, automated screening test on every specimen but save the slow, non-automated confirmatory method only for the 5 to 10% that are positive. Finally, screening methods usually are very sensitive so false negatives are rare, but some screening methods may not be very specific, which may lead to false positive results. Therefore, the confirmatory method must have as close to absolute specificity as is scientifically and realistically possible. With the best confirmatory methods this near-absolute specificity is achieved and any false presumptive positives from the screen are found to be negative when tested by the confirmation test.

We see, therefore, that confirmatory methods need to be very elegant. They must be at least as sensitive as screening methods. Otherwise, true positives will be rejected when run by the confirmation method because they contain less drug than the amount detectable by the confirmatory test, although the amount they do contain was enough to cause a screening positive. In addition, they must be fully specific. If they are not, then a false positive may occur because the specimen is not tested further if the confirmation positive is found. It may, of course, be re-tested by another laboratory if the result is challenged. If the positive is shown at that stage to be due to something other than the drug in question, it can have calamitous consequences for the reputation and financial health of the original testing laboratory.

CONFIRMATION METHODS

At the very least a confirmation method is simply an additional analysis by a method other than the one employed in the screening test. Realistically, however, the method should have the best sensitivity and specificity possible. Therefore, gas chromatography, liquid chromatography, and, particularly, gas chromatography with mass spectrometry (GC-MS) are acceptable confirmation methods. Again, in the context of pre-employment testing, laboratories which meet the very high standards of the National Laboratory Certification Program in the United States have no choice and must use only GC-MS for confirmation.

GAS CHROMATOGRAPHY (GC)

GC may be the most commonly utilized technology within toxicology. There are many reasons for its popularity. Perhaps the foremost reason is the large number of compounds that can be tested. In other words, a skilled analyst can develop a GC-based testing method for an extremely large number of drugs or toxins. It is no exaggeration to state that tens of thousands of GC methods have been published. Further, highly specialized reagents such as monoclonal antibodies are not needed. This increases the universality of the method. GC also has very low detection limits, i.e., trace quantities of toxins can be detected and measured. The detection limit is mainly a function of the particular detector used although some limits are placed on sensitivity by the nature of GC itself. Last, GC can provide inherently good accuracy and precision.

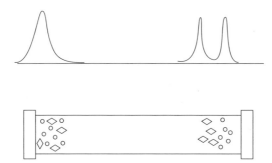

FIGURE 13.1 Principle of partitioning.

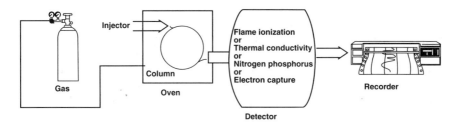

FIGURE 13.2 Schematic illustration of parts of a gas chromatograph.

Principle

In GC a sample is placed on a chromatographic column containing an adsorbent chemical that has variable affinities for the components of a mixture to be analyzed. The sample must be gaseous in its injected form or it must be volatilized within the liner of the injection apparatus. Substances that have very high boiling points and may not, therefore, be compatible with GC analysis, may be rendered GC-compatible by derivatization. Once injected and volatilized the sample is entrained by a moving carrier gas and allowed to interact with the stationary phase that is located on the column.

Each component of the mixture ideally will be delayed to a different degree as it partitions between the moving gas and the stationary column material. Figure 13.1 shows this concept of partitioning with various components of a mixture separating as they move through the column and adsorbing, to varying degrees, with the stationary phase on the walls of the column. The components eventually reach the end of the column where a detector monitors the progress of the run and the elution of each substance. Figure 13.2 diagrammatically shows the components of a gas chromatographic system.

Carrier Gases

The gases employed for the moving phase are hydrogen, helium, or nitrogen. Selection among them is based on economic considerations and performance features exhibited by each carrier gas in a specific system. Only helium, for example, is usually suited for mass spectrometry because the other gases might react with the

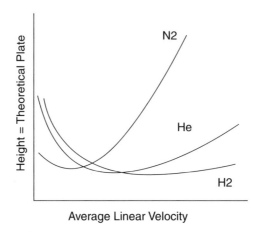

FIGURE 13.3 Van Deemter curve of velocity vs. height equivalent to a theoretical plate.

unknown ions in the hot mass spectrometer detector and render identification more difficult. Helium, however, is very expensive to purchase, especially in highly purified form. Gases also differ in their effect on the column resolution as shown in the Van Deemter curves (Figure 13.3).

This graph shows that N_2 is affected strongly by the carrier flow rate. The HETP (height equivalent to a theoretical plate) increases with flow rate. Conversely, helium and hydrogen are only slightly affected by changing flow rate. The increase in HETP is equivalent to a decrease in resolution by the column. The unique reaction of nitrogen vs. the other two gases is related to its larger molecular size, as a result of which it cannot equilibrate effectively with the stationary phase if the carrier gas is moving rapidly. The smaller gas molecules of hydrogen or helium still can enter the column packing even at relatively high carrier flow rates. They are, therefore, less affected by increasing flow velocity.

Resolution

The most critical feature of a GC column is its ability to resolve the components of a mixture. If two or more components co-elute because they are similar in polarity and the column delays them to the same extent, then it will be very difficult or impossible to identify the components or to quantify them.

Resolution is the term that describes the column's ability to separate compounds. It is calculated in the following manner:

$$R = \frac{2(t_{r2} - t_{r1})}{W_{b1} + W_{b2}}$$

where:

t_{r2} = retention time of compound 1
t_{r1} = retention time of compound 2
W_b, W_{b2} = width at the base for compounds 1 and 2, respectively

Isothermal vs. Programmed Analysis

A GC run can be conducted at a constant temperature (isothermal), or the temperature can be varied during the time course of the analysis (temperature programming). The additional variable of temperature programming may provide enhanced resolution. Characteristics that differ between isothermal runs and temperature programming are

Isothermal
- Retention time very dependent on column length.
- If the column length is doubled, the analysis time doubles.
- If the column length is doubled, resolution increases by 41%.

Programmed
- Retention time is very dependent on temperature.
- Doubling column length increases analysis time only slightly.

Column Types

Early GC columns were completely packed with the partitioning material. The substance would be poured tightly into a tube, typically 1/8 to 1/4 in. diameter, and packed by a method such as filling by shaking or vibrating into place. More commonly today, analysts use capillary columns. In capillary columns the adsorbent is coated by the manufacturer in very thin layers onto the wall of the tube. Most of the interior space of the column is empty. These columns are expensive, but they have the same resolution per unit length as packed columns. However, since capillary columns are very thin, usually 0.2 mm, they can be prepared in very long tubes. Columns of 30 m are often used. The result is that the overall resolution is excellent because the mixture tranverses as much as 30 m rather than the comparatively short packed columns which were popular in the past and averaged about 2 m in length. The packing within columns, whether capillary or packed columns, is a critical factor in determining which substances may be separated and a wide variety of column packings are possible. This is due to the basic nature of the GC process. Substances separate because they have different polarities and the column itself has its own inherent polarity. In general, as polarity increases the retention of a nonpolar substance on the column decreases while the retention of polar compounds increases. This is another manifestation of the rule: like dissolves like.

One of the least polar packings available is 100% dimethylpolysiloxane (Figure 13.4). Because it is nonpolar, it attracts nonpolar substances from the sample. Such nonpolar substances would be expected to be retarded by the column and separated well from each other. Typical of the types of mixtures well separated on 100% dimethylpolysiloxane are mixtures of hydrocarbons and other low boiling materials. All of the major manufacturers market this packing under names that are similar and indicative of the kind of packing. Table 13.1 shows some of the various manufacturers of column packings.

Slightly less polar than 100% dimethylpolysiloxane is 95% dimethyl-5% diphenylpolysiloxane, a packing which is suitable for materials that may have some slight

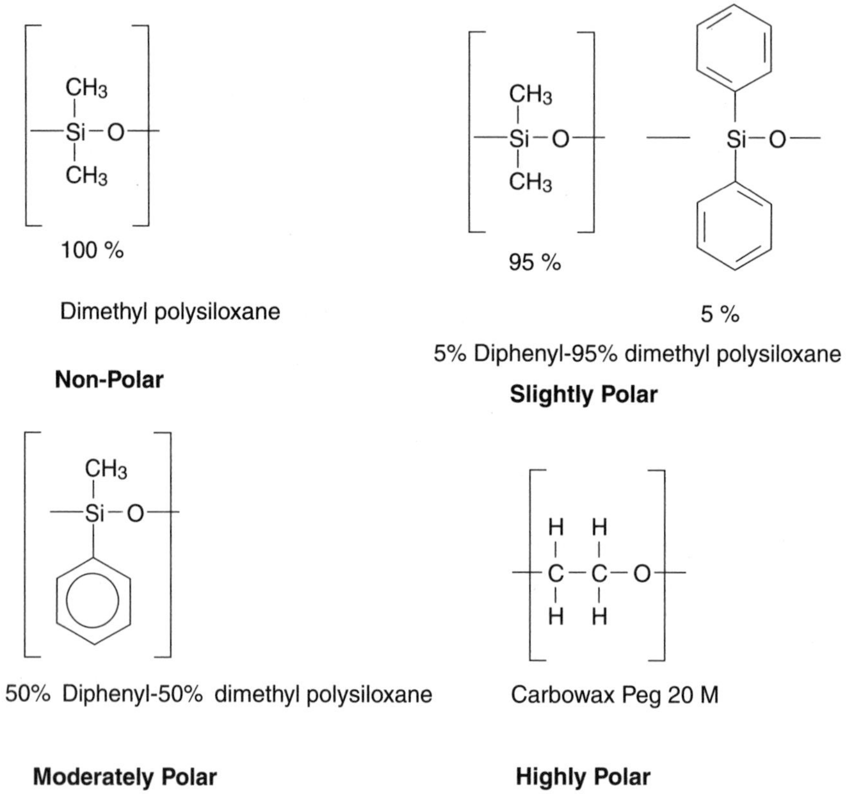

CH₃ → CH_3

$$\left[\begin{array}{c} CH_3 \\ -Si-O- \\ CH_3 \end{array}\right]$$

100 %

Dimethyl polysiloxane

Non-Polar

95 %

5 %

5% Diphenyl-95% dimethyl polysiloxane

Slightly Polar

50% Diphenyl-50% dimethyl polysiloxane

Carbowax Peg 20 M

Moderately Polar   **Highly Polar**

FIGURE 13.4 Stationary phases in gas chromatography.

TABLE 13.1
Manufacturers of Column Packings[a]

Composition	Manufacturer			
	J and W	Supelco	HP	Restek
100% dimethylpolysiloxane	DB-1	SPB-1	HP-1	Rtx-1
95% dimethyl-5% diphenylpolysiloxane	DB-5	SPB-5	HP-5	Rtx-5
50% methyl-50% phenylpolysiloxane	DB-17	SP-2250	HP-17	Rtx-50
Carbowax PEG	DB-Wax	Supelcowax-10	HP-20M	Stabilwax

[a] Stationary phases are of increasing polarity from top to bottom of table.

polar character (Figure 13.4). This packing often is employed to separate drugs of abuse, as well as some aromatics or environmental specimens.

A packing of intermediate polarity is 50% methyl-50% phenylpolysiloxane. Triglycerides or pththalate esters, of intermediate polarity themselves, are separated on this packing. Very polar column packings include 50% cyanopropylmethyl and 50% phenylmethylpolysiloxane or Stabilwax (Carbowax Peg 20M) (Figure 13.4).

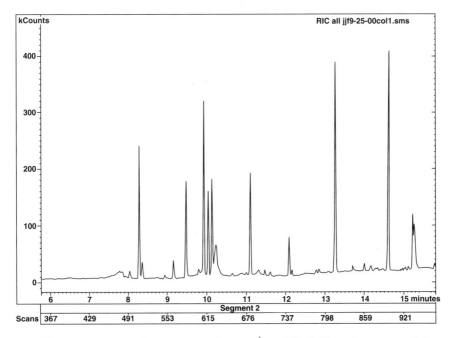

FIGURE 13.5 Separation of components of a test mix on DB-1®. Nonpolar compounds have long retention times.

These highly polar materials are suitable for separations of acids, amines, alcohols, and other highly polar samples.

Figure 13.5 shows separation of several compounds on the very nonpolar DB-1. Decane has a retention time of 13.3 minutes under certain conditions. Undecane and 2,3 butanediol have retention times of 14.6 and 8.3 minutes, respectively. By contrast, decane emerges from the more polar DB-50 packed column at 9 minutes, undecane at 11.5, and 2,3 butanediol at 10 minutes. With all other conditions such as temperature and column length being held constant, the nonpolar compounds have longer retention times on the nonpolar packing. By contrast, the somewhat polar 2,3 butanediol has, as theoretically predicted, a longer retention time on the more polar column. It was stated earlier that peak separation is very important for correct compound identification and accurate quantification. Now one notes that selection of column type is an added means by which an analyst can improve the separation of a particular mixture.

Detectors

Many different kinds of detectors are available for use in gas chromatography. The variety of detector designs is intended to provide differences in the power of the detector with various kinds of samples. It is also possible to split a sample stream so that it can be directed into two different detectors each of which will be specific for certain kinds of substances. Analytic efficiency can be improved in this manner. Following is a description of several detector types and a brief discussion of their strengths, weaknesses, and best applications.

Thermal conductivity detectors. A filament pair is sensitive to cooling by the carrier gas. When a specimen flows past the detector, the cooling rate changes and the detector recognizes this as a specimen. These detectors are inexpensive and respond to almost every known chemical. They are, however, relatively insensitive.

Flame ionization. The sample is burned as it passes the detector. Charged particles result from the burning and are collected for detection. This may be the most common type of detector, is relatively inexpensive, has low detection limits, and reacts to almost all compounds.

Electron capture. These detectors are sensitive to a drop in current associated with the loss of slow electrons as the sample passes the detector and absorbs electrons. Halogenated compounds are especially reactive to electron capture detectors. Their detection limits are much lower than flame ionization and they provide selectivity by not responding to other components of the mixture.

NP detectors. These are a kind of flame ionization detector in which an alkali bead selectively ionizes nitrogen or phosphorous compounds. They have lower detection limits than flame ionization but not as low as electron capture. They also provide selectivity and are advantageous when one wishes to confine attention to nitrogen- or phosphorous-containing compounds.

Mass spectrometer. Described below.

Derivatization

Part of the preparation of the specimen for injection onto the GC may include derivatization, the conversion of the compound of interest into a modified molecule. There are several reasons that justify the added labor involved in conducting the reaction of derivatization. Sometimes the chemical of interest is so polar that it has a very high boiling point and, when heated during chromatography, will char or decompose, rendering the analysis impossible. However, a derivative formed from it may have a much lower boiling point. On other occasions, the molecule to be studied does vaporize but adheres tightly to the column, providing poor chromatographic characteristics, odd peak shape, or other problems. It might be possible to design a derivative that gives sharp peaks. One other reason is for purposes of improving detection quality. For example, halogenated derivatives can be formed which will make the derivative very sensitive to electron capture detectors. Similarly, derivatives can be prepared which increase the molecular mass of fragments formed in a mass spectrometer. With higher mass the fragments can be better recognized and distinguished from low molecular weight background material.

Some Types of Derivatives and Sample Reactions

Silylation
The most widely used derivatives are probably trimethylsilyl (TMS) derivatives. They can be formed from several reagents including N,O-bis(trimethylsilyl) trifluoroacetamide, BSTFA. This is highly reactive and forms stable TMS derivatives that have low boiling points. It has the advantage of reacting quickly and quantitatively under

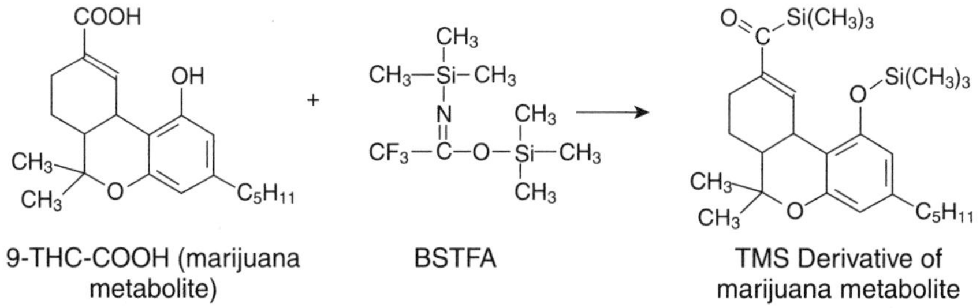

FIGURE 13.6 Silylation of marijuana metabolite.

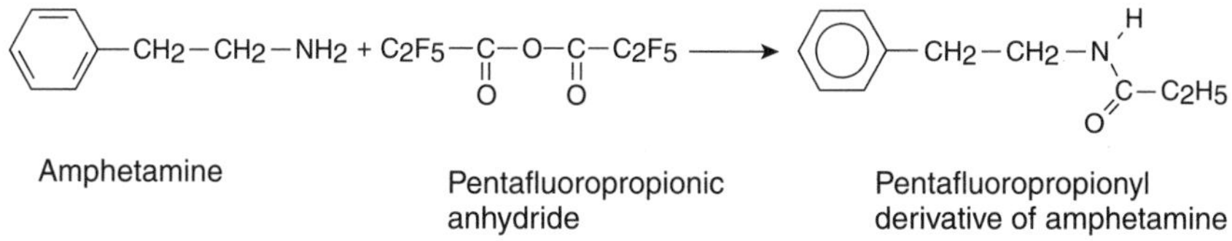

FIGURE 13.7 Acylation of amphetamine with pentafluoropropionic anhydride.

mild conditions and is especially reactive with alcohols, amines, amides, and carboxylic acids. The by-products of the TMS reaction are nonpolar and volatile and, hence, tend to chromatograph well. Figure 13.6 shows the reaction of Δ-9-THC-COOH marijuana metabolite with BSTFA to form a readily chromatographed derivative.

N-methyl-N-trimethylsilyltrifluoroacetamide (MSTFA) is similar in use and behavior to BSTFA. Its by-products are even more volatile than those of BSTFA and it may be preferred when one wishes to assure that there is no interference in the analysis from the by-products of MSTFA derivatization. The presence of water must be cautiously avoided when working with most derivatizing reagents, especially TMS reagents. This is because the hydrogen atoms of water are reactive with these reagents. This reaction can be dangerous. In addition, even small amounts of moisture in the presence of these reagents will quickly inactivate them, a common cause of failure in toxicology analyses.

Acylation

Acylation is the conversion of active hydrogens in some compounds such as hydroxyl, sulfhydryl, and amine, into esters, thioesters, and amides, respectively. It is carried out with a carboxylic acid or derivative of a carboxylic acid. One of the most common acylation reactions is insertion of perfluoroacyl groups, such as trifluoroacyl or pentafluoroacyl groups, onto amino groups. This leads to three desirable results. It reduces the polarity of the amino group, raises the mass of the fragments formed in mass spectrometry, and improves reactivity with electron capture detectors. A disadvantage is that acylation forms highly acidic by-products. Unless these are removed before injection, they can shorten the life of the chromatographic column. The example in Figure 13.7 is acylation of amphetamine to improve its chromatographic properties.

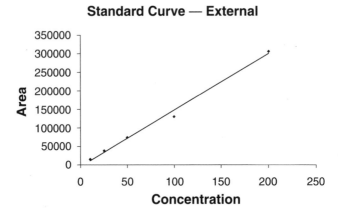

FIGURE 13.8 Calibration curve based on exclusion of internal standard data.

Quantitation with GC

Regardless of the type of detector employed, the various chemical components of a mixture will produce peaks on a recording device. Over a limited range the peak height and the peak area are both proportional to the concentration of the species causing the peak. One can take advantage of this proportionality to measure the quantity of the substance which produced the peak. There are several ways to translate peak height or area into concentration. The two major methods are known as external standardization and internal standardization. These two methods are more commonly applied to peak area rather than height because some variables such as flow rate, measurement of baseline, and others cause more imprecise peak height than peak area.

External Standardization

This method is similar to that used in most analytical methods. Standards are run separately from the unknown specimens and their areas are determined by an electronic integrator. Then, when the unknowns are run, their areas are simply compared to the areas of standards whose concentrations are known. This is analogous to plotting absorbance vs. concentration in spectrophotometry. The following equation may be used:

$$\text{Conc. of unknown} = \text{Conc. of std.} \times \text{area unknown/area std.}$$

External standardization is limited by the linear range of the method. One has to verify separately that the standard and the unknown concentrations are both proportional to the area as integrated. More importantly, one has to be very cautious that all variables in the treatment of the standard and unknown are the same. In other words, volumes injected must be identical, recoveries of sample in pre-treatment steps must be identical, etc. If the analyst, for example, injects 1.0 µL of standard and 1.1 µL of unknown, he/she has unwittingly introduced a 10% error. Note also that an error of such magnitude, 0.1 uL, would be easy to make. If a solvent–solvent extraction preceded the injection, it is also easy to imagine how one could have different recoveries of the analyte from the calibration specimen compared to the unknown specimen.

It is clear, therefore, that external standardization as a quantitative approach is fraught with possible error. Internal standardization is more reliable and is, for most important applications, routinely used.

Internal Standardization

In this method, every sample, calibrator or unknown, receives a specific amount of a third material, the internal standard. The concentration of unknown is then based on the relative signal the unknown gives compared to the signal of the internal standard. As a result, random errors such as those which might be due to variable injection volumes are not important because the inaccuracy in sample volume is offset by a proportional change in the internal standard.

In actual practice one adds internal standard to each standard or unknown and injects the mixture onto the GC. The integrator evaluates the area of all peaks in each sample. Consider the following data from an assay for marijuana metabolite as an example:

Std. Conc. ng/mL	Int. Std. Conc. ng/mL	Component Area	Int. Std. Area	Conc. Ratio	Area Ratio
10	50	15,000	72,000	0.20	0.205
25	50	38,000	71,000	0.50	0.535
50	50	74,000	74,500	1.0	0.993
100	50	130,000	65,500	2.0	1.985
200	50	305,000	75,500	4.0	4.040
Unknown	50	62,000	83,000	Unknown	0.747

If one were not using an internal standard, an acceptable calibration curve might not result. Note that the area for the 100 ng/mL standard is not on a straight line with the other standards. However, the error in that standard is corrected by the internal standard, for we see that the area ratio is in line with the expected value. In other words, the plot of concentration ratio vs. area ratio is closer to a straight line than the plot of concentration vs. component area. This is visually apparent in the two plots in Figures 13.8 and 13.9 and is also confirmed by the regression coefficients for each line, 0.993 and 0.9998, for area not corrected by internal standard and area ratios, respectively. The unknown may have had some error in sample preparation or injection as suggested by the high internal standard area when compared to the average area of the other internal standards, 83,000 vs. a mean of 73,250 for the other samples (excepting the erratic standard). It appears that too much sample was injected. One can calculate the concentration of the unknown from either calibration plot but we know from the foregoing discussion that the result derived from the internal standard method is more likely to have higher accuracy. The calculations, by each method, follow.

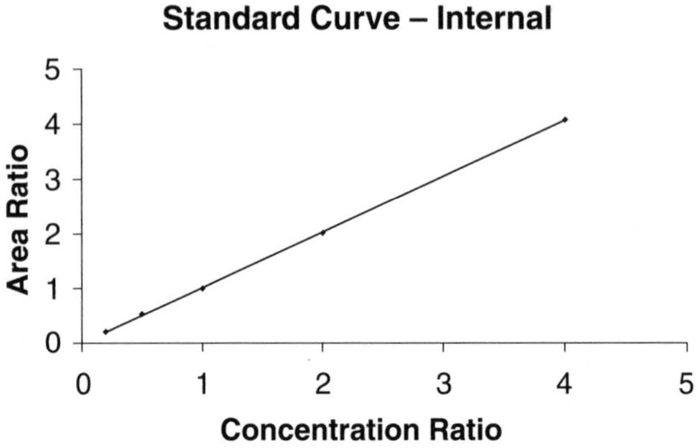

Standard Curve – Internal

FIGURE 13.9 Calibration curve based on inclusion of internal standard data.

Equation of area vs. concentration (from linear regression)

$$Y = Area = 1506.6 \times Concentration - 3609.4$$

For Unknown:

$$62,000 = 1506.6 \times Conc - 3609.4$$

$$Concentration = 43.5 \text{ ng/mL}$$

Equation of concentration ratio vs. area ratio

$$Y = Area \ ratio = 1.0055 \times Concentration \ ratio + 0.0031$$

For Unknown:

$$0.747 = 1.0055 \times Concentration \ ratio + 0.0031$$

$$Concentration \ ratio = 0.7399$$

$$Unknown = 37 \text{ ng/mL}$$

Results show that a significant error $(37 - 43.5) \times 100/37 = 17.6\%$ is encountered by ignoring the internal standard in this example.

Nature of the Internal Standard

In general, the internal standard should be like the compound of interest as much as possible, but be fully distinguishable from it. The reason for this is quite simple. Insofar as the internal standard differs from the compound of interest, to that extent it will tend to behave in a different manner and, therefore, possibly separate from that compound during the extraction or other sample preparation. One wants the substance being measured and the internal standard to stay together but be physically distinguishable when finally measured. The internal standard must not be a compound which might be naturally present in the matrix being measured. For example, isopropanol might seem like a good internal standard for measuring ethyl alcohol in blood. However, if someone drank isopropanol as sometimes happens, then it would be impossible to measure ethyl alcohol in that specimen because one could not distinguish isopropanol in the internal standard from that already present in the specimen. The internal standard must not overlap the substance of interest on the chromatogram or else the integrator cannot determine the area due to each of them. (GC-Mass spectrometer is something of an exception here and will be discussed in the next section.) Finally, it is logical and true that the internal standard must be recovered to the same extent as the unknown in sample preparation prior to chromatography and must not react with any part of the analytic process except for the derivatization step.

GAS CHROMATOGRAPHY-MASS SPECTROMETRY

This is a more powerful technology than gas chromatography coupled to a less sophisticated detector. When GC is hitched to a mass spectrometer as the detector, the sample emerging from the column gives more than a mere nonspecific signal of its presence. It also gives a mass spectrum. The emerging substance is struck by high energy electrons (70 kEv) and fragmented. Usually, a large number of ion fragments are generated and the specific mass, charge, and ratios of these ions constitute something of a fingerprint, which is often uniquely characteristic of just one compound. If a toxicologist wishes to demonstrate conclusively that a particular specimen contained a drug of abuse, it is not enough to show that the specimen produced a peak with a characteristic retention time. There are too many possible compounds in the world to be certain of the identity of a chromatographic peak merely on the basis of its retention time. However, when the suspected identity is supported by both retention time and a characteristic spectrum, then the conclusion that a certain drug is present is usually incontrovertible.

Structure of a GC-Mass Spectrometer

The GC portion of this instrument is essentially identical to any GC. The differences are mainly at the detector end where the mass spectrometer is located (Figure 13.10).

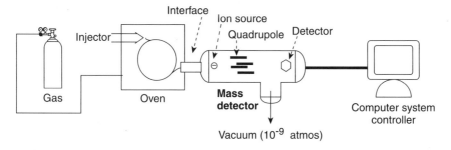

FIGURE 13.10 Schematic of a gas chromatograph-mass spectrometer.

As the carrier gas plus any components of the specimen exit the column together they enter the high vacuum chamber of the mass spectrometer. Electrons strike the molecules and ion fragments are formed. The positive ions so generated are repelled from the ion source and directed toward the detector. As they pass through the quadrupole, one type of mass spectrometric device, most of them strike the rods making up the quadrupole and they are exterminated. In each moment of time only fragments with a specific mass/charge ratio pass through the quadrupole and reach the detector. In this manner, the mass spectrometer is able to distinguish among fragments on the basis of their mass and charge and count their abundance. In turn, the ability of the quadrupole to select among fragments on a continuous basis is determined by a radio frequency field and an electromagnetic field that operate upon it.

An extremely high vacuum must be maintained within the mass spectrometer. If this vacuum is too weak, then gases present in the mass spectrometer space will react with the highly active fragments and new species will form making it impossible to identify substances on the basis of their characteristic mass spectra. Gas molecules present in air in the absence of a high vacuum will also collide with fragments from the sample and deflect their straight line trajectory, which would otherwise allow them to reach the detector at the appropriate time.

If a mass spectrometer is connected to a packed column which has relatively high flow rates of carrier gas, then an interface is needed to prevent the high volume of carrier gas from entering the mass spectrometer and eliminating the vacuum. A number of ingenious devices have been designed for this purpose. Suffice to mention here is that most GC-Mass spectrometry in contemporary toxicology is conducted with capillary columns. They have very low carrier gas-flow rates and the carrier is readily pumped away without requiring a specific interface device.

Derivatization in GC-Mass Spectrometry

For accurate identification and quantification in GC-Mass spectrometry good peak shape is necessary. Some compounds, especially polar ones, do not chromatograph well, i.e., they give broad, asymmetrical peaks. To eliminate this problem a derivatization step is included in the procedure as described above. Derivatization, therefore, which customarily decreases the polarity of the molecule, usually improves the quality of peak shape. In GC-Mass spectrometry, derivatization serves an added function. It increases the mass of the fragments that are formed. To appreciate the importance of this function, look at Figure 13.11, the electron impact mass spectrum

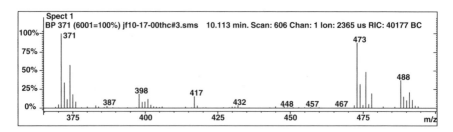

FIGURE 13.11 Mass spectrum of silylated marijuana metabolite.

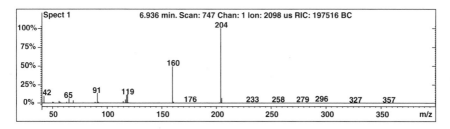

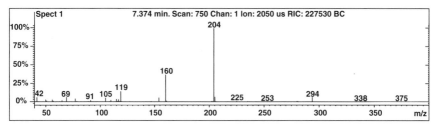

FIGURE 13.12 Electron impact mass spectra of pentafluoroprionyl derivatives of methamphetamine and ephedrine.

of silylated marijuana metabolite. There are many fragments in this spectrum and it has sufficient variety to be easily distinguishable from other compounds. Figure 13.12, however, shows the comparatively simple spectra of pentafluoropropionymethamphetamine and pentafluoropropionylephedrine. The methamphetamine is a drug of abuse whereas ephedrine is a common over-the-counter pharmaceutical. It is very important to distinguish between them. Because their spectra are so much alike it is almost impossible to be certain, on the basis of spectrum alone, that one compound is present and not the other. Their retention times are very close under some conditions, which also complicates matters. Derivatized methamphetamine and ephedrine have heavier fragments than underivatized drugs. The resulting spectra still lack a large variety of fragments. However, those fragments formed are of large mass and, therefore, are removed from the background of small fragments that often complicate the interpretation of spectra. The larger the mass of a fragment the more distinctive it is likely to be and, by extension, the more helpful it will be in the correct identification of a substance.

Quantitation in GC-Mass Spectrometry

GC-Mass spectrometry is capable of providing accurate quantitative results. It is better to use internal standardization rather than external standardization when conducting quantitative GC-Mass spectrometer testing. One of the significant differences between GC-Mass spectrometry vs. GC without a mass spectrometer detector is the nature of the internal standard. With GC-Mass spectrometry, isotopically labeled internal standards may be used. Deuterated standards are available. They differ from unlabeled standards because one or more hydrogen atoms have been replaced with heavy hydrogen, deuterium (hydrogen with atomic mass of two and two neutrons in the nucleus). Such labeled standards have almost the same retention time as

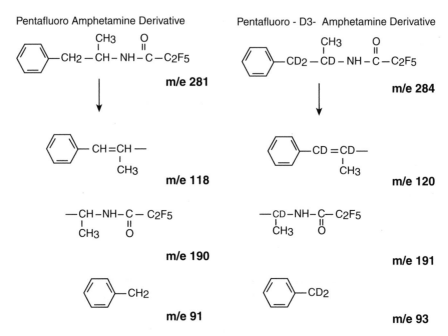

FIGURE 13.13 Acylated amphetamine and deuterated amphetamine.

unlabeled standards and perform in a nearly identical manner during the steps involved in sample preparation. In short, they are the ideal internal standards because of their high degree of similarity to the compound being measured. Again, it is only with GC-Mass spectrometry that such standards may be used because of the ability of the mass spectrometer to recognize the difference in mass. Figure 13.13 shows the pentafluoroacyl derivatives of amphetamine and deuterated amphetamine. Note the differences in mass of each fragment. On the basis of the abundance of the 120 ion, the GC-Mass spectrometer can evaluate the concentration of amphetamine in the sample. On the basis of 118 ion abundance the amount of internal standard can be determined. These substances can be independently measured despite the fact that their peaks have almost identical retention times.

Identification of Unknown Substances by GC-Mass Spectrometry

There are two methods used to identify unknown components of mixtures. The first is by analysis of the fragments formed and then, using a series of rules developed for this purpose, conjecturing about the possible structure and identity of the compound giving rise to those fragments. For example, the molecular weight can be inferred if the molecular ion (the intact molecule with a positive charge) appears in the spectrum. Analysis of the various fragments may or may not lead to a coherent theory about the substance's identity. This depends on the nature of the spectrum and the skill of the analyst. It is far more common to establish identities by the second method simply matching up the spectrum with spectra in a library prepared for this purpose. Each laboratory can make its own library. More commonly, laboratories can purchase libraries such as the Maury, Pfleger, Weber library of drugs which contains about 10,000 drug spectra. The National Institute of Standards and Technology has a mass spectrometer library which runs to over 100,000 compounds.

Computerized matching of spectra can occur very rapidly and programs for mass spectrometers have been written that provide the user with the ten best matches between the substance of interest and the standards present in the library.

There are several different search algorithms for mass spectrometers. In one of these, each fragment in the unknown (or standard) spectrum is evaluated and its abundance is multiplied by its mass. The ten fragments with highest products from this exercise are saved. Other fragments in the spectrum are not considered any further. Each fragment is compared with the same fragment from the standard spectrum. If all 10 fragments from the unknown match the 10 from the standard in the same sequence, i.e., 1 = 1, 2 = 2, etc., we have a perfect match. Great experience is required to effectively utilize this search routine and false identifications can be made easily by an inexperienced individual.

SIM vs. SCAN Modes

When running GC-Mass spectrometry it is possible to set the instrument so that only ions with specific masses will be evaluated. This approach is called SIM or selective ion monitoring. Alternatively, one can SCAN, that is detect and count all ions over a certain mass range. SIM is used for quantitative work. If the instrument is monitoring only 5 or 6 ions, for example, instead of an entire range such as 100 to 400 atomic mass units (amu), then it will focus on the ions of interest for a greater period of time and count more of them. Hence, SIM can have much better detection limits, as low as 1/100th those of SCAN. SIM also provides cleaner spectra because foreign materials that are not of interest to the analyst will not be counted by the detector. SCAN mode must be used whenever one is testing substances of unknown identity. Because the relevant ions are not known prior to the analysis, the investigator has to set the instrument to look at every ion within a realistic range. In this regard, some GC-Mass spectrometer instruments are limited by the range of masses they can detect. Better instruments cover a very wide range of possible masses.

GC-MS of Enantiomers

For purposes of forensic toxicology it is sometimes necessary to identify drugs that are members of an enantiomeric pair. Recall that any molecule with a carbon atom with four different groups attached to it is optically active. The carbon atom with the four different groups is called a chiral carbon. A molecule with a chiral carbon may exist in two different forms: enantiomers and optical isomers. If any two groups (and no more than two groups) on that carbon are switched with each other, the resulting structure is the enantiomer or mirror image of the first structure. This phenomenon of mirror images is a sub-division of the general phenomenon called stereoisomerism.

Enantiomers usually differ in terms of their physiological properties. One of the best examples of this is S-methamphetamine, a potent drug of abuse, and its enantiomer, R-methamphetamine, which does not have abuse potential. It is obviously

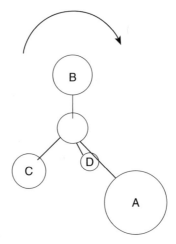

S Form of Enantiomer

FIGURE 13.14 Evaluation of constituents in mass sequence to assign absolute configuration.

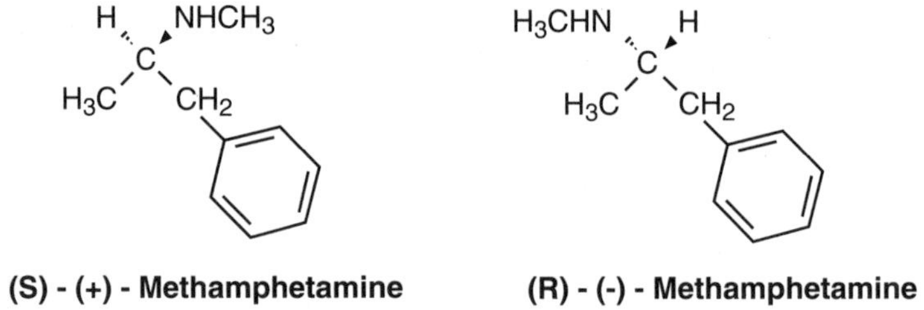

(S) - (+) - Methamphetamine   (R) - (-) - Methamphetamine

FIGURE 13.15 R- and S-methamphetamine.

of great importance to distinguish between pairs of enantiomers. If one's metham-phetamine method is not stereospecific, then a false positive for the drug of abuse could result in a specimen that only contains the decongestant, R-methamphetamine (also known as desoxyephedrine) (see Figures 13.14 and 13.15).

The terminology for optical isomers is illustrated in Figure 13.15. The arrange-ment of groups around the chiral carbon is examined. One "holds" the molecule by the smallest substituent on the chiral carbon, then determines whether the three remaining groups are in clockwise or counterclockwise order in terms of the location of groups on the basis of mass. If the sequence of groups in order of ascending mass is clockwise we are dealing with the S-enantiomer. The R-enantiomer has ascending mass in a counterclockwise direction. This is best explained by an example. Look at (S)-(+)-methamphetamine in Figure 13.15. The largest atom connected to the chiral carbon is nitrogen so we start at that substituent. On each side of the N substituent are carbons connected to the chiral carbon. One of these carbons is, in turn, connected to carbon of a benzene ring whereas the other carbon is part of a methyl group. The carbon with the benzene ring is regarded as having higher priority (greater mass)

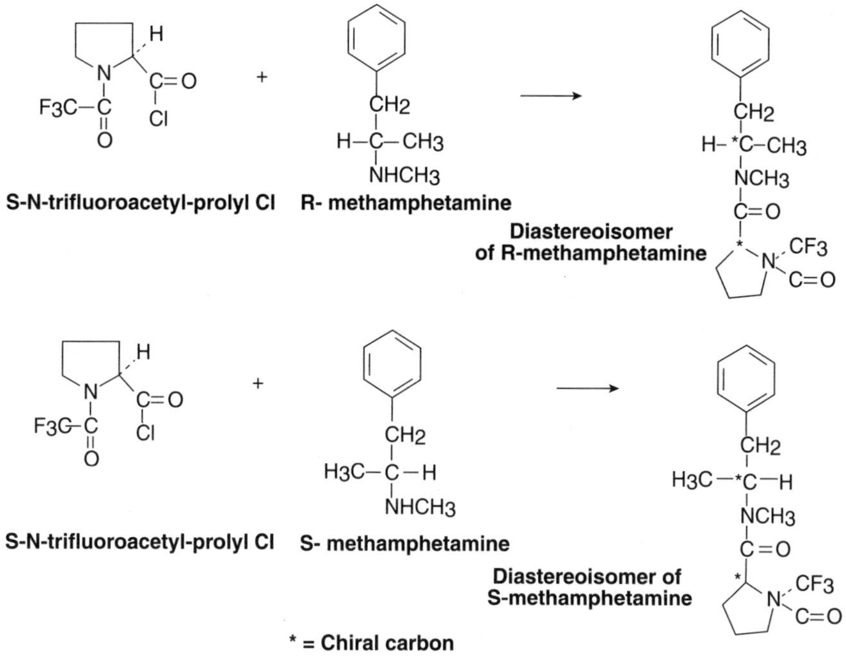

FIGURE 13.16 Derivatization of R- and S-methamphetamine to form two distinguishable diastereoisomers.

than the one that is part of the methyl group. Therefore, the order of descending mass is methylamine, methylphenyl, methyl; a counterclockwise order.

The absolute structures of R- and S-methamphetamine are shown in Figure 13.15 and they illustrate this naming convention.

Most physical and chemical properties are the same for both members of an enantiomeric pair. For example, they will have the same boiling point, the same reactivity in simple inorganic reactions, etc. In complex processes, however, enantiomers may act differently, for example, with enzymes. Since an enzyme is a large molecule and it makes a three-dimensional contact with its substrate, the enzyme can tell whether it is encountering, for example, R- or S-methamphetamine. Only one of these enantiomers will bind tightly in the 3-D active site of the enzyme because of the specific steric demands of that active site. Therefore, R- and S-methamphetamine react differently in enzyme multiplied immunoassay technique (EMIT). Because the EMIT product is designed to detect the S form, antibodies have been prepared against that form and they react quite weakly with the enantiomer, R-methamphetamine.

What about GC-MS of enantiomers? Identification of methamphetamine by GC-MS depends on the retention time of this molecule and the fragmentation pattern that results from electron bombardment. Both of these processes are usually insensitive to the stereochemical differences between enantiomers. Electron bombardment will fragment R and S forms in the same manner. Similarly, the solid phase of a chromatographic column binds equally to the R and S forms of an enantiomeric pair. Therefore, regular GC-MS of methamphetamine will not distinguish R from S.

One can distinguish R- vs. S-enantiomers by GC-MS but only by a significant additional effort. Several methods are employed including the use of a chiral column. In other words, the chromatographic column can be specially selected or specially modified so that it is sensitive to enantiomers. In one type of column, for example, L-valine tert-butylamide is covalently bonded to the polysiloxane backbone of a regular column. The modified packing forms different diastereoisomers as hydrogen bonds to the different enantiomers passing through the column. R- and S- forms have different retention times.

The most common method for GC-MS differentiation of R- and S-methamphetamine is by derivatizing the methamphetamine with a chiral derivatizing agent. For this purpose N-trifluoroacetyl-L-prolyl chloride is frequently used. The derivatizing agent contains a chiral carbon and the drug to be detected also contains a chiral carbon. Therefore, the derivatized methamphetamine contains two chiral carbons. Substances with more than one chiral carbon may have diastereoisomers, i.e., structures that are not mirror images (not enantiomers), but they are stereoisomers of each other. These molecules are distinguishable from each other because some intramolecular forces are slightly different. Diastereoisomers often have different retention times on chromatographic columns and this enables us to distinguish between them. The derivatization reaction of methamphetamine with N-TFA-L-prolyl chloride is shown in Figure 13.16.

OTHER MODES OF MASS SPECTROMETRY

The most common modality in which mass spectrometry is used is in the electron impact mode. In this form high energy electrons strike molecules as they emerge from the gas chromatograph. This occurs in a very high vacuum. As described earlier, mass spectra are produced that are usually quite specific for a particular compound. Electron impact mass spectrometry (EI-MS) is a superb technology that is satisfactory for the large majority of toxicological analyses.

Two other forms of mass spectrometry are available and they provide additional capabilities that are valuable in unique circumstances. The first is chemical ionization-mass spectrometry (CI-MS). In CI, a reagent gas is present at a low pressure within the mass spectrometer. The gas, for example, methane, produces reactive ions such as CH_5^+ that react in a variety of ways with the molecules entering the mass spectrometer from the gas chromatograph. CI is thought of as a soft-energy type of spectrometry in which the molecules under study are fragmented to a lesser degree than in EI-MS. CI and EI generate completely different mass spectra so that complementary information is provided and an additional means of molecular identification is possible. In the case of compounds like amphetamines that have very simple EI mass spectra, CI can be a great help because of added spectral information. Furthermore, many types of molecules, especially heteroatom-containing species like amines and ethers, usually give abundant $(M+1)^+$ ions. Saturated hydrocarbons often provide large amounts of the $(M-1)^+$ ions. In both cases these ions are usually the predominant ion species present and informed speculation about the molecular weight can be conducted.

We saw earlier that the amphetamine class of drugs usually provides very simple spectra by electron impact-mass spectrometry. Identifications are often difficult

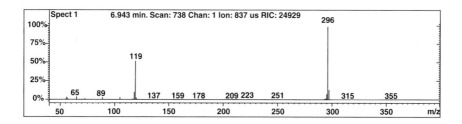

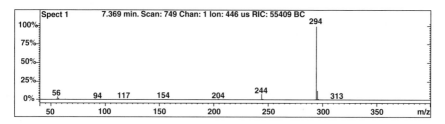

FIGURE 13.17 CI mass spectra of derivatized methamphetamine and ephedrine.

because of the similarities of spectra among these compounds. Figure 13.12 above showed that derivatized methamphetamine and ephedrine were virtually indistinguishable on the basis of electron impact mass spectra. Each of these compounds gave 204, 160, 119, and 91 ions. The ratios of such ions were, moreover, not greatly different between the two compounds. The CI spectra of derivatized methamphetamine and ephedrine are shown in Figure 13.17. When run under identical conditions, derivatized methamphetamine has a large M+1 ion at m/z of 296 whereas ephedrine gives a 294 ion, a different fragment from the 204 found in standard electron impact mass spectrometry. Chemical ionization may, therefore, serve as a tool for clarifying identification of compounds whose electron impact spectra are not sufficiently distinguishing.

A second mode of mass spectrometry is tandem mass spectrometry, also called mass spectrometry-mass spectrometry. In this mass spectrometric modality a specific ion present in a mass spectrum is isolated and subjected to further fragmentation. The pattern that results from this second fragmentation is called a daughter ion mass spectrum. The manner in which a daughter spectrum is generated is variable. In one method, several quadrupoles are arranged sequentially so that the specific ion arising from the first fragmentation is directed into the second quadrupole to the exclusion of all other ions. The second quadrupole then separates the fragments that come from bombardment of the major ion of the first fragmentation. In a different method, the ion trap method, specific energy is applied to the trap that contains all of the ion fragments from the first fragmentation. This results in ejection of all ions other than the ion of interest. This is then further energized to cause its dissociation and formation of a daughter mass spectrum.

Daughter mass spectra are usually not needed because of the typically high specificity present in the first mass spectrum. In some situations, however, they may be helpful. An actual case serves to explain this point. Two decomposed bodies were discovered and some evidence suggested that the manner of death was related to an accident caused, in part, by use of marijuana. It was not possible to demonstrate the

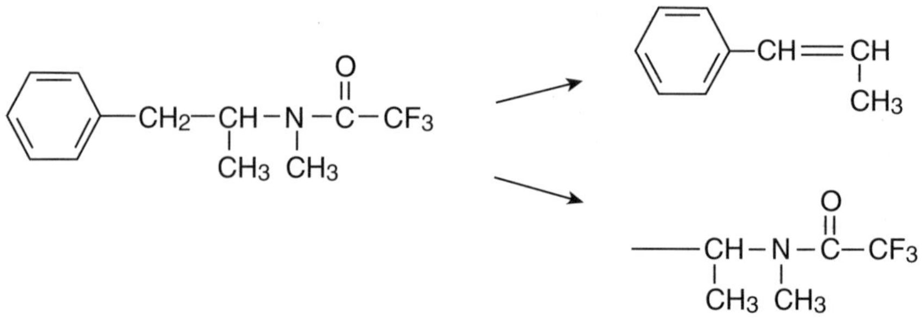

FIGURE 13.18 Structures of derivatized methamphetamine and fragments of its mass fragmentation.

presence of marijuana metabolite in the bodies, however, due to the advanced state of decomposition in which products of decomposition interfered with recognition of the usual mass spectrum of marijuana metabolite. The forensic scientists confronted with this problem were able to solve it by tandem mass spectrometry. A daughter spectrum was generated from the major ion of marijuana metabolite. That daughter spectrum was clean and much less subject to interference from products of decomposition. In circumstances such as these the technique of tandem mass spectrometry can be very useful.

Questions

1. Complete these reactions while showing structures for both reactants and products:

   Benzoylecgonine + MSTFA →

   Methamphetamine + Pentafluoropropionic acid anhydride →

2. Which chromatographic packing would you use for the separation of several compounds, each of which is a moderately polar insecticide?
3. Which chromatographic detector would you use for the detection of several compounds, each of which is a halogenated insecticide present in very low concentration?
4. From the table below, calculate the concentration obtained for the unknown by using the data without the internal standard. Repeat the problem while using the internal standard data to calculate a concentration.

Conc. of Std.	Integrator Response	Int. Std. Cond.	Int. Std. Response
10	10,500	20	20,000
50	41,000	20	16,000
100	99,500	20	20,200
Unknown	60,500	20	23,000

5. Study the chromatogram of Figure 13.6 and calculate resolution on the basis of the peaks at retention times 11.1 and 14.6 minutes.

6. Figure 13.18 shows the structures of derivatized methamphetamine and several fragments formed by its mass fragmentation. Calculate the mass of each and show the structures and mass for each fragment expected from the derivatized deuterated form of the compound. (Assume deuterization is in the locations shown in Figure 13.13.)

Case Study 1: The Abused Child

A 5-year-old boy had a history of six previous admissions to the hospital over a period of 4 months. On each admission he was found to be vomiting, in a state of semi-consciousness, hypoglycemic, and complaining of abdominal pain. A definitive diagnosis could not be made and he was thought to be epileptic on the basis of earlier convulsive episodes. He was given Luminalette for his seizures.

At the present admission this child was fully comatose and was admitted to Intensive Care. He was noted to be bradycardic, temperature was 34°F, and pupils were constricted. The child was cyanotic and underwent a respiratory arrest from which he was resuscitated. Naloxone was administered with a very significant improvement in the patient's vital signs.

If the patient's symptoms were a result of poisoning, what agent among the following is probable?
   a) Methamphetamine
   b) Strychnine
   c) Heroin
   d) Cocaine

(Answer = c) All of the choices given would cause hyperstimulation, which is not consistent with most of this patient's findings. He is manifesting primarily symptoms of physiological depression. These symptoms are consistent with poisoning by heroin. This conclusion is strongly reinforced by the fact that the patient was improved by naloxone, a narcotic antagonist. The earlier report of convulsions by this child may have been due to a different toxin although convulsions may also result from heroin overdose under certain circumstances.

Laboratory screening of the child's urine was positive for barbiturates and opiates, findings that were consistent with the child's symptoms and with his medical history. When the patient regained consciousness, he was questioned by police. The child stated that one of his relatives had forced him, on many occasions, to consume bitter brown and white powders. As a result, the child was placed in protective custody and an investigation was launched regarding the alleged poisoning. A judge ordered that the child's hair be tested for barbiturates and heroin in an attempt to corroborate the child's testimony that he had been subjected to this abusive treatment for a long period.

An 8-cm tuft of hair was cut as closely as possible to the scalp. The hair was cut into 2-cm segments, washed, and enzymatically digested. Any drugs present were then extracted into chloroform, derivatized with pentafluoropropionic acid, and eventually injected into a gas chromatograph-mass spectrometer. The mass spectrometer was operated in the selective-ion monitoring mode in which only ions specific to the substances being sought are measured.

Testing Results

Hair segment	Morphine	6-AcetylMorphine	Phenobarbital
1 (at scalp)	0 ng/mg	0 ng/mg	23 ng/mg
2	0.1	0.2	32
3	0.2	0.3	38
4 (furthest from scalp)	0.3	0.6	31

As seen in the table of results the child's hair revealed the presence of phenobarbital in every segment. This was consistent with his continuous use of phenobarbital. The amounts of phenobarbital also correlated with his therapeutic history. Opiates were also identified in three of the segments that were tested. Based on these forensic laboratory findings, the accused relative of the child was found guilty and sentenced to a prison term.

Questions

Q1. At the trial of the alleged assailant, defense attorneys argued that the finding of opiates in the child's hair was due to the patient's use of antitussive drugs.
   a) This is a solid argument that cannot be deflected by laboratory studies.
   b) Opiates are not found in antitussives.
   c) 6-acetyl morphine is evidence of heroin administration and heroin is absent from pharmaceuticals.
   d) Antitussive drugs would not enter the hair.
Q2. Why is a sensitive analytical method needed when testing hair?
   a) Almost no drug enters hair.
   b) The forms of drugs found in hair are very unusual metabolites.
   c) The amount of specimen is very small compared to the amounts available in biofluids.
   d) Only a very small percent of the drug present in hair can be recovered for testing.
Q3. In the case discussed here, the child's hair specimen was taken 6 weeks after he recovered from the coma. How much of his hair should be drug free?
   a) The 2-cm segment nearest to the scalp only
   b) The first two segments
   c) The segment most distal from the scalp
   d) All of the 8-cm specimen

Q4. How can we rule out external contamination of the hair?
   a) It cannot be excluded and constitutes an inherent limitation of hair testing.
   b) The hair sample is treated in the laboratory so that all drug from outside the body is removed, but no drug from inside the body is removed.
   c) The ions tested in mass spectrometry are indicative of the *in vivo* presence of drugs.
   d) The finding of metabolites in hair is a strong indication that contamination did not cause the positive result.

Answers and Discussion

Q1. (Answer = c) Opiates are present in many antitussive (cough suppressant) medications. They are effective for this purpose because they diminish the coughing reflex. 6-Acetylmorphine is, however, a metabolite of heroin that arises only from heroin and not from other opiates. It is not found in any natural source other than as a heroin metabolite. Its presence is proof of the heroin use.

Q2. (Answer = c) Significant quantities of drug usually enter hair, although for some drugs the quantity is small enough that it does contribute to the analytical challenge. Forms of metabolites present in hair are sometimes different from those found in urine. This fact would not, however, mean that a more sensitive method is needed. Recovery percents are satisfactory for hair testing. The problem with hair testing is that hair is very light in the quantities usually taken for testing. A 100-mg quantity is typically taken. If the concentration of drug or metabolite was the same in hair as in urine, then 100 mg is equivalent to only 0.1 mL of urine, about 2% of the mass of a urine specimen that is usually tested. With hair, we are essentially testing very small quantities and, therefore, need methods with low detection limits.

Q3. (Answer = a) Hair grows at an approximate rate of 1.3 cm (close to 0.5 in.) per month. Although there is some interpersonal variation, one can use this figure to determine the time of drug use based on segmental analysis, i.e., cutting the hair and testing the separated pieces. In the present case, the hair segment nearest to the scalp was, indeed, drug-free. That segment was growing while the child was in protective custody. The other segments all contained drugs and corroborated the charges against the child's assailant.

Q4. (Answer = d) Contamination of hair by drugs present in the environment is a problem with hair testing. A great deal of research has been directed at sample preparation to selectively remove from the sample drugs that are present on the hair by incidental contact. Many methods have been developed that appear to be successful in eliminating external drug. Most of them, however, involve a risk of false negatives by elimination of some internal drug as well. If the laboratory demonstrates the presence of metabolites of drugs, however, this is a strong indication that the person has ingested or injected the drug.

References

Martz, R. et al., The use of hair analysis to document a cocaine overdose following a sustained survival period before death, *J. Analyt. Toxicol.,* 15, 279, 1991.

Rossi, S.S. et al., Application of hair analysis to document coercive heroin administration to a child, *J. Analyt. Toxicol.,* 22, 75, 1998.

14 Metal Analysis (Assay of Toxic Metals)

CONTENTS

Metal testing is a common feature of toxicology testing programs. It is done for several reasons. One of the more common is the monitoring of employees in hazardous occupations where they are exposed to certain metals on a chronic basis at the workplace. Such employees are protected by OSHA and other government bodies which mandate that employees be tested periodically to assure that dangerous levels of toxic metals are not accumulating in their bodies. This type of testing often is performed on urine but is occasionally conducted on whole blood. The workspace is also monitored. If the toxic metal is likely to enter the air space, then air sampling is conducted.

A second kind of metal testing is in the context of clinical toxicology. This is less routine and consists of physicians ordering various blood and urine testing for metals when a patient complains of symptoms that are suspicious for metal poisoning. This latter type of clinical toxicology testing is much less frequent than the routine monitoring referred to above.

The term "trace element analysis" is sometimes used synonymously with metal testing. Trace metals are understood to be those present in quantities less than approximately 1 µg/mL. Thus, calcium, magnesium, and other predominantly light elements are not included in the trace designation. Our discussion here is confined primarily to heavier elements that are more likely to be toxic and are accurately quantified by the methods described in this chapter.

Analytical approaches to metal testing are described in this chapter. Historically, they began with colorimetric tests, mainly for arsenic, which were introduced into forensic practice during the nineteenth century. Colorimetric methods gave way to instrumental methods, the first of which was flame photometry introduced for sodium detection in 1873. Flame atomic absorption spectroscopy came along in 1928 and is still the most commonly used method for testing of metals. The flame was replaced by a graphite furnace in 1959, a change that mainly extended the sensitivity of this new technology, graphite furnace atomic absorption spectroscopy (GFAAS), into the parts per billion range. Other modern and powerful technologies described in this chapter include neutron activation analysis and inductively coupled plasma mass spectrometry (ICP-MS).

EARLY COLORIMETRIC METHODS

Wet chemical methods for metal testing began to appear in the early nineteenth century, especially in response to the widespread use of arsenic for poisoning. From a very modest beginning they progressed in sensitivity and specificity to a point where they are still of great value in modern times. Although they lack the low detection limits characteristic of modern instrumental methods, they are, nonetheless, of use in many forensic applications.

INSTRUMENTAL METHODS

Flame Atomic Absorption Spectroscopy (FAAS)

Theory

A beam of ultraviolet or visible light of highly specific wavelength (specific energy) for the element to be measured is directed through a flame containing the element in the atomic form and in the vapor state. Under these conditions atoms of the element in the ground state will absorb light in proportion to the amount of the element present in the sample. The light source is called a hollow cathode lamp. These devices assure the generation of light of the correct wavelength to excite the element being measured. They achieve this by having the element itself within the lamp being electrically energized with the production of light of the highly specific wavelength. A monochromator is included and it selects the primary excitation wavelength that gives the greatest signal for the element of interest. Standards also are run under the same conditions and unknown concentrations read from a standard curve. A high temperature is required to vaporize the atoms of the sample. This is usually achieved by combustion of air-acetylene (gives 2200°C) or a propane-nitrous oxide mixture (2600°C). Only seconds are needed to complete the measurement step and a sample size between 0.1 and 2 mL is needed. If inadequate specimen is available, it may be possible to dilute the specimen because detection limits are excellent for most purposes and even a diluted specimen is usually well within the analytic range of the instrument. (See Figure 14.1.)

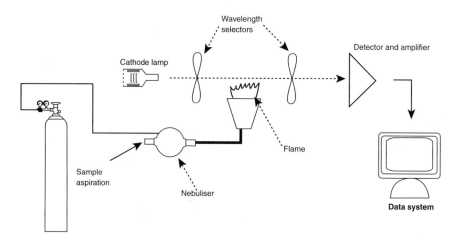

FIGURE 14.1 Sketch of atomic absorption.

Detection limits by FAAS[a]	
As	0.05–0.25 ppm
Ca	0.001–0.005
Cr	0.003–0.005
Mg	0.0003–0.001
Pb	0.01–0.02
Se	0.08–0.1
Sn	0.02–0.09

[a] Amount of element that can be measured with 95% confidence.

The table indicates that sensitivity ranges from selenium (least sensitive) to magnesium (most sensitive). For magnesium, FAAS detects down to 0.0003 ppm (0.3 ppb). This is not an exhaustive list and merely shows some of the relative capabilities of FAAS. A limitation in FAAS is that the tested element must generate resonance lines between 190 and 850 nm as the electrons transit from the ground state of the atom to its preferred higher energy state. Halogens, for example, are poor candidates for this technology because their resonance lines are significantly less than 190 nm.

Possible Problems

FAAS is an excellent technique that has many advantages, such as the simplicity and low detection limits described above. In addition to the excellent detection limits, simplicity of operation, and compatibility with many different metals, it also involves a relatively small capital investment. However, there are several limitations. The technique works primarily for one element at a time. Dual beam instruments make simultaneous measurement of two elements theoretically possible. They must, however, be present in similar concentrations, share the same optimized conditions, and produce no spectral interference. Also, the need described above for at least 0.1 mL means that this is a macro method. In practice, dilution is usually possible, so for all practical purposes, the analyst can often make do with less specimen.

There are also problems which are element specific. When testing for calcium in serum, for example, some salts are formed that will not dissociate under normal conditions of FAAS. This results, of course, in an underestimate of the actual content of calcium within the specimen. One way to circumvent this problem is to add lanthanum chloride which forms lanthanum salts with lower solubility products than their calcium counterparts. Thus, the calcium is liberated and becomes counted by the FAAS.

Graphite Furnace Atomic Absorption Spectroscopy (GFAAS)

Much of the basic theory involved in this technology is the same as that found in FAAS. One major difference is the manner in which the specimen is handled. The sampling module is an automatic pipettor. This device places the specimen in a graphite tube or on a platform within a graphite tube. Atomization of the sample occurs in a graphite furnace heated by electrical current. Two graphite electrodes carry the current to a graphite tube in which the process occurs. The furnace itself is surrounded by argon gas to protect it from oxidation during the test. Analysis occurs in the following steps: desolvation at 120°C, pyrolysis or ashing at 600 to 1500°C, atomization at 1900 to 2200°C, and clean up at 2400 to 2600°C.

GFAAS is about an order of magnitude more sensitive than FAAS. Therefore, background from contamination is a greater problem than found with FAAS. Several methods to eliminate background contamination have been introduced. Zeeman correction is thought to be the best method for correction of errors associated with biofluids such as blood, urine, or serum. Zeeman correction uses a strong magnetic field to separate the signal due to the substance of interest from that due to background. There are several different variations of the Zeeman technique. Transverse Zeeman correction with a pulsed AC magnet is one of the more popular variations.

Neutron Activation Analysis (NAA)

NAA is a radiochemical method drastically different from FAAS because the atomic nucleus is excited rather than the orbital electrons. The specimen is irradiated with low energy neutrons resulting in the production of different radioactive products. The low energy neutrons are usually generated in nuclear reactors but they also may arise from accelerators. Products of neutron radiation emit alpha or beta particles and/or gamma rays or X-rays. Gamma rays or X-rays are usually used when assaying biological materials. A critical feature is that the gamma radiation pattern is specific for each element and may, therefore, be detected precisely and accurately.

The most common biochemical elements, carbon, oxygen, nitrogen, and hydrogen, are not susceptible to activation by neutrons and do not interfere in this process. Potassium, sodium, and chlorine, however, are strongly activated and corrections for these elements need to be made. Two types of NAA are employed. Instrumental

NAA involves measurement of X-rays or gamma rays directly emitted from the irradiated products. Radiochemical NAA, the second type, is a technique in which the radiated products are specially treated to eliminate interferences prior to counting radiation. For example, the specimen may be acid digested and/or solvent extracted. NAA is highly sensitive and, because the nucleus is the site of activation, the physical or chemical state of the specimen is not important. One could use this technology to differentiate among species of an element, e.g., organic vs. inorganic mercury. To accomplish this speciation it would be necessary to separate the species by a method such as chromatography prior to the neutron radiation. Disadvantages of NAA include the difficulty of eliminating some interferences and the high cost of equipment. A nuclear reactor is extremely expensive.

INDUCTIVELY COUPLED PLASMA-MASS SPECTROMETRY (ICP-MS)

ICP-MS is often regarded as the best and most modern method for trace element analysis. Its benefits include a wide linear range of analysis (5 to 6 orders of magnitude), simultaneous multi-element detection, extreme sensitivity (parts per billion or even parts per trillion), and low background interference. ICP-MS is a relatively new technique first introduced in 1978 with commercial instruments available around 1983.

Figure 14.2 shows the basic design of ICP-MS. Briefly, a peristaltic pump transfers the specimen to a nebulizer in which the sample solution is aerosolized. The aerosol is then entrained by argon gas which carries it to the ICP torch. In the torch the extremely high temperature plasma vaporizes and ionizes the sample. Ions are then directed into the mass spectrometer where they are detected and counted on the basis of their mass-to-charge ratio. The nebulizer produces the aerosol by forcing the argon carrier through a small capillary and into a spray chamber. A high percent of the sample may be lost during this transfer so other more efficient transfer devices, such as direct injection, have recently been designed. The ICP torch has

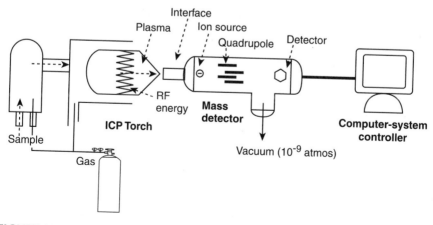

FIGURE 14.2 Illustration of ICP-MS.

three concentric quartz tubes with a coil carrying high frequency radiowaves (27 or 40 MHz), in the range of 1 to 3 kw. Radio frequency energy acts on the argon in the middle tube altering the magnetic dipoles of the molecules and producing energetic collisions among the argon atoms. A plasma with temperature exceeding 6000°K results. The reason for the three concentric tubes design is that the outer tube carries argon which can act as a coolant layer to prevent the torch from melting at such high temperatures.

Perhaps the greatest technological challenge is to transfer the ions formed in the plasma from a region of several thousand degrees Kelvin and one atmosphere pressure into one with a high vacuum and low temperature, the region of the mass spectrometer. This is achieved with an interface in which the sample passes through a 0.5 mm orifice that is cooled by refrigerated water. On the detector side of this orifice, mechanical pumps draw the pressure down to 1 torr. The sample then passes through a second cone into the high vacuum chamber of the detector. A quadrupole located in this chamber separates ions on the basis of mass and charge. The quadrupole consists of four precisely manufactured gold or stainless steel rods about 9 in. long. They generate a radio frequency sweep and an electric field enables only a single species to traverse the quadrupole field and reach the counter per unit time. By continuously varying the radio frequency sweep and the electrical field, ions of different masses and charges can be evaluated. The quadrupole is a low-cost mass detector that is quite efficient although limited in its resolution to about 0.8 amu. After the ions have been separated by the quadrupole, they are detected by an electron multiplier.

Performance

Over 50 elements have good to excellent detection limits by ICP-MS. These limits approach 0.01 ng/mL (ppb range). Eight elements (carbon, chlorine, fluorine, nitrogen, oxygen, phosphorus, silicon, and sulfur) have high detection limits (above 10 ng/mL) because they have high ionization potentials and, therefore, a low degree of ion formation in the plasma torch. For all practical purposes, several elements can be analyzed at the same time. Many laboratories conduct analyses for arsenic, cadmium, antimony, tellurium, thallium, lead, and bismuth, in one single analysis.

Specimen Preparation

The usual sample preparation consists of dilution or digestion with strong mineral acid and then direct aspiration of the resulting mixture into the plasma. Additional routine steps, such as protein precipitation or filtration through filters with very small pores, often are included. For some elements, such as mercury, hydrochloric acid is chosen over nitric acid for specimen digestion. This is necessary due to the loss of volatile nitrates which occurs if nitric acid is employed for mercury compounds. Internal standards often are added to unknown specimens in order to compensate for variation introduced from irregular recoveries during specimen digestion, uneven aspiration rate, and other sources of imprecision.

For analyses conducted in blood, urine, and plasma, sample preparation is easier than described in the previous paragraph. Dilution of the biofluid with a matrix agent is often the only necessary step. This matrix agent consists of a detergent and a buffer. The detergent, for example, Triton-X-100, improves aspiration efficiency and lyses red cells in the case of whole-blood testing. This will, of course, liberate any trace elements which are erythrocyte bound. Buffer is frequently used for the purpose of maintaining protein and metal ions in solution.

Interferences

There are three types of interference in ICP-MS and a close examination of their nature is useful for a fuller understanding of the overall technology of ICP-MS. Isotopic interference arises when isotopes of two different elements have about the same mass/charge value. One common example of this phenomenon is $^{58}Fe^+$ and $^{58}Ni^+$ which have mass/charge of 57.9333 and 57.9353, respectively. These m/e are too close to be distinguished by a quadrupole ICP-MS which has resolution limit of about 0.8 amu. Note, however, that a high-resolution, magnetic sector instrument can distinguish these two despite their close m/e ratios. It is often possible to circumvent this type of interference in a quadrupole instrument by judicious selection of isotopes. For example, zinc has several isotopes of which ^{64}Zn is the most abundant. This isotope, however, is interfered with by ^{64}Ni. One can measure the amount of nickel by targeting ^{60}Ni and calculate the total nickel present in the sample by the known abundance of the isotopes of nickel. After this is known, the amount of zinc may be corrected for nickel and an accurate result for zinc is achieved.

A second kind of interference is known as polyatomic ion interference. This type of interference is due to recombinations that occur in the intense heat of the plasma. Molecular ions formed in this manner include $^{35}Cl^{16}O^+$, $^{40}Ar^{12}C^+$, and $^{40}Ar^{35}Cl$. These interfere with ^{51}V (vanadium), ^{52}Cr (chromium), and ^{74}As (arsenic), respectively. In addition, argon forms a dimer, $^{40}Ar^{40}Ar$, which interferes with ^{80}Se (selenium). This particular type of interference can be reduced or eliminated by adding small portions of organic solvents or nitrogen, which are known to suppress polyatomic ion formation in the plasma. Other methods are also available. This type of interference is virtually nonexistent at m/e greater than 82, resulting in larger elements being better candidates for this type of measurement.

A third kind of interference is that due to doubly charged ions. This is especially prominent for elements with low ionization potentials in which the +2 species is thermodynamically favorable. Thus, $^{48}Ca^{2+}$ predictably interferes with the test for $^{24}Mg^+$. Again, selection of the appropriate isotope will often eliminate this type of interference in a manner analogous to that described above for isotope interference.

REFERENCES

Chan, S. et al., Technical and clinical aspects of spectrometric analysis of trace elements in clinical samples, *Clinics Lab. Med.,* 18, 615–629, 1998.

Delves, H.T., Atomic absorption spectroscopy in clinical analysis, *Ann. Clin. Biochem.,* 24, 529–551, 1987.

Hook, G.R. et al., Analytical approaches for biomedical elemental analysis, *J. Am. Coll. Nutrit.,* 4, 599–612, 1985.

Hsiung, C.S. et al., Minimizing interferences in the quantitative multielement analysis of trace elements in biological fluids by inductively coupled plasma mass spectrometry, *Clin. Chem.*, 43, 2303–2311, 1997.

Nuttall, K.L. et al., Inductively coupled plasma mass spectrometry for trace element analysis in the clinical laboratory, *Ann. Clin. Lab. Sci.*, 25, 264–271, 1995.

Veillon, C., Trace element analysis of biological samples, *Analyt. Chem.*, 58, 851A–866A, 1986.

Questions

1. Make a table that lists flame atomic absorption, flameless atomic absorption, inductively coupled plasmas, and neutron activation analysis. Under each heading list the detection limits, the strengths, and the limitations of each of these techniques. Also describe the appropriate commercial situation in which each would be ideal.
2. Which of the above techniques is best suited for an application in which only an extremely small specimen is available?
3. Explain the importance of Zeeman correction in flameless atomic absorption spectrophotometry and how this technology works.
4. Which of the technologies described in this chapter would be least affected if the specimen is decayed due to exposure to acidic soil for a long time?
5. Explain how each type of interference occurs in ICP-MS and what can be done to negate its impact.

Case Study 1: The Magic Bullet

Neutron activation analysis has been described as an extremely elegant and sensitive method for metal analysis. One of the most intriguing applications of NAA occurred in the context of the assassination of President John Kennedy in 1963. Although this is more a forensic than a toxicological example of NAA, it is worth describing because it shows, perhaps more clearly than other applications, the power and pitfalls of metal analysis. The use of NAA in this critical murder case shows that sometimes the actual analysis, as difficult as it may be, is less complex and challenging than the subsequent interpretation of test data.

President John F. Kennedy was assassinated in Dallas, Texas, on November 22, 1963. The Warren Commission was convened to investigate his murder. After several months of deliberation they concluded that the president was the victim of a lone assassin, Lee Harvey Oswald. This conclusion was widely assailed. One of the Commission's most controversial conclusions was that a single bullet had struck the president and Governor Connally, a bullet that had changed course with remarkable frequency during its journey from the assassin's gun to its eventual resting place on the governor's stretcher. If the president and the governor were struck by different bullets, then more than one assassin had to be involved because photographic evidence indicated that the two victims had been hit almost simultaneously, too close together in time for Oswald to have fired twice. Critics derisively called this bullet the "magic bullet" because of its seemingly impossible and convoluted trajectory. An additional problem with the magic bullet was the fact that it was in perfect condition, despite allegedly passing through two bodies and striking several bones. Was it possible, therefore, to analyze fragments of this one bullet and show chemically that they all were identical in chemical composition?

NAA was called upon to analyze bullet fragments from the governor's wrist, the president's brain, and the nearly pristine round found on the governor's stretcher. To establish that the single bullet theory was plausible, the fragments from all these sources would have to be identical in composition. In addition, it would have to be demonstrated that identical composition is unexpected. In other words, control bullets, when tested, should be found to have different compositions.

Dr. Vincent Guinn conducted the testing and evaluated bullets made for Mannlicher-Carcano rifles, the type of weapon traced to Oswald. Surprisingly, the antimony content of these bullets was found to be highly variable; that is, one might be able to identify a specific bullet for this weapon on the basis of its antimony content. Most bullets within a lot made for other weapons are not distinguishable due to homogeneity of the manufacturing process. Bullets within a lot are usually carbon copies of each other. Mannlicher-Carcano bullets are different because, it is claimed, every bullet has a different content of antimony. Antimony, which is added to bullets to improve their hardness, ranged from 20 to 1200 ppm and the exact amount could be established reliably by NAA. Guinn went on to claim that the stretcher bullet and the fragment from Governor Connally's wrist had antimony equal to 820 ppm. Again, this meant that the fragment in the governor's wrist may have come from the bullet found on the stretcher. To extend the chain of reasoning, because the stretcher bullet was a Mannlicher-Carcano, then the bullet fragment from the wrist was also made for Mannlicher-Carcano rifles. What Guinn's interpretation of the NAA data seemed to prove was that Mannlicher-Carcano bullets differ among each other in their antimony content, a difference which is sufficiently large so that a specific bullet can be traced. Furthermore, the bullet which came from the governor's wrist was identical to one found on the stretcher. NAA also showed that the two bullet fragments from the president's head matched each other, hence only one shot hit his head.

NAA was effective in allowing for a nondestructive and sensitive analysis of several metals in the bullets and fragments. Copper and silver were also tested but the data were not of value because the apparent heterogeneity found for antimony was not present for copper or silver.

Dr. Guinn's data were presented by him to the House Select Committee on Assassination in 1977. That group was impressed with his findings but, nevertheless, eventually concluded that the president had been the victim of a conspiracy involving more than one assassin.

Since the time of Guinn's testimony before the House Committee, several scientists have come forward to point out problems with his conclusions. The issue is very complex because interpretation is based on several important factors: antimony content in the bullet fragments found in the victims and at the crime scene, antimony differences among typical bullets made for this weapon, and variations in antimony within a particular bullet. Wallace Milam and Arthur Snyder were among the critics who noted that antimony in a control bullet equaled 983, 869, 882 ppm in three sections but 358 ppm in a fourth section of the bullet. A different control bullet had antimony equal to 363 to 441 ppm in three pieces but 667 ppm in a fourth. Therefore, the bullets were less identifiable than originally believed simply because the antimony content not only varied from bullet to bullet but also within each bullet. The within-bullet variation may be due to the addition of molten metal to the bullet mold in an irregular manner so that complete mixing of the bullet components during manufacture does not occur.

Arguments about the interpretation of NAA data in the assasssination of President Kennedy continue, despite the fact that this pivotal event in American history occurred over 36 years ago. One important conclusion which appears justified on the basis of NAA testing is that no evidence was found proving the presence of a bullet or bullet fragment with a substantially different metal content than Mannlicher-Carcano bullets. This is consistent with the single bullet theory but does not prove it.

15 Alcohols

CONTENTS

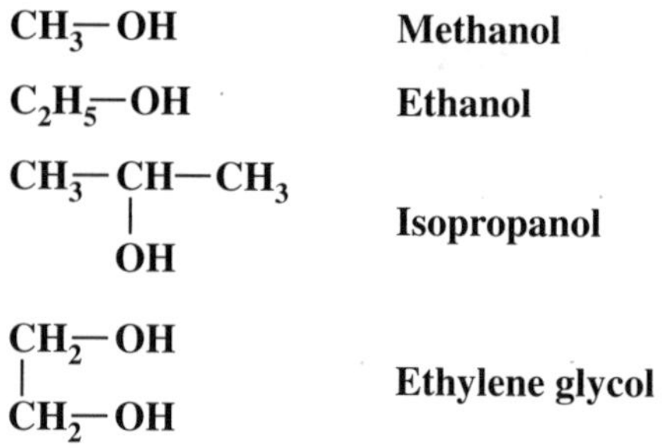

$$CH_3\!-\!OH \qquad \textbf{Methanol}$$

$$C_2H_5\!-\!OH \qquad \textbf{Ethanol}$$

$$\underset{\displaystyle \overset{\displaystyle |}{OH}}{CH_3\!-\!CH\!-\!CH_3} \qquad \textbf{Isopropanol}$$

$$\underset{\displaystyle CH_2\!-\!OH}{\overset{\displaystyle CH_2\!-\!OH}{\displaystyle |}} \qquad \textbf{Ethylene glycol}$$

FIGURE 15.1 Alcohols of clinical importance.

Alcohols are organic chemicals that have hydroxyl groups. There are an extremely large number of such compounds based on the simplicity of this definition. However, only a small number of the low molecular weight alcohols are encountered clinically (Figure 15.1). They include methanol, ethanol, isopropanol, and very rarely, n-propanol or butanol. One other alcohol of great clinical interest is the dihydroxy-alcohol, ethylene glycol.

One of the major effects of the alcohols is central nervous system sedation. Their capacity to induce this effect is approximately proportional to their molecular weight. As molecular weight increases, the net effect of the polar hydroxyl group on molecular polarity becomes less significant and the contribution of the nonpolar aliphatic chain becomes more important. The alcohol molecule, therefore, becomes less polar as molecular weight increases. Nonpolar molecules penetrate the blood–brain barrier more freely and are, thereby, more toxic to the CNS. The general rule is that the higher the molecular weight of an alcohol the greater its toxicity. An exception is methanol. It is more toxic than other low molecular weight alcohols despite its relative polarity. Methanol's toxicity, however, is due to its conversion to toxic metabolites.

ETHANOL

Ethanol or ethyl alcohol occupies a unique place among human toxins. It is the most widespread and heavily consumed drug in human experience. Found in beer, wine, and other alcoholic beverages, ethanol has been used by humans since the earliest recorded history and, undoubtedly, even earlier. It is a clear, colorless, pleasant smelling liquid with a density of 0.78 g/mL.

MECHANISM OF ACTION

The properties of alcohol are well-known, producing a loss of equilibrium and a sense of euphoria and loss of inhibition. These effects are produced by an action on the brain, primarily within the reticular activating system. Euphoria is an early effect of alcohol because the neurons within that structure appear to be more sensitive to alcohol than other parts of the brain. It is interesting to speculate that humankind's heavy involvement with alcohol is accidently due to the "euphoria center" being among the first structures affected. It is hard to imagine that anyone would drink if the earliest result was loss of motor control with euphoria a late-occurring phenomenon.

TABLE 15.1
Effects of Blood Alcohol Concentration

Concentration (g/dL)	Common Effect
0.01–0.05	No obvious impairment, small reduction in reflex action
0.03–0.12	Euphoria, loquacity, decreased inhibitions, decrease in judgment and control, decrease in fine motor control, and start of sensory-motor impairment
0.09–0.25	Emotional instability, impaired perception and memory, reduced visual ability, impaired balance
0.18–0.30	Dizziness, diplopia, decreased muscular coordination, slurred speech
0.35–0.50	Coma, anesthesia, severely depressed reflexes, respiratory and circulatory collapse possible, death possible

Although the precise mode of action is unknown, it is thought that alcohol targets the neuronal membrane where it disrupts normal neuron-to-neuron communication possibly by affecting ion transport or, alternatively, by disrupting the orderly architecture of the membrane. Many experiments confirm that alcohol fluidizes membranes. Fluidization is a term for the change in normal membrane structure that arises from alcohol's invasion of the neuronal membrane. The major effect of this transient phenomenon is disruption of the neuron's natural ability to send impulses in a coherent manner to other neurons. Drunkenness is the manifestation of this phenomenon occurring simultaneously within many disparate neurons.

Ethanol does not affect the entire brain at the same time. Its depressive action happens in a descending order from the cortex to the medulla. The correlation of alcohol concentration with symptoms of alcohol is better than the correlation found with most other substances. Table 15.1 relates blood alcohol concentration and commonly observed effects.

Table 15.1 shows that alcohol concentrations between 0.35 and 0.50 g/dL are associated with a risk of death. There is, however, high variability in the concentrations found among persons who apparently died from alcohol overdose. The concentrations observed depend to a great extent on the person's drinking history. There are some case reports of patients who were treated in emergency departments and discharged with blood levels of alcohol greater than 0.70 g/dL. Such individuals have developed extreme tolerance to the acute effects of alcohol.

ALCOHOL PHARMACOKINETICS

Absorption

Due to its high water miscibility, alcohol readily passes through intestinal mucosa and enters the blood fairly quickly. Some alcohol (about 20% of the dose on an empty stomach) is absorbed through the stomach but the major site of absorption is the small intestine. Therefore, food present in the stomach at the time of drinking will delay the critical transfer of alcohol to the intestine and, all else being equal, will result in a smaller peak concentration being reached.

Alcohol absorption through the stomach helps to explain the difference between men and women in their tolerance to alcohol. It has been shown that the sexes differ in the amounts of metabolizing enzymes they possess within the stomach wall. Men have higher quantities of alcohol-oxidizing enzyme so that the alcohol, while passing through the stomach into the blood, is converted to metabolites (which are not CNS depressants). Women have lesser amounts of these enzymes so more of the alcohol reaches the blood as unmetabolized alcohol. This phenomenon also explains why women are affected by alcohol not only more extensively than men but sooner after drinking. Other factors relating to absorption are concentration of alcohol and presence of carbonation. Thus, the most rapid absorption occurs when alcohol is at 20 to 30% concentrated. The presence of carbon dioxide within the beverage, as in sparkling wines or mixed drinks made with carbonated mixers, decreases the time needed for the alcohol to enter the blood. This effect is thought to be due to the pressure of carbon dioxide which promotes the release of foodstuffs from the stomach to the intestine.

Distribution

After absorption, alcohol is distributed uniformly throughout the body into the various organs in proportion to the water content of each. This also is related to the high water miscibility of alcohol. Alcohol distributes partly into the alveoli of the lungs and the average ratio of alcohol in the blood to that in alveolar air is 2100/1. Because of this proportionality it is possible to estimate blood alcohol by measuring breath samples collected from individuals who have been drinking alcohol. One is also aware of alcohol consumption by the alcoholic breath of the drinker, although the content of the breath is significantly more complex than a mere mixture of air and alcohol. Alcohol also crosses the blood–brain barrier readily. The ratio of blood alcohol to CNS alcohol may be as high as 1:0.9.

Alcohol readily crosses the placenta in a pregnant woman, a phenomenon that may cause a potentially serious disorder known as fetal alcohol syndrome.

Metabolism

The fates of alcohol include excretion into the urine unchanged, exhalation from the lungs unchanged, and excretion without metabolism through the skin. However, the major part of an alcohol load, at least 90%, is metabolized by the liver. The enzymes involved are located in the soluble fraction of the liver but also, to a smaller degree, in the kidney, stomach, and lung. The enzymatic steps are shown in Figure 15.2.

The first step, catalyzed by alcohol dehydrogenase, is the rate-determining step. The second reaction, acetaldehyde oxidation, occurs much more quickly. Therefore, acetaldehyde is formed slowly and dissipated rapidly. Only small amounts are present at any one time in the blood. This is fortunate for the drinker because acetaldehyde is much more toxic than alcohol itself. It is also worth mentioning here that inhibitors of acetaldehyde dehydrogenase are available. One of them is marketed under the name Antabuse (generic name is Disulfiram). This compound has some value in the treatment of alcoholism. When patients take Antabuse, they are inclined not to drink

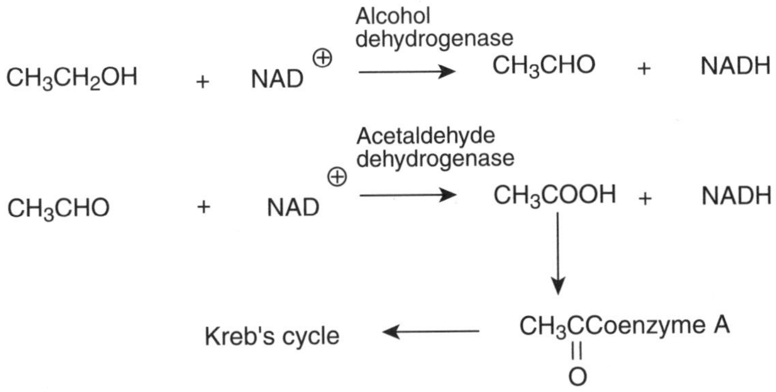

$$CH_3CH_2OH \quad + \quad NAD^{\oplus} \xrightarrow{\substack{\text{Alcohol} \\ \text{dehydrogenase}}} CH_3CHO \quad + \quad NADH$$

$$CH_3CHO \quad + \quad NAD^{\oplus} \xrightarrow{\substack{\text{Acetaldehyde} \\ \text{dehydrogenase}}} CH_3COOH \quad + \quad NADH$$

$$\text{Kreb's cycle} \longleftarrow \underset{\underset{O}{||}}{CH_3C}\text{Coenzyme A}$$

FIGURE 15.2 Biochemical conversion of alcohol to acetate.

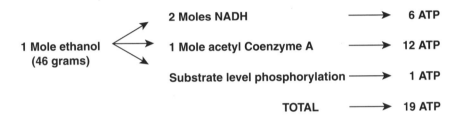

	2 Moles NADH ⟶	6 ATP
1 Mole ethanol (46 grams)	1 Mole acetyl Coenzyme A ⟶	12 ATP
	Substrate level phosphorylation ⟶	1 ATP
	TOTAL ⟶	19 ATP

19 ATP x 7.3 kcal/mol = 138.7 kcal/mole alcohol

FIGURE 15.3 Caloric equivalent of alcohol.

because the return to drinking behavior precipitates a fearful bout of nausea as the concentration of acetaldehyde within the blood achieves toxic levels. Alcohol dehydrogenase is not entirely specific for ethanol. It has some activity in the breakdown of other low molecular weight alcohols as well. The final product of alcohol metabolism is acetic acid, which may be combined with coenzyme A to form acetyl coenzyme A, the major substrate for the Krebs cycle.

Alcohol is very calorigenic, as manifested by well-known figures as high as 200 kcals/cocktail. That alcohol provides high energy to the body is demonstrated in Figure 15.3 which traces the large amounts of energy-rich adenosine triphosphate (ATP) that arise from alcohol.

Two of the bad effects of alcohol, fatty liver and hypoglycemia, can be traced to the large quantity of NADH (reduced nicotinamide adenine dinucleotide) that results from alcohol metabolism. Figure 15.4 shows aspects of intermediary metabolism, and represents some of the critical reactions in which NADH participates. It also clarifies the relative balance of specific reactions that depends on the ratio of the two forms of NAD^+: the oxidized and reduced forms. Note that fat synthesis is favored in the presence of high quantities of reduced NAD^+ (NADH), as is found during alcohol metabolism. Further, during times of low glucose ingestion, such as long after eating, gluconeogenesis occurs with production of glucose from substrates such as lactic acid, glycerol, and amino acids. Many of these reactions require

Ethanol metabolism depletes NAD

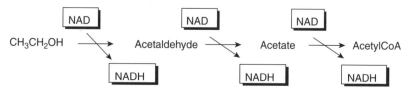

Gluconeogenesis requires NAD supply

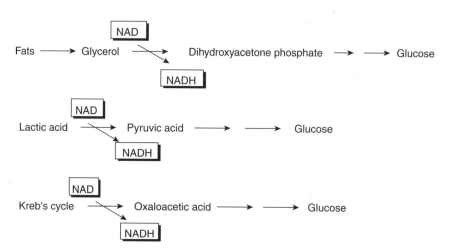

FIGURE 15.4 Aspects of intermediary metabolism relating to NAD⁺-NADH balance.

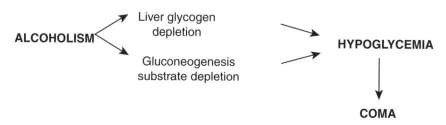

FIGURE 15.5 Hypoglycemia and alcoholism.

oxidized NAD⁺ to form glucose. Because reduced NADH is, however, the prevailing form of NAD under these conditions, glucose synthesis will be retarded and dangerous degrees of hypoglycemia may be reached (Figure 15.5). This is particularly likely in chronic drinkers who depend on alcohol for most of their calories. Such persons will be expected to have depleted glycogen stores resulting from poor dietary habits and some degree of liver disease. If liver glycogen is low and gluconeogenesis is impaired, the stage is set for severe depression of blood sugar. Normal blood sugar is approximately 70 to 110 mg/dL. At levels below 20 mg/dL coma is usually present.

The metabolic pathway shown is the major pathway, especially in non-dr'
or occasional drinkers. Two other possibilities for ethanol metabolism are k ,
It may be oxidized by hydrogen peroxide and the enzyme, catalase. A third syste
also exists. This is the mixed-function microsomal oxygenase system. Enzymes of
this system oxidize ethanol with molecular oxygen and NADPH (reduced nicotinamide adenine dinucleotide phosphate). (See Chapter 6 on biotransformation.) Catalase and the microsomal oxygenase system both lead to acetaldehyde as the first
product of ethanol oxidation. Importantly, the microsomal oxygenases are subject
to induction. These enzymes are believed to be activated extensively in experienced
drinkers and serve to explain the more rapid clearance of alcohol from the blood of
alcoholics compared to non-drinkers.

Elimination

Alcohol is eliminated by liver metabolism at a constant rate until a relatively low
level is reached beyond which the elimination continues but at a rate which depends
on the concentration. This Michaelis-Menten type of elimination kinetics is illustrated in Figure 15.6 and is due to the fact that customary quantities of imbibed
alcohol produce relatively high blood concentrations which saturate the available
enzymes. The Km or Michaelis constant (recall that this constant is the substrate
concentration at which the reaction velocity is one half of the maximum velocity)
equals approximately 10 mg/dL. The Vmax or maximum rate of alcohol elimination
averages 23 mg/dL/hr but has a wide range, dependent, among other factors, on the
drinking experience of the subject.

Some alcohol is eliminated into the urine unchanged. Tests for urinary alcohol
are sometimes conducted to determine whether the subject has been drinking
recently. Employers, for example, may wish to test urine because it is much easier
to collect than blood. Urine alcohol, however, estimates blood alcohol in only the

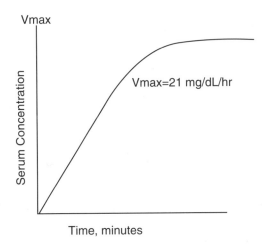

FIGURE 15.6 Change in alcohol blood concentration with time.

most approximate manner. The urine:blood alcohol ratio has been shown to range from 1.10 to 2.44, mean = 1.44.

Calculations on Blood Alcohol and Elimination

The concentration of alcohol in blood may be estimated from a standard pharmacokinetic relationship:

$$Cp\ (g/L) = D(g) / (Vd(L/kg) \times W(kg))$$

This equation assumes that the ingested alcohol has been absorbed but not metabolized. Vd, volume of distribution, in this formula ranges from 0.62 to 0.90 in adult males and from 0.46 to 0.86 in adult females. Average values are 0.70 for men and 0.60 for women. The fat–water partition coefficient for alcohol is 0.018, so alcohol is extensively excluded from adipose tissue. The higher Vd for alcohol in men vs. women is due to the higher total body water or lower body fat in men compared to women. Middle-aged men have an average of 61% total body weight as water whereas women of the same age have 52% body weight as water.

An example of the application of the above equation follows.

Estimate the blood alcohol concentration in a 200-lb. man who consumes 3 drinks, each of which contains 1.5 oz. of 80-proof whiskey.

Solution:

$$3\ \text{drinks} \times 1.5\ \text{oz./drink} = 4.5\ \text{oz.}$$

$$4.5\ \text{oz.} \times 28\ \text{g/oz.} = 126\ \text{g}$$

$$80\ \text{proof} = 40\%\ \text{alcohol}\ (\text{pure alcohol} = 100\% = 200\ \text{proof})$$

$$126\ \text{g} \times 0.40 = 50.4\ \text{g alcohol}$$

$$Cp = 50.4\ \text{g} / ((0.70) \times 200\ \text{lbs}/2.2\ \text{lbs/kg}) = 0.792\ \text{g/L} =$$

$$792\ \text{mg/L} = 79.2\ \text{mg/dL}$$

Remember that this calculation is limited by the use of an average Vd. There is an unfortunately large interindividual variation in actual Vd. It is also limited because absorption of alcohol is not instantaneous and metabolism begins as soon as alcohol starts to traverse the drinker's liver, or even sooner in the stomach of the drinker.

It is often desirable to calculate a person's blood alcohol at a time other than when the specimen was drawn. For example, someone who appears to be drunk at work may claim he was not drinking on the job but rather drank the previous night while at home. If a test is done at noon at the place of employment and it shows a blood alcohol of 0.200%, it is almost impossible to contend that the employee did all his drinking the previous evening.

In a different scenario, people charged with DUI may be injured and blood collection is delayed for several hours after the time of the accident. On such occasions one does not know exactly what the blood alcohol was when the subject was driving. Prosecutors claim that the defendant had higher blood alcohol while driving, and the measured value decreased due to metabolism between the discontinuation of driving and the specimen collection. Defense lawyers, on the contrary, claim their clients were still in the absorptive phase after the accident and their blood alcohol increased by absorption into the blood subsequent to the accident.

Is it possible to accurately estimate blood alcohol at some time other than when the specimen was drawn? In actual practice this estimate is frequently made but not without extreme risk of significant inaccuracy! If the subject is metabolizing only alcohol and no further absorption is occurring, one can easily calculate an earlier blood alcohol using the Vmax given earlier of 23 mg/dL/hr. A problem, however, arises because the rate of decline in blood alcohol, like the volume of distribution, has a wide inter-individual variability. Social drinkers eliminate alcohol with a rate between 11 and 19 mg/dL/hr, non-drinkers vary from 8 to 16 mg/dL/hr, and alcoholics clear alcohol at a rate of 21 to 39 mg/dL/hr. This approximately fourfold difference makes it very difficult to select the rate for use in calculations in a particular case. In terms of estimating the rate of absorption, one also encounters difficulty based on, once again, inter-individual differences. One study showed that 72% of subjects who drank whiskey reached a peak serum concentration within 45 minutes, but 20% required an additional half an hour before the peak was achieved. In addition, the form in which the alcohol was found could make a threefold difference in the rate of absorption. Such findings suggest that the practice of estimating blood alcohol at a time other than at specimen collection is very approximate indeed.

Alcohol Toxicity

Acute

The well-known signs of acute alcohol overdose include ataxia, slurred speech, altered perception and equilibrium progressing to stupor, total loss of equilibrium, and coma and respiratory failure. Symptoms are associated with the region of the brain most affected. The frontal lobe mainly is affected at low alcohol blood level. Above 100 mg/dL, the parietal lobe is affected; motor skills and sensory behavior are targeted primarily at this point. Above 300 mg/dL, the cerebellum and occipital lobe of the cerebrum are affected.

Supportive care is the hallmark of treatment of ethyl alcohol overdose. Laboratory help is critical. Glucose, magnesium, potassium, and fluid deficiencies are common and IVs may need to be started to treat deficiencies of these materials once laboratory studies have confirmed such shortages. Nutritional deficiencies may also be present and treatment with thiamine, pyridoxine, and vitamins C and K is common. In cases of very severe overdose the physician may elect to initiate hemodialysis.

Chronic Toxicity

With long-term use alcohol is deleterious to several organ systems (Table 15.2). Esophageal varices arise from impaired hepatic circulation due to cirrhosis. Gastric lesions and ulcers are often found. Pancreatitis, often fatal if it is of the hemorrhagic

---

TABLE 15.2
Some Medical Effects of Alcohol

Trauma
Pancreatitis
Ruptured esophageal varices
Hepatic failure
Aspiration pneumonia
Pneumothorax
Rhabdomyolysis and myoglobinuria
Seizures
Wernicke's encephalopathy
Korsakoff's psychosis
Subarachnoid hemorrhage
Supraventricular arrhythmias
Cardiomyopathy
Hypoglycemia
Acid-base abnormalities
Electrolyte abnormalities
Withdrawal syndrome

---

variety, is associated with alcoholism. It may arise from hyperstimulation of pancreatic secretions and/or obstruction of pancreatic ducts.

Higher doses of alcohol depress cardiovascular function. Intracellular myocardial lesions are found. Alcoholic cardiomyopathy is well-known and congestive heart failure and hypertension are caused, to some extent, by excess alcohol consumption. Liver disease may be the most common disorder related to alcoholism. Fatty liver is a common but reversible condition. Cirrhosis is found in 8 to 20% of long-term alcoholics. Its associated progressive deterioration in liver function may culminate in liver failure, hepatic coma, and death.

The CNS is the system most severely affected. In cases of very heavy drinking, the alcoholic may develop behavioral disturbances that resemble paranoid and schizophrenic psychoses and physical changes. The physical signs include extreme and irreversible incoordination, partial paralysis, and other severe manifestations of loss of cerebellar function. Wernicke's encephalopathy and Korsakoff's syndrome are two disorders related to alcohol abuse and both involve physical and mental impairment.

ALCOHOL TESTING

There were over 43,000 automobile-related deaths and 1.6 million serious injuries in the United States in one recent year. Associated financial losses are estimated at greater than $96 billion. Between 50 and 75% of such accidents are alcohol related. This figure, more than anything else, highlights the importance of alcohol and alcohol testing.

Testing for blood alcohol is common because of the established relationship between drinking and driving. In the United States alcohol is the only abused substance whose blood concentrations are explicitly regulated in relation to the operation of a motor vehicle. It also is illegal to drive under the influence of any substance known to impair driving ability. However, the amounts of such materials that cause impairment are subject to controversy compared to alcohol for which levels are defined exactly. In most states the legal limit is 0.1%, which also equals 100 mg/dL of blood alcohol. In almost half of the states, the limit is lower at 0.08%. By a recent federal mandate all states must enforce a 0.08% limit by 2003. It is important to recognize that a conviction for driving under the influence is possible without a blood alcohol level. A law enforcement officer can conduct a physical test of coordination at the point where the driver was stopped. If, in the opinion of the officer, the driver does not pass, the driver can be arrested. This is true whether the driver used alcohol or other mind-altering substances. (Drivers have also been arrested who were suffering stroke or other physical disability which superficially resembled drunk driving!) The point is, however, that convictions are much harder to obtain without physical evidence in the form of a blood level that exceeds the legal limit.

Testing Methods

Gas Chromatography

The reference method for ethanol testing is gas chromatography. This method has excellent sensitivity, although such large amounts of alcohol usually are found in the blood of a drinking subject that detection limit is not an issue. More importantly, GC has high specificity. It is important if a conviction for DUI is to be based primarily on a laboratory result that the result be unassailable in court. The laboratory must not confuse alcohol with a different substance. GC provides this ability.

Head space GC, in which the specimen is vaporized offline, i.e., alcohol enters the airspace or head space above a blood sample within a vial, is a preferred method of GC. In head space analysis, the analyst warms the blood specimen in a vial and then withdraws a sample of the vapor above the blood. This is injected into the GC. An advantage of head space analysis is that the chromatographic column lasts a long time because only a gas sample is injected. The vast majority of the blood's components remain in the liquid phase and are not injected. More importantly, for a substance to be identified as ethanol, it must not only have the correct retention time but also be subject to volatilization at moderate temperature. Few materials in whole blood meet this last criterion. Thus, head space analysis provides very high specificity. A substance will not be recognized as ethanol unless it has the appropriate retention time and also is vaporized under the low temperature conditions used in collecting the head space. Chromatographic columns used for alcohol analysis are very polar. Carbowax columns are frequently employed for this purpose. The choice of internal standard for the analysis is, as always, important. N-propanol is customarily used because it behaves like ethanol and virtually is never found in whole blood.

Photometric Analysis

A very common method for alcohol assay is spectrophotometry. For this test, reagents are manufactured that use the same reactions found in the human body for alcohol metabolism. In other words, the reagent contains the alcohol dehydrogenase enzyme and NAD+. NADH, which absorbs light at 340 nm, is produced in an amount proportional to the concentration of alcohol within the sample. The advantage of this method is that it may be automated, and it is, therefore, low in cost and rapidly completed. Two criticisms have been leveled at the spectrophotometric method. The first is that alcohol dehydrogenase is not 100% specific for ethyl alcohol. In fact, the specificity of this enzyme depends on its source. In the past the enzyme was collected from sources that produced nonspecific alcohol dehydrogenase. It cross-reacted with methanol or isopropanol as much as 30%. Manufacturers, however, searched for better enzymes and today have forms of this enzyme which approach 100% specificity toward ethyl alcohol. It also is important to mention that cross-reaction to another alcohol does not eliminate the inherent importance of a positive finding. If, for example, a result of 150 mg/dL was found and the patient or driver had been drinking rubbing alcohol, we would conclude that both his level of driving impairment and his medical risk were greater than if the result was due to ethyl alcohol alone.

The second problem associated with the spectrophotometric method is that one must precipitate the protein from the specimen, a step that increases the labor of the test and could diminish the precision of the analysis. Some laboratories, in order to reduce the time and effort involved in the analysis, have elected to run serum instead of whole blood and, therefore, are not truly providing a result for blood alcohol. The difference is very significant. A blood specimen has lower alcohol concentration than a serum collected simultaneously from the same subject. The serum is approximately 12 to 20% more concentrated with alcohol. In other words, a serum alcohol of 110 mg/dL, for example, is 12 to 20% greater than the result from blood alcohol in the same individual. A result of 110 mg/dL on serum is probably less than 100 mg/dL, the usual legal limit if blood had been tested. This is important because the law is written in regard to blood and not serum alcohol.

Breath Testing

Because there is often a need to estimate alcohol in a subject's blood in the field rather than in the laboratory, methods have been designed that rapidly evaluate the amount of alcohol present in breath. The great advantage of breath alcohol is that venipuncture is unnecessary. Although there is, once again, an inter-individual variation in the relationship between blood and breath alcohol, the average correlation may legally be applied to everyone.

The history of breath testing may be traced back to 1847 when Bouchardt first demonstrated the presence of alcohol in human breath after consumption of wine. With the advent of legislation prohibiting driving under the influence of alcohol efforts soon focused on effective means for measurement. The Uniform Vehicle Code of 1980 specified that "alcohol concentration shall mean either grams of alcohol per 100 milliliters of blood or grams of alcohol per 210 liters of breath." These figures arose from the above-described ratio of 2100:1. This pronouncement established the legitimacy of breath testing.

Instruments used for breath testing are based on oxidation-reduction, infrared absorption, or gas chromatography. The simplest method, that found on the Breathalyzer 900 or Photoelectric Intoximeter, is oxidation-reduction. In one instrument 52.5 mL of alveolar air are delivered to the reagent system, 0.025% potassium dichromate in 50% sulfuric acid. The reaction which occurs involves the reduction of dichromate by ethanol, which is accompanied by a decrease in the yellow color of potassium dichromate and is detected at 410 nm. The specimen volume, 52.5 mL, is 1/40 of 2100 mL (the volume of alveolar breath equivalent to 1.0 mL of blood). Thus, the alcohol result is multiplied by 40 and this result equals milligrams alcohol per 1 mL of blood. A second multiplication times 100 gives alveolar alcohol equivalent to 0.1 L of blood, that amount which is the reference point regarding DUI legislation.

Infrared absorption occurs as the energy of vibration or rotation of a covalent bond increases. The energy absorption is wavelength-specific depending on the nature of the bond undergoing the change. Ethanol molecules absorb infrared energy in the 2 to 5 μm range. Some other materials such as acetone may also absorb in this area. However, instruments such as the Breathalyzer 2000 will detect the presence of interferents and signal that interference occurred in that particular analysis. Newer instruments can distinguish acetone from alcohol by a better optical system with a dual filter. Alcohol is quantified at 3.48 μm and acetone is detected at 3.39 μm.

Portable gas chromatographs are the third instrumental mode for remote breath alcohol testing.

METHANOL

Methanol is a common industrial solvent with applications as a paint thinner, antifreeze, brake fluid, and many other uses. It has been used as a beverage by those who are unaware of its high toxicity.

Methanol, not surprisingly, is physically similar to ethanol. It is absorbed rapidly, distributes in bodily tissues in proportion to their water content, and has a volume of distribution very close to that of ethanol, 0.6 to 0.7 L/kg. The lethal dose is approximately 1 g/kg, which makes methanol approximately 4 times as toxic as ethanol, for which we may approximate the lethal dose at around 4 g/kg. These figures are highly dependent on the metabolism of the drinker and many other factors.

METABOLISM

Like ethanol, methanol is oxidized in two stages, first to an aldehyde and then to an acid. The specific products of metabolism are formaldehyde and formic acid (Figure 15.7). The same enzymes that are responsible for ethanol metabolism also attack methanol but they have a higher Km for methanol. As a result, ethanol and methanol, when present together, will not be metabolized at the same rate. The rate of ethanol metabolism is seven times faster. Methanol metabolism involves a slow reaction with several enzymes and folate as co-enzyme. Formic acid is produced and then degraded to carbon dioxide and water. However, because this reaction is very slow, formic acid will accumulate to significant amounts in severe methanol overdose. Because hepatic conversion of methanol to formic acid is much slower than ethanol conversion to acetic acid, other pathways of methanol disposal such as urinary excretion, pulmonary elimination, etc. will make a larger percent contribution to methanol excretion than that observed for ethanol.

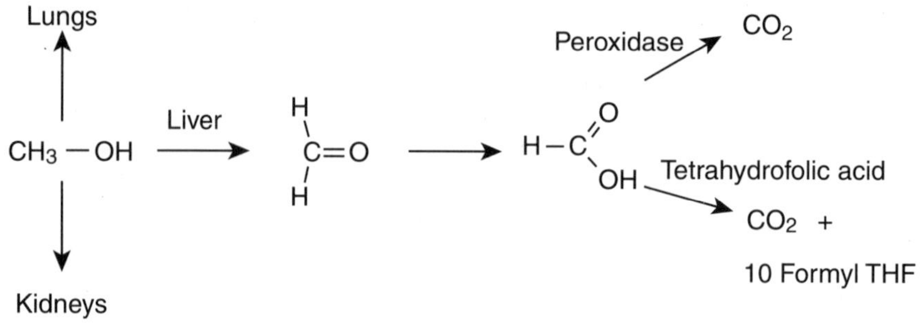

FIGURE 15.7 Methanol metabolism.

Toxicity

Methanol poisoning is characterized by euphoria, loss of inhibitions, muscle weakness, and eventual coma and convulsions, if the overdose is of sufficient severity. Formic acid is a cause of metabolic acidosis due to its inherent acidic nature. In addition, it happens to inhibit cytochrome oxidase and thereby reduces cellular respiration. This leads to an accumulation of lactic acid which only serves to exacerbate the evolving acidosis. In severe poisoning vision is affected, with 43% of patients experiencing blurring of vision and 11% suffering blindness. This is due to two phenomena: first, the methanol enters the vitreous humor extensively because of the extremely aqueous nature of that medium and, second, retinol dehydrogenase, an enzyme involved in normal vision, is able to nonspecifically oxidize methanol to formaldehyde. Relatively large amounts of neurotoxic formaldehyde, therefore, are found within the immediate vicinity of the optic nerve. Severe neurologic effects occur in acute methanol exposure. For example, degeneration of neurons in the parietal cortex was noted in 86% of methanol fatalities in one study and 14% of methanol-intoxicated patients had documented brain hemorrhage in another study. Last, unlike ethanol, methanol causes significant renal damage in acute overdose. Renal tubular degeneration is found with elevated exposure.

Treatment

The methanol-poisoned patient should be forced to vomit, unless a contraindication to vomiting exists. Lavage may be undertaken as an adjunct or replacement for emesis. Reversing the acidosis should be the main concern of therapy. Infuse sodium bicarbonate while monitoring blood pH for response to this therapy.

Ethanol is a semi-specific antidote for methanol poisoning. Ethanol may be given because it will tie up the enzymes that would otherwise serve the deleterious function of converting methanol to its more toxic metabolites. Infuse ethanol at a rate approximating 125 mg\kg\hr while testing for blood ethanol. Adjust the rate of infusion so that the blood ethanol level remains below 100 mg/dL. Because methanol and ethanol are both toxic to the CNS, one cannot provide this antidote in an unlimited manner. If the methanol overdose is severe (indicated by a blood methanol above 25 mg/dL or based on severity as judged by clinical symptoms), then the above therapies should be supplemented with hemodialysis.

Somewhat novel therapies are also possible. A relatively new inhibitor of alcohol dehydrogenase, 4-methylpyrazole, may be given. This antidote has the same effect and same mechanism of action as ethanol. An important difference, however, is that 4-methylpyrazole is not a CNS depressant. Therefore, the danger of extreme CNS depression from the combination of methanol and ethanol is reduced. This is an expensive therapy with a dose of 4-methylpyrazole costing $2000. Alternatively, a folate analog, calcium leucovorin, has been tried on the theory that it will stimulate the elimination of the major toxin, formic acid. It may do so by enhancing the folate-dependent degradation of formic acid (Figure 15.7).

Testing

Methanol overdose is, fortunately, a rare event. This creates a problem, however, for the hospital laboratories in place to help physicians treat poisonings and other medical disorders. The problem is that the laboratory will not be able to conduct the test in an economical or competent manner if it is ordered infrequently. Many laboratories do not offer the measurement of blood methanol for this reason. Some offer to estimate methanol by testing serum osmolality. Osmolality is the concentration of osmotically active particles in serum. In this method one measures and calculates osmolality and attributes the difference between calculated and measured osmolality to methanol, if the history or physical findings are strongly suggestive of methanol overdose. The estimate is carried out in the following way:

1. Calculate an expected osmolality from this formula:
   Calculated osmolality = $(1.86 \times$ serum sodium + serum glucose/18 + blood urea nitrogen/2.8)/0.93.
   (Glucose in mg/dL, urea in mg/dL, sodium in meq/L)
2. Measure osmolality on actual serum from specimen.
3. Methanol (mg/dL) = 2.6 (measured osmolality-calculated osmolality).

This procedure estimates methanol and is approximately correct provided that no other cause of elevated osmolality is present.

Gas chromatography with head space sample preparation is, as with GC for ethanol, a method with superb sensitivity and specificity. It is not rapid, however, and personnel require significant training to be able to perform the analysis reliably. It is, therefore, poorly suited for STAT use. Despite being the best method analytically for performing this test, it is not compatible with real world needs for hospital-based testing.

A third possibility for methanol measurement is based on the enzyme, alcohol oxidase. This nonspecific enzyme oxidizes several low molecular weight alcohols to the corresponding aldehyde. Formaldehyde is formed from methanol. This reaction is linked to that of formaldehyde dehydrogenase, an enzyme which specifically oxidizes formaldehyde. As the second reaction proceeds, NADH is produced and detected at 340 nm in proportion to the concentration of methanol in the sample. This

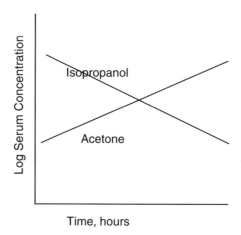

FIGURE 15.8 Decline in isopropanol is correlated inversely with a rise in acetone during isopropanol metabolism.

is a theoretically sound method and does have excellent analytical characteristics. Again, there is the problem of infrequent need for methanol testing, so it is difficult to keep such a method readily calibrated and available with stable reagents, etc.

ISOPROPANOL

This alcohol is found in many consumer products primarily as a cosmetic base and also is used as a disinfectant. Persons with heavy drinking habits will consume rubbing alcohol (70% isopropanol) if they are desperate and, for whatever reason, cannot obtain ethanol.

PHARMACOKINETICS

Isopropanol is readily absorbed and distributed extensively within the body. It is only slightly less polar than ethanol and enters the CNS to cause depression. It is metabolized by alcohol dehydrogenase but the product of this reaction is not an acid but a ketone, acetone. This is expected based on the fact that isopropanol is a secondary alcohol. As isopropanol is cleared from the blood by metabolism, the concentration of acetone in blood rises (Figure 15.8).

TOXICITY

Isopropanol is 2 to 3 times as potent as ethanol in relation to CNS depression. The following table shows its effects:

50–100 mg/dL	Inebriation
>150	Coma possible
>200	Fatal without rapid intervention

Symptoms associated with isopropanol overdose include hypotension, mild acidosis, hypoglycemia, and signs of alcoholic stupor.

THERAPY

Gastric evacuation may be attempted if there is reason to believe the ingestion was recent. Infusions should be started if laboratory findings confirm an electrolyte or acid-base imbalance. If hypoglycemia is present, infuse glucose with constant monitoring of blood sugar. Hypotension is sometimes the major life-threatening aspect of the overdose. Fluids usually are required and pressor drug therapy is needed in more severe cases. If the overdose is extreme, hemodialysis should be considered.

TESTING

Isopropanol may be tested for directly by gas chromatography or it may be estimated by the method described under methanol, i.e., on the basis of the difference between calculated and measured osmolality. If gas chromatography is employed, the same factors apply as stated earlier. The method is excellent analytically but not suited to producing rapid results for use in an emergency situation. If osmolality difference is used, the equations are the same as described under methanol except for the last equation. That is, after the difference between measured and calculated osmolality is found, that difference is multiplied by 6 to give the estimated isopropanol in mg/dL.

ETHYLENE GLYCOL

Among the several glycols used commercially, ethylene glycol is of greatest toxicologic interest because it is the major ingredient in automotive antifreeze. It is a colorless, somewhat viscous (and, therefore, of low volatility) and sweet-tasting liquid. There are many case reports of children who drank bottles of it left in garages and pets will lick it up when spills form on garage floors. Adults, either desperate for its alcoholic effects or with suicidal intent, have been known to ingest large quantities.

METABOLISM

The relatively complex pathway of ethylene glycol metabolism is important for understanding the toxicity of this compound. The molecule is systematically oxidized one carbon at a time. When the first carbon is fully oxidized, the second will undergo a two-step oxidation (Figure 15.9). One intermediate, glyoxylic acid, is converted to formic acid or to oxalic acid. The enzyme central to this oxidative pathway is, once again, alcohol dehydrogenase.

TOXICITY

The range of symptoms associated with ethylene glycol overdose is more diverse than that found with poisoning by most other alcohols. This is due to the variety of

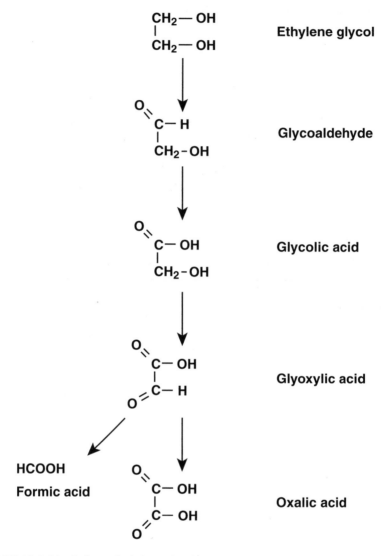

FIGURE 15.9 Metabolism of ethylene glycol.

metabolites, the duration of the metabolic process, and the production at the end of metabolism of oxalate crystals:

Stage 1	<12 hours	Inebriation, nausea, paralysis, acidosis, possible coma
Stage 2	12–24 hrs	Elevated heart and breathing rates, pulmonary edema, renal failure
Stage 3	24–72 hrs	Pain in sides, renal tubular necrosis

The aldehyde products have many metabolic effects including inhibition of oxidative phosphorylation, glucose metabolism, and protein and nucleic acid synthesis. Oxalic acid, the final metabolic product, binds to calcium to form calcium oxalate crystals. In addition to causing hypocalcemia, which leads to tetany, the calcium oxalate crystals may cause mechanical damage to tissue. Renal failure is possible. Acidosis may be severe because several different acids are formed. One of them, formic acid, has been identified as an inhibitor of cytochrome oxidase. The resulting decrease in oxidative phosphorylation is an independent cause of metabolic (lactic) acidosis. One other finding in ethylene glycol overdose is a high anion gap. This means that there are more anions than are readily accounted for. A useful formula has been developed:

$$\text{Anion gap} = Na^+ + K^+ - \left(HCO_3^- + Cl^-\right)$$

Under normal conditions this calculation gives a result of 7 to 17, a normal anion gap. The cause of the normal gap is that more anions, such as phosphate, proteinate (negatively charged protein molecules), etc. are left out of the formula than are cations. If the gap is elevated, it means that additional anions are present in the blood from some source. In the case of ethylene glycol poisoning the source is negatively charged metabolites of ethylene glycol. Measurement of the anion gap, therefore, is useful in confirming poisonings of this type.

THERAPY

Treatment of ethylene glycol overdose is similar to that for methanol poisoning. Acidosis is one of the most severe complications, so sodium bicarbonate is given and blood gases are monitored to guide the pH adjustment back to normal. Ethanol has the same benefits as described for methanol as it continues behaving as a competitive inhibitor and, therefore, forces some of the ethylene glycol to be excreted without being metabolized. Hemodialysis should be initiated if the overdose is severe. Hypocalcemia may be life-threatening and infusions of calcium are likely to be necessary. The serum calcium should be watched closely as calcium is corrected. Ionized calcium is a better test for this purpose than the total calcium. Last, the recently introduced and specific inhibitor of alcohol dehydrogenase, 4-methylpyrazole, has been shown to be beneficial in treatment for this overdose.

TESTING

Crystalluria

Calcium oxalate crystals are usually found in ethylene glycol poisoning. They may be absent in mild poisoning so the test is not 100% sensitive. However, it is a fairly specific test because the crystals are readily recognizable and are not found from almost any other cause. Calcium oxalate monohydrate and calcium oxalate dihydrate crystals are known (Figure 15.10). The latter form, the dihydrate, are more specific for ethylene glycol poisoning. Seeing them in urine is virtually specific for this poison.

Gas Chromatography of Ethylene Glycol

Methods for GC of ethylene glycol have been published. This analysis can work well but ethylene glycol is a highly polar material and its chromatography is somewhat more difficult than that of the other alcohols discussed above.

Enzymatic Assay

Ethylene glycol reacts with several enzymes. Alcohol dehydrogenases from some species of microorganism react much more specifically with ethylene glycol than with ethyl alcohol. Assays have been designed based on using these enzymes.

Problems and Questions

1. Using information provided in this chapter, estimate the toxic dose of isopropanol in g/kg of body weight.
2. An analysis of alcohol was conducted by the photometric method. Ten microliters of serum were mixed with 4.99 mL of reagent containing enzyme and cofactor (NAD^+). After incubation the absorbance change at 340 nm was found to equal 0.50. Calculate the concentration of alcohol in the specimen in mg/dL, in g/L, in mg%, and in absolute percent. What would be a reasonable estimate of the blood alcohol in this specimen? (Millimolar absorption coefficient of NADH is 6.22.)
3. Alcohol is determined by the GC method with head space analysis and n-propanol as internal standards. Areas under the curve were found as indicated:

Standard or Unknown	Ethanol Area	N-Propanol Area
50 mg/dL	23,000	51,000
100	44,500	50,000
200	82,100	54,200
Unknown	60,300	53,400

Graph these data and determine the alcohol concentration in the unknown.
4. Estimate the methanol concentration in a specimen from the following data:
   Serum sodium = 145 meq/L
   Serum glucose = 90 mg/dL
   Serum BUN = 25 mg/dL
   Measured osmolality = 360 mosm/kg
5. A 50-year-old woman who weighs 145 lbs. drank 4 10-oz. glasses of beer (beer was 4% alcohol). Calculate her blood alcohol at peak concentration. Estimate her blood alcohol 3 hours after discontinuation of drinking, assuming that she is a moderate drinker.

6. A child is brought to the emergency department with a blue coating around his mouth. His parents bring along a can of antifreeze, which is also blue in color. They suspect that the child drank some antifreeze. A laboratory result for ethylene glycol was reported as 90 mg/dL of blood. Discuss.

Case Study 1: An Infant with Multiple Admissions

At 5 weeks of age a male child who had earlier done well on infant formula, became limp, lethargic, and mildly comatose. Although afebrile, he was admitted to the hospital to rule out sepsis. Noteworthy findings included moderate acidosis and a serum bicarbonate of 18 meq/L. Ultrasound of the head and EEG were normal. No infection was diagnosed nor were any other causes apparent for his acidosis. He was discharged after 3 days. The child was re-admitted 2 days later with respiratory distress and weakness. Laboratory data for this admission are as noted:

pH	7.35	Sodium	140 meq/L
PCO_2	29 mm	Glucose	200 mg/dL
pO_2	48 mm	Blood urea N	50 mg/dL
HCO3$^-$	16 mmol/L		
Organic acids	Normal		

Since the child's acidosis and other symptoms were unexplained he was transferred to another hospital. Other laboratory studies were ordered. A very high serum osmolality of 585 mosm/kg was noted.

At this time possible diagnoses include which of the following?
   a) Ethylene glycol poisoning
   b) Methanol poisoning
   c) Congenital metabolic disease
   d) Ethanol poisoning

All of these possibilities are feasible although they would not appear to be likely. The osmolality is so greatly elevated that it could only be explained by amounts of one of these toxins which would be well above the fatal range. Using formulas developed for estimating ethylene glycol or methanol from osmolality (see text) would suggest concentrations of 821 mg/dL for methanol or 1959 mg/dL for ethylene glycol, if that were the offending agent. Lethal blood levels are reported variously as 100 to 200 mg/dL for ethylene glycol and 100 to 300 mg/dL for methanol.

Congenital disease appears unlikely (although not impossible) because the child has an entirely healthy 2-year-old sister and he has been tested for organic acidurias, possible causes of the observed metabolic acidosis. Finally, ethanol rarely causes significant acidosis.

A blood sample from the child was tested for volatiles and gave a result of 1148 mg/dL of methanol, an extremely high concentration. At this point the child was started on folic acid and IV ethanol. He was also evaluated for optic damage because methanol is known to cause severe visual problems including blindness. No optic atrophy was found. The child was placed in protective custody and criminal charges were filed against his parents.

Questions

Review of this case suggests several intriguing questions. The methanol result is so high as to strongly suggest a laboratory error. Can this be ruled out? If the result was really this high why was the child's acidosis not more severe and why were other symptoms minimal? Also, why was the child treated with ethanol and folate?

Q1. What is the most common method for methanol analysis?
   a) Enzymatic analysis
   b) Gas chromatography
   c) Liquid chromatography
   d) Calculation based on osmolal gap
Q2. How could laboratory error be ruled out?
   a) Repeat the test.
   b) Have other laboratories verify the result.
   c) Test the specimen by different methods.
   d) Review all aspects of specimen handling and repeat the entire procedure.
   e) All of the above.
Q3. Why is folate helpful for methanol overdose?
   a) It prevents a vitamin deficiency that may occur due to malabsorption.
   b) It prevents megaloblastic anemia.
   c) It increases the rate of conversion of formic acid to carbon dioxide.
   d) It provides nonspecific metabolic support.
Q4. Assuming that the result was correct, how did the child survive?
   a) Children have extreme resistance to acidosis.
   b) This patient did not accumulate the toxic metabolite, formic acid.
   c) There was a defect in this patient's conversion of methanol to formal-
      dehyde.
   d) The clinical problem was recognized early enough for normal treatment
      to prevent severe sequelae.

Answers and Discussion

Q1. (Answer = b). The most common method for methanol analysis is gas
   chromatography, usually by head space. Enzymatic methods are available.
   Because reagents for enzymatic methods are not very stable they should

be used soon after preparation, a factor which is not compatible with the low volume of testing usually done for methanol. Calculation by osmolal gap is usually very approximate and quite nonspecific. It should not be regarded as an adequate method for methanol analysis.

Q2. (Answer = e) The result reported in this case, 1148 mg/dL, is so extreme as to provoke skepticism. The fact that the patient was still alive and, indeed, in no immediate danger of death, only heightens the dubious nature of the result. Laboratories must take all steps to assure their customers of their findings' validity. It is good laboratory practice to verify unusual results before reporting them. The review must include analytical aspects of the result (the actual test) as well as other quality assurance aspects. Is there any chance that the specimen was mixed up? Is there a possibility that methanol was inadvertently added to the specimen during processing? In the present case these errors were ruled out because high methanol was found in several specimens and its elimination from the blood was followed by serial testing of the patient. Misidentification of methanol was not possible because the laboratory ran multiple test methods including gas chromatography, an enzymatic method, calculation based on osmolal gap, and gas chromatography-mass spectrometry. All methods were in good quantitative agreement. The laboratory was acutely aware of the skepticism which would greet their findings and they prepared for that response in a very judicious manner.

Q3. (Answer = c) Injury and death due to methanol are primarily due to its major metabolite, formic acid. Formic acid is an oxidized product of methanol metabolism. Ethanol is employed as an antidote because it competes with methanol for metabolic enzymes and effectively reduces the amount of toxic metabolite. It could be said that ethanol reduces the concentration of formic acid by inhibiting its formation whereas folate reduces the concentration of formic acid by expediting the conversion of formate to carbon dioxide and water.

Q4. (Answer = b) This child did not accumulate toxic amounts of formic acid. Formic acid was measured and the amounts were less than customarily found in low level methanol exposure. It is not entirely clear why this patient did not accumulate toxic levels of formic acid. However, the child's formula is supplemented with folate at a level twice that of breast milk. High concentrations of folate in the diet will catalyze the conversion of formic acid to nontoxic products.

Reference

Wu, A.H. et al., Definitive identification of an exceptionally high methanol concentration in an intoxication of a surviving infant: methanol metabolism by first order elimination kinetics, *J. Forens. Sci.,* 40, 315–320, 1995.

Case Study 2: Patient with Convulsions

A 42-year-old man was lying in bed with vomitus in the area where he lay. His brother, who discovered him, recalled seeing his brother staggering several hours earlier and slumping to the ground several times. Upon arrival at an emergency department, the patient was foaming at the mouth and convulsing strongly. He had no response to deep pain. When examined, the patient was noted to have dilated and sluggish pupils. Periodically his breathing stopped and the attending physician decided to intubate him. Laboratory testing for routine chemistries and arterial blood gases showed only mild elevations of liver enzymes. Over the next 24 hours the patient slowly regained consciousness and was extubated after 1 day. He was kept for 1 further day in the hospital for evaluation of a fever of 101.2° which spontaneously resolved. At the end of his second hospital day he was discharged.

The most likely agent causing his symptoms is
   a) Pesticide exposure
   b) Aspirin
   c) Ethyl alcohol
   d) Acetaminophen

Although this patient's signs are not especially specific, they are consistent with extreme intoxication. One cannot be certain on the basis of the information presented so far. Still, it is very unlikely that clinical findings as significant as convulsions would be unaccompanied by corroborating laboratory evidence if the cause of the convulsions was aspirin, pesticides, or acetaminophen. Alcohol ingestion, however, could give these findings without significant elevations in routine laboratory testing. This patient's serum, when tested for ethyl alcohol by a reliable enzymatic method, gave a result of 648 mg/dL!

Questions

Q1. How can intoxication from ethanol be distinguished from that due to methanol or ethylene glycol?
   a) The patient appears inebriated only if the agent is ethyl alcohol.
   b) Ethyl alcohol does not usually cause a severe acidosis.
   c) The distinction can be made only if history is known.
   d) Clinical and routine laboratory findings are identical; only laboratory alcohol testing will allow for identification.
Q2. The usual serum concentration given as lethal for ethyl alcohol is
   a) 100 mg/dL
   b) 1 g/L
   c) 1 g/dL
   d) 400–500 mg/dL

Q3. Survival from a very high serum ethyl alcohol level
   a) Relates to tolerance
   b) May relate to induction of a second or third catabolic pathway
   c) Is usually a sign of chronic alcoholism
   d) All of the above
   e) None of the above

Answers and Discussion

Q1. (Answer = b) Methanol and ethylene glycol intoxication are usually more serious because of a life-threatening metabolic acidosis; severe acidosis usually does not accompany ethanol overdose. The CNS findings and general appearance of intoxication are, however, likely to be similar in these overdoses. There may be a difference in the perception of the smell of alcohol depending on which specific agent the victim ingests. Recognition of this difference is somewhat subjective on the part of the treating physician.

Q2. (Answer = d) Most tables listing the effects of ethyl alcohol vs. the serum concentration state that death occurs at a serum alcohol concentration around 400 or 500 mg/dL. It is important to remember that high subjective variability is built into this figure. One study of a large number of decedents who were positive for alcohol in the postmortem blood had average alcohol concentrations of 290 mg/dL. Other factors may have contributed to their deaths.

Q3. (Answer = d) Persons who drink heavily on a habitual basis develop high degrees of tolerance to alcohol's effects. This tolerance is based centrally, i.e., receptors in the brain appear to become downregulated in their sensitivity to alcohol. In addition, enzyme induction eliminates alcohol more rapidly in tolerant individuals. Vmax for elimination, when measured in alcoholics, may be as great as three times the figure found for nondrinkers.

Reference

Wells, D.J. and Barnhill, M.T., Unusually high ethanol levels in two emergency medicine patients, *J. Anal. Toxicol.*, 20, 272, 1996.

FOR FURTHER READING

Anon., Isopropanol, *IARC Monogr. Eval. Carcinog. Risks Human,* 71(5), 1027–1036, 1999.
Baker, R.C. and Kramer, R.E., Cytotoxicity of short-chain alcohols, *Annu. Rev. Pharmacol. Toxicol.,* 39(4), 127–150, 1999.
Bosse, G.M. and Matyunas, N.J., Delayed toxidromes, *J. Emerg. Med.,* 17(4), 679–690, 1999.
Egbert, P.A. and Abraham, K., Ethylene glycol intoxication: pathophysiology, diagnosis, and emergency management, *Am. Nephrol. Nursing Assoc. J.,* 26(3), 295–300, 1999.

Henderson, G.I. et al., Ethanol, oxidative stress, reactive aldehydes, and the fetus, *Front Biosci.*, 4(4), D541–550, 1999.

Hillbom, M., Oxidants, antioxidants, alcohol, and stroke, *Front Biosci.*, 4(5), e67–e71, 1999.

LaKind, J.S. et al., A review of the comparative mammalian toxicity of ethylene glycol and propylene glycol, *Crit. Rev. Toxicol.*, 29(4), 1999.

Lieber, C.S., Ethanol metabolism, cirrhosis, and alcoholism, *Clin. Chim. Acta*, 257(1), 59–84, 1997.

Mantle, D. and Preedy, V.R., Free radicals as mediators of alcohol toxicity, *Adverse Drug React. Toxicol. Rev.*, 18(4), 235–252, 1999.

Puddey, I.B. et al., Alcohol, free radicals, and antioxidants, *Novartis Found. Symp.*, 216(4), 51–62, 1998.

Schenker, S. and Hoyumpa, A.M., New concepts in dietary intervention in alcoholic liver disease, *J. Lab. Clin. Med.*, 134(5), 433–436, 1999.

Thurman, R.G. et al., Mechanisms of alcohol-induced hepatotoxicity: studies in rats, *Front Biosci.*, 4(4), e42–e46, 1999.

16 Toxic Gases

CONTENTS

CARBON MONOXIDE

This deadly gas is one of the major causes of toxin-related deaths, amounting to at least 5000 deaths per year. Approximately 70% of these deaths are suicides. The figure of 5000 does not include victims of fires despite the fact that the majority of deaths in fires are thought to be due to gases, especially but not solely, carbon monoxide. Thermal injury is a less common cause of fire-related death.

Carbon monoxide (CO) is very common in the environment and usually arises from incomplete oxidation of reduced carbon. In the presence of sufficient heat and oxygen most carbon compounds will be fully oxidized to carbon dioxide. However, if heat and/or oxygen is deficient, carbon compounds are oxidized to a lesser degree, either to elemental carbon or carbon monoxide. An example is the automobile engine burning hydrocarbons. If a car is caught in traffic, the engine is running slowly and gasoline may not be fully oxidized. Some carbon monoxide will be formed and drivers may experience headaches as the carbon monoxide builds up in their environment. The headache may arise from additional causes as well in this scenario. Carbon monoxide poisoning also is related to the slow traffic that enables the gas to enter the vehicle rather than being dispersed. Part of the problem, however, is the failure of complete oxidation in the first place. Recently, the risk of carbon monoxide poisoning from automobile engines has lessened. Federal mandates in the United States require refineries to add compounds such as methyl tert-butyl ether to gasoline. This additive causes a more complete oxidation of the gasoline with less CO emitted from the engine. Carbon monoxide has been described as the "silent killer" and it does, indeed, have insidious properties. It is odorless, invisible, tasteless, and non-irritating. There are many examples of patients who were treated for carbon monoxide exposure without a correct diagnosis being made.

The most typical situation in deaths due to carbon monoxide is exemplified by the famous tennis star, Vitas Gerulaitis, who was killed by carbon monoxide poisoning. Gerulaitis was sleeping in a hotel room located next to a room containing the heater for the hotel swimming pool. The heater was malfunctioning resulting in incomplete oxidation of fossil fuels and dispersion of carbon monoxide into the surrounding area, including Mr. Gerulaitis' room. This is the most common scenario of CO death. Inadequate venting of devices that burn fossil fuels leads to the transfer of the gas to areas where people are sleeping, resulting in their deaths.

OTHER SOURCES OF CO

Many low level industrial sources of CO exist causing it to accumulate in the atmosphere to the extent of 0.001%. Most of this is carried high into the atmosphere where it is oxidized to carbon dioxide. Tobacco products produce CO, especially in cigarette smokers. The cigarette smoke contains 5% CO, which is responsible for 1.9% carboxyhemoglobin (HbCO) in the blood of an individual who smokes 1 pack per day. Carboxyhemoglobin is the complex formed when CO binds with hemoglobin (Figure 16.1) within the red blood cell. Pipes and cigars contain a higher concentration of CO in their smoke than cigarettes perhaps because they burn at a lower temperature. Fortunately for the cigar smoker, most of this CO is not absorbed because the common practice on the part of cigar and pipe smokers is not to inhale.

Curiously, methylene chloride is also a source of CO as the methylene chloride is metabolized by the body. If a person is exposed to CH_2Cl_2 for 2 to 3 hours, the blood achieves a HbCO concentration between 5 and 15%. A healthy person could tolerate this level of exposure with only mild effects. Someone with pre-existing cardiac or pulmonary disease could experience severe problems because of it. The normal amount of HbCO in blood is approximately 1% and the source of this is absorption of atmospheric CO but it also arises from the metabolism of endogenous hemoglobin.

TOXICITY

CO has multiple toxic properties. The major one is the displacement of oxygen from hemoglobin because the oxygen carrier, hemoglobin, has a much stronger affinity for CO than it does for oxygen. Recall that the human body has an intense dependence

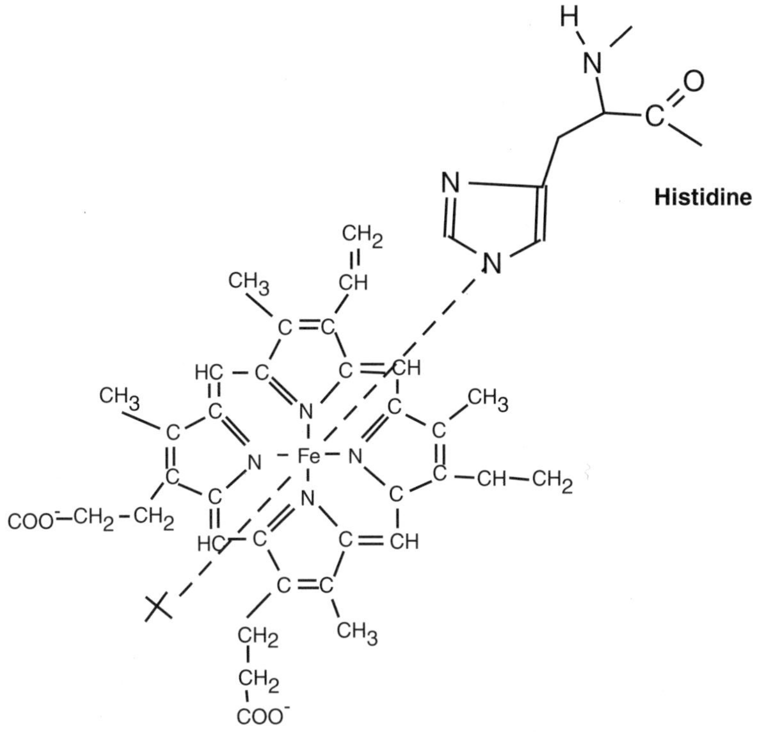

FIGURE 16.1 Heme and its binding site for carbon monoxide. Iron is located centrally between the nitrogen atoms while X marks the site for carbon monoxide, opposite the histidine binding site of the protein moiety.

on hemoglobin for transport of oxygen to tissue. Without oxygen, cells cannot complete the metabolic degradation of carbohydrate and other foodstuffs. The small amount of energy that cells derive from anaerobic respiration will not sustain life and cells die without the oxygen brought to them by hemoglobin. It has been conjectured that cellular death from oxygen deprivation is the proximate cause of death for the vast majority of human beings, the remote cause being heart failure, stroke, or myriad other events that lead to the cessation of oxygen supply. Such is the absolute requirement for oxygen that survival without it is impossible. It is also important to note that very little oxygen can be carried through the blood without hemoglobin. The solubility of oxygen in blood is very limited and, therefore, 98% of oxygen delivery to tissues occurs through the intermediacy of hemoglobin.

An equation which describes the equilibrium of HbCO and HbO_2 in the presence of oxygen and CO is

$$pO_2/pCO = 240 \times HbO_2/HbCO$$

For example, if the partial pressure of CO was 1/240 of the partial pressure of oxygen, then this equation tells us that the resulting ratio of HbO_2 to HbCO is 1:1,

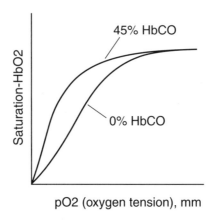

FIGURE 16.2 Hemoglobin–oxygen dissociation curve.

or 50% of the hemoglobin would be bonded to CO and the remainder to oxygen, at equilibrium. This would provoke serious symptoms. Under usual conditions at sea level the partial pressure of oxygen is 21% of 760 torrs or 159.6 torrs. Therefore, the partial pressure of CO needed to produce a condition of 50% carboxyhemoglobinemia is only 150 torrs/240 = 0.625 torrs.

The major toxicity of HbCO is the displacement of oxygen with the resulting failure to adequately oxygenate tissue. In addition to this, however, HbCO causes a left shift in the hemoglobin dissociation curve, a phenomenon which also leads to reduction of tissue perfusion and, therefore, intensifies the level of hypoxia. This effect is explained in the following manner.

Figure 16.2 shows the dissociation curve of hemoglobin. One will note that the curve on the left is found when the HbCO concentration rises. Analysis of this graph leads us to conclude that a left shift results in a higher percent of oxygen being bonded to hemoglobin for a given partial pressure of oxygen. This is disadvantageous within the tissue because the more oxygen remaining bonded to hemoglobin the less will be released to perfuse the tissue. In conclusion, high HbCO fails to oxygenate tissue for two reasons. Much of the hemoglobin carrier will be occupied by CO rather than oxygen and, in addition, a left shift occurs. A left shift is associated with less release of oxygen from hemoglobin deep in the body.

Two other effects of CO are its binding to myoglobin, another oxygen carrier protein, and its capacity to inhibit cytochrome oxidase. Each of these will also diminish the overall level of oxidative respiration within the body, although the impact of CO on the binding of hemoglobin to oxygen remains quantitatively the major effect of CO.

The higher the concentration of HbCO in the blood the greater the morbidity associated with CO exposure. However, the concentration of HbCO, in turn, depends on two factors. Both the amount of CO in the ambient air and the length of time during which the victim is exposed are logically related to the eventual concentration of HbCO. This is demonstrated in the curve in Figure 16.3. Data from that curve are derived from the equation given here:

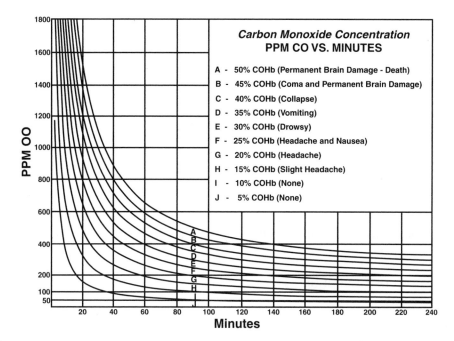

FIGURE 16.3 Carbon monoxide blood concentrations vs. time and severity of exposure. (Adapted from Leitkin, J. and Paloucek, F., *Poisoning and Toxicology Handbook,* Lexicomp, 1996. With permission.)

$$\% \text{ HbCO} = 6 \text{ L/min} \times \% \text{CO} \times \text{minutes of exposure}$$

This equation states that the percent of carboxyhemoglobin achieved in the blood is proportional to the amount of CO in the environment and the duration of exposure. Both of these factors would be expected to be important. One additional factor is represented in the equation, the tidal volume. This is the amount of air entering and leaving the lungs with each minute. An average tidal volume is 6 L/min. Logically, one would expect that an individual's capacity to inspire air would relate to the degree of normal oxygenation and also the degree of poisoning when the inspired air contains a toxin like CO. An example of the use of this equation is the following:

If a person with normal pulmonary function is exposed to 1% of CO for 10 min, what concentration of HbCO is reached?

$$\% \text{HbCO} = 6 \times 1 \times 10 = 60\%$$

METABOLISM OF CO

Approximately 1% of an inspired dose of CO is metabolized to carbon dioxide. The main path of elimination, however, is pulmonary exhalation. The half-life of CO excretion from the blood is related to oxygen pressure within the blood and is about 4.5 hours under normal conditions. If the victim is treated with 100% oxygen, the

TABLE 16.1
Relationship between HbCO Blood Level and Symptoms

%HbCO	Signs
<10	No symptoms
10–30	Headache, exertional dyspnea, dizziness
30–50	Confusion, nausea, vomiting, syncope, tachypnea
50–60	Syncope, possible coma and/or convulsions
60–70	Probable coma, depressed cardiac and pulmonary function
70–80	Respiratory failure, death imminent
>80	Death unless immediate intervention

half-life of HbCO drops to 80 min. and it drops further to 23 min. under 2 atmos. of pressure. Treatment with greater than 1 atmos. pressure is referred to as hyperbaric therapy.

SYMPTOMS OF CO POISONING

There is an approximate relationship between the blood level of HbCO and symptoms. These are described in Table 16.1.

It is difficult to correlate blood levels with clinical findings exactly because the duration of exposure, that is, how long the patient has experienced the elevated blood level of HbCO, is critical. Blood levels are also subject to misinterpretation if the patient has been exposed to air or oxygen between the time of poisoning and the time blood was collected for testing. In that case some of the HbCO will already have been eliminated and the result the laboratory gives on blood collected later will underestimate the severity of poisoning.

CO has many effects on the heart. In animal experiments it has produced ventricular arrhythmias and in humans it has caused anginal pain and electrocardiogram irregularities. CO is known to cause gradual deterioration of myocardial function and subjects with impaired cardiac function are at increased risk of injury from exposure to CO. When death occurs from CO the immediate cause is believed to be myocardial ischemia. Complete recovery is possible after CO exposure, especially if the victim has experienced only low levels of exposure. However, permanent impairment is the rule after high level exposure. Neurological testing demonstrates neuropsychiatric damage, personality deterioration, and sensory impairment months or years after the time of exposure.

CARBON MONOXIDE TESTING

Physical Signs

CO imparts a cherry pink discoloration to the skin. It is blotchy in character and is virtually pathognomonic of carbon monoxide. It is due to the inherent color of carboxyhemoglobin which absorbs light at wavelengths different from the absorption maxima of oxyhemoglobin.

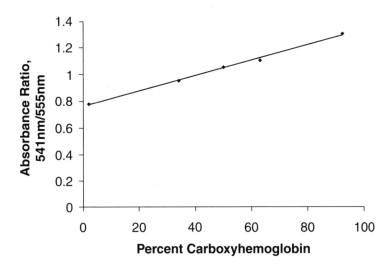

FIGURE 16.4 Spectrophotometric method for measurement of carbon monoxide. Sample calibration curve.

Photometric Method and Automated Versions

The absorption of light in the visible range by carboxyhemoglobin is the basis of tests for CO in blood. A rapid test may be conducted by adding 1 part of 0.01 M ammonia to 20 parts blood and noting the pink color which develops. This is suggestive of the presence of HbCO. To confirm the presence of HbCO, one evaluates the absorption of light at 541 and 555 nm, near the absorption maxima for carboxyhemoglobin. A problem occurs insofar as oxyhemoglobin absorbs light in the same region and, without some additional treatment, would cause a massive interference. However, oxyhemoglobin, but not carboxyhemoglobin, can be reduced by sodium dithionite. This reduction of oxyhemoglobin to deoxyhemoglobin is accompanied by a spectral shift for oxyhemoglobin only. As a result, a simple method is available in which the specimen is reduced with sodium dithionite and its absorbance is determined at 541 and 555 nm. The resulting ratio is proportional to the percent carboxyhemoglobin in the specimen. A standard curve, such as that shown in Figure 16.4, is prepared and used to evaluate the percent of carboxyhemoglobin in an unknown. This analysis can be conducted in an automated manner by several instruments including the Co-oximeter manufactured by Instrumentation Laboratories.

THERAPY

The goal of CO therapy is to improve oxygenation especially of the vital organs, the heart and brain. Oxygen treatment is the mainstay of therapy. The amount of oxygen is estimated by clinical presentation with some guidance being provided by the laboratory's measurement of HbCO (Table 16.2).

The advantage of hyperbaric oxygen is that it shortens the half-life of HbCO as described earlier. It also supersaturates the blood and tissues with oxygen and thereby

TABLE 16.2
CO Therapy

Laboratory Result (HbCO)	Intervention
<15%	Rest patient and assure that he/she is removed from CO source
15–40%	Give 100% oxygen
>40%	Give hyperbaric (2–3 atmos pressure) oxygen

transfers some oxygen to tissue. At 2.5 atmos. of oxygen the dissolved oxygen is 5.6 vol. %. This compares with 0.2 vol. % under normal conditions. Therefore, hyperbaric oxygen means that the dissolved oxygen is 25 times greater than normal and the percent of oxygen supplied by this route is perhaps 20% of the body's normal needs. On the other hand, hyperbaric therapy is not without risk. Decompression sickness (the bends) can occur and oxygen toxicity is a possibility.

CYANIDE

Cyanide has, perhaps, the most macabre history of any toxin. It was used in the mass poisoning of the religious followers of the demented yet charismatic James Jones in his South American refuge, Jonestown. This tragic event, which occurred in 1978, resulted in the deaths of 900 persons. After forcing his followers to drink a light beverage heavily laced with potassium cyanide, Jones committed suicide by shooting himself.

Cyanide has been used as a means of legal execution in many states and was possibly chosen for this purpose because of its rapid action and, therefore, alleged humane character. California was one of those states that executed the condemned in the gas chamber. Cyanide was used by a murderer in the Chicago area who managed to contaminate Tylenol tablets with large amounts of sodium cyanide. This was perpetrated in the 1980s and the murderer has never been apprehended. Probably the most infamous application of cyanide as a vehicle of death was in the extermination camps which dotted Eastern Europe during the Second World War. It is estimated that over 6 million Jews and others were killed with this deadly gas.

Cyanide appears in many forms. Among the most lethal is hydrogen cyanide gas. Cyanide arises from the combustion of many compounds including silk, nylon, solid plastics, polyurethane, and melamine resins. It is present in salts such as sodium and potassium cyanide, which have already been mentioned. Cyanide is found in many plants, especially in the seeds of apple, pear, and apricot. These are known as cyanogenic plants because the cyanide is in the form of an organic compound and is liberated as toxic cyanide only after metabolic action (see Chapter 25 on plants). Cyanide even arises from the metabolism of some pharmaceuticals. For example, nitroprusside is a medication given for control of blood pressure. One of its metabolites is cyanide. In some patients this metabolite may have caused fatalities because the patient's health was undermined already and/or because the patient produced an abnormally large amount of cyanide in his metabolism. There are many other odd ways in which cyanide reaches human environments. One example is the illicit manufacture of phencyclidine (PCP). KCN is sometimes used in this process and is converted to cyclohexane carbonitrile. This final compound is often found in street-level PCP.

TOXICITY

Cyanide binds tightly to ferric ion, Fe^{3+}, in cytochrome oxidase as well as over 40 other enzymes. Its binding to cytochrome oxidase is especially problematic because this action shuts down the electron transport system, preventing the final step in the oxidation of NADH by molecular oxygen. See Figure 16.1 for the structure of cyanide bound to heme, a prosthetic group of both hemoglobin and cytochrome oxidase.

The poisoned organism is reduced to a dependency on anaerobic metabolism which is insufficient to meet its energy needs. The net effect is equivalent to total anoxia. An overwhelming lactic acidosis occurs quickly and death is very rapid if the dose is sufficiently high. There is no defect in oxygen transport in cyanide poisoning. Therefore, the blood may be fully oxygenated initially. The symptoms of hypoxia without cyanosis are suggestive of cyanide poisoning. Death may occur very rapidly. In one case of cyanide poisoning via contamination of a cold remedy, the victim was dead before his body hit the ground. In terms of speed of action, HCN gas is faster than the salts of cyanide because it enters quickly through the extensive pulmonary area, whereas the salts have to be absorbed, a characteristically slower process.

If the cyanide dose is small, its toxicity is manifested as headache, dizziness, tachypnea, and tachycardia. Large doses cause apnea, seizures, and death. Initially, cyanide stimulates chemoreceptors in the carotid and aortic bodies causing tachycardia and tachypnea. The progressive hypoxia eventually leads to CNS anoxia and associated convulsions. The immediate cause of death is often respiratory arrest.

THERAPY

There are effective antidotes for cyanide if they are provided to the victim in a timely manner, a very difficult thing because of the rapid onset of cyanide action. The design of an efficacious cyanide antidote is an interesting example of combining knowledge from several different areas of human study. One area is biochemistry which shows that there is an endogenous pathway for the disposal of cyanide:

$$CN^- + S_2O_3^{2-} \rightarrow SCN^- + SO_3^{2-}$$

In this pathway the enzyme rhodanase reacts with thiosulfate (a product of amino acid metabolism) and cyanide and produces thiocyanate and sulfite. The thiocyanate is excreted into the urine. This pathway is easily overwhelmed and can in no way keep up with the large amounts of cyanide present in a poisonous ingestion. Two other relevant findings are the discoveries that both amyl nitrite or methylene blue are helpful in reducing the severity of cyanide poisoning. Eventually, it became clear that these two compounds have a common mechanism, the conversion of hemoglobin to its oxidized form, methemoglobin, which functions as a "cyanide sink." Methemoglobin has a ferric ion and so can compete with the ferric ion of cytochrome oxidase for cyanide. It is possible by using these hemoglobin-oxidizing agents to easily produce much more methemoglobin than the entire bodily content of cytochrome oxidase. In fact, the amount of cytochrome oxidase in the body is much less than the amount of hemoglobin. The cyanide antidote, therefore, was prepared with three ingredients: amyl nitrite, sodium nitrite, and sodium thiosulfate. It works to produce the reactions shown as follows:

$$\text{Hemoglobin} + \text{Amyl or sodium nitrite} \rightarrow \text{Methemoglobin}$$

$$CN^- + \text{Methemoglobin} \rightarrow \text{Cyanomethemoglobin}$$

$$CN^- \text{ Cytochrome oxidase} + \text{Methemoglobin} \rightarrow \text{Cytochrome oxidase} + \text{Cyanomethemoglobin}$$

$$\text{Cyanomethemoglobin} + \text{Thiosulfate} \rightarrow SCN^- + SO_3^{2-} + \text{Methemoglobin}$$

Amyl nitrite can be administered by inhalation and so it starts working quickly. This is followed by intravenous injection of sodium nitrite, which causes a much greater conversion of hemoglobin to methemoglobin. Methemoglobin combines with cyanide either free in the blood or already complexed with cytochrome oxidase. Cyanomethemoglobin is the product of these steps. The reason for the inclusion of the last ingredient, sodium thiosulfate, is that the previous reactions have some reversible character. One needs to eliminate the cyanide from the body to ensure that it will not re-bind with cytochrome oxidase. This can be done by using thiosulfate to form thiocyanate which then is excreted into the urine.

This antidote is toxic in its own right and must be administered very carefully. Formation of methemoglobin is associated with reduced ability to oxygenate tissue that can actually exacerbate the problem one is trying to solve. However, the patient can tolerate fairly high levels of methemoglobinemia but it must be kept below 50% of total hemoglobin. Nitrites also cause vasodilatation so there is a risk of hypotension which also must be avoided and watched for very carefully.

Oxygen itself has some therapeutic value. It can displace cyanide from cytochrome oxidase and restore enzyme function. The oxygen also may non-enzymatically bring about the conversion from reduced to oxidized cytochrome and get the electron transport system running again.

A new approach to cyanide poisoning is using hydroxocobalamin (Vitamin B_{12a}) as antidote. This compound combines with cyanide to form cyanocobalamin (Vitamin B_{12}) and the vitamin is excreted by the kidney. Studies in animals suggest that this method would be as effective as the one described above but involves less hazard to the patient. Up to now hydroxycobalamin has not been approved for use in the United States.

LABORATORY TESTING

Because cyanide is a rapidly acting poison, laboratory testing may be limited to postmortem evaluation. However, there is a good correlation between blood level of cyanide and severity of exposure. The correlation is not perfect and results are sometimes misleading because what really matters is not the blood level but the concentration of cyanide deep in the cell at the enzyme binding site. As was true for CO, the duration of poisoning is also an important factor. Nevertheless, blood levels of cyanide are interpreted in the following manner:

Interpretation	Cyanide Concentration
Normal, nonsmoking	0.016 µg/mL
Normal, smoking	0.041
No symptoms	<0.200
Tachycardia	0.50–1.0
Stupor and agitation	1.0–2.5
Coma, possible fatality	>2.5

These correlations were found when whole blood, not serum, was tested. Cyanide concentrates in the red cells. Only 1% of the total cyanide is in the plasma portion of blood.

A classical method for cyanide testing involves the Conway microdiffusion apparatus. This is illustrated in Figure 16.5. In the outer part of the well the specimen is acidified and hydrogen cyanide is formed. As a gas it diffuses into the mid-part of the apparatus where it is trapped by alkali as cyanide anion. An aliquot from the middle portion is mixed with chloramine T, phosphate buffer, and pyridine barbiturate. A chromophore with absorption maximum at 580 nm is formed in proportion to the cyanide concentration in the specimen.

Reaction in outer ring: $CN^- + H^+ \rightarrow HCN$

Reaction in inner ring: $HCN + NaOH \rightarrow Na^+ + CN^- + HOH$

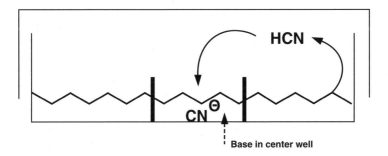

FIGURE 16.5 Conway diffusion apparatus viewed from the side.

TABLE 16.3
Properties of Toxic Sulfides

Compound	BP	Density	TLV	Odor Threshold
H_2S	−61	1.192 g/mL	10 ppm	0.0047 ppm
CS_2	46	1.260	10	0.1 ppm
CH_3SH	43	0.90	0.5	0.0016 ppm
C_2H_5SH	95	0.5	N/A	N/A

NA, data not available.

This method works well but takes a long time to perform. There are very few ways to speed up the diffusion step and this is the reason it cannot be used in emergency medicine.

A product which is suitable for rapid analysis has been developed and marketed under the name Cyantosno. It is paper-based with reagents pre-soaked into paper. The specimen is added and a color change is noted in a very short time. The detection limit is 0.2 μg/mL, which is low enough to make the product clinically valuable.

SULFIDES

Several gases composed of sulfur and other elements are industrially important and potentially toxic (Table 16.3).

Hydrogen sulfide arises from many sources in nature and in industry. Its characteristic rotten egg odor is well-known and it is found as a by-product of coal coking and petroleum refining. One of the most notorious cases of hydrogen sulfide poisoning was an episode in Mexico in 1950. A flare intended to oxidize hydrogen sulfide to sulfur dioxide as it arose out of natural gas became extinguished. Twenty-two people were asphyxiated and died in their sleep.

Hydrogen sulfide is a product of putrefaction and is, as a consequence, often found in high concentrations in sewers. Because of this and also that it is heavier than air, there have been a number of fatalities in which workers died when descending ladders into sewers where they suddenly encountered lethal build-ups of hydrogen sulfide.

Hydrogen sulfide is also employed in the tanning industry. A tragic incident occurred in Chicago involving this gas in 1977. Seven people were killed in a tanning factory, most of them instantly, when sulfuric acid was accidentally mixed with an inorganic sulfide in large quantity. Hydrogen sulfide was the toxic product of this rapid reaction.

TOXICITY OF SULFIDES

Hydrogen sulfide has two major toxic actions. The first is a depressant effect on the CNS. A result of this effect is paralysis of the respiratory center and death. The second is inhibition of cytochrome oxidase in a manner very similar to the effect of cyanide. H_2S is actually a more potent inhibitor of cytochrome oxidase than is cyanide.

Carbon disulfide has some toxic features in common with H_2S. It attacks the CNS and the cardiovascular system. However, it has its own uniquely toxic character in causing a peripheral neuropathy with cranial nerve damage (see Chapter 10 on neurotoxins). Curiously, it is also atherogenic in experimental animals.

THERAPY

The cyanide antidote kit is effective with H_2S poisoning. The nitrites within the kit convert hemoglobin to methemoglobin which becomes an agent for binding hydrogen sulfide before it can bind cytochrome oxidase and cause death. Sulfmethemoglobin is formed by the reaction between methemoglobin and either H_2S or hydrogen sulfide anion and this substance is excreted into the urine as such or as nontoxic metabolites.

LABORATORY TESTING

Hydrogen sulfide is like cyanide in the sense that many victims will die too soon for laboratory evaluation to be of any help. However, testing for sulfide ion in blood may help to make the diagnosis for those who are less disabled. An ion-selective electrode has been developed for measurement of sulfide ion. Because this electrode is not completely specific to sulfide to the exclusion of all other ions, it is necessary to pre-treat the specimen and isolate sulfide. This has been done, in one method, with Conway microdiffusion cells. Concentrations of sulfide ion found in H_2S deaths ranged from 1.7 to 3.75 µg/mL.

HYDROCARBONS

By definition these are compounds which contain only carbon and hydrogen. Many such compounds have been identified in the natural world, a good number of which are found in crude oil. They include the aliphatic alkanes, alkenes, and alkynes, which differ among each other in regard to the saturation of the carbon atoms. The most common members of this class are methane, ethane, propane, and butane. All members of this category are very abundant in the industrial world. The aromatic hydrocarbons include benzene and the many compounds derived from benzene.

Halogenated hydrocarbons and organohalide insecticides are similar to hydrocarbons in some chemical and toxicological properties; however, they also have unique toxicological traits and will be discussed in a separate section of this text.

CHEMICAL CHARACTERISTICS

From the viewpoint of toxicology the important features of hydrocarbons are molecular weight, volatility, surface tension, and viscosity. All of these traits are related to intermolecular bonding which, for this class of very nonpolar molecules, is weak van der Waals-type attractions. It is characteristic of van der Waals attractions to increase in magnitude with molecular weight. Van der Waals forces are thought to be due to temporary distortion of the molecule's electron cloud which gives the molecule a short-lived dipole character. Two hydrocarbon molecules with temporary dipoles are

TABLE 16.4
Some Normal Alkanes

Name	Formula	Melting Point (°C)	Boiling Point (°C)
Methane	CH_4	−183	−162
Ethane	CH_3CH_3	−172	−88.5
Propane	$CH_2CH_3CH_3$	−187	−42
Butane	C_4H_{10}	−135	−0.5
Octane	C_8H_{16}	−57	126

attracted temporarily to each other. This phenomenon, when extended to the entire population of molecules in a hydrocarbon sample, is responsible for intermolecular attractions that dictate the boiling and melting points of the compound. Therefore, to a first approximation, the higher the molecular weight of the hydrocarbon (the larger and more distortion prone the electron cloud), the higher its boiling point, the lower its volatility, the greater its viscosity and surface tension. These important physical characteristics, therefore, correlate with molecular weight. See Table 16.4 in which alkane molecular weight is shown to be a close function of boiling point.

Volatility is the ability of a substance to vaporize, that is, convert to a gaseous form. Surface tension describes the adherence, i.e., cohesiveness of molecules along a liquid surface (creeping ability). Viscosity, another important property, is resistance to flow through a calibrated orifice. It is sometimes described as resistance to stirring and is measured in Saybolt seconds universal (SSU). For example, at SSU less than 60 a substance has low viscosity and there is a high risk of inhalation and aspiration. If these compounds enter the stomach they may be transferred to the lung by forming a vapor, and then cross into the blood from the lung. If SSU is greater than 100, on the other hand, it is not likely to be aspirated. Hydrocarbons with low viscosity and high volatility, that is, those of low molecular weight, can be ingested and then spread over mucosal surfaces posing a significant danger of aspiration. On the contrary, hydrocarbons with high molecular weight are less mobile. If they should happen to be ingested, they are more likely to remain as inert masses within the gastrointestinal tract and are not volatile enough to go from the stomach to the lung. The worst scenario is one in which a victim is exposed to large quantities of a compound with high volatility, low viscosity, and low surface tension. Such a substance can be breathed directly into the lungs or aspirated from the gastrointestinal tract. The effect of its low surface tension is that it will not be likely to stay in a "safe" bodily area as a result of some weak molecular attraction to that tissue. Lacking even weak binding to that tissue, it may migrate to the lungs and thence into the blood.

TOXICITY

Table 16.5 shows the major effects of aliphatic exposures with the two major forms of toxicity, CNS damage and pulmonary aspiration. In the table the substances are listed in ascending order by molecular weight. Their volatilities and viscosities are approximated. As expected, these two properties usually are related inversely to each other.

TABLE 16.5
Toxicity of Components of Petroleum

Component	Volatile Yes/No	Viscous Yes/No	CNS Toxicity	Pulmonary Toxicity
Gases	Y	N	High	No
Benzine	Y	N	High	No
Gasoline	Y	N	High	Mod.
Naphtha	Y	N	High	Mod.
Kerosene	N	N	Mod.	High
Mineral oil	N	N	No	High
Lubricants	N	Y	No	No

When aspirated, hydrocarbons immediately irritate the oral mucosa and bronchial tree. Coughing, choking, and gasping result. Pulmonary air may be replaced by the hydrocarbon which causes cyanosis. As the gas spreads to the lower bronchial tree, hypoxia intensifies and bronchospasm may occur. Hydrocarbons within the lung have the capacity to directly destroy the lung tissue and this leads to inflammation, necrotizing bronchopneumonia, and formation of hyaline membranes. Bloody sputum and hemorrhagic pulmonary edema may progress to shock and cardiorespiratory arrest in severe cases.

Hydrocarbons entering the blood either through the lung or from the GI tract (the latter is uncommon) become toxic to the central nervous system. One of the major mechanisms of such toxicity is attack on the large lipid component of neural tissue, especially myelin. Because hydrocarbons are lipid solvents they will undermine the normal structure of the nervous tissue. The most common physical findings are headache, ataxia, blurred vision, dizziness, lethargy, and/or stupor. These findings are due to acute exposure to hydrocarbons. Persons exposed on a chronic basis, e.g., through occupational exposure, have more serious symptoms. These include neurobehavioral and intellectual impairment. Also observed are neuroasthenia, personality disorders, and sensory-motor peripheral neuropathy.

It is also possible to discuss toxicity in relation to the mode of exposure. If hydrocarbons are ingested, they are usually not well absorbed. Exceptions to this statement include some aromatic hydrocarbons and natural oils which are absorbed from the stomach. When ingested, they may produce CNS depression, seizures, and some degree of renal and liver impairment. Although it was stated that aliphatic hydrocarbons are poorly absorbed, large ingestions do result in some degree of systemic absorption. This may lead to hemolysis, bloody diarrhea, and low levels of liver or kidney injury.

If aspiration is the route of entry, the symptoms described above are found. These can all develop rapidly, within the first day of exposure. Fever and tachypnea are also noted. Patients who have inhaled hydrocarbons often have seizures, encephalopathy, and cardiac arrhythmias. A special case is known as "sudden sniffing death" and is found in individuals who abuse hydrocarbons, a practice called "huffing." In this disorder, the victim's myocardium is sensitized to catecholamines by the inhaled hydrocarbon. This sensitization renders the heart very prone to arrhythmias, even fatal ventricular fibrillation, which has been responsible for the sudden deaths of many recreational inhalers of solvents. On some occasions the inhaler was surprised by a sudden change, e.g., the unexpected appearance of a parent while he was huffing, and this surprise elicited an endogenous release of catecholamines leading to his death.

THERAPY

If the exposure was by ingestion no specific treatment is usually necessary. In particular, do not induce vomiting of a volatile, nonviscous hydrocarbon. Of course, if the hydrocarbon has insecticidal properties it may be necessary to try to limit exposure.

If the hydrocarbon was aspirated, give supplemental oxygen, and aerosolized bronchodilators if the patient is suffering from bronchospasm. Do not give epinephrine as a bronchodilator because it is a catecholamine and may conduce to the sudden sniffing death described above. Corticosteroids have been given to reduce the bronchial inflammation but this is sometimes problematic. They may alter the tracheal flora in favor of Gram-negative organisms.

If the hydrocarbon is inhaled, the patient is sometimes hyperactive and sedative medication may be needed. If the patient is seizing, anticonvulsant medication should be considered. However, seizures from these sources are usually brief and benign and it is usually better to withhold anti-seizure medicines.

LABORATORY TESTING

Gas chromatography can be used to identify the specific hydrocarbon ingested, although this information will often be available from history. A strong correlation between the amount of hydrocarbon exposure and the blood level does not exist nor is the probable outcome very predictable from the blood level. One other limitation is that the laboratory testing will probably take a long time because only a few laboratories do this kind of testing. Finally, the treating physician is better guided in handling the patient by clinical signs including cough, choking, lethary, chest sounds, cyanosis, tachypnea, fever, and leucocytosis.

Questions

1. Calculate the percent of hemoglobin in a person's blood after the individual has had a long-term exposure to carbon monoxide at an ambient concentration of 1000 ppm.
2. What percent of oxygen is released from oxyhemoglobin in the liver if the ambient partial pressure of oxygen in the liver is 20 mm and there is zero carbon monoxide present? What is the percent oxygen released if the carboxyhemoglobin is 45%?
3. Compare the dangers to a person who swallows 50 mL of benzene vs. the hazards associated with swallowing 50 mL of dodecane.

4. A measurement of carbon monoxide is made by the photometric method and the following data are collected:

%CO	A_{541}	A_{555}
20% standard	0.134	0.167
100% standard	0.640	0.512
Unknown	0.430	0.420

Calculate the saturation of carbon monoxide in the unknown.

Case Study 1: Hazards of Heating

A 20-year-old white woman and her husband were found unconscious in their mobile home. While being transported to the hospital they received 100% supplemental oxygen. Upon arrival they were both described as disoriented, restless, and combative. The woman was on a ventilator which she activated 26 times each minute. Carbonaceous material was found in her nose and oropharynx. No burns were observed. Her blood carboxyhemoglobin level was 7%. Peripheral cyanosis was seen in her nail beds. Findings from her abdominal examination were consistent with a 28-week pregnancy. No fetal movement could be detected by ultrasound and fetal heart sounds were absent. On the following day spontaneous labor began and a 1 kg stillborn female fetus was delivered. Gross autopsy of the fetus revealed bright red discoloration of the skin and internal organs. Carboxyhemoglobin level in the fetus was 61%. It was later discovered that the usual heater in the mobile home was broken and a portable propane heater was being used to provide heat on a temporary basis. The propane heater was in need of maintenance work and burned inefficiently with the release of large amounts of carbon monoxide.

Questions

Q1. Which of the following is a major factor affecting this woman's blood carboxyhemoglobin level?
   a) Co-existing pregnancy status
   b) Therapy enroute to the hospital
   c) The woman's age
   d) Her combative, disoriented, restless behavior in the hospital
Q2. What factor contributed to greater toxicity to the fetus than the mother?
   a) Slower rate of CO elimination
   b) Delayed response to therapeutic maneuvers
   c) Greater left shift
   d) All of the above

Q3. What was a specific clue to the mother's diagnosis?
     a) Restless, combative presentation
     b) Peripheral cyanosis in nail beds
     c) Carbonaceous material in nose and oropharynx
     d) Frequency of ventilator activation

Answers and Discussion

Q1. (Answer = b) The aggressive therapy which she received enroute to the hospital was, undoubtedly, a major factor in the relatively low carboxy-hemoglobin result she manifested on testing. The elimination of carbon monoxide from the blood depends greatly on the concentration of oxygen because the two gases are competing for hemoglobin. Under normal conditions (standard pressure of air) the elimination half-life of carbon monoxide is 4 to 6 hours, whereas this half-life is reduced to 1 hour in the presence of 100% oxygen. The patient's laboratory result of 7% carboxy-hemoglobin is inconsistent with her symptoms, including her unconscious state when first found in the mobile home. This small concentration of carboxyhemoglobin is expected to produce only minor symptoms such as headache. When found after a period of 100% oxygen therapy, however, the result has no basis for interpretation in relation to clinical findings.

Q2. (Answer = d) The risk to a fetus in the event of CO exposure is even greater than the risk to the pregnant woman. In the first place fetal car-boxyhemoglobin rises more slowly than maternal carboxyhemoglobin, but it eventually reaches a level at which carboxyhemoglobin is about 10% higher than the maternal level. In addition, the rate of carboxyhe-moglobin elimination from the fetus is slower. The maternal rate of elim-ination can be enormously increased by supplemental or hyperbaric oxygen. Benefits of these therapeutic maneuvers to the fetus are much less pronounced. Another factor working to the disadvantage of the fetus is that the left shift is more significant with hemoglobin F than with the hemoglobin A found in the mother. As a consequence of all of these factors, it is suggested that pregnant patients who have been exposed to CO should be treated more aggressively and for longer periods than would be appropriate for a nonpregnant individual.

Q3. (Answer = c) Most of these suggested responses are consistent with CO poisoning but they are not specific. Peripheral cyanosis or frequent acti-vation of a ventilator could arise from many different causes of hypoxia. Her behavior is especially uninformative and merely indicates an erratic state of mind probably due to an organic or drug cause. The observation of carbonaceous material, however, strongly suggests that she was in the presence of incomplete combustion. When heating devices malfunction they produce carbon monoxide and carbon as incomplete products of oxidation of fossil fuels.

Reference

Farrow, J. et al., Fetal death due to nonlethal maternal carbon monoxide poisoning, *J. Forens. Sci.,* 35, 1448–1452, 1990.

Case Study 2: A Fatal Midnight Swim

On a July evening a group of teenagers decided to go for a midnight boat ride on a small freshwater lake. They motored about 500 yards to the middle of the lake and two of the party, a boy and a girl, jumped into the lake from the rear of the boat. The rest of the group stayed onboard because they found the water too cold for swimming. The boy who jumped in for a swim requested that the motor be left running in order "to warm the cold water" in which they were swimming. After 10 min he felt tired and cold and climbed back on board. While he watched his female companion in the water he observed her diving under the water. She did not re-surface immediately and he became alarmed. He called 911 to summon help. The conversation was recorded and, upon subsequent analysis, it was noted that his breathing rate was 40 breaths a minute.

The remains of the girl were not recovered until 5 days later. Her body was at a depth of 50 ft and lividity was noted to be pink and posterior. Full rigor was present.

Evidence presented so far suggests that the cause of death is probably:
   a) Hypothermia
   b) Trauma
   c) Carbon monoxide
   d) Drug overdose

None of these causes can be unequivocally ruled out on the basis of the given information. However, hypothermia is highly improbable because the swim was too brief in duration. Although temperatures are not given, it seems reasonable to infer that the lake was not very cold based upon its geographic location and the time of year. The finding of an elevated breathing rate in the surviving swimmer and the observation of pink lividity in the decedent are strongly suggestive of carbon monoxide poisoning.

Autopsy found no evidence of trauma. Lungs were heavy and filled with congestion and edema. The brain had a pink discoloration. Toxicology testing was negative for all drugs but a low concentration of alcohol was found. Methemoglobin was negative but carboxyhemoglobin was positive at 51% in the femoral blood and 62% in the heart blood. Subsequent testing of the boat and engine showed that exhaust gas vented at the water level when the boat is idling. At speed the exhaust is vented underwater through the propeller as well as at the water surface. The concentration of carbon monoxide in the air space immediately behind the engine and just above the water surface was greater than 100 ppm.

Questions

Q1. What level of carboxyhemoglobin would be expected from exposure to 100 ppm of carbon monoxide for 2 hours?
  a) 5%
  b) 24%
  c) 7.2%
  d) 72%

Q2. Which of the following is not a source of carbon monoxide?
  a) Automobiles with obstructed exhaust systems
  b) Boats with enclosed cabins
  c) Charcoal heaters
  d) Wood fire at a campsite

Q3. What other factors may have contributed to the absorption of carbon monoxide?
  a) The exercise activity of the swimmers
  b) The temperature of the water
  c) The fact that the episode happened at night
  d) Racial origin of the victim

Q4. Which of the following is an aspect of CO toxicity?
  a) CO displaces oxygen from receptors of the cytochrome oxidase system.
  b) CO competes with oxygen for binding sites on hemoglobin.
  c) CO causes a left shift in hemoglobin dissociation curve.
  d) All of the above.

Answers and Discussion

Q1. (Answer = c) This answer may be found by scrutinizing Figure 16.3. It can also be determined from calculation using the formula:

$$\% \, HbCO = 6 \, L/min \times \% \, CO \times minutes \, of \, exposure$$

Q2. (Answer = d) The critical concept in relation to carbon monoxide generation is that it arises where fossil fuels are burned incompletely or exhaust gases are allowed to accumulate. Automobile exhaust used to be a common source of carbon monoxide especially if the engine was not operating efficiently as, for example, in congested traffic. With modern catalytic converters and gasoline additives, much less carbon monoxide is present in automobile exhaust. An open fire at a campsite would be the least suspect among the sources listed because the fire should have an ample supply of oxygen to guarantee that the products of combustion are fully oxidized to carbon dioxide rather than carbon monoxide. Further, the products of combustion would have no opportunity to accumulate.

Q3. (Answer = a) A major factor in carbon monoxide absorption is the breathing rate. If an individual is exercising, he/she will have elevated respirations and is expected to inhale more carbon monoxide. If the water is cold, this makes a small contribution toward heightened absorption because blood flow is increased as one mechanism for dealing with hypothermia. For some ethnic groups, varieties of hemoglobin are present that bind carbon monoxide with slightly more avidity. This may possibly elevate carboxyhemoglobin as well.

Q4. (Answer = d) Carbon monoxide's mechanism of toxicity is multifactorial. Its major action is competition with oxygen for hemoglobin binding. It is also toxic, however, by provoking a left shift in hemoglobin dissociation. Therefore, at a specific partial pressure of oxygen, more hemoglobin is oxygen bound. The result of this left shift is a reduced level of tissue perfusion. Within the mitochondria of the cell carbon monoxide will interfere with electron transport by displacing oxygen from receptors of the cytochrome oxidase system.

This case illustrates the intense affinity of carbon monoxide for hemoglobin. Despite the open air environment and the relatively unlimited availability of air, the decedent had sufficient exposure to carbon monoxide to cause her death.

Reference

Jumbelic, M., Open air carbon monoxide poisoning, *J. Forens. Sci.,* 43, 228–230, 1998.

Case Study 3: The Boy with the Fingernail Remover

A 2-year-old, 26-lb. boy was brought to the emergency department because of profound lethargy. Ten hours earlier he had been found with an empty bottle of *Super Nail Nail Off*, a preparation used to remove sculptured fingernails and known to contain 98 to 100% acetonitrile. Thirty milliliters of the contents of this bottle appeared to have been ingested by the child or spilled onto his person. In the emergency department he was noted to be pale and barely responsive to deep pain. His pulse rate and respirations were elevated and his blood pressure was low. Extremities were cool and a slight cyanosis was observed. Laboratory studies showed the following:

Arterial pH	6.95
Partial pressure of CO_2	11 mm
Partial pressure of O_2	114 mm
Serum bicarbonate	4 meq/L
Creatinine	70.7 μmol/L

Chest X-ray was normal and the ECG showed a sinus tachycardia.

The child was immediately given oxygen at 10 L/min by face mask. Bicarbonate infusion and fluid resuscitation were started. He was admitted to ICU and electrolytes and arterial blood gases were monitored and corrected. The patient responded to this supportive care and was discharged on the 3rd hospital day without any residual symptoms.

What was the proximate probable cause of the presenting symptoms?
   a) Chloroform
   b) Cyanide
   c) Carbon monoxide
   d) Hydrogen sulfide

This case could be diagnosed on the basis of history although the presentation was also classical for the specific toxin, cyanide. It was believed that acetonitrile in the nail remover was the only chemical to which he was exposed. Acetonitrile is also known as methyl cyanide (CH_3CN) and is metabolized to hydrogen cyanide. Initially, acetonitrile is oxidized to a cyanohydrin intermediate followed immediately by degradation to HCN plus an aldehyde. All of his symptoms are characteristic of cyanide poisoning. An important difference between acetonitrile and direct cyanide poisoning is the fact that the cyanide appears gradually as a metabolic product. Unlike the situation of abrupt exposure to pure HCN gas or cyanide salts such as NaCN, the symptoms have a slow onset and the prognosis is usually much better. Whole blood cyanide in this patient was 231 μmol/L (231 μg/dL) 12 hours after ingestion, 69 μmol/L 48 hours after ingestion, and 15 μmol/L 12 hours after that. Although acetonitrile is much less toxic than cyanide and this patient survived a large exposure, there are cases in the literature in which patients died from cyanide overdose brought on by methyl cyanide exposure.

Questions

Q1. The lethal dose of cyanide is close to 1 mg/kg. How much was this child exposed to if he ingested the full 30 mL and it was stoichiometrically converted to CN? (Specific gravity of acetonitrile is 0.786 g/mL.)
   a) 15 mg
   b) 2.1 g
   c) 1 kg
   d) 14.95 g
Q2. Why was this patient's bicarbonate much below normal?
   a) Excretion into the urine due to a renal effect from the cyanide
   b) Loss of carbon dioxide in compensation for the metabolic acidosis
   c) Respiratory acidosis due to slowing of respirations
   d) Metabolic acidosis due to inhibition of aerobic oxidation
Q3. Direct cyanide measurement is not usually available. What is a fairly specific laboratory finding that is a substitute for cyanide testing?

  a) Severe depression of arterial pH
  b) Lactic acidosis
  c) An abnormal arterial-venous oxygen saturation gradient
  d) Elevated anion gap
Q4. What other substances are toxic via conversion to cyanide?
  a) Sodium nitroprusside
  b) Amygdalin
  c) Calcium cyanamide
  d) All of the above
  e) None of the above
Q5. Some patients have been treated effectively for cyanide poisoning with
    hydroxycobalamin. The mechanism of its action is
  a) It converts hemoglobin to methemoglobin which serves as a cyanide sink.
  b) It binds cyanide and converts it to vitamin B_{12}, hydroxycobalamin.
  c) It binds cyanide and converts it to vitamin B_6.
  d) It expedites the excretion of cyanide as thiocyanate.

Answers and Discussion

Q1. (Answer = d) Thirty mL of methyl cyanide weigh 23.6 g. Methyl cyanide
    has molecular weight equal to 41 g/mol. Assuming complete conversion
    to cyanide anion (MW = 26 g/mol) 14.9 g of cyanide anion are formed
    from 23.6 g of methyl cyanide. This child is 26 lbs. or 11.8 kg and,
    therefore, 12 mg is a potentially fatal dose of cyanide. He survived,
    however, more than 1000 times this amount in the form of a cyanide
    precursor.
Q2. (Answer = d) Cyanide inhibits aerobic respiration and the body shifts to
    anaerobic metabolism in an attempt to maintain life. Lactic acid is pro-
    duced in large quantities and it consumes bicarbonate.
Q3. (Answer = c) All of the choices offered in this question are correct in the
    sense that they usually are noted in cyanide exposure. Most of them are
    at best, semispecific, with the exception of (c) an abnormal oxygen gra-
    dient. This occurs because oxygen is not removed from arterial blood in
    the normal way for oxidative respiration. When the blood reaches the
    venous side, therefore, it has an abnormally high content of oxygen, i.e.,
    the gradient between oxygen in the veins and oxygen in the arteries is
    below normal.
Q4. (Answer = d) The three substances listed here, as well as many others,
    are cyanogenic. Sodium nitroprusside is a medication for hypertension
    and some patients have become cyanide toxic by using it. Calcium cyan-
    amide is a fertilizer and amygdalin is the chemical from apricots that is
    allegedly effective in treating cancer, a specious claim as shown by numer-
    ous studies.
Q5. (Answer = b) Hydroxycobalamin is a promising new antidote for cyanide
    poisoning that converts cyanide to an active form of vitamin B_{12}. This

antidote has less toxicity than the classical antidote because it does not rely on the production of another toxin, methemoglobin, for its effectiveness.

Reference

Caravati, E.M. and Litovitz, T.L., Pediatric cyanide intoxication and death from an acetonitrile-containing cosmetic, *JAMA*, 260, 3470–3473, 1988.

Case Study 4: Two Traffic Fatalities

Two teen-aged men, an 18- and 17-year-old, were the driver and passenger, respectively, of a vehicle which suddenly crossed the median of a 4-lane highway. It then collided with a minivan, leaving the driver of that vehicle seriously injured. The occupants of the first vehicle were declared dead at the scene of the accident. An aerosol spray can was found within the vehicle. Autopsy the following day showed that the driver died from a hinge fracture at the base of the skull, and the passenger suffered transection of the brain stem.

If this accident was related to a toxic chemical what substance might possibly be involved?
   a) Ethyl alcohol
   b) Carbon monoxide
   c) Freon
   d) Barbiturates

None of these suggestions can be unequivocally ruled out up to this point. Carbon monoxide is unlikely, however. If the accident was caused by a sudden reaction to a toxin, as appears likely, CO is an improbable suspect. CO characteristically produces a gradual onset of action. Ethyl alcohol is, of course, implicated in numerous accidents. The only evidence suggesting a cause different from alcohol is the finding of the aerosol container within the vehicle. To elucidate the exact identity of an involved toxin, laboratory testing would be needed.

Headspace gas chromatography was carried out on blood and urine to search for the presence of alcohols or freon (from the aerosol container). Difluoroethane (DFE) was used as a standard for comparison with volatile components present in the blood or urine of the decedents. DFE is a new form of freon recently introduced as a propellent and intended to replace ozone-depleting chlorofluorocarbons. DFE, also known as halocarbon 152A, is a colorless and odorless gas used as a refrigerant as well as a propellent in aerosol products.

GC testing revealed alcohol at 13 mg/dL in the driver's blood and no alcohol in the passenger's blood. DFE was found in the blood of both decedents, 78 mg/dL in the driver and 35 mg/dL in the passenger.

Questions

Q1. Why is headspace GC preferable to other kinds of GC for this application?
   a) It is the only sample preparation method that resolves volatile components.
   b) It is the only sample preparation method that leads to a detector response.
   c) It provides additional specificity because only volatile components of the specimen will be analyzed.
   d) It raises the detection limit of the analysis.

Q2. What interpretation is given to the alcohol finding in the driver's blood?
   a) It is too low to support a role for alcohol in this accident.
   b) It is impressive and suggests that alcohol was probably involved in the accident.
   c) No conclusions can be drawn without greater knowledge of the exact analytical method.
   d) Irrespective of whether it was the cause of the accident the driver was driving in an intoxicated state.

Q3. What interpretation is given to the DFE finding in the driver's blood?
   a) It is probably erroneous because the analysis cannot be done correctly by GC.
   b) The results are not high enough to suggest impairment.
   c) The results are high and similar to concentrations found for other inhalants that have been found in fatal accidents.
   d) At these levels a small degree of impairment is expected but some additional factor must have contributed to the accident.

Q4. How could DFE be responsible for a very abrupt loss of control in a vehicle?
   a) The driver was probably sedated to the point of losing consciousness.
   b) The driver may have had a cardiac arrest.
   c) DFE can cause seizures which would have caused instantaneous loss of control.
   d) DFE's known effects are not compatible with sudden accidents.

Answers and Discussion

Q1. (Answer = c) In headspace analysis the specimen is heated at a low temperature and volatile components enter the airspace above the sample in a sealed vial. Only the vapor is injected. Therefore, only volatile components of the blood enter the chromatographic column. Volatile components are a small fraction of myriad possible components within blood. Analysis by another method in which the whole blood is injected results in many peaks being produced. Such methods are less specific and the chances of a false identification are increased. Resolution and detector response are not related to the specimen preparation method. Finally, headspace does not raise the detection limit. Generally, it can lower the detection limit by permitting more sample to be injected.

Q2. (Answer = a) The alcohol result, 13 mg/dL, corresponds to consumption of approximately 1 drink in an average person. It would normally have little or no effect on control of a motor vehicle.

Q3. (Answer = c) Controlled experiments have shown that the amounts of DFE found here do not arise from incidental exposure to freon as would occur by occupational exposure or everyday use as, for example, hair sprays. These levels are very high and require direct aspiration by a user in the practice referred to as "huffing." Many accidents have occurred in which the drivers were found to have inhalants in their blood in this concentration range. It is reasonable to conclude that the cause of the accident was driving under the influence of an abused substance that contributed significantly to the collision of the vehicle with another car.

Q4. (Answer = b) The driver may have been impaired in a manner very similar to that provoked by alcohol. In that case, he simply may have fallen asleep or lost control of the vehicle due to muscular incoordination. An interesting additional possibility is that the driver may have had a cardiac arrest. There are many incidents on record in which persons abusing hydrocarbons and other inhalants died from an intractable arrhythmia caused by inhalant abuse. These compounds have an ability to sensitize the myocardium to catecholamines. When this happens a sudden surprise or any cause of mild excitation could increase circulating catecholamines (epinephrine is one such compound), which could then lead to loss of normal cardiac conduction.

Reference

Broussard, L.A. et al., Two traffic fatalities related to the use of difluoroethane, *J. Forens. Sci.,* 42, 1186–1187, 1997.

17 Insecticides

CONTENTS

Insecticides are very beneficial to mankind because they help to control vector-borne diseases such as malaria, improve agricultural productivity, and reduce the angst which many forms of insects visit upon "picnicking man." Ideally, they should be entirely species-specific or, at least, specific to invertebrates. This is, of course, not the case. Some insecticides are much more lethal to insects than to higher forms of life. Nonetheless, because they are harmful to all forms of life, at least to some degree, exposure to them can be fatal and they must be discussed in texts on toxicology.

ORGANOCHLORINE INSECTICIDES

The chlorinated hydrocarbon group of insecticides is large and includes what is possibly the most controversial compound of the twentieth century, DDT, dichlorodiphenyltrichloroethane (Figure 17.1). It was synthesized 125 years ago in 1874 but its ability to eliminate insect pests was not recognized until 1939. That recognition led to the 1948 Nobel prize for the responsible scientist, Dr. Paul Mueller, a Swiss chemist. Mueller discovered the potency of DDT while screening for insecticides for the JR Geigy Company.

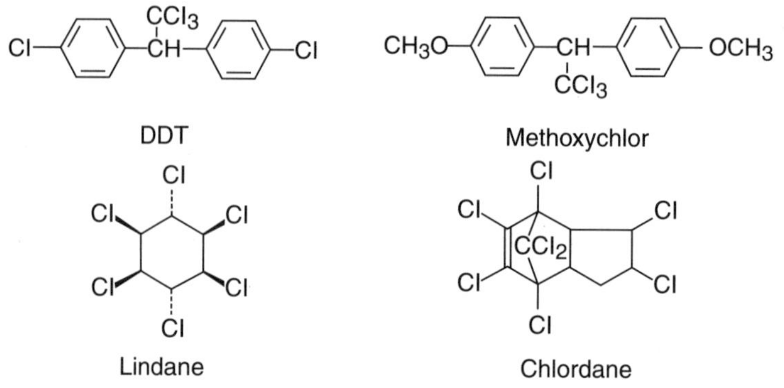

FIGURE 17.1 Structures of some organochlorine insecticides.

TABLE 17.1
Relative Selectivity of DDT

Organism	LD_{50} (mg/kg)
Honeybee	1.7
Lab rats	113
Japanese beetles	205
Bullfrogs	2000

CHEMISTRY

Table 17.1 lists important members of this category together with their structures and LD_{50}s. DDT (1,1,1-trichloro-2,2-bis(p-chlorophenyl) ethane) controlled a wide variety of insects including flies, mosquitoes, and body lice and, thus, helped to reduce the incidence of malaria, typhus, and other endemic diseases. It also appeared safe for humans and was cheap to manufacture. After the publication of *Silent Spring* by Rachel Carson, however, DDT went from a public saviour to the object of profound scorn. Many believe, however, that Carson's indictment was inaccurate or at least exaggerated.

In humans neurological signs including seizures occurred at 22 mg/kg but long-term occupational exposure to 42 mg/day produced no demonstrable neurological deficit. No toxic effects have been demonstrated on human blood, liver, skin, immunological behavior, or reproductive capacity. IARC (International Agency for Research on Cancer) labels DDT as a possible carcinogen although the vast majority of studies on the topic show no relation between DDT and cancer.

DDT and some other organochlorine insecticides act upon the nervous system, mainly on the transmission of impulses through the axon. They induce rapid and repetitive firing of the neuron. In a short time this leads to paralysis. How they cause this effect is not clear but recent research suggests that they interfere with the movement of ions through neuron membranes by delaying the closing of sodium channels, slowing the opening of potassium gates, inhibiting neuronal ATPase which controls repolarization, and blocking calcium ion transport into the neuron. An interesting property of DDT is that it has little effect above 30°C which is a factor relating to the difference in response between insects and warm-blooded mammals to DDT.

BENZENE HEXACHLORIDE (HEXACHLOROCYCLOHEXANE)

This organochlorine insecticide has the distinction of being the oldest chlorinated hydrocarbon insecticide, having been synthesized by Michael Faraday in 1825.

There are 16 possible stereoisomers of hexachlorocyclohexane. One of them, known as the gamma isomer, is also called lindane. Lindane is a neurotoxin to insects and has LD_{50} of 3.8 mg/kg in the cockroach, 1.0 mg/kg in the housefly, and in the thousands of mg/kg for most laboratory animals.

Lindane and cyclodiene insecticides act by a different mechanism from DDT. They do not manifest the temperature sensitivity shown by DDT. As a consequence, they are less selective toward insects than DDT. Lindane is an excitant that antagonizes the neurotransmitter, GABA, and the uptake of chloride ions The natural neuroexcitant, picrotoxinin, is structurally similar to lindane and acts by a similar mechanism.

CYCLODIENES

This group, which includes dieldrin, endrin, chlordane, and heptachlor, dates back to 1945. These compounds are highly lipophilic, a characteristic found throughout the organochlorine family. Unlike other organochlorides, however, they are less selective toward insects and have relatively low lethal doses for fish, birds, and mammals. They are even more persistent in the environment than many other members of the organohalide group. The half-life of aldrin in soil is 1–4 years, dieldrin, 1–7 years, and heptachlor, 7–12 years. These compounds are more like lindane than DDT in terms of the mechanism of their toxic behavior.

CAGE STRUCTURES

The insecticides, chlordecone and mirex, were discovered in the 1950s and found to be effective for the control of fire ants in the southern United States. They are very stable in the environment and their mechanism of action is not clearly known. Kepone (chlordecone) was thought to have an LD_{50} in rats of 95 mg/kg. However, with chronic exposure the LD_{50} is only 1.5 mg/kg, which makes kepone among the more severely poisonous compounds from the perspective of cumulative toxicity.

SYMPTOMS OF ORGANOCHLORINE POISONING

Exposure to organochlorine compounds is manifested by nonspecific signs such as nausea and vomiting, and apprehension. More specifically, there are central nervous system symptoms in high dose exposures. Behavioral changes are noted as well as disturbances in sensation and equilibrium, and depression of vital centers. Large exposures may cause convulsions and coma. In a manner similar to the actions of hydrocarbons, these compounds can sensitize the myocardium to catecholamines, which may lead to fatal ventricular arrhythmias.

THERAPY

There is no specific therapy for organochlorine overdose. Supportive care and treatment of symptoms are the mainstays of therapy. Gastric decontamination is usually beneficial if it can be initiated in a sufficiently rapid time frame. Anticonvulsants, especially diazepam, are usually effective for convulsions caused by this group of compounds.

ORGANOPHOSPHATE INSECTICIDES

Among the most widely used insecticides are the organophosphates, phosphoric acid or thiophosphoric acid esters of a variety of alcohols (Figure 17.2). Research in Germany during the 1930s and 1940s led to the synthesis of many of these compounds some of which, e.g., parathion, are still in use today.

TEPP, tetraethylpyrophosphate, was developed in 1944 and became the first widely used organophosphate insecticide. It was initially tried in place of nicotine to kill aphids. However, it had a short environmental half-life being readily hydrolysed

Name	Structure	LD_{50}	Half-life
TEP	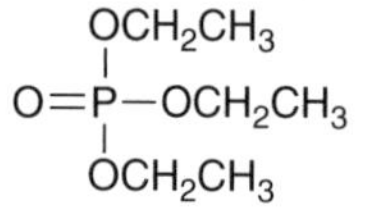 $O{=}P$ with OCH_2CH_3, OCH_2CH_3, OCH_2CH_3	>1600 mg/kg	>1,000,000 hrs
Dichlorvos	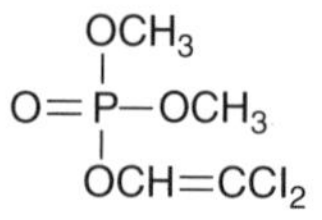 $O{=}P$ with OCH_3, OCH_3, $OCH{=}CCl_2$	80 mg/kg	48 hrs
Parathion	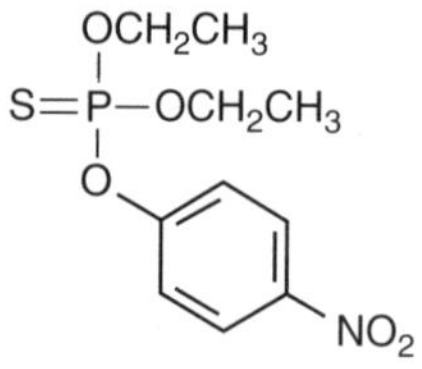 $S{=}P$ with OCH_2CH_3, OCH_2CH_3, O—(aromatic ring)—NO_2	14 mg/kg	3120 hrs
Malathion	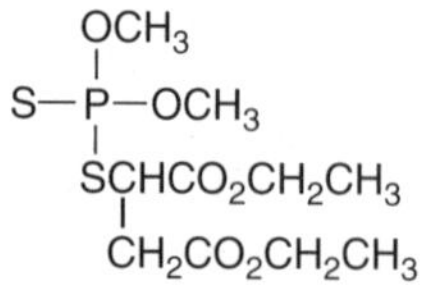 S—P with OCH_3, OCH_3, $SCHCO_2CH_2CH_3$, $CH_2CO_2CH_2CH_3$	1375 mg/kg	variable

FIGURE 17.2 Structures and toxicological properties of several organophosphate insecticides.

in water. As a consequence, it frequently disappeared from the environment before it had an opportunity to exert its insecticidal activity. It is also quite toxic to mammals. The search continued for better compounds and eventually led to the production of parathion and malathion. Parathion became a popular insecticide due to its stability in water vs. the instability of TEPP. However, even this stability was limited, a desirable feature because persistence in the environment beyond the time needed for insecticidal activity leads to other undesirable actions. This persistence feature was the major driving force for the acceptance of the organophosphates because the organochlorine compounds lasted too long in the environment. It becomes clear that duration is a critical feature; the insecticide must last long enough to kill insects but not so long that it has additional toxicity to humans.

CHEMISTRY

Organophosphates interfere in the normal behavior of acetylcholinesterase, an enzyme which cleaves acetylcholine within the synapse of many neurons. Figure 17.3 shows the normal mechanism of acetylcholinesterase action in which the neurotransmitter, acetylcholine, binds to a serine residue of acetylcholinesterase. An intermediate acetylated enzyme is formed. Water rapidly splits acetate off of this intermediate and acetylcholinesterase is regenerated and ready to cleave the next molecule of acetylcholine. Figure 17.3 also shows that an available organophosphate, such as paraoxon, can interfere with this process by forming a phosphorylated enzyme in place of the normal acetylated intermediate. The phosphorylated intermediate may, as is found for the natural intermediate, undergo hydrolysis. The problem is that this hydrolysis

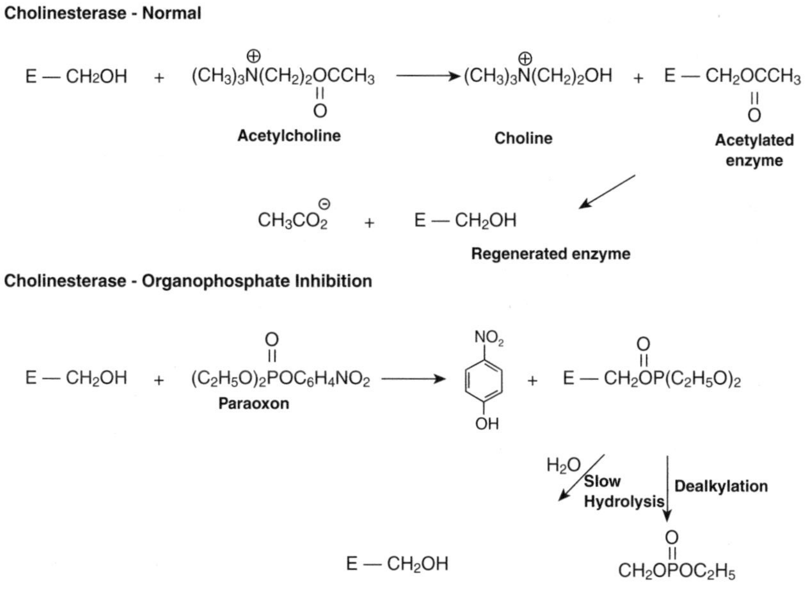

FIGURE 17.3 Outline of normal and inhibited acetylcholinesterase action.

is very slow and, while it is taking place, the enzyme molecule is not available for its normal function, the metabolism of the neurotransmitter, acetylcholine. Finally, the figure shows that an "aging" process occurs in which the phosphorylated intermediate is oxidized to a compound that is not capable of hydrolysis and this product is permanently phosphorylated. In that case irreversible inhibition has occurred.

A great deal is known about the nature of acetylcholinesterase. Its active site contains a serine residue at amino acid 203. The side-chain oxygen of serine is electronegative and made even more so by the neighboring electron-rich nitrogen of the imidazole of histidine 447. This imidazole nitrogen forms a hydrogen bond to serine 203 increasing the electron density around serine's side-chain oxygen. As is true of most enzymes, the amino acid sequence in the active site is critical. The rings of phenylalanine 295 and 297 form an acyl pocket which attracts the acetyl group of the substrate, acetylcholine. Organophosphates, such as paraoxon, are designed to simulate the structure of acetylcholine and bind in the enzyme's active site.

The inhibition of acetylcholinesterase by organophosphates may be clarified further by explaining the process in terms of classical organic reaction mechanisms. Serine 203 and hydroxide anion attack the rear of the tetrahedral phosphorus to effect an alkaline hydrolysis and to expel the weak nucleophile (and good leaving group). The rate of this process is promoted by anything that increases the positive character of the phosphorus. An example would be a neighboring oxygen rather than a sulfur. This explains why paraoxon is more toxic than parathion (relative LD_{50}s: paraoxon, 2; parathion, 14).

PHYSIOLOGY OF CHOLINERGIC ACTIVITY

Why is inhibition of the enzyme acetylcholinesterase detrimental to normal physiology and why does its inhibition cause the signs and symptoms observed? The basic concept is that some neurons conduct impulses through nerve circuits that depend on acetylcholine for a continuous uninterrupted flow of the nerve signal. These are called cholinergic neurons. Synapses, spaces between neurons, are bridged by a stream of acetylcholine in cholinergic neurons (Figure 17.4). If acetylcholine is not formed or does not cross the synapse or does not bind to specific receptors on the postsynaptic side, the impulse is stopped. This is referred to as anticholinergic activity, i.e., the actions induced by acetylcholine-based cholinergic neurons are prevented from happening. The opposite is an exaggerated degree of activity in these neuron types. This might happen if too much acetylcholine was sent across the synapse. It could also happen if acetylcholinesterase was inactive and the acetylcholine that carried the impulse was not inactivated in a normal manner. This would mean that the postsynaptic neuron would be in a state of continual excitation known as a cholinergic reaction. Organophosphate insecticides are one of several agents capable of causing this cholinergic state. The opposite, anticholinergic activity, can also constitute a medical emergency and we shall encounter many natural and synthetic agents that cause anticholinergic responses.

It is important to understand something of nerve physiology in order to understand the clinical findings and the actions of available antidotes for organophosphate poisoning.

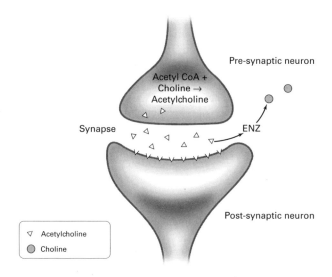

FIGURE 17.4 Chemistry at the cholinergic synapse. ACh = acetylcholine, ACE = acetylcholinesterase, X = postsynaptic receptor.

The human nervous system is made up of central and peripheral nervous systems. In turn, the peripheral nervous system is divided into autonomic and somatic nervous systems. The autonomic system includes sympathetic and parasympathetic systems which generally oppose one another. For example, the sympathetic system increases heart rate, dilates bronchi, and decreases secretions, whereas the parasympathetic decreases heart rate and stimulates gastrointestinal function. If patients are poisoned by an organophosphate insecticide or some other cholinergic agent, they will exhibit a series of symptoms represented by the mnemonic, SLUDGE, which represents **S**alivation, **L**acrimation, **U**rination, **D**efecation, **G**astrointestinal motility, and **E**mesis. All of these actions are due to the fact that target organs are innervated by a nerve circuit that employs acetylcholine. Under continuous stimulation (cholinergic response), the target organ overreacts and its particular activity occurs on a continuous basis. Urination occurs because constriction of the sphincter muscle is prevented while the detrusor muscle is constricted. There is increased GI motility because motility involves peristalsis which involves smooth muscle in the GI tract which, in turn, is supplied by a nerve that depends on acetylcholine for impulse transmission. One other symptom of cholinergic exposure is meiosis, pinpoint pupils. All of the symptoms of cholinergic poisoning can be traced to the specific actions of neurotransmitters, in this case, of acetylcholine.

CHARACTERISTICS OF ORGANOPHOSPHATE POISONING

Signs and symptoms of excess organophosphate exposure are due to persistent acetylcholine stimulation of two kinds of receptors: muscarinic and nicotinic. The muscarinic effects are those described above as the SLUD (salivation, lacrimation, urination, defecation) syndrome. In addition, there is usually nausea, sweating, pinpoint pupils, and blurred vision. Bronchoconstriction and increased bronchial secretions are also found and are due to other cholinergic actions.

Nicotinic effects are caused from the action of acetylcholine at autonomic ganglia and skeletal muscle junctions. Muscle twitches, weakness, fatigue, and fasciculations are found. Eventually, skeletal muscle paralysis will occur. Respiratory failure may be the end result of organophosphate action on nicotinic receptors. Because acetylcholine is also a neurotransmitter in the CNS there are manifestations such as depression of respiratory and cardiovascular centers in the medulla. Anxiety, confusion, slurred speech, convulsions, and coma may result from organophosphate effects on the CNS.

THERAPY

The diagnosis of organophosphate poisoning is based on a patient's history and characteristic symptoms. This kind of poisoning is usually, but not always, associated with persons who have industrial exposures, e.g., from working in agriculture (58% of cases). The diagnosis can be confirmed by the patient's response to antidotes and by positive laboratory results in specific tests (see below).

The biochemical lesion that produces symptoms is enzyme inhibition. Therefore, severity usually parallels the degree of enzyme inhibition. Mild poisoning is consistent with 20–50% of normal activity, moderate with 10–20% of normal, and severe poisoning is associated with less than 10% of residual enzyme activity.

Initial management of organophosphate exposure is supportive, including maintaining an airway and conducting suction or other means for removing as much of the poison as possible from the patient's body.

Two antidotes, atropine and pralidoxime (2-PAM, N-methyl-2-pyridaloxime iodide), are available for cholinesterase poisoning. Atropine should be given immediately if severe poisoning is suspected. Atropine is a natural chemical found in many plants. It is a strong anticholinergic agent that antagonizes peripheral muscarinic effects and many but not all of the central cholinergic effects. It will not, however, reverse neuromuscular paralysis associated with respiratory failure in severe poisoning. During the Persian Gulf War (1990–1991) atropine was issued to combatants on the Coalition side because of the fear that the enemy would use poison gas in the form of organophosphates. Strong evidence existed that this enemy had used poison gas in an earlier effort to subdue a minority group within their country. Fortunately, there was no documented use of poison gas during the war.

Pralidoxime is a triumph of organic chemistry inasmuch as it was deliberately synthesized as an antidote for organophosphate poison. When ultimately tested, it was shown to be effective for this purpose although it will not penetrate the CNS readily because it is a polar compound, a quaternary amine. Therefore, it has little or no effect in terms of reversing the central inhibition of acetylcholinesterase. Its primary activity is the reversal of acetylcholinesterase inhibition at the neuromuscular junction, i.e., the restoration of skeletal muscle activity. Thus, pralidoxime cannot be used by itself and is best employed in conjunction with atropine. In fact, the synergistic action of pralidoxime plus atropine together is approximately 45 times as great as pralidoxime alone.

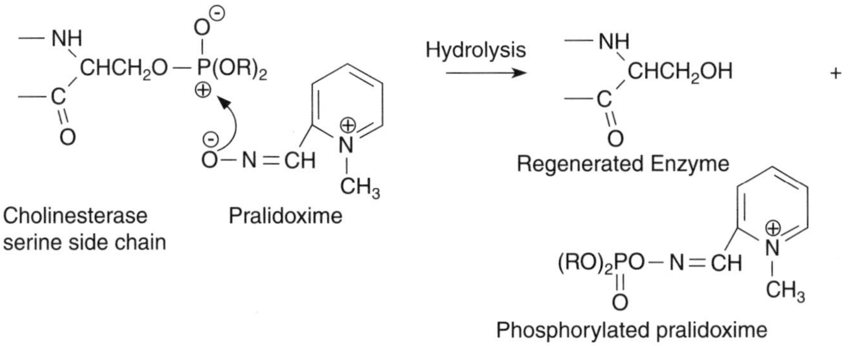

FIGURE 17.5 Attack of the antidote, pralidoxime, on the organophosphate attached to the serine of the enzyme, acetylcholinesterase. The pralidoxime anion displaces the blocking group of the insecticide and regenerates the serine. A product, phosphorylated pralidoxime, is excreted into the urine.

Pralidoxime was synthesized as a strong organic base which was expected to have sufficient strength to hydrolyze the phosphorylated serine, that is, the bond between enzyme and organophosphates (Figure 17.5). One other feature incorporated into the antidote was a group that would enable it to be bound within the enzyme active site. The resulting structure was successful and its anion displaces the blocking group and regenerates the serine hydroxyl. The product, phosphorylated 2-PAM, is then excreted into the urine.

LABORATORY TESTING

When a patient has been exposed to organophosphate insecticides laboratory testing of the specific agent in blood can be conducted by gas or liquid chromatography. A quantitative measurement of the insecticide concentration is of some help in predicting the severity of the exposure. Enzyme testing is, however, much easier and much more informative in guiding therapy and allowing prognostic predictions. As stated earlier, more severe poisoning means more enzyme inhibition. The site of inhibition is at the synapse. It would be extremely difficult to measure enzyme activity at the synapse. However, cholinesterase is also found in red cells and in the serum and the inhibition of the enzyme in either of those tissues, which are easily sampled, is proportional to inhibition at the synapse. Studies show that the red cell enzyme is usually better to measure than the serum form because its levels tend to correlate more closely with clinical effects. This may be due to the fact that the two forms of cholinesterase are not identical and the red cell form is closer to the one found at the synapse in cholinergic neurons. In interpreting enzyme results one must recall that organophosphate poisoning is not the only cause of depression of enzyme activity. Liver disease, malnutrition, and other factors may also lower it.

The usual method for measuring serum acetylcholinesterase activity is by a colorimetric procedure. The hydrolysis rate of butyrylthiocholine is measured in the presence of Ellman's reagent, DTNB (5-5′-dithiobis(2-nitrobenzoic acid). A mixed

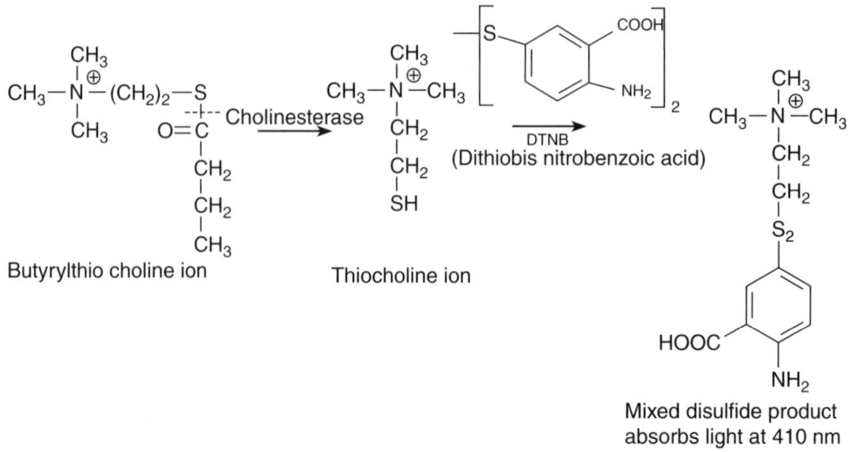

FIGURE 17.6 Scheme for measurement of acetylcholinesterase activity. The rate of reaction equals the micromoles of mixed disulfide formed per minute.

disulfide-colored product is formed that absorbs light at 410 nm in proportion to the concentration of active enzyme. The by-product is mercaptonitrobenzoic acid.

CARBAMATES

Carbamate esters are another important group that also act as acetylcholinesterase inhibitors (Figure 17.7). Furthermore, they react at the enzyme active site by binding to serine 203. However, instead of phosphorylating the enzyme, they carbamoylate it. The result is an inhibited enzyme which is, however, subject to rapid hydrolysis and enzyme regeneration. The bound enzyme is not subject to aging, the phenomenon which led to irreversible inhibition with the organophosphate compounds. Prali-doxime is not an effective antidote.

Because of the features of carbamates, especially the reversible character of the reaction with acetylcholinesterase, it was initially expected that carbamates would be less toxic to humans than organophosphate insecticides. Indeed, the first commercially available carbamate, Sevin (Carbaryl, 1-naphthyl N-methylcarbamate), followed expectations and had the hoped-for low toxicity (LD_{50} = 850 mg/kg). Several of the subsequently developed carbamates, however, had very high toxicity; for example, aldicarb (Temik) has an LD_{50} of 0.9 mg/kg.

Symptoms of carbamate poisoning are similar to those of organophosphate exposure, although the CNS signs are somewhat less. Therapy is also the same as for organophosphate insecticides but pralidoxime is not used because animal studies suggest it may actually be detrimental in treatment of carbamate poisoning.

PYRETHRINS

Pyrethrins are esters of two acids, chrysanthemic acid and pyrethric acid, and three keto alcohols, jasmolone, cinerolone, and pyrethrolone, which are collectively called

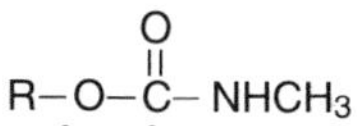

$$O$$
$$\parallel$$
$$R-O-C-NHCH_3$$

General carbamate structure

Name	R Group	LD50, mg/kg
Aldicarb		0.8
Carbaryl	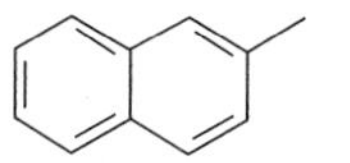	850
Carbofuran	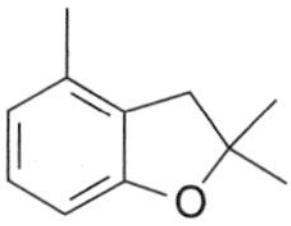	37
Methomyl	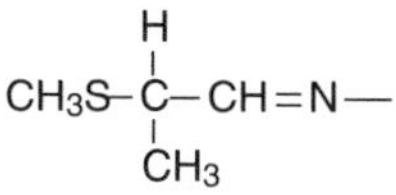 CH₃S-C-CH=N— (with H above C and CH₃ below C)	21

FIGURE 17.7 Structures of some members of the carbamate group of insecticides.

rethrolones (Figure 17.8). They are found in a natural source, chrysanthemum flowers, especially *C. cinerariaefolium*. Their protective effect against insects was recognized by natives of Asia Minor several centuries ago and chrysanthemum oil was spread on the body to ward off body lice. The formulation was known as "Persian insect powder."

Pyrethrins knock down insects very rapidly and have low mammalian toxicity (LD_{50} >1000 mg/kg in rats). Their toxicity mechanism appears to be the same as that of the organochlorine compounds, i.e., they block sodium ion transport within neurons. They are excellent for home use but have been applied only sparingly in agriculture. They are readily hydrolyzed in nature and are also subject to even more rapid decomposition by ultraviolet light, their half-life in bright sunlight being on the order of only a few minutes. These are the reasons for their failure to be effective agricultural agents.

Pyrethrins rarely cause significant morbidity to humans. The fatal dose is thought to be extremely high, 50 g in an average size adult. Contact dermatitis is often reported and more severe hypersensitivity reactions are found in allergic persons. Very high dose ingestion or inhalation has caused nausea, vomiting, muscle paralysis, and death. The very rare fatalities that have been reported were due to respiratory paralysis. Only supportive care is normally necessary for pyrethrin poisoning. Because these compounds are often sold in hydrocarbon solution, the patient may also exhibit signs of hydrocarbon toxicity. Some commercial forms of pyrethrins also contain piperonyl butoxide, which is included as a synergist that inhibits the ability of insects to metabolize pyrethrins by oxidation. Hence, the pyrethrin's

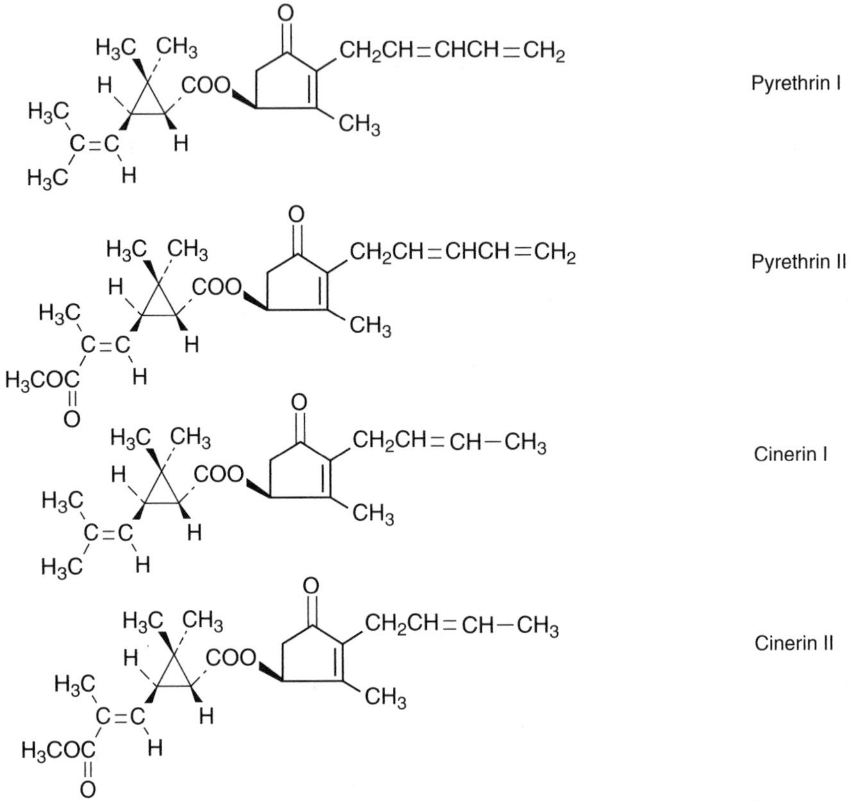

FIGURE 17.8 Some naturally occurring pyrethrins.

insecticidal activity is effectively enhanced. Piperonyl butoxide is even less toxic to humans than pyrethrins. Its estimated LD_{50} is 11.5 g/kg.

Questions and Problems

1. Describe the action of acetylcholine and of paraoxon at the cholinergic terminal.
2. Give the structures of atropine and of pralidoxime. Explain how they are similar and how they differ in regard to their actions in therapy of organophosphate overdose.
3. Review in this chapter the attack of serine 203 and hydroxide ion on the phosphorus of an organophosphate insecticide. Name a less nucleophilic attachment that could be part of the toxin structure. What would be the effect of this attachment on activity?
4. What federal restrictions were issued in the United States in October 1999 to reduce exposure to organophosphates? What evidence prompted these restrictions?

5. Contrast the arguments that have been advanced in relation to the value vs. the toxicity of DDT. These arguments have been made, among other places, in Rachel Carson's *Silent Spring* (anti-DDT), and in *Thrashing the Planet*, by Dixy Lee Ray (pro-DDT).

6. Calculate activity of acetylcholinesterase under the following conditions:

Specimen volume tested	1.0 mL
Absorbance change recorded	0.061 absorbance units/min
Volume of reagent	1.0 mL
Molar absorptivity of chromophore	4×10^3

Note: Activity is in international units = micromoles of substrate reacted per minute per liter of the sample. Molar absorptivity is in L/mol cm.

References

Carson, R., *Silent Spring*, Houghton Mifflin, New York, 1962.
Ray, D.L., *Thrashing the Planet*, Regnery Publ., Washington, D.C., 1990.

Case Study 1: Toddler with Seizures

A 13-month-old child was brought to a local emergency department after his parents found him with an open bottle of a commercial insecticide. Some of the bottle's contents had spilled on the child's face and clothes. At home he had vomited and had a seizure. He became very somnolent while on the way to the hospital and, shortly after arrival there, underwent another seizure. Phenobarbital was administered for the seizures. Activated lavage was conducted followed by treatment with activated charcoal. He was endotracheally intubated when his respirations became labored. Arterial blood gas analysis before intubation gave pH = 6.8; pCO_2 = 77 mm; pO_2 = 121 mm. After intubation his blood gases improved substantially to pH = 7.34; pCO_2 = 41 mm. Other laboratory studies showed hemoglobin at 10.2 g/dL; potassium = 3.5 mmol/L; glucose = 205 mg/dL; and creatinine = 2 mg/dL. The child was transferred to a children's hospital ICU where his condition improved gradually over the next 4 days. He was then discharged home without any apparent residual effects from this poisoning.

What kind of insecticide is likely to have been in the bottle?
   a) Organophosphate
   b) Carbamate
   c) Organochlorides
   d) Pyrethrin

Organophosphates and carbamates have a similar mechanism of action, one in which they inhibit the hydrolysis of acetylcholinesterase. They differ insofar as carbamate inhibition is reversible. Both of them have, as a key feature of their poisoning syndrome, cholinergic action. The patient exhibits the SLUD syndrome, i.e., salivation, lacrimation, urination, and defecation. This patient did not demonstrate this syndrome. Pyrethrins are natural insecticides that are synthesized by plants, especially *Chrysanthemum*. Exposure to pyrethrins produces asthma-like symptoms such as wheezing, shortness of breath, and possible chest pain. It is not at all like this patient's signs. Organochlorides, such as DDT or dieldrin, produce seizures. This patient ingested a scabicide, Kwell™, which is a 1% solution of lindane, gamma hexachlorocyclohexane. Lindane is a member of the organochlorine group of insecticides.

Questions

Q1. What is the major system affected by organochlorides?
   a) CNS
   b) Hepatic
   c) Renal
   d) Cardiac

Q2. What kind of acid-base imbalance did this patient exhibit prior to being intubated?
   a) Metabolic acidosis
   b) Respiratory alkalosis
   c) Respiratory acidosis
   d) Combined respiratory and metabolic acidosis

Q3. This patient's serum lindane concentration was measured and found to equal 0.32 µg/mL. Which of the following is true about serum levels of lindane?
   a) Serum levels of 0.02 µg/mL are associated with the absence of symptoms.
   b) Serum levels above 0.20 µg/mL are sometimes found with coma.
   c) No correlation of any kind exists between serum level and observed effects.
   d) Above 1 mg/mL symptoms are usually found.

Q4. The dose of lindane that causes seizures in children is
   a) 2 g
   b) 2 mg
   c) 2 µg
   d) 200 g

Answers and Discussion

Q1. (Answer = a) Organochlorides primarily affect the central nervous system. The CNS is stimulated, which results in sensory and equilibrium disturbance, involuntary muscle activity, and depression of vital centers. The severity of toxic symptoms is correlated to CNS concentration of these insecticides. They have also been associated, to a lesser degree, with hepatic necrosis. This effect may be found more in laboratory animals than in humans.

Q2. (Answer = d) This patient had a very high partial pressure of carbon dioxide because of depressed respirations and resulting retention of carbon dioxide. The very low pH achieved, however, could not be due to this effect alone. Because some degree of renal impairment existed, as seen in the child's elevated creatinine, acidic waste products of metabolism had probably accumulated. Thus, there also was an element of metabolic acidosis.

Q3. (Answer = b) Several studies show a relation between serum lindane level and symptoms. Coma is often noted if the level exceeds 0.20 µg/mL; 200 ng/mL (0.2 µg/mL) seems like a small serum level. However, in workers chronically exposed to lindane and reaching this level, neurologic abnormalities, electroencephalogram changes, and muscle jerking have been often noted.

Q4. (Answer = a) From several case reports it appears that 2 g of lindane are an adequate amount to cause seizures in pediatric patients. This patient drank Kwell, a 1% lindane solution (1 g lindane per 100 mL of Kwell). This means that 200 mL or approximately 8 oz. would contain enough of this insecticide to cause seizures in children.

Reference

Aks, S.E. et al., Acute accidental lindane ingestion in toddlers, *Ann. Emerg. Med.*, 26, 647–651, 1995.

Case Study 2: The Insidious Concoction

A 46-year-old man was brought by paramedics to an emergency department in coma with generalized seizures and acute respiratory failure. His wife stated that the patient drank a liquid on their patio 8 hours earlier. The patient thought the liquid was alcohol but it actually contained an insecticide. Soon after the ingestion he collapsed, began to seize, sweated profusely, became incontinent, and salivated.

In the emergency department the patient was noted to have trouble breathing and had episodes of seizure activity. He smelled strongly of a pungent, garlic-like odor. Heart rate, blood pressure, and respirations were all moderately elevated. Copious tracheal secretions were noted on physical exam. He was not responsive to physical stimuli. Pupils were pinpoint but reactive to light. Routine chemistry and hematology tests were within normal limits. Arterial blood gases showed the following:

pH	7.53
pCO_2	19 mm
pO_2	149 mm
Bicarbonate	16 meq/L

Routine toxicologic analysis showed no positive findings. CAT scan of the head was normal. ECG showed an elevated heart rate without any other abnormalities.

At this point what is your suspicion about the contents of the unknown liquid?
   a) Pyrethrin
   b) Organohalide
   c) Organophosphate
   d) Carbamate

Among the findings this patient exhibited, cholinergic hyperstimulation was very prominent. The cholinergic signs include salivation, urinary incontinence, tracheal secretions, and sweating. Both organophosphate and carbamate insecticides have a cholinergic mechanism of action, specifically, inhibition of cholinesterase. We can rule out pyrethrins and organohalides which cause different symptoms. We cannot distinguish between the carbamate and organophosphate classes. Carbamates are usually less toxic than organophosphates but there are many exceptions to this statement so that one could not distinguish between them on the basis of severity of poisoning. This patient was poisoned by malathion, an organophosphate. The specific diagnosis was based on finding malathion at 176 µg/mL in gastric contents.

The patient was stabilized, intubated, and given activated charcoal. He then received 2 mg of IV atropine every 30 minutes for 2 hours. He was transferred to the ICU where atropine was continued. One dose of a second antidote, pralidoxime, was also provided. The patient responded well. He became coherent, alert, and had decreased secretions. His condition improved to the point that he was extubated. One hour later, however, he began to deteriorate and to manifest increasing respiratory depression. Hypoxia and respiratory acidosis were noted. In spite of maximum ventilatory support and positive end-expiratory pressure, he remained hypoxemic. He developed a full-blown picture of acute respiratory distress syndrome and died on his 3rd day of hospitalization. At autopsy sections of both lungs showed severely congested dark, reddish-black parenchymal surfaces which exuded blood. This was indicative of severe congestion and edema.

Questions

Q1. What enzyme test is relatively specific for organophosphate poisoning?
   a) Gamma glutamyl transferase
   b) Red cell cholinesterase
   c) Sarcosine dehydrogenase
   d) Lactic acid dehydrogenase
Q2. How do pralidoxime and atropine differ as antidotes?
   a) Atropine is a synthetic material whereas pralidoxime is found in nature.
   b) Pralidoxime is a quaternary amine and cannot, therefore, enter the CNS to relieve CNS symptoms.
   c) Atropine reverses the enzyme inhibition by reactivating the enzyme.
   d) Pralidoxime does not react with the enzyme but antagonizes central cholinergic effects.

Q3. What kind of acid-base imbalance did the patient manifest?
   a) Metabolic acidosis
   b) Metabolic alkalosis
   c) Respiratory acidosis
   d) Respiratory alkalosis
Q4. Which, among the following, is the most toxic organophosphate?
   a) Malathion
   b) TEPP (tetraethyl pyrophosphate)
   c) Parathion
   d) Trichlorfon

Answers and Discussion

Q1. (Answer = b) Both organophosphates and carbamates inhibit cholinesterase. Therefore, a test to measure cholinesterase activity will give a low
   result in the presence of inhibitors. Although the insecticide's target is the
   nerve synapse, it also inhibits cholinesterase in the erythrocyte (RBC
   cholinesterase) and in the serum (pseudocholinesterase). Each of these
   may be measured. If either has less than 50% of normal enzyme activity,
   this is positive for organophosphate poisoning. This patient had severe
   depression of enzyme activity. Red cell enzyme was 1030 U/L (normal =
   3590 to 6666 U/L), while pseudocholinesterase was 100 U/L (normal =
   2436 to 4827 U/L). Of the two cholinesterase assays, the red cell enzyme
   appears to correlate better with clinical symptoms whereas the serum
   enzyme may become abnormal sooner (i.e., it is a more sensitive index
   of poisoning).
Q2. (Answer = b) Atropine and pralidoxime are two antidotes for organophosphate poisoning. Atropine is found in many plant products whereas pralidoxime is a product of synthetic organic chemistry. Pralidoxime was
   designed to react with cholinesterase and reactivate it. Both are effective
   antidotes. However, because pralidoxime is a quaternary amine it cannot
   readily penetrate the blood–brain barrier to enter the CNS. It is effective
   mainly by reversing poisoning at the neuromuscular junction but has
   essentially no effect on cholinesterase within the brain.
Q3. (Answer = d) This patient has respiratory alkalosis which is partially
   compensated by a slightly depressed serum bicarbonate.
Q4. (Answer = b) TEPP is an organophosphate withdrawn from use many
   years ago because of excessive toxicity. LD_{50}s for these compounds are
   as follows: TEPP, 1.1 mg/kg; parathion, 13 mg/kg; trichlorfon, 630 mg/kg;
   malathion, 1375 mg/kg. Thus, this patient was fatally poisoned despite
   the fact that he was exposed to a relatively safe organophosphate. This
   reinforces the old adage dating back to the time of Paracelsus that "the
   dose makes the poison."

Reference

Kass, R., Adult respiratory distress syndrome from organophosphate poisoning, *Amer. J. Emerg. Med.*, 9, 32–33, 1991.

Case Study 3: The Poisoned Pilot

A pilot was spraying crops with the pesticide methomyl from a small commercial aircraft. The plane crashed resulting in the pilot's death. The National Transportation Safety Board (NTSB) launched their customary investigation into the cause of this fatal accident. No mechanical failures in the aircraft could be demonstrated by inspection of the wreckage. The pilot had a good health history and autopsy of his remains failed to reveal any major health trauma such as a heart attack or cerebrovascular accident that might have caused the crash. Weather was excellent during the flight right up to the time of the crash. Unable to demonstrate any other cause for the accident the NTSB requested that toxicology studies be done on the blood of the deceased pilot.

Questions

Q1. To what category of pesticides does methomyl belong?
   a) Organophosphates
   b) Carbamates
   c) Organochlorides
   d) Chlorophenoxy compound
Q2. The pilot's blood was tested by gas chromatography-flame ionization detector and results were confirmed. Which is an appropriate confirmation method?
   a) Gas chromatography-NP detector.
   b) HPLC with ultraviolet spectrophotometric detection.
   c) LC-MS/MS.
   d) It depends entirely on the specific drug found.
Q3. The molecular formula for methomyl is $C_5N_2O_2SH_{10}$. What is the mass of the positively charged parent ion formed by chemical ionization in the mass spectrometer?
   a) 163
   b) 161
   c) 162
   d) 164
Q4. What is an advantage of LC-MS over GC-MS?
   a) Requires no sample derivatization of nonvolatile compounds
   b) Provides a spectrum corresponding to each peak of interest
   c) Allows identification based on retention time as well as spectra
   d) Can be acquired at lower capital cost

Q5. The pilot's blood level of methomyl was found to equal 570 ng/mL. What conclusion can be drawn?
   a) The pilot was impaired by methomyl and it was very likely a contributory factor in the crash.
   b) This is not an impressive amount and it is hard to imagine that such a small quantity contributed to the accident.
   c) The pilot could not have absorbed methomyl while flying so there must be a laboratory error.
   d) The level by itself is not interpretable.

Answers and Discussion

Q1. (Answer = b) Methomyl is a carbamate pesticide first marketed in 1966. Its tradenames are Lannate or Nudrin. The LD_{50} of methomyl is 17 mg/kg in rats. As a cholinesterase inhibitor it provokes headache, dizziness, weakness, tremor, ataxia, and nausea.

Q2. (Answer = c) Any confirmatory method that uses a mass spectrometer as detector will ordinarily give excellent results. To a small extent the method selected does depend on the analyte being tested. For the vast majority of compounds, however, GC and LC, coupled with mass spectrometry, are both suitable methods. LC with photometric detection lacks sufficient specificity and GC with NP detector is extremely sensitive but also lacks ideal specificity. In the original report of this case the positive methomyl finding was confirmed by LC-MS/MS. This technique, also called liquid chromatography-tandem mass spectrometry, uses a liquid chromatograph to separate the components of a mixture. Components then are fed into the first mass spectrometer which filters certain ions for passage into a second mass spectrometer, in tandem with the first. The second mass spectrometer is, therefore, evaluating a highly purified sample. Detection limits and specificity are extremely good.

Q3. (Answer = a) The molecular mass of methomyl equals 162. In chemical ionization the parent ion is the intact molecule plus one proton. Therefore, the parent ion appearing in this situation has a mass of 163.

Q4. (Answer = a) Both GC-MS and LC-MS have mass spectrometer detectors and will, therefore, produce spectra that can be used for identification purposes. At this time the cost of LC-MS is significantly higher than the cost of GC-MS, an older, more established technology. Sample preparation is simplified for LC-MS because vaporization is not necessary. In LC the components of the mixture are dissolved, not vaporized. Vaporizing high boiling components is difficult and is often achieved by derivatizing the components with functional groups that reduce the polarity of the component of interest. This step is unnecessary in LC.

Q5. (Answer = a) Although there is a danger of over-interpreting levels in blood, it is still safe to draw general conclusions. The amount of methomyl in the pilot's blood was quite elevated. This is known by comparison with fatalities in which methomyl was clearly the sole cause of death. Thus, in two suicides, postmortem concentrations were 700 and 1400 ng/mL.[2] Another person who was severely impaired had a blood level of 1600 ng/mL 6 hours after ingesting methomyl.[3] Because the incident under discussion involved the same approximate concentrations, the pilot must surely have been severely affected by the pesticide. The manner in which he became exposed is unknown but the fact that he was exposed appears to be beyond doubt.

References

1. Driskell, W.J. et al., Methomyl in the blood of a pilot who crashed during aerial spraying, *J. Anal. Toxicol.,* 15, 339–340, 1991.
2. Araki, M. et al., Forensic toxicological investigations of fatal cases of carbamate pesticide methomyl (lannate) poisoning, *Nippon Hoigaku Zasshi,* 36, 584–588, 1982.
3. Noda, J., Determination of methomyl by using chemical ionization mass fragmentography, *Nippon Hoigaku Zasshi,* 38, 71–82, 1984.

18 Metals

CONTENTS

ARSENIC

HISTORY

Because metals are natural products their role in poisoning and toxicology goes back to ancient times. Mercury, lead, and arsenic have figured prominently in the history of industrial development and, for arsenic particularly, in the history of crime.

There are many famous episodes involving arsenic. Ironically, one of the best known actually may not have been a case of arsenic poisoning: the alleged murder of Napoleon Bonaparte. Napoleon himself suspected it and asserted, "I die at the hands of my enemies …." Those enemies were not the British who imprisoned him but rather the French monarchy who were most anxious that Napoleon never return to France. Evidence in support of the theory that Napoleon did, in fact, die from arsenic lies mainly in testing of the emperor's hair. Many locks of his hair are still in existence because of the common practice of giving hair to admirers during the early nineteenth century, the time of Napoleon's imprisonment. The evidence from contemporary hair testing is mixed. Some locks show elevated levels of arsenic. The most recent testing tends to suggest that his hair did not have elevated arsenic. Further, any elevations that may have existed are not necessarily evidence of homicide. This is because arsenical pigments were used in the draperies hanging in the emperor's chambers. In the equatorial and humid climate of St. Helena, the island of Napoleon's exile, these pigments would have been acted upon by microorganisms, and vapors rich in organic arsenicals would have resulted. The final judgment of history is not available but it seems that the majority of those who have examined this riddle come down on the side of a natural death. Not only is the chemical evidence ambiguous but the medical conclusion of a large stomach carcinoma was well supported by many witnesses at his autopsy. Finally, some of the expected findings for chronic arsenical poisoning, such as hyperkeratosis and hyperpigmentation were never observed.

FORMS OF ARSENIC

Arsenic exists in many forms in nature. The pure element is uncommon but its multiple forms are widespread. Lead arsenate, $PbAsO_4$, is the most abundant. Many oxides are also found of which the trivalent arsenic trioxide, As_4O_6, is believed to be the specific agent most often employed in arsenic homicides. It is odorless and tasteless, obvious advantages to anyone with murderous intentions. The trivalent forms of arsenic are more toxic largely because they are more fully absorbed after ingestion. Therefore, arsenic trioxide is more toxic than arsenic pentoxide, the latter of which is pentavalent and less subject to extensive absorption. Arsenic trioxide, also called white arsenic, was long thought to be As_2O_3 but is now recognized to have the molecular formula, As_4O_6. Arsine gas, AsH_3, is the most toxic form of arsenic (TWA = 0.05 ppm) although it is far from the most abundant form and is, therefore, not commonly associated with arsenical poisoning. It is a colorless gas formed by the action of acids on arsenic. Organic arsenicals, alkyl arsenates, in which a covalent bond is usually found between the arsenic atom and an aliphatic carbon also exist. Organic arsenic is usually less toxic than arsine or trivalent arsenic

As_4	Elemental
AsH_3	Arsine; reduced
As_4O_6	Arsenic trioxide; oxidized
$AsO(OH)_3$	Arsenic acid
$As(OH)_3$	Arsenious acid
$AsO(OH)_2CH_3$	Methanearsonic acid (organic form)

FIGURE 18.1 Some forms of arsenic.

salts. One major source of organic arsenicals is fish because microorganisms convert arsenic to dimethylarsenate, which seafood accumulates in aquatic life.

SOURCES OF ARSENIC

Arsenic has a large number of industrial uses including the smelting of gold and copper. It has a role in the manufacture of glass and of some alloys. It is an effective insecticide and herbicide; for example, sodium arsenite was used in ant bait, lead arsenate as a general insecticide, calcium arsenate as an anti-snail agent, and copper acetoarsenite as a fungicide. Indeed, it is estimated that 80% of the industrial uses of arsenic today are in the form of pesticides. Arsine gas is used in the semiconductor industry in the production of microprocessors. From these many industrial processes some arsenic finds its way into the environment and, together with arsenic arising from weathering of ores and other natural processes, the total mass of arsenic in soil and water is fairly high. People consume arsenic in food and, to a lesser degree in water, and achieve a total body burden which is estimated to be on the order of 21 mg.

MECHANISM OF ARSENIC TOXICITY

Orpiment and realgar, minerals of arsenic and sulfur, were sought after by the ancients for their pigment qualities and were heavily mined by slaves. They are illustrative of the high stability of the arsenic–sulfur bond. The S–As–S bond angle is 110°, very close to the tetrahedral angle of 109.5°, and, as expected from theory, it is very stable. Therefore, arsenic binds to sulfhydryl groups of many proteins with nonspecific toxic effects. It may, for example, weaken the integrity of structural proteins, or partly inactivate some enzymes. The lethality of arsenic compounds relates also to specific actions at two places in intermediary energy metabolism. Pyruvic acid, a central metabolite which arises from glucose metabolism, is converted to acetyl coenzyme A which enters the Kreb's cycle. A very complex process, catalyzed by pyruvate dehydrogenase, is responsible for the metabolic conversion of pyruvic acid to acetyl coenzyme A. During this conversion, pyruvic acid is first condensed with thiamine pyrophosphate to form hydroxyethyl-thiamine pyrophosphate. Next, dihydrolipoyl transacetylase, an enzyme component of the pyruvate dehydrogenase complex, is acetylated by hydroxyethyl-TPP. Figure 18.2 below shows the action of the transacetylase enzyme containing a 1,3 dithiol, dihydrolipoamide. The adjacent sulfhydryl groups within dihydrolipoamide are especially attractive to

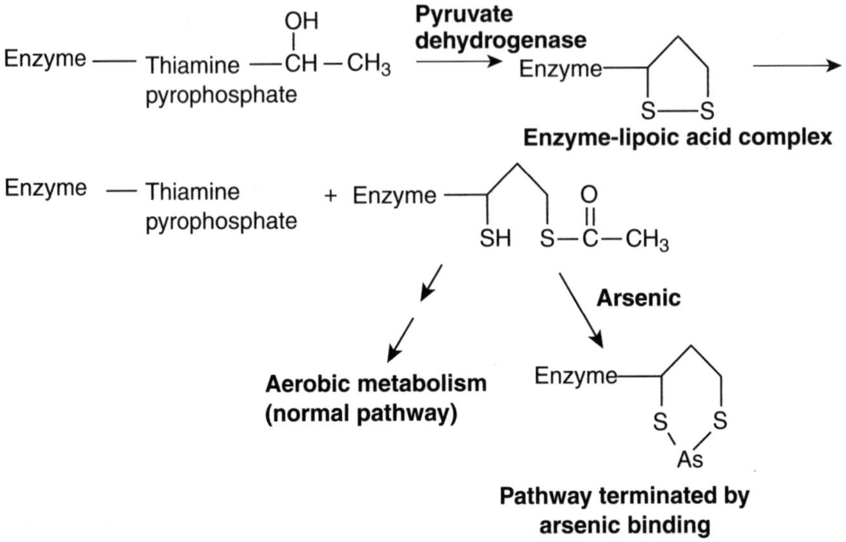

FIGURE 18.2 Binding of arsenic to lipoic acid.

arsenic and a stable compound is formed. This, of course, interferes with the normal action of pyruvate dehydrogenase, which relies for its activity on the preservation of the native state of transacetylase. The interruption in metabolism that occurs is catastrophic. Because over 90% of the biochemical energy used by the organism arises from the Kreb's cycle plus oxidative phosphorylation working together, the inhibition of this process by arsenic has fatal consequences in aerobic organisms.

Arsenates also resemble phosphates in chemical behavior (arsenic and phosphorus are in the same family of the Periodic Table). Thus, arsenates can replace phosphates in several places. For example, in glycolysis the oxidation of glyceraldehyde 3-phosphate to 1,3 diphosphoglyceric acid is followed by the phosphorylation of ADP to ATP while 1,3 diphosphoglyceric acid is converted to 3-phosphoglycerate. If $HAsO_4^{-2}$ is available, it replaces phosphate as the coupling agent, resulting in production of an arseno-phosphoglycerate (Figure 18.3). This product spontaneously dissociates (nonenzymatic) and no ATP is formed. While this reduces the net energy stores of the organism, the deficit is minor compared to the above described action of arsenic at the level of pyruvate dehydrogenase.

This ability of arsenic to behave like phosphate also leads to storage of arsenate in bone, a location in which it may accumulate in a stable manner for a very prolonged period.

SYMPTOMS OF ARSENIC POISONING

After acute arsenic ingestion the most prominent and earliest signs are those of severe gastrointestinal upset such as vomiting, nausea, bloody diarrhea, and intense abdominal pain. A semi-specific sign is the appearance of "rice-water stools" which are masses of gastrointestinal tissue sloughed off from the walls of the GI tract and

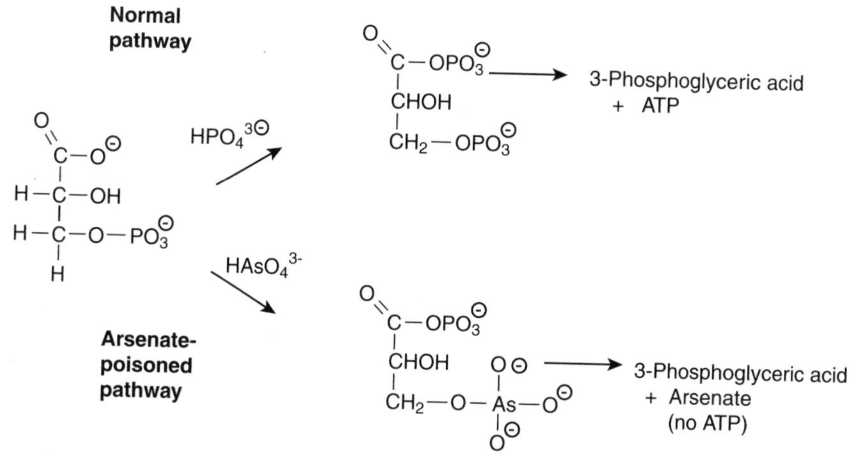

FIGURE 18.3 Mechanism of arsenic interaction with the glycolytic pathway.

egested in the feces. Gustave Flaubert was familiar with arsenic poisoning and describes it very graphically in his celebrated novel, *Madame Bovary*. In the story, the main character, Emma Bovary, overcome by a fit of despondency, purchases arsenic under the pretense of planning to eradicate some rats infesting her home. The ingestion of the white powder by Emma is followed by an acrid taste, a profound thirst, and nausea and vomiting. Her husband, Charles, finds a "fine white gravel" in the basin into which Emma has vomited. This would be a mixture of the poison and tissue fragments produced by the corrosive action of arsenic trioxide. Flaubert describes other symptoms which the unfortunate Emma experiences including an almost imperceptible pulse and convulsions just before her death. Additional symptoms in arsenic poisonings include cardiac depression, cerebral edema, and peripheral neuropathy. Liver and renal failure will eventually occur if the patient has a sufficiently large overdose and survives long enough. These findings are due to arsenic's nonspecific binding to many proteins through available sulfhydryl groups. To a greater degree, however, symptoms are due to toxic action on energy metabolism and the effects of the latter on the function of various organs and tissue types.

Chronic arsenic poisoning has a somewhat different set of symptoms. Hair loss (alopecia) is common. A blush of the skin known as milk rose appearance results from vasodilation of the facial capillaries. Indeed, women would employ arsenical cosmetics in ancient times for purposes of achieving this dubiously beneficial effect. Hyperkeratosis and hyperpigmentation are other effects of chronic arsenic. These symptoms are essentially always associated with chronic arsenic use and can be evaluated in the context of suspected long-term poisoning. Arsenic is also a suspected carcinogen as shown in Table 18.1.

TREATMENT

Immediate treatment of suspected exposure consists of lavage and use of activated charcoal in hopes of reducing absorption. Contaminated clothing must be removed

---

TABLE 18.1
Lifetime Risk of Cancer Death
from Carcinogen Exposure

Low passive exposure to cigarette smoke	4/1000
High passive exposure to cigarette smoke	10/1000
Average home radon exposure	3/1000
Highest 3% of radon-infested homes	20/1000
Exposure to arsenic in average drinking water	1/1000
Drinking highest arsenic-contaminated water	21/1000

---

and affected skin areas washed copiously. Fortunately, antidotes are available for arsenic and they are effective when employed early enough following ingestion. Dimercaprol and penicillamine have been available for many years. Succimer and DMPS (2,3 dimercaptopropane-sulphonate), a water-soluble derivative of dimercaprol, are more recent.

Chelators

Metals have long been known for their ability to bind with reagents known as chelators, organic molecules which form stable complexes with metal ions (Figure 18.4). Chelators are usually water soluble and will, therefore, be readily excreted by the kidney. Chelating agents typically bind one metal with high affinity but they are known to have some degree of nonspecificity, binding several metals with lesser specificity and affinity. For example, EDTA (ethylene diamine tetraacetic acid) has high affinity for calcium but binds strongly with cadmium, lead, iron, and several other metals, as well. The existence of chelators is a boon for the treatment of metal poisoning but one must realize that their use is not without adverse side effects. This arises from the fact that chelating agents do not bind to exogenous metals only but to indispensable metallic cofactors of enzymes (Table 18.2). Insofar as chelators bind to natural metals they interfere with normal metabolic processes.

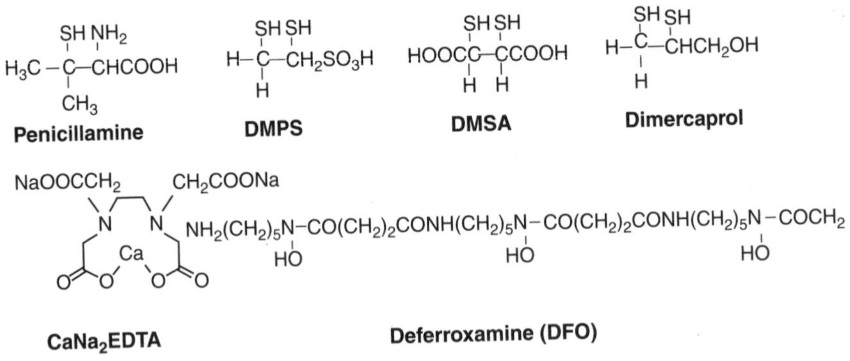

FIGURE 18.4 Structures of clinically useful chelating agents.

TABLE 18.2
Requirements for an Effective Chelating Agent
Binds metals more strongly than tissues
Is highly water soluble
Resists degradation within the blood
Binds tightly to toxic metals
Does not dissociate with pH changes, e.g., in urine
Binds physiologically important metals weakly or not at all
Has little intrinsic toxicity
May be administered orally

Chelating Agents for Use with Arsenic Poisoning

Dimercaprol, also known as British anti-lewisite, was a triumph of organic chemistry because it was designed for the purpose it achieved, treatment of arsenic overdose. Specifically, it was intended to counter exposure to the arsenical poison gas, lewisite. Dimercaprol forms a 2:1 (2 moles dimercaprol to 1 mole of arsenic) complex that is stable and readily excreted from the body. This antidote is potentially toxic and causes many symptoms in patients receiving it, including high blood pressure, elevated heart rate, gastrointestinal problems, and many other symptoms. One way to minimize these toxic effects of antidote administration is to administer it in small doses over a prolonged period. Single large doses are far more likely to lead to antidote toxicity.

TESTING FOR ARSENIC

Blood testing for arsenic is usually not performed because it may not be informative, i.e., blood levels may not be representative of how much arsenic is present in various organs. However, blood arsenic greater than 1000 μg/L (1000 ng/mL) is usually indicative of a fatal level. Urine concentrations are more likely to be helpful. In unexposed persons they should be less than 50 μg/L and, if they exceed 100 μg/L, this is suggestive of chronic exposure. One must be aware of possible dietary effects when interpreting arsenic concentrations. For example, after a meal of seafood, arsenic concentrations in urine may be as high as 1700 μg/L. This elevation is entirely due to diet and it shows the importance of controlling for possible artifacts when conducting testing for metals.

The story of the investigation of Zachary Taylor, twelfth president of the United States, is an excellent illustration of the laboratory evaluation of a possible arsenic poisoning. President Taylor was 66 years old when, in July of 1850, he died of apparent gastrointestinal infection. The president's death was preceded 5 days earlier by the consumption of large amounts of iced milk and cherries. Because his symptoms were consistent with death from natural causes at the time no one appears to have seriously considered the possibility of murder. Not until recently was homicide considered possible. In 1991, several historians and scientists petitioned the coroner of Jefferson County, Kentucky, the county in which President Taylor's remains are interred, to have the body exhumed and investigated. What justification was provided for this rather extreme invasion of the final resting place of the deceased president? In the first place, the symptoms noted, while consistent with death due to infection, are also consistent with arsenic poisoning. Bear in mind that arsenic was a common vehicle for murder in the middle of the nineteenth century as it had been for many centuries preceding that time. From a political perspective, Taylor's assassination would make sense. He was a slave holder who, nevertheless, was sympathetic to the arguments of abolitionists and opposed the admission of new states as slave states. His death would have been welcomed by the pro-slavery faction. In a word, if it could be shown that President Taylor had been murdered, not an unlikely possibility, then American history would need to be rewritten. Permission was granted for the exhumation and testing.

On June 17, 1991, President Taylor's body was disinterred. The process began with sawing of the lead liner of the casket. It was immediately observed that groundwater had reacted with the lead liner over the long period since his death. A small hole was found in the liner. As a result, no soft tissue was left. Only skeletal remains plus some hair and nails were found. Moreover, while hair was available, follicles had decomposed. These findings dictated the appropriate analytic methods. The procedures employed for arsenic detection would have to have low detection limits. In other words, the president's body would have held most of the arsenic, if that was the cause of his death, in soft tissue. Had soft tissue been available, the challenge of detecting arsenic would have been easier. After death from an acute rather than a chronic poisoning, little of the poison is transferred to hair, nails, or bone. The available specimens were adequate but only very sophisticated methods could be used to test them. At this point it is worth emphasizing two aspects of the methodology investigators used. They tested artifacts buried with the president, namely, linen gloves, the shroud, and a pillow within the casket to rule out contamination. Contamination is always a serious issue when conducting metal analyses because of the relative ubiquity of metals in the environment. Second, in view of the special nature of the specimens and the significance of any results, they employed several different laboratories and several different methods of testing. These steps indicate the excellent and professional manner in which this investigation was conducted.

The Kentucky state forensic laboratory performed the Gutzeit test. Hair and nail samples were also sent to the University of Louisville for energy dispersive X-ray microanalysis. Finally, specimens went to Oak Ridge National Laboratory for neutron activation analysis. The Gutzeit test is a spectrophotometric method which was just sufficiently sensitive for this study. In this method, all arsenic present is acid digested to an oxidized form which is then reduced by stannous chloride to arsine. All the arsine gas is trapped and reacted with mercury bromide. This reaction produces a yellow-brown complex which absorbs light in proportion to the amount of arsenic in the specimen. X-ray microanalysis is a technique in which X-ray bombardment causes elements to emit X-rays at specific and characteristic wavelengths the magnitude of which is proportional to the concentration of the element. X-ray microanalysis can quantify the amount of arsenic present and also the amount of mercury. Because the president had been treated with mercury in the form of calomel (mercury chloride) during his last days of life (a common and dubious treatment at that time), it was necessary to guarantee that mercury was not mistaken for arsenic. Neutron activation is the most sensitive method employed. The specimen is irradiated with neutrons which are absorbed into the nuclei of the irradiated atoms. New isotopes are created many of which are radioactive. They decay with the emission of gamma radiation. Again, the decay products and their amounts are characteristic of the content of their precursor elements within the specimen tested. What were the results of testing of specimens derived from President Taylor? The following table shows what was found:

Results of Testing of President Taylor's Remains

Gutzeit test	1.9 µg/g hair or nails	Normal
X-ray microanalysis	1.8% elemental weight	Normal
Neutron activation	< 2.0 µg/g arsenic	Normal

These tests and the entire procedure employed provide convincing evidence that President Taylor was not murdered, at least with arsenic. This history also is very instructive because it shows several of the technologies available for the measurement of arsenic and it also illustrates the correct manner in which to control for the many variables that can undermine the validity of findings in a study of this sort.

LEAD

HISTORY

Lead was one of "the seven metals of the ancient world." Its discovery dates back to at least 3500 B.C. A large variety of lead artifacts are widespread throughout the ancient world. Large-scale use of lead, however, did not occur until the Romans devised an elaborate method of delivering water to their many towns. They manufactured sheet lead in an ingenious manner by rolling and joining pipes to form the basis for their water-carrying system. The amount of lead utilized by the Romans was extraordinary. For example, in building the great aqueduct at Lyons, at least 12,000 tons of lead were used in one section alone. There was a great danger in transporting water in such lead-lined vessels; however, it is believed that the lead absorbed by the citizenry from this source was minor compared to that which arose from a different source. This second source was lead acetate, also called sugar of lead, which the Romans deliberately added to wine to improve its flavor. Lead acetate was also added to prevent wine from spoiling because the lead would inhibit enzymes (and thus prevent growth) in microorganisms that contaminated the wine. It is difficult to determine whether the Romans were fully aware that this practice of consuming wine laced with lead was detrimental to their health. Some were surely aware as, for example, Pliny stated "from the excessive use of such wines arise dangling paralytic hands," and Dioscorides, writing some years before Pliny, stated "wines so treated are most hurtful to the nerves." At the peak of the Roman empire, lead production was estimated to exceed 80,000 tons per year. The resulting debility associated with the extensive exposure to lead is believed by some historians to have been a major factor in the eventual decline and fall of the Roman Empire.

The name given to the constellation of symptoms found among the Romans and due to lead ingestion is saturnine gout. These symptoms are the same as those found in Devonshire colic (England, 1760) and in the Colic Pictonium of late medieval France and indeed in the many episodes down through the millenia in which large groups of people suffered from the harmful effects of lead ingestion, often but not solely, from contaminated wine. Lead symptoms included painful and persistent constipation, abdominal pain (colic), pains in the joints (gout), pains in the extrem-itites starting with wrist drop, headache, blindness, and mental disturbances some-times reaching the extreme of insanity.

SOURCES OF LEAD

Many sources of lead exist in the environment (Table 18.3). Lead may be present in large concentrations in some water and soil samples. In the past, lead was common in children's toys and crayons. Among the major sources of lead, industrially, are storage batteries and sheet metal plants. Before 1975, the average person experienced major exposure to lead from two sources: paint and gasoline. It has been estimated that more than half the lead found within the atmosphere arose from the burning of the tetraethyllead added to gasoline to reduce engine knocking. Lead-based paints were another major source although the transfer of lead from paint to the human body was a much less frequent occurrence. It occurred, nevertheless, in persons who stripped old paint from houses or in children who suffered from pica, a disorder in which the child has a craving for abnormal objects, including paint chips, and puts them in his mouth. Most childhood lead ingestion arose from random ingestion of household dust, often heavily contaminated with lead.

In 1971, the U.S. Congress passed a law limiting the amount of lead in gasoline to less than 1%, and it was further reduced to 0.06% in 1977. The outcome of measures introduced to reduce lead exposure would appear to be excellent as indi-cated by data which contrast the average daily intake of lead in children and adults during the 1980s. In male babies, average lead intake was 45 μg per day in 1980, down to 4.3 μg per day by 1990. In middle-aged men daily lead intake dropped from 84 to 8.5 μg during the same 10-year span.

TABLE 18.3
Sources of Lead Exposure

Occupational	Environmental	Advocational
Plumbing	Lead paint	Pottery making
Auto repairs	Lead-painted houses	Target shooting
Glass making	Leach from plumbing	Soldering of electronics
Printing	Leaded gasoline	Fishing sinkers
Steel welding	Ceramics	Car repair

PHARMACOKINETICS OF LEAD

Under normal conditions, 10% of ingested lead is absorbed in adults; in children this figure may be higher. In terms of absorption through the skin, however, inorganic lead is very poorly transferred whereas organic lead, such as tetraethyllead, readily enters through intact skin. Lead vapor also readily crosses from the alveoli into the blood, a pathway which, in the past, has caused many deaths and high morbidity among those working in lead smelting. Once absorbed, lead salts are rapidly transferred from the blood to soft tissue such as kidney, lung, and liver. Eventually, lead makes its way to hard tissue, teeth, hair, and bone. In these tissues it exists mainly as lead triphosphate. Bone is the major storage site and, as might be expected, lead has a long half-life (greater than 25 years) in the body because of its storage in bone.

MECHANISM OF TOXICITY

In common with other electropositive elements, lead binds to sulfhydryl groups of proteins. Because sulfhydryl groups are widespread in the body, the effects of lead are also widespread. For example, the lead colic pains suffered by many millions down through the ages are due to the paralysis of normal peristaltic motion by lead binding to the proteins involved in peristalsis.

The earliest result of lead poisoning is interference in the formation of heme, the prosthetic group of hemoglobin. Lead interferes with heme synthesis in at least two sites in the biochemical pathway in which succinyl CoA is converted to heme. The first site, as shown in Figure 18.5, is the reaction in which delta-aminolevulinic acid (delta ALA) forms porphobilinogen with catalysis by the enzyme, delta ALA dehydratase. Later in the pathway, protoporphyrin IX is converted to heme by incorporation of ferrous ion, under catalysis by ferrochelatase, a reaction also inhibited by lead. Laboratory investigation of possible lead poisoning can be assisted by evaluation of this pathway; for example, one of the signs of lead poisoning is increased excretion of delta ALA and coproporphyrin. Another sign is accumulation of protoporphyrin IX in red blood cells. The net effect of lead inhibition of this pathway is anemia of the type known as microcytic hypochromic anemia, which is characterized by small, immature red blood cells low in hemoglobin content. This anomaly is detectable by a CBC, a complete blood cell count. Another feature of lead poisoning is the appearance of "basophilic stippling" in which basophils, immature red cells, contain irregular polyribosomes that cause an abnormal appearance referred to as stippling. None of these laboratory features are entirely specific for lead poisoning but usually are found when lead poisoning is present (these are medium sensitivity and medium specificity findings). These results may also be noted in the presence of other disorders such as several inherited diseases.

SYMPTOMS OF LEAD POISONING

Acute or chronic lead poisoning may occur although the acute variety is very rare. It would be found, for example, in a suicidal individual who ingested a lead salt or in a person who had overwhelming exposure to aerosolized lead when sanding lead-based paint from an older home. The first finding in acute exposure is gastrointestinal

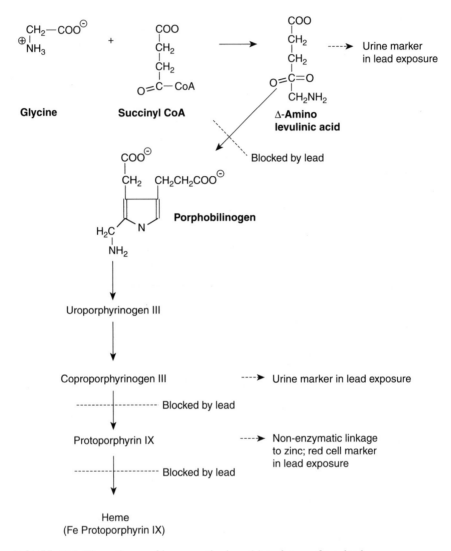

FIGURE 18.5 The pathway of heme synthesis and interference from lead.

upset and inflammation. Renal damage is found if the ingestion is sufficiently large. The victim may die as the end result of cardiovascular collapse. As described earlier, chronic poisoning is manifested by symptoms of red cell deficiency, gastrointestinal disorder, and injury to kidney, nerves, and muscles. One of the earliest signs is anemia with fatigue and weakness. Lead colic, often with extreme pain, is very common. Loss of appetite, constipation, and diarrhea may be found. Other characteristics of lead colic are intestinal spasms and abdominal cramping. Renal damage to the kidneys is primarily related to the proximal tubules, which lose their ability to selectively reabsorb substances from the filtrate. Glucose, amino acids, bicarbonate,

TABLE 18.4
Lead Toxicity in Children

Blood Concentration (mcg/dL)	Effect
>10	Hearing, growth, and IQ deficits
>15	Elevated erythrocyte protoporphyrin
>20	Reduced nerve conduction velocity
>30	Impaired vitamin D metabolism
>40	Depressed hemoglobin synthesis
>60	Colic
>70	Anemia
>80	Renal injury
>85	Encephalopathy
>130	Death

and uric acid appear in the urine in much greater than normal amounts. Eventually, the effects of lead extend beyond the proximal tubules and include the kidney's glomeruli as well. Some of the best known signs of lead toxicity are observed in the form of neurological impairment. These include lead palsy, which is due to demyelination of the median nerve. Because this nerve supplies the extensor muscles of the hand any damage to the nerve results in a "wrist-drop" phenomenon. Extreme neurological damage from lead results in lead encephalopathy in which brain tissue becomes necrotic. Minor symptoms like lethargy are initially present and they proceed to delirium, convulsions, and coma. The mortality associated with lead encephalopathy is reported to equal 25%. Among the survivors of lead encephalopathy there is a 40% incidence of long-term and severe neurological impairment.

TREATMENT OF LEAD INTOXICATION

Ipecac, gastric lavage, or whole bowel irrigation should be used to attempt to reduce the amount of lead absorbed from an exposure. As is true of other electropositive elements lead is amenable to chelating agents and the agent of choice for lead is often EDTA, ethylene diamine tetraacetic acid. One protocol calls for providing EDTA to any patient whose blood lead concentration is greater than 45 μg/dL.

THE LABORATORY AND LEAD OVERDOSE

As described earlier many biochemical aberrations accompany lead poisoning, each of which constitutes a possible way of testing for lead overdose. These tests include urinary coproporphyrin, urinary delta aminolevulinic acid, and erythrocyte protoporphyrin, among others. However, the assay for blood lead is considered to be the best means for accurate evaluation of toxicity. In this regard, the Centers for Disease Control (CDC), have analyzed studies conducted on the harmful effects of lead and, based on those studies, have established threshold values upon which intervention may be based. During the 1960s, up to 50 μg/dL of blood lead was thought to be

TABLE 18.5
Degrees of Lead Elevation

Class	Level	Interpretation
I	<10	Not poisoned
IIA	10–14	Re-screen often, consider prevention
IIB	15–19	Start nutritional and educational intervention
III	20–44	Investigate patient's environment, consider chelation
IV	45–69	Change environment, start chelation
V	>69	Medical emergency

tolerable. Further evaluation of contemporary studies reduced that cut-off to 30 µg/dL by 1970 and 25 µg/dL by 1985. Finally, in 1991, comprehensive review of all data collected up to that time resulted in reducing the cut-off to 10 µg/dL. Above 10 µg/dL CDC claims there is an elevated risk of hypertension in adults and, more importantly, developmental toxicity in children (Table 18.4). This is manifested as diminished IQ, and retardation of growth and hearing acuity. Above 20 µg/dL children show a decrease in nerve conduction velocity. Levels above 30 µg/dL are related to impairment of vitamin D metabolism in children and a distinct increase in systolic blood pressure in adults. The aforementioned lead colic is found when blood lead exceeds 50 µg/dL, while prolonged levels above 100 µg/dL cause encephalopathy in adults and are fatal to children. CDC has recommended that blood lead screening be instituted for children at risk and that the specific response be determined by the degree of lead elevation. (See Table 18.5.)

MERCURY

History

Mercury has been used in human history for at least 3000 years. It has had many applications in both industry and medicine over that time span. One of the industrial uses was in gold mining and refining. Even the ancient alchemists used mercury extensively as they attempted to convert base metals into gold. Before one concludes too hastily that the alchemists were a class of fools, it is salutary to recall that among their number was the celebrated and brilliant scientist, Isaac Newton. Newton, discoverer of gravity and one of the greatest physicists of all time, conducted many alchemical experiments and employed mercury extensively. Further, he had the injudicious habit of tasting the results of his experiments. Did this intense exposure to mercury ever harm Isaac Newton? Many believe that it did because he suffered insomnia, anorexia, memory loss, depression, and paranoia, especially during the years 1692–1693. All of these findings are consistent with the effects of chronic mercury poisoning. Moreover, hairs in the possession of Newton's descendants were tested by neutron activation analysis and atomic absorption spectrophotometry. One hair had 197 ppm of mercury vs. a reference level of 5.1 ppm. By contrast, a child who suffered tremors and hallucinations from mercury exposure had hair levels of

18 ppm. The chemical and physical evidence suggests that Sir Isaac Newton did indeed experience severe deficits from mercury poisoning. However, he recovered sufficiently and when he died in 1727 it was from old age. He had lived to be 85 years old. Perhaps his failure during his later years to imitate earlier successes when he discovered calculus, the nature of light, and the theory of gravitation may have been a residue of the mercury exposure. Perhaps, on the other hand, he had already done enough. Some argue that Newton's malady was an exacerbation of a manic-depressive illness. This contention is based, among other factors, on the observation that he did not report other signs commonly found in mercury poisoning such as GI symptoms, gingivitis, and chronic fatigue. Furthermore, his recovery appeared too abrupt for mercury poisoning. Last, his first recorded breakdown, in 1664, happened at a time which preceded his alchemical experiments. We will never know with certitude whether Newton's illness was mercury poisoning but it is instructive to examine his life with a view to understanding the nature of mercury's effects on the body.

A well-known problem associated with mercury's use in industry was "mad hatter's disease." The manufacture of felt hats involved a process called carrotting, rubbing fur with mercuric nitrate. Subsequently, the fur would be heated and employees were exposed unavoidably to mercury vapor. Workers in this industry were deemed to be mad because they developed some well-characterized symptoms such as tremors, a jerking gait, pathological shyness, and stammering speech. These findings were noted in multiple locations where the carrotting process was used, resulting in eventual recognition of mercury as the causative agent.

Mercury also has been used as a poison and as a medicinal agent. The intriguing case of Benvenuto Cellini illustrates the capacity of mercury to function in both ways. Cellini was one of the giants of the Italian Renaissance. Recognized as an unsurpassed sculptor, he was the first person who was able to produce life-size works in bronze, such as his "Perseus with the Head of Medusa." Cellini was as active in the bedroom as the art studio and he contracted an especially severe case of syphilis when he was 29 years of age. Cellini refused to accept mercury treatment, in common use during the sixteenth century, and tried to "take the wood," that is, to use guaiac.

Guaiac was also an alleged medicinal believed to have curative properties for syphilis. His condition deteriorated, however, to the third stage of syphilis, and he began to exhibit evidence of general paresis. His judgment was greatly impaired by disease and it seemed that syphilis would take his life very quickly. His enemies, however, could not wait even that short period of time and they invited him to a dinner where he was heavily poisoned. He described a sensation of "my stomach on fire," "extreme pain," "the cloth was covered with blood where he lay." We believe the latter comment to refer to bloody diarrhea. Cellini took to his bed and was administered to by a physician who recognized the signs of poisoning with corrosive sublimate, mercuric chloride. His physician noted that the patient lost control over his gastrointestinal tract because his intestines were extensively corroded. Eventually the great sculptor recovered and, contemplating his wretched condition afterward, it occurred to him that he had not experienced any symptoms of syphilis for some time. As it happened, his poisoners had unintentionally provided a sublethal dose which was, however, sufficient to destroy the *Treponema* parasite, the cause of syphilis.

Mercury has, therefore, always been a two-edged sword in the fight against disease. Lewis and Clark, on their famous expedition across America from 1804 to 1806, encountered many hardships, syphilis contracted by their men, being not the least among them. Lewis was an amateur physician, armed with an array of many of the natural remedies popular at the time. He prescribed mercury to his men and they derived short-term benefit from it. Reviews of this practice by modern toxicologists have concluded that the medicine probably did more harm than good in the long term.

One last incident in the history of mercury deserves mention. This famous event illustrated the hazards of organic mercury and its dissemination in the environment in a manner that was not appreciated prior to the event. Starting in 1953 a strange polio-like disease spread among some inhabitants of the small Japanese fishing village of Minamata Bay. Patients suffered from visual field restrictions, ataxic gait, hearing difficulty, and other predominantly neurological signs. At least 2000 victims suffered severe illness, and 51 died. Investigations showed that those most at risk ate a lot of fish and also that fish caught in the bay produced neurological signs in experimental animals that were fed the fish. The causative agent was shown to be thermo-stable and was contained in waste water from a factory manufacturing acetaldehyde and dumping waste water into the bay. Eventually, it was discovered that mercuric oxide, used as a catalyst in the production of acetaldehyde, was converted to methylmercury in the acetylene reaction tank. Since the time of this episode the dangers of organic mercury are more fully appreciated.

TYPES AND SOURCES OF MERCURY

Mercury exists in three forms. Elemental mercury is a liquid metal with a high boiling point and low vapor pressure. The second form is inorganic salts, +1 and +2 charged. Mercurous (+1) salts are found in calomel, mercurous chloride. Calomel had many medical uses in former times including teething powder for which it was used until its adverse effects were publicized in 1948. Organic mercury compounds, the third form, such as methyl mercury, are formed by natural processes.

The major source of atmospheric mercury is off-gassing of mercury from soil and water (Table 18.6). Mercury in water, however, arises from weathering of rocks and from industrial effluents. Primary among the latter are factories producing chlorine or caustic soda, factories involved in mining and ore production, or those making paper or textiles. Mercury released into the environment is usually converted to methyl mercury by soil and water microorgansisms, especially if the pH is low, and then methylmercury is ingested by fish and other water organisms. The average person who does not have a unique source of mercury exposure receives the most amount of bodily mercury from his/her diet. Obviously, fish would be a major source. Predacious fish, such as tuna and swordfish, can have 50 times as much mercury as fish that are lower in the food chain. Despite the potentially high amounts of mercury in fish, the public is protected by FDA regulations prohibiting sale of fish containing more than 1 ppm of mercury.

Another source of mercury is medicinals. Whereas mercury was found in many medicines in former times, it is very limited today. One such drug is thimerosal

TABLE 18.6
Sources of Mercury Exposure

Elemental	Inorganic	Organic
Amalgam preparation	Disinfectant making	Bactericide preparation
Barometer manufacture	Dye making	Drug manufacture
Bronzing	Explosive production	Embalming
Dentistry	Fur processing	Insecticide production
Photography	Tannery work	Histology
Mercury refining	Laboratory research	Farming
Paint manufacture	Taxidermy	Seed handling

(merthiolate), an antiseptic agent added to several medicinal preparations. Another is mercurochrome, a topical antiseptic. Suffice it to say that the availability of mercury from medicinal sources is vanishingly small, especially when compared with its widespread abundance in the past. An interesting source of mercury deserving comment is dental amalgams, approximately one-half mercury by weight. Mercury has been used for dental fillings for over 150 years and is still used for more than 100,000,000 fillings each year in the United States. The mechanical action of chewing releases trace quantities of mercury that are absorbed into the blood. The quantity absorbed, however, is less than 1% of the safe level of mercury and an expert panel of the National Institutes of Health recently concluded that amalgam fillings do not constitute a threat to the population. In spite of this conclusion, there is a segment within the alternative medicine community that believes hypothyroidism arises from mercury released from fillings. They claim that mercury injures the thyroid gland and individuals with fillings should have chelation therapy.

TOXICOKINETICS OF MERCURY

Elemental mercury is readily absorbed through the pulmonary alveoli and transported by the blood to the brain and other organs. Mercury metal is oxidized to mercuric ions in the red blood cells. Mercuric ions are very slowly excreted primarily into the urine with a long half-life of about 60 days. If mercuric chloride is ingested, it dissolves fairly rapidly in the stomach and is quickly absorbed. Wide distribution occurs. This form of mercury is excreted from the bowel, kidney, liver, and skin.

Organic mercury is well-absorbed orally or through the skin and distributes throughout the body. Methylmercury follows the distribution of other forms of organic mercury but with a larger preference for concentrating in blood and in the CNS. Some conversion of organic mercury to mercuric ion occurs in the tissues. The major route of elimination for organic mercury is by the feces. (See Table 18.7.)

SIGNS OF MERCURY POISONING

Many of the findings characteristic of mercury poisoning have been referred to in the historical cases described above. Findings vary with the type of mercury and

TABLE 18.7
Mercury Toxicity

	Elemental	Inorganic	Organic
Route	Inhaled	Ingested	Ingested
Organs	CNS	Kidney	CNS
	Kidney		Kidney
			Liver
Clearance	Renal	Renal	Renal
			Fecal
Symptoms	Tremor	Tremor	Tremor
	Pulmonary		
	GI	GI	GI
	Renal	Renal	Renal
	Acrodynia	Acrodynia	
Treatment	BAL, DMSA	BAL, DMSA	DMSA

whether the exposure is acute or chronic. Thus, acute exposure to elemental mercury may cause bronchial irritation and pneumonia. Metallic taste and gingivitis have been reported. Inorganic mercury may produce severe gastroenteritis, urticaria, and vesication. Severe acute exposures may cause renal and neurological symptoms. Chronic poisoning causes the symptoms found in Isaac Newton, whether his were due to mercury or not. In this regard, elemental or organic mercury is most likely to produce severe neurological findings. Inorganic mercury, on the other hand, is most damaging to the kidney. Its effects on the nervous system are subdued because of its relative inability to cross the blood–brain barrier.

TREATMENT OF MERCURY POISONING

In the case of oral ingestion of inorganic mercury efforts should be directed at rapid removal of the substance from the gastrointestinal tract. This may be accomplished successfully by ipecac-induced emesis and/or lavage. After these steps, activated charcoal should be administered. The patient must be observed for the onset of shock, a common complication from excessive loss of fluids and hemorrhage. Fluid replacement may be adequate to prevent shock from becoming severe.

Chelating agents may be required and are usually helpful in the context of mercury exposure. Alkyl organomercurials, however, do not respond to chelating agents. Most of the common agents, except for EDTA, can be used. Those that have been effective include dimercaprol, penicillamine, DMSA (dimercaptosuccinic acid, also known as Succimer), and DMPS (dimercaptopropane-sulfonate) with the dimer-caprol formerly being the agent of choice in inorganic mercury poisoning. Dimer-caprol enhances the renal elimination of mercury. This therapy is dangerous because kidney damage may occur during the course of treatment. In the absence of other effective treatments, however, it may be necessary. In patients with some degree of renal impairment, it must be employed with great caution. Recent research shows that DMSA and DMPS are both superior to dimercaprol in preventing toxic complications and in limiting the undesirable distribution of inorganic mercury into sites in the CNS and other vulnerable areas.

LABORATORY TESTING AND MERCURY

Cold-vapor atomic absorption spectrophotometry is a common and reliable method for mercury analysis. Many sensitive and elegant methods also exist including neutron activation, X-ray fluorescence analysis, and inductively coupled plasma emission spectrometry. These three methods are slightly superior to AAS under certain conditions. They are all somewhat specialized, however, and limited by significant costs associated with instrument acquisition. Whole blood is an excellent specimen that correlates with total body burden of mercury and with levels of mercury in the CNS. When attempting to evaluate long-term mercury exposure, urine is a better specimen than whole blood. Urine concentrations, however, may correlate poorly with symptom severity while correlating closely with duration and degree of exposure. A confounding factor in mercury testing is a recent meal of seafood. This is likely to transiently elevate urinary concentration. Do not collect samples for mercury analysis for 24 hours after seafood consumption.

IRON

TOXICOKINETICS

Iron is readily absorbed as ferrous ion from the duodenum and jejunum. The transit protein, transferrin, is the vehicle for iron circulation within the bloodstream. In the blood it eventually combines (70%) with protoporphyrin to form heme and then hemoglobin. On average, 25% of iron is in the ferric (oxidized) form within the storage protein, ferritin, or the cellular inclusion, hemosiderin. Less than 0.1% is free in the plasma in the ferric form. Approximately 1 mg/day is lost in the urine or by the desquamation of skin and other cells.

IRON TOXICITY

Iron has a corrosive action on the cells of the gastrointestinal mucosa. This may cause stomach and intestinal ulceration with hemorrhage and coagulative necrosis. The victim will often exhibit hematemesis and bloody diarrhea. Severe gastritis may lead eventually to scarring and possible obstruction of the GI tract. The effect on the cardiovascular system may include a reduction in cardiac output. Damage to the heart and loss of blood volume due to hemorrhage may, collectively, lead to shock. Circulating iron may increase the permeability of capillaries, contributing further to the loss of plasma volume. Additional hematologic abnormalities include depression of the activities of several coagulation factors such as V, VII, IX, and X. Iron also is damaging to the liver as it is absorbed into the mitochondria of hepatocytes. Free radical formation may be one mechanism by which iron injures the hepatic cells. Iron also draws electrons away from the electron transport system, thereby interfering with electron transport and ATP synthesis. This decrease in cellular respiration reduces energy output and hepatocyte necrosis may result.

Iron poisoning has been divided into four stages by various authorities:

I   Immediately after ingestion; vomiting, diarrhea, abdominal pain, pallor, lethargy, low blood pressure; lab findings may include high iron, leucocytosis, hyperglycemia, acidosis

II After 6 or more hours; signs of hypotension, worsening acidosis

III 12 or 24 hours after ingestion; multiple (GI, CNS, cardiovascular) organ failure

IV After 4 or more weeks; gastrointestinal scarring and/or obstruction

TREATMENT

Therapy begins with an estimate of the patient's risk, if this is possible. Calculate the amount ingested, recalling that iron preparations are much less than 100% iron, as shown here:

Ferrous sulfate (hydrate)	20% iron
Ferrous fumarate	33%
Ferrous gluconate	12%
Ferrous chloride (hydrate)	28%
Ferric chloride (hydrate)	20%

Having completed this calculation, refer to the following:

< 20 mg/kg ingested	Minimal or no toxicity
20–60 mg/kg	Mild to moderate
> 60 mg/kg	Possible severe toxicity

Lavage with normal saline or conduct whole bowel irrigation. Treat the patient's symptoms and provide infusions to adjust laboratory abnormalities. Initiate antidotal therapy.

Deferoxamine (Deferoxamine Mesylate, Desferal)

Deferoxamine is a relatively specific chelating agent for iron. It was discovered by Keberle during research on *Streptomyces pelosus*, an actinomycete which binds iron from soil. Deferoxamine from *S. pelosus* binds iron in the ferric form much more strongly than it binds to zinc, calcium, copper, or magnesium. It binds ferric ion at the three N–OH sites, forming an octahedral iron complex. The stability constant of the resulting complex is very high, $10^{30.7}$, which is greater than the affinity of iron for transferrin or ferritin, but not as strong as iron's binding to hemoglobin. When Desferal is given to an iron-poisoned patient the resulting iron-deferoxamine complex, called ferrioxamine, is excreted into the urine and imparts a *vin* rose color to the urine.

Deferoxamine is water soluble, has a molecular weight of 597 Da, and binds ferric ion on a one-to-one molar basis (100 mg Desferal with 9.35 mg iron). Desferal should be given if the laboratory reports a blood iron greater than 500 µg/dL or in the context of appropriate symptoms irrespective of what the laboratory result is. It is difficult to know exactly when the patient ingested the iron and, even if this is known fairly well, other factors may delay or expedite absorption. Therefore, a physician cannot be certain that the blood was drawn at the ideal time for an accurate interpretation of the lab result.

LABORATORY INVOLVEMENT

The measurement of serum iron is clinically helpful to a physician treating an overdose. Thus, toxicity is usually associated with results above 350 µg/dL and there is a 20% incidence of shock if the result is greater than 500 µg/dL. If chelation therapy is started, then the laboratory iron should not be trusted because the chelating agent in the blood will usually interfere with most testing methods.

A test called total iron binding capacity (TIBC) is also available from the clinical laboratory. This is really a measure of the amount of protein, mainly transferrin, present in the blood for purposes of binding iron. Some think that TIBC should be measured to evaluate iron poisoning. The theory is that the iron cannot be dangerous if the amount of iron is less than the ability of the blood to bind to it. In other words, the iron is dangerous when it leaves the blood and enters organs, something which cannot happen when the iron is bound within the blood. Against this theory, however, is the fact that TIBC may be inaccurate, due to analytical interference, in the presence of high iron concentrations. Further, TIBC is definitely inaccurate when chelation has been started so physicians should never order this test once desferoxamine has been given.

LABORATORY TESTING METHODS

Iron may be tested spectrophotometrically after it has been released from binding to transferrin by treating the specimen with acid. Ferric ion is then reduced to ferrous ion and an iron–chromagen complex is formed. Bathophenanthroline or ferrozine are suitable reagents. Whenever a laboratory analyzes for metals, scrupulous cleanliness is required, including washing of glassware with acid.

Questions and Problems

1. President Zachary Taylor was thought to have been poisoned by arsenic. He was tested by the Gutzeit test, by X-ray microanalysis, and by neutron activation analysis. List the advantages and disadvantages of each of these methods for arsenic testing.

2. The contents of a mercury thermometer are spilled onto the floor of a room that is 20×20 feet (W × L) and 8 ft high. The amount of the spill is 1.2 mL of elemental mercury (density = 13 g/mL). When all of the

mercury has evaporated into the room air, will the mercury content of the air be above the permissable exposure limit? The TWA is 0.05 mg/m³.

3. Discuss the carcinogenicity of arsenic.

4. Explain, on a structural basis, the reason why British anti-Lewisite is capable of binding to arsenic.

5. The following tests are used at various times to evaluate lead exposure and lead toxicity. List the value and limitations of each:

    Blood lead
    Urine lead
    Free erythrocyte protoporphyrin
    EDTA challenge

6. Whole-blood lead was tested by flameless atomic absorption spectrophotometry. Working standards were prepared in whole blood from 0 to 900 µg/L. The process involved drying at 110°C, a charring step at 550°C, and atomizing at 2000°C. Absorbance was measured for standards and unknowns:

Absorbance Units	Concentration (µg/L)
0.16	200
0.30	350
0.47	500
0.65	700
0.32	Unknown #1
0.21	Unknown #2

Calculate the unknown concentrations.

Case Study 1: The Case of the Missing Antidote

A 3-year-old boy ingested an unknown amount of a liquid kept in the garage of his home and used for termite eradication. He began vomiting and his parents brought him to the emergency department of a local hospital. At the hospital, he was found to be lethargic with elevated pulse rate and low blood pressure. Fluids and electrolytes were infused. During the next 2 hours he had persistent bloody vomitus and diarrhea. His blood pressure and pulse rate both continued to decline. Gastric lavage was attempted and charcoal was administered. An antidote was not available locally and the emergency department sent for it from another hospital.

At this point a possible identity for the toxin is

    a) Octane
    b) Mercury
    c) Arsenic
    d) 2,4 Dichlorophenoxyacetic acid

It was known that the agent was specifically intended as an insecticide, so arsenic was a strong possibility. Octane could contribute to his symptoms because it may be the solvent for a pesticidal agent. Octane, however, would not, of itself, be expected to cause blood loss. This child's major problem seems to be hemorrhage as manifested by the bloody vomitus and the associated drop in blood pressure. Elemental mercury is not a hemorrhagic agent. The herbicide, 2,4 dichlorophenoxyacetic acid (2,4-D), also has a different constellation of symptoms. Ingestion of 2,4 D causes nausea, diarrhea, vomiting, arrhythmias, and thrombocytopenia. Hemorrhage is not seen with 2,4 D exposure.

Two hours after admission dimercaprol arrived from the other hospital and was delivered intramuscularly to the child. The patient was then transferred to a pediatric ICU in a large medical center. At this time the child appeared to be in shock with irregular pulse, low blood pressure, and pale, cold extremities. Fluids were continued and a dobutamine drip was prepared to support his blood pressure. However, he lapsed into cardiopulmonary arrest. Despite 1 hour of aggressive resuscitative efforts, he expired. The time of death was 5.5 hours after the ingestion.

The cause of death was ruled arsenic poisoning and the manner of death was accidental. Soon after the child's death, his parents filed a lawsuit against the rural hospital that provided the initial care of their son. They claimed that his death was due to the delay in starting the antidote, dimercaprol, a delay which was preventable if the hospital had kept the antidote in stock.

Questions

Q1. What method is most commonly used for arsenic testing?
   a) Atomic absorption spectrophotometry
   b) Neutron activation analysis
   c) The Gutzeit test
   d) The Marsh test

Q2. The child weighed 35 pounds. His total body burden of arsenic was found to equal 113 mg. His blood arsenic concentration was 1.8 mg/L. If the lethal dose of this form of arsenic is 2 mg/kg, what dose of arsenic is expected to be lethal for this child?
   a) 10 mg
   b) 150 mg
   c) 1.2 g
   d) 30 mg

Q3. The pharmaceutical manufacturer recommends that dimercaprol be administered in a dose of 3 mg/kg intramuscularly every 4 hours for 2 days. What, therefore, would be the recommended amount of antidote for this child?
   a) 5 mg Q 4 hrs
   b) 50 mg Q 4 hrs
   c) 150 mg BID
   d) 250 mg TID

Q4. Dimercaprol (MW = 124 Da) reacts with arsenic on a 1:1 stoichiometric basis. By what amount of arsenic would the body burden be reduced when the child was medicated according to manufacturer's directions?
a) 30 mg from each treatment.
b) 90 mg per treatment.
c) 1.2 g.
d) The total body burden would be eliminated in 2 doses of antidote.

Answers and Discussion

Q1. (Answer = a) Laboratories most commonly assay arsenic by atomic absorption spectrophotometry (AAS). The Gutzeit and Marsh tests are colorimetric methods which, therefore, have relatively high detection limits. They were both developed in the nineteenth century and remind us of the common threat that arsenic was at that time and earlier as a vehicle for homicide. Neutron activation analysis is an excellent technology but requires equipment available in only a limited number of locations. In the original report of this case the authors used atomic absorption spectrophotometry. They initially digested specimens from the decedent in a Kjeldahl digestion apparatus using sulfuric, hydrochloric, nitric, and perchloric acids. Products of digestion were reduced with sodium borohydride and the resulting form of reduced arsenic, arsine, was transferred to the flame of the AAS for quantitation.

Q2. (Answer = d) The child's weight, 35 lbs., equals 15.9 kg. Therefore, a lethal amount of arsenic for this patient is 30 mg. The weedkiller was 44% sodium arsenite. This form of arsenic is especially dangerous because arsenic toxicity is related to arsenic's oxidation state and solubility. The 3+ forms (arsenite) are more dangerous than 5+ forms (arsenates) and this specific arsenite is also very soluble.

Q3. (Answer = b) Again, the child's weight is 15.9 kg. A safe level of therapy is delivery of 50 mg of dimercaprol, the amount which was given by the treating physicians. Relevant calculation:

$$15.9 \text{ kg} \times 3 \text{ mg/kg} = 47.7 \text{ mg}$$

Q4. (Answer = a) A 30-mg dose of arsenic should be inactivated by treatment with 50 mg of antidote. Calculation:

50 mg antidote/124 mg/mmole = 0.403 mmole antidote provided

0.403 mmol arsenic $\times$ 74 mg/mmol = 30 mg arsenic eliminated per dose of antidote

The important point is that the child still would be left with at least 70 mg, which is much greater than a lethal dose for this patient. In the survival interval the child could have been medicated twice if the antidote were readily available from the first moment he arrived in the emergency department. Even here, however, sufficient arsenic would have remained in his body to cause his death. Under the most ideal circumstances this patient would have a residual body burden of arsenic of at least 40 mg, a lethal dose for someone of his body size. It would actually be greater than 40 mg because not all of the antidote binds to arsenic under physiological conditions.

As a consequence of this excellent evaluation, the plantiffs were not able to establish that they had been harmed by the failure of the hospital to stock dimercaprol. The case was decided in favor of the hospital. This is an excellent example of the importance of thorough and sophisticated postmortem analysis in forensic toxicology.

Reference

Saady, J.J. et al., Estimation of the body burden of arsenic in a child fatally poisoned by arsenite weedkiller, *J. Anal. Toxicol.*, 13, 310–312, 1989.

Case Study 2: Hazards of a Handy Man

A 33-year-old man was treated at an emergency department for headache, abdominal cramps, and joint pains. The patient described feeling well until approximately 2 weeks earlier when he was working on a renovation job in his older home. The project had consisted of 12 hours of sandblasting paint from a fireplace. During this work he "protected" himself by wearing a surgical mask. The room in which he worked was protected from dust by a canopy he had erected around the fireplace. He stated that viral-like symptoms had begun when he finished the sandblasting. After 2 weeks of worsening illness he decided to seek medical attention.

Physical examination revealed a well-developed young male who was in acute distress and vomited frequently. He complained of weakness and severe abdominal pain. Vital signs were BP, 170/125; pulse, 88; respirations, 16; and temperature, normal. No focal motor or sensory deficits were noted and deep tendon reflexes were normal. Routine chemistry and CBC were within normal limits.

At this time a probable cause of his symptoms is
   a) Viral syndrome
   b) Arsenic poisoning
   c) Aspirin overdose
   d) Lead

Viral illness cannot definitely be ruled out. The progression of his symptoms and their onset after the renovation project are suspicious, however. The findings up to this time are all consistent with acute lead poisoning. In view of the age of the house the paint was most likely to be lead based. The face mask would not provide a significant measure of protection because the sand-blasted particles would be small enough to penetrate it. His efforts to protect the remainder of the house with the canopy would enormously increase his own risk.

There is no history of aspirin exposure and symptoms of aspirin overdose would not last 2 weeks, in any case. Arsenic is not an impossible suggestion, but it is not found in significant quantities in paint.

A blood lead test was performed and the result was 98 µg/dL (normal < 25 µg/dL). Other laboratory findings found in relation to a work-up for lead poisoning were as follows:

Erythrocyte protoporphyrin	68 µg/dL (Normal, <35 µg/dL)
Ferritin	78 ng/mL (Normal, >15 ng/mL)
CBC	Basophilic stippling
	No anemia

Based on these findings, chelation therapy was begun. BAL was administered, 280 mg every 4 hours (4 mg/kg IM) plus 3300 mg of calcium disodium EDTA 50 mg/kg IV daily. Within 2 days the patient was entirely asymptomatic, with return of blood pressure to normal range. BAL was discontinued after 48 hours but the CaEDTA was continued for an additional 3 days. Based on laboratory findings 2 weeks later, a second 5-day chelation regimen with CaEDTA was repeated. Three weeks later (69 days after the exposure) a CaEDTA provocation test was performed. In this test 2 g of CaEDTA are given over the course of a single day, 1 g per 12 hours, IV. A 24-hour urine is collected. The urine lead is divided by the CaEDTA given. In this case the results were 1610 µg urine lead/2000 mg CaEDTA given = 0.80. Treatment should be continued if this ratio is greater than 0.60 or if the 24-hour urine lead >650 µg. Therefore, a third course of chelation was provided. Following the last treatment he remained asymptomatic and all laboratory data returned to normal values.

Days Post-Exposure	Lead (µg/dL)	FEP (µg/dL)	Urine Pb (µg/dL)
15	98	68	
18	15	82	
25	45	95	
36	56	212	
69	43	172	1610

Questions

Q1. Which is true of blood lead testing?
 a) It is most reflective of recent exposure.
 b) Low results do not rule out chronic poisoning.

c) Extraneous contamination is a cause of some false positives.

d) It is not as valuable as urine lead test for chronic exposure.

e) All of the above.

Q2. Which is true of basophilic stippling?

a) It arises from lead's inhibition of an enzyme which results in accumulation of ribosomes.

b) It is the most sensitive indicator of lead overdose.

c) It is a highly specific although relatively insensitive marker of lead.

d) It correlates with lead poisoning more closely than urine or blood lead levels.

Q3. Why is this patient not anemic?

a) Lead is unrelated to anemia.

b) The form of lead to which he was exposed does not inhibit heme synthesis.

c) There was not sufficient time to affect the amount of hemoglobin.

d) His iron levels were very high.

Q4. Why is ferritin measured in lead toxicity?

a) Patients at risk of lead exposure may also suffer from iron deficiency.

b) Some signs of iron deficiency mimic lead intoxication.

c) Lead intoxication increases ferritin.

d) High ferritin is indicative of lead hepatotoxicity.

Q5. Why is the provocation test needed?

a) It is not needed if urine lead testing is conducted.

b) It is necessary because this patient suffered <u>acute</u> lead poisoning.

c) Other tests have high imprecision.

d) Other tests do not evaluate total body burden of lead.

Answers and Discussion

Q1. (Answer = e) The CDC has stated that blood lead is the best overall test for lead exposure. No test is perfect, however, in this context. Because lead is absorbed and then relocated, primarily to bones, a blood lead result may underestimate a significantly earlier exposure to lead.

Q2. (Answer = a) Basophilic stippling (the appearance of spotting on basophils) can be seen in a CBC of some patients with lead overdose. A complicated series of events is responsible for it. An enzyme, 5′ pyrimidine nucleotidase, is inhibited by lead. The cell is, thereby, less capable of elimination of products of RNA degradation. In turn, this causes the aggregation of ribosomes, which is seen as a spotting phenomenon when viewed by a microscope. Stippling of basophiles is a relatively nonsensitive indicator of lead exposure. It is not observed in many documented cases of lead poisoning. It also is nonspecific and is seen in several other disorders, sideroblastic anemia and thalessemia, among them.

Q3. (Answer = c) Finding anemia in the context of lead exposure suggests that the process is chronic, i.e., that the lead exposure has persisted for a long enough interval to affect the concentration of hemoglobin. Since the red cell has a lifetime of 120 days it takes a long time for lead to impact the organism in a manner which manifests as a deficiency of hemoglobin.

Q4. (Answer = b) If lead is present in excess or if iron is deficient, the heme synthetic pathway will be affected. In both situations an elevated erythrocyte protoporphyrin results. The anemia of lead poisoning morphologically resembles that due to iron deficiency. Answer (a) may also be true in many situations for socioeconomic reasons. There is no necessary pathologic correlate, however.

Q5. (Answer = d) In the presence of extremely high blood or urine lead or in the face of significant clinical signs, chelation therapy is clearly indicated. When any of these are less emphatic, the question of conducting chelation is ambiguous. A provocation test helps to show that although blood lead may be moderate, total body burden remains high and chelation would be of benefit to the patient.

Reference

Schneitzer, L. et al., Lead poisoning in adults from renovation of an older home, *Ann. Emerg. Med.,* 19, 415–420, 1990.

Case Study 3: The Fatal Laboratory Accident

A middle-aged woman was admitted to the hospital for evaluation of a 5-day history of progressive loss of balance and speech. Her weight declined 15 pounds over the previous 2 months and she suffered episodes of nausea, diarrhea, and abdominal pain. She appeared thin but anxious in regard to her recent symptoms. Examination showed upper extremity dysmetria and dystaxic handwriting. MRI and CT scan of the head were normal except for the incidental finding of a small meningioma that was determined to be unrelated to her present condition. All results of routine laboratory testing were within normal limits.

The patient, a research scientist, recalled a laboratory accident 5 months earlier in which she had spilled a chemical onto her latex gloves. She cleaned up the spill, recorded its occurrence in her laboratory notebook, and gave it no further thought. At this time the spill became the focus of investigation as the potential cause of her current symptoms.

A possible identity of the toxin causing this woman's findings is:
a) Iron chloride
b) Sodium arsenite
c) Mercury
d) Chlorpromazine, an antipsychotic drug

Iron and arsenic would not be expected to manifest toxicity primarily as CNS symptoms. Further, a large dose of these metals would not penetrate the skin in the form of metallic salts because they have poor dermal absorption. If they did cross the skin, an acute response would be more likely rather than a greatly delayed reaction as in this instance. Chlorpromazine would most likely be in aqueous solution, a form in which it should not penetrate latex gloves. Furthermore, a large quantity would be required to provoke symptoms, much more than the amount that one expects from transdermal absorption. Mercury, however, especially in its organic forms, is toxic in small amounts and causes predominantly CNS findings. This patient was exposed to dimethylmercury during her research 5 months earlier. Studies done on penetration of latex gloves by dimethylmercury showed that such gloves resisted penetration for only about 15 seconds, after which organic mercury compounds readily penetrated them.

Blood and urine specimens were sent for urgent mercury testing while evaluation of other potential causes of her symptoms continued. The patient now experienced tingling in her fingers and progressive difficulty with speech, hearing, walking, and vision.

The laboratory reported whole blood mercury, 4000 µg/L (normal, 1–8); urinary mercury, 234 µg/L (normal, 1–5). Chelation therapy with oral succimer was started (10 mg/kg per 8 hrs). This was initially successful and increased mercury excretion from 257 µg/day before chelation up to 39,800 µg/day after chelation. She then was given an exchange transfusion which further lowered her blood mercury from 2230 µg/L to 1630 µg/L. However, 1 day later, re-equilibration of mercury from other tissues back into the blood again raised the blood level to 2070 µg/L. By the 22nd day after initial onset of neurological symptoms (176 days after exposure), she became completely unresponsive to all visual, verbal, and tactile stimuli. The patient continued to receive chelation therapy and mercury concentrations in urine and blood were continuously monitored. Her comatose state only worsened, however. With the prognosis being extremely poor, her advance directives were carried out. Aggressive intervention was discontinued and she died 298 days after the exposure.

Autopsy revealed many abnormalities in the brain. The cortex of the cerebral hemispheres was diffusely thinned. Many neurons were missing from the primary visual and auditory cortices and some from the motor and sensory cortices. The mercury content of brain was about 6 times the mercury content of blood at the time of death.

Questions

Q1. What analytical methods are feasible for mercury determination in blood and urine?
   a) X-ray fluorescence
   b) Atomic absorption spectrophotometry
   c) Neutron activation analysis
   d) All of the above
   e) None of the above

Q2. Which was not a pathway of exposure in this case?
   a) Inhalation
   b) Ingestion
   c) Transcutaneous absorption

Q3. When this patient's illness was diagnosed, her mercury blood level was 4000 µg/L. Her blood volume was 4.2 L and it is estimated that blood contains just 5% of the total body burden of mercury. Her total body burden can be calculated as
   a) 220 µg
   b) 336 mg
   c) 790 mg
   d) 3.2 g

Q4. Elimination of mercury from hair was studied in this patient by measuring hair mercury and it was found that mercury was transferred from her hair with a half-life of 75 days. Further, the interval between dimethylmercury exposure and hair testing was 150 days. How much mercury did she absorb in milliliters, based on the amounts found in hair (dimethylmercury has a density of 3.2 g/mL)?
   a) 0.44 mL
   b) 0.11 mL
   c) 1.4 mL
   d) 8.9 mL

Q5. What is mercury's normal role in metabolism?
   a) A co-factor for enzymes in energy metabolism
   b) A structural component of metalloproteins
   c) A trace element involved in glucose homeostasis
   d) No known role in human biochemistry

Answers and Discussion

Q1. (Answer = d) All of these methods are capable of specific detection of mercury in biological materials. Neutron activation analysis was not employed in the published study of this case because of the method's limited availability. Atomic absorption spectrophotometry may have been used and would have been an acceptable method for accurately measuring the amounts present in this case. X-ray fluorescence was used for mercury determination in hair.

Q2. (Answer = b) This person appears to have absorbed dimethylmercury in a single laboratory accident. Extensive additional investigation of her workplace and co-workers was unable to detect any other source of this toxin. Because her co-workers were normal for blood mercury a laboratory environmental problem was ruled out. There was no record of any ingestion. Some small amount of inhalation of the toxin is possible even though she conducted the experiment in a hood. It was concluded that most, if not all, of her mercury absorption was by the transcutaneous route.

Q3. (Answer = b) The appropriate calculation is as follows:

$$4.2 \text{ L} \times 4000 \text{ }\mu g/L \times 1/0.05 = 336,000 \text{ }\mu g = 336 \text{ mg}$$

Q4. (Answer = a) The appropriate calculation is as follows:

Body burden estimate $= 336$ mg $\left(\text{previous calculation}\right)$

Density $= 3.2$ g/mL $\left(3200 \text{ mg/mL}\right)$

Thus, 336 mg/3200 mg/mL $= 0.11$ mL

150 days between exposure and test $= 2$ half-lives

Thus, original mercury $= 4 \times 336$ mg $= 1344$ mg

1344 mg/3200 mg/mL $= 0.44$ mL

This shows that the victim absorbed at least 0.44 mL of dimethylmercury. Her actual degree of absorption may have been higher because some of it was presumably exhaled.

Q5. (Answer = d) Mercury is found in blood, urine, bones, nails, and virtually all other tissues. This appears, however, to be incidental to simply living on earth because mercury has not been shown to have any role in human biochemistry.

References

Kulig, K., A tragic reminder about organic mercury, *New Engl. J. Med.,* 338, 1692–1693, 1998.

Nierenberg, D. et al., Delayed cerebellar disease and death after accidental exposure to dimethylmercury, *New Engl. J. Med.,* 338, 1672–1676, 1998.

FURTHER READING

Boening, D.W., Ecological effects, transport, and fate of mercury: a general review, *Chemosphere,* 40(12), 1335–1351, 2000.

Ellis, M.R. and Kane, K.Y., Lightening the lead load in children, *Am. Fam. Phys.,* 62(3), 545–554, 2000.

Hu, H., Exposure to metals, *Primary Care,* 27(4), 983–996, 2000.

Landrigan, P.J. et al., The reproductive toxicity and carcinogenicity of lead: a critical review, *Am. J. Indust. Med.,* 38(3), 231–243, 2000.

Langford, N. and Ferner, R., Toxicity of mercury, *J. Human Hypertens.,* 13(10), 651–656, 1999.

Madden, E.F. and Fowler, B.A., Mechanisms of nephrotoxicity from metal combinations: a review, *Drug Chem. Toxicol.,* 23(1), 1–12, 2000.

Markowitz, M., Lead poisoning: a disease for the next millennium, *Curr. Prob. Pediatr.,* 30(3), 62–70, 2000.

Moienafshari, R. et al., Occupational exposure to mercury. What is a safe level? *Can. Fam. Phys.*, 45, 43–45, 1999.

Myers, G.J. and Davidson, P.W., Prenatal methylmercury exposure and children: neurologic, developmental, and behavioral research, *Environ. Health Perspect.*, 106, Suppl. 3, 841–847, 1998.

Osborne, J.W. and Albino, J.E., Psychological and medical effects of mercury intake from dental amalgam. A status report for the American Journal of Dentistry, *Am. J. Dent.*, 12(30), 151–156, 1999.

Risher, J.F. et al., Updated toxicological profile for mercury, *Toxicol. Ind. Health,* 15(5), 480–482, 1999.

Silbergeld, E.K. et al., Lead as a carcinogen: experimental evidence and mechanisms of action, *Am. J. Indust. Med.,* 38(3), 316–323, 2000.

Simeonova, P.P. and Luster, M.I., Mechanisms of arsenic carcinogenicity: genetic or epigenetic mechanisms, *J. Environ. Pathol. Toxicol. Oncol.,* 19(3), 281–286, 2000.

Van Zyl, I., Mercury amalgam safety: a review, *J. Mich. Dent. Assoc.,* 81(1), 40–48, 1999.

Vig, E.K. and Hu, H., Lead toxicity in older adults, *J. Am. Geriat. Soc.,* 48(11), 1501–1506, 2000.

Zalups, R.K., Molecular interactions with mercury in the kidney, *Pharmaceut. Rev.,* 52(1), 113–143, 2000.

19 Over-the-Counter Analgesics

CONTENTS

INTRODUCTION

This class of compounds deserves special treatment in a text on toxicology because of the extremely widespread use of these drugs as well as their potential dangers. So common are over-the-counter analgesics that we would be astonished to meet someone who claimed to have never used them. Acetaminophen, ibuprofen, and aspirin are the objects of intense marketing efforts on the part of major drug manufacturing firms. Interestingly, aspirin is usually marketed as a combination drug, partly because manufacturers believe that modern users are more likely to be impressed by a formulation containing multiple drugs. Modern advertising campaigns are successful as proved by the many millions in sales of these products. These drugs are potentially dangerous as is discussed in the following pages.

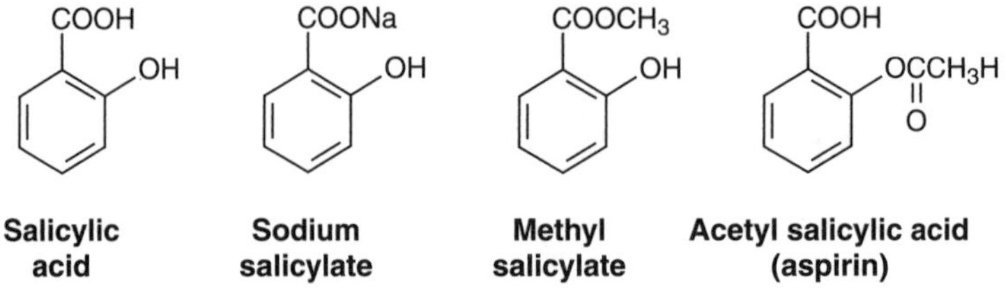

FIGURE 19.1 Salicylic acid and some of its analogs.

SALICYLATES

Willow bark is a plant material which has been known for many centuries for its ability to reduce fever. The active agent in the willow is salicin, a bitter glycoside, which is converted upon hydrolysis to glucose and salicylic alcohol. In 1838, Piria prepared salicylic acid from salicin. Various related structures were made and tested during the nineteenth century and aspirin, which is acetylsalicylic acid, was finally introduced in 1899.

These compounds are among the most common agents involved in poisoning, especially among the young. Although the lethal doses for salicylates are very high (e.g., 10 g of aspirin are fatal to a child in the absence of medical intervention), the relatively ubiquitous nature of these over-the-counter products leads to many incidents of overdose.

These poisonings were even more common prior to 1970 at which time the U.S. Congress passed the Poison Prevention Packaging Act. That act mandated childproof packaging which reduced subsequent incidents of aspirin overdose by about one half. Nevertheless, the frequency with which such overdoses continue to occur is very high, with 10,000 calls about salicylates to Poison Control Centers in a recent year.

FORMS OF SALICYLATES

Salicylic acid is medically active, but it also is very irritating when taken orally. Therefore, esters of salicylic acid with substitution in the carboxyl group, and salicylate esters of organic acids with substitution in the hydroxyl group have been prepared. Salts of salicylic acid also have been synthesized.

The salicylic acid moiety is responsible for most of the activity of aspirin and other salicylates. The substances shown here (Figure 19.1) are converted to salicylate *in vivo*, mainly by esterase enzymes in the gastrointestinal mucosa, red cells, and synovial fluid. These various derivatives of salicylic acid differ only in their potency and toxicity. As salts and esters of salicylic acid at least 40 other forms of salicylate are marketed.

TOXICITY

The response to salicylate overdose is correlated with the dose ingested by the patient and with the blood concentration that is reached. Table 19.1 shows these relationships for a child who weighs 45 lbs.

TABLE 19.1
Relationship of Dose and Blood Concentration in a Child

Dose of Salicylate Ingested (g)	No. Children's Tablets	No. Adult Tablets	Blood (mg/dL)	Symptoms
<3	<37	<9	45–65	Nausea, gastritis, tinnitus, hyperpnea
4–6	50	15	65–90	Hyperpnea, sweating, lethargy, dehydration
6–8	75	25	90–120	Coma, convulsion, cyanosis, respiratory failure
7–10	100	35	>120	Coma, death

For an average adult, the doses and numbers of tablets would be 3 to 4 times greater than shown in the table. The blood concentrations found with each set of symptoms are approximately the same as given for children.

MECHANISM OF TOXICITY

Salicylate toxicity is an excellent example of a disorder in which multiple biochemical abnormalities appear at the same time. In general, most of the signs of aspirin overdose relate to either the respiratory or the metabolic effects of salicylates. One property of salicylates is their ability to stimulate the respiratory center. When stimulated by salicylates, the respiratory center increases the breathing rate and oxygen consumption. Fever occurs and there is an increase in frequency and depth of breathing. The patient exhales carbon dioxide at an exaggerated rate with a consequent drop in blood CO_2. The effect of this on the bicarbonate buffer system is to decrease the hydrogen ion concentration. In other words, respiratory alkalosis (high blood pH due to elevated rate of CO_2 loss) occurs. There is a renal compensation for respiratory alkalosis in which increased excretion of bicarbonate occurs as the body attempts to offset the loss of acid in the form of carbon dioxide. This compensation is not immediate and the patient may not survive long enough to be saved by renal intervention. In addition, the picture of acid-base imbalance gets more complex because of the metabolic effects of aspirin discussed next.

Mechanism of Respiratory Alkalosis

Normal bicarbonate equilibrium:

$$H_2O + CO_2 \rightarrow H_2CO_3 \rightarrow H^+ + HCO_3^-$$

Effect of increased CO_2 loss is to pull the equilibrium away from hydrogen ion (reduce the concentration of hydrogen ion = raise the pH)

$$H_2O + CO_2 \, (drops) \leftarrow H_2CO_3 \, (drops) \leftarrow H^+ + HCO_3^-$$

Salicylates are among a handful of compounds which have the property of uncoupling oxidative phosphorylation (Figure 19.2); that is, they prevent the formation of ATP during the oxidation of NADH in the stepwise process known as electron transport. Oxidative phosphorylation is the cell's major pathway for energy production and any interference with it will be fatal if the obstruction is sufficiently extensive and prolonged. Such is often the case with cyanide or hydrogen sulfide poisoning. The cell reacts to the uncoupling of ATP production from electron transport by increasing the rate of glycolysis, attempting to provide more substrate to the electron transport system to compensate for a slower rate of oxidative phosphorylation. This is a partly successful maneuver which, however, has its own set of complications. Faster glycolysis produces more acids, lactic and pyruvic, which can cause metabolic acidosis (low blood pH due to reduced level of bicarbonate in the blood). The body also reacts to energy depletion by fat oxidation which produces large quantities of ketoacids, acetoacetic acid, and beta-hydroxybutyric acid. The end result is that the acid load in the blood increases many-fold and severe acidosis occurs. The patient may have a mixed acid-base disorder, metabolic acidosis superimposed on respiratory alkalosis. Which direction the pH takes depends, among other factors, on the patient's age. Thus, children develop metabolic acidosis rapidly whereas it is delayed in adults. The respiratory alkalosis may be so brief in children that their presentation is often thought to be a pure metabolic acidosis.

The enhanced rate of glycolysis leads to hypoglycemia. Depletion of glucose in the brain is, in some cases, one of the most debilitating effects of salicylate overdose.

One of the most sensational trials of the decade of the 1970s involved the re-trial of Claus von Bulow for the attempted murder of his wife, Sonny von Bulow, a fabulously rich socialite. Von Bulow was found guilty in the first trial but the verdict was overturned on a technicality. He was acquitted in a subsequent re-trial. The prosecution alleged that Sonny von Bulow was rendered comatose by the covert administration of insulin by her husband, Mr. von Bulow. Laboratory studies showed that Mrs. von Bulow experienced profound hypoglycemia at the time of her hospitalization, the presumed cause of her coma. Experts for the prosecution maintained that only insulin, which von Bulow was charged with injecting into his wife, could have caused such severe hypoglycemia. Experts for the defense, however, argued successfully that salicylates, which Mrs. von Bulow was known to use excessively, were the actual cause of her hypoglycemic coma.

SYMPTOMS

The signs of salicylate poisoning are related to dosage, as shown in Table 19.1 above. We now understand that the early signs including nausea, vomiting, hyperpnea, and headache are a result of stimulation of the central nervous system, which produces respiratory alkalosis as an early finding. The fever and dehydration described in salicylate poisoning are also seen as effects of the hypermetabolic state as the patient's metabolism speeds up in a vain effort to compensate for the reduced output of ATP in association with blockage of oxidative phosphorylation.

Salicylate toxicity may also be described in terms of stages of poisoning:

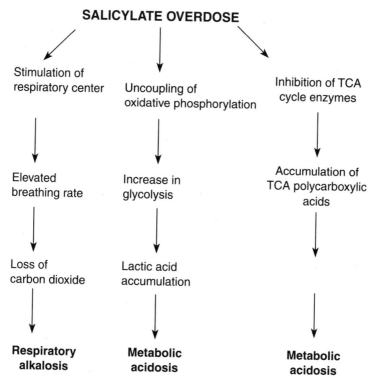

FIGURE 19.2 Biochemical abnormalities in salicylate overdose.

   I   (up to 12 hours post-ingestion). Tachypnea and hyperventilation; alkaline blood pH and alkaline urine

  II (12–24 hours post-ingestion). Shift from alkaline to acid character in blood; coagulation abnormalities may be present

III (>24 hours post-ingestion). Potassium and hydrogen ion excretion; increase in acidosis

TREATMENT

Initial steps in therapy include attempts to prevent further absorption of salicylates from the stomach. Emesis with ipecac or another emetic is usually helpful. Activated charcoal and/or gastric lavage are also of some assistance. Aspirin delays the emptying of the stomach, a feature of this drug which works to the benefit of the patient by allowing the clinician a prolonged opportunity to remove aspirin from the body before absorption is complete. Particularly in the case of an enteric-coated or sustained-release form will the physician have a greater window of time in which to perform emesis or lavage. Supportive measures are critical in therapy of aspirin overdose. Correction of acid-base abnormalities, dehydration, hyperthermia, and hypoglycemia are central to treatment. Dehydration is managed with IV fluids, acidosis is treated mainly with bicarbonate, and seizures, when they occur, are controlled with benzodiazepines.

Enhanced elimination of salicylates is important in large overdoses. If enough bicarbonate is given to maintain the pH of the patient's urine above pH 8, then the salicylate will be excreted more rapidly. This phenomenon is due to the acidic nature of salicylates, which are weak acids with pKa = 3.5. Thus, at urine pH equal to 8 almost all salicylic acid is in the ionized form. As a charged substance, its entry into the CNS is reduced and its re-entry into the blood after passing through the renal proximal tubules is also reduced. Thus, excretion is increased (see discussion in Chapter 3 on ion trapping). Finally, because salicylates are at least 50% dialyzable, dialysis should be undertaken in the case of serious overdoses.

LABORATORY TESTING

Salicylates are drugs for which the serum concentration is related fairly closely to the severity of poisoning. Therefore, it is advisable to measure the salicylate level in all cases of overdose. If the resulting concentration reported by the laboratory is in the mid-range, it can mean a medium dose ingested a few hours ago or a large dose ingested some time ago. In other words, the result is difficult to interpret unless the time of ingestion is known. Done has developed a nomogram (Figure 19.3) which relates the serum concentration to the time of ingestion and estimates the risk on the basis of these two factors. From the Done nomogram we see, for example, that 60 mg of salicylate per deciliter of serum is consistent with moderate overdose, whereas the same concentration at 6 hours post-dose is more likely to be a mild intoxication.

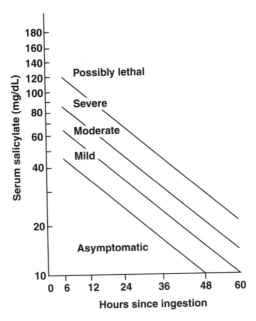

FIGURE 19.3 Done nomogram for aspirin overdose.

The Done nomogram can be helpful but its interpretation and use are confounded by acute vs. chronic salicylate overdose, use of sustained-release tablets, and other factors. Great caution is required when referring to the Done nomogram.

It is easy to test for salicylates and may even be done so at the bedside. Several drops of 10% ferric chloride are added to 1 mL of urine. If a purple color appears, then salicylates are probably present, although a false positive may be given by acetoacetic acid (as in ketoacidosis) or by phenylpyruvic acid (as in phenylketonuria). This test is said to have no false negatives (100% sensitivity), although occasional false positives may be noted. This test should be followed up with a quantitative test from the laboratory. The test used in the laboratory is usually the Trinder test. This is the same as the bedside method described above with the exception that standards are run to make the test quantitative. As was true for the bedside test, sensitivity is very good but specificity is less than perfect. For the most accurate work, high-performance liquid chromatography methods have been developed. They provide excellent results, but are not rapid enough for STAT usage.

ACETAMINOPHEN

Acetaminophen, N-acetyl-para-aminophenol, was first used in medicine in 1893. It was a product of the nineteenth century search for better analgesics and arose from studies based on an earlier discovery that acetanilid had antipyretic actions. Acetanilid itself was found to be excessively toxic but research continued on compounds that were structurally similar in hopes of finding one which shared the medicinal benefits but not the toxicity of acetanilid. The search led first to phenacetin (acetophenetidin) and then to acetaminophen, a major active metabolite of acetanilid and acetophenetidin.

Acetaminophen has analgesic and antipyretic effects similar to aspirin. It differs from aspirin in not having the anti-inflammatory effects of salicylates.

PHARMACOKINETICS

Acetaminophen is rapidly and extensively absorbed from the GI tract, reaching a peak plasma level in about 1/2 to 1 hour. It is extensively distributed throughout bodily fluids. Metabolism occurs predominantly in the liver (see Chapter 6, Biotransformation) and is important in relation to the major toxicity of this drug. Most acetaminophen (90 to 95%) is converted to conjugates. Acetaminophen glucuronide is formed by reaction with uridine (diphospho) acetylglucosamine, and acetaminophen sulfate is formed by reaction with phosphoadenosyl sulfate. To a very minor degree catechols and other metabolites are formed. About 1 to 2% of acetaminophen is excreted into urine as the parent drug. Finally, mixed function oxidases form the highly reactive intermediate, N-acetyl-para-benzoquinoneimine (NAPQI), with 5 to 10% of the acetaminophen. NAPQI is conjugated with glutathione to form nontoxic cysteine and mercapturic acid conjugates and is eliminated unless glutathione stores become depleted. The portion of NAPQI not detoxified to acetaminophen mercapturate binds covalently to critical intracellular molecules, which eventually leads to toxicity and cell death. Although acetaminophen may have other toxic effects, it is this capacity for widespread liver cell necrosis that is its major effect and most toxic possibility.

Alcohol

It has been noted that persons who consume alcoholic beverages and also use acetaminophen have a heightened risk for drug toxicity. The dimensions of this increased risk are very significant, i.e., the toxic dose may be lowered by as much as five-fold. For example, the minimum dose for severe liver damage is estimated to equal 200 mg/kg in an adult. This equals 16 g in an 80 kg (176 lb.) person. Case studies show, by contrast, that alcoholics have suffered severe liver damage after 4 to 6 g of drug for 3 to 4 days. A famous case became the subject of litigation from which the claimant was awarded millions of dollars. He required a liver transplant and won his suit by claiming that the drug manufacturer did not provide adequate warning that wine would increase his risk of using acetaminophen.

This effect of alcohol relates to its ability to affect the amount of toxic metabolite (NAPQI) formed and the rate at which the toxic metabolite is detoxified. Of the two mechanisms, the second is thought to be more prominent, i.e., alcohol depletes glutathione so the patient has a reduced ability to detoxify NAPQI. The other mechanism has some impact, as well. Consumption of alcohol induces the mixed function oxidases. Therefore, alcoholics would be expected to form more NAPQI than individuals who do not drink alcohol excessively.

TOXICITY

Metabolic abnormalities are occasionally observed from acetaminophen use. These include hyponatremia, hypophosphatemia, and elevated transaminases. GI symptoms include vomiting, nausea, diarrhea, and rarely, pancreatitis. There are also rare cardiac problems, and renal injury is sometimes noted.

Acetaminophen overdose sometimes follows four stages:

I Day 1. Major findings are GI irritation; large ingestions may cause metabolic acidosis and cardiac arrhythmias.

II Days 1 to 3. Hepatic toxicity develops; renal failure may occur; hepatic encephalopathy may be found.

III Days 3 to 5. Worsening hepatic necrosis leads to disseminated intravascular coagulation as the shortage of coagulation factors intensifies; other signs of liver failure are noted such as icterus, hepatic portal hypertension, and hepatic encephalopathy.

IV Days 5 to 14. Recovery occurs if patient is treated effectively.

THERAPY

The patient should be decontaminated by providing ipecac and administering lavage within 1 hour of ingestion. Activated charcoal should be given up to 4 hours post-ingestion. The cornerstone of treatment for acetaminophen overdose is the antidote,

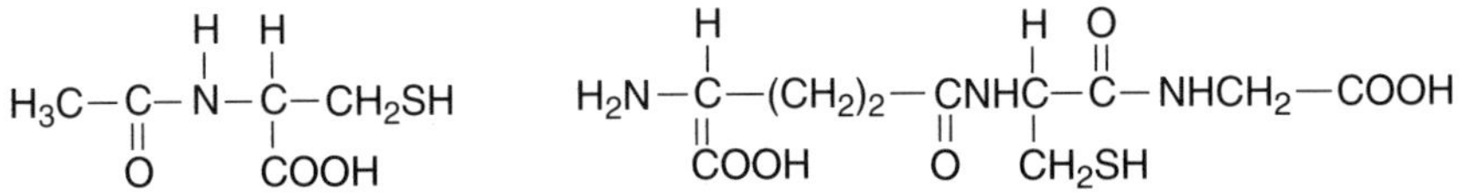

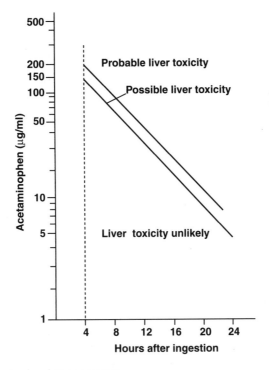

N-Acetyl cysteine   **Glutathione**

FIGURE 19.4 Structures of NAC and glutathione.

FIGURE 19.5 Acetaminophen nomogram.

N-acetyl cysteine (NAC or Mucomyst). This antidote can be traced to studies by Mitchell in 1974 which showed that glutathione has a protective effect on the liver during the metabolism of acetaminophen. A similar protection was afforded by cysteamine, methionine, and NAC but the latter, NAC, is less toxic. In 1985 the FDA approved NAC for antidotal use in acetaminophen poisoning. The entire spectrum of NAC activity is not fully known but it is believed to prevent the binding of NAPQI to hepatocytes, enhance the synthesis of additional glutathione and sulfate, and favor the reduction of NAPQI back to acetaminophen (Figure 19.4). NAC is most effective when given within 8 hours of acetaminophen ingestion. Indications for using it, therefore, are history suggestive of drug ingestion greater than 140 mg/kg or serum drug level above the line on the nomogram (see Figure 19.5).

LABORATORY TESTING

Some hospital laboratories conduct acetaminophen testing on all patients if there is even a remote suspicion of ingestion of this drug. This practice is based on the fact that despite the low incidence of acetaminophen overdoses (0.3% of emergency department visits), the diagnosis is difficult to make on clinical grounds and, if therapy is delayed, the outcome may be devastating.

The serum level is important for estimating the severity of poisoning. Rumack has developed a nomogram similar to that used for aspirin which enables the physician to predict the likelihood of liver damage on the basis of the serum level and the time since ingestion (see Figure 19.5). While nomograms of this sort may be helpful, one must recall that they do not apply in several common situations. These include chronic (vs. acute ingestions) use of sustained-release tablets, and patients who consume moderate to high amounts of alcohol. Interestingly, it is possible to use the nomogram without knowing when the patient ingested the drug. Because acetaminophen is metabolized by the liver, any impairment of hepatic function by the drug will reduce the rate of acetaminophen clearance. In other words, the drug will decline from the blood at a slower than predicted rate. If a laboratory measures acetaminophen in serum at two different times and compares the slopes of the concentration vs. time curves, a slope which is less than that found in the nomogram is indicative of hepatic damage. This method works to some degree but is not as accurate as actually knowing the time of ingestion.

The shortcomings of the Rumack nomogram are illustrated by a true incident in which a patient used a significant quantity of acetaminophen and became symptomatic of possible overdose. He was brought to an emergency department and tested. A call to the local Poison Control Center was made and the physician treating the patient was assured that the patient could be discharged because his blood level was in the safe range, based on the nomogram. The patient went home but returned 2 days later and this time was in fulminant liver failure. The patient died 1 day later. It was subsequently discovered that the patient had a history of alcoholism and was not an appropriate candidate for use of the acetaminophen nomogram.

Acetaminophen may be measured by colorimetric assays, by HPLC, or by immunoassay. The colorimetric assays are not inherently specific so extra steps are included to clean up the specimen to permit adequate specificity. These steps render the method too tedious. HPLC is a superb method but, again, not entirely compatible with STAT testing needs. Most laboratory testing is now done by immunoassay in a very accurate and rapid manner.

IBUPROFEN

Ibuprofen (Figure 19.6) belongs to a class of drugs known as nonsteroidal anti-inflammatory drugs. This large class, generally referred to as NSAIDS, literally includes aspirin although it usually is not included in lists of NSAIDS. Some other commonly prescribed members of this category are oxyphenbutazone (Tandearil), indomethacin (Indocin), sulindac (Clinoril), fenoprofen (Nalfon), and naproxen (Naprosyn). The toxicity of all members of the class is somewhat similar. Because

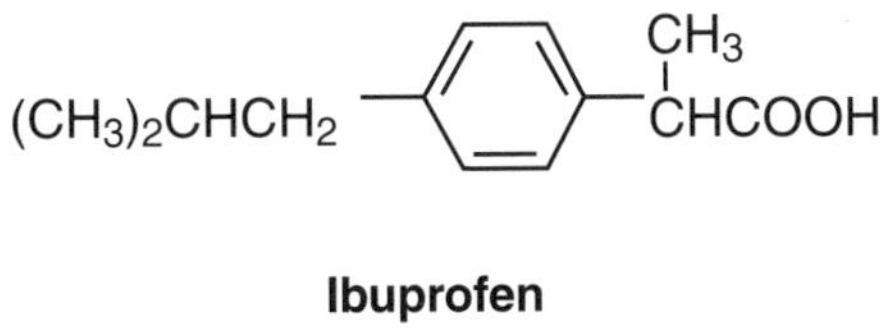

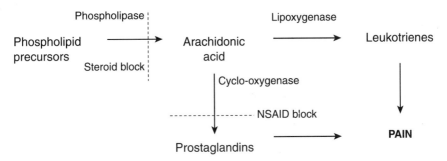

Ibuprofen

FIGURE 19.6 Structure of ibuprofen.

FIGURE 19.7 Mechanism of action of prostaglandin synthesis inhibitors.

ibuprofen is a very commonly used drug and is available over-the-counter, this discussion focuses only on that member of the NSAID group.

MECHANISM OF ACTION

Arachidonic acid is converted to prostaglandins by the enzyme, cyclooxygenase. The prostaglandins are instrumental in provoking the pain response, as well as fever and inflammation. Aspirin, ibuprofen, and other anti-inflammatory drugs exert their beneficial effect by inhibiting cyclooxygenase (Figure 19.7).

TOXICITY

In general, ibuprofen is a very safe drug. In 1991, seven deaths (0.016% of reported exposures) were described by the PCC for ibuprofen or other NSAIDS, excluding aspirin. By contrast, deaths related to aspirin exposure were 0.46% of exposures or 35 times greater than the ibuprofen figure. For acetaminophen, deaths constituted 0.06% of exposures, making acetaminophen much safer than aspirin (in relation to fatalities) but not as safe as ibuprofen. The reader would do well to remember that fatalities are not the only important aspect of drug toxicity. For example, some NSAIDS, while not as likely to cause a fatality as aspirin, may be more likely to induce some other toxic event (such as profound bleeding).

High dosage administration of ibuprofen often results in no symptoms or mild gastrointestinal irritation. In very severe cases metabolic acidosis, hypotension, and renal impairment are reported. CNS toxicity is very rare with drowsiness and lethargy being reported on occasion. Hematologic effects of the NSAIDS include decreased platelet aggregation as a result of inhibition of prostaglandin synthesis within the platelet. Sometimes thrombocytopenia and/or hemolytic anemia may occur. Some patients manifest bleeding disorders, especially with aspirin. If the NSAID is being taken for relief of pain, then patients who experience bleeding disorders should consider acetaminophen. It is also worth mentioning in this context, that the anti-coagulating effects of NSAIDS can be put to good use. Thus, it is currently believed that adults who take one children's aspirin per day reduce their risk of myocardial infarction by about 25 to 35% and their risk of stroke by about 50%.

TREATMENT

Ibuprofen overdose is treated by decontamination as a first step. Ipecac or lavage and administration of activated charcoal are the first interventions to be employed. Supportive therapy is then indicated for any complications which arise from over-dose. There is no specific antidote known for treatment of excess ingestion of this drug and, as mentioned earlier, an antidote usually would not be needed.

LABORATORY TESTING

Serum levels of ibuprofen correlate to some degree with toxicity. A nomogram (Figure 19.8) has been developed for predicting severity of overdose, as is the case with nomograms for acetaminophen and salicylates. Note, however, that ibuprofen overdose is much less dangerous than that of the other aforementioned drugs. As a result, the clinical need for this nomogram is questionable.

There are no commercially available immunoassays for ibuprofen. This is sur-prising in view of the widespread use of this drug. On the other hand, because of the relatively innocuous nature of ibuprofen, physicians will rarely need laboratory help when treating patients exposed to large amounts of this drug.

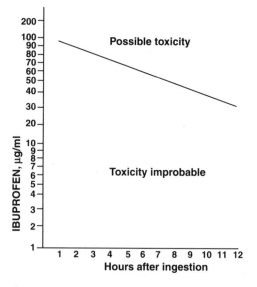

FIGURE 19.8 Ibuprofen nomogram.

Questions and Problems

1. Many different salicylates are therapeutically effective. What are the common structural features required for a compound to have salicylate activity in the blood?

2. Explain why retention of carbon dioxide or accumulation of organic acids have the same effect in the blood in relation to pH.

3. Explain how pH adjustment of the blood might be beneficial in relation to treatment of aspirin overdose.

4. A pediatric patient has a blood concentration of salicylates equal to 40 mg/dL 6 hours after ingestion. A different pediatric patient has this concentration at 48 hours after ingestion. Discuss the relative danger to each child. If an adult had 40 mg/dL of salicylate at 6 hours post-ingestion, what would his prognosis be?

5. A patient has ingested acetaminophen and a blood level of 100 μg/mL is found but the time of ingestion is not known. However, a second blood specimen is drawn 6 hours after the first and this one is equal to 50 μg/mL. On the basis of these results should the antidote be provided? What circumstances might be present that would negate the value of the Rumack nomogram?

6. Explain why ethanol exacerbates the toxicity of acetaminophen.

Case Study 1: Beer and Analgesics

A 43-year-old man was admitted complaining of hallucinations. Five days earlier he had fallen while bicycle riding and sustained a fractured clavicle. At that time his family physician prescribed Tylenol #3 (300 mg over-the-counter pain reliever plus 30 mg codeine per tablet), 1 to 2 tablets every 4 to 6 hours, for 2 days. For the next 3 days he suffered from occasional vomiting, jaundice, and hallucinations. On admission, he was noted to have positive Babinski signs and to be jaundiced. AST was extremely elevated at 8685 U/L; bilirubin was elevated at 13.0 mg/dL; and prothrombin time was 44.2 seconds. A wide assortment of serological tests for viral hepatitis were performed and all were negative. The patient was given extensive supportive care but lapsed into hepatic coma. Relatives mentioned that the patient usually drank about one half a case of beer each day and had taken, for pain relief, 9 Tylenol #3 tablets plus 10 tablets (500 mg each) of another pain reliever the day after his bicycle accident. The patient continued to deteriorate. He experienced a respiratory arrest and died 30 hours after admission.

What was the probable identity of the pain reliever which this patient used?
    a) Aspirin
    b) Ibuprofen
    c) Acetaminophen
    d) Naproxen

This is the classic toxidrome for acetaminophen which produces relatively mild symptoms early on followed by a stage in which symptoms are absent. After 1 to 2 days of apparent recovery, the patient lapses into severe liver failure which leads to death in about 30% of cases. The symptoms associated with ibuprofen, naproxen (similar picture to ibuprofen), and aspirin are quite different, as detailed in other cases found in this chapter. This patient was given Tylenol #3 which contains 300 mg of acetaminophen plus 30 mg of codeine per tablet. On top of these he self-medicated with 10 high-strength (500 mg) acetaminophen tablets. Therefore, he ingested about 7.7 g of acetaminophen in less than 24 hours.

Questions and Discussion

Q1. Which of the following contains acetaminophen?
a) Darvocet
b) Nyquil
c) Excedrin
d) Tylenol #3
e) All of the above

Q2. What was the patient's acetaminophen serum level likely to be when tested on admission?
a) 200 µg/mL
b) 20 mg/dL
c) 50 µg/mL
d) Undetectable

Q3. What is the diagnostic clue that a particular overdose is one of alcohol plus acetaminophen?
a) Very high levels of AST
b) Elevated bilirubin
c) Prolonged prothrombin time
d) Hallucinations

Q4. Why does alcohol intensify the danger of acetaminophen ingestion?
a) Increase in NAD coenzyme from alcohol metabolism.
b) Enzyme induction with synthesis of an abnormally large amount of the toxic metabolite of acetaminophen.
c) CNS depression which slows metabolism of acetaminophen.
d) Alcohol decreases renal excretion of acetaminophen.

Answers and Discussion

Q1. (Answer = e) Acetaminophen is a widely available over-the-counter analgesic. Part of the problem with public education to its dangers is that it is available in many compound medications with other agents. Frequently, people are aware that acetaminophen is dangerous but they do not know that a specific medication found in their homes contains acetaminophen.

Q2. (Answer = d) This patient's acetaminophen level was less than the detection limit of the assay when measured on admission and also a few hours later. This is not surprising despite the fact that his critical condition and ultimate death were attributed to acetaminophen overdose. Most or all of his use of acetaminophen occurred 96 hours before he was tested. If levels had been tested at that time, we would expect that they would have been in the toxic range by the Rumack nomogram. For example, 8 hours after ingestion he was likely to be above 100 µg/mL, a level which predicts probable hepatotoxicity. On the other hand, he may have been in the safe range at that time, according to the nomogram. The co-ingestion of alcohol is a critical factor which greatly increases one's susceptibility to the toxic effects of acetaminophen. The nomogram is unreliable for a patient who drinks alcohol. By the time this patient was tested, most of the acetaminophen had been excreted. Its effects continued, nevertheless, leading to the patient's demise from the irreversible hepatic necrosis set in motion earlier when the acetaminophen concentration was much higher.

Q3. (Answer = a) It is something of a diagnostic challenge, in the absence of a complete history, to distinguish hepatic damage due to acetaminophen or other drugs from that caused by alcohol, viral disease, or some combination of the lot. Extremely high enzyme levels point toward the acetaminophen–alcohol syndrome. On presentation, patients with pure viral hepatitis or alcoholic hepatitis usually have lower levels of enzymes that may eventually rise much higher. They are already greatly elevated in the acetaminophen–alcohol syndrome. In a study of alcoholics who were treated for acetaminophen overdose, 90% of the patients had levels of AST between 3000 and 48,000 U/L.[2]

Q4. (Answer = b) The deleterious effect of alcohol seems to work predominantly by enzyme induction. The toxic metabolite of acetaminophen that does all the harm is NAPQI (N-acetyl-p-benzoquinoneimine). Fortunately, less than 5% of acetaminophen is usually converted to this compound. Alcohol induces two liver cytochromes of the P_{450} system and they increase the proportion of acetaminophen converted to NAPQI. Alcohol is also harmful because it lowers hepatic glutathione levels. It is glutathione which detoxifies NAPQI and, therefore, the liver is less capable of defending itself by the normal detoxification mechanism.

References

1. Johnston, S.C. and Pelletier, L.L., Enhanced hepatotoxicity of acetaminophen in the alcoholic patient, *Medicine,* 76, 185–191, 1997.
2. Zimmerman, H.J. and Maddrey, W.C., Acetaminophen (paracetamol) hepatotoxicity with regular intake of alcohol: analysis of instances of therapeutic misadventure, *Hepatology,* 22, 767–773, 1995.

Case Study 2: Over-the-Counter Analgesics and Pregnancy

A 38-year-old woman with a previous history of four pregnancies from which she delivered three children, presented to the emergency department. She was in the 31st week of her fifth pregnancy and had become despondent. In a suicide attempt the woman ingested 35 g of a common over-the-counter analgesic. On arrival at the hospital, 26 hours after the ingestion, she was lethargic, with slight, generalized abdominal discomfort. Vital signs were normal. Hepatic function tests including aspartate aminotransferase, alanine aminotransferase, and bilirubin were much above normal (see table). Her prothrombin time was grossly prolonged. Arterial blood gases were consistent with metabolic acidosis: pH, 7.10; pCO_2, 15 mm Hg; pO_2, 164 mm Hg; HCO_3, 5.8 mmol/L.

| | Hours After Ingestion | | |
Test	26	42	60
AST	3280 IU/L	6540	13320
ALT	2248 IU/L	4730	4250
Total bilirubin	1.6 mg/dL	3.2	4.3

Arterial blood gases over the following 30 hours showed a continuous moderate acidosis that did not respond to therapy. The patient was promptly treated with an antidote that was maintained at 4-hour intervals.

At this point what is a probable identification of the toxin?
  a) Acetaminophen
  b) Aspirin
  c) Ibuprofen
  d) Naproxen

If this overdose had been with aspirin, the patient would be expected to have other signs such as hyperthermia, tinnitus, and a different blood gas picture (probable respiratory alkalosis or a mixed acid base disturbance) at this stage of her poisoning (26 hours post-ingestion). Ibuprofen usually gives a benign presentation but, on those rare occasions when it is severe, CNS depression and acidosis are common findings. CNS depression was not evident here. This patient was only mildly lethargic and not sufficiently depressed for a significant ibuprofen overdose. The delayed hepatic symptomatology is strongly suggestive of acetaminophen poisoning. Indeed, the patient admitted taking acetaminophen and a serum level at the time of admission equaled 40.4 mg/L.

Fetal distress was evident by absence of fetal movement and breathing. The fetus also exhibited bradycardia. An emergency Caesarian section was performed. A grossly normal female infant was delivered who, however, had extremely poor Apgar scores of 0, 0, and 1 at 1, 5, and 10 minutes, respectively, after birth. The baby was transferred to ICU and treated continuously with the acetaminophen antidote, N-acetyl cysteine. Each patient, mother and child, received intensive supportive care, antidote administration, and hemodialysis. Nevertheless, the baby died 34 hours after birth and the mother expired 66 hours after ingesting the drug.

Questions

Q1. How would one interpret the mother's acetaminophen level of 40.4 mg/L at the time of admission?
   a) It cannot be interpreted from the nomogram because it was determined too late after ingestion.
   b) It is in the toxic range.
   c) It is suggestive of a low risk.
   d) It is not interpretable because of the pregnancy.

Q2. How should one interpret AST, ALT, and total bilirubin results?
   a) Progressive deterioration of liver function
   b) Major toxicity to other organ systems
   c) Stable but serious impairment of hepatic function
   d) Indicative of toxic effects on both mother and child

Q3. Which is true of acetaminophen?
   a) It is contraindicated in pregnancy.
   b) It can cross the placenta.
   c) Its pharmacokinetics are greatly different in pregnancy.
   d) Acetaminophen overdose should not be treated with N-acetyl-cysteine in pregnancy.

Q4. What was the cause of fetal death?
   a) Loss of maternal sustenance
   b) Acetaminophen poisoning and hepatic failure
   c) Acetaminophen poisoning by a mechanism that differs from that in adults
   d) Hemorrhage from acetaminophen overdose

Answers and Discussion

Q1. (Answer = b). Her level of 40.4 mg/L is very high in view of the long time interval between ingestion of the drug and collection of the specimen. The result implied a very high risk of hepatorenal damage and fulminant hepatic failure.

Q2. (Answer = a) These test results are not completely specific for liver disease but in the context of her history and clinical findings they confirm other signs of a poor prognosis. Other sources of AST and ALT may contribute to the enzyme elevations but the major source is most likely hepatic. There is no reason to infer a fetal contribution to this elevation because maternal injury is a sufficient explanation.

Q3. (Answer = b) Acetaminophen is routinely used in pregnancy to treat pain and high temperature. It crosses the placenta and has pharmacokinetic characteristics that are essentially similar to those found in non-pregnant persons. N-acetyl-cysteine is an antidote for acetaminophen that has been used successfully in other reported overdoses in pregnancy to save both mother and child.

Q4. (Answer = c) The baby did not appear to die from loss of maternal support because, at a time when fetal heart rate, breathing, and movement were severely diminished, the mother's vital signs (blood pressure, partial oxygen pressure, etc.) were acceptable. At birth, the baby's acetaminophen was high (37.3 mg/L) and liver enzymes were elevated although less dramatically than those of the mother. Signs of cardiotoxicity, especially elevation of creatine kinase and creatine kinase isoenzyme MB, were very pronounced in the baby. It is possible that the mother's death was a classical acetaminophen demise due to fulminant hepatic failure whereas the baby died from acetaminophen-induced cardiomyopathy.

Reference

Wang, P. et al., Acetaminophen poisoning in late pregnancy. A case report, *J. Reprod. Med.*, 42, 367–371, 1997.

Case Study 3: Pregnancy and Suicidal Intentions

A single 22-year-old woman, pregnant for the first time, came to an emergency department and admitted she had ingested 100 tablets from a bottle of medicine that was present in her home. She acknowledged being depressed and was obviously in great distress. She complained of tinnitus, vomited several times, and was breathing rapidly. Vital signs included respiratory rate at 30 to 40 breaths per minute, pulse elevated at 100/minute, and blood pressure in the normal range. Arterial blood gases revealed a pH of 7.52, pCO_2 of 17 mm Hg, pO_2 of 115 mm Hg on room air, and bicarbonate equal to 12 mmol/L.

What drug is responsible for this patient's symptoms?
   a) Aspirin
   b) Acetaminophen
   c) Ibuprofen
   d) Digoxin

The symptoms manifested by this woman match closely with only one of the choices, aspirin. Tinnitus is a fairly unique finding and aspirin is one of the few drugs that can cause it. Her elevated respirations, resulting in respiratory alkalosis, are also a common finding in the early stages of aspirin poisoning.

An obstetrical consultant evaluated the patient's pregnancy shortly after she was admitted to the hospital. He confirmed the presence of a 32- to 34-week-old fetus with normal cardiac sounds who appeared to be in no immediate danger. The obstetrician believed that the pregnancy should not be interrupted at that time.

The patient's subsequent course included severe agitation requiring restraints and ongoing abnormalities in pH and electrolyte balance for which IV fluids were administered. Her initial salicylate level, drawn 48 minutes after she first presented to the emergency department, was 568 μg/mL. This decreased to 200 μg/mL within 24 hours and further dropped to 44 μg/mL by the end of her 2nd day in ICU.

A fetal monitor was connected at the time of admission to follow the health status of the fetus in response to the aspirin challenge. At 15 hours post-admission the fetus appeared to be doing well. However, the fetus deteriorated rapidly after that time and no signs of life were apparent only 5 hours later. It was decided to await the onset of natural labor. This commenced on the 6th day of hospitalization and a stillborn fetus was delivered by the patient without surgical assistance. The fetal remains were autopsied by the medical examiner and toxicological studies found a postmortem concentration of salicylates at 243 μg/mL in the fetal blood. Liver and brain had very high quantities of salicylates, as well.

The mother recovered from the aspirin overdose and, having received the customary post-natal care, improved rapidly, and left the hospital on the 8th day after admission.

Questions

Q1. Why was the patient's first pH measurement in the alkaline range?
   a) Elevated respirations result in an accumulation of carbon dioxide.
   b) Elevated respirations cause a conservation of bicarbonate.
   c) Aspirin is hydrolyzed to an acid.
   d) Aspirin's effect on the brain is to stimulate the respiratory center and raise the rate of carbon dioxide excretion.

Q2. Which is a true statement in relation to the Done nomogram?
   a) It predicts mild overdose for the mother in this case.
   b) It predicts severe overdose for the mother.
   c) It predicts severe overdose for the fetus.
   d) It cannot be used if the patient is pregnant.

Q3. What blood level is predicted for the mother if the tablets she ingested were 5-grain generic aspirin?
   a) Approximately 100 mg/dL
   b) Less than 40 mg/dL
   c) Over 120 mg/dL
   d) 50 μg/mL

Q4. What factor made the fetus more susceptible to the lethal effects of aspirin?
    a) Immature enzyme system
    b) Reduced ability to compensate for acid-base abnormalities
    c) Higher permeability to salicylates in the CNS
    d) No clear reason

Answers and Discussion

Q1. (Answer = d) A well-established effect of salicylates is to stimulate the respiratory center. The effect of this stimulation is a more rapid breathing rate that leads to enhanced excretion of carbon dioxide. As carbon dioxide decreases, a shift in the equilibrium of the bicarbonate buffer system occurs with a net decrease in hydrogen ion in the blood. A respiratory alkalosis is the first acid-base imbalance in aspirin overdose.

Q2. (Answer = a) The mother's serum level of salicylate was 568 µg/mL or 56.8 mg/dL within one hour of admission. Although the record is not entirely clear, it seems to indicate that this specimen was drawn less than 6 hours after the ingestion. This level is predictive of mild overdose from the Done nomogram. There is always the risk that the nomogram is misleading because the patient may be in the early-absorptive phase. In this case, however, another specimen was drawn just 2 hours later and it was equal to 528 µg/L, slightly less than the first level. This suggests that her peak blood level was near 600 µg/mL. The Done nomogram could not be used for estimating fetal risk because very little is known about fetal risk in relation to aspirin ingestion by the mother. Many limitations exist on the use of devices such as nomograms in assessing severity of poisoning. For the Done nomogram, sustained-release tablets and chronic salicylate overdose are just two of the situations in which the nomogram may not be helpful.

Q3. (Answer = a) Five-grain tablets are also referred to as adult aspirin tablets. A grain is an ancient unit equal to 64 mg. Therefore, 5 grains equals 325 mg; 100 such tablets equal a total aspirin dose of 32.5 g. This is predicted to produce a blood level of about 100 mg/dL and cause severe symptoms including convulsions, severe hyperpnea, and possible respiratory and cardiovascular collapse. Why were the mother's symptoms less severe and her blood level lower (57 mg/dL)? There may be an error in the patient's history so that her dosage was actually less. A second possibility is that she lost much of the drug by vomiting and, in fact, her medical record did show at least several bouts of emesis.

Q4. (Answer = d) The fetus appears to have been more susceptible to the toxic effects of aspirin because fetal death resulted despite a maximum fetal blood level of 243 mg/dL. An adult in this range is usually not even symptomatic. One can only guess as to why the fetus was apparently at greater risk. Cases such as this are rare so that a large body of knowledge about salicylate toxicity *in utero* does not exist. It is reasonable to suspect, however, that a fetus is poorly able to compensate for acid-base abnormalities and compensation is known to be an important factor in reducing salicylate toxicity in adults.

Reference

Rejent, T.A. and Baik, S., Fatal *in utero* salicylism, *J. Forens. Sci.*, 30, 942–944, 1985.

Case Study 4: A Man of Many Pills

A 33-year-old unemployed man was brought to the emergency department one morning after drinking alcohol and ingesting 60 tablets of an over-the-counter pain killer 9 hours earlier on the previous evening. The man also consumed 10 Diclofenac pills (25 mg each).

He was unconscious and in shock. Blood pressure was 54/34 and he had a tachycardia at 122 beats/minute. He was in deep coma with small pupils and he was lacking in spontaneous limb movements or response to painful stimuli. Arterial blood gases showed a severe metabolic acidosis; pH 7.0; pCO_2, 4 kPa; pO_2, 17.8 kPa; and bicarbonate, 9.3 mmol/L. Chemistries were significant for renal impairment: K^+, 5.9 mmol/L; creatinine, 226 μmol/L; urea, 6.3 mmol/L, and glucose, 4.3 mmol/L. Urinalysis was negative for blood, protein, or ketones. His serum ethyl alcohol on admission was 110 mg/dL. Serum Diclofenac was tested for and found to be absent. The patient was intubated and administered activated charcoal via an NG tube. Resuscitation was effected with a combination of crystalloid and colloid. These restored blood pressure and urinary flow. Nevertheless, his acidosis worsened (pH dropped to 6.88) and he manifested cardiac instability. He became very bradycardic (30 beats/minute) and hypotensive. Bicarbonate was slowly infused with improvement in his acidosis. His coma resolved in about 24 hours at which time he was extubated. His acidosis persisted for an additional 12 hours. Eventually, he recovered fully with renal function returning to normal. He was discharged on the 3rd hospital day.

What was the over-the-counter painkiller which he ingested?
   a) Acetaminophen
   b) Aspirin
   c) Ibuprofen
   d) Bufferin

The course of this patient's illness is completely different from the picture expected for acetaminophen overdose. Our patient's major problem is unremitting acidosis and CNS depression. On the contrary, acetaminophen overdose is usually mild at presentation and then proceeds to fulminant hepatic failure if severe enough and not recognized at an early enough stage. Aspirin is similar to the picture here, but hyperthermia and other signs characteristically present with aspirin are missing in this case. Aspirin is also characterized by mixed acid-base abnormality in the early stages in contrast to the clear metabolic acidosis this patient manifested. Bufferin is merely a specific form of aspirin. Ibuprofen is the correct answer and, although it is usually a rather benign drug, in overdoses of this magnitude, it may produce coma and severe metabolic acidosis.

Questions

Q1. To what extent are this patient's co-ingestants, ethanol and Diclofenac, responsible for his symptoms?
   a) Probably not at all.
   b) Diclofenac was contributory to his toxic syndrome but alcohol was not.
   c) Alcohol was contributory to his toxic syndrome but Diclofenac was not.
   d) Both drugs probably exacerbated his symptoms.

Q2. What is generally regarded as a serious overdose of ibuprofen?
   a) Over 10 mg/kg
   b) Over 100 mg/kg
   c) Over 400 mg/kg
   d) Over 1 g per kg

Q3. What are the most common findings in ibuprofen overdose?
   a) Nausea and vomiting
   b) Agitation and hyperthermia
   c) GI disturbance and CNS sedation
   d) Liver inflammation and severe acidosis

Q4. Why was this patient acidotic?
   a) Alcohol-induced ketoacidosis
   b) Acidic metabolites of ibuprofen
   c) Inhibition of electron transport
   d) Reduction of cardiac output

Answers and Discussion

Q1. (Answer = d) Diclofenac is similar to ibuprofen, i.e., it is a nonsteroidal anti-inflammatory. Symptoms of Diclofenac overdose are like those from ibuprofen overdose. It has, however, a very short half-life, 1 hour. One could argue that the effects due to 250 mg of Diclofenac were gone by the time this patient entered the hospital. In fact, laboratory analysis showed the absence of this drug at the time of admission. Alcohol was probably a significant factor in this patient's CNS depression and level of coma. Recall that blood was not drawn for testing for 9 hours after the ingestions. At that time the result was 110 mg/dL of alcohol. Assuming a normal rate of metabolism, this patient probably achieved blood alcohol as high as 300 mg/dL at peak. Such a level would be expected to contribute to CNS depression.

Q2. (Answer = c) Cases have been reported with coma and acute renal failure from ibuprofen overdose but, generally, only if the dose exceeds 400 mg/kg. In a 70-kg adult, therefore, that equals 27 g. Several cases have been reported, however, in which this amount of ibuprofen produced only minor symptoms.

Q3. (Answer = c) Most overdoses are in the range of 100 mg/kg and these produce mild CNS depression and gastrointestinal distress.

Q4. (Answer = b) This patient's acidosis is probably not due to the high alcohol ingestion. In the first place, ibuprofen overdose to this degree has been associated with significant acidosis in many case reports even when alcohol was not a complicating part of the picture. This patient did not have other features that are almost always found in alcohol-induced ketoacidosis, namely, urinary ketones and hypoglycemia. The two major metabolites of ibuprofen are 2-carboxyibuprofen and 2-hydroxyibuprofen and both of these are acids. The acid burden within the blood from these metabolites appears to be a sufficient explanation of the acidosis usually seen in ibuprofen overdose.

Reference

Downie, A. et al., Severe metabolic acidosis complicating massive ibuprofen overdose, *Postgrad. Med. J.*, 69, 575–577, 1993.

CONTENTS

Drugs of abuse could be considered in separate chapters devoted to the specific features each abused drug has, e.g., cocaine could be treated in the chapter on stimulants, heroin with sedatives, etc. Because drug abuse is such a large problem and the specific widely abused drugs are known mainly for their abuse potential, it seems more appropriate to devote a separate chapter to this topic.

The dimensions of the problem of drug abuse are known to all. They are so staggering that many believe that drug abuse is the major problem facing America and much of the world today, greater than the challenges posed by poverty, racial inequality, international peace, and all others. Even those who believe that it deserves lesser status among the scourges of America and the rest of the world would still give it a prominent position among humanity's challenges. Estimates are that over 21 million Americans have tried cocaine, 3.5 million of whom are regular users. The number of regular marijuana users is over 20 million and at least 65 million have tried it once. Among high school seniors, 50% admit to trying marijuana. Drug abuse is not limited to those who are economically or academically deprived. Medical students acknowledge marijuana use among 27% of their group, and cocaine and tranquilizer use by 11 and 10%, respectively. The degree of regular drug abuse on the part of established physicians is between 5 and 10%, not significantly different from that of the population at large. In a recent 10-year period the percent increase in admissions to Emergency Medical departments was about 40%, but the increase in admissions for treatment of drug overdose was close to 100%. Moreover, the percent of all emergency visits which are made for drug overdose is greater than 25%. DAWN (Drug Abuse Warning Network) figures show that 26 metropolitan areas had 5628 drug-related deaths in 1990 and this figure grew by over 33% in just 3 years to 7485, by 1993. It is clear, moreover, that the DAWN statistics underestimate deaths due to drugs of abuse.

Many drugs of abuse also have therapeutic uses. In this chapter we discuss those solely or mainly used abusively rather than medically. This is a difficult distinction. Marijuana, cocaine, and phencyclidine (PCP) clearly belong here. Benzodiazepines and barbiturates are discussed in a separate chapter because, although they have abuse potential, they were designed for clinical use and primarily to serve a valuable medical purpose.

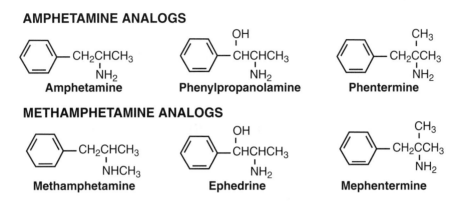

FIGURE 20.1 Amphetamine, methamphetamine, and some of their analogs.

AMPHETAMINES AND DESIGNER DRUGS

Amphetamines are the prototype of this class of drugs. They have sympathomimetic activity (stimulate the sympathetic nervous system) together with strong CNS stimulation. This is a very large category of drugs, some of which are illustrated in Figure 20.1. Throughout this discussion amphetamine will generally be the drug to which reference is made. The reader should recognize that its effects are found in other members of the class as well although to a lesser or greater degree depending on the potency of the specific drug.

HISTORY

Amphetamine was the first member of this class to be synthesized and this was achieved by a German scientist, L. Edeleano, in 1887. Not until 1927, however, were its major physiological effects described when Gordon Alles self-administered amphetamine and reported its induction of euphoria, reduction of fatigue, and increase in alertness. The pharmaceutical giant, Smith, Kline and French, marketed an over-the-counter amphetamine inhaler under the name Benzedrine beginning in 1932. Although it was marketed as a nasal decongestant, it was widely abused. Unfortunately, the American Medical Association promoted amphetamine for many years even claiming that it was an effective therapy for depression, schizophrenia, drug addiction, and many other ailments. Several amphetamine drugs were used widely by combatants of both sides during World War II to increase energy levels and counter the effects of combat fatigue. The U.S. Army dispensed amphetamine to all soldiers during the Korean War and veterans subsequently used this same drug for exam preparation when they became students after the war. Because amphetamine class compounds reduce appetite they have been used for weight control by millions. In one single year, 1967, 31 million prescriptions were written for diet pills in the United States. Many, although not all, were amphetamine analogs.

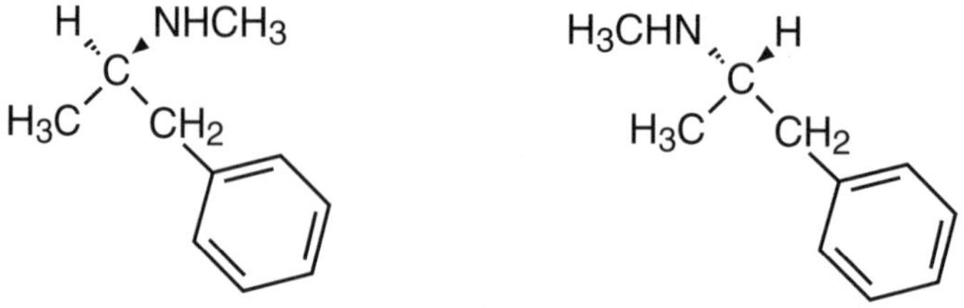

(S) - (+) - Methamphetamine   **(R) - (-) - Methamphetamine**

FIGURE 20.2 Enantiomers of methamphetamine.

DRUG EFFECT

The response to amphetamine drugs is very dose dependent. It also depends on the stereochemical nature of the drug. Because all of these drugs have at least one asymmetric carbon, they may be found in D or L forms. (See Chapter 13 on confirmation methods for a discussion of the nature of optical activity and analysis of different optical isomers.) Whenever optical activity occurs in nature it is almost always true that the activity of the two enantiomers is quite different. For example, dextroamphetamine, D-amphetamine, has approximately four times the potency of L-amphetamine. Similarly, dextro-methamphetamine (Figure 20.2) is highly euphoric whereas levo-methamphetamine has very weak euphoric properties. Different physiological reactions by enantiomers are not surprising in view of the fact that drugs react with large biological receptors. The receptor has a 3-dimensional shape which can distinguish stereochemical, i.e., 3-dimensional features, in a molecule that binds to it. It would be expected to favor tight binding with one enantiomer more than the other because of the spatial arrangements of charged groups within the molecule.

It is characteristic of amphetamines to cause a significant increase in blood pressure, a reflex slowing of heart rate, relaxation of bronchial muscle, and in general, responses which prepare the body for the "fight or flight" reaction. These include elevations in blood sugar, blood flow to muscles, respiratory and heart rate, and pupillary dilation. In the CNS amphetamine acts as a stimulant and causes increased alertness, euphoria, wakefulness, lack of fatigue, decrease of appetite, and increased motor and speech activity.

If taken intravenously, amphetamine provides what is described as a rush or flash, a reaction which has been described as orgasmic in character. A condition of manic paranoia often follows the rush. Amphetamine and related compounds have abuse potential for those engaged in sports because they increase the subjective perception of power and sometimes enable an athlete to complete rudimentary tasks with more speed and strength. However, dexterity usually deteriorates, so results that depend on fine motor skills are liable to decrease rather than improve. There are reports of professional baseball players who accepted amphetamines when they were initially provided to them. With continued use the athletes noticed that their ability to bat and field successfully decreased so they discontinued amphetamine use. Similar anecdotal evidence has been presented in relation to professional football teams.

TOXIC EFFECTS

At higher doses or with prolonged use of moderate doses, amphetamine users experience tremor, restlessness, insomnia, and agitation. Insomnia progresses to complete sleep deprivation, which eventually results in profound sleep when the drug is discontinued. Mental depression and fatigue are aspects of the withdrawal process associated with stopping amphetamine use.

Amphetamine psychosis, a schizophrenia-like state accompanied by visual and auditory hallucinations, paranoia, and aggressive behavior, is often found with high-dose amphetamine abuse. Indeed, the striking similarity of this condition to psychosis and the response of this state to antipsychotic drugs strongly suggest that there is a common denominator in the biochemical abnormalities found in both amphetamine action and psychosis. In very severe poisoning, amphetamines cause intense hypertension, tachycardia, arrhythmias, and fevers. Convulsions may occur followed by circulatory collapse, coma, and death.

High-dose users who become "amphetamine freaks" are a special case. In addition to the psychosis sometimes found, these individuals often undergo the progressive deterioration of mental and physical well-being that is associated with near total dependence on the drug. They experience weight loss, skin sores, infections related to indifference to their health, sometimes including HIV from needle sharing. Most high-dose users undergo progressive social, personal, and occupational deterioration.

The dose of amphetamine associated with different responses is not especially predictable. In some individuals 30 mg has provoked severe responses, but a case is reported in which a patient who had no tolerance to the drug still survived a 200-mg exposure. The acute lethal dose is estimated at 25 mg/kg in adults and 5 mg/kg in children.

MECHANISM OF ACTION

Amphetamine acts on neurons in both the CNS and the peripheral nervous system that employ dopamine, norepinephrine, and/or serotonin (Figure 20.3). These drugs have good lipophilicity and hence readily enter the CNS. Although they interact with several different neurotransmitters, it is believed that their effect in the reward circuit of the CNS is dopamine associated. Effects outside the CNS are mainly due to norepinephrine.

The specific action of amphetamine is to enter vesicles that store neurotransmitters and produce a leakage of the neurotransmitter into the synaptic junction. Thus, the nerve cell transmits its message but in a manner which is excessive and not related to normal physiological reaction.

This amphetamine-induced neurotransmission is terminated when the dopamine or other neurotransmitter is returned to the presynaptic vesicles. However, even here amphetamine may inhibit the re-uptake and thereby intensify the original action of neurotransmitter release.

TREATMENT

Because effects of amphetamines can be very severe it may be necessary to stabilize the patient even before any effort is made to reduce absorption of drugs from the

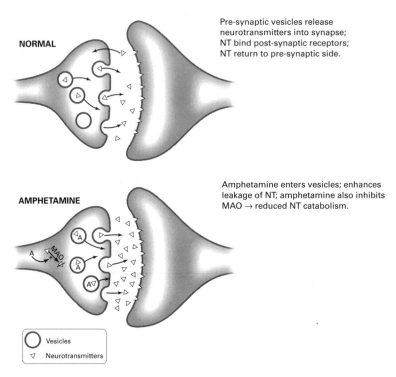

NORMAL

Pre-synaptic vesicles release
neurotransmitters into synapse;
NT bind post-synaptic receptors;
NT return to pre-synaptic side.

AMPHETAMINE

Amphetamine enters vesicles; enhances
leakage of NT; amphetamine also inhibits
MAO → reduced NT catabolism.

Vesicles

Neurotransmitters

FIGURE 20.3 Illustration of the mechanism of amphetamine action.

GI tract. Several drugs are available that reduce the toxicity of amphetamine over-dose. They are not, themselves, without toxicity, so drug selection for treatment may be difficult. Phenothiazines are effective in reducing psychotic manifestations arising from amphetamines. Chlorpromazine, a phenothiazine, also reverses hyperthermia, convulsions, and hypertension due to amphetamine. Despite these benefits and the fact that phenothiazines are direct antagonists to amphetamine, they can enhance toxicity by lowering the seizure threshold. Therefore, they probably should not be used. Diazepam, a benzodiazepine, is preferred. Salicylates also are recommended to reduce fever, an important step in limiting the risk of convulsions.

Efforts to reduce drug absorption are desirable and emesis should be attempted unless contraindicated for some legitimate reason in which case gastric lavage is recommended. It is desirable to enhance amphetamine elimination by acidification of urine. Ammonium chloride is useful for this purpose. Acidification is effective because of the alkaline character of amphetamine. Acidification is so useful that one study showed 3% clearance without intervention to control urine pH whereas 55% elimina-tion of the amphetamine was noted when the urine pH was adjusted from 7 to 5.0.

LAB TESTING

Most testing for amphetamine and related compounds is conducted by immuno-assays. Immunoassay methods are sensitive, but differ in their specificity. Some of them, e.g., fluorescence polarization immunoassay, are highly specific for just amphetamine and methamphetamine. Their cross-reactivity with ephedrine, phenyl-propanolamine, etc. is very low. Other methods have broader class-related specificity. If the goal of testing is to detect only amphetamine or methamphetamine, then FPIA is desirable from the perspective of its specificity. This is the case with drug screening for pre-employment in the SAMHSA (Substance Abuse and Mental Health Services Administration) program. In this program certified laboratories must test only for these two members of the amphetamine class. It is a problem for these laboratories if they use a method that detects other members of the amphetamine class. Conversely, in the context of clinical toxicology, test needs are different. Clinical laboratories need to detect any member of the drug class that might help to explain a patient's symptoms. Clinical toxicology laboratories need a less specific screen. The exact identity of a sympathomimetic amine and its concentration is usually determined by gas chromatography-mass spectrometry. The drugs are derivatized, usually by acylation, and specific ions are monitored. As was mentioned in Chapter 13, exact recognition of each sympathomimetic amine is not easy. Close attention to masses and retention times is needed.

COCAINE

History

Because cocaine is a natural product with strong psychoactive properties, it is not surprising that its history goes back at least several thousand years. Coca leaves (of the plant *Erythroxylon coca,* the source of cocaine) and a chewed wad of coca have been found near gravesites which date to 2500 B.C. As far back as the traditions of the Inca people can be traced, coca was a critical entity in the religion and lives of these people. Prehistoric artifacts such as statues and bells cast in the shape of human faces show humans with their cheeks distended in the act of chewing coca leaves, which have a 1% content of cocaine.

Amerigo Vespucci, the famed explorer, describes the natives chewing coca leaves in 1499. When he asked the Indians why they had coca leaves in their mouths they replied that it prevented them from feeling hungry and gave them vigor and strength. The Inca regarded coca as being of divine origin and so the Spaniards forbade it as a pagan practice when they conquered the Indians. In time, however, the Spaniards discontinued the prohibition on coca in order to get the Indian slaves to work harder in the mines.

Those who have studied the Indian culture have remarked on the absence of any obvious problems from coca use among the Indians. Why this drug, which has caused so much trouble in modern times, was relatively benign when employed by Indian tribes is not clear. It is probable that the low concentrations to which the Indians were exposed spared them from the toxicity associated with more potent cocaine preparations. Just as the introduction of high-potency crack cocaine caused health problems not observed with snorted cocaine salt, so also did the least potent form, coca leaves, probably could be used without any serious sequelae.

In the nineteenth century cocaine was introduced into European society and became an object of scientific study. Angelo Mariani, a Corsican chemist, added

FIGURE 20.4 Erythroxylon coca, the natural source of cocaine. (From Michael Moore, South-western School of Botanical Medicine. With permission.)

cocaine to cough drops and also to his own blend of wine. Among Mariani's warm supporters was the Pope, dozens of European aristocrats, and thousands of physicians. One of these physicians was Sigmund Freud, founder of psychoanalysis. His report, "Uber Coca," describes in glowing terms the alleged medical benefits of cocaine. Another celebrated beverage, Coca Cola, was dramatically embellished by the addition of cocaine. After 1906, cocaine was replaced by caffeine in Coca Cola, a change which probably had little impact on taste but a great effect on medical reactions. A Viennese physician, Carl Koller, discovered that cocaine had anesthetic properties and could be an effective topical anesthetic for surgical use.

The widespread use of cocaine in so many forms inevitably led to abusive use on the part of many people. The dangers of cocaine slowly began to impress themselves on the public awareness. Public concern over cocaine was heightened by the fact that southern employers often gave cocaine to their black employees in order to increase their work output. Once this drug was introduced into a specific group, regardless of that group's ethnic orientation, it spread to other members of the group. Although cocaine was used by black and white, the popular consciousness labeled it more as a drug identified with minority groups. Such a misidentification was bound to hasten the day on which cocaine would be banned.

In the past 15 to 20 years cocaine has continued to be abused by many people. Specific features of modern abuse patterns differentiate it somewhat from earlier times, i.e., cocaine abuse by the rich and famous and in newer and more potent forms, free-basing and crack cocaine.

CHEMISTRY

Cocaine is the same as methyl benzoyl ecgonine (Figure 20.5). It is a weak base with pK of 8.6. It is extracted from coca leaves which are ground into a paste that is about 70% pure cocaine. The cocaine is usually titrated with hydrochloric acid to form cocaine hydrochloride. In this salt form cocaine may be snorted but it cannot be smoked because of the high melting and boiling points of the cocaine hydrochloride salt. As a salt the cocaine would char when heated before it would reach its boiling point. It is, however, very easy to convert cocaine into a smokable form. Two such forms exist: crack cocaine and free base. They are identical chemically but the manner of their preparation is slightly different. Cocaine can be dissolved in water, titrated with ammonia, and extracted into ether. It will, in this manner, be converted to uncharged cocaine base and will, therefore, extract into a nonpolar solvent such as ether. This is known as free basing, a process which is exceedingly

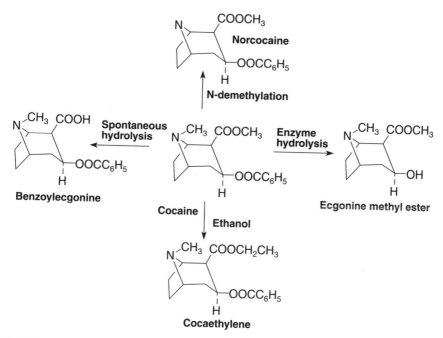

FIGURE 20.5 Cocaine and some metabolic transformations.

hazardous in the hands of an untrained person due, mainly, to the flammable properties of ether. If the alkaline substance used to titrate the cocaine hydrochloride is sodium bicarbonate (baking soda), then the resulting substance is called crack cocaine or simply crack, a name derived from the popping or cracking sound that occurs whenever the crack is heated. Crack is highly pure cocaine but does contain some bicarbonate and a small amount of other impurities.

Cocaine base is potentially more dangerous than the salt because it is uncharged. The absence of a charge means that cocaine base molecules are held together by a relatively weak intermolecular force and, hence, have lower boiling points and melting points than cocaine in the salt form (melting point of cocaine HCl is 195°C while melting point of free base is 95°C). The upshot of all this is that cocaine can be smoked. If it is smoked, then the portal of entry into the body is the vast surface of the lungs rather than the limited area of the nose. This is the primary reason why crack causes more toxicity. Higher blood levels of cocaine are reached when it is smoked. The higher surface area of the lung is one reason but, in addition, cocaine causes vasoconstriction, a further reason why absorption from the nose is limited.

PHARMACOKINETICS

Absorption

As described above, cocaine is readily absorbed through lungs or nose. Nasal application results in peak levels of approximately 100 ng/mL in about 50 to 60 minutes. The rate of uptake into the blood by the nasal route is limited by the small available surface area and vasoconstriction. Cocaine placed in the nose will enter the blood at a diminishing rate because the blood vessels, under the influence of cocaine, constrict and have a smaller surface for cocaine absorption. Cocaine may be ingested, but it rarely is because the slow uptake by this route (peaks at about 90 minutes, 30 minute concentration = 0 ng/mL) discourages abusive use and esterases in the stomach and blood hydrolyze a significant portion of the dose before it reaches the brain. Smoking crack cocaine results in peak levels of 200 to 400 ng/mL in about 5 to 10 minutes. The rapid achievement of peak level by the smoking route may be the major factor responsible for the popularity of crack cocaine. The high blood levels achieved by this manner of exposure explain much of the toxicity currently experienced by crack users. Cocaine toxicity was much less in the decades before 1990, when nasal use of cocaine was the preferred method. Table 20.1 shows that one advantage of the nasal route, from the perspective of cocaine abusers, is the higher bioavailability by this route.

Distribution

Cocaine reaches the brain rapidly due to its lipophilic character. Within 15 minutes, the concentration in the central nervous system is much higher than the corresponding level within the blood. Cocaine may also be readily distributed into the fetus when taken by a pregnant user.

TABLE 20.1
Cocaine Absorption — Findings of Several Studies

Mode of Exposure	Bioavailability	Dose	Peak Conc. (ng/mL)	Time to Peak
Oral (leaves)	n/a	17–48 mg	11–149	0.4–2 (hrs)
Oral (capsules)	n/a	2 mg/kg	104–424	0.8–1.5 (hrs)
Nasal	n/a	n/a	n/a	1–2 (hrs)
Intravenous	n/a	32 mg	308	5 mins
Intravenous	n/a	25 mg	98–349	5 mins
Smoking	n/a	50 mg	203	5 mins
Smoking	70%	42 mg	154–345	5 mins
Nasal	94%	32 mg	40–88	0.4–0.9 (hrs)

n/a, information not available.

Metabolism

Cocaine has a short half-life of approximately 60 minutes. As a result very little cocaine is excreted unchanged in urine. Finding cocaine in urine is an indication that the individual being tested used the drug very recently, within the last several hours. The *in vivo* conversion of cocaine results predominantly in two products: benzoylecgonine and ecgonine methyl ester.

The reaction that produces benzoylecgonine is largely spontaneous and requires no enzyme. It occurs readily in aqueous solution (because of this, cocaine may never be kept in aqueous solutions without rapid conversion to metabolite)! Production of ecgonine methyl ester, on the other hand, is an enzymatic process. Under normal conditions the proportions of metabolic products formed are 1% cocaine, 45% benzoylecgonine, 40% ecgonine methyl ester, and 5 to 10% ecgonine.

In the presence of ethanol a transesterification occurs leading to the production of cocaethylene, the ethyl homolog of cocaine (ethylbenzoylecgonine) and a compound with pharmacological properties similar to those of cocaine. Cocaethylene has a half-life about three times that of cocaine. As a result, some patients who use cocaine and ethanol simultaneously have been found to have low cocaine blood levels but significant toxic symptoms. Concomitant use of ethanol and cocaine definitely produces much more mortality and morbidity than cocaine alone. Cocaethylene also penetrates the blood–brain barrier more readily than cocaine and may explain the subjective perception of a greater high from both drugs than from cocaine alone. It is believed that cocaethylene is metabolized to ecgonine ethyl ester and the appearance of the latter by itself in urine is an indication of concomitant use of both cocaine and ethanol.

Cocaine Elimination

Cocaine has a short half-life and is usually fully metabolized by the time it is excreted. For this reason cocaine, itself, is not usually found in the urine of users. Therefore, manufacturers of screening reagents for cocaine testing usually make their product

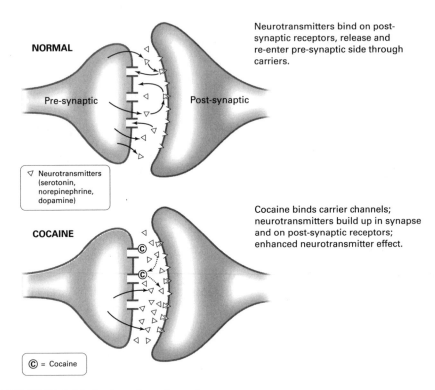

FIGURE 20.6 Mechanism of cocaine action.

able to detect cocaine metabolite and not cocaine. The presence of cocaine within the blood and the prolongation of its toxic effects occur in persons who are genetically deficient in cholinesterases, enzymes involved in cocaine metabolism.

MECHANISM OF ACTION

It will be recalled that amphetamines, which produce effects that are similar to cocaine, work by increasing the release of the neurotransmitters, dopamine, serotonin, and norepinephrine. It might be expected that cocaine will have a similar mechanism (Figure 20.6). Indeed, these same neurotransmitters do have an intensified effect in the presence of cocaine. In the case of cocaine, this is due to the action of cocaine in binding to specific receptors at the site of the synapse and, in so doing, preventing the re-uptake of the neurotransmitters into the presynaptic vesicles. With its re-uptake diminished, the neurotransmitter remains within the synapse and can continuously act to propagate the nerve impulse beyond the time at which it would normally cease to do so.

CLINICAL TOXICITY

Cocaine is a stimulant with actions that are similar to those of amphetamine. Persons who have tried both drugs report that the psychoactive effects of both are very similar. In the CNS, cocaine produces an intense euphoria, but also agitation, seizures, and occasional cardiovascular accidents (strokes). It increases mental awareness and alertness with an associated feeling of well-being and euphoria. Fatigue is decreased and motor activity is increased, but coordination decreases at the same time. Profound physical and emotional depression, such as those noted for amphetamine, are found after prolonged use of cocaine. Cardiac effects are common, including tachycardia and other arrhythmias, hypertension, and myocardial ischemia or infarction. Other effects, such as sweating and hyperthermia, are often noted. The toxic dose of cocaine is estimated to equal 2 mg/kg body weight. Many deaths have resulted from cocaine abuse. When fatalities occur the immediate cause is usually intracranial hemorrhage, myocardial infarction, seizures, and/or trauma.

FETAL EFFECTS

Because cocaine use is very common and it also crosses the placenta easily, the danger of fetal toxicity exists and has received a great deal of attention in the scientific and the popular press. It is known that women who use cocaine during pregnancy have a higher than normal incidence of miscarriage, placental detachment, placental insufficiency, and fetal death late in pregnancy. Cocaine also decreases the birthweight of the newborn. These findings may relate to the known ability of cocaine to induce vasoconstriction. The uterine and placental arteries are constricted and, hence, the fetus receives a reduced amount of blood and oxygen. Babies so affected have the problems listed above. In addition, they may have morphological birth defects. Perhaps the most frequent finding, however, is neurological impairment. "Crack babies" are irritable, tremulous, and unresponsive to normal care. The latter problem is likely to become exacerbated when the child is left in the environment of a mother who is drug addicted and incapable of providing normal maternal interest and care for the baby. The long-term effects of this illness are yet to be determined as larger numbers of children born of cocaine-using mothers are now entering school and growing into the latter stages of childhood.

THERAPY

Decontamination usually is not possible for cocaine overdose except for that small percent of patients who have ingested cocaine or who have attempted to smuggle the drug by "body-packing." In those cases, significant quantities of cocaine may still be entering the body and survival may be related to preventing further uptake.

General supportive care is critical because cocaine has many metabolic effects on the body. Benzodiazepines are helpful for patients with extreme agitation or who are actually in seizure. Vasodilators, such as nitroprusside, help to lower blood pressure. Beta blockers, such as labetalol, are often effective in breaking arrhythmias. There are no known antidotes nor specific treatments that are valuable for enhancing the elimination of cocaine.

LABORATORY ASPECTS

Cocaine is tested very extensively for clinical and forensic purposes. It is one of the substances popularly called the NIDA 5 which the federal drug testing program allows laboratories to test for when screening job applicants prior to employment. Immunoassays are most commonly used for drug screening and are described more fully in Chapter 12 on methods for drug screening. Confirmation of the presence of cocaine and quantitation of the amount of drug are best done by gas chromatography-mass spectrometry. Chapter 13 is devoted to that topic in this text.

A clinician who is treating a patient with cocaine toxicity should not request a blood level for cocaine from the laboratory. The level correlates with severity of overdose only in a very approximate manner and the testing is time consuming so that the result is not likely to be of value by the time the physician receives the report from the laboratory. Overall laboratory support, on the other hand, is of great value in helping a physician to treat a cocaine overdose. Acid-base abnormalities are common in this context and so pH and blood gas studies are critical. Myoglobin and enzyme studies help to assess the patient's status if he develops rhabdomyolysis, a common complication of cocaine toxicity.

The window of detection for cocaine is a subject of controversy. It is generally stated that a patient will be positive in urine testing for about 3 days following cocaine use. For individuals who use cocaine on a heavy and chronic basis, up to 1 week may be needed before that person's urine is no longer positive when tested. Reports have appeared in the literature claiming that sometimes it has required 3 weeks of abstention from cocaine use before some persons returned to a negative urine status. This is a rare claim and very widely contested. An absolute assurance that the subjects of such studies remained drug free during the time of the study does not seem possible.

OPIATES

Opiates is a term referring to compounds derived from the opium poppy, *Papaver somniferum* (Figure 20.7). It also applies to compounds that are either pharmacologically similar or closely related structurally to morphine, the chief opiate found in the poppy. A related word, narcotic, is very similar to opiate and means, strictly speaking, a CNS depressant that has a numbing action. Narcotic has been used in some quarters to refer to any drug subject to abuse and by others to mean, more specifically, a drug that may be abused and is also a depressant. Finally, some experts use the term narcotic interchangeably with opiates. In the present volume this practice is followed, so the two terms, narcotic and opiate, may be regarded as synonymous.

HISTORY OF OPIATES

Because the opium poppy is widespread and contains compounds with high pharmaceutical potency, it is no surprise that the history of opiates is very old. A 6000-year-old Sumerian tablet refers to the poppy as equivalent to "joy" plus "plant," an allusion which, at a minimum, indicates that Sumerians had experience with poppies and were familiar with their essential nature. The famous "Ebers papyrus" of ancient Egypt (1500 B.C.) lists opium from poppies as among the essential 700 medicinal compounds of the old world. By the third century B.C., Theophrastus, the Greek writer, was describing various methods for extracting opium from poppies. The

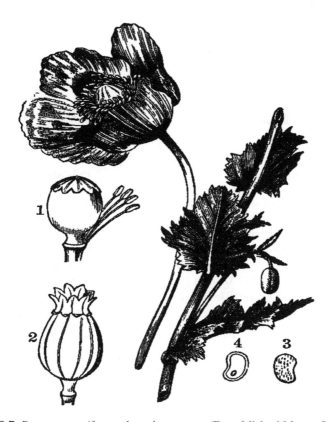

FIGURE 20.7 *Papaver somniferum*, the opium poppy. (From Michael Moore, Southwestern School of Botanical Medicine. With permission.)

Greek god of sleep, Hypnos, and the Roman god of sleep, Somnus, have both been portrayed as carrying containers filled with opium pods, an indication of the widespread knowledge and probable equally widespread use of opium in antiquity. One country, China, had a particularly great impact on the history of opium. Opium started in China as medicinal but in short order, certainly by the sixteenth century, was an object of widespread abuse. Eventually, the Chinese government attempted to stem the tide of addiction by prohibiting the importation of opium from India. Intense smuggling networks developed mainly under the sponsorship of the British East India Company. By 1839 the Chinese decided to strictly enforce the anti-importation laws against opium. England and China went to war, ostensibly because of opium, between 1839 and 1842, and the British were victorious. The real motive behind Britian's war was to force China to open more ports to international commerce for the benefit of British companies. British goals were achieved with the opening of five ports to shipping and Hong Kong was ceded to England.

In 1803, a German chemist, Frederick Serturner, purified opium and isolated morphine. He named it after the Greek god of dreams, Morpheus. In 1832, codeine was purified from opium. (See Figure 20.8.) Alexander Wood perfected the hypodermic syringe in 1853. Ironically, Wood's aim was to reduce opiate addiction by circumventing

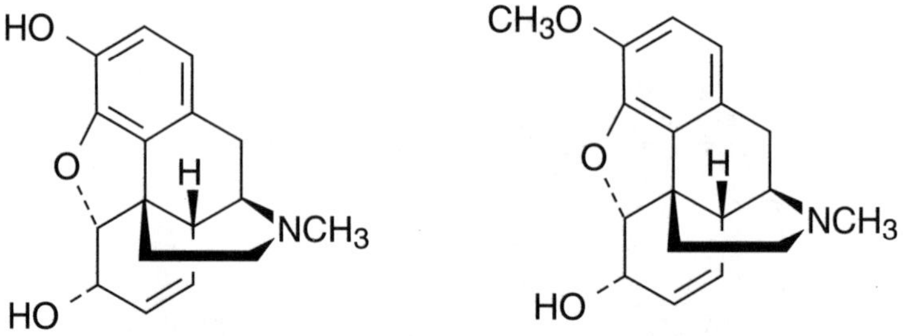

Morphine   **Codeine**

FIGURE 20.8 Morphine and codeine, the naturally occurring opiates.

the oral route of administration. In reality, of course, injection of morphine gives a much greater high and resulted, therefore, in more extensive abuse. Further chemical research on morphine lead to the synthesis of diacetylmorphine or heroin. Bayer marketed this compound in 1898 as a substitute for morphine and, therefore, a step toward reducing addiction. Heroin, of course, was all the more addictive. The introduction of heroin led to a greater worldwide problem of opiate addiction.

CHEMISTRY

Opiates are frequently divided into the naturally occurring, the synthetic, and the semisynthetic (Figure 20.9). The latter are those which are manufactured most easily by using starting materials that are themselves opiates. Only morphine and codeine are found in nature. Synthetic opiates may be prepared by synthesis from non-opiate precursors (see below).

PHARMACOKINETICS

Morphine may be taken orally or by other routes. When ingested, blood levels are less than half those achieved by drug injection. The reason for the low bioavailablility of morphine and some other opiates by the oral route is a significant first-pass metabolism in which large quantities of the drug are metabolized while transversing the liver. Injection of the drug directly from a peripheral site, such as a vein in the arm, enables it to reach the central nervous system before significant amounts of the opiate are metabolized by the liver.

History teaches us that opiates are absorbed extensively by inhalation. Many cultures have made a habit of smoking crude opium. In fact, the ingredients of opium are rapidly and completely absorbed from opium smoke. The onset of drug action is just as rapid when opiates are smoked as when they are injected intravenously.

Crossing the blood–brain barrier is somewhat difficult for morphine and, on average, only 20% of a dose reaches the CNS. This is due to the relatively polar nature of the morphine molecule which, in turn, is attributable to its two hydroxyl groups. By contrast, heroin, or diacetylmorphine, is less polar (the hydroxyl groups have been derivatized, i.e., covered by acetyl groups), and it crosses the blood–brain barrier readily. It is, therefore, 2.5 times as potent as morphine, and IV injection of

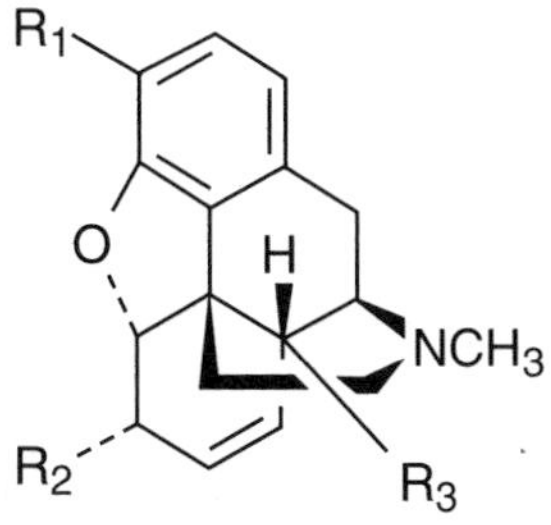

	R₁	R₂	R₃
Hydrocodone	OCH₃	=O	—H
Hydromorphone	OH	=O	—H
Oxycodone	OCH₃	=O	—OH
Oxymorphone	OH	=O	—OH
Heroin	OCOCH₃	OCOCH₃	—H

FIGURE 20.9 Semisynthetic opiates.

heroin causes a rush or flash not experienced by someone using the same amount of morphine. This response is due to the achievement of higher levels of opiate within the brain from the heroin.

Morphine and heroin are rapidly metabolized by the liver and products of metabolism are excreted by the kidneys. Heroin is converted first to monoacetyl-morphine and then to morphine. This conversion is rapid so no heroin will be found in the urine of a heroin user. This means that the presence of morphine in the urine indicates use of morphine or heroin, but it does not specifically indicate which one. One way to determine whether a person's urinary morphine came from morphine or heroin use is to demonstrate the presence of 6-monoacetylmorphine, the inter-mediary metabolite, in the blood or urine. This compound can arise only from heroin. The reverse reaction in which 6-monoacetylmorphine would form from morphine does not occur. Another complication in interpreting drug findings is that codeine is partly demethylated to morphine. Therefore, a finding of urinary morphine may be due to use of a codeine-containing medicine. However, use of morphine or heroin is characteristically associated with large amounts of morphine in the urine vs. small amounts if the morphine arose from codeine use.

MECHANISM OF ACTION

Within the brain, spinal cord, and other organs are opioid receptors, structures which bind natural, endogenous compounds known as endorphin peptide transmitters or

TABLE 20.2
Opiate Receptors

Receptor	Location	Actions	Drugs
Mu	Cerebral cortex, thalamus	Analgesia, respiratory depression dependence	Morphine Fentanyl
Delta	Frontal cortex, limbic system	Euphoria, analgesia, respiratory depression	Enkephalin Endogenous opioids
Kappa	Spinal cord	Spinal analgesia, sedation, physical dependence	Dynorphin Butorphanol
Sigma		Hallucinations, tachycardia, vasomotor stimulation	Phencyclidine Pentazocine

beta endorphins. These endorphins bind to the opioid receptors and, in so doing, they diminish the perception of pain throughout the pain pathway. Narcotics such as morphine or heroin enhance the opioid receptor response by stimulating these receptors in a manner similar to that induced by the natural compounds, the endorphins. The binding of the receptor by the endogenous compound, beta endorphin, or by the exogenous opiate inhibits the release of a specific neurotransmitter. That neurotransmitter is known as substance P in the main afferent pathway for pain. This theory explains the pain suppression conferred by opiates. How does their abuse potential arise? It is believed that opioid receptors exist within the limbic system, the part of the brain related to drug dependence. Binding of opiates within the limbic system, therefore, presumably is associated with the drug dependence that develops within the narcotic user.

At least four kinds of opioid receptors exist: mu, kappa, sigma, and delta (Table 20.2). The mu receptors are associated with most narcotic effects including euphoria, analgesia, respiratory depression, and constipation. They are found mainly but not entirely within the cerebral cortex. Kappa receptors are responsible for analgesia at the spinal cord level, sedation, and miosis (pupillary constriction). Delta receptors are located within the frontal cortex and the limbic system. They have the same function as mu receptors but within a slightly different region. Sigma receptors have hallucinatory and dysphoric (opposite of euphoric) reactions. Most opiates, with the exception of pentazocine, do not bind to sigma receptors.

CLINICAL PRESENTATION

Receptor stimulation causes euphoria, analgesia, sedation, and respiratory depression. Therefore, overdosed patients are in CNS depression which may range from a state of lethargy all the way to deep coma. Dizziness or psychosis are other CNS findings sometimes observed. Patients are usually hypotensive and bradycardic. Heart palpitations are sometimes heard. Gastrointestinal symptoms include nausea, vomiting, and constipation. Pinpoint pupils are a semispecific finding that is usually present. Noncardiogenic pulmonary edema is often noted and, if fatalities occur, postmortem pulmonary edema is usually evident. Severe, acute overdose may result in death. This may be preceded by respiratory depression to the point of apnea,

TABLE 20.3
Comparison of the Toxic Properties of Opiates

Drug	Equivalent Dose (mg)	Therapeutic Concentration (mcg/mL)	Toxic Concentration (mcg/dL)	Lethal Concentration (mcg/dL)
Morphine	10	1–8	10–100	>400
Codeine	120	1–12	20–50	>60
Heroin	3–4	—	10–100	>400
Methadone	8–10	30–100	200	>400
Meperidine	80–100	30–100	500	2000
Hydromorphone	1.5	0.1–3	10–200	>300
Oxycodone	15	1–10	20–500	

myocardial depression, rhabdomyolysis, seizures, and coma. Toxic doses of morphine and other opiates are shown in Table 20.3.

THERAPY

As in many poisonous ingestions emesis should be attempted if the exposure was oral. In fact, opiate ingestions delay gastric emptying, which increases the probable efficacy of this mode of therapy. Gastric lavage should be employed for unconscious patients.

Because the opiates suppress respirations and have many other effects, the opiate-poisoned patient is likely to require immediate attention to vital functions. Thus, assure that respiratory function and cardiovascular action are adequate before other interventions.

For opiates, a class of compounds exist which effectively reverses almost all of the symptoms of opiate overdose. These are opiate antagonists such as naloxone (Figure 20.10).

Naloxone (Narcan) is a pure opioid antagonist, i.e., it has no actions that are additive to those of opiates. By contrast, some compounds such as levallorphan have partial agonist action, which means that it has some morphine-like behavior; for example, it can promote sedation. Naloxone is the antidote of choice for opiate overdose and it dramatically improves respiration in just 1 or 2 minutes. It is also highly potent with 0.4 mg being the usual dose.

When given to a patient whose coma is not due to opiates there is usually no toxicity whatever. For this reason naloxone is often tried for patients with coma of unknown etiology. It has a short half-life of about 60 minutes. It may, therefore, need to be given repeatedly because it is extremely likely to disappear from the blood while the morphine or other opiate is still present. Pure opioid antagonists such as naloxone work by binding to all of the opioid receptors but, after binding, they have no activity, i.e., they do not stimulate the receptor. One problem with opiate antagonist use is that they may provoke withdrawal in overdosed individuals. An additional use for opiate antagonists besides application for adult narcotic overdose is the treatment of respiratory depression in newborns of mothers who have been using narcotics before or during delivery.

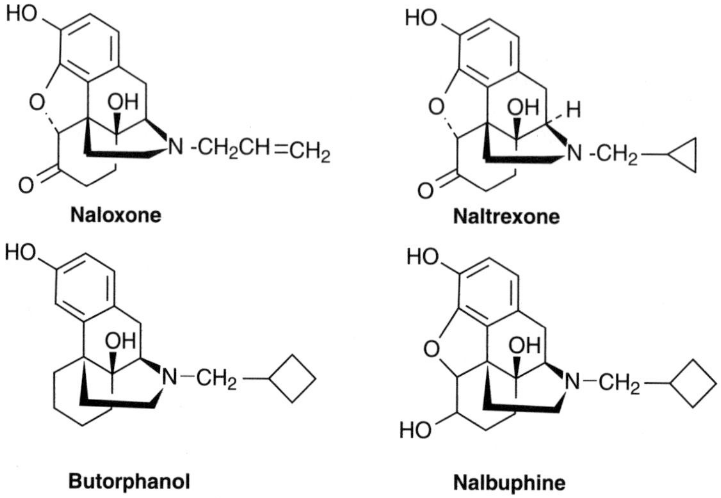

FIGURE 20.10 Structures of opiate antagonists.

Naltrexone (Trexan) is a narcotic antagonist which, unlike Naloxone, may be administered orally because of its excellent bioavailability. It has one added advantage, long duration of action. Only a single daily dose of 50 to 100 mg is needed.

SPECIFIC DRUGS

Hydromorphone (Dilaudid) and Oxymorphone (Numorphan)

These derivatives of morphine, despite being only slightly structurally different from the natural morphine itself, are much more potent. They are effective mu receptor stimulants. Each is used therapeutically for severe cancer pain.

Meperidine (Demerol)

This is a synthetic opiate with a structure that is significantly different from morphine. At one time it was thought to be nonaddictive, a hope which proved to be forlorn as time passed and experience accumulated. It is very popular medically despite having only 10% the potency of morphine. Interestingly, the toxicity of meperidine is usually different from that of other opiates and more like that expected from a stimulant. Tremors, seizures, and delirium are observed. These are apparently due to normeperidine, a metabolite which has a long half-life. Meperidine causes opiate-like symptoms, but these are overwhelmed by the symptoms associated with normeperidine which accumulates to higher amounts.

Methadone (Dolophine)

This drug was developed in Germany during the second World War at a time when Germany was unable to acquire opiates for medical use from the Orient. (See Figure 20.11.) The trade name, Dolophine, was given in honor of Adolph Hitler. Its

$$C_6H_5 \quad N(CH_3)_2$$
$$CH_3CH_2COC-CH_2CHCH_3$$
$$C_6H_5$$

Methadone

$$H_3C \quad OOCCH_2CH_3$$
$$(CH_3)_2NCH_2CH-C-CH_2C_6H_5$$
$$C_6H_5$$

Propoxyphene

FIGURE 20.11 Methadone and propoxyphene.

pharmacological activity is quite close to that of morphine. Thus, it is an effective analgesic, may be taken orally although with reduced potency, and will suppress withdrawal symptoms. This latter property has led to its usage for treatment of drug-addicted persons in methadone maintenance programs. In these programs, orally administered methadone is provided as a substitute for injected heroin. The methadone does not provide a high when given in the program but, ideally, it prevents withdrawal and eliminates the craving for heroin. If possible, the addict can be slowly weaned from the methadone. The degree of success or failure of these methadone maintenance programs is a matter of great controversy.

Fentanyl

Fentanyl is a synthetic opiate which was found to be 80 times as potent as morphine. Its actions are similar to morphine except that high doses cause marked muscular rigidity. It is used for anesthesia and analgesia. Unfortunately, a high incidence of drug abuse from this agent has occurred among healthcare professionals. Based on the high potency of fentanyl, some chemists, seeking to make high profits but avoid legal difficulties, have designed modifications of its basic structure. A series of compounds based on the fentanyl structure were originally synthesized as designer drugs, i.e., they were made in an attempt to circumvent the law because the law was written in language specifically prohibiting certain substances. Because these drugs were new to the scientific, legal, and drug-abuse communities, no statutes existed explicitly forbidding their use. In 1986 the Controlled Substances Analogue Enforcement Act was passed which encompassed substances that were reasonably similar to known drugs of abuse. Thereafter, designer drugs could not be manufactured and sold with impunity.

Among the designer forms of fentanyl marketed by illicit drug dealers are alpha-methylfentanyl and 3-methylfentanyl (Figure 20.12). These compounds are unique for their extremely high potency. For example, the potency of 3-methylfentanyl in laboratory animals is equal to 6000 times that of morphine. The estimated lethal dose in humans is in the microgram range. This compound caused many deaths in the Pittsburgh area in 1988. It was known as "China white" and its unexpectedly high mortality undoubtedly was related to its high potency. Drug addicts would take as much as they thought would be needed to give a high; however, they were taking methylfentanyl, not heroin. Fentanyl compounds behave very similarly to other opiates. They cross the blood–brain barrier and bind at mu receptors. Euphoria and respiratory and CNS depression ensue. Fentanyl overdoses respond to naloxone. However, a deeper depression is commonly noted when fentanyl causes an overdose

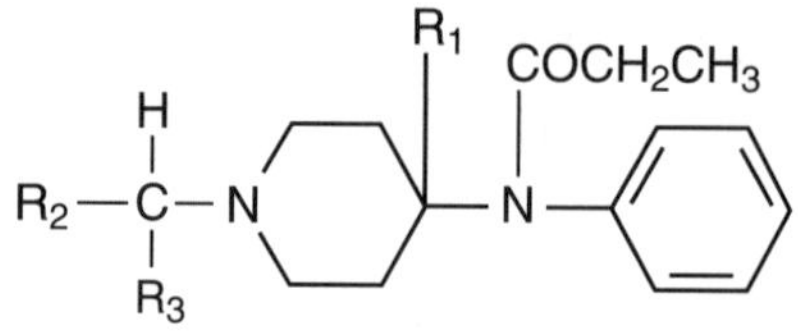

	R1	R2	R3
Fentanyl	H	$C_6H_5CH_2$	H
Alpha methyl fentanyl	H	$C_6H_5CH_2$	CH_3
Sufentanil	CH_2OCH_3	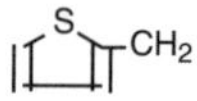 (thiophene)CH_2	H
Carfentanil	$COOCH_3$	$C_6H_5CH_2$	H

FIGURE 20.12 Fentanyl and its derivatives.

in contrast to those provoked by morphine or heroin. Thus, more doses of antidote are likely to be required.

An interesting problem occurs with hospitalizations associated with fentanyl; namely, the laboratory often cannot confirm a physician's diagnosis of opiate overdose because most opiate screens do not react with fentanyl and, even if they did, the drugs are so potent that quantities which appear in the blood and urine are below the detection limits of most assays. Therefore, whenever an opiate poisoning is strongly suspected (and, perhaps, confirmed by patient response to naloxone) and laboratory confirmation is important, specific testing for fentanyl and related compounds should be conducted. Methods with low detection limits such as radioimmunoassay or gas chromatography with sensitive detectors are available and must be used in this context.

MARIJUANA

The term, marijuana, is believed to originate from a Portuguese or Spanish word for intoxicating. It is present in the plant, *Cannabis sativa*, which is also known as hemp. Hemp is commercially valuable for more than marijuana. Its stem yields a fiber which can be made into rope or cloth.

The "Book of Drugs" appeared in China around 2737 B.C. It describes marijuana, alluding to its multiple commercial and medical uses. The Chinese at the time found it to be helpful in gout, malaria, and absent-mindedness. Marijuana appeared in other Chinese literature and, by the beginning of the Christian era, it underwent a period of disrepute during which the ruling classes believed that its beneficial qualities were outweighed by its capacity to undermine the morals of the young. Marijuana also was used heavily in India through the millennia. It also met with condemnations in the popular literature and with large numbers of moralistic groups who urged that it be banned.

Other ancient civilizations, among them the Assyrians, Greeks, and Romans, all used and wrote about marijuana. The celebrated traveler, Marco Polo described an Arabian leader of the 10th century, Hassan Ibn-Sabbah, who wielded power by providing his followers with hashish, an especially potent form of marijuana. Members of his cult were said to be provided with hashish and would then readily murder all opponents. They were known as hashishiyya, from which the term hashish has arisen. The word, assassin, is thought to be derived from their leader, Sheik Hassan. This legend about the assassins was recounted by Alexander Dumas in *The Count of Monte Christo*. The story may be true but hashish would not be likely to excite men to a murderous rage. It would be more likely to sedate them. In that case it may, perhaps, have been provided as a reward after the deed was done.

In colonial America hemp was also important. The Jamestown settlers used it for making rope. The Pilgrims also employed it for making rope, as well as for the manufacture of clothing. Even the father of his country, George Washington, planted hemp among his crops at Mount Vernon. Ironically, hemp was so valuable a raw material in the colonies that Massachusetts passed a law requiring every household to plant hemp. Today, laws are widespread for the opposite purpose.

It appears that recreational use of marijuana in America started to become prevalent during the early nineteenth century. By the twentieth century marijuana use was common along the Mexican border and in the poorest areas of large cities. Harry Anslinger, first director of the Bureau of Narcotics in America, swore to eradicate marijuana and was responsible for some of the distortions in the public mind. Marijuana underwent the usual collection of unscientific and untested contentions about its true nature. Most notably it was believed to provoke vicious behavior and sexual excitation.

Marijuana is today an object of great controversy. Its proponents claim that marijuana use is without any ill effect and they have succeeded to a modest degree in decriminalizing its use in some municipalities.

CHEMISTRY

Marijuana is a preparation from the *Cannabis* plant which, because of its appearance, is commonly called grass. Ganja and sinsemilla, forms of marijuana, come from the flowering tops of the plant. Hashish is a dark resin, rich in the active ingredient, which is prepared by intense drying of the flowering tops of *Cannabis*. Thai sticks are compressed products favored by military personnel during the Vietnam War. The active agent in marijuana is tetrahydrocannabinol (THC) (Figure 20.14). Most marijuana contains about 2 to 6% THC, the amount varying depending on the pedigree of the source plant. Ganja and sinsemilla are about 6 to 7% THC while hashish is up to 12% THC. The most concentrated form, aside from pure THC itself, is hash oil. This substance is extracted from *Cannabis* and contains up to 50% THC.

MECHANISM

Tetrahydrocannabinol receptors have been located and shown to occur naturally in the cerebellum, basal nuclei, and hippocampus of the human brain. Because these

FIGURE 20.13 *Cannabis sativa* plant, source of marijuana and other cannabinoids. (From Michael Moore, Southwestern School of Botanical Medicine. With permission.)

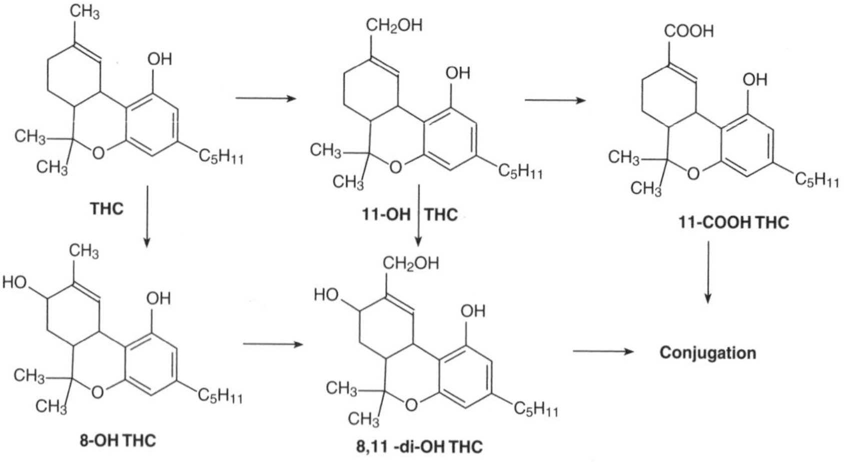

FIGURE 20.14 THC, the active agent in marijuana and aspects of its metabolism.

receptors exist it was reasonable to postulate that endogenous molecules must also exist for the purpose of binding to these receptors under certain conditions. A biochemical found in the human body, anandamide, has been discovered and shown to bind to marijuana receptors in the brain. The euphoria related to marijuana use seems to arise in the following manner. Compounds similar to morphine and called opiopeptins are released from specific neurons called opiopeptin neurons. Having been released, the opiopeptin then goes to a dopamine neuron in the reward circuit and it inhibits the release of dopamine, an event which provides a substantial reward. The role of tetrahydrocannabinol is that it can bind a tetrahydrocannabinol receptor located on the opiopeptin neuron and, in so doing, cause the release of opiopeptins. Naloxone, a narcotic antagonist, is able to prevent the rewarding properties of marijuana. This supports this mechanism because the opiopeptins released by tetra-hydrocannabinol binding are morphine-like. It is also significant that tetrahydrocan-nabinol has some activity in ameliorating narcotic withdrawal.

PHARMACOKINETICS

Marijuana is usually employed in the form of a hand-rolled cigarette containing 1 to 2 g of plant material. With a tetrahydrocannabinol (THC) content of 5% this works out to 75 mg of THC, the active agent. The actual absorbed quantity is highly variable among users. One of the factors which varies is "pacing," a term referring to the ability of the user to hold the smoke in his lungs and absorb ingredients during that time. Studies show that the actual bioavailability of THC ranges from 2 to 20%. Onset of drug action is within a very few minutes, with peak blood levels being reached in about 20 minutes. Effects usually last for approximately 2 hours. Marijuana may be taken orally with peak level and effects occurring on the order of 2 to 3 times more slowly than from smoking.

After absorption, tetrahydrocannabinol is widely distributed especially to organs with high fat content. This is in keeping with the highly nonpolar nature of THC. Tetrahydrocannabinol readily crosses the blood–brain barrier or the placenta in a pregnant woman.

Tetrahydrocannabinol is extensively metabolized initially to an active product, 11-OH-delta-9-tetrahydrocannabinol, then to an inactive one, carboxy-9-THC. Most THC is excreted into the urine as a conjugate with glucuronic acid.

Tetrahydrocannabinol metabolite elimination follows a biphasic model with rapid clearance initially, followed by very slow complete elimination. The early rapid decline of THC from the blood is due to metabolism, excretion, and distribution into fat. There follows a very slow phase in which THC re-emerges from fat stores and is slowly eliminated from the body. It is for this reason that tetrahydrocannabinol users will remain positive by urine testing for relatively long periods of time after discontinuation of drug use. Many studies show that THC will continue to be eliminated in amounts sufficient to provide a positive urine drug test (>15 ng/mL of marijuana metabolite) for as long as 60 days after discontinuation of use. This effect is, as might be expected, especially likely in obese persons who have large fat storage sites for the nonpolar THC. It is dramatically different from the elimination behavior of most other drugs that tends to become negative in testing within 1 week after usage is stopped.

Effects

Mild cannabis use produces relaxation, a sense of well-being, alterations in perception, and impaired memory. Moderate intoxication causes mood swings, significant memory deficits, and depersonalization. Severe intoxication (more than 6 times as much THC as the usual recreational doses) leads to slurred speech, loss of coordination, hallucinations, delusions, and paranoia; anxiety reaching panic proportions can take the place of euphoria, sometimes as a result of a fear that the drug-induced state is permanent. Physical findings found in tetrahydrocannabinol overdose include a dose-related tachycardia, impotence, fine tremor, constipation, nystagmus, bronchial irritation, and hypothermia.

Chronic Effects

Whatever the toxicity of marijuana is, it is generally recognized as being significantly less than all or most other drugs of abuse. In fact, its long-term toxicity is sufficiently low so that efforts to reduce or eliminate penalties for its use have been successful in many places around the world. Nevertheless, it is not totally innocuous.

1. Driving is impaired. In some studies, the frequency of marijuana-associated vehicular accidents is comparable to that of alcohol-related accidents. An added problem is that the impairment lasts long beyond the time the user is subjectively aware of being impaired.
2. Some level of impairment in pulmonary function occurs. Bronchial irritation and inflammation are commonly noted. The picture is similar to that of early emphysema. This chronic effect is absent when a user takes marijuana by the oral route.
3. Pre-cancerous changes are noted in the bronchi of marijuana smokers. Marijuana cigarettes contain more carcinogen than tobacco cigarettes although marijuana is almost always used less frequently than tobacco.
4. Personality changes may occur in marijuana users in which they develop apathetic personalities. They may have a poor work ethic and can be classic underachievers. This constellation of symptoms has been labeled amotivational syndrome. Some have suggested that it is not due to marijuana but rather a personality defect in the drug user. Persons who choose to place a drug at the center of their lives are the same persons most likely to lack normal motivation. The fact that many marijuana users have become much more motivated when drug use was discontinued suggests, however, that the amotivational syndrome is a result of marijuana use and not merely associated with it.

Therapy for Overdose

Decontamination may be useful for the minority of users who ingested the marijuana. Lavage or activated charcoal may be helpful. Benzodiazepines can be given if the patient is severely agitated. Hypotension is usually mild, when present, and may be medically treated. Beta blockers are effective for tachycardia caused by tetrahydrocannabinol.

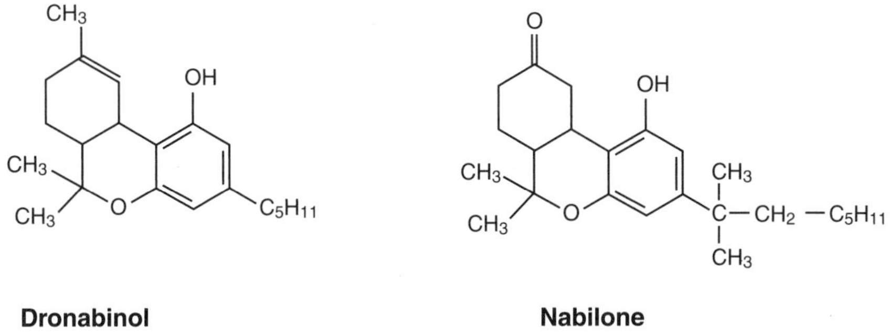

Dronabinol   **Nabilone**

FIGURE 20.15 Medical forms of marijuana.

MEDICINAL USE

There has been a consistent effort on the part of many to make marijuana available for medical use. In 1989 the Drug Enforcement Administration rejected a petition to reschedule marijuana from Schedule I (always prohibited) to Schedule II (available by prescription for medical use). The particular schedule under which a controlled substance is classified is stated in the Controlled Substances Act. Basically, the lower the schedule (I is the lowest) the more a substance is excluded and the less it is perceived to have medical value. Marijuana is claimed to be beneficial for glaucoma and for the nausea associated with cancer chemotherapy. Two synthetic forms of marijuana, nabilone and dronabinol (Marinol), have been marketed by the drug industry. Dronabinol is equal to delta-9-tetrahydrocannabinol and is extracted and purified from *Cannabis* but nabilone is slightly different from marijuana (Figure 20.15.) When these agents are used medicinally they produce the same psychoactive effects as found from marijuana. Overdose, when it occurs, is similar to marijuana overdose. Those who favor selling marijuana itself in place of the pharmaceutical products for medical use claim that marijuana is much cheaper and far more effective for these purposes.

LABORATORY CONSIDERATIONS

Tetrahydrocannabinol and its metabolites may be measured in blood or in urine. When measured in blood serum no relation between concentration and effect exists initially but, after equilibrium is attained, the intensity of effect is proportional to tetrahydrocannabinol plasma level. No reliable relationship exists between urine concentration and behavioral impairment.

Because of the difficulty of obtaining blood specimens and the short window of detection when tested in blood, drug testing programs usually are based on urine rather than blood testing. Urine offers the advantages of large specimen volumes which can be collected without venipuncture and which will remain positive for much longer periods of time after use. Marijuana is, therefore, regularly tested for in urine. The methods used are almost all based on antibodies to the major urinary metabolite of tetrahydrocannabinol, delta-9-tetrahydrocannabinol-carboxylic acid. Government-sponsored testing programs are based on screening tests which, when positive, are followed by confirmation testing. The screening test is positive if the result exceeds 50 ng/mL. Confirmation testing is done by gas chromatography-mass spectrometry. The cut-off for positivity is 15 ng/mL. The reason these numbers are so different is that the immunoassays will react to a small extent with other cannabinoids in urine whereas the GC-MS reacts only with one metabolite. It is possible, therefore, for perfectly calibrated assays to give a result of 50 ng/mL by screening and 15 ng/mL by GC-MS.

PHENCYCLIDINE

Phencyclidine was developed in the late 1950s by Parke-Davis Pharmaceuticals under the trade name, Sernylan, as an anesthetic for intravenous use (Figure 20.16). It provided a semiconscious separation from sensation which was desirable because it spared the patient the deeper CNS depression provoked by other anesthetics. Initially regarded as a good therapeutic agent it was eventually found to be unsatisfactory because some patients had prolonged manic states after being administered phencyclidine. Those patients were the ones who, for various reasons, achieved relatively high blood concentrations of the drug. Phencyclidine is also known as PCP which comes from its chemical name (1-(1-**p**henyl**c**yclohexyl)-**p**iperidine). Phencyclidine first became a street drug during the Vietnam War resistance movements of the late 1960s. In that scenario it was known as PeaCe Pill. Other terms that soon were applied to it included angel dust because it was dusted onto parsley and smoked.

When phencyclidine was determined to be too dangerous for human use as a pharmaceutical, it was relegated to veterinary use. However, even this application was problematic because drug dealers would steal it from veterinary offices. PCP is not widely available today but is popular in certain regions of the United States. Where it is available it comes from clandestine laboratories.

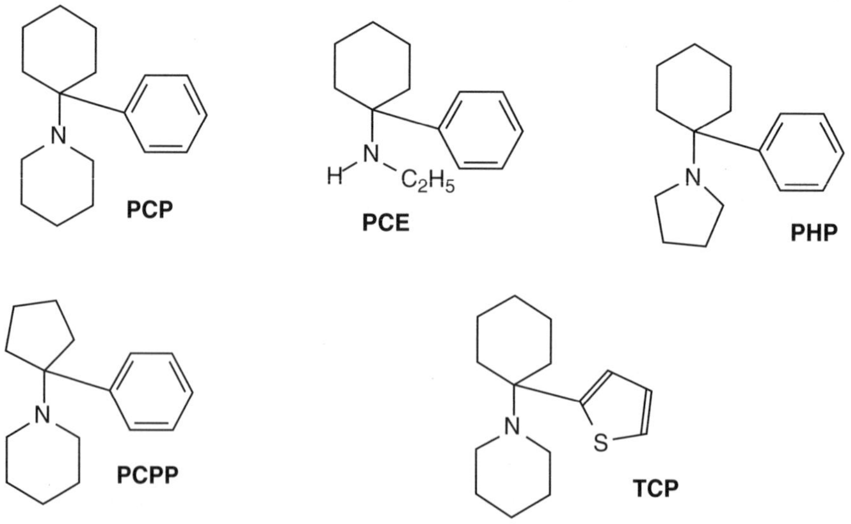

FIGURE 20.16 Phencyclidine and some of its analogs.

Phencyclidine is highly lipid soluble but also is soluble in water and alcohol. It is a weak base with pK of approximately 9.0. Phencyclidine undergoes extensive metabolism and is eliminated predominantly as the monohydroxypiperidine metabolite. Less than 10% of the parent compound is excreted in the urine.

Users smoke, snort, or orally ingest phencyclidine. Response time to inhaled drug is 2 to 5 minutes and 15 to 30 minutes when it is orally ingested. In addition, the dose needed to produce sedation is only 0.25 mg for the intravenous drug vs. at least 10 times as much for ingested drug.

Illicit synthesis of phencyclidine is very simple, so many clandestine laboratories are engaged in this very profitable pursuit. Some of them also are preparing related compounds which have properties similar to phencyclidine. Among these related compounds many are more toxic than phencyclidine. TCP, 1-(1-cyclohexyl) piperidine; PHP, phenylcyclohexylpyrrolidine; PCE, (1-phenyl-cyclohexylethylamine); PCC, (1-piperidonocyclohexanecarbinol) are some compounds being sold on the street as phencyclidine. All of these structures are similar to PCP. Chemists with a criminal bent have synthesized them in hopes of finding molecules which could be sold for a fast profit.

DRUG EFFECTS

Phencyclidine is unpredictable, but the risk associated with its use is accepted by some of the drug-abusing population. It often gives feelings of strength, power, and invulnerability, occasionally to a superhuman extent. A heightened sensitivity to external stimuli, mood elevation, and a detachment from cares of this world are all described features of phencyclidine drug use. Phencyclidine also causes serious perceptual distortions so that it is very hazardous to use it before driving or other activity which requires control of one's body and mind. Persons driving under the influence of phencyclidine have been stopped because of the obviously erratic nature of their vehicular control. These individuals were almost always noted to be sedated rather than manic in their mood. This is because persons who used enough drug to achieve mania would usually not be able to start a motor vehicle.

MECHANISM OF ACTION

Phencyclidine interacts with several neurotransmitter systems including cholinergic neurons. Some of its activities (but probably not too many) are believed to be related to this interaction. More specifically, phencyclidine binds to sigma receptors located in various parts of the brain, most specifically the frontal cortex and the hippocampus. In an unknown manner this binding is thought to be responsible for the analgesic and psychotomimetic activity of phencyclidine. The most specific binding of phencyclidine is to receptors for an excitatory amino acid, N-methyl-D-aspartate (NMDA). Phencyclidine binds to this NMDA receptor and inhibits its normal action. Calcium, sodium, and magnesium movements through certain neurons are, in turn, affected by the status of the NMDA receptor. However, the specific steps by which changes in the flux of these ions are related to the behavioral changes induced by phencyclidine are not yet known.

CLINICAL PRESENTATION

Overdose with phencyclidine is manifested by a variety of physical and psychological signs. Vomiting is common. Ocular signs, including lacrimation, nystagmus, and mydriasis, are found. Tachycardia may be noted. Psychiatric manifestations include violent behavior, psychosis, hallucinations, and paranoia. Laboratory findings may include myoglobinuria, hyperuricemia, hypoglycemia, and acid-base abnormalities. The most severe overdoses are accompanied by respiratory depression, fasciculations, encephalopathy, coma, and seizures.

THERAPY

For oral ingestions lavage or activated charcoal should be attempted to minimize absorption of drug. Medication should be given to control symptoms, e.g., benzodiazepines may be provided for agitation, haloperidol for psychotic behavior, and beta blockers or peripheral vasodilatation for hypertension. Enhanced elimination is possible because phencyclidine has alkaline characteristics. If urine is acidified, the rate of elimination will be enhanced. Although this is theoretically feasible, the advantages of more rapid elimination are often outweighed by the complications associated with the resulting acidosis which complicate the course of therapy. There are no known antidotes for phencyclidine overdose.

LABORATORY CONSIDERATIONS

Phencyclidine can be measured in the blood or urine. There is an approximate agreement between the blood concentration and clinical findings as follows:

Excitation	20–30 ng/mL
Coma	30–100 ng/mL
Seizures, death	>100 ng/mL

Measuring levels is not recommended in overdose because of the very approximate nature of this association and the prolonged delay in receiving results from most laboratories. This delay is due to the esoteric and time-consuming nature of the analysis. An additional problem is that most phencyclidine sold on the street is heavily contaminated with other active agents. Phencyclidine is usually only one of several substances found in street materials which are sold as PCP and which adversely affect the patient.

Phencyclidine is one of the NIDA 5, the drugs which may be tested for in federally certified testing programs for pre-employment. This testing is done on urine and a result >75 ng/mL in the initial test is a presumptive positive. However, a positive will be reported only if the initial test is above this cut-off and the confirming test, GC-MS, is above 25 ng/mL. An interesting feature of phencyclidine usage is that the window of detection is approximately 1 week. Therefore, its presence can be demonstrated in urine considerably longer than most other drugs with the notable exception of marijuana.

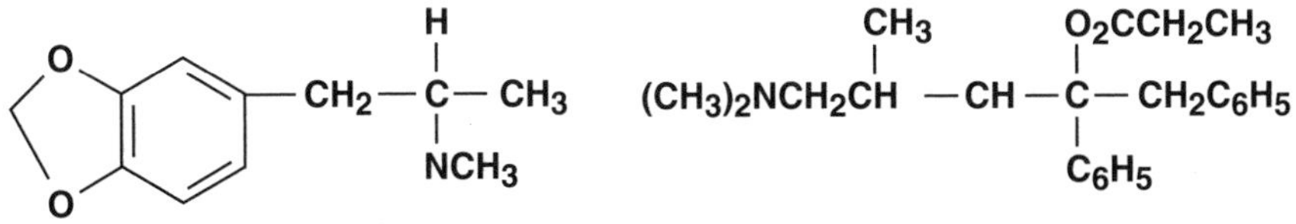

FIGURE 20.17 Absolute structures of two drugs (see Question 2 below).

Questions and Problems

1. For each of the following, list the drug category to which it belongs and describe the characteristics of the toxidrome associated with its overdose:
   Hydromorphone
   Ephedrine
   Phencyclidine
   Tetrahydrocannabinol
   Cocaine
2. Name the compounds depicted in Figure 20.17. Include a stereochemical designation in the name.
3. Describe, for each of the following, the biochemical mechanism of action:
   Phencyclidine
   Tetrahydrocannabinol
   Methamphetamine
4. Make a sketch that shows the process of conversion of cocaine hydrochloride to crack.
5. An automobile driver is stopped while driving erratically. She is tested for drugs and the laboratory report states that she is positive for cocaine metabolite in her urine. She claims that someone else must have added cocaine to her urine and that she is being framed. Discuss.
6. An employee is tested for cause and his urine is positive for marijuana metabolite at a concentration of 59 ng/mL. He denies any usage and suggests that the finding must be due to passive exposure during a recent concert. Discuss.
7. A person was accused of using cocaine and asked for a drug test on her urine 1 week after the alleged time of use. The test was negative. Is this evidence that the accusation is groundless?
8. Show the reaction for the acidification of methamphetamine.
9. Make a table listing the cut-offs for each of the following in the National Laboratory Certification Program:
   Morphine
   Codeine
   Phencyclidine
   Marijuana metabolite
   Amphetamine
   Cocaine metabolite
   Methamphetamine

10. Describe the biochemical and biological basis for the opiate antagonistic behavior of nalorphine.
11. Discuss the statement, "Marijuana is never eaten because it would have no psychoactive effect when eaten. But, if eaten, laboratory tests on urine would be negative."
12. Discuss the statement, "Marijuana should be legal because it has less toxicity than a legal drug, ethanol."

Case Study 1: A Patient with Bizarre Behavior

A 30-year-old man was brought to the emergency department from his hotel where he was found in a comatose state. He reacted only to deep pain and had an absent gag reflex. Pupils were sluggish and his eyes had a fixed stare. Skin was warm and dry. Vital signs were blood pressure, 130/60; pulse, 87; temperature, 38.8°C. Muscles were rigid with spasms. He continuously moved his shoulders and head in an erratic manner. His mood was extremely agitated. The patient was given diazepam which lessened his erratic behavior.

Laboratory testing consisted of routine chemistry and urinary drug screen. Chemistry testing showed the following:

Test	Result	Reference Range
Urine myoglobin	Positive	Negative
Serum CK	125,000 U/L	<200 U/L
AST	2000 U/L	<30 U/L
LDH	1445 U/L	30–150 U/L
BUN	64 mg/dL	10–20 mg/dL
Creatinine	5.5 mg/dL	<1.3 mg/dL

The drug screen was positive.

Which drug was positive in the urine screen?
   a) Valium
   b) Phencyclidine (PCP)
   c) Cocaine
   d) Morphine

The best estimate of the offending toxin in this case is phencyclidine. Valium is, of course, diazepam, the agent administered to treat his symptoms. A comprehensive drug screen would include benzodiazepines, and the Valium (diazepam) might cause a positive. It would be readily recognized that benzodiazepines were not responsible for his symptoms. Morphine is an unlikely cause in this case because it would be expected to produce sedation. Cocaine and phencyclidine are both possible suggestions and do produce a similar picture. The behavioral aberrations are possible from either drug although they are more likely from phencyclidine. The lack of additional signs of stimulation is more consistent with PCP than cocaine and the drug screen did show the presence of PCP only.

All of the chemical abnormalities in the table above are due to rhabdomyolysis, a breakdown of muscle tissue. This is a frequent complication of cocaine or PCP overdose and also arises from other causes.

The patient was admitted to intensive care. He was placed on pancuronium to paralyze him and prevent further muscle damage. Airway suctioning and dialysis were initiated. For the next month the patient underwent treatment and showed progressive improvement with occasional setbacks. Eventually, he was discharged when his liver and renal function returned to normal. Despite an obvious need for it, he refused admission to an outpatient drug treatment center.

Questions

Q1. What causes rhabdomyolysis?
   a) Impurities in the street drug
   b) Extreme agitation by the patient
   c) Hypoxia from the drug of abuse itself
   d) All of the above
   e) None of the above
Q2. Which of the following is not a symptom of PCP overdose?
   a) Ataxia
   b) Depression
   c) Stupor
   d) Catatonic posturing
   e) All of the above are symptoms
Q3. How long will urine remain positive for PCP by screening tests after the discontinuation of regular PCP use?
   a) 1 day
   b) 3 days
   c) 2 weeks
   d) 2 months
Q4. The most severe intoxication with PCP produces so-called Stage III symptoms. The associated blood concentration is
   a) 20 ng/mL in blood
   b) Serum concentration about 50 ng/mL
   c) Serum concentration about 100 ng/mL
   d) None of the above

Answers and Discussion

Q1. (Answer = d) Rhabdomyolysis is a common complication of drug overdose. It is equivalent to destruction of muscle tissue and is manifested by outpouring of creatine kinase (CK) and myoglobin from necrotic muscle cells into the blood. Muscle may be injured by a specific toxic effect due to the drug itself or some unspecified impurity within the mixture. Hypoxia is also a common cause of rhabdomyolysis and it may occur as a side effect from the drug. In this patient, PCP induced a spastic muscle reaction. The prolonged muscle spasms were associated with inadequate blood flow, i.e., a hypoxic state in the myocytes.

Q2. (Answer = e) PCP produces an extremely wide array of symptoms that are greatly dependent on the amount of drug being abused. PCP intoxication has been divided into three types which differ greatly in their manifestations. In Stage I we have a conscious patient who has ingested 2 to 5 mg of PCP. The patient is likely to be agitated and incapable of mentally concentrating. Stage II patients are stuporous or in mild coma. This stage typically is due to a dose of 5 to 25 mg of PCP. Deep coma, tonic-clonic seizures, and possible stroke are found in Stage III. Deep pain response is absent. Over 25 mg of PCP are required to produce this stage.

Q3. (Answer = c) PCP is known to have a larger window of detection than most drugs. Exceptions to this generalization include marijuana, some long-acting barbiturates, and miscellaneous other drugs. Its elimination is prolonged due to its lipophilic character. PCP is stored in adipose tissue from which it re-enters the blood. This recycling between adipose tissue and blood is responsible for PCP positive findings in urine up to 2 weeks after discontinuation of drug use.

Q4. (Answer = c) There is a rough correlation between blood level of PCP and a user's symptoms. To a first approximation, high blood levels are associated with more toxicity. Because PCP acts on the CNS, we should expect that the blood level may not always reflect the concentration of the drug at the active site. The CNS is remote from the blood and drug concentrations are not always in equilibrium between blood and CNS. Recall also that experienced users develop some degree of tolerance so that higher drug concentrations have lesser effects on them than those usually seen in a naive user.

Reference

Milhorn, H.T., Diagnosis and management of phencyclidine intoxication, *Am. J. Fam. Pract.*, 43, 1293–1302, 1991.

Case Study 2: Queen of the World

A 21-year-old college student with a long history of bulimia and intermittent depression was admitted to the hospital in an acute manic state. Four weeks earlier she was started on fluoxetine and desipramine for her depression, suicidal ideation, and eating disorder. The desipramine was discontinued because she experienced an associated dry mouth which was very irritating to her. Four days before the present admission she smoked some drugs with her friends at her college. This made her feel hyperenergetic, euphoric, and severely delusional. She described herself as being "the queen of the world," and she believed that she was in charge of international affairs in the western hemisphere.

What is the cause of her psychiatric symptoms?
   a) Marijuana
   b) Fluoxetine
   c) Desipramine
   d) A drug interaction

This extreme manic reaction was probably due to a drug interaction. The side effects of these drugs taken individually do not usually include such severe personality disorders. Although marijuana can produce hallucinations and other psychiatric manifestations these symptoms rarely are found to the degree exhibited by this patient. Moreover, she acknowledged frequent previous use of marijuana without any adverse effects. She had no earlier episodes of this kind of manic behavior. Desipramine was not likely to be a suspect cause either alone or in combination because she discontinued it 2 weeks before the onset of these symptoms. She also had used desipramine for several years earlier in her life and that usage was not associated with toxic effects.

The patient was admitted and required a seclusion room for behavioral management. Lorazepam and perphenazine were given for agitation and manic excitement. Her mania and grandiose delusions disappeared over a 4-day period. She was not discharged, however, for 36 days because of efforts to treat her depression and bulimia and to achieve total elimination of the initial manic state.

Questions

Q1. Which is true of the difference between fluoxetine and desipramine?
   a) Fluoxetine is an antidepressant whereas desipramine is an antipsychotic.
   b) Both are antidepressants but fluoxetine is a newer drug.
   c) Fluoxetine affects more organ systems.
   d) Toxicity due to fluoxetine is likely to be greater.
Q2. What is the basis for a probable interaction between marijuana and fluoxetine?
   a) Both inhibit serotonin re-uptake.
   b) Both deplete serotonin at the synapse.
   c) Both are primarily cardiotoxic.
   d) Fluoxetine decreases clearance of marijuana and thus prolongs the half-life of marijuana.
Q3. Which is true of marijuana toxicity?
   a) It carries a high risk of lung cancer.
   b) A common side effect is gynecomastia.
   c) It is associated with amotivational syndrome.
   d) It provokes physical addiction.

Answers and Discussion

Q1. (Answer = b) Fluoxetine (Prozac) is referred to as a third-generation antidepressant. It also is known as an SSRI, a selective serotonin re-uptake inhibitor. Its activity is almost exclusively associated with serotonin. Desipramine is a first-generation antidepressant. This class of drugs, which includes amitriptyline, imipramine, nortriptyline, and others, have multiple toxicity. The first-generation antidepressants are much more toxic than fluoxetine and have strong anticholinergic action, cardiotoxicity, and CNS depressant effects.

Q2. (Answer = a) The primary action of fluoxetine is the inhibition of serotonin re-uptake which enhances the concentration of serotonin in the neuron. Delta-9-tetrahydrocannabinol, the major active ingredient in marijuana, has the same potent effect on serotonin. Marijuana and fluoxetine are not regarded as especially cardiotoxic and fluoxetine has no known effect on marijuana pharmacokinetics or metabolism.

Q3. (Answer = c) The toxicity of marijuana is a topic of great controversy. There is general agreement, however, that it is not significantly toxic compared to other recreational drugs. Studies on the tar content of marijuana cigarettes suggest that they are more carcinogenic than ordinary tobacco. This is offset, however, by the smaller absolute amount of smoking by the marijuana user in contrast to the average cigarette smoker. Marijuana sometimes causes gynecomastia in heavy users. Perhaps the most common finding in smokers of marijuana is amotivational syndrome, a lack of normal interest in life, family, career, etc.

Reference

Stoll, A.L. et al., A case of mania as a result of fluoxetine-marijuana interaction, *J. Clin. Psychiat.*, 52, 280–281, 1991.

Case Study 3: Child with Laceration

An 8-month-old girl sustained a ½-in. cut to her upper lip and was brought by her mother to an emergency department for treatment. A cotton pledget with anesthetic was held to the injured area by the girl's mother. After several minutes this pledget was changed to a fresh one and the application to the affected area was repeated. The mother noted that the medication on the pledget was dripping into the child's nose and her daughter was licking her lips. Eventually, suturing was completed and the little girl was discharged. No vital signs were recorded but the mother described her daughter as being tense and wide-eyed.

At home the girl was placed in her crib in which she was found dead 3 hours later. Autopsy showed no anatomical abnormalities nor any indication of natural illness.

What drug may be involved here?
    a) Mercury
    b) Cocaine
    c) Chloroform
    d) Ethanol

The clinical signs are very few in this case although those given are consistent with the identity of the offending agent. What is of greatest importance is the history. TAC, a solution containing cocaine, is commonly used for anesthesia in children. High amounts of cocaine are found in TAC. The child's tense demeanor and wide-eyed status are also common observations in cocaine poisoning. Mercury or chloroform have, especially in the past, been employed for anesthesia or antisepsis but they would not produce the clinical picture seen here.

Questions

Q1. What are the components of TAC?
    a) Tetracycline, adrenaline, cocaine
    b) Tetracaine, adenosine, cocaine
    c) Tetracaine, albuterol, cocaine
    d) Tetracaine, adrenaline, cocaine
Q2. What is a toxic dose of cocaine?
    a) 200 mg in adults
    b) 2 mg
    c) 2 g
    d) 500 mg
Q3. From which of the following is cocaine readily absorbed?
    a) Intact skin
    b) Lacerated skin
    c) Mucous membranes
    d) All of the above
Q4. What is the lethal blood level of cocaine?
    a) 0.1–21 mg/L
    b) >20 mg/dL
    c) >1 g/L
    d) 1–200 mg/L

Answers and Discussion

Q1. (Answer = d) TAC is a topical solution containing 0.5% tetracaine, 0.05% adrenaline, and 11.8% cocaine. Tetracaine is an anesthetic while adrenaline is a vasoconstrictor used here to reduce blood flow. Cocaine has both anesthetic and vasoconstrictive properties. TAC is desirable because it is topical and the patient is spared administration of an anesthetic by needle into an area that may already be painful from the prior injury. Because TAC is applied in a volume of 5 mL the quantity of cocaine in a pledget is 590 mg.

Q2. (Answer = a) It is always difficult to determine safe doses of street drugs because many of them cause harm from an impurity rather than from the alleged main ingredient. Nevertheless, cocaine is not regarded as toxic in amounts less than 200 mg in adults. Street doses are usually in the range of 50 to 100 mg. It is clear that 5 mL of TAC (590 mg cocaine) contain a lethal amount of cocaine even for someone whose body mass is much greater than that of an 8-month-old child.

Q3. (Answer = c) Cocaine will not penetrate intact skin or even abraded, burned, or lacerated skin except to a very small degree. It is, however, absorbed readily from mucous membranes or by inhalation. The manner of this child's exposure led to absorption of significant quantities of cocaine.

Q4. (Answer = a) In one study, 11 patients who died from an apparent overdose of cocaine had blood levels between 0.1 and 20.9 mg/L.[2] Other studies and case reports support the finding that blood levels are highly variable in deaths caused by cocaine. This child had a postmortem cocaine level of 11.9 mg/L in her blood, a result high enough to unequivocally constitute a cause of death.

References

1. Dailey, R., Fatality secondary to misuse of TAC solution, *Ann. Emerg. Med.*, 17, 159–160, 1988.
2. Mittleman, R.E. and Wetli, C.V., Death caused by recreational cocaine use, *JAMA*, 252, 1889–1893, 1984.

Case Study 4: Nature's Purest Food?

A 2-week-old girl was brought to an emergency department by her mother who stated that the baby had become extremely irritable and had vomited repeatedly starting 4 hours earlier. The mother was most alarmed by the baby's pupils which had remained dilated since that time. Examination revealed a normally hydrated and nourished baby who was easily startled by the most trivial stimulus. Her heart rate was 160 beats per minute; systolic blood pressure was 96 mm; respiratory rate, 36 breaths per minute; and she had a normal body temperature. The child also was noted to have a high-pitched cry, dilated pupils with sluggish response to light, increased deep tendon reflexes, and trembling of the extremities.

The mother was certain that the baby was exposed only to her breast milk which she had provided 5 times between 10 a.m. and 2 p.m.

A probable identity for the offending agent is
  a) morphine
  b) alcohol
  c) cocaine
  d) marijuana

If the mother had been using morphine or alcohol, one would expect that the baby's major response, assuming sufficient quantities of either of these reached her blood, would be sedation. Her presentation probably would have been characterized by extreme lethargy with reduced vital signs. The baby's response to marijuana probably would be minor with little or no symptoms exhibited. Cocaine is expected to manifest the signs exhibited by this patient. As a stimulant it is well-known to elevate vital signs and cause hypertension, hyperpnea, and tachycardia as shown by this child.

The mother acknowledged that she used 0.5 g of cocaine intranasally between 10 a.m. and 2 p.m., the same time during which she had breast fed the baby on 5 occasions.

The baby was admitted to the hospital. She received fluids and her vital and neurological signs were watched closely. Her clinical course was marked by a steady but slow return to normal vital signs and she was discharged 4 days later. The state department for family services recommended that the child be permitted to remain with her family after discharge. They chose, however, to subject the mother to close supervision and repeated visits for the child's welfare. When questioned about her drug use during this baby's gestation, the mother claimed that she used cocaine heavily for 2 months until she became aware of the pregnancy. She then discontinued cocaine use but consumed about 2 to 3 alcoholic drinks each day as beer or hard liquor. She smoked 1 pack of cigarettes each day throughout the pregnancy. This level of exposure to alcohol and tobacco did not appear to harm the infant; she was delivered vaginally without problems at 38 weeks of gestation. Nothing abnormal was observed during the time of perinatal observation.

Questions

Q1. How much cocaine was present in the breast milk 12 hours after the mother's last use of cocaine?
   a) 30 ng/mL
   b) 300 ng/mL
   c) 3000 ng/mL (3 µg/mL)
   d) 30,000 ng/mL

Q2. Which of the following symptoms is <u>not</u> typically seen in cocaine exposure?
   a) Tachycardia
   b) Tachypnea
   c) Hypertension
   d) Irritability
   e) All of the above

Q3. What problems are associated with cocaine use during pregnancy?
   a) Increased rate of perinatal complications
   b) Low birth-weight babies
   c) Neurobehavioral abnormalities
   d) All of the above

Q4. Which is true of the transfer of cocaine from the maternal circulation into breast milk?
a) Cocaine is very polar and crosses into milk readily.
b) Cocaine is very polar and should not cross membranes into breast milk.
c) Cocaine is very nonpolar and would not penetrate into milk.
d) Cocaine is very nonpolar and readily crosses cell membranes.

Answers and Discussion

Q1. (Answer = a) Cocaine and benzoylecgonine, the major cocaine metabolite, were measured in the breast milk and the baby's urine. The amount of cocaine in the milk was only 30 ng/mL. It would be difficult to extrapolate this figure to the time during which feeding occurred but, clearly, cocaine in milk at that time was much higher. The baby's urine had benzoylecgonine concentration equal to 900 ng/mL, a significant amount. The cocaine in the urine of the baby equaled 100 ng/mL. The ratio of cocaine to benzoylecgonine in the baby's urine is rather high, suggesting that the cocaine was being metabolized more slowly in the baby than in an adult. Measurement of cocaine in the baby's blood was not determined. The child's total absorption of cocaine was presumably very small, but her young age and small body mass resulted in symptoms clearly due to cocaine despite a very low dose.

Q2. (Answer = e) Cocaine is believed to achieve its effects by blocking the re-uptake of norepinephrine at nerve terminals. This increases norepinephrine levels and predictably causes vasoconstriction with resulting hypertension and tachycardia. Other actions noted in this baby, such as irritability, are related to cocaine's effects on the CNS. Because cocaine is a stimulant its effects are primarily to intensify physiological actions. Massive overdoses, however, result in CNS depression and paralysis of the medulla including respiratory function.

Q3. (Answer = d) Many studies have been conducted in regard to the deleterious effects of cocaine use during pregnancy. Premature deliveries and *abruptio placentae* are among the complications that occur with greater frequency in those pregnancies associated with cocaine use. Babies born to cocaine-using mothers also are at risk for low birth weight. They exhibit many neurological signs such as extreme tremulousness, irritability, and inability to control mood and interact normally with care givers.

Q4. (Answer = d) Cocaine is nonpolar and its metabolite, benzoylecgonine, is significantly polar. Nonpolar molecules readily cross the lipophilic cell membrane. The benzoylecgonine found in the baby's urine arises in small part from the mother's milk but probably more from hydrolysis of cocaine in the baby's circulation.

Reference

Chasnoff, I.J. et al., Cocaine intoxication in a breast-fed infant, *Pediatrics,* 80, 836–838, 1987.

Case Study 5: A Cancer Death?

An 83-year-old woman was found dead in her home. She had been diagnosed earlier with terminal cancer and was being treated for pain relief. Several medicinal patches were noted on her chest. Autopsy showed extensive carcinoma of the stomach with ulceration of her esophagus and spread of her cancer to the lymph nodes in the vicinity of the pancreas. However, based on her known medical history and the absence of other findings at the autopsy, death due to cancer alone was regarded as unlikely.

A possible cause of this patient's death is
    a) Overdose from over-the-counter analgesic
    b) Fentanyl
    c) Morphine
    d) Physical injury secondary to her debilitated state

The observation of three patches on her chest prompted an investigation of their contents. They were found to be 100 μg/hour fentanyl patches. These transdermal patches provide a constant therapeutic serum concentration of the potent pain reliever, fentanyl. They are analogous to intravenous infusions but have the obvious advantages of simplicity of delivery. For long-term therapy of cancer pain they are quite popular. The manner in which they should be used, however, is application of 1 patch every 2 to 3 days. A significant risk exists for an elderly patient who is experiencing great pain to use multiple patches in an accidental or suicidal manner.

Questions

Q1. What are therapeutic and lethal serum levels of fentanyl?
    a) Therapeutic, 2–5 ng/mL; lethal, >12 ng/mL
    b) Therapeutic, 0.1 ng/mL; lethal, >1 ng/mL
    c) Therapeutic, 10 μg/mL; lethal, >100 μg/mL
Q2. What autopsy findings are indicative of opiate-induced death?
    a) A very characteristic skin rash found only in opiate overdose.
    b) A highly specific finding of pulmonary edema.
    c) No very specific indications; the diagnosis is based primarily on laboratory testing.
    d) None of the above.

Answers and Discussion

Q1. (Answer = a) Fentanyl is especially potent with analgesic potency at least 80 times greater than that of morphine. Surgical anesthesia is induced at levels of 2 to 5 ng/mL, while deaths are associated with serum concentrations greater than 12 ng/mL. Fentanyl patches containing 10 mg release 100 μg/hour for over 72 hours. It can be calculated that 3 patches with 10 mg each should produce a serum concentration of 10 ng/mL. This woman's postmortem serum level was 25 ng/mL, somewhat higher than expected. The larger value may indicate that she had been using the excess number of patches for several days or that, due to her age or disease status, her metabolism of fentanyl was compromised.

Q2. (Answer = c) Death from opiate overdose is a situation in which the physical findings are very few and quite nonspecific. Pulmonary edema is often noted but it is not specific. As with many other drug-related deaths the cause of death in this case must be established by history and laboratory findings.

Case Study 6: The Theft of Fentanyl

The extreme dangers associated with fentanyl in relation to its high potency are illustrated by another case in which an individual appears to have appropriated a fentanyl patch in an illicit manner and paid for it with his life.[2]

A 31-year-old male went fishing with a friend one morning. Several hours into this enterprise he fell to the ground. He then described feelings of nausea, weakness, and dizziness. Shortly thereafter he became comatose and exhibited grunting breathing sounds. EMS personnel were summoned and, on arrival, observed the patient tachycardic with elevated blood pressure at 210/110. His respirations faded to 2/min and he became cyanotic. Eventually he experienced cardiac arrest from which he could not be resuscitated. Autopsy did not show any natural disease nor signs of trauma. Toxicologic studies, however, found fentanyl at 15 ng/mL plus small amounts of several other drugs. Death was attributed to a fentanyl overdose.

Investigation into the origin of the fentanyl in this case revealed that the decedent had a history of drug abuse and was employed, at the time of his death, in a funeral home. Further, it was discovered that he had been involved in the handling of the body of a woman who died from cancer. That woman was known to have two fentanyl patches on her body at the time her remains were transferred to the funeral home from a nursing home. The patches were never located and are believed to have been removed and employed abusively by the funeral parlor employee.

Fentanyl is one of the most widely abused drugs by some members of the healthcare professions, including personnel working in anesthesiology. Analysis for this drug may be difficult and it must be tested for by specific, sensitive methods. Routine methods of opiate analysis are not sufficient for detection and confirmation of fentanyl use.

References

1. Edinboro, L.E. et al., Fatal fentanyl intoxication following excessive transdermal application, *J. Forens. Sci.*, 42, 741–743, 1997.
2. Flannagan, L. et al., Fentanyl patches left on dead bodies. Potential source of drug for abusers, *J. Forens. Sci.*, 41, 320–321, 1996.

FOR FURTHER READING

Aderjan, R.E. and Skopp, G., Formation and clearance of active and inactive metabolites of opiates in humans, *Therapeut. Drug Monitor,* 20(5), 561–569, 1998.

Albertson, T.E. et al., Methamphetamine and the expanding complications of amphetamines, *West. J. Med.,* 170(4), 214–219, 1999.

Ameri, A., The effects of cannabinoids on the brain, *Prog. Neurobiol.,* 58(4), 315–348, 1999.

Andrews, P., Cocaethylene toxicity, *J. Addict. Res.,* 16(3), 75–84, 1997.

Brust, J.C., Acute neurologic complications of drug and alcohol abuse, *Neurolog. Clin.,* 16(2), 503–519, 1998.

Cami, J. et al., Cocaine metabolism in humans after use of alcohol. Clinical and research implications, *Rec. Devel. Alcohol,* 14, 437–455, 1998.

Church, M.W. et al., Effects of prenatal cocaine on hearing, vision, growth, and behavior, *Ann. NY Acad. Sci.,* 846, 12–28, 1998.

D'Apolito, K., Substance abuse: infant and childhood outcomes, *J. Pediatr. Nurs.,* 13(5), 307–316, 1998.

Deutsch, S.I. et al., Neurodevelopmental consequences of early exposure to phencyclidine and related drugs, *Clin. Neuropharmacol.,* 21(6), 320–332, 1998.

Keller, R.W. and Snyder-Keller, A., Prenatal cocaine exposure, *Ann. NY Acad. Sci.,* 909, 217–232, 2000.

Li, J.H. and Lin, L.F., Genetic toxicology of abused drugs: a brief review, *Mutagenesis,* 13(6), 557–565, 1998.

Moore, C. et al., Determination of drugs of abuse in meconium, *J. Chromatog. B Biomed. Sci. Appl.,* 713(1), 137–146, 1998.

Nzerue, C.M. et al., Cocaine and the kidney: a synthesis of pathophysiologic and clinical perspectives, *Am. J. Kidney Dis.,* 35(5), 783–795, 2000.

Stein, M.D., Medical consequences of substance abuse, *Psychiat. Clinics N. Am.,* 22(2), 351–370, 1999.

Volles, D.F. and McGory, R., Pharmacokinetic considerations, *Crit. Care Med.,* 15(1), 55–75, 1999.

Woods, J.R., Maternal and transplacental effects of cocaine, *Ann. NY Acad. Sci.,* 846, 1–11, 1998.

21 Sedatives and Hypnotics

CONTENTS

The terms sedative and hypnotic are equivalent to central nervous system depressants. More specifically, a sedative is a substance that diminishes environmental awareness and physical activity. A hypnotic is an agent that induces sleep. Sedatives and hypnotics are, logically, considered together because no agent is capable of inducing sedation without also conducing to more profound sedation, i.e., sleep. A third category also may be included here: the group of drugs known as tranquilizers, or relievers of anxiety. Again, there is a subtle difference between sedation, anxiety relief, and sleep induction. They are, nevertheless, so closely linked that the grouping of these agents into different categories is, to some degree, artificial.

All of these agents depress the central nervous system and produce progressive, dose-dependent alterations in behavior which are described as being depressant in action. Their actions lie on a continuum which is represented in Figure 20.1. We see

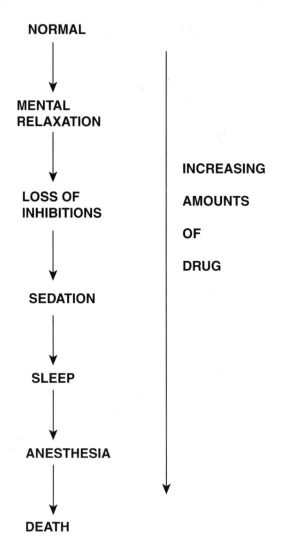

FIGURE 21.1 The stages of behavioral sedation.

from this figure that the first stage of sedation is anxiety relief. This progresses to disinhibition, a more extensive form of mental relaxation, and then to extreme sedation. The end stage of this process happens with overdose of these agents. It is depression of the respiratory and cardiac centers within the brain. With depression of these areas their respective end-organs, the diaphragm and the heart, stop functioning and death quickly intervenes.

The classes of agents that provoke this response include bromides, barbiturates, minor tranquilizers (especially benzodiazepines), miscellaneous drugs, alcohols, and anesthetics. All of these classes are discussed in this chapter except anesthetics and alcohols which are considered elsewhere.

PRINCIPLES OF CNS DEPRESSANTS

Although these classes of drugs are different in many ways there are some features common to all agents that behave as CNS depressants:

1. The effects of CNS depressants are additive. In other words, a barbiturate taken with alcohol causes a reaction comparable to taking only alcohol or only barbiturates but in larger quantities. Because the mechanisms of action of these compounds are similar, it should be no surprise that the end result of dosing with multiple agents is an intensified action.
2. Effects of CNS depressants are additive with the mental state of the user. Persons who wish to enter a drug state are more likely, by virtue of their specific intentions, to do so. Although the physiological basis of this phenomenon is unclear, it is known to be real on the basis of many observations of persons using these drugs.
3. Depressant effects of these drugs are often supra-additive, i.e., the observed effect is greater than predicted. In some cases, this is due to one drug inhibiting the metabolism of a second so that both drugs achieve higher blood and brain concentrations than would be predicted from simple pharmacokinetic models. In other cases, the second drug delays the elimination of the first drug. Other mechanisms are also known.
4. CNS depressants are antagonized by stimulants. Although this would appear to be intuitively obvious, in actuality the nature of this antagonism is unpredictable. Someone intoxicated with a depressant will be temporarily aroused by a stimulant. However, when the stimulant is metabolized, the patient's depression may deepen beyond previous stages. Remarkably, one of the breakthroughs in treatment of barbiturate overdose was discontinuing the previous therapy of giving the barbiturate overdose victim a stimulant. After years of unintentionally doing harm in this way, it was finally recognized that this particular therapy was doing more harm than good.
5. General depressants depress all neurons within the brain. How is this statement compatible with the common observation that low doses of depressants produce a state of excitation or euphoria? This is because an early effect of these drugs is depression of inhibitory neurons, or disinhibition.
6. In acute, i.e., one-time, use depressants cause depression that is then followed by a return to normal behavior. In chronic, and especially high-dose, use discontinuation is not followed by a return to normal behavior. The patient becomes hyperexcitable, a state known as drug withdrawal. The term physical dependence is sometimes used to describe a drug's capability of producing withdrawal symptoms when it is discontinued after prolonged and heavy usage. The withdrawal may be severe enough to cause coma or death.
7. CNS depressants produce tolerance. This is a state in which the user needs progressively larger amounts of drug to achieve the same response. Such

tolerance is often due to changes in which metabolizing enzymes are induced that clear the drug more rapidly. A second mechanism of tolerance is a neuronal change in which the brain's response to the drug is dampened. In the first type of tolerance the user requires larger doses to achieve a certain mental and physical state but the blood levels remain the same. This is true because the dose and elimination rate both increase. In the second kind, the dose and blood levels are higher but the effects of the drug are no greater than previously noted at lower blood levels.

8. Cross tolerance occurs. This means that a drug will produce tolerance, not only to itself, but to other members of the CNS depressant category.

HISTORY OF CNS DEPRESSANTS

The earliest sedatives were plant products. Many plants have sedative actions and their use for this purpose was undoubtedly somewhat haphazard and often dangerous. Slightly more scientific were bromides which were introduced into medicine in 1857. At one time they were employed in huge quantities and used as anticonvulsants as well as sedatives but were not prescribed as hypnotics. Bromides were taken only because nothing better was available. They are very toxic; their sedation is associated with extreme drowsiness and they commonly cause severe GI distress. Sedation also takes weeks of medication before this desired effect begins. One reason for the severe side effects of bromide therapy is the very large doses required. Three to five grams are therapeutic and extreme intoxication is found at only slightly higher amounts.

Barbiturates were synthesized in the nineteenth century. In 1864 Adolph von Baeyer prepared barbituric acid from malonic acid and urea. Barbiturates were found to have medical properties in the early twentieth century when barbital was marketed as a hypnotic in 1903. Phenobarbital was introduced into medicine in 1912. Barbiturates and bromides were almost the only sedative agents available until the 1950s when several miscellaneous agents including meprobamate, glutethimide, and ethchlorvynol were introduced. These drugs are very similar to barbiturates in effect, toxicity, etc.

Benzodiazepines were synthesized in the laboratory in 1933. They were studied for medical effects and it was observed, serendipitously, that their major action was mental not physical. They tamed the laboratory monkeys. The taming observation led to trials of these compounds as anti-anxiety agents and they have been used mainly in this role since 1960.

BARBITURATES

CHEMISTRY

Acids, such as malonic acid, with two carboxyl groups, may react with urea and form cyclic diureides, such as barbituric acid (Figure 21.2).

If the hydrogens at positions 5 are replaced with alkyl or aryl groups the resulting compound will have hypnotic activity. The carbonyl at position 2 has acidic character

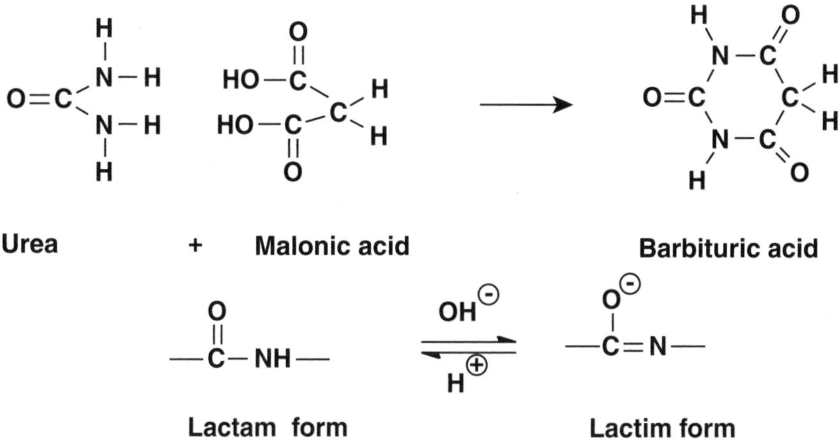

FIGURE 21.2 Formation of barbituric acid and lactam-lactim equilibrium.

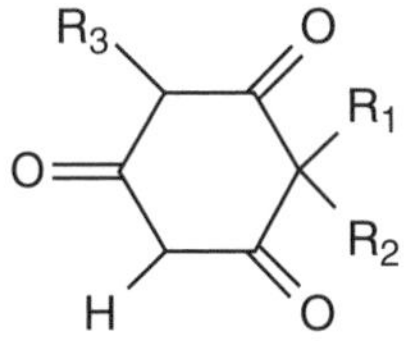

Barbiturate Drug	R1	R2	R3
Amobarbital	Ethyl	Isopentyl	H
Butabarbital	Allyl	Isopropyl	H
Pentobarbital	Ethyl	1-Methylbutyl	H
Phenobarbital	Ethyl	Phenyl	H
Secobarbital	Allyl	1-Methylbutyl	H

FIGURE 21.3 Common barbiturates.

because of keto (lactam) enol (lactim) tautomerization in relation to its location between the two electronegative amido nitrogens. The enol (lactim) form is favored in alkaline solution.

Sodium, and other salts of barbiturates, are readily prepared. Barbiturates, in the acid form, dissolve in nonpolar solvents to a greater degree than in water. This is a property found in many CNS depressants. (See Figure 21.3.)

Structural changes among barbiturates which increase lipid solubility also decrease duration of action, decrease time to onset of activity, accelerate metabolic degradation, and increase hypnotic potency. Introduction of polar groups (e.g., hydroxyl, carboxyl, amino) into alkyl side chains eliminates hypnotic activity. Methylation of the barbiturate nitrogen atoms increases the affinity of the barbiturate for lipid molecules which, as explained above, tends to decrease their duration of action. Methylation of the nitrogen atoms is also a step included in barbiturate analysis (see below). Interestingly, a phenyl group at C5 or one of the nitrogens greatly increases the anticonvulsant properties of the molecule. Phenobarbital is much more potent as an anticonvulsant than as a sedative due to this structural feature. Thiobarbiturates (C doubly bonded to S replaces C doubly bonded to O) are more lipid soluble than oxybarbiturates because the electronegativity of sulfur is near that of carbon; thus, the CS bond is almost nonpolar. This leads to a very rapid onset of action for thiobarbiturates, a short duration of action, and greater potency than oxybarbiturates.

MECHANISM OF ACTION

There are several features of barbiturate mechanism of action that are shared with other CNS depressants. The major common feature of barbiturates and benzodiazepines is that they increase chloride channel patency within neurons. The larger the number of open chloride channels the less excitable the membrane of the neuron. In turn, the inhibited neuron, with its membrane downregulated, is less reactive to a stimulus. Barbiturates bind to the membrane and allow more chloride to enter the neuron. Benzodiazepines are somewhat different in action. Benzodiazepines also increase chloride entry by opening channels. However, with the benzodiazepines an additional entity must be active. GABA, gamma aminobutyric acid, and the benzodiazepine must bind simultaneously for the chloride entry effect.

PHARMACOKINETICS

One of the interesting features of the barbiturates is their highly variable half-lives. Thiopental has a redistribution half-life of only 3 minutes. For secobarbital and several others the half-life is 24 hours. For phenobarbital it is 4 to 7 days. Thiopental is given intravenously as a general anesthetic for surgical use because it depresses breathing for several minutes. Thiopental is highly lipid soluble and penetrates into the CNS rapidly. It induces sleep within seconds. Longer-acting barbiturates are more water soluble and reach the CNS more slowly. The action duration of barbiturates is dependent on three processes: redistribution, metabolism, and excretion. Thiopental is redistributed from the brain to muscle and fat within 3 minutes. This leads to the end of its activity. Thereafter, thiopental is slowly metabolized in the blood. Some of it re-enters the brain during this time which causes a sedated but not unconscious state. All barbiturates, especially the more water-soluble ones, have their actions terminated to a large extent by metabolism and renal elimination.

TOXICITY

Barbiturates have a long and illustrious history as poisonous substances. In Europe from 1950 to 1970 they were a more common vehicle for suicide than all other methods combined. Many famous celebrities, including Marilyn Monroe, died from barbiturate overdose. The role of barbiturates in suicides has declined more or less in proportion to their decreasing use as popular sedatives. They still occasionally appear as the means to a suicidal end. For example, a religious cult, Heaven's Gate, committed mass suicide in California in 1997. Several dozen members of this group died from an overdose of phenobarbital and alcohol.

The adverse effects of barbiturates are almost identical to those caused by alcohol. They include drowsiness and impaired intellectual and motor performance and judgment. Blood pressure and heart rate decline. Hypothermia is a potentially serious problem following toxic ingestions of barbiturates. It results from depression of the thermoregulatory center in the brain and increases the risk of shock and hypoxia. In severe overdose, respiratory and cardiac function are paralyzed and death results.

THERAPY

Treatment of barbiturate overdose is largely supportive. Decontamination with activated charcoal in multiple doses is advisable if the patient is likely to be in the absorptive phase. Hemoperfusion has been effective in removing barbiturates if the form of the drug is long acting. Patients may require prolonged ventilatory assistance, which can be life-saving because respiratory depression is the most serious consequence of overdose. Hypotension also is commonly found and is very serious. Administration of intravenous fluids is the initial therapy for this problem. Pressor agents may be necessary in supporting blood pressure if intravenous fluids alone are not adequate. After recovery, withdrawal is possible and medication to treat seizures is often necessary.

LABORATORY TESTING

If a patient is suspected of barbiturate overdose, the concentration of barbiturates in the blood can be measured. There is an approximate correlation between the concentration and effect (Table 21.1).

It is important to state that this table applies to short-acting barbiturates. The toxic and lethal concentrations of barbiturates depend on the subclassification of the drug (Table 21.2).

Several methods are used to measure barbiturates. Thin-layer chromatography or immunoassay is used to test urine and determine whether the patient has been exposed to barbiturates. TLC is somewhat slow for emergency medical applications.

TABLE 21.1
Correlation of Barbiturate Blood Concentration and Effect

Concentration (mcg/mL)	Effect
<6	Normal and alert
6–10	Drowsy
11–17	Stuporous
20–24	Stage 2 coma
>24	Stage 4 coma

TABLE 21.2
Barbiturate Class vs. Toxicity

	Therapeutic Concentration (mcg/dL)	Toxic Concentration (mcg/dL)	Lethal Concentration (mcg/dL)
Short-acting	10–100	700–1000	>1000
Intermediate-acting	10–500	1000–3000	>3000
Long-acting	1000–4000	4000–8000	>8000

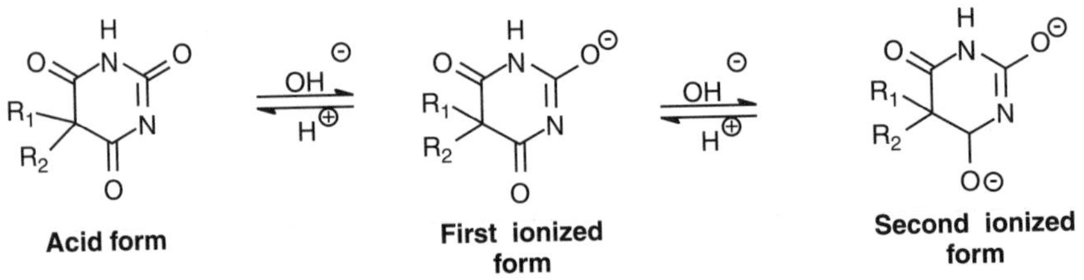

FIGURE 21.4 Changes in barbiturate structure with titration.

Immunoassay is rapid but is, like TLC, not quantitative in urine. Because these methods are only qualitative, a patient may be positive for barbiturates by these tests without the barbiturate being the actual cause of the patient's coma. Although either of these methods may be performed on serum, they are more commonly used with urine.

A classical method for barbiturate detection is based on the ultraviolet absorbance features of these drugs. Figure 21.4 shows the structural changes barbiturates undergo with pH adjustment. There are three possible structures for 5,5 disubstituted barbiturates and two possible structures for 1,5,5 trisubstituted barbiturates. The latter have one less enolizable hydrogen and so have just a single ionized form.

Barbiturates have characteristic UV spectra and their spectra change in a predictable manner when the drug is titrated. Because of this it is possible to extract the barbiturate from blood or urine and determine absorbance behavior at several different pH levels. A barbiturate is present if the following conditions are met:

In pH 9.9 solution, an absorbance maximum occurs at 238–240 nm.
At pH 14, a maximum occurs at 252–255 nm and a minimum occurs at 234–247 nm.
Isosbestic points (lines cross) occur at 227 and 247 nm.

This method is very specific for barbiturates although less than 100% specific. It may be conducted in a quantitative manner. A disadvantage of the method is that it does not specify which barbiturate is present. This is not a minor concern. A quick check of the table above shows that significant variation exists in the lethality of barbiturates. For example, note that a lethal amount of a short-acting barbiturate is equal to the therapeutic concentration of a long-acting barbiturate.

One of the best methods for barbiturate detection and quantification is gas chromatography. GC with a flame ionization detector or a mass spectrometer is able to accurately measure a wide variety of barbiturates. One of the more popular ways to conduct the chromatography is to convert the barbiturates to their methyl derivatives. This may be accomplished easily by preparing the sample and dissolving it in a methylating agent such as tetramethylammonium hydroxide just prior to injection. When the specimen is injected into the gas chromatograph the barbiturates are instantly methylated within the hot environment of the injection port liner. The methylated derivatives of the barbiturates are less polar and yield, therefore, better shaped chromatographic peaks.

MISCELLANEOUS SEDATIVES

Because sedative drugs are medically valuable but known sedatives all have significant toxic potential, the pharmaceutical industry has tried for many years to develop less toxic sedatives. Drugs which have arisen from this effort include chloral hydrate, ethchlorvynol, methaqualone, meprobamate, and glutethimide. Each has a small to medium position in medical practice. It is well to recall that they are all similar to some degree and that the basic principles listed for CNS depressants at the beginning of this chapter apply to them as well.

Chloral Hydrate

This is a very old drug first made by Justus von Liebig in 1832. It is the 2,2,2 trichloro derivative of acetaldehyde. In the body, chloral hydrate is reduced to 2,2,2 trichloroethanol. Indeed, trichloroethanol is also a hypnotic but is irritating in this form. It is, therefore, marketed as triclofos sodium, the monosodium salt of the phosphate ester of trichloroethanol. The combination of chloral hydrate and ethyl alcohol is called knockout drops, or Mickey Finns. Studies show that this combination is, indeed, more potent than either drug alone but not nearly as dangerous as suggested by a menacing name like knockout drops.

The lethal dose of chloral hydrate is quite high, approximately 10 g. One gram is a common dose to relieve insomnia. The symptoms and treatment of chloral hydrate overdose are the same as those for barbiturate intoxication.

Ethchlorvynol

This drug, known by the trade name of Placidyl, is a sedative-hypnotic with rapid onset and short duration of action. It also has anticonvulsant and muscle relaxant properties. Its use is somewhat limited by side effects including dizziness, nausea, vomiting, hypotension, and facial numbness. Severe overdose is characterized by prolonged and deep coma, respiratory depression, hypotension, bradycardia, and hypothermia. Like chloral hydrate, the lethal dose is very high at approximately 15 g. Lethal blood concentrations are also very high, in the range of 140 mg/L.

Methaqualone

Methaqualone (Quaalude or Sopor) is a 2,3 disubstituted quinazolinone. It has a very wide spectrum of pharmacological activity encompassing sedation, anticonvulsant, antispasmodic, local anesthetic, and antihistaminic properties. This drug acquired an undeserved reputation as an aphrodisiac, a property which is guaranteed to promote the sales of any substance. In reality, as a CNS depressant, it is more likely to have the opposite effect. Like other depressants, however, it causes euphoria, and this drug developed a large following. In the 1970s it was heavily abused, trailing only marijuana and alcohol in frequency of abusive use. Due to many fatalities it was removed from the legitimate market in 1984.

Meprobamate

Said to be the first molecule to which the name tranquilizer was given, meprobamate (Equanil, Miltown) spawned a new generation of attitudes toward pharmacology. The public came to believe that ordinary, decent folk could find relief from anxiety by using ethical pharmaceutical agents. Drug use was, for the first time, regarded as a legitimate and effective means for relieving the ordinary anxieties of everyday life.

This belief was somewhat illusory with meprobamate for this drug is really not significantly different from barbiturates. It is primarily a sedative that provides some euphoria and relief from anxiety but definitely not as its major activity. Meprobamate has no striking advantages over barbiturates. Its half-life is longer than the intermediate acting barbiturates. It also is fetotoxic and must be avoided especially during the first trimester of pregnancy.

Meprobamate is less of a respiratory depressant than barbiturates and so suicides with this drug are much less common.

Glutethimide

Glutethimide (Doriden) is a piperidinedione whose structure, shown in Figure 21.5, is strikingly similar to the barbiturates. It was introduced in 1954 and very quickly rose to the sixth most heavily prescribed hypnotic. Physicians were under the mistaken impression that it was significantly different from the barbiturates because it was not represented as being from the same class. However, in time it was recognized as having the same addictive potential as well as relatively low therapeutic indices, which made it a hazardous drug in general medical practice.

Symptoms of acute glutethimide poisoning are similar to those of acute barbiturate poisoning. Respiratory depression is less severe, but this beneficial finding is offset by the fact that circulatory failure can be more severe. The hypnotic dose is 0.5 g and 5.0 g will cause severe intoxication. Death may occur from 10 g. The therapeutic index is unfavorable for widespread and careless use.

Benzodiazepines

Barbiturate deaths were very commonplace in the 1950s and 1960s. As a result, an intense search was ongoing within the pharmaceutical industry to find a safer alternative. Chlordiazepoxide (Librium) was the first of the benzodiazepines (1965) to be marketed as a sedative and an anxiolytic. Diazepam (Valium) followed soon after chlordiazepoxide and became even more popular. For many years diazepam was the

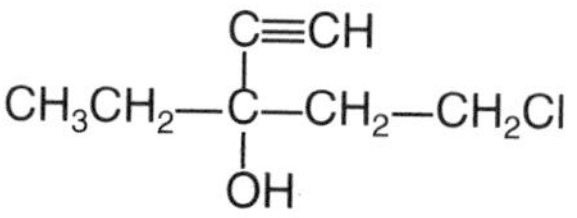

Ethchlorvynol (Placidyl)

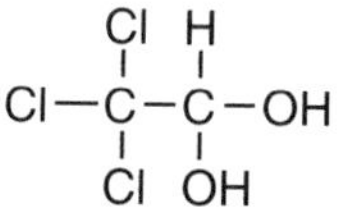

Chloral hydrate

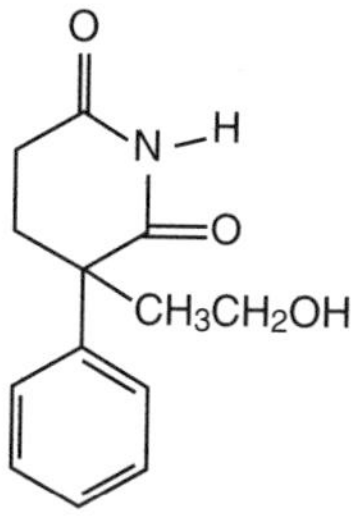

Glutethimide

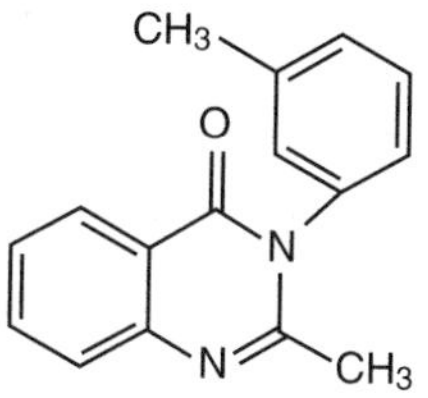

Methaqualone

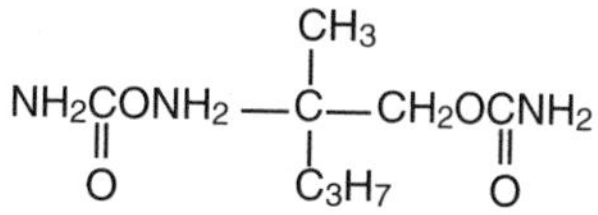

Meprobamate

FIGURE 21.5 Structures of some non-barbiturate sedatives.

most widely prescribed drug in the United States. One hundred million prescriptions were written each year for benzodiazepines during the 1970s. As the danger of abuse became more clear, physicians cut back and by the mid-1980s only 70 million prescriptions were written each year. By 1999, 28 different benzodiazepines were available worldwide; 13 of which were available by prescription in the United States. Most of these are taken to relieve anxiety. Temazepam (Restoril) and triazolam (Halcion) are exceptions that are primarily taken as sleeping pills. Clonazepam (Clonapin) is the only benzodiazepine marketed mainly for the treatment of seizures. Other indications for which benzodiazepines are somewhat effective are panic disorder and as muscle relaxants.

CHEMISTRY

The first generation of benzodiazepines were diazolobenzodiazepines. They have the basic three-ring structure shown here for diazepam (Figure 21.6). Further

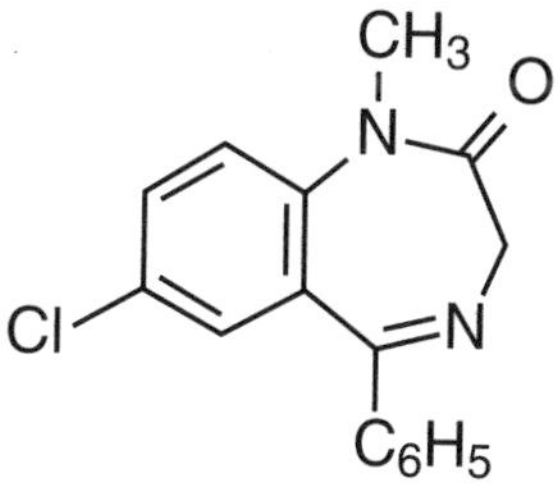

Diazepam (Valium)

FIGURE 21.6 Diazepam (Valium), a representative first-generation benzodiazepine.

Alprazolam   **Midazolam**   **Triazolam**

FIGURE 21.7 Alprazolam (Xanax) and other more recent benzodiazepines.

research led to the introduction of a second generation of benzodiazepines, triaz-olobenzodiazepines, with a four-ring system. A major example of this category is alprazolam (Figure 21.7).

PHARMACOKINETICS

These drugs are extensively absorbed when taken orally and achieve peak blood concentrations in about 1 hour. Benzodiazepines become highly protein bound after absorption. Many of them are metabolized and excreted into bile from which they may undergo reabsorption back into the blood. Most of them also are highly fat soluble. These three factors — protein binding, biliary recirculation, and fat storage — are major reasons why benzodiazepines often have very long half-lives.

METABOLISM

It is an understatement to say that benzodiazepine metabolism is complex (Figure 21.8). These drugs are extensively metabolized to myriad products. Some metabolic intermediates, such as oxazepam, which arises from metabolism of diaz-epam and other benzodiazepines, is itself an active pharmacological agent. Some benzodiazepines, such as chlordiazepoxide, excrete almost none of the parent com-pound in urine. It is, therefore, almost impossible to identify the specific benzodi-azepine that a patient may have ingested on the basis of urine analysis only.

Benzodiazepines, like the barbiturates, have been subclassified on the basis of duration of action (Table 21.3).

The importance of metabolic pathways is that they determine the duration of action and also the nature and severity of withdrawal which starts when the drug is discontinued. Some benzodiazepines are conjugated rapidly, an event which sets them up for fast elimination because the glucuronide is very polar and easily excreted from the kidney. Others are oxidized before glucuronidation. The oxidized forms resist conjugation and remain active in the body for long periods. Benzodiazepine withdrawal is very severe for some patients. If the withdrawal is based on a short-acting benzodiazepine, then symptoms begin fairly rapidly after drug discontinua-tion. For the longer-acting benzodiazepines the patient may have as much as a week

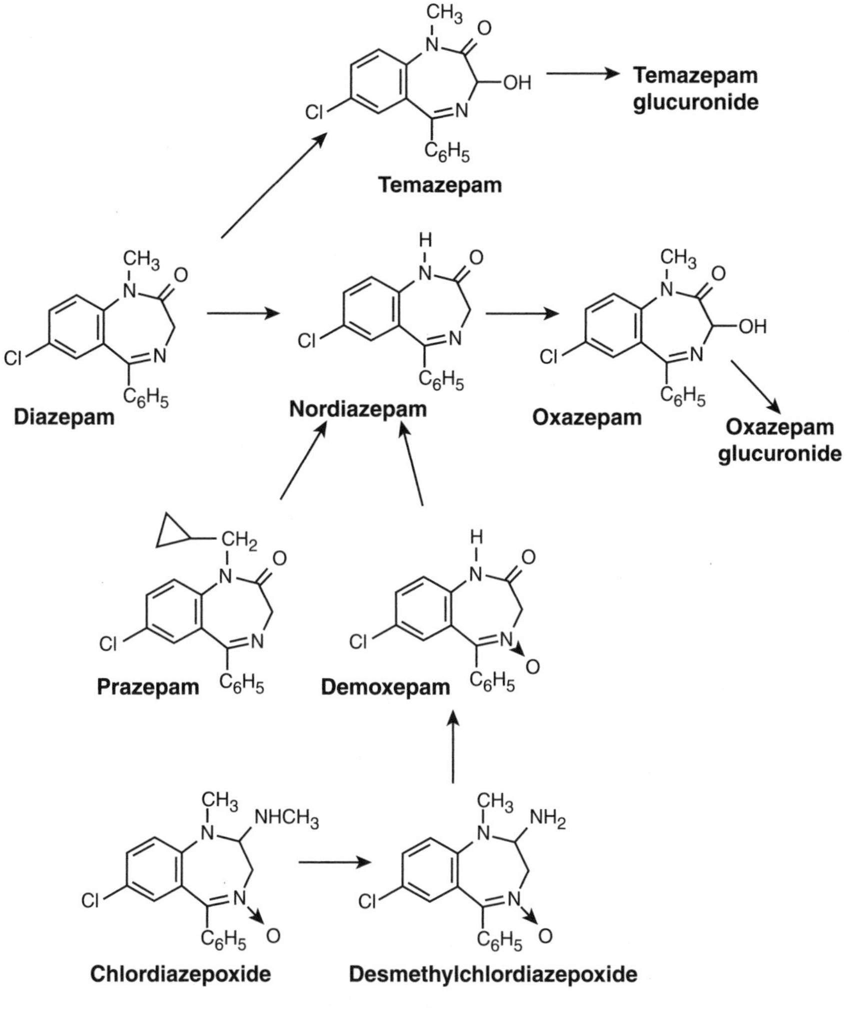

FIGURE 21.8 Partial scheme of benzodiazepine metabolism.

TABLE 21.3
Categories of Benzodiazepines

Class	Half-life	Examples
Short acting	1–8 hours	Triazolam, Midazolam
Intermediate	Approx. 1 day	Lorazepam, Oxazepam
Long acting	Up to several weeks	Chlordiazepoxide, Diazepam, Flurazepam

of symptom-free activity after stopping medication before withdrawal symptoms will begin. It is, therefore, important to know which benzodiazepine a patient used in order to treat his/her overdose and withdrawal.

TOXICITY

Benzodiazepines have many adverse effects including light-headedness, drowsiness, lethargy, and ataxia. At higher doses impairment of mental and physical function is noted. The signs of organic brain dysfunction observed with other CNS depressants are also found with benzodiazepines. Benzodiazepines also have significant drug interactions with other depressants, alcohol being the most common.

There is substantial disagreement in regard to the ability of benzodiazepines to cause fatalities. Whatever the exact extent of their lethality, they are clearly much safer than barbiturates. Posindex, generally a very authoritative source, states that there are no reported deaths for benzodiazepines when taken alone. This is definitely an exaggerated claim. During the 1960s there were 5.9 deaths per million prescriptions for benzodiazepines in Europe contrasted with 69 to 176 per million for barbiturates. Flurazepam was the most commonly reported benzodiazepine associated with fatalities. For flurazepam there were 90 deaths per million prescriptions. At the other extreme, medazepam was never reported to cause a fatality despite having been prescribed over one million times. Some of the cases of benzodiazepine fatalities were undoubtedly multiple overdoses (at least one additional agent), but a study in Great Britain reported 891 deaths in England during the 1980s and, in all cases, benzodiazepines were the sole agents found in the decedent.

Once thought to have limited abuse potential it is now recognized that many benzodiazepines are heavily abused by individuals with an inclination toward depressants as the preferred vehicle for abuse. Moreover, abuse of benzodiazepines is a serious health problem partly because of the long half-lives some of them possess and the associated prolonged therapy that withdrawal entails.

THERAPY

Therapy for benzodiazepine overdose is similar to that provided for intoxication with other CNS depressants. Efforts initially should be addressed toward reducing absorption by conducting gastric lavage or charcoal administration. Thereafter, therapy is largely supportive. One important difference exists, however, between benzodiazepines and other CNS depressants. For benzodiazepines an antidote is available, flumazenil (Figure 21.9). This antidote is structurally similar to benzodiazepines and

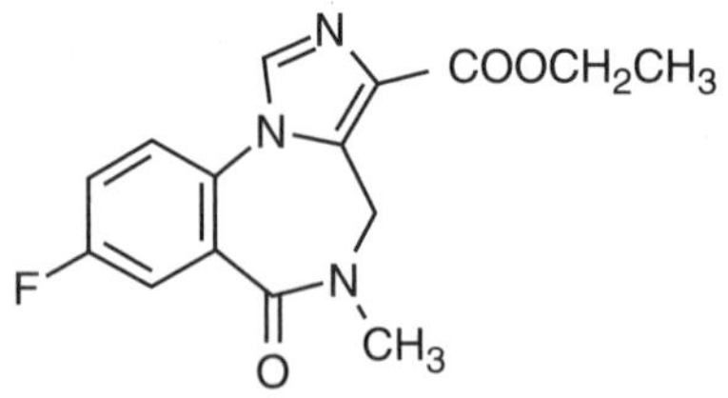

Flumazenil

FIGURE 21.9 Structure of flumazenil, a benzodiazepine antagonist.

binds at the same site within the neuron. When it binds to the neuron, it displaces benzodiazepines without triggering the change in chloride channels caused by active benzodiazepines. Flumazenil reverses benzodiazepine-induced coma in a manner similar to the effect of naloxone on opiate overdose. The antidote is, however, not without problems including:

Possible withdrawal seizures in the chronic benzodiazepine abuser
Breakthrough seizures in patients with underlying seizure disorder
Seizures in tricyclic antidepressant overdose because tricyclics lower seizure
    threshold
Cardiac arrhythmias in patients with multiple drug overdose

LABORATORY TESTING

Benzodiazepines are often tested for by screening methods performed on urine. Thin-layer chromatography or immunoassays are the most common methods for screening. Because this is a large class of drugs, some members of the class are detected more effectively than others. There are multiple reasons for this. In the first place, these drugs vary widely in their potency (see Table 21.4; e.g., alprazolam is 100 times as potent as chlordiazepoxide). As a result, very small doses usually are administered for some of these drugs (Table 21.4). At such small doses, these drugs produce low concentrations of urinary metabolite and thus, are hard to detect. To detect as many members of the benzodiazepine family as possible, reagent manufacturers target their antibody for a metabolite that is common to many benzodiazepines, usually oxazepam. If a specific benzodiazepine does not produce oxazepam as a metabolite, then that drug will probably not be detected at low levels. An exception is a situation in which the drug's metabolites, despite not including oxazepam, are sufficiently like oxazepam that substantial cross-reactivity occurs. A third reason which makes benzodiazepine assay difficult is that greater than 99% of the urinary metabolites are conjugated with glucuronic acid. These conjugates do not react as well with the assay antibody as unconjugated metabolites. It has been estimated that, due to the three foregoing reasons, only 50% of urines that actually contain benzodiazepines are positive in screening immunoassays. One testing product, Triage (Biosite Corp.), is more sensitive in benzodiazepine screening because it contains two antibodies, and they are both directed at the glucuronide conjugates of benzodiazepine metabolites.

Immunoassays are quite different in their ability to detect different benzodiazepines. For example, the detection limit for lorazepam is 400 ng/mL by Triage but 20,000 ng/mL by cloned enzyme donor immunoassay (CEDIA). Conversely, the detection limit for nordiazepam by Triage is 1000 ng/mL vs. 75 ng/mL by CEDIA.

Confirmation of benzodiazepines can be conducted by high-performance liquid chromatography or by GC-MS. In the latter method a sample-preparation step must be included in which the glucuronic acid is cleaved from the metabolite. Enzyme or acid hydrolysis can achieve this. The benzodiazepines must also be derivatized and trimethylsilylation is a common method for derivatizing benzodiazepines.

TABLE 21.4
Comparison of Benzodiazepine Potency

Drug	Therapeutic Dose (mg)
Chlordiazepoxide	25
Clonazepam	2
Diazepam	5
Flurazepam	15
Lorazepam	1
Alprazolam	0.25

Questions and Problems

1. Describe the eight principles of CNS depressants.
2. Draw structures for dimethylsecobarbital and the trimethylsilyl derivative of oxazepam.
3. Discuss structure vs. reactivity for barbiturates.
4. List 3 problems with the ultraviolet spectrophotometric method for barbiturate analysis.
5. Many laboratories test for methaqualone in their routine panel for drugs in urine. Is this a reasonable policy?
6. Explain why some benzodiazepines have long half-lives and others have short half-lives. What is the significance of half-life in relation to withdrawal?
7. Contrast benzodiazepines and barbiturates with respect to lethal doses.
8. List at least three reasons why false negatives might occur in screening tests for benzodiazepines.
9. An absorption spectrum in the ultraviolet region for a serum specimen was similar to the known spectrum for phenobarbital. The concentration of phenobarbital may be determined on the basis of change in absorbance at pH 10 vs. pH 13 at 260 nm. Find the concentration of phenobarbital in an unknown from the following data:

	A_{260} nm	
	pH 10	pH 13
20 mg/L std	0.31	0.45
80 mg/L	0.18	0.64
Unknown	0.26	0.47

Case Study 1: The Automobile Accident

A 30-year-old male became involved in an argument with his girlfriend. In a mood of depression he swallowed 41 tablets of a prescription medication and drove off in his truck. Thirty minutes later he was treated by paramedics at the scene of an automobile accident where his pick-up truck struck three other vehicles. Examination of the accident scene suggested that the crash had not been severe. The truck that he was driving was only slightly damaged and its steering wheel was not bent nor was the windshield cracked. Nevertheless, the truck driver was comatose and required intubation.

Neither 4 mg of naloxone nor 25 g of dextrose were effective in relieving the coma. His blood pressure was 120/70. Pulse was elevated at 114 and respirations were 30 and shallow. Physical examination found that he had an abrasion to his right forehead. Pupils were constricted and minimally reactive to light. His neck was supple and no deformities were noted. Breath sounds, cardiac exam, and abdominal exam were all within normal limits. Neurologically, however, the patient had no gag reflex nor response to painful stimuli. His Glascow Coma Scale was 3.

Gastric lavage was conducted but no tablet fragments were recovered. Activated charcoal and magnesium sulfate were given. A CT scan of the head was normal. Laboratory data were as follows:

Hemoglobin	16.7 g/dL
Hematocrit	49.1%
Sodium	139 meq/L
Potassium	3.3 meq/L
Chloride	105 meq/L
Bicarbonate	19 meq/L
Glucose	73 mg/dL
Blood alcohol	251 mg/dL

Based on the history and findings what is the likely identity of the pills that he swallowed?
   a) Morphine
   b) Alprazolam
   c) Phenobarbital
   d) Aspirin

The key feature of this patient's presentation is the profound coma in the absence of other physical or laboratory findings. Any of these drugs could cause a coma but, if it had been provoked by morphine, the patient should have responded to the naloxone. Phenobarbital is suspect but the comatose state began very early after the drug ingestion. Phenobarbital does not usually cause coma so rapidly. Alcohol was an exacerbating factor, but the timing is still not right for designating phenobarbital as the causative agent. Alprazolam, a benzodiazepine, would act more rapidly than phenobarbital and could be responsible for this coma. Indeed, the driver's girlfriend subsequently stated that he had ingested 41 half milligram tablets of alprazolam.

The patient received 1 mg of flumazenil, an antidote for benzodiazepine overdose. Five minutes later he sat up in bed and could be extubated. His coma score was now rated at 15. One hour later, however, he relapsed into a coma and was reintubated. With further flumazenil administration he recovered fully and was discharged 1 day later. His drug screen was positive for benzodiazepines and tetrahydrocannabinol.

Questions

Q1. Which is true of the Glascow Coma Scale?
 a) The deepest coma is indicated by a score of 1.
 b) A shallow coma is indicated by a score of 15.
 c) The score is unaffected by neuromuscular paralysis.
 d) The score is related only to coma caused by head trauma.
Q2. Which is true of flumazenil?
 a) It reverses the effects of alcohol on the CNS.
 b) It increases the metabolism of benzodiazepines.
 c) It enhances the elimination of benzodiazepines.
 d) It competitively inhibits the activity of benzodiazepines at their recognition site on the cerebral GABA receptor complex.
Q3. Which of the following should not be a form of treatment for this patient?
 a) Ventilatory assistance
 b) Administration of activated charcoal plus a cathartic
 c) Emesis followed by hemoperfusion
 d) Flumazenil
Q4. Which of the following is true of alprazolam testing?
 a) The major metabolite in urine is 4-hydroxyalprazolam.
 b) Drivers stopped for DUI and found positive for alprazolam had blood levels over 100 µg/L.
 c) Screening tests for alprazolam have a small incidence of false negatives.
 d) There is a close correlation between blood concentration and impairment.

Answers and Discussion

Q1. (Answer = b) For medical management and estimation of prognosis it is desirable to have a method for evaluating the severity of a coma. The Glascow Coma Scale (GCS) is commonly regarded as the best means for doing this. Three critical items are considered: eye opening, motor response, and verbal response. For each of these a score of 1 is given for no response. Higher numbers are assigned to a greater reaction. For example, no eye opening is 1 point and spontaneous eye opening is 4 points. Scores for the three categories are summed. Therefore, the deepest coma has a score of 3 (one for each category). The best score is 15 and this is correlated with a very light coma. The GCS was developed to assess brain injury from trauma but it has been found to be of some value in assessing prognosis in coma of other causes as well. Medical treatment of a comatose individual, such as sedation or neuromuscular paralysis, renders the GCS of lesser value in monitoring the recovery of a comatose patient.

Q2. (Answer = d) Flumazenil appears to affect the actions of a small number of drugs in addition to benzodiazepines, their primary target. Alcohol is, however, not among those affected. Flumazenil has no effect whatever on the metabolism or elimination of benzodiazepines. It competes with the active drug, such as alprazolam, at the receptor site but does not have the drug's pharmacological action on the receptor.

Q3. (Answer = c) Emesis is contraindicated in this patient who is in a deep coma and at risk of aspiration by vomiting. Hemoperfusion has no proven value for alprazolam overdose. Flumazenil is a specific antidote that logically should be provided for benzodiazepine-induced coma. Some physicians rarely or never will employ flumazenil because of the generally mild course of benzodiazepine intoxication. In the present case, however, it brought a rapid end to the patient's coma and resolved the question of the patient's actual diagnosis. His response to flumazenil supported the original suspicion that his crash injuries were minor. Without flumazenil a very extensive work-up would have been necessary because of the possibility that his injuries were the actual cause of the deep coma.

Q4. (Answer = b) Those driving under the influence of alprazolam usually have concentrations exceeding 100 µg/L although the range found in one study was 8 to 642 µg/L. The major urinary metabolite is alpha-hydroxyalprazolam (17%) while 4-hydroxyalprazolam is only 0.3%. False negatives for alprazolam are common because it is a triazolobenzodiazepine and not that similar structurally to oxazepam, the compound usually used to make antibodies for screening assays. In addition, patients usually take this potent compound in small doses (1 to 4 mg/day). The correlation between blood concentrations and physical effects is not strong for benzodiazepines.

References

Burkhart, K.K. and Kulig, K.W., The diagnostic utility of flumazenil (a benzodiazepine antagonist) in coma of unknown etiology, *Ann. Emerg. Med.*, 19, 319–321, 1990.

Drugs and Driving Committee, American Academy of Forensic Sciences Toxicology Section, Washington, D.C., 1993.

Weinberg, A.D. et al., Oxazepam overdose associated with ethanol ingestion: treatment with a benzodiazepine antagonist, *Am. J. Crit. Care*, 3, 464–466, 1994.

Case Study 2: A Girl with Epilepsy

A 17-year-old white girl was brought to an emergency department. Twelve hours earlier she had ingested 2.3 g of a medication that she had taken daily for many years for her seizure disorder. She was supposed to take 150 mg/day but, in a fit of despondency, she took an amount that equaled 46 mg/kg or about 15 times the prescribed daily dosage. Her heart rate was elevated at 100 beats per minute, blood pressure was 126/70, and respirations were shallow and irregular. She was in a coma and responsive to deep pain only. Laboratory results were as follows:

Sodium	143 meq/L
Potassium	4.6 meq/L
Chloride	113 meq/L
Total CO_2	25 meq/L
Arterial pH	7.29
pO_2	91 mm
pCO_2	52 mm

What drug may be responsible for her symptoms?
   a) Phenobarbital
   b) Secobarbital
   c) Diazepam
   d) Alprazolam

Any of these four choices could cause the profound sedation this patient experienced. Only phenobarbital, however, among the choices here, is prescribed routinely for epilepsy. The girl's parents stated that she took 2.3 g of phenobarbital, and blood testing revealed a serum level of 120 mg/L, 12 hours after she had ingested the capsules.

Treatment consisted of intubation and mechanical ventilation. She was lavaged; 90 g of activated charcoal plus 30 g of magnesium sulfate were then instilled. The charcoal-magnesium sulfate therapy was repeated every 4 hours for 48 hours, 12 treatments in all. This repetitive charcoal treatment sometimes is called gastrointestinal dialysis. The patient also was alkalinized by infusion of 180 meq/L of sodium bicarbonate to hold her arterial pH at 7.5. Following are the patient's serum barbiturate levels during the GI dialysis procedure:

16 hours post-ingestion	116 mg/L
21 hours	86
26 hours	70
33 hours	36

The patient recovered consciousness fairly quickly. She was extubated, alert, and oriented 24 hours after the ingestion and was discharged on the 4th day of hospitalization. There were no remaining ill effects.

Questions

Q1. What is the calculated half-life of phenobarbital in this patient as she underwent the GI dialysis?
   a) 2 hours
   b) 10 hours
   c) 20 hours
   d) 50 hours

Q2. What are the kinetics of elimination under gastrointestinal dialysis?
   a) Zero order
   b) First order
   c) Second order
   d) Not enough data to determine
Q3. What acid-base disorder is the patient suffering from?
   a) Metabolic acidosis
   b) Metabolic alkalosis
   c) Respiratory acidosis
   d) Respiratory alkalosis
Q4. How does 120 mg/L compare with the lethal blood level of phenobarbital?
   a) It is well below the lethal amount.
   b) It is very close to the lethal amount.
   c) It is above the usually quoted fatal blood level.
   d) There is no correlation between levels and outcome for phenobarbital.

Answers and Discussion

Q1. (Answer = b) The appropriate calculation is

$$k_e = \text{elimination rate constant} = \ln\left(C1/C2\right)/(t2-t1)$$

$$= \ln\left(116/36\right)/(33-16)$$

$$= 0.069 \text{ hr}^{-1}$$

$$t_{1/2} = \ln 2/k_e$$

$$= 0.693/0.688 = 10.1 \text{ hours}$$

Because the rate of elimination is logarithmic, any set of data can be used to do this calculation. We have used the first and last 2 data sets. During the first 4 hours of hospitalization, prior to the onset of repetitive charcoal treatment, the half-life was found to be 69.3 hours for phenobarbital. Therefore, GI dialysis with charcoal is very effective in lowering the half-life and speeding elimination of the drug.

Q2. (Answer = b) When a graph of natural log of concentration vs. time is made, the resulting line is straight. This means that concentration is declining logarithmically or the rate of decrease is a function of the concentration of drug. This is the definition of first order kinetics.

Q3. (Answer = c) The findings of lowered pH in the presence of elevated pCO_2 are indicative of respiratory acidosis. The bicarbonate is at the low end of normal, which is consistent with partial compensation. This is the classical arterial blood gas picture in barbiturate overdose because the drug sedates the respiratory center and slows the breathing rate. Carbon dioxide accumulates and induces respiratory acidosis.

Q4. (Answer = b) Acute fatalities that appeared to result from phenobarbital alone had blood levels between 78 and 116 mg/L. In one study, a range very close to this was found in patients with severe coma who, nevertheless, survived. There is an approximate correlation between blood levels and outcome, and this patient's blood level is indicative of a possible fatality in the absence of rapid medical intervention.

References

Mofenson, H.C. et al., Gastrointestinal dialysis with activated charcoal and cathartic in the treatment of adolescent intoxications, *Clin. Pediatr.*, 24, 678–684, 1985.
Sunshine, I., Chemical evidence of tolerance to phenobarbital, *J. Lab Clin. Med.*, 50, 127–133, 1957.

Case Study 3: Innocent by Reason of Temporary Overdose?

A 54-year-old man who sometimes drank heavily also suffered from depressive episodes and had overdosed on drugs on several occasions. His physician wrote a prescription for triazolam (Halcion) for insomnia with instructions that the man should take one tablet each day. In a probable suicide attempt the man ingested 25 tablets from the bottle. He vomited soon thereafter, however, and fell asleep only to awaken the following day with confusion and mild amnesia as the only apparent after-effects. During the day he consumed a large quantity of whiskey. At night he visited an elderly neighbor whom he had befriended. As they conversed he placed a silk scarf around his neighbor's neck and strangled her to death.

During their investigation of the murder, police questioned the man who confessed that he was the murderer. Corroborating his confession was the fact that he claimed to have burned the scarf on the windowsill of his home and the sill was observed to be charred when the police subsequently investigated it. A number of issues came up at the man's trial, including the fact that he had no history of violence and was, by the testimony of many neighbors, a person of "exemplary character." It was clear that the deceased victim was a close friend of her murderer who had been of much help to her on many occasions. The man had no motive. All the testimony strongly supported the fact that the deceased and her confessed murderer had never argued, including on the night of the murder.

The jury, despite the exculpatory testimonies, found the defendant guilty by a unanimous decision. Defense counsel pleaded with the jury to recommend a verdict of manslaughter rather than murder because of the peculiar circumstances surrounding this murder. These circumstances included the above-mentioned facts of the relationship plus the testimony of a defense psychiatrist who stated that the accused may have been a victim of drug automatism. That is, his actions were, at least in part, robotic, and he had no free will because of a very high dose of benzodiazepines followed by alcohol throughout the following day, the day of the murder.

The court decided that the murderer should be sentenced to life imprisonment, They discounted the possible effect of the benzodiazepine, partly because the triazolam would, it was thought, have been eliminated by the time of the murder. It was further believed that elimination being completed the triazolam overdose could have played no part in the murderer's state of mind at the time of the crime. Although some jurors were hesitant, a life sentence was meted out. The undecided jurors were influenced by the judge who ruled that manslaughter should not be permitted as a lesser verdict.

An appeal was lodged on behalf of the murderer on grounds that the judge exceeded his authority in preventing consideration of the lesser offense of manslaughter. The Court of Appeals subsequently ruled that there was at least some element of diminished volition on the part of the murderer and, therefore, the sentence was reduced to 10 years.

This case illustrates an important concept in toxicology: namely, all toxic injury is not limited to physical damage but may also extend to behavioral effects. This murder was perpetrated, at least in part, because of the toxic effects of a drug or drugs (alcohol plus triazolam). A body of expert opinion actually believed that the defendant should be fully acquitted. There was a similar case in the United States in which a woman also committed an act of murder.[2,3] The victim was the murderer's mother. A trial was conducted and the alleged murderer was acquitted. She claimed that the drug caused her to kill her mother. Two experts testified at the trial that triazolam had contributed to her violent behavior. Not only was the woman acquitted but she brought suit against the manufacturer of triazolam, Upjohn Pharmaceuticals, alleging that they did not provide adequate warning that a violent act could be committed under the influence of this drug. She was the beneficiary of an out-of-court settlement in an amount of several million dollars.

Questions

Q1. The court decided that the drug use was not material in the case of the 54-year-old murderer because it had been eliminated from the defendant's body. Is this probable?
   a) It has a short half-life and was cleared by the time of the crime.
   b) They were incorrect because of the known long half-life of triazolam.
   c) Even if the drug had been fully cleared, behavior effects may linger.
   d) The amount of triazolam was not sufficient to have this great an effect on behavior.
Q2. What adverse effects are possible according to the product insert for triazolam?
   a) Schizophrenic reactions
   b) Infrequent renal failure
   c) Confusion, bizarre behavior, agitation, hallucinations, depersonalization
   d) Euphoria and togetherness

Q3. What is true about withdrawal phenomena for triazolam?
   a) No withdrawal is provoked by this drug.
   b) A severe withdrawal syndrome may occur only after several months of therapeutic use.
   c) Symptoms similar to those of withdrawal from alcohol may occur even after 1 week's use.
   d) Medium dosing does not require gradual tapering of drug use.
Q4. Which is a physical effect of triazolam overdose?
   a) Ataxia
   b) Apnea
   c) Coma
   d) All of the above

Answers and Discussion

Q1. (Answer = c) The average half-life of triazolam is 3.5 hours and may be as short as 1.7 hours. If one assumes that the man ingested 25 tablets of the smallest dosage form, 0.125-mg tablets, the blood level might indeed be very low at the time of the murder. In all probability the blood level was still significant. But even if it the concentration was close to zero the drug could have significant residual behavioral effects. Intense withdrawal symptoms are possible in view of the large amounts of drug eliminated by this man. Therefore, the pharmacokinetics of this drug are not irrelevant in this case.

Q2. (Answer = c) The *Physician's Desk Reference*[4] and the product insert both refer to mental and behavioral changes that include, but are not necessarily limited to, those listed in answer c. An intensification of depression and suicidal ideation are also possible. These effects are usually dose related but have been noted even in low dosage. Importantly, it is very difficult to separate out the cause of bizarre behavior when it occurs with a user of triazolam. Bizarre behavior may be caused by or at least related to drug use. On the other hand, the patient may have an underlying psychiatric disorder that is, alone or synergistically with the triazolam, responsible for the behavior.

Q3. (Answer = c) Convulsions, tremor, cramping of muscles and the abdomen, sweating, vomiting, insomnia, dysphoria, and perceptual disturbances may all occur in triazolam withdrawal. These symptoms also are found from barbiturates or alcohol. Withdrawal effects are likely to be more severe after long-term and/or heavy use but may arise from as little as 1 week's use of the drug.

Q4. (Answer = d) Triazolam is, like other benzodiazepines, a relatively safe drug from the perspective of physical symptoms of overdose. In the case described above the patient awakened the morning following a large overdose and was able to be physically active during the day. He experienced confusion and, of course, his behavior was uncharacteristically aggressive. Although triazolam usually causes mild physical symptoms of overdose, there are case reports of major toxicity including apnea and coma. Some deaths have been reported.

References

1. Medawar, C. and Rassaby, E., Triazolam overdose, alcohol, and manslaughter, *Lancet,* 338, 1515–1516, 1991.
2. Brahams, D., Confidentiality of Upjohn's triazolam documents, *Lancet,* 338, 243, 1991.
3. Oswald, I., Safety of triazolam, *Lancet,* 338, 516–517, 1991.
4. *Physician's Desk Reference*, 50th ed., Medical Economics Co., Montvale, NJ, 1996.

22 Stimulants

CONTENTS

Stimulants are a diverse group of chemicals that have in common the ability to excite the CNS when they are taken in moderate to large amounts. Some of them, notably amphetamine and cocaine, are well-known as drugs of abuse. They are discussed as such in Chapter 20 of this text. Other sympathomimetic amines, less subject to abuse, are discussed here. In addition, compounds in the stimulant category described here include analeptics (drugs that have restorative qualities) such as methylphenidate, picrotoxin, and pentylenetetrazol. Also of importance as stimulants are the xanthines: caffeine, theobromine, and theophylline. Finally, we will discuss camphor, a stimulant with local anesthetic properties.

Most stimulants will cause some degree of hallucination or sensory misperception in severe overdose. If they provoke hallucination as one of their most prominent features, they are discussed in the chapter on psychedelics rather than here as stimulants. Among compounds that are primarily psychedelic in character are MDA (3,4-methylenedioxyamphetamine) and DOM (2,5-dimethoxy-4-methylamphetamine).

SYMPATHOMIMETIC AMINES

These compounds are derivatives of amphetamine that were synthesized in an effort to reduce the addictive and abusive properties of amphetamine while retaining some medical value for treating narcolepsy, hyperactivity, and obesity. Prominent among these compounds are those illustrated in Figure 22.1.

Perhaps the major use of these compounds has been in weight-reduction programs (Table 22.1). Most of them are, indeed, appetite suppressants (anorectants). Sympathomimetic amines derive their anorectic activity via a central catecholamine mechanism. They are indirect alpha-adrenergic stimulants. They also have a weaker beta-adrenergic stimulatory component. Data on the effectiveness of phenylpropanolamine, the member of this category that is available over the counter (Accutrim, Dexatrim), are ambiguous in relation to anorexic activity and show it to be only weakly anorexic.

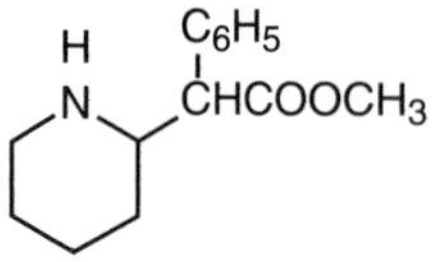

Methylphenidate

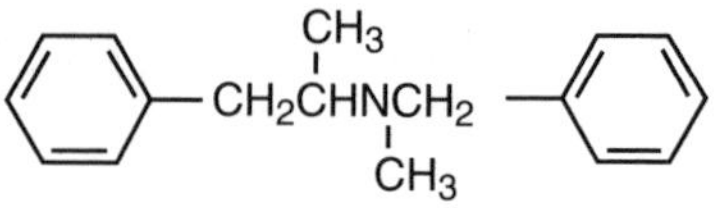

$C_6H_5COCHN(C_2H_5)_2$
       |
       CH_3

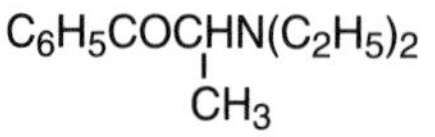

Diethylpropion

Benzphetamine

$C_6H_5 - CH_2CNHCH_3$
          |
          CH_3

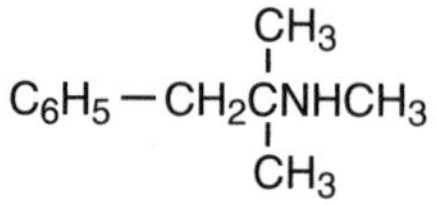

Mephentermine

FIGURE 22.1 Amphetamine-related anorectic drugs.

Studies also show that weight loss from use of these medications is only on the order of 1 lb. per week. Such studies also show that weight loss depends more on the patient's relationship to his/her diet counselor, previous history of weight loss activities, etc. rather than history of anorexiant use. The actual drug involvement appears to be a minor factor in eventual success or failure. Use of these drugs for weight control has been beset with numerous problems. Tolerance develops to the anorectic actions and users find that they must take larger doses to continue to suppress their appetites. Because the drugs cause some level of euphoria, users may be consciously or unconsciously increasing their usage levels to achieve this effect. With the onset of tolerance to euphoria, users also are inclined to take more drug. It appears that tolerance to convulsions and toxic psychosis is less prominent so that users of these drugs may be continuously increasing their doses to maintain appetite suppression and euphoria but, at the same time, their risk of severe toxicity is increasing.

As a consequence of the great danger associated with this class of compounds, some states have banned their prescription use for control of obesity. In addition to abuse potential, patients using these drugs in the prescribed manner usually complain of anxiety, tremulousness, palpitations, and vascular headache. Phenylpropanolamine at doses of 85 mg/day caused hypertension in 33% of healthy young people. Encephalopathy, angina, ventricular dysrhythmias, and even myocardial infarction have been reported in phenylpropanolamine use. Obviously, phenylpropanolamine is contraindicated in those with pre-existing hypertension or with a history of atherosclerotic vascular disease.

Caffeine and phenylpropanolamine were marketed together in many over-the-counter preparations for weight control prior to 1983. The FDA banned their sale as combination products because of research showing that hypertension was more severe with both drugs than from using either of them alone.

Methylphenidate (Ritalin) is a sympathomimetic amine that is regarded as a mild stimulant. It is readily absorbed and distributes preferentially to the CNS. It is well-known for its use in the treatment of attention deficit disorder (ADD). ADD is a condition, primarily in children, characterized by short attention span, restlessness, and emotional lability. Methylphenidate is believed to be helpful in more than 80% of such patients. Disadvantages to its use include appetite suppression that may

TABLE 22.1
Drugs for Weight Control

Agent	Narcotic Class	Comparative Health Effects (phenylpropanolamine = 1)
D-amphetamine	C-II	4
Methamphetamine	C-II	4
Phenmetrazine	C-II	4
Benzphetamine	C-III	3
Diethylpropion	C-V	2
Phentermine	C-IV	2

interfere with the normal growth of the child. The use of a stimulant to treat hyperkinetic children at first appears paradoxical. In animal studies, however, amphetamine compounds accelerate behavior that is slow in the absence of drug while suppressing some rapid behavior patterns. Perhaps the sedative action of methylphenidate in hyperactive children relates to acceleration of "slow rate" behavior or an improved balance of behavioral forces. In any event, this drug is clearly of benefit in improving the learning and memory skills of many children.

Overdose of methylphenidate or one of the sympathomimetics used as diet aids can cause the same symptoms found in overdose of amphetamine. Because they are generally less potent drugs, however, larger doses are needed to cause the same effects found with amphetamine or methamphetamine. Therapeutic use can cause restlessness and irritability, sweating, and insomnia. Mild overdose is associated with confusion, hypertension, tachypnea, and tachycardia. Significant overdoses may cause delirium, severe tachycardias, arrhythmias, and hyperpyrexia. Without intervention, large overdoses have caused convulsions, coma, and death.

METHYLXANTHINES

Three methylxanthine alkaloids are present in nature and have stimulant properties. A fourth methylxanthine, aminophylline, is equivalent to 2 moles of theophylline with 1 mole of ethylenediamine. Because it is just 78.9% theophylline it is less potent than theophylline. These compounds are widespread in food materials including coffee, cocoa, tea, chocolate, and many soft drinks (Table 22.2). All of them stimulate the CNS, relax smooth muscle, stimulate cardiac function, and cause diuresis. Theobromine's ability to cause these effects is less than that of theophylline and caffeine so it is not used medicinally.

CAFFEINE

Caffeine is rapidly absorbed after oral administration, reaching peak serum levels in about 45 minutes. It becomes widely distributed throughout the body. Demethylation within the liver is the major pathway for caffeine metabolism. Other methylxanthines including theophylline, theobromine, and paraxanthine are products of its metabolism that appear in the urine (Figure 22.2). Less than 10% of a caffeine dose

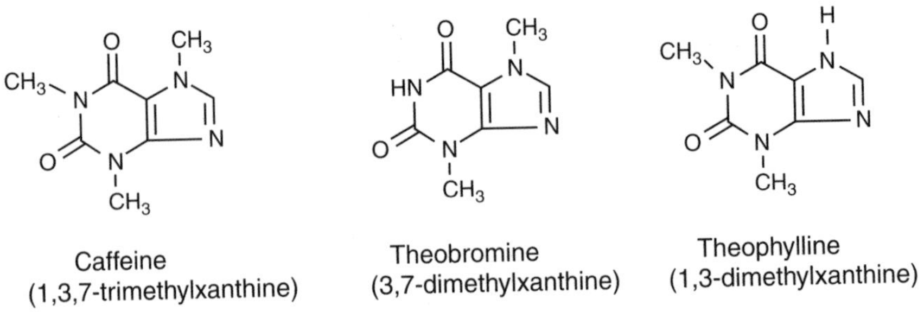

| Caffeine | Theobromine | Theophylline |
| (1,3,7-trimethylxanthine) | (3,7-dimethylxanthine) | (1,3-dimethylxanthine) |

FIGURE 22.2 Caffeine and other pharmacologically active methylxanthines.

TABLE 22.2
Caffeine Content

Food/Beverage	Amount in 6-oz. Cup (mg)
Cocoa	8–20
Coffee	72–210
Decaffeinated coffee	2–5
Cola drinks	35–55
Non-cola soft drinks	<35
Tea	25–110
Coffee beans	1–2% caffeine by weight

TABLE 22.3
Relative Activity of Methylxanthines

	Caffeine	Theophylline	Theobromine
CNS excitation	High	Moderate	Low
Cardiac excitation	Low	High	Moderate
Coronary dilation	Low	High	Moderate
Smooth muscle relaxation	Low	High	Moderate
Diuresis	Low	High	Moderate

is excreted as caffeine. In adults the half-life of caffeine is 3.5 hours, an important factor in deciding when to have the day's last cup of coffee. Caffeine ingested late in the day may cause an insomniac effect because substantial quantities may still remain in the CNS at bedtime. The half-life is much longer in neonates, and is estimated to equal as much as 100 hours.

Caffeine has numerous physiological effects. At the level of the cerebral cortex it appears to clarify the thinking process, reduce sleepiness, and permit sustained intellectual activity and psychomotor activity. In large amounts, however, restlessness, nervousness, and irritability are the result. Very high doses (>1 g) cause sensory disturbances, tachypnea, and muscle fasciculations. Caffeine is capable of gastrointestinal injury. It stimulates gastric acid and pepsin secretion. In high amounts, taken on a chronic basis, gastric mucosal erosions occur. Many coffee drinkers experience heartburn and this symptom arises from a reduction in the tone of the lower esophageal sphincter that, in turn, leads to acid reflux.

In common with the other methylxanthines, caffeine has a potent effect on the cardiovascular system. With large ingestions tachycardia, dysrhythmias, and extra-systoles are noted. The observed increase in heart rate is believed to be associated with small increases in blood pressure, force of contraction, and cardiac output.

Caffeine toxicity is also manifested by many symptoms. The term "caffeinism" has been applied to a syndrome of long-term excessive caffeine use. Patients with this condition exhibit headache, delirium, palpitations, and tachycardia. Often, there are gastrointestinal complaints, muscle twitches, psychomotor agitation, and possible arrhythmias. The lethal dose of caffeine is highly variable but 3 g was reported as a cause of death in at least one case. The commonly published lethal dose is 150 to 200 mg/kg (about 15 g for a 150-lb. man). Blood levels greater than 25 µg/mL also are regarded as in the toxic range, but a good correlation between blood level and toxicity does not exist.

Although the major exposure of most people to caffeine is in the form of beverage coffee, caffeine also has at least two medical applications. It is available over-the-counter as an aid for the prevention of sleep and has been employed for this purpose by generations of students. Vivarin™ and No-Doz™ are two such products. Some neonatalogists employ it in the treatment of apnea of prematurity. It is superior to theophylline in some ways, i.e., a much greater half-life that allows for less frequent dosing. Caffeine also has a wider therapeutic window; for example, there is a larger gap between doses that provide therapeutic benefit vs. those associated with toxicity. Blood levels are of some value in this application and the following guidelines are recommended:

Therapeutic	8–14 µg/mL
Toxic	>30 µg/mL
Fatal	>80 µg/mL

Caffeine is also sold in many over-the-counter diet pills. What, if any, value it has in this context has been the object of substantial controversy.

THEOPHYLLINE

Theophylline is a methylxanthine that finds its most common medical application in asthma therapy. It was once thought that it worked by inhibiting cyclic AMP phosphodiesterase activity. This theory was disproven when it was demonstrated that the concentrations of drug required to achieve this purpose were not attainable *in vivo*. Further, more potent phosphodiesterase inhibitors have been shown to be ineffective in asthma treatment. In overdoses, however, part of theophylline's actions probably are due to phosphodiesterase inhibition. Currently, the mechanism of action of theophylline is believed to be antagonism of the activity of adenosine. Because adenosine modulates histamine release and, therefore, causes constriction of respiratory smooth muscle (bronchoconstriction), theophylline, by antagonizing adenosine, causes a bronchial muscle relaxation. Theophylline also causes a release of catecholamines. Epinephrine and norepinephrine are, therefore, quite elevated in overdoses with theophylline.

Normal metabolism of theophylline consists of oxidation to 1,3 dimethyluric acid and/or demethylation to 3-methylxanthine or 1-methyluric acid. A small percent is eliminated as theophylline. In very young babies theophylline is partly metabolized to caffeine, a reaction that does not occur in older children or adults. Because of this, it is advisable to perform analyses for both theophylline and caffeine when conducting drug monitoring of the very young who are being treated with theophylline. The reactions of theophylline metabolism involve the cytochrome P_{450} mixed-function oxidase system. Therefore, many factors alter theophylline clearance by changing the available quantities of these enzymes. Cigarette smoking or barbiturates may shorten theophylline half-life by 50%, whereas some medicines such as erythromycin, ciprofloxacin, and propranolol inhibit theophylline metabolism.

The toxicity of methylxanthines is mainly in association with an excess of their normal therapeutic actions. Their stimulatory actions can reach the extreme, causing cardiac and/or respiratory arrest. Theophylline also has a notorious GI irritation believed to reside in its direct stimulation of the chemoreceptor trigger zone. Thus, nausea and vomiting are common findings in any level of theophylline overdose. Restlessness, excitation, and insomnia are symptoms of mild overdose with the methylxanthines. Perceptual distortions, such as seeing lights or hearing noises, may be experienced. Headache and dizziness are often reported in overdose. At the cardiovascular level, tachycardia may progress to ventricular fibrillation and cardiopulmonary arrest. These are due to the aforementioned excess secretion of catecholamines by theophylline. The catecholamines stimulate the myocardium and this effect is aggravated by hypokalemia, hypercalcemia, hypophosphatemia, or metabolic acidosis. Convulsions and coma may precede death. One of the unusual characteristics of theophylline overdose is that major symptoms may be the first indication of the overdose. Often, nausea and vomiting are the first signs but, on occasion, generalized seizures occur without any other sign of overdose.

Theophylline overdose is clearly a life-threatening emergency and therapy must be initiated as promptly and energetically as possible. Ipecac should not be used, but lavage must be attempted for ingestions that happened during the previous hour. Activated charcoal with cathartic is usually desirable. Hypotension can be treated with intravenous fluids. Seizures can be treated with diazepam or phenobarbital. Lidocaine may be required for arrhythmias. In serious overdoses, hemodialysis is helpful in enhancing elimination, but charcoal hemoperfusion is three times faster in reducing the body burden of theophylline. The pharmacokinetics of hemoperfusion are described in a case at the end of this chapter. Blood levels are helpful in the evaluation and treatment of theophylline overdose. They should be run every 2 hours until a decrease is observed and then every 4 hours until a level of 20 μg/mL is achieved. Interpretation of levels is based on the fact that patients with acute exposures usually tolerate up to 90 μg/mL whereas those with chronic overdose experience toxicity at lower levels (greater than 40 μg/mL). The fact that many patients appear to be quite stable mandates the need for blood testing. It indicates that the patient may be in serious jeopardy despite appearances to the contrary. A 5-year study of 300 patients showed that blood concentration above 80 µg/mL is predictive of major toxicity and suggests that charcoal hemoperfusion should be started. Another study refined this value and concluded that if theophylline goes above 60 µg/mL or clinical status is deteriorating, then hemoperfusion should be started while the patient is stable. Supportive therapy must usually be extensive. A rough correlation exists between blood level and toxicity for the methylxanthines. For caffeine, blood levels below 15 µg/mL usually are not associated with toxicity. Fatal levels have been reported in the range of 1600 µg/mL. For theophylline, physicians are advised to medicate the patient so that blood concentrations equal 10 to 20 µg/mL. Some patients are toxic at these concentrations, so recently this therapeutic range has been adjusted and 5 to 15 µg/mL is now regarded as the appropriate range for the control of asthma. Theophylline is employed for asthma therapy because it dilates the bronchi. This effect is presumed to be due to its ability to relax smooth muscle.

CAMPHOR

Camphor is a compound with stimulant properties on the cerebral cortex. It is found in many pharmaceutical products (Table 22.4) because of the many additional properties that it possesses. Among its uses are as a preservative, antipruritic, topical rubifacient, cold remedy, and antiseptic.

Camphor is not highly toxic and has a minimum lethal dose of approximately 50 mg/kg. However, because it is widespread in the consumer market, present in large quantities, and can be absorbed through intact skin, a significant number of poisonings are found.

Nausea and vomiting are the usual first findings in camphor overdose. From there the customary findings in stimulant overdose are noted. These include confusion, restlessness, delirium, and possible hallucinations. Muscular excitability proceeds to

TABLE 22.4
Some Compounds Containing Camphor

Product	% Camphor
Absorbine Pain Lotion	10
Ben Gay Children's Rub	5
Campho-Phenique Liquid	10.85
Heet	3
Mustarole	4
Vick's VapoRub	4.75
Vick's Vaposteam	6.2
Sloan's Liniment	5

Note: The U.S. FDA ruled in 1983 that medicinal products may not contain more than 11% of camphor.

tremors and then epileptic-type seizures. Seizure onset can be sudden, without any previous signs that seizures are imminent. They can be followed by depression after the seizure and then coma. If there is a fatal outcome, it is usually due to respiratory depression. Patients who have been poisoned by camphor can be diagnosed partly on the basis of the customary signs of stimulant exposure. History may be helpful if parents or others report an unusual exposure to a pharmaceutical product. Because such exposures normally are large in amount, the odor of camphor is usually detectable in urine or on the breath. This odor has been described as organic and pungent in nature. If blood testing is conducted, a level of 14.5 mg/L is ominous and suggests the danger of imminent seizures.

Camphor exposures should be treated with lavage and activated charcoal. Supportive care should include benzodiazepines or barbiturates for seizures. If they are refractory, then pentobarbital may be effective. Hemodialysis has been shown to be ineffective in decreasing blood levels; however, hemoperfusion with resins has been successful in enhancing the rate of camphor elimination.

Questions

1. What are the advantages and disadvantages of treating obesity with sympathomimetic amines?
2. Discuss the use of methylphenidate as treatment for attention deficit disorder. How can a drug classified as a stimulant cause a depression of hyperactivity in children?
3. Contrast the use of caffeine and theophylline as treatments for pulmonary problems in infants. What toxicity is associated with each and how can laboratory data be helpful in avoiding toxicity?
4. What are the toxic features of camphor and where is this compound found medically?

Case Study 1: The Hazards of Dieting

An 18-year-old woman ingested eight over-the-counter diet pills. Two hours later she felt ill and went to an emergency department for evaluation of a headache and generalized malaise. Her BP was 140/90 and pulse 52. No neurological abnormalities were noted. Because of her history of the diet pill ingestion, gastric lavage was attempted. She was discharged only to return soon after with generalized convulsions. She was lethargic but awake and aware of herself and her surroundings. She was admitted to the hospital and 1 day later she abruptly lost all brain stem reflexes. A spinal tap revealed that her CSF was grossly bloody. Evaluation by electroencephalogram resulted in an isoelectric profile. Carotid angiography revealed that her intracranial vessels were not filling with blood in a normal manner. She was placed on respiratory support but, after a long interval of flat brain waves, that support was withdrawn and she was pronounced dead.

What is a possible identification for the diet pills?
a) Phenylpropanolamine
b) Diethylpropionate
c) Thyroxine
d) Fenfluramine

All of the suggested answers are marketed alone or in combination with other agents as diet medicines. Diethylpropionate and fenfluramine, however, were never sold in the United States as over-the-counter drugs. Because they have a modest abuse potential, both required a prescription. Fenfluramine was removed from the market in 1997 when a number of patients were found to have cardiac injury that appeared to be related to use of fenfluramine. Thyroxine is not a diet drug although it has been used in that manner by some persons. This is a great mistake because of thyroxine's high potency and the fact that any weight loss it provokes is mainly lean body mass. Thyroxine also requires a prescription.

Phenylpropanolamine is available as an over-the-counter appetite suppressant. It is fairly effective for this purpose but has many side effects including rapid tolerance, insomnia, and occasional irregularities of cardiac rhythm. On rare occasions it causes major toxicity as related in the present case.

Questions

Q1. What adverse effects have been reported for phenylpropanolamine?
a) CNS stimulation
b) Hypertension
c) Abuse potential
d) All of the above
Q2. How does phenylpropanolamine resemble amphetamine?
a) Pharmacologically similar but structurally in a different class.
b) Stereoisomers of each other.
c) Optical isomers of each other.
d) Phenylpropanolamine is a hydroxylated form of amphetamine.
Q3. Which of the following items of evidence helps to rule in a drug as the cause of this patient's symptoms?
a) Absence of signs of chronic hypertension on autopsy.
b) Brain evaluation did not show a bleeding source such as an aneurysm or an atrioventricular malformation.
c) Relation of drug use to appearance of symptoms in time.
d) All of the above.

Answers and Discussion

Q1. (Answer = d) Phenylpropanolamine is classified as a sympathomimetic amine. This is a large class of compounds that includes drugs with very high abuse potential such as amphetamine and methamphetamine as well as numerous analogs of these compounds. They have the classical pharmacological properties of stimulants. All of the features listed here are common to this class of drugs.

Q2. (Answer = d) Phenylpropanolamine is very similar to amphetamine and differs from it merely by the presence of a hydroxyl group on the carbon adjacent to the benzene ring. However, it does not have the same molecular formula as amphetamine and is not an isomer of it. (See the structures of sympathomimetic amines in this text.)

Q3. (Answer = d) It is rare for this particular response to occur in sympathomimetic amine usage. Cerebrovascular accidents are usually associated with hypertension, cerebral malformations, or chronic degenerative disease in the central nervous system. Therefore, among the probable causes of this patient's stroke, phenylpropanolamine overdose is far down the list. Nevertheless, her death was eventually attributed to phenylpropanolamine exposure because no other proximate cause could be determined and her drug use was close in time to the occurrence of this catastrophic event. In addition, there are a number of other published cases of stroke arising from moderate consumption of sympathomimetic amines.

Reference

McDowell, J. and LeBlanc, H., Phenylpropanolamine and cerebral hemorrhage, *West. J. Med.,* 142, 688–691, 1985.

Case Study 2: The Excitable Baby

A 4-month-old baby girl who weighed 10 lbs. was brought to a hospital by her distraught parents who found the child with an empty bottle of an over-the-counter medication. The bottle had contained about 30 Tri-Aqua pills. On evaluation, the child was found to be irritable with elevated breathing and heart rate. Physical exam revealed hyperresponsiveness to any stimulation with increased muscle tone and hyperactive deep tendon reflexes. Therapy was started with the administration of Ipecac. Upon receipt of this emetic the child vomited coffee ground emesis. Laboratory studies were immediately initiated and they revealed the following:

pCO_2	18 mm
pH	7.45
K	2.6
HCO_3^-	13
Glucose	323
Theophylline	31
Chest X-ray	Normal

The child was provided IV fluids, NG suction, antacids, and benzodiazepines for her hyperstimulation status. Dialysis for the elevated theophylline was considered but was eventually deemed to be unnecessary because it was only modestly above the therapeutic range. All of the patient's aberrant laboratory findings normalized over the following 6 days of hospitalization, although the hyperexcitability and tachycardia persisted for over 2 days past the time of the ingestion.

Which of the following drugs was probably in the Tri-Aqua pills?
  a) Caffeine
  b) Aspirin
  c) Morphine
  d) Theophylline

The bottle of Tri-Aqua contained caffeine pills each of which contained 98 mg of caffeine. The symptoms of caffeine overdose are very consistent with the hyperactive appearance of this patient. Morphine is not possible because it is not an over-the-counter medication nor does it provoke signs of hyperstimulation. Aspirin does cause some of this child's findings but the overall picture is, in many respects, different from aspirin. Theophylline seems to be a likely suspect because it is a stimulant and the patient had a high theophylline level. The theophylline level is, however, not impressive and serum concentrations greater than 40 mg/L or higher would be expected for this degree of hyperstimulation. The observed theophylline arose as a metabolite of caffeine.

During her hospitalization both caffeine and theophylline drug levels were frequently measured in this patient. Because her physicians were mainly concerned about possible theophylline toxicity, they ordered that theophylline be tested serially and, if possible, that it be confirmed by a second test method. The laboratory, accordingly, ran both enzyme immunoassay and high-performance liquid chromatography methods. The following data were recorded:

Specimen Number	Enzyme Immunoassay (mg/L)	HPLC (mg/L)
1	9.2	12.4
2	13.6	31
3	13.4	32
4	10.7	24

In view of the marked discrepancy between these two methods a third, different HPLC method was attempted and recovery experiments were run in an effort to unravel this mystery. The third method gave results of 6.7 and 9.1 mg/L for specimens 2 and 3, respectively. It was eventually determined that the first two methods were erroneous and the third method, which gave the lowest answers, was correct.

Questions

Q1. An erroneously high HPLC result would most likely result from
   a) A problem with the instrument detector
   b) An interference from a metabolite of the analyte
   c) An improperly labeled standard
   d) Another medicinal taken at the same time

Q2. What is the best HPLC method modification to prevent co-elution?
   a) Change the flow rate
   b) Change the type of detector
   c) Change the mobile phase
   d) Change the column

Q3. Are theophylline and caffeine concentrations valuable in caffeine overdose?
   a) Both are critical.
   b) Neither is valuable.
   c) Only theophylline is needed because it is a more toxic drug.
   d) Only caffeine is needed because it is present in larger amounts.

Q4. How did this child's ingestion compare with a lethal dose of approximately 100 mg/kg?
   a) Far below a fatal dose
   b) Almost a fatal dose
   c) Just above a fatal dose
   d) Manyfold greater than the estimated fatal dose

Answers and Discussion

Q1. (Answer = b) Any of these possible answers are feasible but interference from a metabolite is most likely. Metabolites are structurally similar to the drug being tested and it is entirely possible, sometimes probable, that they will react in a manner similar to the test substance. In the case being discussed, paraxanthine, a metabolite of caffeine, co-eluted with theophylline and contributed to the area under the curve (Figure 22.3). The instrument's result was effectively equal to paraxanthine plus theophylline. Also, as a result of its structural similarity, paraxanthine cross-reacted in the immunoassay with the anti-theophylline antibody. It is quite unusual, however, for two test methods to be affected to such a large degree. The erratic HPLC method gave results that were up to 500% too high while the enzyme immunoassay had errors of up to 380%.

Q2. (Answer = c) Neither the detector nor the flow rate will have any significant effect on the co-elution of these two compounds. If the column were changed, it would probably separate the two compounds. Although this step could be taken, it would be easier to change the mobile phase. In this case, conversion to a more acidic mobile phase led to a separation of theophylline from caffeine.

Q3. (Answer = b) Neither serum concentration is of much clinical value. The correlation between concentration and clinical symptoms is extremely

Retention Time	Mobile Phase 1 (min.)	Mobile Phase 2 (min.)
Theobromine	2.7	3.3
Theophylline	3.7	5.8
Paraxanthine	3.7	5.2
Internal standard	4.2	6.7
Caffeine	9.0	11.0

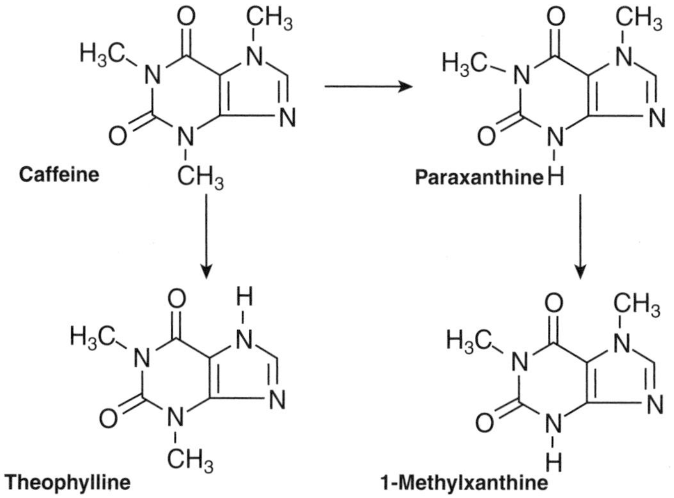

FIGURE 22.3 Aspects of caffeine metabolism.

variable for caffeine and could, therefore, be misleading. Treating the symptoms is usually sufficient in cases of this sort. It also seems that amounts of theophylline present in caffeine overdose usually are quite low. Thus, despite the potential toxicity of theophylline, it is not likely to be a problem in caffeine overdose.

Q4. (Answer = d) This child's weight is 4.5 kg and she ingested 30×98 mg = 2940 mg of caffeine. This is equal to 650 mg/kg, far in excess of the estimated lethal amount. She was saved, therefore, because of rapid and effective medical intervention. It is also possible that she absorbed it poorly or that the ingested amount was overestimated.

Reference

Fligner, C. and Opheim, K., Caffeine and its dimethylxanthine metabolites in two cases of caffeine overdose: a cause of falsely elevated theophylline concentrations in serum, *J. Analyt. Toxicol.*, 12, 339, 1988.

23 Anticholinergic Drugs

CONTENTS

INTRODUCTION

This chapter is devoted to drugs that have anticholinergic properties (Table 23.1). This is a large group of compounds with many pharmaceutical applications. Thus, included

TABLE 23.1
Examples of Drugs With Anticholinergic Activity

Antihistamines	Antidepressants
Brompheniramine	Amitriptyline
Chlorpheniramine	Desipramine
Diphenhydramine	Doxepin
Anti-Parkinsonian drugs	Gastrointestinal agents
Benztropine	Atropine
Procyclidine	Homatropine
Trihexyphenidyl	Scopolamine
Antipsychotics	Ophthalmic drugs
Chlorpromazine	Atropine
Promazine	Cyclopentolate
Triflupromazine	

among substances with anticholinergic properties are antihistamines, anti-Parkinsonian drugs, antipsychotic agents, antidepressants, gastrointestinal antispasmodics, and some ophthalmic drugs. It is remarkable, therefore, that drugs with such diverse and useful medical properties would share the characteristic of being anticholinergic.

ANTICHOLINERGIC ACTIVITY

It will be recalled that the cholinergic neuron employs acetylcholine to conduct the nerve message across the synapse. If this process is enhanced, the resulting effect is described as cholinergic. Conversely, any interference with this activity is referred to as anticholinergic activity. This can occur in the CNS or at peripheral nerve receptors. Some anticholinergic agents block transmission at the so-called muscarinic sites only, others at nicotinic sites, and some at both. Quaternary anticholinergics, because they are highly polar molecules, do not enter the CNS and exert their effects primarily at peripheral sites.

In the discussion of insecticides it was mentioned that the SLUDGE syndrome (salivation, lacrimation, urination, defecation, gastrointestinal action, emesis) is characteristic of cholinergics. To some degree the anticholinergics produce the opposite set of symptoms. They depress salivation (dry mouth), reduce sweating, increase body temperature, dilate pupils, and increase heart rate. Those that reach the CNS also cause drowsiness, mild euphoria, amnesia, fatigue, delirium, and mental confusion. An expression devised to describe the anticholinergic syndrome is "hot as Hades, red as a beet, mad as a hatter, blind as a bat, dry as a bone." Alternatively, the mnemonic STUD represents this syndrome: Slowed bowel motility, Tachycardia and raised Temperature, Urinary retention, and Desiccation of skin.

ANTIHISTAMINES

Antigens, such as pollen, bee venom, viral protein, and numerous others, elicit immune responses ranging from mild nasal congestion to potentially fatal anaphylactic shock. Histamine, a chemical produced in many human tissues, is the biochemical mediator of many of these responses. The specific actions of histamine include constriction of bronchial smooth muscle in the lung, venous constriction, increase in capillary permeability, and several other actions. Histamine binds to so-called Histamine 1 (H1) or H2 receptors to produce these effects.

Because histamine release is such a common occurrence in a multitude of human afflictions, histamine antagonists, or antihistamines, are among the most widely used medicinal agents. They are especially useful for treating allergies and for controlling the symptoms of viral ailments like colds and influenza. The public employs these agents on a regular basis and a large variety of them are available on an over-the-counter basis. As a result of their common use, people develop an attitude of indifference toward the potential toxicity of these drugs. In spite of public perceptions, however, antihistamines are dangerous in overdose and some fatalities have been associated with their use.

CHEMISTRY

Figure 23.1 shows the structures of histamine and several of its antagonists. Terfenadine (Seldane) and loratidine (Claritin) are second-generation antihistamines (Figure 23.2). They cannot cross the blood–brain barrier and thus lack the sedative

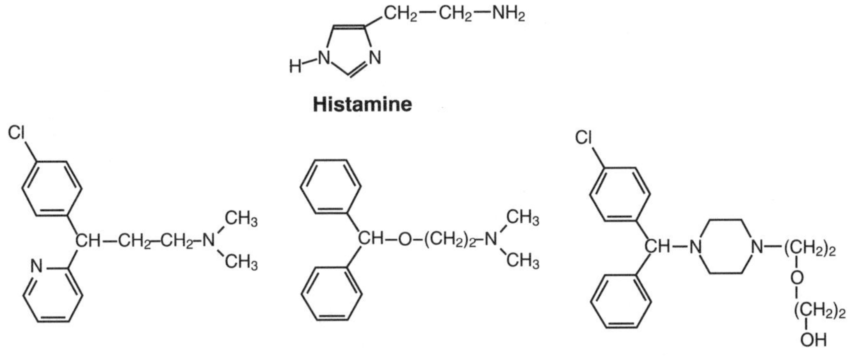

FIGURE 23.1 Histamine and some first-generation antihistamines.

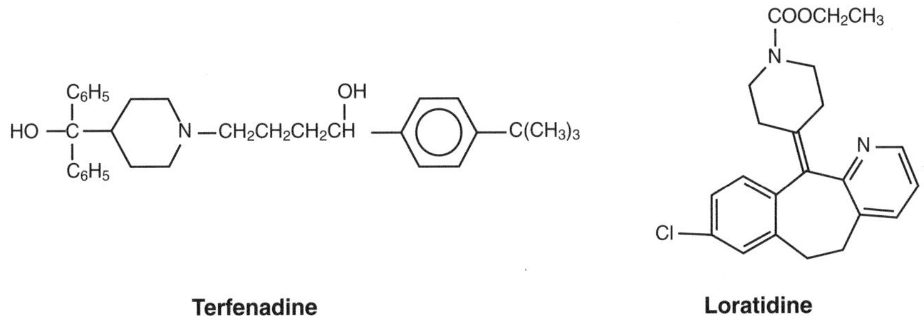

FIGURE 23.2 Some recent antihistamines.

properties common to first-generation agents such as chlorpheniramine. The sedative potency of the earlier drugs is so significant that some of them, such as diphenhydramine, are independently marketed as hypnotics. The introduction of the second-generation compounds was a great breakthrough in drug research, particularly because many of these drugs must be used chronically by allergy sufferers. In chronic usage the soporific effects become intolerable for many patients.

TOXICITY

Antihistamines have sedative properties which may be described as low to moderate in potency. Their anticholinergic actions are moderate to high in intensity. A small number of them, e.g., pyrilamine, are classified as having a high potential for GI upset. The sedation antihistamines provoke can reach severe degrees including coma and death in extreme overdose. Surprisingly, children have a paradoxical stimulation reaction to antihistamines. Rather than depression, children may experience hallucinations, tonic-clonic convulsions, and hyperpyrexia from high dose antihistamines.

TREATMENT

The classical methods to reduce drug absorption are helpful with antihistamines. Because an additional effect of anticholinergics is a delay in gastric emptying, the physician has more time than usual to prevent uptake of these drugs from the GI tract into the blood.

An antidote, physostigmine, is available for anticholinergics (Figure 23.3). Physostigmine is a naturally occurring alkaloid found in Calabar bean (ordeal bean) which has potent cholinergic properties. It grows on the banks of streams in West Africa and was once used by native tribes as an "ordeal poison" in trials for witchcraft. As a cholinergic, it might be expected to be helpful in reversing the effects of anticholinergic overdose. It is the only reversible acetylcholinesterase inhibitor without a charged quaternary amine function. It is, instead, a tertiary amine that is less polar. It will, therefore, enter the CNS. Thus, it will reverse anticholinergic actions in the CNS and in the peripheral nervous system.

This is a difficult antidote to employ and must be used with extreme caution. If too much is given or if the diagnosis of anticholinergic poisoning is not correct, then the antidote will induce a cholinergic crisis provoking the SLUD syndrome and other symptoms of cholinergic poisoning. However, in the appropriate context, it is

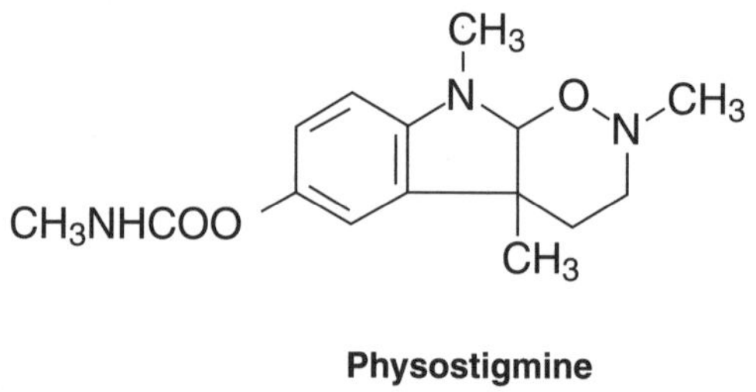

Physostigmine

FIGURE 23.3 Physostigmine.

a valuable aid in therapy. Because 1 to 2 mg are infused slowly over 5 min, the clinical effect is short-lived (20 to 60 min) so multiple doses may be needed. As stated, physostigmine should only be provided when anticholinergic overdose is a certainty. Both peripheral and central signs must be present. The patient should show central signs including agitation, myoclonus, seizures, and hallucinations. Peripheral signs also must be present such as mydriasis, hyperthermia, dry skin and mucosa, decreased bowel sounds, tachycardia, and urinary retention. Note that the antidote is given primarily to reverse the life-threatening complications of anticholinergic overdose such as coma, seizures, respiratory depression, hypotension, and severe arrhythmias.

ANTIDEPRESSANTS

Depressive illness is a mood, or affect, disorder in contrast to schizophrenia, which is a thought disorder. Depressive episodes are said to be characterized by dysphoria, that is, a loss of interest or pleasure in all or most of a person's usual activities. Organic or functional depression is an unexplained phenomenon in which the subject develops a profoundly pessimistic state in the absence of identifiable stimuli. That is, no life circumstance, i.e., death of a close friend, exists as a natural explanation for the behavior. Other aspects of functional depression commonly observed include suicidal ideation, feelings of helplessness and worthlessness, anorexia, and fatigue. Some patients suffer from bipolar depression, a state in which one oscillates between profound depression and mania. During the manic phase, the patient experiences essentially all of the feelings that are the opposite of depression. They are euphoric, excessively enthusiastic, extremely self-confident, sociable, and may even be subject to delusions of grandeur.

A clinical entity known as reactive or endogenous depression is a mood of sadness which overcomes most people for temporary periods during their lives. It is not psychotic in nature and the cause of the depression is usually recognizable. Psychological counseling can be effective therapy for reactive depression. However, the medications that are useful for functional depression (of complex or unknown cause) are not indicated for reactive depression. Those medications, to be discussed in this chapter, include tricyclic and newer antidepressants, and monoamine oxidase inhibitors.

AMINE THEORY OF DEPRESSION

In 1965 it was suggested that functional depression might be related to some imbalance of neurotransmitters within the brain (Figure 23.4). The evidence for this theory arose from several quarters. Reserpine, for example, is a chemical that induces severe depression and also depletes CNS stores of serotonin and norepinephrine. Second, available antidepressant drugs were known to potentiate the neurotransmitter activity of serotonin and norepinephrine. Third, some individuals with genetic predisposition toward depression also have hypofunctioning in respect to serotonin and norepinephrine release. Last, actual correlations were noted between increases in mood and increases in drug-induced release of these neurotransmitters. It seems, therefore, that some compelling evidence, as just described, supported the amine theory of depression. Problems and inconsistencies remain. One of these is that administration

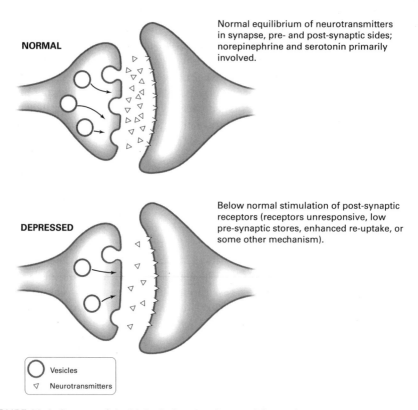

NORMAL

Normal equilibrium of neurotransmitters in synapse, pre- and post-synaptic sides; norepinephrine and serotonin primarily involved.

DEPRESSED

Below normal stimulation of post-synaptic receptors (receptors unresponsive, low pre-synaptic stores, enhanced re-uptake, or some other mechanism).

○ Vesicles
▽ Neurotransmitters

FIGURE 23.4 Cartoon of the biological amine theory of depression.

of antidepressants causes an almost immediate response in neurotransmitter levels whereas a patient will not experience relief of depression for several weeks. It is also puzzling that cocaine and amphetamine increase the levels of biological amines without having any antidepressant action (however great their euphoric potential).

It appears that the role of serotonin and norepinephrine levels in depression is beyond controversy. The exact nature of this interaction, however, is yet to be fully understood.

THERAPY FOR DEPRESSIVE ILLNESS

The major pharmaceutical means for treatment of depression consist of the following: tricyclic antidepressants, second-generation cyclic antidepressants, third-generation antidepressants (selective serotonin reuptake inhibitors), and monoamine oxidase inhibitors.

Tricyclic Antidepressants (TCA)

These compounds have a structure containing a 3-ring core (Figure 23.5). They can be effective in relieving depression and have been shown to block the reuptake of norepinephrine and serotonin into presynaptic terminals. Drawbacks include their

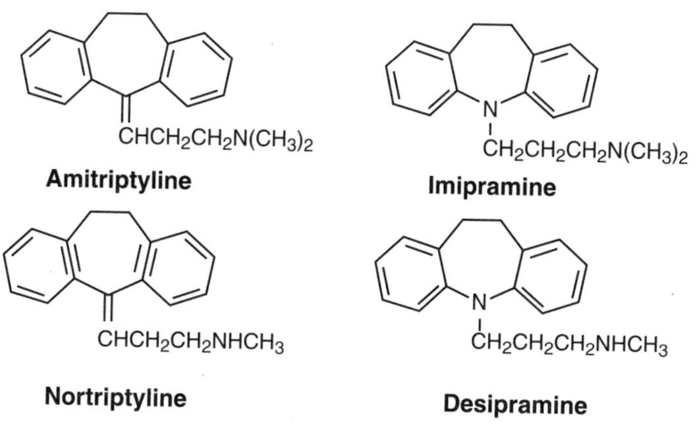

FIGURE 23.5 Some first-generation tricyclic antidepressants.

very slow onset of action, failure to be therapeutically effective in some patients, troublesome side effects, and severe toxicity in overdose. Somewhat surprisingly, these drugs relieve depression in the sick but do not produce euphoria in the healthy. Therefore, they have no abuse potential.

Toxicity

Even at therapeutic levels, the TCAs cause anticholinergic reactions such as hypotension, dry mouth, and blurred vision. Drowsiness, confusion, and motor incoordination are also commonly noted. In many patients profound sedation is experienced. Orthostatic hypotension, in which the patient experiences dizziness when rising from a recumbent position, occurs. This is due to a drop in blood pressure. TCAs have a very significant cardiotoxicity. They depress the heart but also cause cardiac arrhythmias. Characteristic of these arrhythmias is that they lead to ventricular fibrillation, and possible cardiac arrest and death. They are extremely difficult to treat.

TCAs are recognized as very toxic drugs and a quick review of the data provided in Chapter 1 shows that they are listed second, behind analgesics, as the group of drugs associated with the most deaths. Their reputation for toxicity is due to two factors. In the first place, they are inherently dangerous with a wide range of toxic reactions. A second and important additional factor is that they are used to treat many patients who are disposed toward suicide.

In addition to their own toxicity, TCAs have dangerous interactions with other drugs. In particular, they potentiate the effect of alcohol. Many cases are on record of victims of alcohol plus TCAs who died from respiratory depression. In some of these cases the amounts of alcohol consumed were not high. Other drug interactions, such as with medications for high blood pressure, arthritis, or epilepsy, also occur and have dangerous consequences.

Laboratory Testing

There are two situations in which testing for TCAs might be desirable. The first is therapeutic drug monitoring and the second is evaluating a symptomatic patient for possible overdose with TCAs.

Therapeutic Monitoring

If a drug has significant potential toxicity, as is the case with TCAs, a physician should give the minimum dose that will control a patient's symptoms. Accordingly, many physicians will start with a small dose and increase it until the patient receives adequate relief. The problem with TCAs is that several weeks pass before patient and doctor can decide that the dose needs to be raised. Several such cycles of progressively raising the dose and waiting for response might be necessary. This is too long a process for realistic usage. An alternative is to give the drug and measure its concentration in blood. If the concentration is within a therapeutic range, then the patient is usually being dosed in the best manner. Therapeutic ranges are as follows:

Drug	Dose
Nortriptyline	50–150 ng/mL
Imipramine + desipramine	150–300 ng/mL
Amitriptyline + nortriptyline	100–250 ng/mL
Doxepin	Mean approx. 110 ng/mL

If the patient is below the therapeutic range, then a higher dose must be prescribed. This system is useful although the correlation between blood level and clinical effect is not perfect and some patients are toxic within the therapeutic range. Others require a blood level above the therapeutic range for relief of symptoms. It also is noteworthy that patients receiving imipramine or amitriptyline must be measured for two drugs: the one given and the second, which is an active metabolite of the first. For example, patients receiving imipramine convert it to desipramine, a metabolite that also has antidepressant actions. Having two drugs in the blood (drug + metabolite) complicates matters and makes interpretation of concentrations more difficult. As a result, many psychiatrists will prescribe nortriptyline, the metabolite of amitriptyline, and a drug available by itself for treatment of depression. A final point about therapeutic monitoring of TCAs is that the absolute concentrations being measured are quite low, well below 1 mcg/mL. This limits the number of methods that can be used for this purpose because many analytic methods have detection limits that are too high. Furthermore, if immunoassays are used, they cannot adequately distinguish among the closely related structures of the TCA group.

Testing for Suspected Overdose

Many physicians will order testing for TCAs if overdose is suspected. For example, urine screens may be performed to see if TCAs are in the urine. This has limited clinical value because the amount in the urine is poorly correlated with the amount of drug present at receptor sites where the toxic effects are occurring. In addition, someone using the drug therapeutically will be positive by a urine test even though he has not had an overdose and his symptoms may be due to some other toxin. Blood levels may also be measured in the context of possible TCA overdose. Many physicians think that severe overdose can be detected on the basis of high concentrations of TCA in the blood. This is sometimes mistaken. Blood level may be low in a severe poisoning and vice versa. It also has been shown that patients presenting

TABLE 23.2
Chromatographic Separation of TCAs on HP-5 Columns

Compound, TFA-tricyclic	Retention Time (mins)	Major Ions
Amitriptyline	10.12	58
Doxepin	10.20	58
Imipramine	10.27	234, 58
Nortriptyline	11.04	232
Desipramine	11.19	208
Protriptyline	11.20	191

to emergency departments with TCA overdose could be reliably evaluated on the basis of altered mental status, seizures, arrhythmias, and ECG findings. Blood levels are not necessary.

Measurement of TCAs for therapeutic monitoring usually is done by gas or liquid chromatography. It is not easy to separate these compounds because of their very similar molecular structures and resulting similarity of chromatographic mobility. If GC-MS is used, one can take advantage of the different ions which are formed. Table 23.2 comes from a GC-MS method used for testing TCAs. In this method a relatively nonpolar column is used and the tricyclic antidepressants are converted to their trifluoroacetyl derivatives by reaction with trifluoroacetic anhydride.

Note that all 6 TCAs emerge from the column over a span of just 1 minute and 8 seconds. Some are very close, e.g., desipramine and protriptyline have virtually the same retention time. They can be distinguished from each other, however, because the monitored ions are distinct. In other words, desipramine does not produce a 191 ion and protriptyline does not make a 208 ion. The method is, nevertheless, challenging and narrow chromatographic peaks must be formed if one is to successfully measure amitriptyline in the presence of doxepin by use of the same 58 ion.

Second-Generation Antidepressants

Because of the widely recognized toxicity associated with TCAs, extensive pharmaceutical research was conducted to find better and safer antidepressants. A group of compounds were introduced that included amoxapine, trazodone, nomifensin, and maprotiline. They were represented as being of greater safety and were called second-generation antidepressants (Figure 23.6).

Toxicity

Early optimism about the alleged safety of the second-generation drugs eventually gave way to recognition that their true safety was probably not significantly different from that of the TCAs. When toxic characteristics were studied, no differences were found in the CNS depression or the cardiotoxicity of the first- vs. second-generation antidepressants. Some studies even contended that the second-generation compounds caused more fatalities and had a wider range of adverse reactions. Toxic effects

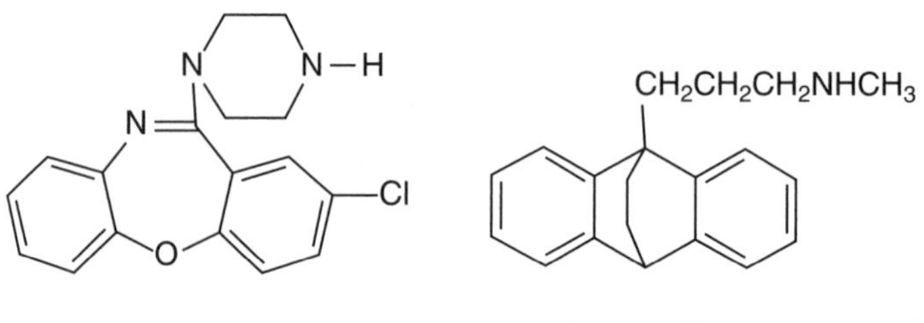

Amoxapine   Maprotiline

FIGURE 23.6 Maprotiline and amoxapine, representative second-generation antidepressants.

Fluoxetine (Prozac)   Sertraline (Zoloft)

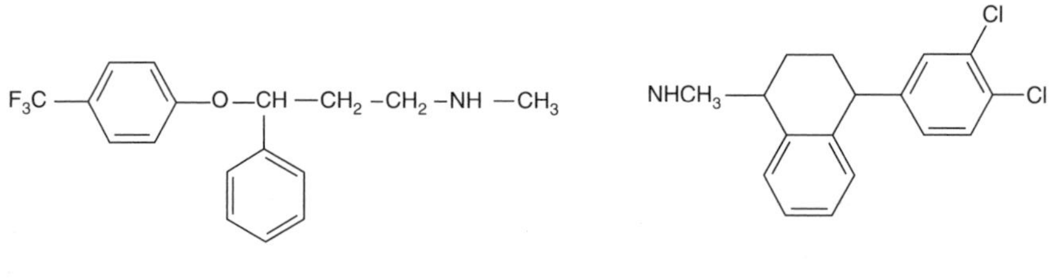

FIGURE 23.7 Representative third-generation antidepressants.

reported for the second generation included hypotension, drowsiness, constipation, fatigue, vertigo, arrhythmias, renal failure, coma, and rhabdomyolysis. Many psychiatrists used these drugs extensively when they were first introduced but eventually prescribed them less frequently as it became clear that they did not satisfactorily address safety issues raised by the first-generation TCAs. Only minor improvements are now thought to exist. As an example, amoxapine has a lower sedating effect and less anticholinergic action than TCAs. The safety issue was not resolved and so the search continued for better drugs.

Third-Generation Antidepressants

Two members of this class are fluoxetine (Prozac) and sertraline (Zoloft) (Figure 23.7). The former has become well-known in the public mind and has been the object of much discussion in the popular press. Prozac was released in the late 1980s and was classified as the first of a set of compounds known as SSRIs, selective serotonin reuptake inhibitors. Fluoxetine and sertraline are the most widely prescribed antidepressants by a wide margin, although fluoxetine tends to be employed for less severe depression. They are much more expensive than the TCAs (as much as 30 times greater cost per tablet) but it has been argued that overall healthcare costs associated with their use actually may be lower because they have so many fewer toxic effects. The SSRIs are serotonin selective but, despite their inactivity toward norepinephrine, they still function as antidepressants. It is believed that their lack of activity toward norepinephrine is responsible for their safety and, in particular, the absence of cardiovascular toxicity.

Toxicity

Adverse reactions with fluoxetine include nervousness, anxiety, motor agitation, and sexual dysfunction. In very severe overdose, coma, tachycardia, and cardiac arrhythmias have been reported. These signs are also found in TCA overdose but a much larger ingestion of fluoxetine usually is required to cause an equal degree of toxicity. Blood levels of fluoxetine found in overdose cases are very high if significant symptoms are present. It clearly has a much wider margin of safety than TCAs.

Sertraline also is at least as safe as fluoxetine. One study of patients treated for sertraline overdose in emergency departments showed that 25% of such patients had no symptoms whatever. Patients who consumed 160 times the therapeutic dose had minor presenting symptoms. Some patients manifested the serotonin syndrome. This is a recognizable set of symptoms found with serotonin hyperactivity and includes tachycardia, hypertension, hyperthermia, tremors, skin flushing, and, in severe cases, coma.

Monoamine Oxidase Inhibitors (MAOI)

As the reader will recall, the amine theory of depression states that depression is essentially due to a depletion of specific neurotransmitters, especially norepinephrine and serotonin. Tricyclic, and other antidepressants, work by rebuilding stores of these compounds. It was observed in 1952 that iproniazid, administered to patients for tuberculosis, was an effective antibacterial but also had mood-elevating effects in patients. Biochemical studies then showed that it was also an inhibitor of monoamine oxidase. Eventually, it was recognized that iproniazid's ability to inhibit monoamine oxidase may be the reason that it elevates mood. When amine breakdown is delayed, amine stores will increase. Because the neurotransmitters related to depression are amines metabolized, in part, by monoamine oxidase, inhibition of this enzyme should help cure depression. This theory proved to be correct and enzyme inhibitors have had some therapeutic potential in depression.

A first generation of MAOIs were designed and employed for a short time. They were problematic because their efficacy was poor for severe depression. In addition, they caused serious drug interactions with some other medications that also depended on monoamine oxidase for clearance. Some foods were also a problem, especially cheeses. Vasoactive amines present in cheese, especially tyramine, would not be cleared from the blood after ingestion of cheese and they provoked dangerous increases in blood pressure. A number of deaths occurred in patients who used these drugs and also ate cheeses. As a result, use of the first-generation compounds was soon discontinued.

Further biochemical research led to a key discovery; namely, two subgroups of monoamine oxidase, types A and B, exist. MAO-A is found in norepinephrine and serotonin nerve terminals of the brain and several other organs. MAO-B is found in neurons (usually dopamine secreting) in the brain and in blood platelets. Importantly, the older MAO inhibitors are irreversible and nonselective and inhibit both A and B forms of MAO (Figure 23.8). Because MAO-A is mainly responsible for the

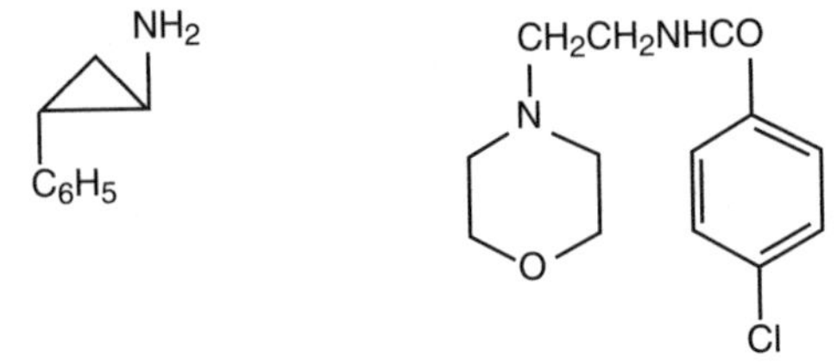

Tranylcypromine   **Moclobemide**

FIGURE 23.8 Tranylcypromine (early MAOI) and moclobemide (selective MAOI).

antidepressant activity whereas MAO-B causes most of the unwanted effects, an agent selective toward A only would be very desirable. Such agents are now available, one of the foremost being moclobemide. It is a short-acting, selective, reversible inhibitor of MAO-A.

Toxicity

Newer MAOI are less toxic than the first-generation compounds, but their overall toxicity is still described as being significant. This is partly due to the fact that they are not 100% specific for monoamine oxidase but also inhibit some other, necessary enzymes. They also delay the metabolism of potential toxins such as barbiturates, alcohol, cocaine, and anticholinergics.

Their major toxicity, however, continues to be hypertension. Natural catecholamines are hypertensive and their levels are elevated during therapy with these compounds. Cardiovascular abnormalities and liver disease also have been observed. A unique problem which occurs with MAOI is a severe withdrawal syndrome, which often includes hypertensive crises and orthostatic hypotension.

ANTIPSYCHOTIC DRUGS

TERMINOLOGY

The term psychosis refers to an impaired ability to recognize reality. It is characterized by behavioral aberrations, i.e., incoherent thinking, delusions, and hallucinations. Often, psychoses are divided into brain syndromes (e.g., drug intoxication), affective disorders such as depression, and schizophrenia. Many terms have been used to refer to drugs that have some effect in psychoses. Major tranquilizer is one such inexact term. In this context, major is contrasted with minor which stands for those agents that merely relieve anxiety. Antischizophrenic or neuroleptic are other terms employed to describe agents with antipsychotic action. The best term appears to be antipsychotic because it best approximates the actual purpose of these agents, although it has the disadvantage of lacking any more specific pharmaceutical reference.

HISTORY

Schizophrenia has presumably been with us since the dawn of human life on Earth. Bizarre methods of treating it constitute a sad and notorious history that lasted until

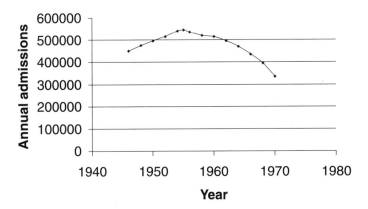

FIGURE 23.9 Trends in admission of patients to psychiatric care facilities.

the middle of the twentieth century. In 1956 a remarkable transformation occurred. Effective drug therapy for psychosis was first introduced and, with it, a reversal in a previously well-established trend. Figure 23.9 shows the increase in the number of institutionalized psychiatric patients during the years before 1956 and the unanticipated decline after that time. Such was the impact of drug therapy with antipsychotics that most mental patients could be treated on an outpatient basis. Study of this figure also shows that the incidence of schizophrenia in the general population is 0.5 to 1%. In a country the size of the United States this equals about 1.5 to 3 million affected individuals, a staggering national problem.

Antipsychotics were discovered when a French surgeon introduced promethazine into anesthetic practice to deepen surgical anesthesia. In 1952 a second member of this drug class, the phenothiazines (Figure 23.10), was added to presurgical medications to reduce the anxiety associated with an impending operation. This drug was chlorpromazine and it was noted quickly that chlorpromazine profoundly altered the patient's mental awareness. Patients receiving this drug became quiet, sedated, and very uninterested in their surroundings. The traits they demonstrated are known as neuroleptic behavior and the drugs causing the state sometimes are referred to as neuroleptics.

Given the reaction of the presurgical patients, chlorpromazine was tried in patients with mental illness. It was found to be effective in ameliorating schizophrenic episodes and preventing relapses. Subsequent research produced a large class of similar compounds with variable potencies and small differences in the specific toxicity associated with each.

MECHANISM OF PSYCHOSIS

Many theories exist to explain schizophrenia but the leading hypothesis is the dopamine theory. Simply stated, the dopamine theory asserts that antipsychotic medicines antagonize the actions of dopamine and are effective for this reason. Schizophrenia, in turn, is due to functional overactivity of dopamine or an increased sensitivity of dopamine receptors in selected neuronal pathways. Evidence for this theory includes the fact that drugs which block dopamine receptors are clinically useful in a dose-related manner in treatment of schizophrenia. Furthermore, it has been shown that schizophrenic persons have more dopamine-binding sites than normal.

Side Effects

Phenothiazine antipsychotics have very substantial side effects found in a high number of patients who use them. This is because they block all dopamine receptors and dopamine is involved in numerous pathways in the brain. Specific effects include

Acute dystonia	Facial, neck, and back spasms
Parkinsonism	Limb rigidity, shuffling gait, slow movement
Akathisia	Motor restlessness
Tardive dyskinesia	Involuntary movements of the face, trunk, and extremities

These effects are collectively termed extrapyramidal symptoms. They arise when dopaminergic receptors in the striatum within the basal ganglia of the brain are blocked by phenothiazine drugs. Such symptoms become much more severe in overdose situations.

Toxicity

Autonomic Nervous System

The antipsychotic class of drugs has potent anticholinergic activity and alpha-adrenergic blocking activity. The anticholinergic actions, symptoms of which have been described above, are variable among the phenothiazines. Thioridazine is one of the strongest in this regard whereas haloperidol, a butyrophenone type of compound, is one of the weakest anticholinergics. The alpha-adrenergic blocking effects are manifested by a number of symptoms, with orthostatic hypotension and reflex tachycardia among the most significant. Reflex tachycardia is an increase in heart rate in response to the perception of a drop in blood pressure.

Cardiovascular

Reflex tachycardia has already been mentioned as a cardiovascular effect. In addition, antipsychotic drugs have an action which is similar to that of quinidine, a cardiac drug. This quinidine-like effect decreases atrio-ventricular nodal conduction causing heart block and ventricular arrhythmias. There may be numerous abnormalities in the electrocardiogram. When patients die from phenothiazine overdose, ventricular fibrillation or cardiac arrest is the usual cause. These deaths can be very sudden and in close proximity to the time of dosing with the drug.

Central Nervous System

All levels of the CNS are involved in phenothiazine overdose, again because of the widespread distribution of dopamine receptors in the CNS. Antipsychotics depress the reticular activating system (RAS), the part of the CNS which controls wakefulness. Depression of the RAS, therefore, provokes a sedation reaction.

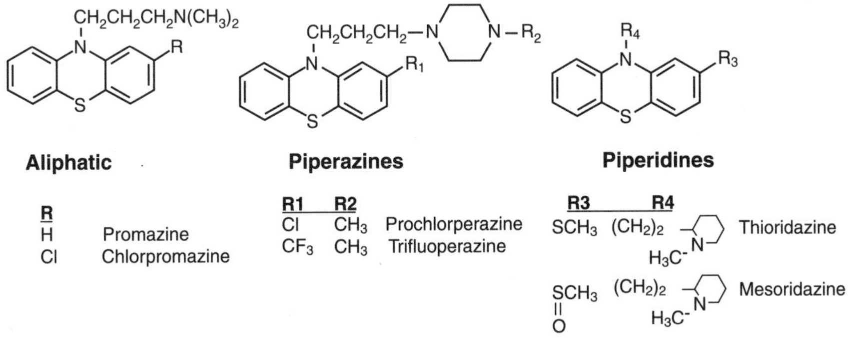

FIGURE 23.10 Structural features of the classes of antipsychotic drugs.

TABLE 23.3
Summary of Phenothiazine Toxicity in Relation to the Three Most Affected Areas

Central Nervous System	Extrapyramidal Symptoms	Autonomic Nerve System
Sedation	Dystonia	Miosis
Ataxia	Akinesia	Constipation
Slurred speech	Hypersalivation	Blurring of vision
Coma	Tardive dyskinesia	Urinary retention
Possible seizures	Spasm of larynx	ECG abnormalities
		Hypotension
		Renal failure

Coma may occur from overdose, especially in children. Unlike the coma of barbiturates, the patient is more likely to exhibit tremor, spasms, and dystonic reactions. Other effects on the CNS sometimes observed in overdose with antipsychotics are respiratory depression, vasomotor depression (leading to hypotension through vasodilatation), and impairment of temperature regulation. Hypo- or hyperthermia may result and there are cases in which either has been fatal (Table 23.3).

TREATMENT OF OVERDOSE

An unusual aspect of antipsychotic drugs is that they are prescribed in widely variable doses. Patients take chlorpromazine in doses ranging from 25 to 5000 mg/day and haloperidol from 0.5 to 30 mg/day. Toxic and lethal doses are also very variable. Published case studies refer to fatalities that apparently resulted from as little as 1.4 g of chlorpromazine. Note that this is less than the daily dose taken by some patients.

As with any overdose, stabilization of vital signs is the first step taken in therapy. Supporting blood pressure may need to be the first vital sign to be stabilized. Fluids are provided and norepinephrine or dopamine may be needed. If arrhythmias are present, lidocaine or phenytoin is usually helpful. Phenytoin is also beneficial in treating seizures, a common finding in phenothiazine overdose. The anticholinergic reaction, which is usually substantial with many phenothiazines, can be treated with physostigmine. This antidote is discussed in greater depth above.

LABORATORY TESTING

It is not a customary practice to measure serum concentration of antipsychotic medications as a means of improving the therapy of patients taking these drugs. One reason is lack of a good correlation between such levels and patient response.

It is also not valuable to measure antipsychotic levels as a means for assessing severity of overdose. Many clinical indications provide a better index of the degree of poisoning. No one has shown, for example, that therapeutic measures for responding to these poisonings may be guided by serum concentrations of antipsychotic drugs.

Simple urine tests are available which will alert a physician that phenothiazines are present in the urine and may be a contributor to the clinical picture that his/her patient is presenting. The Forrest test is one such urine test used to screen for phenothiazines. Mix 5% ferric chloride, 20% perchloric acid, and 50% nitric acid in proportions of 5:45:150. Add 1 mL of this reagent to 10 mL of a urine specimen or mix smaller amounts in the same proportions. Shake gently and check the color against a positive control. Phenistix™, a urine-testing product of the Ames Company, may also be used for this test.

Questions

1. Describe the symptoms found in anticholinergic overdose. What additional symptoms are found in phenothiazine toxicity and why do these compounds (phenothiazines) have the other toxic properties in addition to anticholinergic activity?
2. Why are antihistamines active as sedating agents? What is the characteristic of the most recent antihistamines that reduces their sedative properties?
3. Describe antidotes that have activity against anticholinergic agents. Under what clinical circumstances should such antidotes be employed?
4. Compare and contrast the first- and third-generation antidepressants. Why are the most recently introduced less toxic?
5. Discuss laboratory measurement of antidepressant concentration. What methods are most commonly employed? Under what clinical conditions should these tests be ordered?
6. Describe the theory of tricyclic antidepressant action and contrast it with the theoretical basis for the action of monoamine oxidase inhibitors.

Case Study 1: Fits and Starts

The patient, a 67-year-old woman in a coma and with occasional seizures, was brought to the emergency department. Her pulse was elevated and temperature also was raised at 39.3°C. Blood pressure was low at 60/35. She was a known schizophrenic whose dose of antipsychotic medication had been recently increased due to an adverse change in her symptoms of psychosis. She was experiencing more hallucinations and confusion. On admission her laboratory results were as follows:

Hemoglobin	9 g/dL
Sodium	151 mmol/L
Potassium	4.7 mmol/L
Urea	27.6 mmol/L
Creatinine	287 μmol/L
CK	11,200 U/L
LD	929 U/L

Arterial blood gases showed a metabolic acidosis: pH = 7.15; pCO_2 = 2.57 KPa; pO_2 = 14.9 KPa; HCO_3 = 6.9 mmol/L.

If these symptoms are due to the patient's medication, a probable causative
   drug is
   a) Fluoxetine
   b) Imipramine
   c) Lithium
   d) Trifluoperazine

All of the drug choices are psychoactive medications. The first three, however, are used primarily in depression. Moreover, overdose of any of these antidepressants is not manifested by the symptoms shown by this patient. Trifluoperazine is an antipsychotic commonly provided to schizophrenic patients. Excessive dosing, especially in the presence of certain predisposing factors, can cause this syndrome. Those risk factors include physical exhaustion, dehydration, and concurrent organic brain disease.

The patient's antipsychotic medications were immediately discontinued. She was treated with dantrolene to reduce muscle spasm and fever. Fluid replacement and bicarbonate were provided to correct electrolyte abnormalites and acid-base imbalance. Diazepam was given to control seizure activity. She was intubated, placed on a ventilator, and transferred to the Intensive Care Unit. After 5 days of generally supportive care she returned to her normal status and was discharged.

Questions

Q1. This patient manifested a well-known complication of phenothiazines called
   a) Cholinergic crisis
   b) Neuroleptic malignant syndrome
   c) Serotonin syndrome
   d) Steroid hypersensitivity

Q2. Why is her creatine kinase elevated?
   a) Due to hyperthyroidism.
   b) Specific damage to myocardium.
   c) Hypertonicity of skeletal muscle is part of the syndrome.
   d) Direct muscle damage by a myopathic toxic factor.
Q3. Why are her urea and creatinine abnormally high?
   a) Muscle damage
   b) Dehydration
   c) Drug-induced liver disease
   d) Cardiac damage
Q4. What is the mainstay of therapy?
   a) Discontinuation of the drug
   b) Muscle relaxants
   c) IV fluids
   d) All of the above

Answers and Discussion

Q1. (Answer = b) Neuroleptic malignant syndrome is a constellation of symptoms including high temperature, skeletal muscle spasms, autonomic nervous system dysfunction, and partial coma. Cholinergic crisis is not seen
because phenothiazines are anticholinergic. The other suggested choices
for this question are not feasible.

Q2. (Answer = c) Prolonged muscle spasms deprive the muscle tissue of
adequate oxygen and other nutrients. The resulting myocyte necrosis leads
to release of creatine kinase and other chemicals from myocytes into the
circulation. Hyperthyroidism, when it occurs, is associated with depressed
creatine kinase, not elevated amounts.

Q3. (Answer = b) Dehydration, caused by the elevated body temperature,
would be expected to raise creatinine and especially urea. Muscle damage
is also likely to be a contributing factor to the creatinine elevation. Liver
function abnormalities may be present in neuroleptic malignant syndrome
but they are not manifested by urea or creatinine elevations.

Q4. (Answer = d) All of the suggested answers are correct. IV fluids and
muscle relaxants will diminish the severity of symptoms in this disorder.
Antipyretic (fever-reducing) agents are also helpful. The critical component of therapy, however, is recognition and discontinuation of the offending agent, the phenothiazine drug.

Reference

Kausar, S.A. et al., Fits and starts, *Postgrad. Med. J.,* 74, 687–688, 1998.

Case Study 2: The Little Girl who Fibbed

A 4-year-old girl was admitted to a community hospital emergency department 4 hours after a suspected ingestion of her father's pills. The bottle had contained 35 pills, 20 mg each, which were now missing and could not be found any place else in the house. Nevertheless, the little girl steadfastly denied taking the pills. In spite of her denials she started acting with profound anxiety and displayed abnormal jerking movements 3 hours after the start of the missing pill incident. She then underwent a spell of unresponsiveness during which she appeared unable to recognize verbal or tactile stimuli. This prompted her parents to rush her to the emergency department. On arrival, her vital signs included an elevated pulse rate and mild hypotension. She continued to manifest moderate psychomotor agitation with dyskinetic, erratic jerking motions. A comprehensive laboratory work-up including chemistry, hematology, and urinalysis gave results all within normal limits. Chest roentgenogram was normal and ECG showed a sinus tachycardia.

The child was treated with 30 g of activated charcoal through an NG tube. She vomited profusely and capsule fragments were noted in the vomitus.

What was the probable nature of the pills which the child ingested?
 a) Amitriptyline
 b) Digoxin
 c) Fluoxetine
 d) Aspirin

Although the clinical picture is not completely clear, it suggests a medication which is relatively benign when taken in overdose. The history implies strongly that the child ingested all 35 tablets, and fluoxetine is the only one of these choices which, when taken in that amount, could conceivably produce such mild effects. In fact, even a relatively safe drug like fluoxetine would be expected to cause more serious symptoms than those displayed by this patient because of the number of capsules and the age and size (36 lbs.) of the child.

Over the following 24 hours the child improved and cooperated well with the nursing staff and other caregivers. She manifested a mild tremor and a slight dyskinesia but no other findings. Her heart rate was elevated for approximately 4 days and, on the 4th day of hospitalization, she was discharged. Some time later her mother was contacted for follow-up. She reported that her daughter had continued to appear "hyped up" for about 2 weeks after the exposure to fluoxetine and then returned to normal. The little girl continued to deny any role in the loss of her father's pills.

Questions

Q1. The volume of distribution for fluoxetine is variously reported as 11 to 88 L/kg. What is Vd in this child if a blood specimen collected at admission gave a fluoxetine level of 3080 ng/mL?
 a) 8 L/kg
 b) 14 L/kg

      c) 80 L/kg

      d) 231 L/kg

Q2. What is the proposed mechanism of action of fluoxetine and similar drugs?

      a) Dopamine inhibition

      b) Selective serotonin reuptake inhibition

      c) Inactivation of cholinesterase

      d) Depletion of norepinephrine

Q3. What is one reason for the greater popularity of fluoxetine vs. tricyclic antidepressants?

      a) Greater safety of the former

      b) Higher cost for tricyclics

      c) More gradual onset of action by fluoxetine

      d) Ability to give fluoxetine orally vs. need to dispense tricyclic antidepressants intravenously

Q4. Which is <u>not</u> true regarding treatment of fluoxetine overdose?

      a) Hemodialysis is not likely to be of benefit.

      b) General supportive care is the mainstay of treatment.

      c) Occasional seizures are observed and diazepam is helpful when this happens.

      d) Calcium gluconate has antidotal properties in this situation.

Answers and Discussion

Q1. (Answer = b) The child's weight equals 16.3 kg. She ingested 35 capsules $\times$ 20 mg/capsule = 700 mg. Her fluoxetine blood level on the admission specimen was 3080 ng/mL (3.08 µg/mL = 3.08 mg/L = 3080 ng/mL).

$$Vd = 700 \text{ mg}/3.08 \text{ mg/L}$$

$$= 227 \text{ L}/16.3 \text{ kg} = 13.9 \text{ L/kg}$$

Q2. (Answer = b) Fluoxetine (Prozac), sertraline (Zoloft), and several other newer antidepressants are classed as SSRIs, i.e., selective serotonin reuptake inhibitors. They act fairly specifically to block serotonin uptake and have minimal action on other neurotransmitters.

Q3. (Answer = a) A very clear edge goes to SSRIs vs. tricyclic antidepressants. There are many reported tricyclic antidepressant fatalities vs. numerous SSRI overdoses with mild outcome. In fact, data from Poison Control Centers show that tricyclic antidepressants ranked first in number of fatalities as a percent of overdoses. Fluoxetine is many times the cost of tricyclic antidepressants for purchase, but some studies find that they are effectively cheaper because their use is associated with such a relatively low cost for treatment of overdoses. Both drugs have a slow onset of pharmacological activity and both are taken orally.

Q4. (Answer = d) The drug manufacturer states that hemodialysis is not beneficial for treatment of fluoxetine overdose. This would be expected in view of the high volume of distribution of fluoxetine. Supportive care (airway maintenance, supplemental oxygen, and ventilatory support) with cardiac monitoring is often the only therapy needed. Diazepam has been employed successfully when seizures were observed. Neither calcium gluconate nor any other compound is known to possess antidotal properties for fluoxetine overdose.

Reference

Feierabend, R., Benign course in a child with massive fluoxetine overdose, *J. Fam. Pract.,* 41, 289–291, 1995.

Case Study 3: A Patient with Cardiac Abnormalities

A 35-year-old woman who was suffering from depression and was in a coma was brought to an emergency department. She had been on several medications for this illness prior to this hospitalization. Her vital signs included elevated pulse, mild hypotension, and hypothermia at 32°C. She was intubated for hypoxemia. Electrocardiogram was significant for sinus tachycardia, enlarged QRS interval, and markedly prolonged QT interval. Her creatine kinase was elevated at 2780 U/L (normal < 250 U/L). The MB fraction of creatine kinase, the isoenzyme of cardiac origin, was less than 10 U/L. Her stomach was lavaged and charcoal was administered. She went on to show ventricular tachycardia with severe hypotension. For this she was defibrillated. Over the next 36 hours she demonstrated recurrent ventricular tachycardia with hypotension. These did not respond to lidocaine nor bicarbonate but did respond to frequent cardioversion. Over the following 5 days she gradually improved and could be removed from mechanical ventilation on her 7th day of hospitalization.

Which of the following drugs might be implicated in her disorder?
a) Thioridazine
b) Fluoxetine
c) Amitriptyline
d) Salicylates

This lady eventually admitted ingesting 1000 mg of thioridazine. This is a phenothiazine class drug which has antipsychotic ability and has been used to treat psychosis and depression. The major aspect of its toxicity is usually cardiovascular with the patient having refractory arrhythmias as in the case described here. Fluoxetine (Prozac) is an antidepressant that is usually quite mild in overdose. Amitriptyline is a tricyclic antidepressant structurally similar to thioridazine and could cause the symptoms described here. Typically, the tricyclics cause a more complex picture than the one described although they could not absolutely be ruled out without additional information from history or the laboratory.

Questions

Q1. What is a therapeutic dose of thioridazine?
a) 2 mg/day
b) Up to 800 mg/day
c) Less than 100 mg/day
d) One gram, TID

Q2. What causes thioridazine toxicity?
a) Anticholinergic effects
b) Sodium-channel effects (quinidine-like)
c) Beta-adrenergic receptor blocking effect
d) All of the above
e) None of the above

Q3. What is the significance of this patient's MB fraction < 10 U/L?
a) The patient has severe heart disease.
b) MB is an isoenzyme of creatine kinase which relates to liver disease.
c) Creatine kinase is probably from skeletal muscle and not from heart.
d) The MB fraction is significantly elevated when the patient has experienced a CNS bleed.

Q4. Which is not likely to be beneficial in treatment of thioridazine overdose?
a) GI decontamination and charcoal
b) Cardiac pacing and DC defibrillation
c) Physostigmine
d) Hemoperfusion

Answers and Discussion

Q1. (Answer = b) In adults the maximum recommended therapeutic dose is 800 mg/day of thioridazine. Remarkably, this patient suffered severe disease from just 1 g (1000 mg). However, cases of fatalities have been reported from even less (900 mg in one report).[1] Conversely, other cases in which patients survived as much as 16,000 mg have been reported.[2] In general, coma and cardiac arrhythmias are usually associated with doses greater than 2 g of thioridazine.[3] All of these case reports highlight the great variability associated with reactions to this drug and the difficulty of treating depressed patients with the appropriate amount of drug.

Q2. (Answer = d) Thioridazine causes multiple pharmacological effects. Usually, the anticholinergic effects are seen first. Subsequently, beta-adrenergic, sodium-channel blocking, and calcium-channel blocking properties exert themselves. The clinical symptoms resulting from these multiple pharmacological properties are sedation, Parkinsonian symptoms, and tardive dyskinesia in the CNS. Anticholinergic reactions are also noted.

Q3. (Answer = c) Thioridazine may cause both cardiac and muscle toxicity among a wide constellation of other findings. The enzyme, creatine kinase, is elevated whenever muscle damage occurs. One specific isoenzyme, creatine kinase MB, is especially concentrated in cardiac muscle tissue. Therefore, the elevation of MB in the blood is a sign of cardiac involvement. MB must be greater than 3% of total creatine kinase to indicate heart damage rather than skeletal muscle. We can conclude in this case that this small amount of MB suggests that there is no myocardial necrosis. On the other hand, there is probably significant muscle damage and the cause of this damage is myoclonus.

Q4. (Answer = c) Efforts to decontaminate this patient are worthwhile and should be attempted. Some of the toxin may be removed if time of ingestion was sufficiently recent. Hemoperfusion may be helpful but is not commonly practiced in most centers. Cardiac pacing is said to be the most effective treatment for thioridazine overdose in patients with ventricular tachycardia. It increases the baseline heart rate and stabilizes conduction. Physostigmine is an anticholinergic antagonist and may be helpful in reducing the anticholinergic aspects of toxicity. However, it has many side effects and is difficult to control, so its application should be limited in this context.

References

1. Le Blaye, I. et al., Acute overdosage with thioridazine: a review of the available clinical exposure, *Vet. Hum. Toxicol.,* 35, 147–150, 1993.
2. Schmidt, W. and Lang, K., Life-threatening dysrhythmias in severe thioridazine poisoning treated with physostigmine and transient atrial pacing, *Crit. Care Med.,* 25, 1925–1930, 1997.
3. Annane, D., Near fatal case of self-poisoning with thioridazine, *Inten. Care Med.,* 22, 1463–1464, 1996.

Case Study 4: Delayed Catastrophe

A 38-year-old woman was brought to the emergency department at 9 p.m. by her mother, who stated that her daughter had taken 25 of the mother's antidepressant tablets 2 hours earlier. The patient was alert with only slight abnormalities in vital signs. These included pulse of 125 per minute and respirations at 28 per minute. Bowel sounds were hypoactive. ECG showed a sinus tachycardia and QRS duration of 0.10 seconds. Ipecac was given by mouth and emesis contained some pill fragments. The patient was closely observed for the next 6 hours in the emergency department. During this time she slowly improved and was awake and alert and able to walk unassisted to the bathroom. She was then (3:30 a.m.) transferred to the psychiatric emergency department for further evaluation. All vital signs were now approximately normal. At 5 a.m. a psychiatrist examined her and noted that her speech was slurred, her gait unsteady, and she was fearful, agitated, and hallucinating. During the following 2 hours her vital signs collapsed with respirations becoming labored, blood pressure dropping precipitously, and pulse becoming irregular. Despite efforts at cardiac resuscitation, she died at 6 a.m., 11 hours after ingestion of the drug.

What was the drug which caused this woman's death?
   a) Desipramine
   b) Acetaminophen
   c) Fluoxetine (Prozac)
   d) Digoxin

This is a diagnostic dilemma because the patient's presentation is very unusual. An important point is that the drug was identified by the mother as an antidepressant. This allows us to rule out digoxin and acetaminophen as possible causes. They could be ruled out in any case because they are known to produce symptoms at great variance from those seen here. Of the remaining two choices, fluoxetine and desipramine, the former is relatively benign and would be under less suspicion than desipramine, a drug that has caused many deaths. Last, there are a number of case reports in the literature of patients who have improved significantly after a desipramine overdose and then abruptly reversed course with marked increase in symptom severity. Desipramine, a first-generation tricyclic antidepressant, was measured by the laboratory on a specimen drawn 3 hours postdose and again on a postmortem specimen. The first specimen had 20 ng/mL and the postmortem specimen was 8600 ng/mL.

Questions

Q1. What is the expected lethal plasma level of desipramine?
   a) >15 ng/mL
   b) >100 ng/mL
   c) >1000 ng/mL
   d) >10,000 ng/mL
Q2. Why was the first specimen so low for desipramine compared to the postmortem specimen?
   a) Desipramine is known to be absorbed very slowly.
   b) Desipramine takes days to become effective.
   c) There may have been a laboratory error in the first specimen.
   d) In overdose the anticholinergic effects of tricyclic antidepressants slow absorption from the gut.
Q3. How can we rule out a second dose of desipramine while the patient was in the hospital?
   a) Drug unavailable to the patient.
   b) She was under constant observation.
   c) This drug is known to display this kind of behavior.
   d) All of the above.

Q4. Which are common signs of tricyclic antidepressant overdose?
a) Tachycardia
b) Agitation
c) Seizures and coma
d) All of the above
e) None of the above

Answers and Discussion

Q1. (Answer = c) Case reports show that plasma levels greater than 1000 ng/mL have been correlated with seizures, arrhythmias, coma, cardiac arrest, and death. Levels of 20 to 160 ng/mL are within the therapeutic range. Importantly, the levels are very poor predictors of prognosis for several reasons. In the first place, metabolism and half-life are highly variable, with as much as a 40-fold difference found among patients. In addition, free drug concentration varies 5-fold with pH changes that are observed in ill patients. Last, because TCAs have very high volumes of distribution, the fraction of total drug in the blood is small and measurements made in blood are not necessarily predictive of total body burden.

Q2. (Answer = d) Among the toxic effects of tricyclic antidepressants, anticholinergic activity is one of the earliest to occur. This inhibition of nerve transmission across cholinergic synapses includes GI peristalsis. Therefore, it makes sense that the presence of desipramine would slow its own absorption. Desipramine is not absorbed especially slowly except in overdose. It is true that desipramine takes days to weeks before patients note therapeutic benefit from it. This delay in efficacy is not, however, related to any delay in uptake.

Q3. (Answer = d) In view of the dramatic change in this patient's disease course, which occurred after she appeared to be improving, it is logical to suspect that she took a second dose of desipramine. She may have. This was doubted in the published case report because the patient was watched closely and was dressed in a hospital gown in which she could not hide any drugs. Furthermore, there are many similar reports of this type of dramatic downturn in a patient's illness when desipramine was overdosed. It is, therefore, reasonable to believe that all of her symptoms were related to the original dose.

Q4. (Answer = d) The major problem with tricyclic antidepressants is that they are not sufficiently specific. They interfere with many different neurotransmitters. As a consequence, three major organ systems are affected in the event of TCA overdose. These are the autonomic nervous system, central nervous system, and cholinergic neurons. All of the symptoms listed in this question are possible.

Reference

Callaham, M., Admission criteria for tricyclic antidepressant ingestion, *West. J. Med.*, 137, 425–429, 1982.

24 Psychedelic Drugs

CONTENTS

The category of drugs that are thought of as mind expanding are so well-known today and are composed of such a large variety of compounds that they surely deserve a separate section for discussion. Some of them are more commonly taken for euphoria rather than hallucinatory effects. Such drugs are discussed separately under drugs of abuse. Still others are primarily stimulants that have some hallucinatory character. They are also discussed separately, in the chapter on stimulants. Those discussed here are primarily hallucinatory.

Various names have been given to these drugs. They have been called hallucinogens. Although the drugs that are the subject of this chapter can cause hallucinations that term is a bit narrow as a designation for these compounds because they have many other properties. Psychotomimetics is another term used to describe these drugs because they, on some occasions, produce mind states reminiscent of psychotic behavior. Here again, however, the term psychotomimetic is neither entirely accurate nor of sufficient diversity to truly capture the mental states these compounds may create. Psychedelic is a word that was created specifically to describe the behavioral reactions these drugs produce. As a new term it can mean whatever its originator wants. What was intended by it is a concept of agents that alter sensory perception and also have unique mind-expanding properties. Users of these compounds have an enhanced awareness of sensation and a self-perception of clarity although with a decreased control over one's environment. The personality of the user is often divided into two persons. One person is a passive spectator who witnesses the divided persona in the act of receiving the distorted sensory perception. These two parts of one ego are the observer and the participant. The user believes that he is free from the doubts and misperceptions of normal mortals and, during the brief period of drug participation, shares a gift of clarity and insight. At the same time, the psychedelic drug user lacks the ability to make even the simplest distinctions such as that between himself or herself and the outside world. This leads to a false sense of unity with the whole of creation, a false perception of absorption into the cosmos.

CHEMISTRY AND CLASSIFICATION

Most of the psychedelic chemicals resemble neurotransmitters and/or are thought to derive their properties from an ability to bind specific receptors of important neurotransmitters involved in normal cognition. They may be conveniently classified on this basis:

1. Anticholinergic psychedelics
2. Catecholamine analogs
3. Serotonin-like psychedelics
4. Psychedelic anesthetics

ANTICHOLINERGIC PSYCHEDELICS

These compounds block acetylcholine receptors on the postsynaptic membrane, as discussed earlier in this text (Figure 24.1). Although they occupy the receptors, they do not activate the receptors. As a result, they are anticholinergic rather than cholinergic. Among their effects are intoxication, amnesia, and delirium. Like the other members of the psychedelic group, effects are not limited to mental changes. Atropine and scopolamine have the well-known anticholinergic properties of depression of salivation and sweating, increases in body temperature and heart rate, and pupillary dilation plus blurring of vision. On occasion they have been used as anti-ulcer medications because they block the secretion of stomach acid.

The CNS effects of these drugs are of greatest interest. Low doses of scopolamine produce mild euphoria, sleepiness, amnesia, fatigue, mental confusion, and delirium. Larger amounts of atropine are required for the same degree of effect because it is less capable of crossing the blood–brain barrier. In actuality, they do not expand the mind. They can provoke sensory misperception, a hallucination-like state, but the mental experience associated with their use is more likely to be described as confused and mind-scrambling. Large doses of atropine or scopolamine cause a psychotic-like experience. Delirium and confusion are the dominant symptoms. As a consequence, they

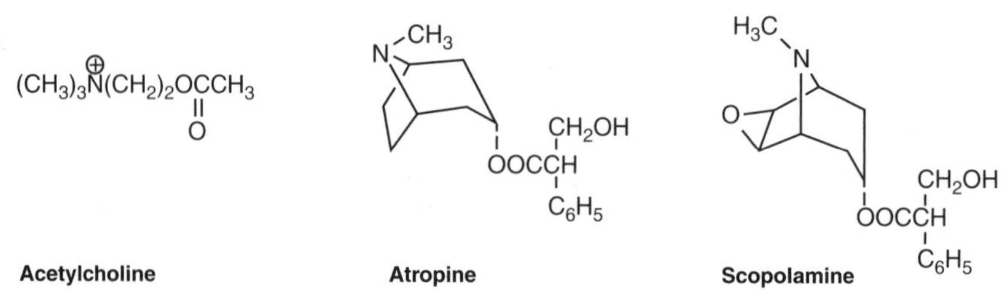

FIGURE 24.1 Anticholinergic psychedelic drugs.

are not used as psychedelics on a repetitive basis. Sometimes young people will take them after they have been misinformed as to the nature of the drug-using experience. Once they have tried them, however, they are not likely to try them a second time.

CATECHOLAMINE ANALOGS

Amphetamines and cocaine resemble this category of drugs inasmuch as they induce a psychosis with delusions, hallucinations, and sensory disturbance, when they are taken in high doses. A case could be made for covering them at this point. Because they are more commonly thought of as euphoriants, however, they are covered in the chapter on drugs of abuse. The other members of this group are shown in Figure 24.2. For them a psychedelic reaction is more prominent than a euphoriant

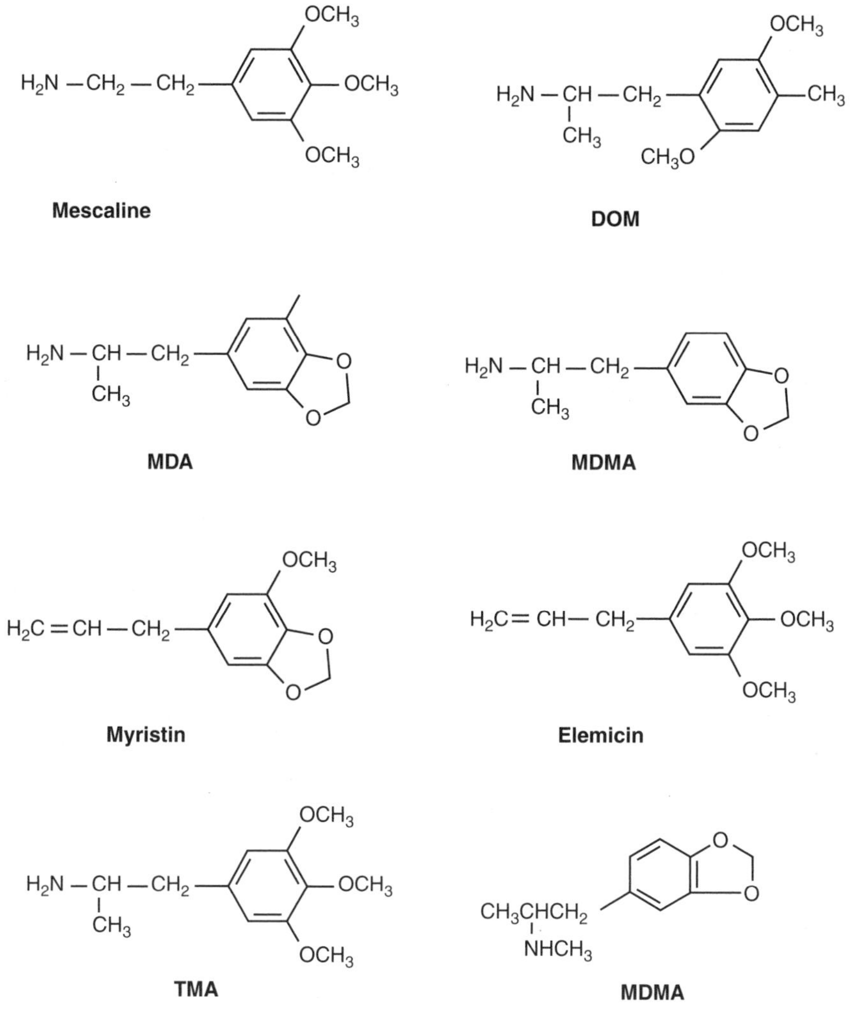

FIGURE 24.2 Psychedelic catecholamine analogs.

response and they belong, therefore, in the discussion of psychedelics. Perusal of the members of this group of catecholamine analogs in Figure 24.2 readily shows their structural relationship to both amphetamine and to norepinephrine. A marked feature of the compounds that are psychedelic is methoxy substitutions on the benzene ring. For reasons that are unknown this structural feature appears to heighten the psychedelic character of the compound. It is believed that these compounds bind at adrenergic receptors, i.e., those that employ norepinephrine as neurotransmitter. In addition, however, they appear to affect serotonin neurotransmission. Their psychedelic properties may relate to an interaction at the physiological locus that connects adrenergic neurons and serotonergic neurons.

Mescaline

Peyote is the name of a cactus, also called *Lophophora williamsii*, found in the southwestern part of the United States and in Mexico. Morphologically, it consists of a crown plus a long root. The crown may be cut away and dried and it will become a brown-colored disk. This is known as a mescal button and contains the psychedelic agent, mescaline (3,4,5-trimethoxyphenyl-ethylamine), in a quantity of about 50 mg. Peyote is a component of the religious practices of many Native Americans. Many states permit its use in the context of such religious expressions. The U.S. Supreme Court, however, has ruled that states may prohibit the use of peyote without infringing on the constitutionally guaranteed freedom of religious expression. Near the end of the eighteenth century, mescaline was identified as the hallucinogenic principle of peyote. Knowledge of the structure of mescaline, which was obtained in 1918, led to the synthesis of mescaline derivatives that also were psychedelic.

Mescaline is absorbed rapidly and produces a psychedelic state that lasts for approximately 9 to 10 hours. It is not especially potent and hallucinogenic doses are about 5 mg/kg orally. Over half of a mescaline dose is excreted as the parent drug with acidic compounds constituting the major percent of its metabolites. Pharmacological manifestations of its use include classical symptoms of adrenergic stimulation, hypertension, tachycardia, hyperthermia, mydriasis, and other stimulatory signs. Psychedelic symptoms include hallucinations, anxiety, tremors, and impairment of color and space perception. The hallucinations usually involve bright lights, geometric designs, and strange animals and people.

Overdose of mescaline is characterized by hypertension, chest pain, bradycardia, vomiting, mydriasis, and tachypnea. CNS symptoms include ataxia, tremor, and possible coma. Hallucinations may proceed to psychotic manifestations. The extreme hyperactivity that often is noted leads to myoglobinuria and rhabdomyolysis.

Other Derivatives

In general, the structurally related catecholamines DOM, MDA, TMA, MMDA, and DMA have the adrenergic effects and the hallucinatory effects of mescaline. They are, however, more potent.

DOM (STP = serenity-tranquility-peace; 4-methyl-2,5-dimethoxy-amphetamine) is one of the synthetic analogs of mescaline. It belongs to the group called designer drugs. DOM is 100 times more potent than mescaline. Therefore, doses of just 3 mg will produce euphoria followed by hallucinations. Like many compounds that arise primarily from illicit laboratories DOM is marketed with a very wide range of quality and purity. Because it is potent there have been many overdoses. These are associated with tremors that may progress to seizures. Some deaths have been documented. DOM usage is not widespread because of an understandable fear of the repercussions of its use.

MDA (3,4-methylenedioxy-amphetamine), MMDA (3-methoxy-4,5-methylene-dioxyamphetamine), and TMA (2,4,5-trimethoxy-amphetamine) are all quite similar to mescaline and, like DOM, are products of the efforts to circumvent existing drug laws by marketing agents not specifically banned because they came into existence after some of the laws were written (designer drugs). In general, their effects and toxicities are very similar to mescaline.

MDMA (3,4-methylenedioxy-methamphetamine, "Ecstasy") is allegedly able to cause both euphoria and self-awareness. It was first synthesized in 1912 in Germany. Although intended as an appetite suppressant, its hallucinogenic properties prevented its use as an anorectic. In the 1950s it reappeared, this time as an aid for psychotherapy. Over the objections of some psychotherapists who believed that MDMA was clinically valuable, the FDA placed the drug on Schedule I in 1985. Since 1985 it has essentially disappeared from psychotherapy but has been accepted into illicit use on a grand scale. For example, in one university, 24% of the student body admitted to using it at least once in 1991. One of the venues in which its use is most popular is during "raves," huge dance parties also characterized by extreme music and a wide assortment of other drugs. Users take about 2 mg/kg and boost this amount with an additional 1 mg/kg after 3 hours. They take the drug in many ways. It is ingested, injected, snorted, or smoked. When taken orally, the onset of activity is approximately 30 to 45 minutes. MDMA affects serotonergic and dopaminergic neurons in the CNS. It enhances serotonin release on the presynaptic side as well as inhibiting the serotonin reuptake. These activities appear to cause a stimulating effect, a euphoria, and a seeming ability on the part of the user to experience reduced inhibitions and congeniality with others. In fact, the psychological effects alleged for MDMA are remarkable. Enactogenesis, a sensation that all is well with the world and empathogenesis, a feeling of emotional closeness to others, are some of its claimed effects. It also enhances the senses of touch, taste, vision, smell, and proprioception.

In animal studies, including primate work, MDMA damaged serotonergic neurons in a reversible and also in an irreversible manner. In humans, analyses of spinal fluid have shown reductions in serotonin metabolites in MDMA users. From this, it may be inferred that the number of serotonin neurons is decreasing. In primates, the LD_{50} of MDMA is 22 mg/kg. Case reports on adverse reactions show altered mental status, tachycardia, and tachypnea. Acute renal failure, cardiovascular collapse, hepatic failure, disseminated intravascular coagulation, and malignant hyperthermia also have been observed. In some cases, profound psychosis has occurred in acute exposure.

Defenders of MDMA claim that many or all of these findings may be due to contaminants that undoubtedly are present in the strange concoctions that find their way into the rave scene. The FDA has not been convinced, however, so MDMA remains under severe restriction in the United States.

Myristin and elemicin are both found in the spices nutmeg and mace. They are derived from seeds and seed coats of *Myristica fragans*, the nutmeg tree, that grows mainly in India and parts of the Caribbean. Nutmeg is a popular home remedy for gastrointestinal upset, arthritic disorders, and sometimes for psychiatric conditions. It also has been employed as an abortifacient. To achieve a euphoric and hallucinatory effect from these sources the user must ingest large quantities. One to two teaspoons are brewed in water from which the active chemicals are extracted. As much as 15 g of nutmeg is taken in some cases. Ingesting elemicin and myristicin from nutmeg in this manner leads to many unpleasant side-effects such as vomiting, nausea, and tremors. Furthermore, the accompanying hallucinations are often of impending doom or other such frightening scenarios. These toxic side-effects usually convince a user not to repeat the experience. There is evidence that myristicin and elemicin are not the only psychoactive agents found in blood after ingestion of nutmeg but that normal metabolism of these compounds produces MMDA and TMA. Both of these, as described above, have psychedelic properties. Nutmeg oil, approximately 10% by weight of the entire nutmeg, also contains several compounds that have some level of psychedelic activity. Included in the oil are eugenol, borneol, saffrole, and linalol.

SEROTONIN-LIKE PSYCHEDELICS

This group of drugs includes lysergic acid diethylamide (LSD), psilocybin, psilocin, dimethyltryptamine, and bufotenin. Their effects derive from their interference in normal serotonin activity. This neurotransmitter is involved with increasing a person's sleep time and reduces feeding, aggression, and sex. Because the structures of members of this group of psychedelics are similar to serotonin it has been theorized in the past that mental illness is related to aberrations in serotonin metabolism. Such abnormal mental states are believed by some to lead to changes in serotonin levels.

Lysergic Acid Diethylamide (LSD)

LSD is the prototypical member of this category (Figure 24.3). One should note that LSD has some structural characteristics that resemble serotonin. It also is proven that LSD antagonizes some of the actions of serotonin. Further, LSD actually decreases the discharge rate of serotonin neurons. Recent research has shown that LSD binds to the serotonin-2 receptor, a specific subtype. This binding is associated with an agonist action, i.e., LSD stimulates serotonin activity. The stronger the binding to the serotonin-2 receptor the greater the psychedelic reaction. Having bonded to the serotonin-2 receptor, a cascade of neural reactions occurs including interaction with other neurons, especially adrenergic (catecholamine-based) neurons. The final psychedelic response may start with serotonergic neurons but appears to involve other types as well in its complete expression. One theory states that the pontine raphe, a major area of central serotonin activity, acts as a kind of filtering station for the evaluation and classification of incoming sensory stimuli. It screens perceptions as a prelude to their deeper evaluation by higher brain centers. LSD and other serotonin-related psychedelic agents prevent the occurrence of this early stage of filtering. The effect would be an overload of sensory input that would overwhelm

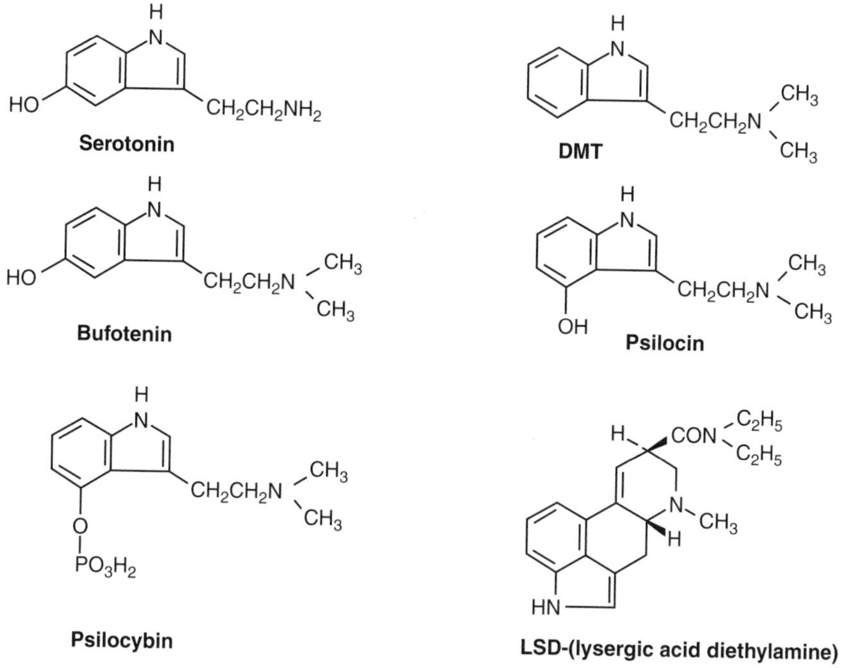

FIGURE 24.3 LSD-like psychedelic drugs.

customary abilities of discrimination. Theories that relate LSD's action to serotonin also derive support from the observation that LSD-psychoses can be treated with neuroleptics. These drugs are known to block serotonin receptors. The most recent drugs of this type are selective serotonin-2 antagonists. Cyproheptadine, clozapine, and risperidone are members of this category. Although the FDA has not approved this application yet, it is believed that these drugs would be helpful in the management of LSD overdose and bad trips.

LSD has an interesting history that begins at least 2000 years ago. At that time it was used in religious ceremonies among at least two peoples. The ancient Eleusinians are thought to have placed lysergic acid amides at the center of their ceremonies in a holy potion called kykeon. The native peoples of Mexico clearly included seeds of the morning glory plant in their religous rites. Morning glory (see below) contains LSD. In the Middle Ages there were periodic outbreaks of ergotism, mass poisonings in which fungi infested rye and other grains (Figure 24.4). These epidemics were also known as St. Anthony's fire because the victims of ergotism complained of intense burning sensations in the extremities. *Claviceps purpurea* was the responsible fungus that excreted ergot, a mixture of alkaloids containing several active agents. Among the many components of ergot are ergotamine, ergocristine, ergosine, ergocornine, bromocriptine, ergonovine, and methylsergide. Many of these pharmacologically active substances are derivatives of lysergic acid. They are not hallucinogenic as such but are easily converted into psychedelic compounds (Figure 24.5). Properties of the ergot alkaloids include vasoconstriction and uterine contraction. These account

FIGURE 24.4 Rye plant infested with *Claviceps purpurea*. (From Michael Moore, Southwestern School of Medicinal Botany. With permission.)

for their use in medieval times to induce abortion and for their modern application in the treatment of migraine headache.

Through much of the first half of the 20th century Sandoz Laboratories, a Swiss drug firm, researched the properties of ergot in their efforts to develop new therapeutic agents. Work with laboratory animals failed to demonstrate any unusual properties of LSD so it was basically ignored. By accident, Albert Hofmann, one of the leaders in pharmaceutical research at Sandoz, discovered the psychoactive propeties of LSD while studying ergot in 1943 (Figure 24.5). Hofmann vividly described his reaction to LSD:

> Objects and the shape of my associates in the laboratory appeared to undergo optical changes…. In a dreamlike state I left for home…. I drew the curtains and immediately fell into a peculiar state similar to drunkenness, characterized by an exaggerated imagination. With my eyes closed, fantastic pictures of extraordinary plasticity and intensive color seemed to surge toward me. After two hours this state gradually wore off.

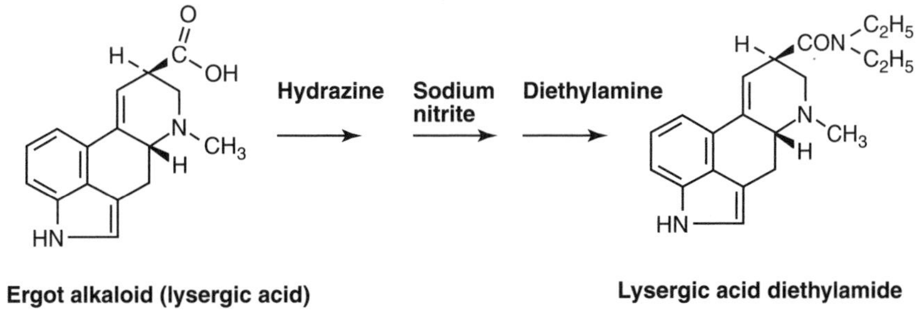

Ergot alkaloid (lysergic acid)   **Lysergic acid diethylamide**

FIGURE 24.5 Synthesis of LSD from ergot.

Hofmann surmised that this was a drug reaction, related in some manner to his work in the laboratory. He, therefore, tested this suspicion by deliberately ingesting some LSD. The dose that he chose was 250 µg, an amount he believed might be too small for any effect but it would be a good place to begin. It was fortunate for Hofmann that he selected this quantity. Most drugs would have no effect at 250 µg but this was equal to 4 to 5 street doses of LSD. Hofmann again recorded his experiences and stated, among other experiences, "My ego seemed suspended in space, from where I saw my dead body lying on the sofa. Acoustic perceptions, such as the noise of water gushing from a tap or the spoken word, were transformed into optical illusions." In this manner Hofmann recorded the phenomenon of synesthesia, exchange among senses, in which a perception proper to one sense is detected by a different sense.

Hofmann and others continued to study LSD. It was believed for some time that it would be a help in research on psychosis and also in the therapy of the psychotic patient. By 1965, however, the federal government in the United States reviewed the LSD record up to that time and decided that its pharmaceutical benefits, if indeed there were any, were outweighed by its abuse potential. It was classified in Schedule I of the Controlled Substances Act, a step which severely limited its availability and declared that it had no medical benefits.

LSD is currently moderately popular. About 8% of Americans respond to surveys by stating that they have used LSD at some point in their lives. Not surprisingly, the 18- to 25-year-old age group acknowledged the highest rate of use (14%). The illicit market provides LSD as a powder, tablet, or material dried onto a support (paper, sugar cubes, postage stamps). Street doses range from 20 to 200 µg and sell for $3 to $10.

LSD has primarily psychological effects but there are some physiological reactions as well. Body temperature is raised, a tachycardia and hypertension are usually noted, and dizziness (even ataxia) and drowsiness are perceptible by a user who is not hopelessly distracted by the psychological effects. The hallucinatory experience depends on dose, as expected, but also on the user's personality, his expectations, previous LSD and other drug experience, and the setting in which the drug use occurs. Apparently an important aspect of the setting is the nature of one's companions who are present. "Trips" include alterations in mood and emotion, laughter and sorrow (even simultaneously), and euphoria and dysphoria. The major reported findings are perceptual changes, visual hallucinations and sensory distortions.

LSD provides up to 12 hours of such distorted reactions from a single ingestion. Its half-life is about 3 hours and it is metabolized extensively with only 1% of a dose being excreted as unchanged LSD. In view of this extensive biotransformation and the very small doses that are used, it is clear that LSD analysis is a great challenge. Urinary quantities following customary levels of dosage are only in the range of one ng/mL. Blood concentrations are even lower and very sensitive methods are needed for laboratory analysis.

LSD has a very high therapeutic index so that a fatal amount is approximately 150-fold greater than a hallucinatory dose. In view of its potency, however, this means that dimethyltryptamine (DMT) is still very dangerous with a lethal amount being only 0.2 mg/kg.

DMT is a natural compound that is extraordinarily similar to serotonin in structure. It produces psychedelic effects similar to those of LSD and also shares the property of binding to serotonin receptors. DMT is found in snuff that is used in various parts of the world. For example, cohoba is a type of snuff made from South American beans that contains DMT. Another example is yopo, a West Indian snuff. The reaction experienced from these forms of snuff is partly hallucinatory and DMT is, in turn, largely responsible for this. Bufotenin, another serotonin-related psychedelic, is also found in these forms of snuff. DMT resembles LSD to a large degree in terms of the nature of the psychological response of the user. It differs from LSD in at least two ways: it is not absorbed from the oral route and must be inhaled or snorted, and it provides only about a 1-hour drug experience.

DMT Derivatives

Psilocybin is 4-phosphoryl-DMT and psilocin is 4-hydroxy-DMT (see structures in Figure 24.3). They are found in more than one dozen species of mushrooms from three genera: Psilocybe, Panaeolus, and Conocybe. As was true for mescaline and other psychedelics, these mushrooms have been incorporated into religious ceremonies. *Psilocybe mexicana* is known as "magic mushroom" and has been used for centuries by the native peoples of Mexico.

Pure psilocin and psilocybin have only 0.5% the psychedelic potency of LSD. They are ingested directly from the mushrooms that are eaten without any specific preparation. Some species, e.g., *Psilocybe semilanceata*, are low in content of these materials so that the required dosage is up to 40 mushrooms whereas others, such as *Psilocybe cyanescens*, provide a hallucinogenic dose in just 2 to 5 mushrooms. The mushroom eater must be especially diligent in correctly identifying the species in order to avoid a toxic dose of psychedelic agent as well as avoid selection of the wrong species entirely. Within the bloodstream psilocybin is hydrolyzed to psilocin by dephosphorylation. Therefore, the active agent is psilocin, irrespective of which is ingested. Tolerance to this drug and other psychedelics can be very high and occurs after a short period of usage. Cross-tolerance occurs among LSD, mescaline, and psilocin. This suggests that they all have the same target organ within the CNS.

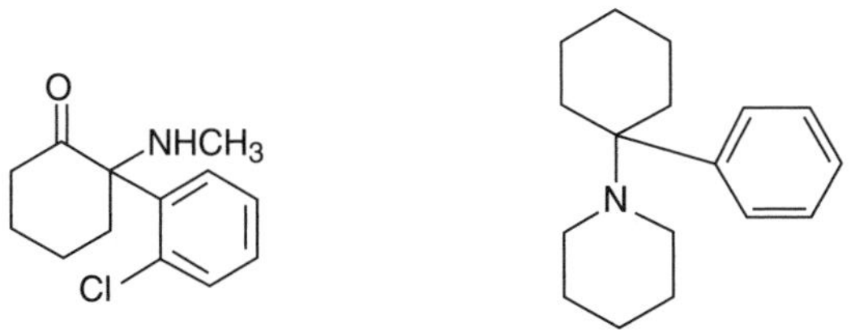

Ketamine   **PCP (phenylcyclohexylpiperidine)**

FIGURE 24.6 PCP and ketamine.

Morning Glory Seeds (Ololiuqui)

South American Indians employ morning glory seeds as psychedelic agents which have become enveloped into their religious rites. The seeds are eaten directly and, some time afterward, the priests enter a trance-like state characterized by hallucinations. Albert Hofmann, the Sandoz scientist who discovered the psychoactive potential of LSD, was the first one to analyze the morning glory seeds. He found that they contained several ingredients, the major one of which appeared to be lysergic acid amide. This substance is a powerful psychedelic compound and has 10% of the potency of LSD in this regard. Recalling the extreme potency of LSD indicates to us that lysergic acid amide is also very active. Besides the hallucinatory actions of this amide it has significant physiological actions including nausea, vomiting, headache, hypertension, mydriasis, and drowsiness.

PSYCHEDELIC ANESTHETICS

There are only two compounds in this category and one of them, phencyclidine, was discussed under drugs of abuse. The other compound is ketamine (Figure 24.6).

Phencyclidine was introduced into medicine as an anesthetic. However, patients with high blood levels of this drug reported unusual reactions such as disorientation, delirium, and hallucinations. As a result phencyclidine and its analog, ketamine, were referred to as dissociative anesthetics, meaning that users of these drugs felt removed or dissociated from others and from the environment. The user often becomes agitated but euphoric. He loses inhibitions but may become rigid and speechless. In overdoses the subject frequently lapses into a coma and, if he survives, undergoes a long period of confusion or even psychosis that may last up to several months. Ketamine can produce the same spectrum of physiological and psychological reactions although it has less potency as a psychedelic agent.

Questions

1. What is the chemical reason for the psychedelic properties of scopolamine? Describe the features of scopolamine overdose.
2. Compare the structural similarities among the catecholamine analogs. What is the most widely held theory for their psychedelic character?

3. What is the relationship between LSD and ergot? Use structural formulas in your answer.
4. Contrast the psychedelic potency of LSD and morning glory seeds. What is the structure of the main ingredient of the seeds?
5. Compare ketamine and phencyclidine. What is the current status of each in medical usage in the United States?

Case Study 1: The Rave Party

A 19-year-old man was brought to an emergency department and then transferred to a tertiary level burn center. He sustained a severe burn injury from an explosion of a gasoline can within his car; 31% of his body surface was burned including 4% as third degree (full thickness skin burns). Although the history preceding the burn injury was unclear it was known that the man had been at a rave party just before the accident. At the time of admission the patient was paranoid and required high doses of sedative to calm him. Soot was found in his trachea indicating some level of burn injury to his airway. He also displayed edema of the pharynx so he was intubated in order to guarantee a patent airway. He had proteinuria and hemoglobinuria although his total urine volume was adequate. Surgical excision of burn tissue with application of grafts was started 48 hours after admission.

On his 5th hospital day he developed a fever and tachypnea. He went into respiratory failure. His urine also was noted to be a dark green color. This was thought to be due to oxidation of the urinary hemoglobin and some of the drugs that were being administered including propofol for sedation. Chest roentgenograms were consistent with widespread infection. His urine output and total hemoglobin both decreased. Further surgery for his burns was postponed while attention focused on treatment of his infection. Aggressive fluid therapy was effective and surgery was resumed on the 9th day of hospitalization.

On the 14th hospital day his urine again appeared discolored and his temperature increased. Signs of renal failure were evident including creatinine of 444 μmol/L and urea of 55.8 μmol/L. Dialysis was instituted and his renal function eventually improved.

He was approved for discharge after 4 weeks. At that time, however, he suffered a grand mal seizure and lapsed into coma. CT scan of the head was consistent with cold abscesses or multiple small infarcts. He recovered on antibiotic therapy and was discharged on anticonvulsant therapy 10 weeks after the original burn injury.

What drug did this man use at the rave?
   a) Cocaine
   b) Methylenedioxymethamphetamine
   c) Marijuana
   d) Heroin

There is very little clinical information that would enable one to answer this question. Most of his treatment within the hospital was for his burn injury. However, he was paranoid at the time of admission. He also suffered a seizure several weeks after admission. At rave parties, such as the one he attended, drug abuse is almost universal. Although any drug is possible, Ecstasy, or methyl-enedioxymethamphetamine (MDMA), is commonly abused at raves. Further-more, there are reports of Ecstasy causing cerebral infarcts even several weeks after use and some research shows mental impairment in association with chronic Ecstasy abuse. Paranoid behavior following MDMA abuse is common. In point of fact the patient admitted heavy consumption of MDMA at the rave plus 2000 mg of amphetamine ingestion over the preceding 48 hours. He also acknowledged that he used MDMA regularly and consumed as many as 15 pills per day over the previous 1.5 years.

Questions

Q1. Which is not seen in MDMA abuse?
  a) Paranoia and psychoses.
  b) Euphoria and feelings of closeness.
  c) Hyperpyrexia.
  d) Sympathomimetic effects.
  e) All of the above are seen.

Q2. Which complication in this patient's burn injury may be related to MDMA?
  a) Cerebral infarct
  b) Shock
  c) Acute respiratory distress
  d) Widespread infection

Q3. How did MDMA cause or contribute to renal failure?
  a) Amphetamine-like drugs are inherently nephrotoxic.
  b) Tubular damage results from rhabdomyolysis that is induced by hyper-thermia.
  c) Disseminated intravascular coagulation (DIC)is caused by MDMA and DIC causes renal failure.
  d) All of the above are possible.

Q4. What is the usual dosage of MDMA?
  a) 1 to 2 mg
  b) 10 to 20 mg
  c) 100 to 200 mg
  d) 1 to 2 g

Answers and Discussion

Q1. (Answer = e) Abusers of MDMA claim that the drug causes a euphoria that is common to many abused drugs. They also allege that it makes one feel a spirit of togetherness that is ideal for parties because it breaks down interpersonal barriers. Interestingly, this experience of closeness commonly is followed by paranoia in overdose. Hyperpyrexia is so common that raves regularly provide a "cooling off" area that is heavily air-conditioned for use by those especially affected by hyperthermia. The expression "chill out" has entered the vernacular from this practice. Sympathomimetic effects are virtually universal with MDMA use. These include hyperactivity, sweating, mydriasis, tachycardia, and dry mouth. It is not surprising that sympathomimetic effects would be observed in view of the close relationship of MDMA to other sympathomimetics.

Q2. (Answer = a) As stated above there are reports of cerebral infarcts and other brain injury from chronic MDMA abuse. This patient would be expected to be especially at risk because his level of use was extremely high. All of the other problems he experienced are commonly found in association with major burn injury. They are probably related to MDMA in this case only indirectly. That is, the burn injury might not have occurred in this case if the patient had not been under the influence of drugs when it happened.

Q3. (Answer = d) The literature reports that responses a, b, and c have been seen in amphetamine-analog overdose. In this case, DIC was excluded by repeat CBC testing. The patient did experience hyperthermia, as is found commonly in MDMA overdose. Therefore, this patient may have suffered rhabdomyolysis that, in turn, led to renal failure. The diagnosis of rhabdomyolysis is difficult to make in the presence of burn injury because the burn itself will cause the production of markers that are otherwise indicative of rhabdomyolysis. Last, MDMA may be directly harmful to the kidney and may be a cause of interstitial nephritis.

Q4. (Answer = c) The usual dosage is 100 to 200 mg in the form of MDMA hydrochloride. Thus, this patient's admission that he regularly used up to 15 tablets a day meant that he ingested 1.5 to 3 g per day.

Reference

Cadier, M.A. and Clarke, J.A., Ecstasy and Whizz at a rave resulting in a major burn plus complications, *Burns,* 19, 239–240, 1993.

Case Study 2: An Unusual Complication

A 32-year-old Native American man drank ceremonial tea containing a herbal compound. He then experienced a period of hallucinations and incoordination. Several hours later, however, he experienced shortness of breath that progressed to respiratory distress. He collapsed and was brought to an emergency department by his family. At the hospital his vital signs were very poor and included bradycardia and shallow respirations. He lapsed into a coma and efforts to resuscitate him were not successful.

Autopsy was carried out and 45 mL of blood were found in his stomach plus quantities of blood in the duodenum and in the lungs. Extensive hepatic fatty infiltrates existed that were consistent with chronic alcohol consumption. Most significantly, 4 lacerations, each 1 cm in length, were found at the gastroesophageal junction.

What are the expected drug findings in his postmortem blood and urine?
a) Cocaine
b) Mescaline
c) Psilocin
d) Amphetamine

The history on this patient is strongly suggestive of mescaline. Because he was a Native American and the agent that caused his hallucinations and incoordination was ceremonial, mescaline was strongly suspected. Cocaine and amphetamine are not used by his people in a ceremonial manner nor are his symptoms especially consistent with use of these substances. Psilocin might be suspected as well. The reason that mescaline is a more likely answer here is that psilocin is usually ingested in the form of the whole mushroom without any extraction into a liquid form. In actuality, postmortem studies found mescaline in blood at 0.48 mg/L and in urine at 61 mg/L. Tiny amounts of chlordiazepoxide were also detected but no ethanol nor any other drugs were detected. The cause of death was certified as mescaline intoxication.

Questions

Q1. How did mescaline contribute to this death?
a) Respiratory arrest from mescaline's central effect.
b) Cardiac arrest due to a specific mescaline-associated cardiotoxicity.
c) Bleeding into the lung from ruptured blood vessels secondary to mescaline-induced vomiting.
d) Mescaline is hepatotoxic in the setting of chronic alcoholism.
Q2. The decedent's vitreous fluid urea nitrogen and glucose were normal. How should this be interpreted?
a) The time of death was very recent.
b) Diabetes may have been a factor in his death.
c) Renal malfunction and diabetes were not related to his death.
d) Mescaline was absent from vitreous fluid.
Q3. What is the significance of his postmortem concentrations of mescaline?
a) They are extremely high and suggestive of a direct lethal effect of mescaline.
b) They are in the range found for normal use and suggest that mescaline was indirectly involved in the person's death.
c) The blood level is normal for a mescaline user but the urine level suggests sustained usage.
d) The finding of chlordiazepoxide suggests a lethal drug interaction.

Answers and Discussion

Q1. (Answer = c) Mescaline is not the cause of many drug-related deaths. When there are deaths in which the decedent had used mescaline, the relationship is often obscure or incidental. In the present case the decedent had four esophageal lacerations known as Mallory-Weiss lacerations. He bled extensively from them, with blood appearing at several locations within the GI tract. The immediate cause of death appeared to be aspiration of blood into the lungs that led to respiratory failure. Mescaline causes vomiting of such force that lacerations are a result. Mescaline is a strong emetic. Other emetics, such as ipecac, also have caused Mallory-Weiss lacerations. A possible cardiotoxic effect of mescaline cannot be ruled out. The decedent's history of alcoholism may be a contributing factor in undermining the normal strength of his vascular walls.

Q2. (Answer = c) Vitreous fluid displays good stability because it is located in an anatomically isolated region. It resists putrefactive changes. Vitreous urea nitrogen will be elevated if renal failure occurred before death. This finding could be significant when blood values are not elevated but putrefaction has begun. Similarly, glucose concentrations in blood change rapidly after death but if they are elevated in the vitreous fluid, this is indicative of premortem hyperglycemia.

Q3. (Answer = b) The trace quantity of chlordiazepoxide is very likely of no significance. The blood level of mescaline is similar to values reported in the literature after controlled mescaline ingestion. For example, 12 subjects given 500 mg of mescaline hydrochloride had 3.8 mg/L at 2 hours postingestion and 1.5 mg/L at 7 hours postingestion. The decedent had 0.48 mg/L at an unknown interval after ingestion. This strongly suggests, therefore, that he was not ingesting a uniquely high amount of mescaline. This death was an indirect result of mescaline use.

References

Charalampous, K.D. et al., Metabolic fate of mescaline in man, *Psychopharmacologia,* 9, 48–63, 1966.

Noite, K.B. and Zumwalt, R.E., Fatal peyote ingestion associated with Mallory-Weiss lacerations, *West. J. Med.,* 170, 328, 1999.

Case Study 3: The Child with the Imaginary Rats

A 2-year-old toddler was taken to a medical center by his parents because he was crying uncontrollably, was highly agitated, and complained of seeing rats that were not visible to anyone else in the room. At the emergency department the child vomited several times. He was noted to have mild hypotension and a moderate elevation of temperature. Pulse rate was 148/min and respirations were 32/min. The remainder of the physical examination was normal and no laboratory abnormalities were found. Diazepam was given and the child was kept overnight for observation. The parents admitted that the child might have gotten into some hallucinatory substance which their friends had left at the house. The child was discharged in an asymptomatic state and the county Department of Human Services was contacted for follow-up to assure that the child's welfare was not neglected.

What was the probable identity of the offending material?
   a) Mescaline
   b) LSD
   c) Psilocybin
   d) Cocaine

None of these possible answers can be unequivocally ruled out. Mescaline and psilocybin are very unlikely simply because of their relative scarcity and that they provoke significant additional signs. Mescaline causes significant gastrointestinal upset beyond that which this child experienced in the brief case history described. Psilocybin causes muscle weakness, no signs of which were reported here. Cocaine is always a possibility but hallucinations are not the most prominent feature of cocaine use. LSD is the agent which this child ingested and that resulted in the hallucinations he experienced.

Questions

Q1. What dose of LSD is typically employed for a psychoactive effect?
   a) 50 µg
   b) 0.5 µg
   c) 50 mg
   d) 500 µg
Q2. What is a common analytic method for LSD?
   a) Thin-layer chromatography
   b) Ultraviolet spectrophotometry
   c) Gas chromatography-mass spectrometry
   d) Gas chromatography-thermal conductivity detector
Q3. Which of the following is an oral form of LSD in common use?
   a) Sugar cubes
   b) Tablets
   c) Powder
   d) Postage stamps impregnated with LSD
   e) All of the above
Q4. Which is not a common feature in the presentation of patients who have overdosed on LSD?
   a) Paresthesias
   b) Diaphoresis
   c) Ataxia
   d) Bradycardia

Answers and Discussion

Q1. (Answer = a) LSD is among the most potent of all drugs and a quantity of just 50 µg is enough to provide even an experienced user with a 6-hour trip.

Q2. (Answer = c) Among the choices provided here only gas chromatography-mass spectrometry has sufficient sensitivity to measure LSD in body fluids. Even with GC-MS, assay of LSD in blood is difficult because the amounts usually found (0.1 to 0.2 ng/mL in non-overdose) are at the limit of detection for many GC-MS methods. Determination of LSD in urine is less of a challenge because more specimen is available and higher concentrations of the drug are found in urine. Average users may have 2 to 5 ng/mL of LSD in urine. The important point to remember is that many common methods of urine screening will not detect LSD even in overdose. This is because most of those methods have inadequate sensitivity and others, for example, common laboratory drug screens, may not look for LSD.

Q3. (Answer = e) All of these dosage forms have been employed by LSD users. Because LSD is so potent it is virtually impossible to handle a customary dose (100 µg) of LSD or any substance without trapping it in a pill or tablet that also contained other fillers. Two of the more popular forms are sugar cubes in which the LSD is present in a sucrose cube and postage stamps. The fact that one can get a psychoactive dose by merely licking the LSD from a stamp shows how little of the drug is needed for a high.

Q4. (Answer = d) Although hallucinations are a prominent response to LSD, the overall physical findings are similar to those from a stimulant overdose. Temperature, heart rate, and blood pressure are elevated. The mental status in adult intoxications is characterized by anxiety or panic, paranoia, illusions, time and visual distortions, and profound disorientation. The term, synesthesia, has sometimes been employed to describe the state of LSD users in which they smell colors, hear visions, see sounds, and experience similar sensory misperceptions.

Reference

Schwartz, J.G., LSD intoxication, *J. Fam. Prac.,* 27, 550–551, 1988.

25 Plants

CONTENTS

In the nineteenth century and earlier, that time in history before most drugs were discovered, plants accounted for over 90% of all poisonings. They are still involved in many modern poisonings but the figure is estimated at 6% of all poison exposures and the vast majority of plant poisonings are minor. A few plants, however, contain especially toxic chemicals.

Why are plants poisonous? On some occasions, when animals are injured by exposure to plants, it is an accident of nature. A chemical is a normal biochemical to the plant but is accidentally deleterious to an organism of another species. However, the major reason for the poisonous character of many plant biochemicals appears to be an evolutionary response by plants for self-protection. In a sense, plants are deliberately poisonous. Their toxicity to humans and other animals is an example of natural selection. In other words, plants that were toxic to animals would not be eaten by animals and would, therefore, survive. Thus, many animals, especially grazing farm animals, are killed when feeding on certain plants.

Plant poisonings are found most commonly in children. Sometimes they occur in adults who mistake poisonous plants for edible ones. The current trend toward natural foods has lead to people buying or cultivating natural products including plants that are often toxic. At times poisonings occur when people deliberately smoke or ingest plants known to provoke hallucinations, as has often been reported for Jimsonweed. One other route of poisoning is not from the plant itself but from insecticides sprayed onto the plant. The insecticides persist and are still present when the victim comes into contact with the plant.

The variety of toxic chemicals produced by plants is incredible. It is difficult to attempt to organize myriad plant toxins in an understandable manner. The goal here will be to describe the most common types of plant poisonings, show the many chemical structures found in plant poisons, and categorize the major plant toxins into classes based on the general group to which they belong. To that end plant poisons will be described as cardiotoxins, neurotoxins, etc. Mushrooms will be described separately.

PLANT RECOGNITION

It is very difficult to recognize specific plants without specialized training. Only skilled botanists can make identifications based solely on written descriptions that refer to the shape of leaves, the texture of stems, etc. Black and white illustrations are slightly better in helping one to recognize plants. Color pictures are more helpful and are available from several online and other computerized sources. For a true capability of recognizing poisonous plants one needs to actually go to botanical gardens and other natural settings and see each plant in a wild environment. This is not always easy to do, so many alternative sources are available which provide illustrations that, despite the aforementioned shortcomings, are helpful in learning to identify plants. A search for plant poisons by an Internet Search engine will find many excellent sources. One of the best, in this author's opinion, is a Poisonous Plant Database at http://chili.rt66.com/hrbmoore/HOMEPAGE/HomePage.html

Once the user brings up the database, specific sites can be selected. An excellent one, which provides multiple illustrations of a wide variety of poisonous plants, is Poisonous Plants (University of Pennsylvania) at http://chili.rt66.com.hrbmoore/Resources/ImagesOther–A–c.html

THE MOST COMMON PLANT EXPOSURES

Based on calls to Poison Control Centers the following are the 10 most common plant exposures, arranged in order of descending frequency of contacts with the Poison Control Centers (Table 25.1). It is important to recognize that this is a list of frequency of contact and not a list of severity. Fortunately, most of the following cause only minor symptoms.

PHILODENDRON

These common houseplants are often sampled, especially by children, and with benign outcome. There may be mucosal enlargement or GI irritation. Some individuals experience a contact dermatitis. Philodendron contains high amounts of calcium oxalate crystals, but these do not cause significant complications as have been observed with other calcium oxalate-containing plants. The more benign course may be due to the manner in which the crystals are located inside the plant tissue.

TABLE 25.1
Most Common Plant Exposures

Scientific Name	Common Name
1. *Philodendron* spp.	Philodendron
2. *Dieffenbachia* spp.	Dumbcane
3. *Capsicum annuum*	Pepper
4. *Euphorbia pulcherrima*	Poinsettia
5. *Ilex* spp.	Holly
6. *Phytolacca americana*	Pokeweed
7. *Crassula* spp.	Jade plant
8. *Ficus benjamina*	Weeping fig
9. *Brassaia* spp.	Umbrella tree
10. *Toxicodendron radicans*	Poison ivy

DIEFFENBACHIA

These houseplants are also known as dumbcane. Chewing of plant tissue causes rapid onset of severe pain and swelling. Within the plant are sharp calcium oxalate crystals which are needlelike and capable of being fired like projectiles. As the victim chews on the leaves, he is exposed to penetration of the oral mucosa by the calcium oxalate crystals and also is exposed to proteolytic enzymes found in the vicinity of the crystals in the dumbcane (Figure 25.1). The enzymes act like the proteolytic enzyme, trypsin, and also provoke the localized release of histamine and bradykinin. Severe exposures may progress to profuse salivation, loss of speech (hence the name, dumbcane), and even respiratory difficulties. Fortunately, extensive exposure is rare because the immediate onset of symptoms causes the victim to stop ingesting the plant.

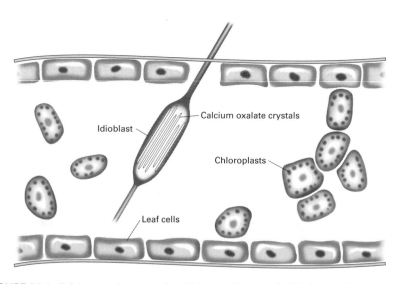

FIGURE 25.1 Calcium oxalate crystals within an idioblast of a Dieffenbachia leaf.

CAPSICUM

All of the common peppers, i.e., chili pepper or red pepper, are included within this genus. The active agent has been isolated and is sold in sprays as mace or dog repellents intended for self-protection. Pepper contains capsaicin and its derivatives, dihydrocapsaicin, nordihyrocapsaicin, homocapsaicin, and homodihydrocapsaicin. These alkaloids may work by causing the depletion of substance P from nerve terminals. Substance P stimulates sensory nerve endings and the inhibition of this effect, as can happen when red pepper depletes substance P, causes local pain. Patients report burning or stinging and pain. Nausea and vomiting accompany oral exposure. Long-term effects are usually not found.

EUPHORBIA (POINSETTIA)

A report of a fatality from Poinsettia in 1919 resulted in exaggerated fears in regard to this plant's toxicity. Innumerable cases of exposure followed by mild findings have lead to a contemporary attitude that Poinsettia is relatively innocuous. The original report appears to have involved misidentification of the responsible species. No symptoms or minimal nausea and vomiting have been associated with modern incidents of Poinsettia ingestion.

ILEX (HOLLY)

Children often eat the attractive red berries of this plant when it is displayed during the Christmas season. Symptoms are usually mild nausea, vomiting, or abdominal cramping. There are many chemicals in the Holly berry and the exact causative agent of these symptoms is not known.

PHYTOLACCA (POKEWEED)

All parts of this plant contain the toxins phytolaccine, a potent GI irritant, and Pokeweed mitogen, which causes mitosis of lymphoid cells. When served in salads by restaurants, the plant is boiled twice, a process which usually inactivates the poisons. The typical response to ingestion of unboiled pokeweed is severe nausea, vomiting, and cramping. The most serious outcome is hemorrhagic gastritis resulting from large ingestions. Lymphocytosis occurs about 2 to 4 days after exposure, and the white cell count returns to normal within 2 weeks without producing any toxic outcome.

CRASSULA (JADE PLANT)

No toxin has been isolated from this species, and it is generally regarded as being entirely innocuous.

SPATHIPHYLLUM (PEACE LILY)

These are common houseplants with large, glossy leaves containing calcium oxalate crystals. Mild symptoms, similar to those seen with exposure to dumbcane, are found. Minimal gastrointestinal symptoms are also noted.

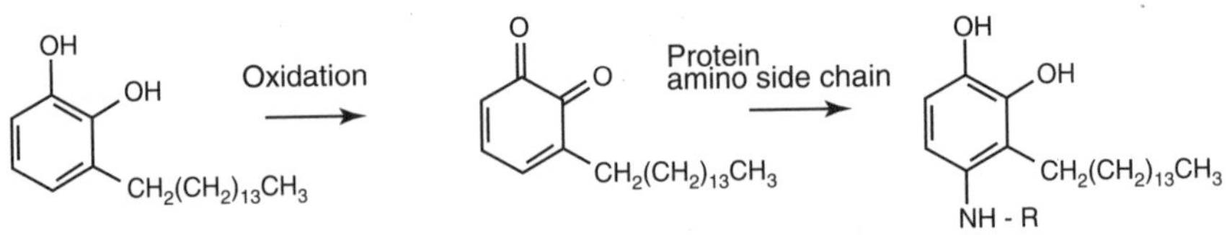

FIGURE 25.2 Conversion of uroshiol into a contact allergen.

BRASSAIA (UMBRELLA TREE OR RUBBER TREE)

These plants contain two potential toxins: calcium oxalate and falcarinol. It resembles Philodendron insofar as they both contain calcium oxalate, which does not appear to cause problems when ingested from either of these sources. Some individuals experience dermatitis when exposed to the other poison, falcarinol.

TOXICODENDRON (POISON IVY)

This genus, which includes Poison Ivy, Oak, and Sumac, is well-known for causing a common form of contact dermatitis. The oily material visible in these plants is called toxicodendrol and contains urushiol, a mixture of catechols (Figure 25.2). They penetrate skin and bind to endogenous proteins at which point they behave as antigens, producing an allergic response.

FATAL PLANTS

While the above 10 plants were listed merely on the basis of frequency of exposure, the following are grouped together as posing severe danger (Table 25.2). Fortunately, just as the most common exposures are usually mild, exposure to the very dangerous plants is rare.

TABLE 25.2
Potentially Fatal Plants

Plant	Toxin	Fatal Dose
Akee	Hypoglycin	1 fruit
Apple seeds	Amygdalin	50 seeds
Castor plant	Ricin	1 bean
Death cap	Amanatin, Phalloidin	1 mushroom
Jequirity	Abrin	1 bean
Oleander	Oleandrin	1 leaf
Stone fruit	Amygdalin	30 kernels
Hemlock dropwart	Oenanthetoxin	1 root
Yew	Taxine A and B	50 needles

TOXIC PLANTS CLASSIFIED BY AFFECTED ORGAN SYSTEM

Most plant toxins affect more than one organ system in the human body. It is somewhat artificial, therefore, to classify plants and their toxins on the basis of their major effect only. Nevertheless, efforts to do so are helpful because they bring some measure of organization to what is otherwise a hopelessly complicated area. In addition, although most toxins have multifaceted effects, they will usually cause death by a well-defined mechanism that acts primarily on one organ system within the body.

GASTROINTESTINAL

Nausea, vomiting, abdominal pain, and diarrhea are probably the most common findings from plant ingestions. A review of the most common 10 plant poisonings, above, will show that most of these 10 plants affect the GI tract. Many other plants also affect this area and some of the more significant are the following.

Yew (*Taxus Canadensis*)

This is a very common ornamental hedge. All parts of Taxus except the red fruit contain poisons, taxine A and taxine B. Within 1 hour after consumption this plant causes severe gastroenteritis which may be followed by convulsions, shock, coma, and death. It also is classed as a cardiotoxin because it causes decreased atrioventricular conduction which may lead to uncontrollable bradycardia. The toxic properties of the plant have been recognized from earliest times and it has been employed as an abortifacient by many women. Unfortunately, it has no selectivity in terms of specifically inducing abortion so many women died from its generalized toxicity.

Castor Bean (*Ricinis Communis*)

This plant contains ricin, a potent cellular protein toxin. The protein is a dimer in which the two subunit chains are linked by a single disulfide bond. The B-chain binds to cell surface glycoproteins and thereby facilitates the entry of ricin into the cell. Once within, ricin acts on the 60s ribosomal subunit inhibiting protein synthesis which eventually causes the death of the cell. The outline of ricin structure is schematically represented in Figure 25.3. The seeds containing the toxin can be swallowed whole without injury. If, however, the seeds are chewed and the toxin is released, then severe gastroenteritis results. Death may occur although the fatal dose of ricin is much higher when taken orally than when injected. Ricin is absorbed poorly from the GI tract. A famous case of ricin poisoning involved Georgi Markov, a Bulgarian ex-patriate who was working as a broadcaster in London. In 1978, he was stabbed in the thigh with an umbrella and developed severe gastroenteritis and died in a few days. Autopsy revealed a tiny metallic sphere, less than 1 mm in radius, embedded in his thigh. The sphere was empty but was capable of holding 0.28 mm^3 of material. Postmortem experimentation strongly supported the hypothesis that Markov was a victim of ricin poisoning that had been administered to stop his

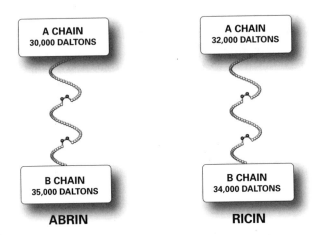

FIGURE 25.3 Structures of two toxalbumins, ricin and abrin.

anti-Communist broadcasts. Fatal ingestions of ricin cause a gastroenteritis which is hemorrhagic and proceed to more severe symptoms of CNS depression, cardiac dysrhythmias, coma, and death.

Rosary Pea (*Abrus Precatorius*)

The toxin produced by this plant, abrin, is extremely similar to ricin, a toxalbumin protein capable of causing inhibition of protein synthesis. All parts of the plant are toxic with the seeds containing the highest quantity of toxin. The toxins have similar structures and modes of action. Further, if the seed is ingested without chewing, most of the toxin will not be released and symptoms, if any, may be mild. *Abrus* also contains other potentially toxic components, glycyrrhizin, abric acid, and N-methyltryptophan, the significance of which is not yet understood.

Cardiovascular

Many plants are toxic to the heart. Their modes of action are not uniform except for causing heart injury. Several plants, however, are similar in producing cardiac glycosides, highly potent toxins which contain a sugar bonded to a steroid moiety with an unsaturated lactone at carbon 17.

Lily of the Valley (*Convallaria majalis*)

Convallarin and convallotoxin are two toxins found in this common garden plant. Reference to Table 25.3 shows that convallotoxin has an LD_{50} of 0.08 mg/kg, the smallest value among the figures given. This is equal to only 5 mg for a person who weighs 140 lbs. (62 kgs). Despite the inherent potency of *Convallaria* toxin, however, overdoses are not always fatal because the concentration of the toxin in the plant is low. Convallotoxin and other cardiac glycosides act by inhibiting the enzyme, Na$^+$K$^+$ATPase, which increases ATP. They thereby act on the heart muscle, the myocardium, to increase contractility and will support a failing heart especially in congestive heart failure. For those glycosides employed medicinally, overdose is common because the therapeutic and toxic doses are close (narrow therapeutic index). Intoxication with *Convallaria* causes bradycardia and heartblock (uncoordinated heartbeat) progressing to fibrillation and cardiac arrest. Lily of the Valley is similar in morphology to wild garlic and some deaths have resulted when it was mistaken as such and made into a soup.

CARDIAC GLYCOSIDES

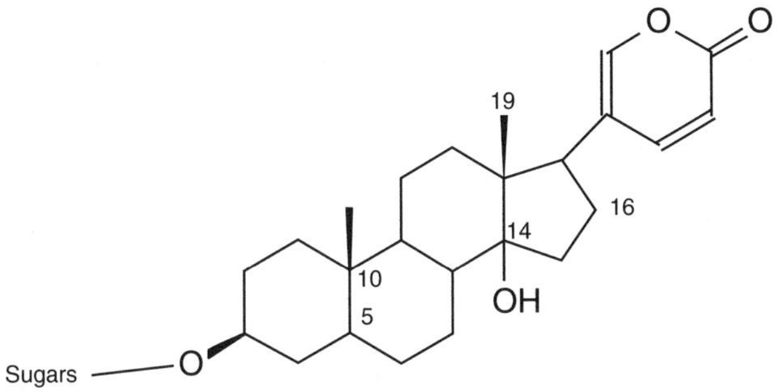

FIGURE 25.4 Overall cardiac glycoside structure.

TABLE 25.3
Some Cardiac Glycosides

Compound	Plant Source	Sugar	Substitutions	LD$_{50}$ (mg/kg)
Digitoxin	*Digitalis*	Digitoxose		0.33
Oleandrin	*Nerium*	Oleandrose	16 beta OAc	0.20
Scillarin A	Scilla	Rhamnose, glucose	delta 4	
			6-memb. ring[a]	0.15
Hellebrin	*Helleborus*	Rhamnose, glucose	5 beta OH	
			10 CHO, 6-ring[a]	0.10
Convallotoxin	*Convallaria*	Rhamnose	5 beta OH;10 CHO	0.08
Thevetin A	Thevetia	Thevetose	10 CHO	0.89

[a] Addendum to cardiac glycoside structure

Foxglove (*Digitalis Purpurea*)

The medicinal properties of digitalis have been known since at least the thirteenth century, but it was not accepted into medical practice until William Withering, in 1785, wrote his medical epic, "An Account of the Foxglove and Some of Its Medical

Uses: With Practical Remarks on Dropsy and Other Diseases." Despite the title, Withering was only vaguely aware that digitalis had an action on the heart. It was not until the twentieth century that digitalis became a regular part of therapy for congestive heart failure. Digitoxin, as shown in Table 25.3, is a major glycoside present in digitalis but not the only one. Gitoxin, gitalin, and digoxin are also present. Withering described the signs of digitalis poisoning when he wrote, "...in very large and quickly repeated doses, occasions sickness, vomiting, purging, giddiness, confused vision, objects appearing green or yellow,...slow pulse, cold sweats, convulsions, syncope, and death." Ingestion of wild foxglove causes the same signs and toxicity as overdose of digitoxin or digoxin medicines. Digoxin has been very valuable in medicine, but while it has saved many lives, it also has produced significant toxicity. Because the drug is excreted by the kidney, toxicity is most likely when a patient's renal function deteriorates. An antidote, digoxin-binding antibody, has been synthesized for treating digitalis overdose by binding the drug in blood with a specific antibody. This antidote also is somewhat effective against the other cardiac glycosides described here because of the strong similarity in structures.

Many murders have, undoubtedly, been committed with digitalis as the vehicle of death. An interesting one was that of Seraphine de Pawr who was murdered by her lover, Dr. Edmond de la Pommerais, in 1861. Her death was initially regarded as natural. However, de la Pommerais pressed for insurance money with excessive zeal and the insurance company, therefore, pressed for an investigation with equal zeal. The decedent was exhumed and found to have died from digitalis, a difficult point to prove at the time. De la Pommerais was convicted of murder and sent to the guillotine in 1864.

Oleander (*Nerium Oleander*)

Oleander poisoning is based on a cardiac glycoside which, as with the other members of this class, causes predominantly GI and cardiac symptoms. Ventricular ectopy and cardiovascular collapse are the main findings. A middle-aged man ingested a handful of oleander leaves and manifested myriad cardiac symptoms. Included among these were bradycardia, arrest of the sinoatrial node, and junctional escape. The patient recovered. Part of his therapy was digoxin-specific FAB antibody fragments. As mentioned earlier, all plant cardiac glycosides respond to some degree to this antidote despite the fact that it was designed specifically for digoxin. In addition, assay methods created for digoxin also react with the other plant materials described here. This also is due to structural similarities which cause the antibody used in the assay method to cross-react with all cardiac glycosides. Oleander is so potent that persons have suffered serious injury merely from roasting meat over an open fire while the meat was skewered on a twig of this plant. In further testimony to its potency it has been shown that bees sometimes use oleander pollen for their honey and honey prepared in this manner is poisonous.

Monkshood (*Aconitum Napellus*)

This plant also is known as wolfsbane. It is used by some as an herbal medicine under the name of aconite (Figure 25.5). A case is reported in which the patient

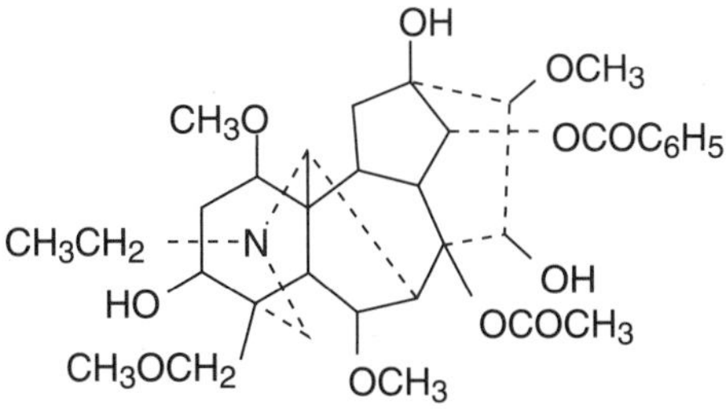

FIGURE 25.5 Aconitine, a potent cardiotoxin.

experienced cardiac failure because of heavy application of the aconite externally as a chest ointment. Two alkaloid toxins are present: aconine and aconitine. Upon ingestion cardiac and neurologic symptoms are observed. Arrhythmias similar to those found from digitalis are found, although the particular cardiac toxin is not a glycoside. Fatal doses are as small as 5 ml of aconite tincture or 1 g of plant material. The roots of aconite may be mistaken for radish. On one occasion, several French army recruits died from eating Monkshood while on a training exercise during World War I. A celebrated murder involved a plant mixture containing Monkshood which Dr. George Lamson fed to his brother-in-law. The poison was contained in a cake. Lamson's motive was greed, the transfer of the victim's money to Lamson's wife. Suspicion fell on the doctor and at his trial his ego got the better of him. He proudly proclaimed how he had fooled the victim and, with cunning intellect, selected a virtually untraceable poison. This was true at the time for the murder occurred in 1882. Despite his effective guilty plea and confession, Lamson was condemned and executed soon thereafter.

Black Hellebore (*Helleborus Niger*)

This plant is also known as henbane. The entire plant is poisonous and contains hellebrin, helleborin, and saponins. It is a GI irritant, but its major effect is cardiotoxic and death occurs from cardiac arrest. A case has been published in which a patient was poisoned with henbane and appeared in an emergency department for treatment of abdominal pain and vomiting. Because no cause was apparent the patient was given supportive care and discharged. He returned several hours later with complaint of increasing paralysis. In short order he began to convulse and expired. Police investigation revealed that he had been poisoned by a friend who had contracted AIDS for which he blamed the decedent.

Death Camas (*Zygadenus Venenosus*)

The cardiovascular toxins found in this species are also different from the glycosides. They are referred to as grayanotoxins and include veratrine and zygadenine. They cause bradycardia and hypotension as well as several cholinergic symptoms, namely, salivation, lacrimation, rhinorrhea, and emesis. Death camas has been mistaken by campers for onion because it has an onion-like bulb. Indeed, two cases of poisoning with this plant involved children who roasted the bulbs on a bonfire and ate them.

Azalea (*Rhododendron Aborescens*), Rhododendron (*Rhododendron Ponticum*), Mountain Laurel (*Kalmia Latifolia*)

These common plants share many properties including their omnipresent nature and the specific poison, andromedotoxin. This toxin causes GI distress, respiratory difficulty, and bradycardia. Some wild birds eat these bushes which renders their flesh harmful to eat.

ANTICHOLINERGIC POISONING

As described in the chapter on anticholinergic poisons, these substances interfere with the propagation of the nerve impulse in the very many cholinergic synapses present throughout the body. It also is pointed out in that chapter that anticholinergic behavior is characteristic of many drug classes. It is found in many plants, a sample of which are described in the following.

Deadly Nightshade (*Atropa Belladonna*)

A characteristic of these plants is that they derive their poisonous nature from the same toxins, three chemicals which possess a tropane nucleus and are only slightly different from each other in molecular structure. They are atropine, hyoscine (scopolamine), and hyoscyamine.

All parts of *Atropa* are dangerous with roots, leaves, and berries containing the highest content of toxic alkaloids. As stated earlier the toxins of *Atropa* have an anticholinergic action, which means that they primarily paralyze the parasympathetic nervous system. The name "belladonna" means beautiful woman and refers to the practice during the Renaissance of placing an extract of *Atropa* on the eyes in order to achieve dilated pupils, regarded by many at the time as being an attractive feature. Poisoners of the middle ages were known to employ this plant in murder. Such was the widespread use of it for this purpose that it was named *Atropa* from Atropos, oldest of the Three Fates, who cuts the thread of life.

Jimsonweed (*Datura Stramonium*)

Jimsonweed is also called thorn apple, stinkweed, and Devil's trumpet. It has an unpleasant odor and contains the three tropane alkaloids shown above. Symptoms of Jimsonweed poisoning include the anticholinergic ones described earlier and also loss of sight, involuntary motions, and delirium. Severe cases may proceed to convulsions, coma, and death. The name Jimsonweed is a corruption of Jamestown weed and refers to the fact that many soldiers died from eating this plant when famine broke out in 1666 in the early American colony, Jamestown, Virginia. The affected soldiers were attempting to quell Bacon's rebellion. A shortage of food lead to scavenging among the fields for something to eat. Hence, the tragic, chance encounter with Datura.

Mandrake (*Mandragora Officinarum*)

In addition to atropine and hyoscyamine, mandrake also contains mandragorin. It was considered a plant that promoted fertility and had aphrodisiac properties probably

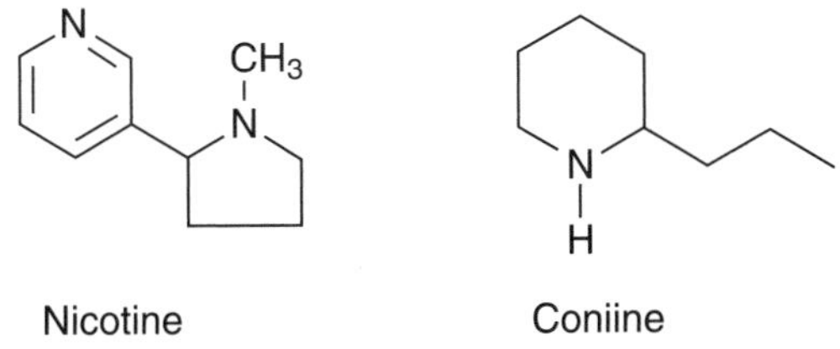

FIGURE 25.6 Nicotine and coniine.

because the large root is thought to resemble the male organ. It also was associated with witchcraft and women were executed in seventeenth century Germany for possession of mandrake, an indication in the minds of some people that they were witches.

Atropine Poisoning in the Scarlet Letter?

The famous American novel by Nathaniel Hawthorne, *The Scarlet Letter*, describes the adultery of Hester Prynne with the Reverend Dimmesdale. Dr. Chillingworth, Hester's husband, may have slowly poisoned Dimmesdale, as retribution, with atropine. Hawthorne was known to be familiar, perhaps even an expert, with the dangers of some plant species. It may have been his hidden plot within a plot that Dimmesdale was, in fact, murdered with atropine at the hands of Chillingworth. The argument is based on several points. First, Chillingworth, the physician, had the motive and the knowledge. Second, Hawthorne describes poisonous plants in the novel. Third, the symptoms from which Dimmesdale suffered were consistent with the known characteristics of atropine. The possible truth of this suggestion reminds us of the common nature of poison, including poisoning with plants, that occurred in colonial times.

NEUROLOGIC TOXICITY

Poison Hemlock (*Conium Maculatum*)

The toxins found in this plant are piperidine alkaloids, coniine, and gamma coniceine. These toxins are fairly potent with gamma coniceine having an LD_{50} of 12 mg/kg. They act at the neuromuscular junction to block the nerve impulse. The primary lethal consequence of this activity is respiratory failure. They also produce what are called nicotinic effects: salivation, mydriasis, and tachycardia at first, followed by bradycardia (Figure 25.6).

Was Socrates Executed with Hemlock?

Plato, the great Greek philosopher, describes the death of Socrates in his dialogue, *Phaedo*, written around 360 B.C. The dialogue does not actually identify the poison used to carry out the execution. However, Plato describes the jailer giving Socrates

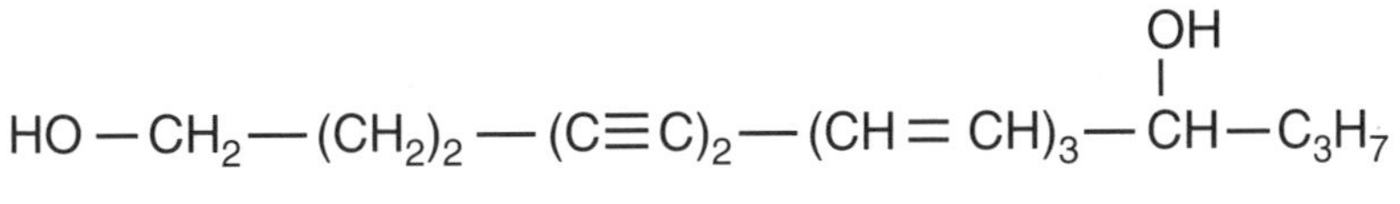

$$HO-CH_2-(CH_2)_2-(C\equiv C)_2-(CH=CH)_3-\overset{\overset{\displaystyle OH}{\displaystyle |}}{CH}-C_3H_7$$

FIGURE 25.7 Structure of cicutoxin.

poison and instructing him to walk about until his legs are heavy. Sometime later Socrates reports no sensation in his legs and, eventually, in the upper part of his body as well. Because some of his symptoms are consistent with the known actions of hemlock and it was known to be used for official executions in the ancient world, it is likely to have been the cause of Socrates' death. With the consumption of hemlock there passed "the wisest, and justest, and best of all men whom I have ever known" (words of *Phaedo*).

Water Hemlock (*Cicuta* spp.)

Water hemlock is a weed commonly found along lakes and streams. This plant is sometimes confused with poison hemlock because they belong to the same family and have similar appearances. The toxin in water hemlock, however, is cicutoxin, whose primary activity is on the brain and spinal cord (Figure 25.7). Cicutoxin is highly potent and is often fatal. In one study 30% of patients exposed to cicutoxin died. It causes rapid onset of status epilepticus, which is difficult to treat and resists the customary anticonvulsant therapy. It is believed that cicutoxin causes seizures by overstimulating central cholinergic pathways.

Curare (*Chondrodendron Tomentosum* and Other Genera)

Curare and similar neuromuscular blocking agents are found in several different plant types and have been used for centuries by the Indians along the Amazon and Orinoco Rivers in South America. The Indians tip their arrows with this poison which paralyzes the skeletal muscles of their prey. Death results from paralysis of the pulmonary structures resulting in respiratory failure. Plants containing curare are not indigenous to the United States. Curare blocks nicotinic receptors without stimulation at skeletal neuromuscular junctions resulting in weakness and paralysis. Although curare is potent when administered intravenously, it has no activity when ingested. Curare has several pharmacologic uses; the principal one is promoting muscular relaxation in general anesthesia.

CYANOGENIC PLANTS

The term cyanogenic indicates that a plant material is able to form cyanide under certain conditions, especially as a result of metabolism. Most cyanogenic substances are glycosides; that is, a carbohydrate moiety is part of their structure. Fortunately, the cyanogens are rarely found in the edible fruit portion of the plant but rather are more likely to be located in leaves, stems, bark, and seed pits. Common cyanogenic plants include apple, apricot, cherry, peach, and black cherry. Because the toxic principle formed in these plants is actually cyanide, the symptoms and treatment are the same as they are for cyanide poisoning.

Hydrangea (*Hydrangea Paniculata*)

Hydrangea contains hydrangin and amygdalin, two cyanogenic glycosides (Figure 25.8). Concentrations are not very high and symptoms usually found from ingestion of this plant are limited to nausea and gastroenteritis. The cyanide antidote should be employed if the patient shows signs of cyanide toxicity.

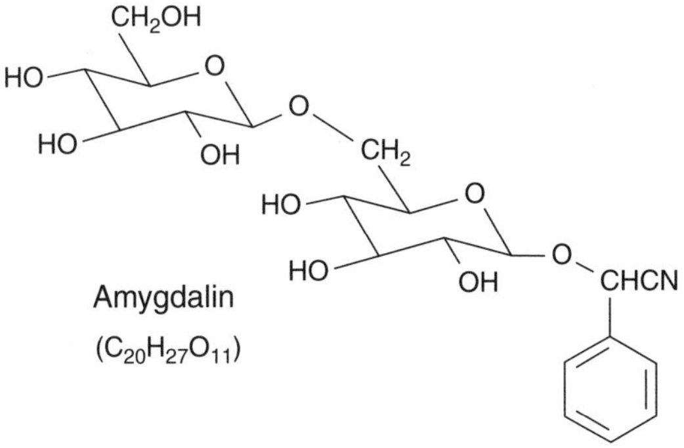

Formation of hydrocyanic acid from amygdalin:

$$C_{20}H_{27}O_{11} + 2H_2O \longrightarrow 2C_6H_{12}O_6 + C_6H_5CHO + HCN$$

FIGURE 25.8 Structure of amygdalin and formation of HCN from amygdalin.

Apricot

This fruit contains amygdalin (as does apple, peach, plum, cherry, and almond). The structure and biochemical pathway of amygdalin are shown in Figure 25.8. It will be noted that the aglycone portion, the molecule without the carbohydrate moiety, is hydrocyanic acid. Interestingly, amygdalin has become celebrated as an alleged cancer cure and is most commonly referred to as laetrile. Laetrile is more likely to cause harm rather than benefit. Consumption of 48 apricot kernels caused lightheadedness and sweating in one patient. Symptoms subsided after ipecac-induced emesis. A similar quantity in another patient caused severe disorientation which was successfully treated with the cyanide antidote. In a third case, 12 bitter almonds caused more serious manifestations including coma, lactic acidosis, and pulmonary edema.

Cassava (*Manihot Esculenta*)

This is a common dietary material in many parts of the world. It contains a cyanogenic glycoside known as linamarin (Figure 25.9). Normal elimination mechanisms, including the conversion of ingested cyanide to thiocyanate, protect those who eat cassava from the cyanogenic glycosides. However, illness and fatalities have

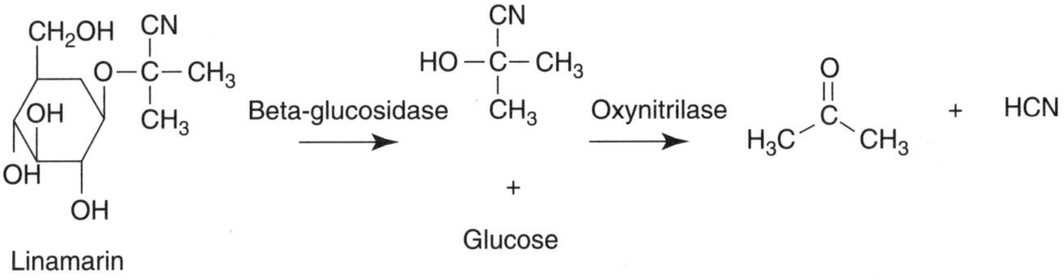

FIGURE 25.9 Formation of HCN from linamarin.

occurred in victims who ate large amounts of cassava. Two forms of nutritional neuropathies have been described in which cyanide from cassava is believed to be part of the pathological mechanism. They are tropical ataxic neuropathy (observed in Nigeria), and epidemic spastic paraperesis (seen in parts of equatorial Africa).

HEPATOTOXIC PLANTS

Akee (*Blighia Sapida*)

Akee, when unripe, contains hypoglycin A (Figure 25.10), a compound believed to be teratogenic and a cause of toxic hypoglycemic syndrome (also called Jamaican vomiting sickness). Akee is a staple in the diet of the people of Jamaica, British West Indies. It is safe when the raw fruit or the spoiled aril (as poisonous as unripe fruit) is avoided. It is believed

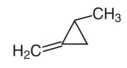

FIGURE 25.10 Hypoglycin.

that the metabolite of hypoglycin, methylene cyclopropane acetic acid, causes malformations and stunted growth in animals and stillbirths as well as severe malformations among humans. Symptoms of akee poisoning are similar to those of insulin overdose and include severe hypoglycemia, convulsions, coma, and death.

SOLANACEOUS PLANTS

This is a large category of plants, as many as 1700 species, that contains solanaceous alkaloids. These glycoalkaloids contain three sugar molecules attached to a steroid-like aglycone portion. Many solanaceous alkaloids contain the same basic aglycone but differ in the number and type of carbohydrate molecules.

Solanine occurs in the common potato, *Solanum tuberosum*, usually at levels less than 10 ppm, a concentration that can increase to 500 ppm when potatoes are green or in those that are injured or sprouting. Levels above 20 ppm are dangerous. Hungry people have died from eating such potatoes. Solanine is a cholinesterase inhibitor. As such it causes cholinergic symptoms such as salivation, trembling, progressive weakness, and paralysis. Solanine contains the aglycone, solanidine, and a unique trisaccharide, solanose. Acid or enzyme hydrolysis converts solanine to solanidine plus the three sugars, D-galactose, D-glucose, and L-rhamnose (Figure 25.11).

MUSHROOMS

"There are old mushroom hunters and there are bold mushroom hunters. But there are no old, bold mushroom hunters." This is an ancient saying that suggests to the modern reader the hazards associated with collection and ingestion of wild mushrooms.

There are many species of edible mushrooms. There are also, however, a large variety of poisonous ones, recognition of which is difficult (Figure 25.12). It is for this reason that many experienced individuals misidentify mushrooms. Only about 10% of the time do victims of mushroom poisoning appear in emergency departments with the specific causative mushroom identified.

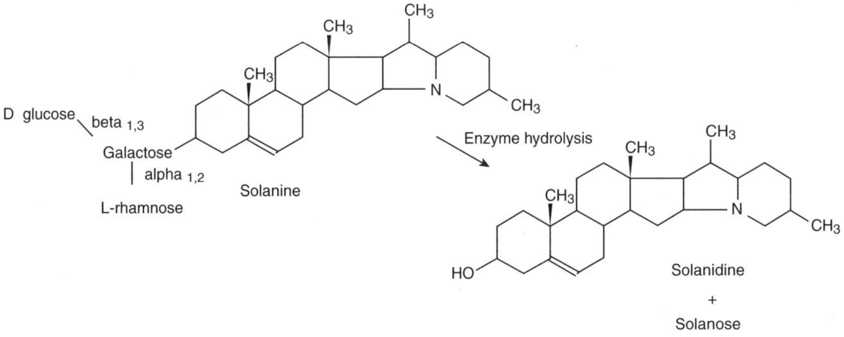

FIGURE 25.11 Synthesis of solanidine from solanine.

FIGURE 25.12 Some poisonous plants. *Aconitum napellus* contains aconitine. *Atropa belladonna* and *Hyocyamus niger* both contain cholinergic alkaloids atropine, scopolamine, and hyoscyamine. *Convallaria majalis* contains a cardiac glycoside. *Taxus brevifolia* is a source of taxine.

Many factors relate to selection of mushrooms for eating. In the first place, everyone should know that only experienced mycologists can safely pick mushrooms in the wild. Even the degree of toxicity of a given species varies from one locale to the next. Emergency departments should try to make an accurate identification when the patient states that he has eaten some suspect mushrooms. This is true because some species are especially toxic, with up to 60% fatalities associated with their ingestion while others have rarely, if ever, been implicated in a fatal ingestion.

Furthermore, the onset of very serious symptoms may be delayed and patients mistakenly discharged only to return in a much more morbid condition at a later time. The danger of mushroom poisoning is only exacerbated by the fact that old wives tales abound in relation to methods, virtually all of them ineffective, for recognizing dangerous mushrooms. In general, because some toxins can be partially or fully inactivated by cooking, some small measure of safety is provided by never eating raw mushrooms collected in the wild.

CATEGORIES OF MUSHROOMS

Cyclopeptide-Containing Varieties

Amanita and *Galerina* are genera of mushrooms from this first category and they account for 95% of all mushroom-associated fatalities (Figure 25.13). Toxins from some members of these genera, e.g., Amanita phalloides (Death cap) or Amanita virosa (Destroying angel) produce nonspecific symptoms initially and then a quiescent phase which appears to be the onset of recovery. In 2 or more days, however, the patient enters a stage of hepatic and renal failure which usually leads to death. Hepatic failure is manifested by many biochemical signs the most ominous of which is hypoglycemia indicating that reserves of glycogen are essentially depleted.

The toxins from Amanita are cyclic peptides including amatoxins (cyclic octapeptides), phallotoxins (cyclic heptapeptides), and virotoxins (cyclic heptapeptides). Phallotoxins act earlier than amatoxins. Their mechanism of action relates to interruption of actin polymer formation and impairment of cell membranes. More severe damage is due to the slower acting amatoxins. Alpha amanatin interferes with RNA polymerase II and so prevents the transcription of DNA. Amatoxins are eliminated slowly from the victim in urine and stool and can be detected by high-performance liquid chromatography. They are exceedingly potent with 10 mg being a lethal dose in average-size subjects. (See Figure 25.14.)

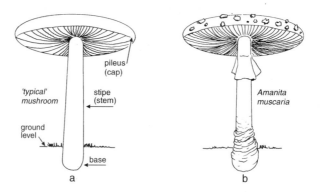

FIGURE 25.13 Illustration of a generic mushroom vs. the appearance of the highly toxic *Amanita* spp. Morphological differences between harmless and harmful mushroom species are often very subtle.

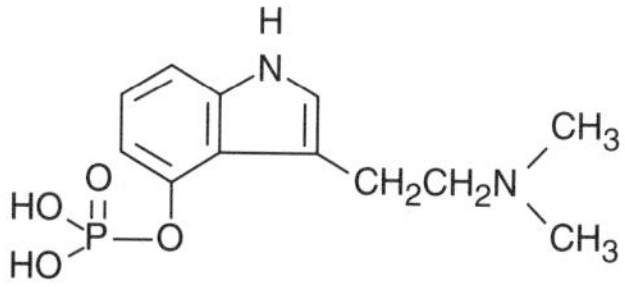

Psilocybin (*Psilocybe* sp.)

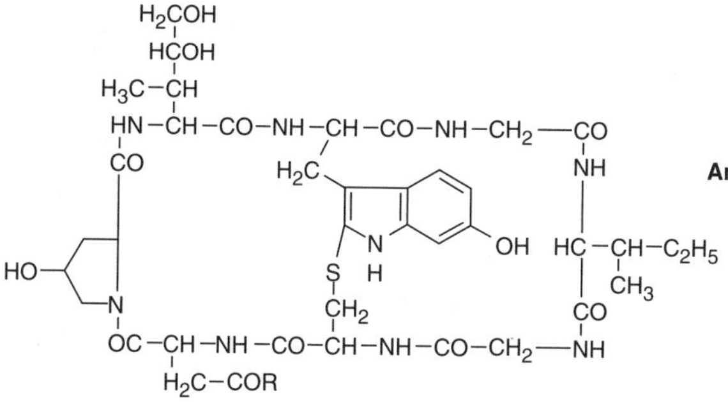

Amanitin (*Amanita* sp.)

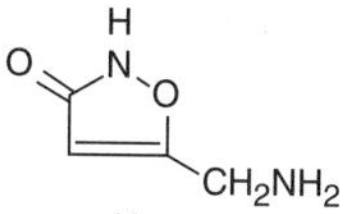

Muscimol (*Amanita muscaria,* etc.)

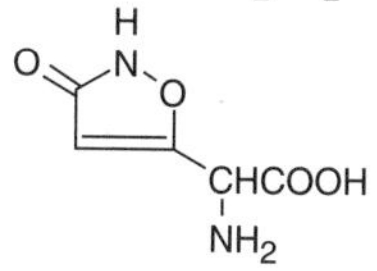

Ibotenic acid (*A. muscaria*)

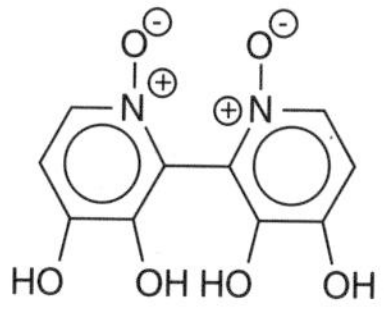

Orellanine (*Cortinarius* sp.)

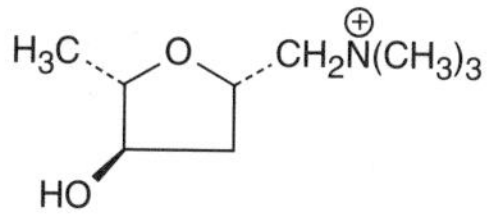

Muscarine (*Clitocybe* sp.)

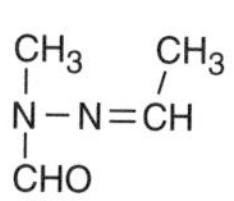

N-methyl-N-formyl hydrazone (*Gyromitra* sp.)

FIGURE 25.14 Structures of some mushroom toxins.

Thioctic acid (alpha-lipoic acid) has been credited with antidotal behavior toward *Amanita* species. This is not fully proven and the mechanism of its proposed activity is not known. Penicillin at high concentration and silibinin, an extract from the milk thistle, are both thought to inhibit alpha-amanitin hepatic uptake. They are components of some therapeutic schemes, but their beneficial action is doubted by some experts. Cimetidine also has been suggested as a remedy for amanatin because it is a potent P_{450} cytochrome system inhibitor.

In severe poisoning where the clinical course has progressed to the point of hepatic encephalopathy, liver transplant may be the only recourse to save the patient. There are, indeed, several published case reports of patients saved from Amanita poisoning while in fulminant hepatic failure by liver transplant.

Monomethylhydrazine-Containing Mushrooms

Mushrooms of the genus, *Gyromitra*, contain gyromitrin. This is equal to N-methyl N-formyl hydrazone which readily hydrolyzes to N-methyl N-formyl hydrazine plus acetaldehyde. A second, slower hydrolytic step leads to monomethylhydrazine. Hydrazine has the peculiar property of binding to pyridoxine (vitamin B_6), thereby inhibiting pyridoxal phosphate-mediated enzymatic reactions.

Gyromitra, unlike many other species, is easily recognized. Persons ingesting it experience GI upset and, in large ingestions, seizures and hepatorenal failure. Mortality may be as high as 40%.

Because the toxin interferes with pyridoxine activity, exogenous pyridoxine may be beneficial as an antidote. This category of mushrooms is a good example of regional differences in poison content because the *Gyromitra* are reputed to be edible and safe when collected in the western United States but not in other areas.

Muscarine-Containing Mushrooms

Clitocybe species mushrooms contain muscarine. This compound exerts a cholinergic effect on the patient that is characterized by the SLUD syndrome: salivation, lacrimation, urination, and defecation. The symptoms are limited to the peripheral nervous system because the toxin is a quaternary ammonium compound that is too polar to cross the blood–brain barrier. Morbidity from this toxin can be severe, but mortality is almost unknown and there is an antidote, atropine, which reverses the effects of the toxin.

Coprine-Containing Mushrooms

The genus, *Coprinus*, contain the toxin, coprine. This is an amino acid which is metabolized to L-aminocyclopropanol, a metabolite that functions as an inhibitor of the enzyme, acetaldehyde dehydrogenase. Disulfiram is a synthetic drug that has the same effect as L-aminocyclopropanol. Disulfiram is taken with the intention of blocking acetaldehyde dehydrogenase. It is an effective treatment in a small number of alcoholics because consumption of alcohol will cause an accumulation of acetaldehyde and resultant nausea. Therefore, coprine metabolite has a disulfiram-like effect. If the patient eats *Coprinus* and also drinks alcohol, severe nausea results. Some tachycardia, nausea, and vomiting are noted, even in the absence of alcohol consumption.

Ibotenic Acid- and Muscimol-Containing Mushrooms

Amanita gemmata, A. muscaria (fly agaric), and *A. pantherina* all contain isoxazole derivatives. Ibotenic acid and its decarboxylated metabolite, muscimol, are found in this group. Ingestion of these species is followed by fairly rapid development of hallucinations, delirium, and seizures. The 3-dimensional structure of muscimol is quite similar to that of gamma-amino butyric acid (GABA), a neurotransmitter. Symptoms observed are those found in GABA activation so it is a reasonable hypothesis that muscimol activates GABA receptors. The activation is characterized by opening chloride channels, which results in the inhibition of neuron function. While muscimol opens chloride channels and thus inhibits function, benzodiazepines bind at a nearby site in GABA neurons and they close the chloride channels. This, of course, produces the opposite effect of neuronal activation. Benzodiazepines are effective antidotes for ingestion of these varieties of mushrooms.

Psilocybin-Containing Mushrooms

Psilocybe species are often deliberately eaten for their capacity to induce hallucinations. They contain indoles, psilocybin and psilocin (the metabolite of psilocybin), which promote LSD-like behavior (but with 100-fold lower potency). Within 1/2 hour of ingestion, hallucinations occur and may be accompanied by hyperkinesis, ataxia, and seizures.

Psilocybe species are common in the southwestern United States, Mexico, and Central America, where they have long been employed in religious ceremonies. Popularly they are known as magic mushroom or shrooms.

Psilocin is chemically similar to the neurotransmitter, serotonin. It enters the synapse and affects the presynaptic release of serotonin, leading to a decrease in serotonin. The concentration of serotonin at the postsynaptic receptor is decreased and activity in the neuronal circuit declines. The hypothesis that psilocin reacts in a manner identical to LSD is supported by the finding that tolerance to LSD is caused by use of psilocybin.

Gastrointestinal Toxin-Containing Mushrooms

A very large and diverse number of toxins which cause gastrointestinal distress are found in many mushrooms. The number actually runs into the hundreds and symptoms are referrable to the GI tract. Morbidity can be significant, but fatalities are very rare.

Orelline and Orellanine-Containing Mushrooms

These toxins are bipyridyl compounds found in the *Cortinarius* species. They cause renal damage of the tubular type, usually interstitial nephritis. Glomerular damage is usually not found. The victim initially experiences nonspecific symptoms including headache, chills, anorexia, and nausea. Oliguric renal failure occurs as long as several weeks after the ingestion. No specific therapy is known, but deaths are very rare and renal function is eventually recovered in about one half of exposed patients.

TABLE 25.4
Some Mushroom Species and their Target Organs

Species	Organ	Time of Symptom Onset
Phalloides	Liver	Up to 24 hours
Gyromitra	Liver	Up to 12 hours
Cortinarius	Kidney	Up to 14 days
Coprina	Autonomic nervous system	0.5 hours
Pantherina	Central nervous system	0.5–3 hours
Psilocybe	Gastrointestinal system	0.5–3 hours

Questions and Problems

1. If you have Internet access, run a search of plant poisons. List at least three sites that provide helpful illustrations of poisonous plants.
2. Make a table that lists the name and the structure for the major toxin found in each of the following plants:
    Capsicum
    Pokeweed
    Brassaia
    Azalea
    Hellebore
3. Make a table for poisonous mushrooms that includes the following categories:
    Name
    Toxin name
    Toxin structure
    Organ system(s) affected
    Antidote
    Therapy
4. Search Medline, the National Library of Medicine database, for these topic headings: plants, overdose, case studies. Summarize the major aspects of at least one study that you locate from your search.

Case Study 1: The Bold Mushroom Hunter

A 32-year-old man collected mushrooms from his girlfriend's lawn in the southern United States. As a child he had frequently collected mushrooms under the directions of cousins who had learned to recognize them in their native Italy. After sauteeing the mushrooms in butter he consumed them. Twenty hours later he arrived at an emergency department complaining of nausea and vomiting. He was given gastric lavage. Activated charcoal was provided in an attempt to bind any particles remaining free in the GI tract. He appeared to be improving. Nevertheless, 1 day later liver abnormalities were noted by elevated hepatic enzymes and prolonged prothrombin time. His AST rose to 7892 U/L and ALT reached 5326 U/L (normal for both is less than 35 U/L) and prothrombin time reached 60 seconds (normal < 15 seconds). As his symptoms worsened he was transferred to a tertiary care facility. Over the following 3 days, he experienced renal failure, hypofibrinogenemia, coagulopathy, acidosis, hypoglycemia, encephalopathy, and fulminant hepatic failure. He died on the 7th day after ingestion of the mushrooms.

What kind of mushrooms are most likely to be implicated in this case?
   a) *Amanita muscaria*
   b) *Omphalotus illudens*
   c) *Amanita phalloides*
   d) *Psilocybe* spp.

Psilocybe mushrooms contain hallucinogenic agents so the major manifestation of their exposure is likely to be hallucinations. *Omphalotus*, also known as Jack O'Lantern, primarily causes gastrointestinal symptoms. Sweating and nausea also are sometimes noted. Whereas this type of mushroom may cause some degree of liver toxicity manifested by elevations of liver enzymes, such elevations are minor. Jack O'Lantern also produces symptoms rather early, typically 3 to 5 hours after ingestion. The delayed onset seen in the present case is not characteristic of *Omphalotus* nor of most mushrooms. *Amanita muscaria* has as its toxic agents ibotenic acid and muscimol. They usually cause confusion, dysarthria, and staggering gait. Symptoms are also seen fairly rapidly, on the order of 2 hours after ingestion. The patient in this case ate *Amanita phalloides*, also known as Death Cap. It is believed to be responsible for 90% of deaths associated with mushroom poisoning; 20 to 30% of patients who eat this species just once die as a result.

Questions

Q1. Why is the liver especially susceptible to *Amanita* poisoning?
   a) Rich blood supply
   b) Site of glycogen storage
   c) High rate of protein synthesis in hepatocytes
   d) Major site of drug metabolizing activity
Q2. Which is not usually effective in treatment of *Amanita* ingestion?
   a) Hemoperfusion
   b) Gastric lavage and charcoal treatment
   c) Liver transplant
   d) Fluids and electrolytes to maintain hydration and balance
Q3. Which is not a common reason for mushroom poisoning?
   a) Difference in appearance of same species in different climates.
   b) Picker does not know that mushrooms can be poisonous.
   c) Important anatomical feature is missing when the mushroom is classified before eating.
   d) False reliance on cooking as a means of detoxifying the mushroom.

Q4. Which is an indication that a liver transplant is needed?
a) Markedly prolonged prothrombin time
b) Hypoglycemia
c) Gastrointestinal hemorrhage
d) All of the above
e) None of the above

Answers and Discussion

Q1. (Answer = c) Amanitins are cyclic octapeptides that interrupt protein synthesis and cause cell death. They bind with a subunit of RNA polymerase II and interfere with mRNA synthesis. Hepatocytes, because they have a high rate of protein synthesis, are a primary site for amanitin's deleterious action. The rich blood supply is a small factor in increasing the liver's vulnerability. For some toxins the liver's role as a drug metabolizing organ is a contributing factor toward toxicity. In this case, however, it is not a factor because amanitin is toxic in its native form and does not require conversion to a toxic form.

Q2. (Answer = a) Hemoperfusion has been attempted in *Amanita* poisoning but was not found to be effective in reducing severity of poisoning. Supportive therapy and decontamination are very helpful. Liver transplant, if achieved, can be life-saving because liver failure appears to be the major cause of death for many patients poisoned with this species of mushroom.

Q3. (Answer = b) Virtually all individuals who collect mushrooms are aware that some species are poisonous and even involve a high risk of death. They are, nevertheless, confident of their ability to recognize the small percent (less than 2.5%) of poisonous species. Problems occur when these pickers do not realize that the same species may have morphological variations in different regions which render their identification difficult. In addition, the mushroom might be only partially picked so that a structure is left behind and that structure is indicative of a poisonous nature. For example, *Amanita phalloides* has a cup at the base (called the volva) which allows some to recognize it. This cup is often left behind in the soil if the mushroom is broken at the stem when picked. Finally, some toxins are inactivated by cooking, but this is not the case with amatoxins. Despite their generally large body of knowledge about mushrooms, some collectors are under the illusion that mushrooms are toxic only when eaten raw.

Q4. (Answer = d) Because liver transplant is such an extreme surgical intervention it is critical to utilize it as intelligently as possible. Therefore, selection of patients is of prime importance. Those with fulminant hepatic failure or very likely to experience fulminant failure are candidates. Further, they can be recognized by the signs listed here as well as hypofibrinogenemia, acidosis, and significant increase in ammonia after high elevation of liver enzymes.

References

O'Brien, B.L. and Khuu, L., A fatal Sunday brunch: Amanita mushroom poisoning in a Gulf Coast family, *Am. J. Gastroent.*, 91, 581–583, 1996.

Yamada, E.G. et al., Mushroom poisoning due to amatoxin, *West. J. Med.*, 169, 380–384, 1998.

Case Study 2: The Mass Casualty or "Bugs All over Me"

Eleven teenage boys and girls were brought to an emergency department over a 4-hour period one mid-afternoon in September. They were acquaintances from school who were at a party together. All 11 displayed various stages of agitation and delirium. Ten of the teens were hallucinating and several described seeing bugs all over them and throughout the room. They were disoriented and babbling incoherently. Physical examination revealed elevated pulse rate in all (up to 180/minute in one case), dilated pupil size, and agitation requiring restraints for 6 of the 11 patients. All were noted to have slight tachycardia, dry skin, and decreased bowel sounds.

One patient was disoriented but not agitated, and she received oral charcoal in the emergency department. The rest were given charcoal by NG tube. Nine of the 11 were judged to be sufficiently disoriented after several hours that they required admission. The other two were hallucinating when admitted to the emergency department but recovered there and did not require admission for further observation. After admission the 9 patients received primarily supportive care and were discharged after 2 days.

What is a possible toxin involved in this poisoning?
   a) Atropine from a plant
   b) Gamma hydroxybutyric acid
   c) LSD
   d) Mescaline

The actual toxins in this case were atropine, scopolamine, and hyoscyamine, three anticholinergic alkaloids found in Jimsonweed (*Datura stramonium*). These teenagers were erroneously informed by a friend that Jimsonweed causes pure hallucinations without any other effects. They ingested between 1 and 4 seed pods (each pod contains about 100 seeds and each seed contains about 60 μg of atropine). Approximately 8 hours after the ingestion they began appearing in the emergency department. The other suggested answers above also could cause the agitation and hallucinations observed in these patients. Gamma hydroxybutyrate is more likely to produce sedation, however. None of these other possibilities provoke the anticholinergic syndrome seen here. These physical signs, including mydriasis, tachycardia, dry skin, and decreased bowel sounds, are characteristic of atropine and other anticholinergic agents. They are not found from ingestions of the other listed agents.

Questions

Q1. The volume of distribution of atropine is 2.3 L/kg. What is the expected blood level for one of these patients, a 160-lb. 15-year-old boy, who ingested 2 pods of *Datura* seeds?
a) 72 µg/L
b) 5 mg/L
c) 130 ng/L
d) 50 µg/dL

Q2. A mnemonic is often suggested as a means of remembering anticholinergic symptoms. Which of the following is not part of the mnemonic?
a) Mad as a hatter
b) Dry as a bone
c) Blind as a bat
d) White as a sheet
e) Hot as Hades

Q3. Where does Jimsonweed rank in frequency of poisoning compared to other plants?
a) First
b) In the top 10
c) Not in the top 20
d) Very common because of the attractive appearance of the pods

Q4. Which is not an advisable step in treatment of Jimsonweed ingestion?
a) Volume resuscitation with crystalloid fluids
b) Control of agitation with phenothiazines or butyrophenones
c) Temperature reduction with evaporative cooling
d) Decontamination by administration of charcoal

Answers and Discussion

Q1. (Answer = a) The boy weighs 73 kg.
Calculation

$$\text{Two pods contain 200 seeds} \times 60 \text{ µg atropine each} =$$

$$12{,}000 \text{ µg or 12 mg of atropine.}$$

$$Vd = dose/Cp; \quad Cp = \text{blood concentration} = Dose/Vd$$

$$Cp = 12 \text{ mg}/2.3 \text{ L/kg} \times 73 \text{ kg} = 72 \text{ µg/L}$$

Q2. (Answer = d) The patient is not as white as a sheet and is, in fact, not pallid by any stretch. In the mnemonic the wording is red as a beet. The redness is due to hyperthermia and anticholinergic agitation. Dry as a bone and hot as Hades also refer to the effects of hyperthermia which, in turn, is an anticholinergic effect.

Q3. (Answer = c) Despite the common distribution of *Datura stramonium*, Jimsonweed poisoning is uncommon. Poison Control Center data for 1993 recorded only 318 cases among a total of 94,725 poisonings from all plants. Part of the explanation for this low rate of exposure is the relatively unappetizing appearance of the pods which are not likely to attract very many children. In addition, it is probable that many poisonings are mild enough so that they are not reported by people who have an additional motive for not reporting them: The plant is being ingested as an abused substance.

Q4. (Answer = b) Volume repletion will be necessary because the patient becomes dry from the hyperthermia. Again, the hyperthermia is usually quite severe and simple cooling blankets or mild antipyretic agents may not be sufficiently effective. Aggressive temperature reduction may be necessary. This can be achieved by evaporative cooling with water and fans. Decontamination by administration of charcoal is usually effective because charcoal has been shown to bind most anticholinergic agents. Control of agitation is critical because many patients are aroused to the point at which they harm themselves. Muscle injury is common in this context so the patient needs to be medicinally calmed. Phenothiazines and butyrophenones are drugs employed for this purpose in many situations. They are, however, themselves anticholinergic. While possibly calming the patient they also may intensify the anticholinergic crisis. Benzodiazepines are preferred in this context. Midazolam is a benzodiazepine that penetrates the blood–brain barrier rapidly and is, therefore, a good choice for atropine poisoning.

Reference

Tiongson, J. and Salen, P., Mass ingestion of Jimsonweed by eleven teenagers, *Del. Med. J.*, 70, 471–476, 1998.

Case Study 3: Much-Delayed Poisoning

A 78-year-old woman had a single meal of mushrooms with her son and grandson. A week later she developed nausea, vomiting, dizziness, malaise, and joint pain. As symptoms worsened she decided to seek medical attention and was admitted to the hospital 11 days after ingesting the mushroom meal. Her laboratory results showed several gross abnormalities as indicated here:

BUN	48 mg/dL
Creatinine	20 mg/dL
LD	508 U/L
Potassium	6.8 mmol/L
Uric acid	15 mg/dL
C-reactive protein	35.5 mg/dL

In addition, her blood pressure was elevated and her arterial blood gases showed metabolic acidosis. Her urine output was only 50 mL/day. Renal biopsy showed acute tubular necrosis, and acute renal failure was diagnosed.

What kind of mushroom was ingested by the patient?
- a) *Agaricus campestris* (meadow mushroom)
- b) *Coprinus comatus* (shaggy mane)
- c) *Morchella angusticeps* (black morel)
- d) *Cortinarius orellanus*

Cortinarius spp., which contain orellanine, a nephrotoxin, were identified in this case by an expert mycologist. This type of mushroom also would have been strongly suspected on the basis of the symptoms this woman manifested. The others who shared this meal with her also experienced renal failure. The other mushrooms listed above are all classified as edible.

The patient was treated with steroids which alleviated her symptoms. She was then given hemodialysis and required such treatment for the 1 year following the onset of symptoms. At the time that the case was reported she continued to be in need of maintenance dialysis.

Questions

Q1. Why are this patient's urea and creatinine elevated?
- a) Liver toxicity and inability to metabolize them
- b) Renal disease and inability to excrete them
- c) Cardiac injury and reduced perfusion
- d) CNS toxicity with associated multiple organ failure

Q2. What is the major feature of *Cortinarius* toxicity?
- a) Gastrointestinal irritation
- b) Kidney disease
- c) CNS disturbance
- d) Cardiac arrhythmias

Q3. Why is presentation for medical help delayed?
- a) The toxin slowly and specifically inhibits protein synthesis in renal tubular cells.
- b) The toxin undergoes transformation in three steps to an active form.
- c) The toxin has a low binding affinity for a hepatic receptor and takes a long time to reach toxic levels at the receptor surface.
- d) The toxin changes membrane permeability, and the effects are gradual in onset.

Q4. What is the chemical nature of the toxin?
- a) An organophosphate, like malathion
- b) An anticholinergic agent. like atropine
- c) A dipyridyl, like paraquat
- d) An organohalide

Answers and Discussion

Q1. (Answer = b) *Cortinarius* causes renal failure, and this results in a decrease in the normal filtering action of the glomerulus in the kidney. As filtration slows waste materials such as urea and creatinine pile up in the blood. This mushroom may also cause, less commonly, disease in other organs. In most cases, the accumulation of waste products is due primarily to a renal effect.

Q2. (Answer = b) *Cortinarius* contains orellanine which has a specific affinity for the renal tubular cells. Ultraviolet light reduces orellanine to orelline which is nontoxic. The toxin is quite stable and can be detected in renal biopsies for up to 6 months after ingestion. Approximately 50% of patients ingesting *Cortinarius* develop acute renal failure. Of these, one half experience irreversible disease requiring permanent dialysis or kidney transplant.

Q3. (Answer = a) It is believed that orellanine enters the brush border region of the proximal tubular cells and inhibits protein synthesis. Thus, effects are delayed until the number of functioning nephrons is too small to meet physiological needs. This process appears to take at least 4 days. During that 4-day or more interval the patient may be asymptomatic or may be suffering from the gastrointestinal effects of *Cortinarius*. The toxin does not require transformation to an active form. Nothing is known about hepatic effects of this toxin and, if they exist, they are likely to be minimal.

Q4. (Answer = c) Orellanine is 3,3-4,4 tetrahydroxy 2,2 dipyridine-dioxide. Chemically it is structurally similar to paraquat (1,1-dimethyl-4,4′-bipyridylium chloride). However, orellanine appears to attack primarily the kidneys whereas paraquat mainly causes lung damage.

Reference

Horn, S. et al., End-stage renal failure from mushroom poisoning with *Cortinarius orellanus*: report of 4 cases and review of the literature, *Am. J. Kidney Dis.*, 30, 282–286, 1997.

Case Study 4: A Child with Green Emesis

The patient, a 4-year-old boy, took a nap in mid-afternoon. Two hours later his father attempted to awaken him but could not do so. The father also noted that his son had vomited some green material. The child was then brought to an emergency department. Vital signs on this 46-lb. boy were within normal limits. His pupils were noted to be small and reactive, and his gaze was described as disconjugate. Upon neurological exam the child displayed slow reaction to painful stimuli in the upper extremities and withdrawal in the legs. All laboratory testing including routine tests plus toxicology screens were within normal limits and chest and abdominal radiographs were normal.

The child was lavaged and treated with activated charcoal. For the first 2 hours at the emergency department he became progressively less responsive. After this time, however, he started to become oriented and spoke with his parents. The child stated that he ate, just before napping, 10 leaves of a plant that grew in the backyard of his home. These leaves were later estimated to weigh about 3 g each. He was kept for observation for an additional 24-hour period and then was discharged. At that time there were no residual signs of his toxic exposure.

The toxic plant may have been which of the following?
a) *Amanita phalloides*
b) Jimsonweed
c Poison hemlock
d) Dieffenbachia

Amanita is the toxic form of mushrooms. There is a delayed reaction to this toxic ingestion and patients do not feel sick for 8 or more hours after eating *Amanita*. Jimsonweed is a common plant often deliberately eaten to provoke hallucinations. It causes a severe anticholinergic syndrome not similar to the clinical picture seen here. Poison hemlock is the herb this child ingested. Hemlock contains coniine and gamma-coniceine (850 µg of gamma coniceine per gram of leaf) which block nerve transmission at the neuromuscular junction. In sufficient quantity they cause death by respiratory failure. Dieffenbachia discharges calcium oxalate crystals into the oral cavity and produces intense inflammation within the mouth.

Questions

Q1. The median lethal dose in mice is 12 mg/kg for gamma-coniceine, the most toxic and abundant alkaloid in hemlock. Assuming that humans have the same LD_{50} what fraction of a lethal dose did this child ingest?
a) 10%
b) <1%
c) 92%
d) 53%

Q2. Water hemlock is a related species of toxic plant. It contains
a) Coniine
b) Cicutoxin
c) Atropine
d) Oleander

Q3. Why did this patient have such relatively minor symptoms?
a) Small dose
b) Vomiting after ingestion
c) Gastrointestinal decontamination
d) All of the above
e) None of the above

Answers and Discussion

Q1. (Answer = a) For this child who weighs 46 lbs. or 21 kg, a median lethal dose is 12 mg/kg × 21 kg = 252 mg. He recalled eating 10 leaves which have an estimated weight of 3 g each or 30 g. There are 850 μg of gamma-coniceine in each gram of leaf or a total of 25,500 μg (25.5 mg) of toxin in the total ingestion. This is close to 10% of a median lethal dose and explains why the child's poisoning was relatively mild.

Q2. (Answer = b) Water hemlock is similar in morphology to poison hemlock and belongs to the same family of plants. The toxin of the former is, however, much different in structure and action. It acts primarily on the CNS and causes, among other reactions, seizures. Coniine, a toxin of poison hemlock, is not found in water hemlock. Atropine is found in many plants. Oleandrin is an extremely potent cardiac glycoside found in the oleander plant.

Q3. (Answer = d) Review of the case indicates that all of these items are true and all should conduce to a relatively benign response. Indeed, in accidental ingestions, the amount of plant material is usually less than found in this case because of the repulsive odor from the plant, its bitter taste, and the rapid onset of a burning sensation after placing material from it in the mouth. On the other hand, it caused fatalities, such as in the alleged execution of the great philosopher, Socrates, when used as a means of offical executions because the toxin was concentrated into an elixir.

Reference

Frank, B.S. et al., Ingestion of poison hemlock (*Conium maculatum*), *West. J. Med.,* 163, 573–574, 1995.

26 Snake Venoms

CONTENTS

Snake venoms are an important area in toxicology. This is true not merely because of their inherent variety and complexity but also because they appear to offer research opportunities for better understanding of physiological processes and as possible means for medical benefit. In the latter context, many venoms are studied for a potentially beneficial role in stroke and other disease processes.

The statistics regarding snakes and their venoms are impressive. It is said that 3000 species of snakes are found worldwide; 300 of which are poisonous. The poisonous ones are in the following families: Elapidae (cobra, mamba, and others); Hydrophidae (sea snakes); Viperidae (true vipers and pit vipers, including rattlesnakes);

and Colubridae (boomslang, mangrove, and other Asiatic varieties). In North America there are 45,000 snakebites in a typical year. Only about 20% of these are from poisonous snakes, however, and only a handful of these, perhaps a total of just 12 to 15, cause death. Some of the poisonous bites are not dangerous because the snake bites its victim without envenomating the victim (dry bite). This occurs approximately 20% of the time. The major reason for the high survival rates following snakebite in North America is not the lack of potency of the venom but rather its relatively slow action. If medical care is provided, administration of antivenin is usually curative. However, without treatment, it is estimated that 75% of rattlesnake bites would be fatal. The vast majority of fatal bites are associated with alcohol intoxication, other drug abuse, and/or careless activity on the part of the victim. If the victim is sober and nothing happens to inhibit his access to medical care, then the outcome is usually good. Some of the world's most dangerous snakes are in Australia and yet deaths from snakebite are rare in that country because of a comprehensive program for the preparation of antidotes and making them available on a widespread basis. In some parts of the world, however, snakebite is a common cause of death. Annual fatalities from this cause in select nations are as follows: Southeast Asia, 2500; Burma, 1000; India, 15,000; and Brazil, 1500.

In this chapter we limit the scope of this extensive topic to Crotalids, representative of American snakes, and cobra, representative of foreign species. The major goal of this discussion is an examination of the biochemical and pathological aspects of venom. We also discuss current concepts of therapy for snakebite.

More than 98% of all envenomations in the United States are caused by Crotalids (family Crotalidae, pit vipers, or new world vipers). They possess triangular-shaped heads, elliptical pupils, and a single row of subcaudal scales. They are known as pit vipers because they have infrared, heat-sensitive pits. Such pits enable them to locate prey, strike accurately, and even determine from the size of the prey how much venom to release. It is critical for the snake to conserve venom because it takes approximately one month to completely replenish the venom supply should it be dispensed fully in one large strike. The family Crotalidae has three genera: Crotalus, Sistrurus, and Agkistrodon. The first two genera possess rattles and are more commonly called rattlesnakes.

PATHOPHYSIOLOGY OF CROTALID BITES

Snake venom is among the most complex of biochemical mixtures. Unlike plant poisons that usually consist of 1 or at most 2 to 3 specific compounds, snake venom of a given species usually contains a large number of components. The list of substances in Crotalid venom shown in Table 26.1 is not an exhaustive compendium of all the actual components, despite the fact that it runs to 19 different substances.

The activity of different components of snakebite with respect to causing pathological events is not fully understood. However, in an approximate manner, certain constituents of the venom can be related to the overall damage associated with envenomation. Tissue damage at the bite site is usually the first manifestation of the attack. The venom component collagenase is intended to break down the integrity of the tissue and permit the venom to penetrate more deeply into the victim. Toxin

---

TABLE 26.1
Some Constituents of Crotalid Venom

Acetylcholinesterase	L-amino acid oxidase
Arginine ester hydrolase	Collagenase
Deoxyribonuclease	Hyaluronidase
Lactic dehydrogenase	Metalloproteinases
Myotoxin - a	NAD nucleotidase
5' Nucleotidase	Phospholipase A2
Phospholipase B	Phospholipase C
Phosphomonoesterase	Phosphodiesterase
Ribonuclease	Thrombin-like enzyme
Veriditoxin	

---

components that are hemorrhagic damage or increase the permeability of capillary endothelial cells and other components of vessel walls. The impact of this hemorrhagic and histiolytic activity is the transfer of blood and fluid into tissues surrounding the bitten region. Patients develop swelling at the site. Discoloration and hemorrhagic blebs (dark, fluid-filled blisters at the spot of the bite) develop. Swelling can become extreme and continue for several days. On occasion, bites to the tongue have resulted in life-threatening edema and airway obstruction.

TISSUE DAMAGE

Metalloproteinases are now known to promote tissue necrosis in the area of the bite. Their enzymatic action involves cleavage of protumor necrosis factor-alpha with release of active tissue necrosis factor-alpha (TNFA). TNFA is an inflammatory activator that induces macrophage differentiation, release of inflammatory mediators such as interleukins, and other typical activities found in the inflammatory response. The venom metalloproteinases are, therefore, intimately involved in the severe pain experienced from the bite. They also contribute to the degradation of extracellular matrix proteins. Not surprisingly antivenin can limit this process because it contains factors specifically prepared against the metalloproteinases. Inhibition of snakebite pathology at this stage, however, requires early administration of antivenin. Because the inflammatory process is started by the venom but perpetuated partly by the victim; however, administration of antivenin cannot completely interrupt inflammation.

MUSCLE DAMAGE

In addition to the action of metalloproteinases, another venom factor that contributes to tissue necrosis is myotoxin-a (MA). MA leads to necrosis of skeletal muscle by its direct action in increasing intracellular calcium. MA opens voltage-sensitive calcium channels leading to enhanced sodium-calcium ion exchange and, thereby, a higher calcium concentration in the cell. Other mechanisms are also believed to be active in raising cytoplasmic calcium. The end result of elevated cellular calcium is activation of enzymes that are damaging to muscle, exaggerated muscle fiber contraction, and eventual muscle necrosis. Other venom components also are myopathic, among them an enzyme called veriditoxin. The myopathic character of venom may be exerted locally as when a bite directly into muscle occurs, or remotely, as when myopathic factors diffuse to a remote area where rhabdomyolysis is then observed. The molecular nature of MA is not fully worked out. It is known, however, that it is a polypeptide just below protein dimensions at molecular weight 4100 Da. It does not behave as a good antigen and, as a result, polyvalent Crotalid antivenin is only mildly protective against MA. In summary, the muscle necrosis caused by snake venom is difficult to deal with therapeutically. This is due to the low quantity of anti-MA in antivenin as well as to the fact that other venom components are also myopathic.

COAGULOPATHY

Blood clotting is a process that constitutes a very common target for venoms of many different snake genera. Not only do venoms of many snake species interfere in the normal clotting cascade but they do so in a large variety of ways.

Defibrination (the depletion of fibrinogen and fibrin) without disseminated intravascular coagulation (DIC) is the most common coagulopathy of North American pit vipers. Defibrination may occur from the action of fibrinolysins, venom components that directly destroy fibrinogen. Venom also may contain thrombin-like enzymes that remove a fibrinopeptide from one end of fibrinogen resulting in an abnormal fibrin chain. Normally, one function of thrombin is to activate Factor XIII. The abnormal thrombin substitute found in venom does not activate Factor XIII, which leads to production of fibrin that is not cross-linked. Collectively, the coagulopathic venom components (fibrinolysins and thrombin-like enzymes) deplete fibrinogen, the clot precursor. They also cause a lack of intravascular clots, elevated fibrin degradation products, and prolongation of clotting time. DIC, disseminated intravascular coagulation, is often regarded as the ultimate catastrophe in coagulation. This is uncommon in snakebite. Sometimes, however, the coagulation cascade is activated by direct envenomation into a blood vessel (most snakebites are into skin or muscle). DIC is a major complication of snakebite that is believed to be rare but may be common in victims who die before medical care has been provided.

PLATELET DEFICIENCY

Venom is able to induce thrombocytopenia. A possible mechanism for this is the injury to platelet membranes by phospholipases present in venom. Alternatively, platelets may become aggregated under the influence of some venom component. It is common to find thrombocytopenia and defibrination in bitten patients. Laboratory studies that confirm these two events are prolonged coagulation time, low fibrinogen, high fibrin degradation products, and low platelet counts. These laboratory findings are also found in the context of DIC, but in snakebite they do not usually mean that DIC has occurred. Severe thrombocytopenia from snakebite is associated with some degree of spontaneous hemorrhage. Bleeding is otherwise uncommon in snakebite, even in the presence of extensive defibrination.

CARDIOTOXINS

A myocardial depressant protein is found in the venom of at least some species of rattlesnake. It is of low potency, however, and does not, by itself, lead to significant hypotension from reduced cardiac output. Hypotension may occur following snake-bite. It is more likely to be due to anaphylactic shock or adult respiratory distress rather than a venom-based myocardial depressant.

NEUROTOXINS

Neurotoxic activity is found in Crotalid venom but tends to be less pathologically significant than other aspects of rattlesnake venom toxicity. Mojave rattlesnake produces a neurotoxin that causes weakness and paralysis. In severe cases, the neurotoxin can cause paresthesias, diplopia, and even respiratory failure. More commonly, neurologic signs are limited to tingling and numbness of the tongue, fingers, and bite location. Its mechanism appears to be calcium channel blockade in presynaptic neurons as a result of which neurotransmitters, usually acetylcholine, cannot be released at the motor end-plate.

The timber rattlesnake has a venom constituent that causes myokimia, subcutaneous muscle movements that resemble the motion of a worm. The mechanism of action of this venom neurotoxin is believed to be the same as that of the Mojave rattlesnake neurotoxin.

ELAPID VENOM

Most or all of the toxic components of Elapid venom are protein or polypeptides. For Naja Naja cobra 94% of the solid composition of venom is made up of protein. Further, most of the toxic properties that have been explained are traced to a protein component of venom protein composition.

NEUROTOXIN

A neurotoxin isolated from Elapid venom is regarded as primarily responsible for the lethality of bites from these snakes (Table 26.2). It acts on nerve and muscles to cause paralysis. Biochemical characterization reveals a single-chain polypeptide with 16 different amino acids and 62 total amino acid residues with molecular weight approximately 7000 Da. It is rich in basic amino acids and has an isoelectric point of 9.4. Four cystine bridges cross-link the polypeptide chain. These cystine groups provide part of the critical 3-dimensional shape because it has been demonstrated that neurotoxic activity is lost when they are reduced but restored when they are re-oxidized. A central loop, containing mainly basic linkages, is believed to be the active site of the toxin.

The neurotoxin of the common cobra (a different Elapid) is similar to that just described for other Elapids. It has a molecular weight of 6000 Da and contains about 50 amino acids. Cobra neurotoxin also has isoelectric point (pI) at 9.4.

TABLE 26.2
Summary of Symptoms Due to Cobra Neurotoxin

Paralysis of respiration
Anoxia from decreased activity of respiratory mechanisms
Vertigo from central effects of venom
Ptosis, strabismus, and speech incoordination
Intercostal paralysis (decrease in outward rib movement)
Shallow breathing
Muscle weakness, especially proximally
Shock

Cobra venom acts in a paralyzing manner similar to that of curare, a non-depolarizing acetylcholine antagonist. Besides the curare-like action at the neuromuscular junction an action on the respiratory center in the brain also provokes convulsion and paralysis of the center. Flaccid paralysis occurs from Elapid envenomation. This is manifested by strabismus, convulsions, drowsiness progressing to coma, and death from complete respiratory collapse. The LD_{50} of isolated neurotoxin from Cobra (Naja Naja) is 0.1 mg/kg. This is impressive potency and death may be very rapid. Laboratory mice die in 15 seconds from intravenous venom. In one documented human death the victim, a Sri-Lankan woman, died in 15 minutes. Besides the inherent potency of the venom an additional factor that contributes to rapid action is the relatively small molecular weight of the toxin as a result of which it rapidly diffuses to its target site in the body.

CARDIOTOXIN

A cardiotoxic factor isolated from Naja Naja cobra venom causes a sharp drop in blood pressure. In monkeys this factor, at 3 mg/kg intravenous, caused rapid ventricular fibrillation followed by death. The cardiotoxin depolarizes all membranes affecting skeletal, cardiac, and smooth muscle. In the mammalian heart it is extremely toxic and causes a rapid onset of circulatory failure and systolic arrest.

Biochemical studies of cobra cardiotoxin show it to be a heat-stable protein with isoelectric point of 12.0. This protein retains 50% of its biochemical activity when heated at 85°C. It is also ultraviolet labile and is 100% inactivated by 15 minutes exposure to ultraviolet light. Cardiotoxin has some structural features that are reminiscent of neurotoxin. It is a single-chain polypeptide of approximately 58 amino acid residues. Molecular weight is about 6400 Da, and basic amino acids predominate. Like neurotoxin it has four intramolecular disulfide crosslinks. Although highly potent the lethality of cardiotoxin is estimated to be only 5% that of neurotoxin. As suggested earlier, it is not truly cardiospecific but is more of a general cell membrane poison. Its irreversible depolarizing activity on cell membranes is potentiated by phospholipase A, another component of cobra venom. While the major effect of cardiotoxin is on the heart, it also intensifies the damaging effect of neurotoxin.

LYTIC FACTOR

Direct lytic factor (DLF) is a protein from cobra venom that is able to rupture red blood cells. This is a curiously weak effect by the DLF alone, but it is extremely magnified by phopholipase A and even more by phospholipase A plus calcium ion. The actual mechanism of hemolysis appears to be a lytic action of the phospholipase enzyme on structural components of the cell membrane. Phospholipase attacks these components and, in doing so, it undermines the integrity of the membrane leading to its rupture. The point is that some parts of the membrane structure are partially hidden from the enzyme. DLF seems to expose these parts to the enzyme, thereby enhancing the lytic action of the enzyme.

DLF is also a very basic protein with molecular weight in the range of 7000 Da, and, in common with the earlier described venom constituents, has four disulfide bridges in a single chain. It is relatively heat stable and resists tryptic digestion. While apparently much weaker overall than neurotoxin or cardiotoxin it is, nevertheless, described as the major cytotoxic factor in cobra venom.

HEMOLYSIN

Hemolysis is a lytic factor that is distinguished from DLF. It promotes the loss of hemoglobin from erythrocytes. It appears that the major activity of hemolysin is due to its content of the enzyme lecithinase A. Two steps are involved in the hemolytic action of venom. In step 1, lecithinase A catalyzes the hydrolysis of lecithin, a phospholipid in the red cell membrane. The product of this reaction is called lysolecithin. In step 2, lysolecithin, known to be highly hemolytic, acts on erythrocyte stroma to destroy membrane integrity and cause leakage of hemoglobin.

Hemolysin is a weak component of venom. By itself, it can kill a bitten animal, but large doses are needed. Many agents also inhibit the lecithinase A enzyme by stabilizing the membrane and preventing the formation of an active complex between cobra venom and lecithin. Hemolysin was shown to be stable to boiling provided that the pH remained neutral. Some Elapid venoms also contain lecithinase C as part of their hemolysin fraction. This enzyme also attacks lecithin but forms a diglyceride plus phosphocholine.

VENOM ACTION ON COAGULATION

As described above in relation to Crotalid venom, many components in the venom of numerous species of snakes have some action on the coagulation process. Venom may inhibit coagulation or promote an inappropriate coagulation activity. *Bothrops* have a Factor X activator, and a thrombin-like activity that promotes the conversion of fibrinogen precursor to fibrin clots. Russell's viper shares one of these activities with *Bothrops*, the Factor X activator. *Crotalus terrificus*, by contrast, has only the thrombin-like activity.

Venom coagulin is a name that has been given to a coagulation-promoting factor from venom. This factor has some features in common with thrombin, and its activity is also promoted by calcium ion. Unlike thrombin, however, coagulin retains activity

TABLE 26.3
Comparison of Some Venom Components

Toxin	Source	LD$_{50}$	pI	Molecular Weight Da	Amino Acids
Neurotoxin	Cobra	0.1 mg/kg	9.4	6000	50
Cardiotoxin	Cobra	3 mg/kg	12	6400	56
DLF	Cobra	Rel. weak		7000	65
Coagulin	*Bothrops*	0.25 mg/kg	6.6	36000	350

at high temperature, up to 70°C for 20 minutes. Venom coagulin is quite potent and 0.25 mg/kg was lethal in rabbits.

ASPECTS OF THERAPY FOR SNAKEBITE

Immediate Care

There are many misconceptions about first aid for snakebite. One is that therapy is almost impossible unless the snake can be identified. Although it is helpful to identify the species responsible for the bite, heroic efforts to capture the snake should not be undertaken. This involves an associated risk of further envenomation and may delay the start of professional medical care.

If the snake is dead, then its remains should be kept for identification. It must be handled with extreme care because even dead snakes have been responsible for transferring venom. Immobilization of the victim, if possible, and rapid transfer to a hospital are the most important aspects of immediate care. The need for immobilization of the bite victim is demonstrated by radiotracer lymphoscintigraphy experiments in which injected tracers were transferred through the body more rapidly after a short walk. Nevertheless, immobilization must be avoided if walking is the only way in which the victim can reach medical care.

Many texts still recommend that incision, tourniquets, and suction be employed as first line means of restricting venom distribution. These steps are analogous to lavage of an orally ingested toxin and, when first suggested, appear to be logical ways of diminishing the impact of the bite. Recently, a re-examination of these therapies questions their value. Tourniquets induce vascular compromise and their dangers might logically outweigh their benefits. For example, there are cases in which tourniquets caused arterial thrombosis in snakebite victims. Newer studies show no efficacy from tourniquets and it is now recommended that no band of any kind be placed on the extremity of a Crotalid victim.

Incision followed by suction is also a protocol that seems to be logical in reducing the distribution of venom. In fact, early experiments supported this position by demonstrating some small loss of venom into a suction device. However, the hazards of this procedure often outweigh any small benefit. Numerous possible complications include damage to muscles, nerves, and tendons, in addition to hemorrhage. Infection becomes a more serious problem from the cutting device and from oral flora. Some patients have even required neurosurgery to repair self-inflicted injury following a dry bite. The current weight of professional opinion is opposed to incision, suction, and/or tourniquets.

Cryotherapy was recommended in the past in the belief that cold temperatures would decrease venom enzyme activity and slow the host inflammatory response. For a long time snakebite kits contained ethyl chloride, Freon, or other temperature-lowering agent. A modern re-examination of these former therapies fails to show any benefit and, on the contrary, further tissue necrosis results when they are employed.

Extraction kits are available that allow suction of the venom through the bite wound itself. No additional incision is needed. When used immediately, they may provide some very small benefit, but the victim still has a critical need to receive immediate care.

Hospital Treatment

The physician must examine the wound for evidence of envenomation and order laboratory studies including CBC, platelet count, fibrinogen, and prothrombin time. Evidence of actual envenomation may include some or all of the following: pain, swelling, discoloration, proximal lymph node tenderness, nausea, vomiting, hypotension, and/or laboratory indication of coagulopathy, hypofibrinogenemia, or thrombocytopenia. Actual envenomation can be ruled out only if repeat laboratory studies and physical examination are negative. Even then, caution is necessary for small children or those with bites to the leg because physical signs may be delayed in these patients. On the other hand, if envenomation has occurred the patient should be admitted.

Fluid Replacement
Hypotension following snakebite is common. It is associated with vomiting or hemorrhage secondary to coagulopathy or thrombocytopenia. Fluid resuscitation in the form of crystalloid administration should be commenced and continued for a prolonged period.

Wound Care
The region of the bite should be cleaned thoroughly. Measurements at several points along the affected limb or other involved area should be taken to follow the probable course of subsequent swelling and to monitor the need for additional therapy. Some experts have suggested prophylactic antibiotic administration because of the extensive collection of microorganisms found in the mouths of snakes. In fact, however, infection from snakebite seems to be rare. This may be due, in part, to an antibacterial property of the venom itself. Therefore, antibiotics ought to be withheld unless there is clear evidence of infection as a complication of the bite.

Medications

Pain Relief
Very significant pain is present at the bite site and in the immediately surrounding region. Intravenous narcotics should be provided. A unique problem with morphine

in this context is that it causes some release of histamine. The physician might mistake this for an anaphylactic reaction to antivenin and inappropriately withhold the needed antivenin. Fentanyl is a narcotic that provides excellent pain relief but does not induce histamine release. Because fentanyl does not confuse the issue of possible anaphylaxis it is the preferred narcotic for pain relief from snakebite.

Steroids

Steroids were once thought to be beneficial as suppressors of inflammation in snakebite. Current thinking is that they are not helpful.

Blood Products

Because coagulopathy is one of the major complications of Crotalid envenomation, selective use of blood products might seem to be an effective response. Surprisingly, fresh frozen plasma and cryoprecipitate do not, by themselves, raise fibrinogen or correct the venom-induced coagulopathy. Antivenin is far more effective for this purpose. Platelet administration is also much less effective in treatment of thrombocytopenia than antivenin therapy. Packed red-cell transfusions are sometimes helpful in treating the hemorrhage associated with snakebite in children.

Antivenin

This is the mainstay of snakebite therapy. Several forms of antivenin are available. One of the most common for treatment of rattlesnake bites is Wyeth Pharmaceutical's polyvalent Crotalidae antivenin. This material is made up mostly of antibodies derived from horses that have been immunized with venom from several species of *Crotalus* and from *Bothrops atrox*. The antivenin has several beneficial effects (Table 26.4). It often constitutes a life-saving measure. In view of the time frame and manner of antivenin therapy, however, it could not be expected to eliminate all complications of snakebite. For example, prevention of local tissue necrosis at the site of the bite is not possible with antivenin.

When to Treat with Antivenin

Because most physicians do not see many snakebites and the use of antivenin is not without its own set of risks, one must be very careful in the decision to administer it. Some signs that it should be used in a particular case are swelling that is progressing rapidly; significant coagulopathy, defibrination, and thrombocytopenia as seen from laboratory studies; signs of neuromuscular toxicity; and shock. In addition to deciding that the patient would benefit from antivenin, the physician must confirm that he/she is not a strong candidate for anaphylaxis. The Wyeth kit

---

TABLE 26.4
Some Beneficial Antivenin Activities for Snakebite

Stop progression of swelling
Reverse coagulopathy
Reverse thrombocytopenia
Counter muscle weakness caused by paralysis

---

includes a small sample in a separate vial that is intended for skin testing. Before administration of large amounts of antivenin, therefore, the physician injects a small quantity intradermally. A positive test result is the appearance of erythema and a wheal at the site of injection within 20 minutes of injection. A positive finding means that the snakebite victim is presumably allergic to the antivenin. This does not absolutely rule out the use of the antivenin but indicates that complications from its use are much more likely. The potential risk to the patient must be weighed more carefully against its benefits for a patient who has a positive skin test to antivenin. Finally, it should be mentioned that a negative skin test does not guarantee that a patient will not experience an immunological reaction, such as anaphylaxis, when a large dose of antibody is provided as in treatment with antivenin. To guard against the possible onset of anaphylaxis during antivenin administration, resuscitation capability must be available where the patient is being treated. An epinephrine drip, antihistamines, airway supplies, and corticosteroids should be ready in case they are needed.

Serum sickness is a common disorder in patients who are treated with medical products of equine origin. In particular, serum sickness is common when equine-derived antivenin is administered for snakebite. In one study 10 vials was the median dose required to provoke mild serum sickness and 15 vials caused more serious serum sickness. This is to be compared with the fact that the average victim of snakebite in the American Southwest receives 35 vials of antivenin and higher doses are not rare in the more severely ill. Therefore, nearly 100% of patients receiving antivenin will subsequently develop serum sickness. Serum sickness is manifested usually by a rash, fever, malaise, and arthralgia (flu-like symptoms) starting about 1 to 2 weeks after the exposure to antivenin. More serious cases of serum sickness involve nephritis and/or bronchospasm.

F(ab) Fragments

Because of the high incidence of adverse immune reactions to antivenin there is great interest in therapeutic products that might be less antigenic. Recall that immunoglobulins are composed of four polypeptide chains folded by disulfide bridges. It is possible to enzymatically cleave immunoglobulin into two antigen binding (Fab) fragments and one (Fc) complement-binding fragment. Because the Fc fragment is more responsible for hypersensitivity reactions, administration of Fab alone might still bind antigens in the venom but be less likely to produce serum sickness or other unwanted immunological responses. This is an area of ongoing research.

Questions

1. In what areas of the world are snakebites the greatest problem regarding human mortality? What medical intervention would probably be most effective in reducing snakebite deaths in these areas?
2. List at least 5 components of Crotalid venom and, for each, describe its effects on the physiology of the snakebite victim.
3. What is the major difference between the venom of Crotalids vs. the venom of Elapids?

4. What are the biochemical nature and pathological effects of cobra cardiotoxin?
5. Discuss the classical first aid for snakebite and recent thinking about the
   desirability of this type of intervention.
6. What are the advantages and disadvantages of antivenin for snakebite?

Case Study 1: A Hazardous Profession

A 43-year-old professional snake trainer was demonstrating how to handle a
snake at a show in the Sea Aquarium of Myrtle Beach, South Carolina. Suddenly,
he suffered a bite to his right thumb. He immediately stopped the show and
drove himself to the nearest hospital, arriving in the emergency department
15 minutes after the bite. At this time he complained of severe pain and nausea.
He was pale and sweating and his thumb was noted to be swollen. Vital signs
on admission revealed elevated pulse rate, respirations, and blood pressure. His
respirations were labored. Initial laboratory studies are as follows:

Test	Result	
CBC	WNL	
Platelets	WNL	
Prothrombin time	WNL	2 hrs later = 15.1 seconds (INR = 1.56)
Partial thromboplastin time	WNL	
Fibrinogen	WNL	
Fibrin degradation products	WNL	
AST	57 U/L	
LDH	211 U/L	
Creatine kinase	WNL	
ALT	77 U/L	
ECG	WNL	

Note: WNL = within normal limits; INR = international normalized ratio.

Over the next 90 minutes the patient had worsening neurologic signs including bilateral ptosis (drooping of eyelids), dysphagia, and generalized flaccidity
and confusion. He received supplemental oxygen, but his blood showed declining
oxygen saturation in spite of the enhanced delivery of oxygen. Two hours after
the bite he was endotracheally intubated and placed on mechanical ventilation.

At this point what was the probable identity of the snake that bit him?
   a) *Crotalus terrificus*
   b) *Sistrurus* spp.
   c) African spitting cobra
   d) King Cobra

It is difficult to be certain of the identity of the snake on the basis of the small amount of information presented up to this time. What is most impressive about this patient's presentation, however, are its neurological aspects. The major concern appears to be a developing paralysis as evidenced by the patient's ptosis, flaccidity, and failing respirations. Although he may have other problems, a progressive respiratory paralysis appears to be present and this would point to an Elapid, specifically a King Cobra. As an aside, one would expect such an exotic snake to be displayed at a sea aquarium show. The first two choices above are rattlesnakes, for whom neurotoxins are not the major toxin present. The third choice, the African spitting cobra, is an interesting species that belongs to the cobra family and is capable of delivering venom through the air. This form of delivery typically is much less damaging than venom deposition from fangs, however. Furthermore, the spitting cobra has little or no neurotoxin. The major problem from an encounter with this species is local swelling and necrosis.

This patient knew, of course, that he was bitten by a 14 ft-long King Cobra. He reported this fact to the ED staff. They responded appropriately by initiating a search for a source of antivenin to King Cobra bites. The Poison Control Center in Columbia, South Carolina, was contacted and they were aware that the local zoo maintained an inventory of Thai Red Cross King Cobra antivenin. This material was sent to the patient's bedside and was administered intravenously starting at 2 p.m. At this time it was 3 hours and 45 minutes after the envenomation. Within 2 hours the patient had improved greatly. He was alert and could move all extremities. No neurological abnormalities remained except a palsy of one area that resolved over the following hour. Two hours later the patient, believing himself to be fully cured, extubated himself. He remained in ICU overnight. The following morning his laboratory studies showed a slight prolongation of the prothrombin time (13.3 seconds, INR = 1.22) and a mild elevation of white cells at 15,900 mm^3. The patient then signed out of the hospital against medical advice.

Questions

Q1. Which of the following are not found from cobra bite?
a) Cranial nerve palsies.
b) Dysarthria.
c) Drowsiness.
d) Respiratory paralysis.
e) All of the above are found.
Q2. What interpretation should be given to the elevated prothrombin time 4.5 hours after the bite?
a) It is not significant because it is a minor elevation.
b) It is indicative of abnormally rapid blood coagulation.
c) It means that coagulation is inhibited.
d) There might be a laboratory error because the INR is at variance with the result in seconds.

Q3. What is the expected outcome from bites of this species without medical care?
a) Death from respiratory paralysis in 1 hour
b) Death from respiratory paralysis in 24 hours
c) Eventual recovery with significant morbidity
d) Death from the cardiotoxin after a mean survival time of 48 hours

Q4. The neurotoxin of King Cobra
a) May produce presynaptic neuromuscular blockade only.
b) Could be partly reversed by acetylcholinesterase inhibitors.
c) Could be partly reversed by anticholinergic agents.
d) Acts in a paralytic manner opposite to that of curare.

Answers and Discussion

Q1. (Answer = e) All of the symptoms listed are usually seen in cobra bite. They are effects of the cobra neurotoxin. Cranial nerve palsies are manifested by ptosis, ophthalmoplegia, blurred vision, diplopia, dysphagia, increased secretions, and facial muscle weakness. A worsening condition is shown by flaccid paralysis, loss of deep tendon reflexes, coma, and respiratory paralysis.

Q2. (Answer = c) Prothrombin time (PT) is one measure of normal coagulation. When it is prolonged, blood coagulation takes longer indicating that at least one factor required for coagulation is defective. For many years normal prothrombin time was highly variable from one laboratory to the next and even from one batch of PT reagents to the next. The INR was developed around 1990 and attempts to eliminate the former variability in the manner of reporting for this test. With the INR all laboratories use 1.0 as the mean of the reference range. With this patient both the earlier reporting method (seconds) and the newer INR show an abnormality. Hence, the two tests are in agreement that the patient's blood is taking an excessive amount of time to coagulate.

Q3. (Answer = b) Most patients die from respiratory paralysis in about 1 day. Despite the potency of the cardiotoxin, cardiac effects are not usually seen, perhaps because of the earlier action of the neurotoxin. A fatal outcome is not inevitable from cobra bites. For example, a man who kept a large collection of pet snakes claimed that he had been bitten several times in less than a year by a Black Pakistani cobra. All of these bites had resolved without specific treatment.[2]

Q4. (Answer = b) Antivenin appears to be the best agent for treating cobra bite. However, acetylcholinesterase inhibitors have been shown to reverse the paralysis caused by cobra neurotoxin. Because the neurotoxin produces presynaptic or postsynaptic neuromuscular block it is not surprising that acetylcholinesterase inhibitors would reverse cobra neurotoxin effect to some degree. This presumably arises from maximizing the effect of the available acetylcholine at the neuromuscular junction.

References

1. Gold, B.S. and Pyle, P., Successful treatment of neurotoxic King Cobra envenomation in Myrtle Beach, South Carolina. *Ann. Emerg. Med.,* 32, 736–738, 1998.
2. Britt, A. and Burkhart, K., Naja Naja Cobra bite, *Am. J. Emerg. Med.,* 15, 529–531, 1997.

Case Study 2: The Persistent Snake

A 36-year-old man was bitten on a finger of his right hand while working at a construction site in the western United States. The snake attached itself to the man's hand and refused to release its grip. Great effort was needed to physically remove the snake, after which the victim cut the bite site with a razor blade and sucked the venom out as much as possible. He was then taken by co-workers to the emergency department of a local hospital where his chief complaint was pain and swelling of the right hand and arm. He also described numbness of the mouth and hand. Fasciculations were observed on the right hand. Laboratory studies at the time of presentation gave the following results:

Fibrinogen	83 mg/dL	(N = 200–400)
Fibrin split products	>1000 ng/mL	(N = < 250)
Platelets	80,000/mm³	(N = 130,000–400,000)
PT	WNL	
PTT	WNL	

Note: WNL = within normal limits.

What species of snake may be responsible for this strike?
  a) Western diamondback rattlesnake
  b) King Cobra
  c) Mojave rattlesnake
  d) Boa constrictor

Again, one can only hazard a guess about the identity of the offending agent. The fact that the incident occurred at a construction site in the United States suggests that the snake was probably a rattlesnake. The cobra is very unlikely and the Boa constrictor is not the answer because it is a nonvenomous species of snake. The Boa is notorious because of its great size and, as a result, it has no need for venom to kill prey. The probability of the snake being a rattlesnake is enhanced by the specific presentation. Although there are some symptoms suggestive of a neurotoxin those findings are not the major part of toxicity up to this time. Rather, the coagulopathy evidenced by depletion of fibrinogen and excess formation of fibrin products plus the thrombocytopenia are consistent with a rattlesnake. Comparing the two rattlesnake species, the Mojave rattlesnake is ruled out because experience with this species shows that it has, unlike many other rattlesnakes, a significant neurotoxicity. As it happened, the victim and his co-workers were familiar with this kind of snake and definitely identified it as a Western diamondback rattlesnake.

The patient received six vials of investigational Fab antivenin. An adverse reaction occurred and it was necessary to continue medicating the victim with antivenin at a slower rate. Six more vials were administered over an 18-hour period. At this time his fibrin split products were still elevated but all other laboratory results were in the normal range. He was discharged at 36 hours post-envenomation and returned 24 hours later for re-evaluation. Physical exam was unremarkable so blood was drawn for studies and he was again discharged. After he left, it was found that his PT was over 200 seconds, PTT greater than 300 seconds, fibrinogen less than 50 mg/dL, and fibrin split products greater than 1000 ng/mL. Because of this grossly abnormal coagulation profile it was decided to re-admit him. He could not, however, be reached at this time. This patient returned for a final visit 6 days later at which time he was slowly improving. His coagulation profile was still abnormal but much better than on the previous testing.

Questions

Q1. What complications are associated with self-treatment by incising the wound area?
a) Incision of nerves, tendons, and other structures
b) Transfer of venom to other areas
c) Potential delay in initiation of antivenin therapy
d) All of the above
e) None of the above

Q2. How does one interpret a prothrombin time above 200 seconds?
a) Slight inhibition of the clotting process
b) Severe inhibition of clotting with high risk of bleeding
c) Slight increase in rate of blood clotting
d) Severe increase in clotting tendency with associated risks of thrombosis

Q3. This patient was treated with Fab. What are the advantages of this material over whole antivenin?
a) Absolute prevention of serum sickness.
b) Larger number of species for which the antivenin is effective.
c) Probable reduction in anaphylaxis or other immune response to therapy.
d) Fab is more stable in storage.

Q4. A patient is bitten by a snake and subsequently does not respond when treated with antivenin. The most likely reason is
a) The antivenin is administered too rapidly.
b) The antivenin is outdated.
c) Venom from the specific kind of snake was not used in preparing the antivenin.
d) Antivenin treats only one type of snake toxin.

Answers and Discussion

Q1. (Answer = d) It is generally a bad idea to apply first aid in the form of slicing a wound area. Many patients who have done so had a subsequent need for neurosurgery or other complex intervention. There is also the danger, as occurred in this case, of transferring the venom to another susceptible area. The patient's perception of numbness around the mouth is clearly due to sucking the venom. This act did not necessarily worsen the situation but it could have.

Q2. (Answer = b) The finding of very abnormal coagulation test results 4 days after the envenomation was surprising. It indicated the great impact of the venom on normal coagulation and the possibility that relief by antivenin might be temporary.

Q3. (Answer = c) Horses are inoculated with venom and the resulting immunoglobulins are isolated. This produces classical antivenin. Additional steps, including digestion with the enzyme papain followed by affinity purification, give a product called Fab, fragment antigen binding. This is more potent than regular antivenin and, more importantly, it is less likely to provoke an antigenic response from the recipient. As described in the text these responses run a wide range of severity and are very common because of the large quantities of foreign antibody that are used.

Q4. (Answer = c) All of the suggested answers are at least remotely possible. However, the most likely is that venom from the species of snake involved in the bite was not used to prepare the antivenin. This is possible if the victim has no idea what species bit him. Because there is some degree of cross-reactivity among species the antivenin usually provides at least partial relief. No response is possible, however, and the most likely reason is that the antivenin was prepared for a different species.

References

Clark, R.F. et al., Successful treatment of crotalid-induced neurotoxicity with a new polyspecific Crotalid Fab antivenom, *Ann. Emerg. Med.,* 30, 54–57, 1997.

Cole, M., Cerebral infarct after rattlesnake bite, *Arch. Neurol.,* 53, 957–958, 1996.

Guisto, J., Severe toxicity from Crotalid envenomation after early resolution of symptoms, *Ann. Emerg. Med.,* 26, 387–389, 1995.

Index

C

N

Appendix 1

NORMAL LABORATORY REFERENCE VALUES

Test Name	Metric Units	S. I. Units
Alanine aminotransferase (ALT)	10–40 U/L	0.15–0.70 ukat/L
Albumin	3–4.4 g/dL	30–44 g/L
Alkaline phosphatase (ALP)	40–110 U/L	0.6–1.7 ukat/L
Amylase	50–120 U/L	0.8–2 ukat/L
Aspartate aminotransferase (AST)	10–35 U/L	0.15–0.50 ukat/L
Bicarbonate	22–26 meq/L	22–26 mmol/L
Bilirubin, total	0–0.4 mg/dL	0–17 umol/L
Calcium	8.5–10 mg/dL	2.1–2.6 mmol/L
Chloride	100–108 mmol/L	100–108 mmol/L
Cholinesterase	5–12 U/mL	5–12 kU/L
Creatine kinase	60–250 U/L	1–4 ukat/L
Creatinine	0.6–1.5 mg/dL	53–133 umol/L
Glucose	70–110 mg/dL	3.9–6.1 mmol/L
Gamma glutamyl transferase (GGT)	1–80 U/L	1–80 U/L
Lactic acid	0.5–2.2 mmol/L	0.5–2.2 mmol/L
Lactate dehydrogenase	110–210 U/L	1.8–3.5 ukat/L
Lipase	30–190 U/L	0.5–3.2 ukat/L
Magnesium	1.4–2 meq/L	0.7–1.0 mmol/L
Osmolality	280–296 mOsm/kg	280–296 mmol/kg
pCO_2	35–45 mm Hg	4.7–6.0 kPa
pH, arterial	7.35–7.45 units	7.35–7.45
pO_2	80–100 mm Hg	10.7–13.3 kPa
Potassium	3.4–4.8 mmol/L	3.4–4.8 mmol/L
Protein, total	6.0–8.0 g/dL	60–80 g/L
Sodium	135–145 mmol/L	135–145 mmol/L
Thyroid stimulating hormone	0.5–5 mIU/L	0.5–5 mIU/L
Thyroxine	4.5–11 ug/dL	58–140 nmol/L
Triglycerides	40–150 mg/dL	0.45–1.69 mmol/L
Urea nitrogen	8.0–25 mg/dL	2.9–8.9 mmol/L
Uric acid	3–7.5 mg/dL	200–450 umol/L

Appendix 2

Estimated Toxic Doses and Blood Concentrations for Some Drugs

Drug	Lethal Dose	Lethal Blood Concentration
Acetylsalicylic acid	16.0 g	3.4 mg/mL
Amitriptyline	4.0 g	9.0 ug/mL
Caffeine	50.0 g	80.0 ug/mL
Chloral hydrate	25.0 g	270.0 ug/mL
Chlorpromazine	2.0 g	3.0 ug/mL
Diphenylhydantoin	2.8 g	112.0 ug/mL
Doxepin	3.0 g	9.0 ug/mL
Ethchlorvynol	11.0 g	36.0 ug/mL
Fenfluramine	2.0 g	6.5 ug/mL
Imipramine	0.6 g	5.0 ug/mL
Lidocaine	0.25 g	25.0 ug/mL
Meprobamate	25.0 g	225.0 ug/mL
Methapyrilene	750.0 mg	12.0 ug/mL
Methsuximide	10.0 g	18.0 ug/mL
Methylenedioxy-amphetamine	1.0 g	2.0 ug/mL
Methyprylon	8.0 g	76.0 ug/mL
Nicotine	25.0 g	29.0 ug/mL
Nitrazepam	250.0 mg	9.0 ug/mL
Nortriptyline	1.5 g	0.7 ug/mL
Pentobarbital	4.0 g	37.0 ug/mL
Phencyclidine1	20.0 mg	3.0 ug/mL
Phenobarbital	6.0 g	78.0 ug/mL
Propoxyphene	5.0 g	11.0 ug/mL
Propranolol	3.0 g	8.0 ug/mL
Quinidine	5.0 g	45.0 ug/mL
Secobarbital	4.0 g	21.0 ug/mL
Thiopental	6.5 g	21.0 ug/mL

Glossary

abortifacient An agent that is able to induce abortion

abruptio placentae Early detachment of a normally placed and functioning placenta; problematic because associated with hemorrhage

acute A problem which is associated with a relatively sudden onset

adipose tissue Tissue which is dedicated primarily to lipid metabolism

afebrile Absence of fever; presence of normal body temperature

akathisia Feeling of restlessness with urgent need to move; perception of muscular quivering

akinesia Partial or complete loss of muscle movement

alcoholic cardiomyopathy Damage to muscle tissue of the heart from heavy use of ethanol

alopecia Loss of hair

amnesia Memory loss especially failure to be aware of one's identity

analgesic A medication that relieves pain perception

aneurysm Pathologic dilatation of a blood vessel in a localized area due to congenital defect or weakness; rupture risk is very high

anginal Disease characterized by sense of suffocating pain; usually refers to angina pectoris, severe chest pain from hypoxia

anion gap Difference between sodium ion concentration and sum of chloride plus bicarbonate; a clinically useful entity

anorexia Loss of interest in eating

anoxia Total or near total deprivation of oxygen

anticholinergic Impeding the action of nerves which employ acetylcholine; normally, blocking impulses in parasympathetic nerves

antioxidant A substance which prevents oxidation reactions; such reactions are believed to be involved in aging, carcinogenesis, and other processes

antipsychotic A substance which is effective in treating psychosis; especially medications which affect neurotransmitters related to rational behavior

antispasmodic A substance that relieves spasm of muscles

Apgar score A system of scoring an infant's apparent physiological condition one minute after birth; maximum score is 10; low scores require immediate medical intervention

apnea Interruption in breathing; multifactorial and temporary or permanent

arrhythmia Absence of normal cardiac rhythm; usually a pathological interference in discharge or conduction of cardiac impulses

arterio-venous gradient The normal change in a physiological parameter between arteries and veins

aspiration Drawing in or out by suction; often refers to transfer of stomach contents to lungs

ataxia Lack of normal muscular coordination; especially noted when voluntary muscle motion is attempted

atelectasis Collapse and airless condition of the lung often caused by obstruction from foreign bodies or excessive secretions

atrioventric malformation A structural abnormality that relates both to an atrium of the heart and to a ventricle

atrophy Loss of tissue mass as a result of disuse

AV block A failure of nerve conduction attributable to both atrium and ventricle

Babinski sign The extension of the great toe rather than toe flexing in response to stroking of the sole of the relaxed foot

basophilic stippling The appearance of spotting in basophilic cells that is seen in certain diseases

beta blocker A substance that interferes with nerve transmission in certain autonomic pathways; also called beta adrenergic blocker

bezoar A concretion or solid precipitate that forms, for example, as several pill fragments coalesce within the stomach

bioavailability The percent of a total dose that reaches the bloodstream; intravenous administration of a dose results in 100% bioavailability

bowel sounds Those sounds that emanate from the intestine in relation to normal muscle movement and that are usually detected by stethoscope

bradykinin A plasma polypeptide with nine amino acids that arises from trypsin action on a blood globulin

brain stem reflexes Responses that occur to external stimuli from sections of the brain other than the cerebellum and cerebrum

bronchoconstriction Change in the degree of opening of the bronchus in which the diameter is reduced

bronchodilator A medicinal agent that reverses bronchoconstriction and expands the bronchus

bulimia Hunger experienced shortly after eating; refers also to the eating disorder in which the victim retches after eating to prevent weight gain

canaliculi A small channel, used commonly for the very small bile-carrying structures in the liver

cardiac arrest Sudden loss of circulation due to cessation of heart motion

cardiac glycoside A potent drug which has a carbohydrate moiety and cardiac activity

cardiopulmonary arrest Sudden loss of both circulation and ventilatory functions

carotid angiography The investigation of carotid (neck) arteries with dyes to determine whether blood flow to the brain is compromised by carotid blockage

catatonic posturing Maintaining a fixed posture with refusal to talk or move

centrilobular Pertaining to the middle portion of a lobule (a small portion of an organ)

cerebral edema Excessive amount of tissue fluid present in the cerebrum

cerebrovascular accident A stroke; a loss of some CNS function due to interruption of normal blood circulation in the brain

cholestasis A liver condition in which normal bile flow is interrupted to some degree

chronic A long-lived condition as contrasted with acute or recent onset

cinesthesia A hallucinatory-like response in which sensations are mixed in regard to their source; e.g., one smells sound, one hears color, etc

cirrhosis A chronic condition in which normal cells are replaced by connective tissue

CNS Central nervous system; brain plus spinal cord

coagulative necrosis Necrosis or cell death that results when tissue coagulation occurs and cells are deprived of bloodflow

coagulopathy A pathologic condition in which blood coagulation is abnormal

coma A deep stupor that usually arises from injury to the brain; may be due to head trauma, circulatory compromise, drug overdose, etc.

congestion The presence of an excessive amount of tissue fluid or blood in an organ

congestive heart failure Condition in which heart muscle is weakened and output of the heart is reduced; venous stasis occurs and peripheral edema is found

CT scan Computerized tomography scan; radiologic technique in which various depths of tissue are imaged in succession

cyanogenic A substance that gives rise to cyanide by metabolism or some other process

cyanosis The appearance of blue or gray skin due to the presence of unoxygenated hemoglobin in large quantities in the blood

decontamination Any process intended to remove a toxin from the blood or GI tract

deep tendon reflexes Reflected action or movement that is elicited from a deep tendon skeletal muscle movement from a blow to its tendon of insertion and related to innervation from single synapse; e.g., knee jerk response

defecation Egestion of fecal material from the body

defibrillation Interruption of fibrillation of the heart by administration of drugs or by other means such as electrical stimulation

delirium Mental confusion and disorientation, often with illusions and hallucinations

depersonalization An altered perception of oneself; strange or unreal feelings about oneself

dermatitis Inflammation of the skin as seen by itching, redness, and skin lesions

dialysis Transfer of a solute through a membrane; medically used to refer to the process of treating blood to remove waste material by equilibration across a semipermeable membrane

diaphoresis Extensive sweating

diplopia Double vision in one or both eyes

disconjugate gaze Lack of coordinated movement of both eyes while gazing at a single object

disseminated intravascular Altered blood coagulation with widespread clotting within the vascular coagulation system; secondary to many other conditions

distal tubule Kidney structures within each nephron that conduct filtrate beyond the proximal tubules

dyskinesia Abnormal voluntary movement

dysmetria Inability to control the range of motion in a normal manner; rapid, forceful, uncontrolled motions often indicating cerebellar dysfunction

dysphoria Depressive feeling without any recognizable explanation

dyspnea Shortness of breath

dystaxia Partial lack of control of muscle motion

dystonia Lack of normal muscle tone; hypotonicity or hypertonicity

ECG Electrocardiogram; record of the heart's electrical activity

edema Excessive tissue fluid in part of the body; may be generalized or localized

emesis Vomiting; multifactorial causes including nervous, drug-induced, gastric, or systemic in origin

emphysema Chronic lung disease in which the air spaces beyond the terminal bronchiole are enlarged and alveolar walls are partly destroyed

encephalopathy A disorder characterized by some abnormal function in the brain

endotracheal Within the airway

esophageal varices Twisting and dilatation of the veins that surround the esophagus

euphoria Absence of anxiety and positive feeling of elation; exaggerated feeling of wellness

fasciculation Small and local muscle contraction that is visible through the skin and is due to spontaneous contraction of a number of fibers supplied by a single nerve

first pass metabolism That portion of drug metabolism which occurs when a dose is absorbed and transits the liver for the first time

gag reflex Gagging and vomiting due to irritation of the rear of the oral pharynx

GFR Glomerular filtration rate; expression of the efficiency of the renal glomerulus

gingivitis Inflammatory condition of the gums

glomerulus Part of the renal nephron in which filtration of the blood occurs

gynecomastia Female-like mammary glands in a male; condition that sometimes arises from drug-induced changes in sex hormone metabolism

hallucination A perception that is not related to reality

heartblock A failure in the normal conduction of the nerve impulse through the heart; usually atrioventricular heart block

hematemesis Production of vomitus that contains blood

hemoperfusion Pumping blood through a device that treats it in a specific manner; usually exposure of blood to a filter or exchange resin within the device for the purpose of removing a toxin from the blood

hemorrhage Loss of blood in an abnormal manner; external or internal bleeding

hepatic Pertaining to the liver

hepatitis Inflammatory disease of the liver

hepatocytes The cells within the liver parenchyma responsible for most hepatic function

histamine A chemical released during cell injury and causing many pathologic responses

huffing The practice of inhaling hydrocarbons and other solvents that provokes a brief period of euphoria; breathing in from a rag or other device

hyperbaric Oxygen pressure that is greater than normal

hyperkeratosis Excessive growth of the cornea or of the horny layer of the epidermis

hyperkinesis Excess physical activity and muscle motion; often seen in children in association with minimal brain dysfunction

hyperpyrexia Greatly increased body temperature; usually an increase of 4 degrees centigrade or more above normal temperature

hyperreflexia Reflex responses that are exaggerated and clearly above normal

hypertension Elevated tension; usually blood pressure that is greater than normal systolic and/or diastolic

hyperuricemia Above normal blood concentrations of uric acid; symptomatic of gout, renal disease, or other disorders

hypnotic An agent that induces sleep

hypoactive Below normal activity; often bowel sounds that are reduced

hypochromic Red blood cells that are deficient in hemoglobin

hypofibrinogenemia A lower than normal amount of the clotting precursor, fibrinogen, in the bloodstream

hypoglycemia A lower than normal amount of glucose in the blood

hyponatremia Depressed level of sodium in blood

hypotension Blood pressure that is below the established reference range

hypothermia Body temperature that is significantly depressed

hypoxia Literally, low oxygen content in inspired air; hypoxemia is the reduction of oxygen in blood

inflammation Response to injury or tissue damage that is localized and protective; A reaction which occurs on the part of some cells to injury; characterized by swelling, pain, erythema (redness)

intravenous Delivery of a drug or other agent directly into the blood as by a needle

intubation Placement of a tube as, for example, a nasogastric tube; an aspect of therapy for removal of stomach contents, and other purposes

ischemia Localized and usually temporary interruption of blood flow to an organ or an area resulting in oxygen deprivation to that area

isoelectric Possessing equivalent electrical potentials

jaundice Yellowing; yellow appearance of skin and superficial structures usually resulting from an elevated level of hemoglobin degradation products, especially bilirubin; often due to hepatic disease

junctional escape The pacemaker action of atriventricular tissue in place of normal pacemaker action from a higher priority tissue

ketoacidosis A metabolic acidosis or below-normal pH due to an excess amount of ketoacids in the blood; arises from diabetes and other causes

Korsakoff's psychosis Personality disorder often caused by alcoholism and characterized by disorientation, muttering, delirium, illusions, insomnia, and hallucinations; physical signs are also common

lacrimation Tearing; excess tears as, for example, cholinergic activation

lavage Washing; removal of contents from the gastrointestinal tract often performed for purposes of toxin removal

lethargy Fatigue; commonly refers to profound feeling of weakness brought on by some pathological means

lividity The quality of being black and blue; postmortem, it is the discoloration of dependent parts of the body from gravitation effect on blood

lymphocytosis An above-average concentration of lymphocytes (white blood cells) in the blood; may occur from multifactorial causes

malaise A sick feeling; a vague feeling of discomfort

manic state Period of mental disorder associated with expansive emotional feelings, hyperirritability, loquacity, and increased motor action

MAOI Monoamine oxidase inhibitors; substances that interfere in the action of monoamine oxidase, an enzyme involved in amine catabolism

meiosis Constriction of the pupil of the eye; pupillary aperture less than about 3 mm in an adult

meningioma A type of brain tumor; usually a hard, slow-growing tumor that occurs along the meningeal vessels and erodes and thins the skull

metabolic acidosis Biochemical abberation in which the pH of the blood is below normal and blood bicarbonate is also reduced; multifactorial

metabolic alkalosis Biochemical abnormality in which the pH of the blood is above normal and blood bicarbonate is also elevated

microcytic Small cells; especially small red blood cells often found in nutritional deficiencies and occasionally due to drug reactions

miosis Contraction of pupils to abnormal degree; typically less than 3 mm in size

MRI Magnetic resonance imaging; imaging technique of recent development and very powerful for evaluation of some neurological illnesses

muscarinic Refers to actions that are similar to those of the chemical muscarine; such actions mimic acetylcholine action at some cholinergic synapses, such as many in the autonomic nervous system

mydriasis Dilation of the pupil of the eye; pupillary aperture is greater than approximately 6 mm in an adult

myocardial infarction Necrosis of some myocardial cells as a result of the interruption of blood flow through the coronary arteries to the heart muscle

myocardium The muscle tissue of the heart wall that provides the structure for heart beat

myoclonus Clonic (relating to variable spasms) contraction of a muscle or group of muscles

myoglobinuria The presence of myoglobin in the urine in above normal (> 5 ng/mL)

amounts; often due to toxins that poison muscle

myopathy A pathological condition or disease of muscle

necrosis Death of cells; necrotic tissue is devoid of biochemical activity

nephron The functional unit of the kidney; each kidney has several million nephrons each containing a glomerulus and tubules

neuroleptic malignant A disorder sometimes caused by phenothiazine usage; syndrome characterized by high body temperature, muscle spasms, autonomic dysfunction, partial coma, and other symptoms

neuropathy A pathological condition of nerve tissue; impairment in the normal function of nerve cells

NG tube Nasogastric tube; a structure that communicates between the stomach and the upper part of the alimentary canal

nicotinic Refers to actions similar to those of the chemical, nicotine; found in some cholinergic synapses in the CNS and ANS

nystagmus Movement of the eyes in any direction that is usually constant, involuntary, and cyclical; may be occupational, infectious, or drug induced

obtunded Lack of normal response to pain and other stimuli; dullness or blunting of normal reactions

organic brain disease Disease of anatomic or physiological origin in contrast to psychiatric illness that is undefined; group of diseases that relate to impaired brain function

oropharynx Middle part of the pharynx; lies between soft palate and upper part of the epiglottis

orthostatic hypotension A decrease in blood pressure that accompanies a change in posture; may be indicative of drug exposure or organic illness

pallid Presence of pale skin; indicative of circulatory impairment or other disorder

pancreatitis Inflammatory illness of the pancreatic gland

paraparesis A condition of partial paralysis that affects the legs

paresis Partial paralysis; also a brain disease caused by syphilis and manifested by progressive dementia, tremor, and speech disturbance

paresthesias Numbness, tingling, and other abnormal sensation for which there is no obvious cause; found in some neurological illnesses

perinatal Around the time of birth; relating to the time of birth

peristalsis Contraction of longitudinal and circular muscle fibers around bodily tubes; moving, wave-like motion

pharmacokinetics "What the body does to a drug," the sum total of the metabolic changes, kinetic factors, and so on, for each drug

phase I reactions A type of metabolic reaction; hydroxylation, oxidation, etc. that is from phase 2 or conjugation reactions

plegget A small, flat section of gauze or absorbent cotton (also, pledget)

pneumonitis Inflammatory condition of the lung

pneumothorax A break in the chest wall or in the visceral pleura that covers the lung; the resulting gas that enters through the orifice

portal hypertension Elevated blood pressure due to congestion within the liver

positive end expiratory A therapeutic manouver in which a ventilator is set to provide air pressure into a patient's lungs at the end of each expiratory cycle; intended to pre-collapse of the lung

potency The ability of a drug to exert a large physiological effect from a small dose; also a comparative term, e.g., morphine is more potent than aspirin because the same degree of pain relief is achieved from less drug

pressor A substance that raises blood pressure;

prognosis The probable outcome; a prediction in relation to a patient's severity of illness

prothrombin time One of the laboratory tests related to clotting time; thromboplastin and calcium are added to decalcified plasma and the time measured until clots form; one of the tests of liver function

proximal tubule Part of each nephron that is nearest to the glomerulus

pulmonary edema A transfer of serum fluid into the air spaces and the interstitial tissue of the lung

reactive pupils The response of the central opening in the iris to stimulation by light; the normal partial closure in bright light

renal Pertaining to the kidney

renal medulla That part of the kidney that is internal and removed from the outer layers; the region of each kidney containing nephrons

respiratory acidosis An abnormally low blood pH in which partial pressure of carbon dioxide is elevated

respiratory alkalosis An abnormally elevated blood pH in which partial pressure of carbon dioxide is reduced

respiratory arrest Stoppage of the breathing movement; interruption of air flow into the lungs

respiratory center An area in the medulla oblongata of the brain which controls breathing rate; it is sensitive to blood concentrations of oxygen and carbon dioxide

resuscitation Restoring a comatose patient to full consciousness

reticular activating system That part of the brain responsible for alertness; a focus for some drugs; part of the brain that initiates and maintains wakefulness

rhabdomyolysis Destruction of muscle tissue resulting from factors such as the toxic effect of a drug, viral illness, etc.

rhinorrhea A watery secretion emanating from the nose

rigor Usually refers to the stiffness noted in corpses for an interval following death

roentgenogram An image produced from X rays or gamma rays

sedation Calming; the reduction of anxiety

seizure A sudden attack; usually refers to an epileptic event; disordered brain activity causing muscular incoordination

sepsis The state of having pathological microorganisms growing within the bloodstream

serological Relating to serum; usually, a reference to tests of specific antibodies within blood or blood serum

serotonin syndrome A constellation of symptoms noted in patients who have excess serotonin usually from a medication that interferes with normal serotonin metabolism

shock A syndrome in which a disturbance exists in regard to normal oxygen supply to tissue and return of blood to the heart

sinus tachycardia Uncomplicated rapid heartbeat; elevated heart rate in an appropriate setting, e.g., during exercise

sinusoid A very small blood vessel but slightly larger than a capillary; found in organs such as the liver

somnolent Profound sleepiness; trance-like state

spasms Involuntary muscle motion that is often sudden or convulsive in character; clonic spasms are alternating between relaxation and contraction whereas tonic spasms are sustained

SSRI Selective serotinin reuptake inhibitors; these drugs specifically are limited to action on serotonin rather than other neurotransmitters; contrast with other drugs that act on multiple neurotransmitters

stupor Some degree of unconsciousness; may be mere lethargy or reduced awareness or feeling

subarachnoid hemorrhage Bleeding below the arachnoid membrane; i.e., bleeding below the middle of the three membranes that cover the brain and spinal cord

suicidal ideation Contemplation of self-destruction; planning or consideration of suicide

sympathomimetic Like sympathetic nerve action; drugs that mimic the neurotransmitter of the sympathetic nervous system, typically, norepinephrine

syncope Loss of consciousness specifically associated with inadequate flow of blood to the brain

syndrome A constellation of symptoms that is correlated with a disease or other impairment

systolic pressure Blood pressure that is present at the moment when the ventricle contracts; the maximum blood pressure in the cardiac cycle

tachycardia A rapid heart rate

tachypnea An elevated breathing rate; nervous tachypnea is about 40 breaths per minute

during hysteria and other conditions

tardive dyskinesia Slow and automatic stereotypical motions that may be confined to single muscle groups; seen in use of certain drugs such as phenothiazine antipsychotics

teratogenic Capable of causing birth defects

theriac A term for antidote; largely archaic at the present time

tinnitus The perception of a ringing sound in the ears unrelated to one's surroundings; associated with some overdoses such as aspirin

tolerance The development of resistance to the effects of a drug so that larger amounts are needed to achieve the same pharmacological effect

tonic-clonic Both tonic and clonic spasms; alternating between sustained and relaxed muscles

topical On the surface of the body; e.g., drugs that are applied to the skin

toxidrome A syndrome related to exposure to a potentially poisonous substance

transdermal Across the skin; absorption of a chemical through the skin

transection Cutting across a long axis; severing of a structure by a parallel cut

tremor Quivering; uncontrolled actions of opposed muscles that provoke involuntary movements

ulceration An open lesion on skin or mucous membrane; pus formation on an ulcer

urticaria Skin reaction in which very itchy eruptions appear; often due to contact with an external irritant, drugs, neurogenic factors, etc.

vasoconstriction Constriction, or decrease in internal diameter of a blood vessel

vasomotor Regulation of blood vessel wall contraction; a reaction resulting from contraction of these circular muscles that results in enhanced or diminished blood flow to specific areas

ventilator An instrument of variable complexity that replaces the normal physiological ventilation of the lungs

ventricular ectopy An arrhythmia arising from the cardiac ventricle and often associated with chest pain and loss of consciousness

ventricular fibrillation